Landscapes of Communism

Landscapes of Communism

A History Through Buildings

OWEN HATHERLEY

THE NEW PRESS

NEW YORK
LONDON

First published in Great Britain by Allen Lane, Penguin Random House UK, 2015
Published in the United States by The New Press, New York, 2016
Distributed by Perseus Distribution

LIBRARY OF CONGRESS CATALOGING-IN-PUBLICATION DATA

Hatherley, Owen, author.
Landscapes of communism : a history through buildings / Owen Hatherley.
pages cm
Includes bibliographical references and index.
ISBN 978-1-62097-188-8 (hardback)—ISBN 978-1-62097-189-5 (e-book)
1. Communism and architecture—Europe, Eastern—History. I. Title.
HX520.H38 2016
720.947'09045—dc23 2015032819

The New Press publishes books that promote and enrich public discussion and understanding of the issues vital to our democracy and to a more equitable world. These books are made possible by the enthusiasm of our readers; the support of a committed group of donors, large and small; the collaboration of our many partners in the independent media and the not-for-profit sector; booksellers, who often hand-sell New Press books; librarians; and above all by our authors.

www.thenewpress.com

Composition by Jouve (UK)
This book was set in Sabon MT Pro

Printed in the United States of America

2 4 6 8 10 9 7 5 3 1

Dla Agatki, z miłością
'Socjalistyczna Stolica – Miastem Każdego Obywatela –
Robotnika, Chłopa i Pracującego Inteligenta!'

Contents

. . . it was inappropriate to build it, and it would also be inappropriate to demolish it

Deng Xiaoping on Mao's Mausoleum[1]

Introduction: Socialism Isn't

> We intend to tell you what socialism is. But first we must tell you what it is not – and our views on this matter were once very different from what they are at present. Here, then, is what socialism is not.
>
> . . . a society where ten people live in one room – a state that possesses colonies – a state that produces superb jet planes and lousy shoes – one isolated country, a group of underdeveloped countries – a state that employs nationalist slogans – a state which currently exists – a state where city maps are state secrets – a state where history is in the service of politics . . .
>
> That was the first part. But now listen attentively, for I will tell you what socialism is. Well, socialism is a really wonderful thing.
>
> *Leszek Kołakowski, 'What is Socialism?' (1956)*[1]

COMMUNISTS OF HAMPSHIRE

For several decades, my grandparents were members of the Communist Party of Great Britain. I'm not now going to regale you with stories about their strange habits and political delusions, or denounce their decision from the lofty heights of hindsight. I'm not going to retrospectively tell them off. Instead, I'm going to describe where they lived, and what this said about them and what they believed. For the last thirty or so years of their lives they lived in a small semidetached early-twentieth-century house in Bishopstoke, a suburb not far from the Eastleigh Railway Works, on the outskirts of Southampton. From the outside the house was nondescript; it was what was inside that made this noticeably different from any other of these houses for railway clerks. A framed print of Salisbury Cathedral was on the living-room wall, as were several paintings of northern rural scenes. A polished wood and glass cabinet displayed hardback sets of Bernard Shaw, Shelley, Dickens, and a complete bound set of the CPGB's *Labour Monthly* from 1945 to 1951. The books on the other shelves were divided between children's books, books on ornithology, and political books – *The Socialist Sixth of the World*, *New China: Friend or Foe?*, the Marxist literary critic and Spanish Civil War martyr Christopher Caudwell, the Stalinist and biologist J. B. S. Haldane – which all seemed to end in 1956, not, I think, because of the suppression of the Hungarian Revolution or the Secret Speech in which Khrushchev revealed (some of) the crimes of Stalin, but because that was the year they had their first child, at which point they dropped out of active communist politics.

You probably wouldn't have noticed any of this if you were to visit, but you would definitely have noticed the huge plate glass window at the edge of the living room, giving a complete view of the garden. They would usually sit here and watch for birds. The garden itself had been transformed from a small suburban patch into something more wild. A green path ran between two dense thickets of tall, bright plants, with paths running through them and a bench placed somewhere unexpected in the middle; at the end of it was a shed, which we were discouraged from visiting, as Grandad used this as a quiet place, away from children and their din. Here, heaps of compost and tangles of wisteria gave way almost imperceptibly to an overgrown alleyway, which led to a churchyard and a huge, slate-grey Victorian church, whose clang you could hear from inside the living room. These, I'm afraid, are the people I think of when I think of communists, and for most of my life, this entirely private place they created was the most extensive I had experienced that had been made, created, tended, by communists.

So I've often wondered, in the last few years, what they would have made of certain other spaces that had been created by communists, in those countries where they were the unquestioned ruling power rather than a small party that was a tiny minority just about everywhere outside of South Wales and Central Scotland (both so far away from Southampton they might as well have been abroad). I wondered what they would have made of Šeškinė, on the outskirts of Vilnius, Lithuania, where grey prefabricated towers with balconies at unlikely angles are cantilevered over vast, usually empty public spaces. Would they have liked it? Had they lived there, would they have tried to make gardens in those in-between spaces? Would they have been impressed by the technology and the extent of the amenities? I wondered what they would think of MDM, the centre-piece of rebuilt Warsaw, where absolutely immense neo-Renaissance blocks are decorated with giant reliefs of musclebound workers. There was no imagery like that in their books or on their walls. Would they have identified with it? Would it have made them feel powerful, or would they have felt as if power was aiming to intimidate and crush them? What would they have made of the Moscow Metro, with its staggeringly opulent gilded halls? Would they have considered all this grandiose display something that was best for a distant, recently feudal country, or would they have wanted the same at home? They never visited the communist-ruled states of Europe and Asia, so I don't know, and I never got the chance to ask. They would almost certainly have found the homes there worse than a semi on the outskirts of Eastleigh, but would they have contrasted them favourably, at least, to the places they came from – to the slums of Portsmouth, or rural Northumbria, respectively? I'm not sure, but of all the communist-built places I have seen in the last few years, I can only think of a handful where I can be absolutely sure they would have found something to their satisfaction – the old towns of Warsaw, Gdańsk, and St Petersburg, which were meticulously reconstructed after the war. I suspect they'd have preferred them to the starker lines of rebuilt Southampton or Portsmouth, but they might have reflected on the fact that these were mere replicas of cities from a pre-revolutionary past, not visions of the future.

For the last five years I have been visiting these places. It was not by choice, at first; I began doing so because I began a romantic relationship with a woman who lived in Warsaw, a city levelled during the war, and because of that a capital city whose built fabric is, probably more than any other in the European Union, almost entirely a product of the Soviet era. We explored that city together, and found things in it that neither of us expected. And from there, the two of us found we could get trains with the greatest of ease to Berlin, Prague, Budapest, Vilnius, Kiev, Moscow and elsewhere, throughout the region that was once called the 'socialist camp'. To someone brought up in a family of committed Marxists in an environment formed by post-war Western social democracy and then by triumphant and triumphalist neoliberal capitalism, this was a parallel world, where a version of the marginal ideology I had grown up surrounded by had taken power and had remade space in its own interests. For her, it was a journey around places which she had usually slotted away at the back of her mind as dark, disturbing, 'Eastern'; to get on a train westwards to Berlin, Prague or even Paris was one thing; to go east, to Kiev and Moscow, quite another. Neither of us found what we were expecting; partly because we well knew we were not the first to make these journeys.

COUNTER-REVOLUTIONARY TOURISM

There is a large and mostly disreputable history of those from Western Europe going East to see what they want to see and finding it. In the 1920s, and especially in the 1930s, sundry now-ridiculed communists, Fabians, pacifists and the merely curious visited the USSR, most of them returning from their heavily choreographed, meticulously prepared trips to proclaim: 'I've seen the future and it works!' The West German poet and thinker Hans Magnus Enzensberger, who had travelled in the Eastern Bloc, the USSR and Cuba and married a Russian writer, called them *tourists of the revolution*, a very specific type – bourgeois writers in search of 'concrete utopias'. 'No one who returns from a sojourn in socialism is a genuine part of the process he tries to describe . . . no propaganda action, no walk through the cane fields and schools, factories and mines, not to mention a few moments at the lectern and a quick handshake with the leader of the revolution, can deceive about the fact' – but those writers who were aware of this were prone to upset their hosts. They were met with the *delegacja*, a system of tightly planned itineraries, which still prevails in North Korea. Yet he recommended that the Western left travel to the 'East' nonetheless, but in so doing bear in mind what the *delegacja* wouldn't be showing them, and to take the effort much more seriously. Most of the 'tourists' couldn't speak Russian, Polish or Czech (or, later, Mandarin or Vietnamese – perhaps the international left's longer-running love affair with Cuba partly comes from the relative ease of learning Spanish), and they were reliant on the pre-provided contacts.

This meant that their accounts were, by their very nature, superficial – to give an extreme example, George Bernard Shaw saw lots of food and well-fed people so assumed that the Western news stories of famine must have been mere propaganda.[2] By the time Enzensberger was writing in the 1960s, tourists of the revolution had long since forsaken Eastern and Central Europe in order to partake of more exotic, non-European revolutions. What was starting to happen, especially after the tanks were sent in to crush 'socialism with a human face' in Czechoslovakia in 1968, was a newer thing that could be called the *tourism of civil society*. This time, rather than going to meet workers and look at the building of dams, Metros and collective dining facilities, the Westerners were off to meet dissident novelists, to ponder man's folly, to flagellate themselves for their foolishness, and to fall back in love with liberal democracy, adultery and, eventually, capitalism.[3] Most recently, the tourism has been directed towards the relics of the USSR and its satellites, to half-ironically admire the edifices left by a civilization which it is hard to imagine died as recently as twenty-five years ago, where the former Bloc becomes what Agata Pyzik calls a 'toxic Disneyland', whose remnants are documented by aesthetic 'scavengers'.[4] It's this last form – tourism of the counter-revolution, maybe – which is closest to what this book will be undertaking; although the motivations here are at least slightly different.

One of the most common ways of dismissing 'communism' is to point to its monolithic modern architecture, and one of the most common ways of dismissing modern architecture is to point to its association with Soviet communism. In the UK, for instance, blocks commissioned by no one more radical than a constituency Labour Party are habitually described as 'Soviet' if they are repetitious and use reinforced concrete. Meanwhile, as the historian Norman Davies recently put it, in the USSR beautiful historic cities like Tallinn were surrounded by what are now 'museums to the mistreatment of the proletariat'; and it is probably these blocks, seen on the way from the airport en route to a holiday in Prague, Kraków or Riga, that people mean when they talk about 'commieblocks'. Nothing is seen to discredit the entire project of building a non-capitalist collective society more than those featureless monoliths stretching for miles in every direction, and their contrast with the irregular and picturesque centres bequeathed by feudal burghers or the grand classical prospects of the bourgeois city. This, it is implied, is what people were fleeing from when they pulled down the Berlin Wall; the implication when the example is applied to the other side of the Iron Curtain is that there was something a little totalitarian about the mass housing of social democracy, or perhaps about any attempt at planning and modernity: the 'Architecture of Stalinism', as the right-wing architectural historian David Watkin called it.

Except, and here is where the story gets complicated, these 'totalitarian' spaces with their endless blocks on blocks weren't the architecture of Stalinism at all.[5] Architecture in the Soviet Union (and, later, its Central/Eastern European client states) followed a strange zigzag over the course of its existence. After 1917, for around fifteen years Modernist architecture was dominant, either in the dynamic forms of Constructivism or in block-like public housing set in parkland (as, indeed, it was in social democratic Berlin, Prague and to a degree Warsaw). From the early 1930s until the mid-1950s, a reaction set in whose rationale sounds, to the untrained ear, remarkably similar to that advanced in the 1970s and 1980s on the other side of the Curtain. Modernism was inhuman, technocratic, tedious, repetitious, constricting; instead the appeal was to tradition, history, ornament, hierarchy, beauty – the city as a composition, not as repetition. During that period of reaction, modern architects were often persecuted if they didn't follow the new line.[6] Practically the first thing Nikita Khrushchev did on succeeding Stalin was cancel this new eclectic architecture, which in a later era would be called 'Postmodern', favouring instead a return to functional mass housing, after a period that built office blocks as palaces while most workers lived a family to a room in converted 'kommunalkas'. Churned out in massive amounts, prefabricated by specialized factories, these new blocks accommodated the huge population increases caused by a late industrial revolution, and stretched for miles around every major 'socialist' city. In the most authoritarian countries, the 1980s saw the clock go backwards again – in the late Brezhnev years in the USSR, in the last dregs of East Germany and in the maniacal projects of Ceauşescu's Romania, classical details and traditional streets made an unexpected return. The architecture that accompanied the very worst of Stalinism was almost always a matter of columns, marble, ornament, variety, and a paradoxical embrace of the historical city that often entailed destroying its 'real' built fabric.

This isn't interesting solely as a question of architectural historiography, a way of wielding a version of Godwin's law against people who don't like modern buildings. What is perhaps worth doing now, with those regimes twenty-five years dead, is assessing and exploring their most obvious legacy, and what will soon, as those who lived through them begin to age and depart, be their only easily explorable legacy outside of the museums, libraries and archives – their buildings. What sort of cities did the communists build, what sort of buildings did they expect people to live in, what places to work in, what places to meet, what did they do that was different from the capitalist norm, compared either with the age of social democracy or with the neoliberal era of the last thirty years? Was (is) there something in it that suggests ways of building cities outside of capitalism? It is a question worth asking, as a seemingly endless economic crisis reveals ever more ragingly the insanity of a world system geared largely towards maximizing profit for a small group of people, seemingly impervious to any protest or reform. The same appeared to be obvious in the 1930s, when a financial crisis resulted in fascism and world war, during which my grandparents and many people like them joined a Communist Party. The conventional wisdom, and frankly most of the historical evidence, is that they failed wholly and utterly in their attempt to build a better alternative, especially by comparison with the attempt to tame capitalism that dominated Western Europe from the 1950s to the 1980s. However, they left rather a lot behind in the process, and there are perhaps few better ways to judge a (new) society than by walking through its architecture.

Conventional wisdom would also once have argued that a book on communist architecture was a risible idea, fit only for the parodic world of *Boring Postcards* and *Crap Towns*; yet recent years have seen something of a flurry of coffee table books on the subject. From the careful, scholarly documenting of the pre-Stalinist years in Richard Pare's *The Lost Vanguard*, to the melodramatic Brezhnev/Gorbachev-era, late-socialist schlock of Frédéric Chaubin's *CCCP: Cosmic Communist Constructions Photographed*, to individual volumes on Stalin's neo-Byzantine skyscrapers (Gabriele Basilico's *Vertiginous Moscow*), Slovakia (Hertha Hurnaus's *Eastmodern*), Bulgaria (Nikola Mihov's *Forget Your Past*), or Yugoslavia (Armin Linke's *Socialist Architecture: The Vanishing Act*), or the attempt to catalogue the whole region in Roman Bezjak's *Socialist Modernism* (photographically probably the best of the bunch), photographers have led the way; in art, too, the likes of Jane and Louise Wilson, Nicolas Grospierre or Cyprien Gaillard could all be found creating works on these stark, bleak and bare monolithic landscapes. Most of them are mute, blankly presenting the ruins, devoid of much in the way of context or history, let alone politics. What they do is present the fascinating relics of a vanished civilization, which just happens to be at the same time an actual civilization where hundreds of millions of people live and work – as Agata Pyzik recently put it, 'the former USSR is not an alien terrain and obsolete ecology. It's populated by ordinary people, whose lives were thoroughly scattered and jeopardized by both the collapse of the communist economy and the introduction of capitalism. Western intellectuals can behave like it was a playground for their alternative tourism, and perhaps there's nothing objectionable in this per se – but even the most intellectually valuable of those projects can seem either exploitative or miss the importance of context.'

At the same time, as Pyzik also notes, there has been a revived interest in Bolshevism as politics, which comes curiously from philosophers more often than historians. According to voguish philosophers – Alain Badiou, Jodi Dean, Slavoj Žižek, among others – after thirty years of continuous defeat, the left needs to look again at Lenin and his party for pointers as to actually winning their battles, and think about what it might actually mean to go on from there to taking power and trying to construct actual alternatives. Yet they often seem to stop there, as if pointing out the very fact of a formerly marginal group of intellectuals and factory activists taking power nearly a century ago was enough, and what they did next is of lesser importance. So these two sides, the aesthetes and the philosophers, have little to do with each other, and it wouldn't necessarily be better if they did, as the left already has more than its share of both. They do point to something hugely important by reminding us of the fact that revolutionary change both in politics and in the city is possible. But at this point, the bodycounters come in, carrying their Black Books, to remind you that any such attempt is a direct route to the Gulag. If you're a Marxist – let alone a Leninist – you have, inevitably, to answer this question.

At this point, I will put my cards on the table. Authors who are obviously fascinated with communism often have a tendency to disavow it, and even more so those who are fascinated by its aesthetics; something which is also true of those fascinated by other unpleasant regimes. Why, they ask, when enjoying looking at the buildings of Alexey Shchusev (or for that matter Albert Speer) do we worry that we might be suspected of being Stalinists (or Nazis) when nobody assumes that enthusiasts for the classical architecture of Athens, Rome or Washington DC are also enthusiasts for the slave societies that built it? That amoral neutrality is a position sometimes genuinely held,[7] but more often it serves to more or less ineptly mask a real conviction, which usually reveals itself inadvertently.[8] I will try to avoid this by being as honest as possible about the political convictions lying behind this book, and what I think about the state(s) that constructed these buildings. This does not, incidentally, mean that the remarks on architecture are completely determined by those convictions; appalling regimes do sometimes commission architectural masterpieces, sympathetic regimes have been known to construct the shoddiest dross. Franco's Spain built a lot of interesting architecture. So before I go any further, I ought to make clear what I think the Soviet Union and its empire *was,* and how this related to what they built. This is a book about power, and what power does in cities. What was that power?

BUILDING SOCIALISM, SOCIALIST BUILDINGS

Landscapes of Communism centres on the products of a very peculiar society, one whose emergence, status and collapse are still in certain respects unresolved and unexplained. As it is written from a communist perspective – at least in the sense in which the word was used in *The Communist Manifesto* – it is necessary that I say exactly what I think 'communism' was, and what effect that had on the environment communists made. Regardless of the banal Cold War commonplace that the Soviet experience was directly the result of the thought of Karl Marx and Friedrich Engels – the notion that as soon as private property is abolished a big scary state will 'inevitably' step into the resultant vacuum – it is clear that Soviet societies veered greatly from what was predicted by the (extremely few) Marxist writings that suggested what the post-capitalist society would be like: that is, a 'free association of producers', democratic, libertarian and open.

Marx's and Engels' writings on cities and urban space were sparse indeed, but the first decree of the Bolshevik government would have major implications for both. Land nationalization was practically the first thing instituted upon the October Revolution. Whether it resulted in 'socialism' or despotism, it meant the possibility of a new spaciousness, a completeness, the treatment of any given site as a potentially blank slate, and the possibility that town plans could be completed without the obstruction of any private interests. However, the urban space that was now officially communally owned was an unexpected one. The second professedly socialist state – the first, which fitted the plan much more, was the short-lived Paris Commune of 1871 – occupied the space of the Russian Empire, proverbially the most 'backward' of the great powers. Marx and Engels had envisaged that socialist revolutions were most possible, or most desirable, in Britain, France and Germany, even in the United States, where an economy of abundance rather than scarcity could be redistributed.[9] When a revolutionary situation emerged in 1905 in the Russian Empire, with a huge wave of strikes and the setting up of 'Soviets' (workers' councils, a form of direct democracy elected in factories) from Łódź to Vladivostok, certain thinkers began to imagine that revolution could instead break out in capitalism's weakest link. In the Russian Empire, 'combined and uneven development' had created a society where a mass working class in unusually high-tech factories coexisted with a feudal, rural autocracy, and a bourgeoisie which relied on that autocracy to protect it from the proletariat – a society whose ruling class was so weak that working-class organizations were capable of overthrowing it more easily.[10] Their example, however, could inspire revolution elsewhere, in the more developed capitalist countries. The last years of the First World War brought a wave of revolution, where 1917 in Russia broke that 'weakest link', but the socialist revolutions in stronger links like Germany, Austria and Hungary in 1918–19 were all neutralized by either military defeat or Social Democratic compromise.

The disastrous consequences if Europe and the USA didn't follow Russia were pointed out early on by the Russian Mensheviks. Within a couple of years of the revolutionary seizure of power in October 1917, a Communist Party found itself presiding over a society that was hardly 'ready' for socialism – the ruthlessly fought Civil War of 1918–21 meant the workers' party found itself ruling a country where the urban working class barely existed, and large industrial cities like St Petersburg, Moscow and Kiev emptied at a rapid rate. What urban workers were left began to resist the state power the Bolsheviks had accumulated, in the strike wave and Kronstadt mutiny of early 1921, both of them failed attempts to return to the original ideal of direct 'Soviet democracy'.[11] Whether that was even plausible by then is doubtful – eight years of war had led to de-industrialization, militarization and famine, meaning that some kind of coercion and centralization was unavoidable even with the best of intentions. Restrictions were placed on democracy, the press and freedom of assembly, although cultural life was much more relaxed – in fact, there were twelve years of artistic, literary and scientific ferment, a decade comparable to the Renaissance in its intensity and wide-ranging effects. It was also an exceptionally fertile time for architecture, and speculation on the future of cities.

There was something to build on here, to some degree – there is, especially in the work of Engels, a sharp critique of urban planning as it existed in the nineteenth century. Napoleon III's town planner, Baron Haussmann, with his boulevards clearing the workers' quarters of Paris, was a particular target, as were the philanthropic housing schemes of the period.[12] And Marx and Engels did argue in *The Communist Manifesto* that communism should obliterate the division between city and country, something which planners in the Soviet 1920s took seriously – the urban planner and Trotskyist Mikhail Okhitovich imagined the future socialist metropolis as something resembling Los Angeles, a series of road and rail networks trailing light industry along an endless suburban territory mixing agriculture, collective public buildings and detached houses.[13] There was also the legacy of the great utopians, who were published in large numbers under the new Bolshevik government: the new Commissariat of Enlightenment made sure that Thomas More's *Utopia*, Campanella's *The City of the Sun* and the works of Charles Fourier envisaging communal live–work environments, the dissolution of the family and rivers of lemonade were all issued in editions of hundreds of thousands. So although the 'fathers of scientific socialism' had little to say on the subject, the 1920s saw a huge debate about what the socialist city, and a socialist architecture, should be like. This took place not just in the revolutionary state, but in all of the former imperial capitals of (broadly conceived) Eastern Europe – Moscow/St Petersburg, Berlin and Vienna, where the aftermath of an incomplete revolution meant that Social Democrats held power in most big cities throughout the 1920s and early 1930s.

These three former imperial capitals and the lands they once commanded run through this book, as the centres of debate and the centres of power. After 1945, this is where 'communism' happened, Vienna aside – though that city still bears several signs of its long post-war Soviet occupation, and has been a one-party city-state of Austria's relatively leftist Social Democratic Party for seventy years. This meant that the system was overdetermined from the start by the imperial legacy – as many argued, 'socialism' in countries like Czechoslovakia or Hungary resembled the Hapsburg Empire's revenge, with the persistence of its paradoxes, double-talk and intricate bureaucratic hierarchies.[14] The Austrian, Russian and, until its rapid industrialization, the Prussian Empire were all serf economies,[15] with the Russian Empire and the Polish–Lithuanian Commonwealth both actually reinforcing this in the 'second serfdom' of the early-modern era, crucial to economies based on exporting agricultural produce to the West – and all were much less urban than their Western contemporaries. When in the eighteenth century they came to plan cities, in the era when French intellectuals flocked to pay tribute to their 'enlightened despotism', they favoured expanses of space that would have been impossible under most capitalist conditions (though the intricate apparatus of banking and real estate set up by Haussmann and Napoleon III was a very good attempt). Nevsky Prospekt and the Palace Square in St Petersburg, Unter den Linden, the Gendarmenmarkt and the Forum Fridericanum in Berlin, the Ringstrasse and the Hofburg in Vienna: all were on an enormous scale, where an effect of awe and intimidation at a sheer exorbitance of space is created – especially impressive bearing in mind that these were usually urban islands dotted around a rural expanse.

These would each have major, if contrasting, effects. All were cosmopolitan, multi-ethnic empires that were nonetheless strongly centralized, with power and ideas flowing from the centre to the periphery, and all favoured some version of grids, axes and tall tenement blocks in their cities. The provincial capitals bequeathed by the Hapsburgs are by some way the most impressive, with the nineteenth-century quarters of Budapest, Zagreb, Ljubljana, Bratislava, Prague, Kraków and Lviv, among

The Tsar's grand boulevard, Nevsky Prospekt, St Petersburg (1959 postcard)

others, built with a remarkable eye for ease, verdancy and order; the cities of the Tsars and the Kaisers were mostly lesser versions of the same, usually somewhat more grim, industrial and chaotic, with less obvious signs of careful planning. Regardless, these were all rejected *in toto* in the revolutionary 1920s. All were considered examples of a class architecture, a class planning, encapsulated in the way that the ornamented classical or Baroque façades of the ubiquitous tenements masked courtyards within courtyards, where each layer further in was poorer than the last – a territory of Potemkin cities, where the opulence of the boulevards reflected nothing about the real lives and the real poverty experienced inside. These are now, of course, the very places that the tourists flock to.

Post-revolutionary Moscow, Leningrad and Berlin favoured a modernized version of the planning of the English garden city movement. Small houses or low-rise flats, with no 'fronts' or 'backs', in open green areas, designed without appeal to tradition and precedent, without ornament, but with keen and precise attention to colour, geometry and proportion. They can be seen in the suburbs of Berlin, in estates like the Horseshoe Settlement or the White City (which have recently been beautifully restored), and in Moscow districts like Usachevka and Dombrovka (which have not). Social Democratic councils, co-ops and trade union building societies built similar things on a smaller scale in Prague, Riga, Warsaw and Łódź. These were all quite light on ideology – no commemoration of the struggle in the names, no declarative statuary, no explicit statements of politics via architecture, although a great deal was implicit in their total rejection of the 'dishonesty' in imperial city building. In the USSR, architecture pivoted between the creation of reproducible types and specially designed objects, divided between warring factions of Constructivists, who favoured smooth, machine-made, elegant solutions, and Rationalists, whose equally Modernist structures aimed at an expressive, unique effect. And while housing in Social Democratic cities was still based around single-family houses and flats, some of the few new buildings erected in Soviet cities were designed for a more radically communal lifestyle with shared canteens, libraries and gyms built as part of blocks of flats which often lacked private kitchens, such as the Narkomfin 'semi-communal' House or the fully Communal House for the Textile Institute, both in Moscow.

Tenement courtyards, St Petersburg

Montwiłł-Mirecki Estate, Łódź, built by the Polish Socialist Party in 1928

Yet the former imperial centre that was most militant in its city planning and its architecture in the inter-war years was actually Vienna, and the Hapsburg capital's experiment in socialist planning was probably the most extensive of the three, at least before Stalin's mega-projects in the 1930s. It might not later have been part of the 'Bloc', but Vienna is a major part of its prehistory. The 'Austro-Marxists' who controlled Vienna after the chaotic, revolutionary years of 1918–19 and who would keep control until 1934, when they were bombed out by the 'Austro-Fascist' regime elected by rural Austria, had a far larger housing programme than the Bolsheviks or the German Social Democrats, and they concentrated not on the virginal outskirts but on the inner city.

Unlike in the USSR, land could not be nationalized in its entirety, so the Viennese programme was based on direct expropriation of dozens of city centre sites, additionally funded by both a Luxury Tax and a Housing Tax; the programme hit private landlords hard, and accordingly landlords would form the backbone of Austro-Fascism. Rents were frozen at between 2 and 4 per cent of the average worker's income. Between 1925 and 1934, 60,000 flats were built.[16] Vienna favoured high-density, inner-urban 'superblocks', partly out of necessity, the embattled city building where it could, but also reflecting a faith in the metropolis that was grounded in imperial urbanism; most of its architects had been students of Otto Wagner, Emperor Franz Joseph's architect of imperial modernization. It's very telling that the Social Democrats called the concentration of superblocks along the wide expanse of the Gürtel 'the Ringstrasse of the Proletariat'. That very Ringstrasse had been the object of the Modernists' scorn ever since it was built, a grandiose and pompous 'Potemkin city'. The Viennese tried to claim imperial grandeur and pomp for the working class, seeing Modernism, at least implicitly, as an aesthetic of poverty.

So the average Viennese superblock breaks all the new Modernist rules being set up in Moscow and Berlin. They follow the street pattern, with a 'block and courtyard' system not massively unlike that of the nineteenth century (although the courtyards are far larger and without further flats in their interior), and they are not oriented to the sun. There is a lot of greenery, but it is mostly inside, not outside, with blocks not set 'in space', but within a tight urban grid. Interestingly, they thus have few, if any, of the features that 1960s critics of Modernism like Jane Jacobs considered to be inherent flaws of planned, municipal housing projects. Yet there's more happening here, too, in the architecture; a continuation of the ornamental, figurative and symbolic design of pre-war Vienna, just as it was being abandoned by Modernists and neoclassicists alike.[17] The easiest place to see this is in the largest and most famous of the superblocks, Karl-Marx-Hof, designed by Karl Ehn in 1927. The design is Modernist, in a sense, as there is no obvious historical referent, but is monumental and epic, not matter of fact and functional. Most photographs concentrate on the series of grand archways in the centre of the complex, with a park in front and flagpoles on top. But look closely at those archways and you'll notice sculpted figures in the niche of each – realistic, figurative and vaguely allegorical statues, their thin, attenuated form in some sort of lineage with the willowy figures of the Vienna Secession. The marble doorways and the ornate light fittings also speak of something much more traditional in its values than, say, Moscow's Usachevka housing scheme or the Horseshoe estate in Berlin the same year, while at the same time the socialist values are far more explicit.

Another difference with 1920s Moscow and Berlin might explain what all the sculptures are doing there. The great Modernist estates were often built using Taylorist methods – that is, using the scientific management of labour, where each movement of the worker is precisely measured and regulated, as on a production line; and were, when possible, built with the newest technologies in steel and concrete, and if possible made from prefabricated parts. Vienna's avoidance of this was largely because of the direct-labour programme the council used, meaning that they tried to provide as much work as possible, in a city which suffered from high unemployment after the collapse of its empire. Not only did the new buildings partake visually in traditional forms, but they used fairly traditional methods, not least in the way that they employed sculptors and craftsmen on almost every project. This seeming abundance actually had a 'functional' purpose. The rhetorical, or ideological, import of the decorative elements is clear enough, but the very fact of their existence was testament to a curious fusion of 'useless' elements for a 'useful' end, i.e. keeping the city's artisans in work – a real 'workerism' rather than an invocation of the worker, and a presaging of the many curious methods that could be employed to create full employment. The peak of this approach might be in the staggering Engelsplatz, where the architect Rudolf Perco managed to invent most of the motifs of Soviet 'Socialist Realism' several years early, from the sense of massive scale, symmetry and pure, domineering mass, to the use of weirdly squat athletic sculptures, here of naked proletarian athletes.

The Soviet Commissar of Transport, Lazar Kaganovich, probably the Party leader with most influence over architecture in the 1930s, once criticized the Karl-Marx-Hof – 'a fine Marxist house indeed, especially since we know that Marx fought consistently for high technology, while here we heat with cast-iron stoves' – rather rich, given that most Soviet workers were at that point living in overcrowded converted kommunalkas, or in tents and even holes in the ground at mega-projects like the new town of Magnitogorsk.[18] Yet it must surely have influenced what the Soviets did next. Kaganovich declared in 1932 that all the attempts at founding an entirely new socialist school of town planning were foolish and distracting, and turned to a definition of socialism as, to misquote Herbert Morrison, 'what Soviet governments do' rather than what anyone else might have thought it was. The replanning of Moscow, the renamed Leningrad and the likes of Magnitogorsk would now follow imperial precedent – organized around wide streets and big squares, with tall tenements hiding layers of courtyards inside, all built super-fast using 'shock-work', or, as it was known under capitalism, piece rates.[19] The

Socialist City turned out to be an only slightly modernized but even more spacious and authoritarian spin on the urban planning of Haussmann's Paris, or imperial Vienna, Berlin and St Petersburg. But when it came to the actual style of this, it was Vienna that was emulated. The sculptures, the flagpoles, the symmetrical axes, the sense of monumentality and pride: all of these were hijacked by the Bolsheviks from the Social Democrats of Austria. If you've ever visited the huge Stalinist projects like the mid-1950s Stalinallee in East Berlin, it can be disconcerting to visit the Engelsplatz in Vienna, built nearly thirty years earlier by a popular, democratically elected council – only the lack of a boulevard for the military parades to go down stops it feeling like a precise prototype.

In terms of architectural detail, meanwhile, some strange strictures took hold. Although the nineteenth-century city was being revived, nineteenth-century details were out – only capitalism before it became 'decadent' was considered worthy of plunder, so Renaissance and Mannerist motifs appeared in the strangest places. The strangely neo-Victorian tastes of Stalinism implied a longing for the sort of places that the

The wintry monumentalism of Engelsplatz, Vienna

revolutionaries had grown up with, that symbolized the lushness of the imperialism they were once pledged to destroy.[20] Like Victorian architecture, and like that of Red Vienna, the architecture of (actual) Stalinism was paradoxically craft-oriented – a sudden proliferation of mosaic, majolica and marble, after a decade of concrete and glass. To work out how this was justified, we need to turn to the complex, disturbing shifts in the USSR at the turn of the 1930s.

Both culturally and politically, the screws were put on around 1929, with a clampdown on trade unions,[21] a 'cultural revolution' against the pluralism of the previous decade, and the imprisonment or exile of the Bolshevik Party's own opposition. A breakneck programme of industrialization and urbanization would form the material basis for this new regime, which both supporters and enemies called 'Stalinism'. The most complete attempt to analyse the society that resulted at the time was, unsurprisingly, made by the revolution's most famous exiled leader, Leon Trotsky. In the 1936 study *The Revolution Betrayed: What is the Soviet Union and Where is It Going?* he ridiculed the idea that the USSR had created socialism, but at the same time noted the prodigious industrial revolution that *had* been created, that gave it the highest growth rate in the world in the 1930s – at the cost, he pointed out, of sweated labour and extremely low-quality products. He argued that a bureaucratic 'caste' had usurped power and governed in its own interest. The resultant state could only end in the victory of one of its contending classes – either the bureaucracy, realizing that 'privileges have only half their worth if they cannot be transmitted to one's children', would consolidate their de facto rule by taking de jure control of the economy and turning themselves into real private owners; or, in a tellingly spatial metaphor, workers who reluctantly allowed the rulers to act as 'the watchman of their own conquests' would 'inevitably drive out the watchman as soon as they see another possibility', and launch a revolution against them.[22]

Within a couple of years, this argument was already being threatened by other dissident Marxists, also often in Trotskyist organizations. For the Italian thinker Bruno Rizzi the bureaucracy was a ruling class like any other; 'the owners are the bureaucrats . . . it is they who control the economy, it is they who reap the benefits, just as is normal for any exploiting class . . . the workers count for nothing in the control of society, further they have no share in the receipts of surplus value, and what is still worse, have no interest in defending this alien nationalized property. The Russian workers are still exploited and the bureaucrats are their exploiters. The nationalized property of the October Revolution now belongs as a whole to the class which directs, exploits and defends it: it is class property.'[23] Moreover, Rizzi saw in the actual built form of the Soviet Union much evidence of this – a new form of bureaucratic despotism that recalled the slave-built projects of ancient dynasts, symbolized by the pyramidal Palace of the Soviets in Moscow, planned from 1932 on and intended to be taller than the Empire State Building, topped by a colossal gesturing figure of Lenin. These buildings were themselves the refutation of Stalin's claims to 'communism'. 'Instead of a State which dissolves itself into an economic administration from below, there is a State which has been inflated by the bureaucratisation of the economy controlled from above. The Palace of the Soviets, 360 metres high, will remain a symbol of this period and the "Bastille" of the bureaucratic world.'[24] It was never completed.

What was this new architecture? The rightward turn in Soviet aesthetics was given the term Socialist Realism, a phrase which made some degree of sense in literature or art – in that it is easy to say what a realist novel or a realist painting is – but in architecture its looseness as a concept was especially glaring. If you read early accounts of what Socialist Realism was, you can see that the general ethos is perhaps applicable to architecture. Its least crass exponent, Maxim Gorky, described it thus: 'Socialist Realism looks upon being as doing, and regards existence as a creative activity, the object of which is the uninterrupted development of the most valuable individual gifts of men in order that they may conquer the forces of nature, achieve health and long life and enjoy the great good fortune of living on an earth which man, in conformity with the incessant growth of his needs, wants to exploit in its entirety as the magnificent dwelling-place of mankind united in one great family.'[25] The sense of grandiosity, the vague and windy humanism and the talk of 'magnificent dwelling places' had some concrete results; as did Gorky's insistence that 'it is not enough to depict already existing things – we must also bear in mind the things we desire and the things which are possible of achievement.'[26] Socialist Realist architecture is full of grand archways, passageways, triumphal routes – aimed at instilling the feeling that you are always about to *arrive at something*.

A typical attempt to define the 'Soviet Approach to Architecture' from the Stalinist period stresses several things that were not part of Soviet architecture in the Modernist period – the creation of a total artwork, a 'synthesis of other arts with architecture, by which we mean the unity of architecture, painting and sculpture', an adherence to tradition, and an embrace of the elusive concept of 'national form', encompassing both the distinctly Russian silhouettes of the new architecture, reflective of the new centrality of 'Great Russia' in Stalinist rhetoric[27] – and, alongside, various appliquéd references to the local cultures of the Soviet Union's Asian republics. 'Soviet architecture believes', wrote Karo Alabian, chair of the Union of Architects in 1939, 'that no progress is possible that is not based on what is progressive and valuable in the past', and architecture, 'like all our culture, is national in form and socialist in content. By this we mean neither exotics nor imitation of national styles from the past, but the creation, in each of our national republics, of an architecture that derives organically from the traditions, customs, life conceptions and climatic conditions of the given nationality.' His example of this is the Exhibition of Economic Achievements in Moscow.

Best known by all and sundry simply by its Russian abbreviation, 'VDNKh', this is a space something between a fairground, a trade fair and an architectural exhibition, where grand, often pyramidal, symmetrical neo-historical frontages smothered in sculpture, ornament and rhetoric led to functionalist halls showing off technological innovations and produce from the various republics. 'Uzbekistan' borrows patterns

The Exhibition of Economic Achievements, Moscow (1969 postcard)

from medieval Samarkand, 'Karelia' has a wooden pediment complete with wooden statues, and the grandest, 'Ukraine', plunders the Baroque styles popular under Catherine the Great. The notion of 'national form' thus displayed would be particularly important when Stalinist architecture, like Stalinism itself, was exported to and imposed upon the new client states of Eastern Europe after 1948.[28] But VDNKh itself also said something fundamental about the way that the Stalinist city worked, in that it was essentially pictorial, a matter of mere façades and picturesque arrangements, with sheds behind them; they didn't need much that was really functional, bar a big roof under which to put exhibits on cattle breeding, new implements and machine tools, or, later, model Vostoks and computers. Self-described in its official guidebook as a 'city within a city', where there are 'no secrets from our foreign guests',[29] VDNKh is the Soviet Union as it wanted to be seen, an endlessly fascinating ideological and technical ragbag full of hope and absurdity, ranging from its first decorative national pavilions to the later Modernist glazed and patterned plastic boxes, and liberally sprinkled with the most iconic Soviet sculptures, such as Vera Mukhina's *Worker and Kolkhoz Woman* or the *Space Obelisk* commemorating the cosmonauts. In among them are lakes, fountains – such as the Friendship of Peoples fountain, guarded by gold figures of Slavic and Central Asian peasant women – and lots of activities, now somewhat attenuated to kebab stalls and cat-grooming exhibitions. This was and is a popular approach to urban space, and local branches of VDNKh can be found in Kiev (a remarkably finely wrought neo-Baroque park of monumental façades) and Tbilisi (where Modernist architecture and shimmering Futurist mosaics have taken over). In each case, they take the format of the International Expo, with its eye-catching, circus-like, festive approach to architecture, and try and make it permanent. It is all, to a degree unusual in twentieth-century architecture, a matter of pure spectacle and surface. Real human needs can't be served by it, only 'demonstrated'.

The first sign of de-Stalinization was a speech, followed by a decree, on 'architectural excess', delivered by the formerly loyal henchman Nikita Khrushchev in 1954, giving some sign of how central this new opulent architecture was to Stalinism. The historians and Polish exiles Isaac Deutscher and Moshe Lewin both argued that Khrushchev's dismantling of the Gulags, his renunciation of bloody purges, his attacks on privilege and wage differentials, and the restoration of law made the system something other than 'Stalinist'.[30] For Lewin, the USSR was a failure largely only if judged by its own standards, as an attempt at 'socialism'. By any other definition, it was a remarkable success. Going from a mostly illiterate, mostly rural expanse to an industrial world power that scared the hell out of the United States was always a weird definition of failure. But Lewin proceeded to analyse in detail the system that resulted from the era of 'stagnation' under Leonid Brezhnev. The worst of Stalinism was long since over, a system where nobody was certain of his own position (bar Stalin himself) had been replaced with its near-opposite, where the entire nomenklatura system was engineered to make sure as few people as possible were removed from their posts. Stalin's monumental, professedly solid architecture embodied a hugely unstable 'quicksand society'. Post-Stalinist 'stagnation' favoured something a little lighter.

If Vienna is the unacknowledged father of the Socialist Realist empire style, so Stockholm was the absent parent to the architecture of the post-1956 Thaw. According to the trade unionist and economist Rudolf Meidner, Sweden had by the 1970s come closer than anywhere else to the

Well-scrubbed social democracy in Vällingby, Sweden

achievement of a classless society,[31] something which had the later, unintended side effect of making its private capitalist concerns very rich; IKEA, he notes, owed its success to providing furniture for housing built under the famous 'Million Programme'. Like the Eastern Bloc, Sweden did not actually have 'social housing', but an entire apparatus of regulated and public housing – housing built by the several municipally owned building companies, housing run by tenant-owned co-operatives, and rigorous rent control for what was left in private hands. Anyone could get on the waiting list and after a few years get a choice of flats, which would pass out of their 'possession' on death.[32] The intent was straightforwardly egalitarian – to avoid any divide between rich and poor areas – and entire towns were designed on that basis.

The most famous of these, and the one which was borrowed from most compulsively by architects elsewhere, is Vällingby, on the outskirts of Stockholm. It knows how important it is, and today appears almost as a mid-century-modern theme park, with all its cute and dynamic neon signs and jaggedly decorative details left in place, something which is rarer in its Eastern followers. Its residential areas around the town centre are in remarkably good shape today, with lines of tenements interspersed with tower blocks to the street. There are winding paths connecting towers and low-rise blocks, with dense little thickets of tall trees in between. The effect is similar to the interspersing of buildings with nature that you can find in Polish or Czech architecture in the 1960s, only without the same sense of a mad rush to complete buildings, without the sloppy execution; though the dominance of land nationalization (Swedish municipalities and governments were highly aggressive in buying and acquiring previously private land to plan settlements on) and even the techniques (prefabrication using panels) were similar. Yet the relative affluence of Swedish social democracy meant that their town planning was careful and unhurried, and hence much more truly 'planned' than that of the 'planned economies'. Perhaps Swedish neutrality made it an easier place to borrow from than, say, the US or the UK. But it also calls into question the necessity, if the results were the same but better, of the sacrifices and upheavals of the Soviet version of socialism.[33] When we walked around Vällingby, Agata's enjoyment of it was tempered by irritation, that the 'West' had seemingly done socialism better than the 'East', and had conserved it, preserved it and, here in Sweden, even extended it. Was 'communism', then, really only ever a more repressive, shoddier mirror image of social democracy, or did it point somewhere else?

For those dissidents who considered themselves socialists – and at first, these were many – the answer to this question was that the Soviet societies had removed vested interests from their economies much more decisively, which meant that they provided the preconditions for socialism, which was not the same thing as being socialist. The most famous of these analyses was Rudolf Bahro's *The Alternative in Eastern Europe*, published in the mid-1970s in samizdat, a massively ambitious attempt to explain the Soviet Bloc on Marxist grounds. It drew heavily on the notion of the 'Asiatic mode of production', which Marx wrote about in the unpublished notebooks later collected as the *Grundrisse*. Marx argued, following Adam Smith, that Ancient Egypt, India, China and other non-European societies had developed a uniquely extensive and unchanging form of despotism that stemmed from the hydraulic works needed to irrigate the fields – which necessarily had to be carried out under a society where there was no private property in land and where the irrigation works themselves were controlled by an educated bureaucratic caste.

Though somewhat too trusting of the factual veracity of this 'mode of production', Bahro applied it to the USSR, which, especially during the Stalin years, appeared to confirm the 'Asiatic' thesis, with its absence of private property, its quasi-priestly bureaucratic caste, its gigantic public works (lots of them 'hydraulic' slave labour schemes like the White Sea Canal), and its more recent tendency to stabilize into a 'stagnant', unmoving society. Its architecture also reflected this, both in its 'Stalinist' and its Modernist variants. Stalinist architecture, like that of Ancient Egypt, was superstitiously despotic – the pyramids, he noted, 'certainly did not rest on exploitation by way of private property, and no more so the monuments of Stalinism, which began with the mausoleum in which Lenin was mummified like a Pharaoh'.[34] Equally puzzling was East Germany's obsession with the 'hallowed' prefabricated concrete panels out of which it built nearly everything, where this symbol of industrialization was insisted upon even in areas that had abundant and cheap traditional building materials that would have been far more genuinely 'functional'.

One common factor in critiques of 'communism' from the left in the 1960s and 1970s was the attention to the effects of prefabrication and repetition in the massive estates that fully urbanized and housed the population of these usually newly industrialized countries. The frequently jailed Czech playwright Václav Havel, in the days when he described himself as a socialist,[35] argued that the new Modernist housing estates of the post-Stalin Bloc were designed to replace public, civic (one could say 'collective') life with a depoliticized private sphere of thousands of identical single-family units, where 'people today . . . fill their homes with all kinds of appliances and pretty things . . . they turn their main attention to the material aspects of their private lives. The authorities welcome and support this spillover of energy into the private sphere. In the interests of the smooth management of society, society's attention is deliberately diverted from itself, that is from social concerns.'[36] In architecture, the result of this new obsession with privacy was not individualism but uniformity: 'It would be to the greatest advantage of a centrally directed system of production if only one type of prefabricated panel were constructed, from which one type of apartment building would be constructed; these buildings in turn would be fitted with a single kind of door, door handle, window, toilet, washbasin and so on, and together this would create a single type of housing development constructed according to one standardized urban development plan, with minor adjustments for landscape, given the regrettable irregularity of the earth's surface.'[37] A similar point about the uniformity of centrally planned housing was made by the Soviet dissident Roy Medvedev, who also faced (house) arrest for his loyal opposition.

Medvedev noted that the proverbial 'dead hand' of central bureaucracy in Moscow meant that a housing estate could end up looking identical in places as distinct as Kiev and Tashkent, but he also claimed that the nomenklatura had far less concrete power than other historical ruling groups like the clergy, the aristocracy, or the bourgeoisie.[38] In the 1970s, the Party contained several distinct groups, none of whom could explicitly argue their position, given the insistence on a public consensus: neo-Stalinists, 'party democrats' (among which Medvedev counted himself), Christian socialists, Westernizers, and an amorphous bureaucratic mass mainly interested in maintaining its own position. Within fifteen years this former ward of the KGB was working as an adviser to the General Secretary, Mikhail Gorbachev, himself a 'party democrat', bent on *glasnost* (openness) and *perestroika* (reconstruction). What is staggering when reading Medvedev today is the realization that almost all of what he advocated came to pass, and that exactly what the bureaucracy feared happened – the floodgates were opened, and the entire edifice collapsed with unprecedented swiftness. From 1985 onwards, bit by bit, the press was freed, dissidents living and dead were rehabilitated, competitive elections were introduced, history was no longer officially falsified, and the government forswore suppressing any countries that wouldn't follow 'The Line' (as they had in Czechoslovakia in 1968, to the protests of even the most cravenly Stalinist Western communist parties). Within four years the entire system fell.

However disliked or hated these systems were, historically speaking the protests against them in 1989 were small, the rulers giving up without a fight – committing suicide, in essence.[39] Two analyses of this conundrum were useful when writing this book: one by the Soviet-trained Marxist economist Hillel Ticktin, another, more a bon mot, by the Slovenian celebrity intellectual Slavoj Žižek. Ticktin's work, best summarized in the 1991 *Origins of the Crisis in the USSR*, was a total dismantlement of the pretences of the Soviet economy. There was no planning, only a 'command economy' in which an arbitrary target was set and then ineptly run towards. The economy ran on barter and graft more than money, the rouble was a fiction, flats and cars were allocated on the basis of connections and good behaviour; and, perhaps most importantly, there was no political force holding the economy up. Feudalism worked because it satisfied the aristocracy and kept the peasants just quiet enough; capitalism does much the same in a different way, by creating great privilege for the owners of the means of production and holding out the *possibility* of social advance for those who work for a living. The Soviet economies satisfied neither – the bureaucracy was aware of how much less privileged it was than the Western ruling class, the workers were well aware of the drudgery and misery of 'their' system. It rested on an uneasy compromise, best encapsulated in the famous quip: 'We pretend to work, and they pretend to pay us.'

Like Havel or Medvedev, Ticktin used housing as a useful example of the problems that its professed socialism caused for the Soviet economy. 'The same problem', he wrote, 'that may appear as one of many difficulties in capitalism is of crucial moment in the Soviet system. The production of poor quality housing under capitalism is a fact of life that may increase the profits of the construction companies. In the USSR, it leads to enormous costs of repair, problems of replacement, and to an absorption of resources that the system cannot afford . . . at all times the poor quality of the Soviet product constitutes a contradiction of the system'.[40] That is, the Soviet economy was incredibly wasteful, but, unlike capitalism, it hadn't figured how to make waste and failure *profitable*. The endemic low productivity and low quality of goods were explained by Ticktin as a consequence of the bureaucracy's fear of the workers – they would not push workers as hard as they would be pushed in the West, and with full employment an intrinsic part of the system they were not threatened with the sack; but then it could not offer workers the consumer goods or the dream of social advancement as incentives to coax them into raising productivity. All this was compounded by the knock-on effects of the oil crisis and the arms race, both of which were major impediments against reform. For Ticktin, trying to come up with a definition of Soviet society was pointless, as it assumed that it was a stable, definable social formation rather than a cul-de-sac produced by the failure of the Russian Revolution to spread to the West, extended in time and space largely because of Soviet victory in the Second World War. The only logical ends to it were those that Trotsky posed: either the workers would revolt, or the bureaucracy would attempt to seize legal and financial control of the means of production – to become owners. And the workers were already revolting – Solidarity in Poland had 10 million members in 1980–81, on a programme that demanded an end to bureaucratic privilege, a reliable welfare state, and a system of workers' self-management. By the late 1980s, a miners' strike was spreading across the USSR.

Except *both* of the possible endings to the Soviet system happened. 'The ultimate irony', writes Slavoj Žižek, 'is that the two opposite outcomes predicted by Trotsky seem to have combined in a strange way: what enabled the nomenklatura to become the direct owners of the means of production was the resistance to their political rule, whose key component – at least in some cases (Solidarity in Poland) – was the workers' revolt against the nomenklatura.'[41] The nomenklatura made an alliance not so much with the workers, but with the mafia, the forces behind the black market that had thrived under a system of shortages and requisites. These two groups embarked on a series of privatizations executed with astonishing ruthlessness and corruption, with state-owned enterprises sold to new private owners for less than 1 per cent of their estimated value on the world market. The transformation of the bureaucracy into a capitalist class was no longer political speculation, but accomplished fact – 'converting power into property', as it was unambiguously called.[42]

The extent and violence of the change were vast, to a degree still barely understood in the West – the huge industrial concerns bought for peanuts, the increase of unemployment from 1 per cent or less to a quarter or more of the population within a year or two, the refusal in many cases to even pay workers, the cutting off of basic services like electricity and hot water, the suppression of the Russian parliament by tanks in 1993, drastic falls in living standards across the entire Bloc – when relatively cushioned as in East Germany it meant mass dependence on unemployment benefit and depopulation as workers drifted to the West, when at its most brutal, as in Ukraine, Georgia or the Russian Federation, living standards fell by 50 per cent and rates of 'excess deaths' reached heights not seen since Stalin. Everywhere, life expectancy fell, causing a demographic crisis. Only a handful of former 'communist' countries have returned to the levels of GDP per capita they had in 1989, and fewer still, such as Poland, have surpassed it.[43] The result is that paradoxically, given the official odium, the built environment of communism is often ubiquitous, as little has been built to replace it for the mass of the population – their needs are no longer important, as the housing market, as ever, serves those who can afford to pay. In 'second tier' cities especially, Soviet-era buildings are as ubiquitous as Victorian buildings are in Britain – fittingly, as both were the result of industrial revolution. Only where war has levelled them, as in Grozny, or where enough was built before 1945 to overshadow them, as in Budapest, can they be ignored.

SPEAKING SOVIET, SPEAKING ARCHITECTURE

This book uses the term 'communism' as a matter of convenience. I do not consider that these societies fit the description in any meaningful sense. Nobody, not even Stalin, ever seriously argued that 'communism' had been built in the USSR. Yet competing terms like 'Stalinism', 'state socialism', 'state capitalism' or just the 'Soviet' system don't really work either. To call shabby, undemocratic but hardly totalitarian societies like 1960s–1980s East Germany, Bulgaria, Hungary or Poland 'Stalinist' trivializes the hecatombs of Stalin's actual rule. 'State socialism' suggests we take this society at its word that it had established 'socialism', despite the evidently shaky nature of that assertion – absence of private property is not socialism, as Ancient Egypt or the Ottoman Empire made abundantly clear. 'Soviet' is specific, and I will use it frequently, but it's still a strange term: its literal meaning is 'council', describing the organs of direct democracy that were meant to supplant parliaments and parties, and only after some time did it come to designate solely the successor to the Russian Empire, its satellites and their system.[44] Rudolf Bahro's 'non-capitalism' is, though a purely negative term, also of some use, as it suggests a system which had not quite become something distinctive, which had defined itself negatively but not positively. Bahro also, more ironically, used the term 'really existing socialism', in scare quotes to mark the gap between the ideal and the reality. This no-longer existing system is still sometimes called retrospectively 'real socialism', a term which is useful when the bitterness of its irony is clear – which it isn't always.

Throughout this book these terms will slip out of control here and there, much as do the subjects under discussion. Either way, we have a system founded upon a 'planned' or 'command' economy, depending on who you believe, which has full nationalization of all (or almost all) land and industry, in which private interest has no role whatsoever in urban and regional planning, a system which was in theory either a 'people's democracy' or the 'dictatorship of the proletariat', and in practice either the dictatorship of one dubiously sane individual or the dictatorship of functionaries; one which oscillated culturally between relative freedom and ideological conformity, between internationalism and practically atavistic appeals to local tradition.

The paradoxical nature of architecture in the Soviet Bloc, with its sharp, sudden zigzags of official style – from Modernism to classicism to Baroque to a bizarre despotic Rococo to Modernism to Brutalism and back – has long puzzled historians. The best definitions were made by the late Soviet architectural historian Vladimir Paperny, who called the Stalinist style 'Culture Two', contrasting it with the future-oriented 'Culture One' of Modernism. The two were wholly and utterly opposed, something he explored through a series of stark dichotomies. Culture One was obsessed with *movement*, wanting its cities to be fast, instant, disposable, dynamic; Culture Two was equally fixated with *immobility*, preferring its buildings to be monumental, solid, massive, immovable. Culture One built *horizontal* blocks of flats, long, low and linear; Culture Two opted for the *vertical*, creating skylines of spires and state offices which rose, step by step, like pyramids and ziggurats.[45] He was writing this under Brezhnev, during a regime that may actually have been an amalgam of both cultures, with a proliferation of heraldic public spaces combined with seemingly endless, non-hierarchical prefabricated housing estates. Because of this animated, argumentative quality, for Paperny the architecture of the Soviet era was always, to use a phrase from eighteenth-century France, an *architecture parlante*, a speaking architecture – one that constantly tells you about the state it represents. This, at least, will be our hope while exploring it, that this rhetorical, verbal architecture may be able to tell us something new about the vanished society it housed.

So in this book we will look at what is there, *as it is now*. How it has aged, and how it has become (or hasn't become) integrated with the cityscape of real capitalism. In so doing, we will search for the distinctive spaces that a non-capitalist society made which a profit-driven society could not. There won't be much on stadiums, factories, hotels, office blocks, schools, hospitals, markets and private villas, interesting as they often are, as these are found in any industrial system. Instead we will have a chapter each on the spaces that were, I'll argue, unique to this place, its ideology and its economy. These are, respectively, the 'magistrale', the huge ceremonial boulevards that were built in all the larger 'socialist' cities; the 'microrayons' (or 'microregions'), the vast housing estates that were often the size of entire cities in themselves; the 'social condensers', the public buildings where collective ideology was supposed to be inculcated; the declarative 'high buildings', the often meticulously crafted skylines that spoke of these societies' unity, hierarchy or coherence; urban rapid transit, a field that was surprisingly often the most impressive showcase of all; the historical reconstructions indulged in by regimes which claimed, paradoxical as it may sound, to be uniquely capable of preserving the national heritage; the many memorials to themselves built by regimes that were obsessed with the judgement of history; and the improvisations that a rather less mediated people's power has created in these buildings both during and after the existence of the 'People's Democracies'.

We will veer across a huge and diverse territory, and one chosen to some degree by accident. This is a book about cities, so there is nothing of the potentially fascinating and contrasting landscape of the countryside, where both Stalinism and neoliberalism have had drastic effects; it is a book about landscapes that still exist, too, so the temporary, and brutal, landscapes of construction sites and labour camps are of course absent, and that absence should be borne in mind. Given that both myself and my partner are freelances, where we have visited has been dictated by cash and convenience, either by where we could travel to easily and cheaply from Warsaw, or where we had work assignments. So there is unsurprisingly a lot of Poland, as we were living there half the time; there is what I hope will be regarded as decent coverage of the western Soviet Union, a little less of East Germany, Czechoslovakia, Bulgaria and Yugoslavia, only the capitals of Hungary and Romania, and nothing at all of that ex-Maoist anomaly, Albania. Exorbitant visas and overpriced hotels meant that the two geographically closest non-Polish places to us in Warsaw – the Republic of Belarus and Russia's Kaliningrad Oblast – went unvisited, as did the more distant southern Yugoslav republics of Montenegro, Bosnia-Herzegovina, Macedonia and Kosovo, and the ex-Soviet republic of Moldova. Absent too, for reasons more financial and practical than geopolitical, is almost all of ex-communist (or even currently communist-ruled) Asia – Siberia and the independent ex-Soviet states of the Caucasus (bar Georgia) and Central Asia, as are North Korea, Vietnam and Laos, let alone Cuba. Non-European communisms will feature largely in an epilogue on the world's most successful and still professedly socialist economy, presided over by a Communist Party. So this is an attempt to tell a story of the communist landscape, but it is certainly not *the* story. It is, by and large, a record of what we found on what were usually unplanned walks, usually for our own pleasure.

We follow the borders as they existed before 1989, but that is not to say that the differences between Serbia and Eastern Germany, Latvia and Slovenia, Ukraine and the Czech Republic, are not genuinely huge – they are, topographically, culturally, religiously and aesthetically. Yet all have mostly lived under exceptionally similar historical forms. The 'end of communism' here is often described as a 'return to liberal democracy', but this is mythical. Few had major experiences with democratic government before 1989 – though most were 'officially' democratic after their emergence from war and empire in 1918, full parliamentary democracy endured longest (from 1918 to 1939) in interwar Czechoslovakia, until 1933 in Germany and untill 1934 in Latvia and Estonia, while it was finished off in Lithuania and Poland by military coups in 1926. Entirely free elections had barely been held at all in Yugoslavia, Romania, Bulgaria and Hungary. And aside from Germany, Czechoslovakia and scattered cities of the Hapsburg or Russian empires like Budapest, Warsaw, Łódź, St Petersburg and Riga, or mining areas like Silesia and eastern Ukraine, little of this territory was industrial. All these countries had a legacy of serfdom and latifundia until the First World War, after which most more or less quickly became right-wing agrarian dictatorships; almost all faced a much more horrific experience during the war than was normal in Western Europe, let alone the United States.[46] After 1945, when communist-dominated coalitions won elections in Czechoslovakia, Bulgaria and Yugoslavia or came to power by ballot-rigging and terror in Poland, Romania, East Germany and Hungary, they played host to an equally dictatorial 'non-capitalist industrialization' – and after 1989 outright, untempered neoliberalism, this time acclaimed by popular vote. Because of this, bunching them together will not, I hope, be as insulting as it may initially seem. I mention the above not as a way of arguing that these places were or are 'backward', or congenitally committed to 'despotism', or anything similarly stupid – but to make clear that, historically, they share a great deal more than divides them.

This is a profoundly uneven landscape, full of holes into which you can easily fall, full of paradoxes, where nothing is what it seems. To give an example: on our first trip to Bulgaria, Agata and I emerged in the city of Ruse from a trundling 1970s train into an astonishing, breathtaking ballroom of a railway station, one which any European capital would be jealous of, with a magnificent, double-height central hall, lit by gilded chandeliers and framed with marble arcades. Outside, we found that most of the station building, with its neoclassical colonnades forming a square, was battered and derelict, with smashed TVs and other detritus left among the pillars, under the iron '1954' sign that commemorated the station's opening. The square didn't connect with anything, only with a grim, low-ceilinged underpass, under an impassable road lined with crumbling high-rises. We tried to find Nikolaevska, the street we were staying in, and were pointed onto a street which, when we finally found a street sign, was named after Maxim Gorky. It was only after some time of struggling down a potholed, barely lit road of garages, high-rise estate open space and rotting nineteenth-century villas that we realized we were

Welcome to Bulgaria: Ruse

on the right street after all. The next day, we woke up in our hotel and found that we were actually in a very conventionally attractive area of lush and leafy fin-de-siècle squares, all newly pedestrianized and tarted up with EU money. We had been given a lesson in 'combined and uneven development'.

This is a book that reads history through buildings. It is meant to be read as such, and I intend it as much as possible to be a potentially useful book, one which hopefully can be read both by traveller and inhabitant in describing these spaces. But as a book by an English writer, with no grounding in this place, and a reliance mostly on translated sources, it will be of necessity *superficial* – a book about surfaces, and about the many political and historical things that can be learned from surfaces, especially in states as obsessed with surface as these. Accordingly it's unavoidably a partly touristic book; in his study of English travel writers of the 1930s, Paul Fussell writes that a traveller is someone who hasn't reserved hotels in advance, and speaks French; 'a tourist is one who has hotel reservations, and does not speak French'.[47] Aside from living in Warsaw and a couple of examples of using people's spare rooms, all hotels were booked well in advance. And although this book documents almost entirely trips embarked upon with a Pole who does speak French (and, more importantly, Russian), they are recounted by an *Angol*. I'm also keen here not, as in the well-mannered fashion of most English writers, to devote myself to a particular national cause (generally before 1945 this was the Russian cause, since then the Polish or, less often, the Czech), which means that there may be an uneasy combination of argumentative historical exposition and contemplation of buildings.

Anyone who, understandably, eventually tires of this and wants a wider insight into the culture of this territory is advised to read Agata Pyzik's *Poor but Sexy*, a far more sweeping, personal, informative and often bitterly funny historico-cultural essay on the area's past and present contradictions.[48] In mitigation, this book will not involve just my own pontification, but also some input from others who do know it from inside, those who I have spoken to, corresponded with, walked with and read – though here, too, the reader should be cautious. Writers, especially travel writers, are prone to finding the interlocutors they want, or who resemble them, and the people cited here may give the wholly unrepresentative impression that the former Eastern Bloc is populated entirely by broadly left-wing aficionados of twentieth-century architecture. Nonetheless, the fact that such people exist at all is illuminating. At this point the time is long overdue to descend into the maelstrom of socialist architecture, to submerge into the Metros, to walk the magistrale, to go to milk bars in the microrayons. Who knows what we might find?

I

Magistrale

After the uprising of the 17th June
The Secretary of the Writers' Union
Had leaflets distributed in the Stalinallee
Stating that the people
Had forfeited the confidence of the government
And could win it back only
By redoubled efforts. Would it not be easier
In that case for the government
To dissolve the people
And elect another?

Bertolt Brecht, 'The Solution' (1953)[1]

MARCHES INTO PARADES (AND BACK)

One of the most notorious images of public space under the Soviet system was of enormous parades going down wide streets, progressing inexorably to similarly gigantic squares, where they would be watched, saluted and subsequently harangued by Party and military leaders. I have in my possession a children's book from the Polish People's Republic, *Idzie Wojsko* (*The Army's Going*), which explains the army's role to young people, solely by showing cartoons of these parades. 'The tanks come in threes, as far as the eye can see.'[2] Not merely do you see soldiers in their identical uniforms marching in formation, but exhibits of military, and sometimes even non-military, technology – tanks, missile carriers, tractors, aeroplanes. Well into the 1980s, ordinary people were expected to join these parades, and attendance was considered compulsory. The spaces that they went down – those boulevards wide enough for tanks – had not, in most cases, existed already in the capitalist city. They had to be created. This chapter is about a series of boulevards which were carved through cities between the 1930s and 1980s, most of them with the express intention of serving as the conduit for these parades. Soviet lexicography had a specific name for such streets, perhaps deriving from its reluctance to call them by the suspiciously bourgeois name of boulevards. They were called 'magistrale', and they were, along with the squares they led to, the most loaded and declarative public spaces in the Bloc.

There are, unsurprisingly, antecedents for the magistrale, often in cities that are laid out on a blank slate by absolute monarchs. Unter den Linden is such a street, a four-lane highway that was planned on a field of linden trees (hence the name) at the turn of the nineteenth century, as Berlin went from being a Prussian garrison town to the capital of an empire. Nevsky Prospekt in St Petersburg is a more spectacular example, created a few decades earlier as the main artery of Peter the Great's new capital on the Baltic Sea. Lacking the spine of trees along the middle that marks Unter den Linden, even with the filigrees and glass of its late-nineteenth-century commercial buildings it is a harsher, more unforgiving space, leading directly to the immense parade ground of the Palace Square, and with the cruel spire of the Admiralty visible as its termination. Both of these are spins on the Baroque planning that came with the Counter-Reformation, when the Catholic church and the surviving Catholic states aimed to create spaces that would be both awesome and terrifying, beautiful and intimidating. The magistrale is not, it should be noted, quite the same as the similar typology of the *Ringstrassen* – the monumental multi-lane ringroads that encircle Vienna, Pest and Kraków, most of them created by knocking down medieval city walls and then building on their foundations. Moscow's Garden Ring is a *Ringstrasse*, and an extremely impressive one, but for all its monumental Stalinist architecture it is not a magistrale. A magistrale is a straight line from A to B, a linear passageway that could only have been created by the new precision that came with the Enlightenment. But, again, Nevsky Prospekt and Unter den Linden were planned on virgin territory. How do you make such a thronghfare out of a space that has already been built upon? The answer was pre-emptively provided in Baron Haussmann's

Paris, whose ramrod-straight clearings such as the Boulevard de Sébastopol or the Boulevard Saint-Michel are so obsessively rectilinear that the trees are sculpted sharp to be in keeping.

What 'the vandalism of Haussmann' did, according to Marx, was to rob Paris both financially, via an intricate system of speculation and financial corruption, and aesthetically, by 'replacing historic Paris with the Paris of the sightseer'. But it wasn't just about graft, flânerie and tourism. As Marx also pointed out, the boulevards had several very real functions – they were meant to push the poor out of potentially lucrative city centre areas (hence their appeal to other bourgeois governments in Europe as 'slum clearance' – the likes of Shaftesbury Avenue or Charing Cross Road are London's shabbier attempts), and they were meant to provide free-fire zones in the case of urban uprisings: it would now be difficult to build barricades and there would be few places to hide. It has been argued that it was the attachment to barricade-fighting that did for the military prospects of the Paris Commune, whose fighters were annihilated by the much better armed and more tactically ruthless army of Versailles. To see what artillery can do to a demonstrating crowd, just put 'Nevsky Prospekt' into Google Images. You'll find a photograph taken during the 'July Days' in 1917, a series of insurgent street demonstrations that were suppressed by the Provisional Government. The organized march of Bolshevik workers has been blown into its component parts – thousands of frightened people, scattered this way and that, ducking and running from the bullets, with bodies lying in the middle of the boulevard. The Bolsheviks did not make the same mistake when they seized power three months later – the seizure of completely unsymbolic spaces like the telephone exchanges and the railway stations proved more decisive than the famous attack on the Winter Palace, which lies at the end of Nevsky Prospekt. But within a couple of decades the (already obsolete) model of the grand street as the artery for public protest and revolution would be supplanted by its mutation into the grand street as the artery for revolution's performance, for its ossification into a spectacle of order – the demonstration becomes the parade. The magistrale is the built form of that change.

This will not be the last time that we find that Karl Marx and Friedrich Engels wouldn't have been impressed with the urban interventions of the governments invoking their good name. But, as we've seen, it was not the

Communist Party of the Soviet Union that began this trend, but the more moderate Austro-Marxists of 'Red Vienna', with their attempt to transform the Gürtel into the '*Ringstrasse* of the Proletariat' via huge, monumental and symmetrical apartment blocks. The Gürtel is long and relatively straight, enough to push it close to being a magistrale. The difference with Parisian practice is that rather than their being displaced elsewhere while the new boulevard accommodated the wealthy, the new street was lined with high-quality and extremely low-rent housing for the working class. This would sporadically be the case with the real magistrale, although they may have displaced as many people as they rehoused. Workers definitely weren't given flats on the first Soviet street that really befits being called a magistrale – Tverskaya, renamed during the Soviet period Gorky Street, Ulica Gorkogo. Tverskaya was a fairly ordinary Moscow shopping street; observers in the nineteenth century were often disappointed by its lack of Petersburgian grandeur. A Soviet guide quotes one G. Belinsky thus: 'a traveller will look in vain for the main or best Moscow street . . . he will be directed to Tverskaya, and once there, will be surprised to find himself amidst a crooked and narrow street going up the hill. One house runs out forward into the street as if to see what is taking place there while another draws several steps back.'[3] So as to provide a less disappointing Moscow for the sightseer, the street was gradually rebuilt during the 1920s and then much more emphatically in the 1930s, when it was widened from 19 to 50 metres.[4] It became the street through which the tanks and other pieces of military hardware travelled on their way to assemble at the annual parades in Red Square. It is, then, the emblematic space of Stalinist power.

Get out at Tverskaya Metro station – passing 1990s murals of what Tverskaya looked like until the 1920s, a sweet-looking provincial street, with little domes, spires, two storeys at the most – and you can see what this involved straight away. First, that pretty and irregular little street has become a monster, a wide, six-lane highway, lined by considerably less pretty buildings. These (mostly apartment) blocks are as much as seven storeys high, and are hierarchical in their construction. A rusticated base of irregular, purple-brown tufa stone to the pedestrian, interspersed by closed arcades. The storeys of flats – for the higher ranks of the nomenklatura from the very start – are arranged into slightly stepped tiers, themselves demarcated by Ionic columns and symmetrically arranged

The magistrale of Gorky Street, Moscow (1955 postcard)

balconies for a mere handful of the flats. At one corner is a large pediment, for no particular reason. This is this book's first direct sighting of the architecture of the Stalin period, and it is a usefully typical one – hulking, traditionalist, heavy in its materials. However, right away you can step out of this into the spaces that were built by the regimes before and after, because you will be walking past Pushkin Square. Here, the poet presides over the Izvestia Building. The first time I visited Moscow, this was entirely covered by a huge canvas car advert; the third, it was under a giant canvas picture of a nineteenth-century Secession building; but the second time, only its drab 1970s extension was covered, so I got a good look.

Izvestia (*News*) was the newspaper of the St Petersburg Soviet in the revolutions of 1905 and 1917, and gradually became a newspaper of state under the Bolshevik regime. Its HQ, designed in 1926 by Grigori Barkhin, speaks vividly of the first decade of 'Soviet power'. It is as light as the construction quality could handle, its concrete mass broken up with large expanses of glass, an early use of the rhetoric of political and actual 'transparency'. Porthole-shaped windows are at one end of its asymmetrical composition; a Constructivist clock at the other. Perpendicular to this is the Rossiya Cinema, built as one of the first new Modernist buildings under Khrushchev, in the late 1950s, designed by Yuri Sheverdyaev and opened in 1961. It is graceless compared to Izvestia, but noticeably much more light, optimistic and active than those hulking apartment blocks on the main street – the structure is arranged around a swooping concrete roof, connected to a glass box, covered like almost everything else by very large canvas advertisements. What you might notice more than these, though, is a reminder of 'combined and uneven development' – several one-storey classical palazzos of the early nineteenth century, fragments of a city where, as Walter Benjamin once put it, 'the village plays hide and seek.' In fact, Benjamin found something close to Tverskaya's model already in the 1920s, before it was reconstructed – 'if you step through one of the high gateways – they often have wrought-iron gates, but I never found them closed – you find yourself on the threshold of a spacious settlement. Opening before you, broad and expansive, is a farmyard or a village'.[5] The main difference is that he finds the squares empty of 'profaning' monuments.

Get back onto the boulevard and continue along it, and the contrast couldn't be greater. The blocks have become positively megalomaniacal – rising to ten storeys at the centre, these neo-Baroque apartments, largely designed in the mid-1930s by a reformed Modernist and one-time 'proletarian architect', Arkady Mordvinov, and then given extra storeys after 1945, are designed with a faintly obsessive attempt at creating variety from floor to floor, much as late-imperial architects like Edwin Lutyens in England had the aim to 'get up a building without repeating yourself'. Lutyens, and some of his contemporaries, used the contrasting treatments of their neoclassical edifices as a way of playing semi-private architectural jokes – styles that couldn't have gone together historically, elements overemphasized for the sake of effect or incongruity, the classical orders deliberately mixed and confused; Gothic or Baroque skylines with sober classical detail. Only this is that late-Victorian/Edwardian Beaux Arts architecture with all the irony extracted. It is the Beaux Arts under conditions of terror, Lutyens at gunpoint. You probably shouldn't laugh (and, at one time, you definitely couldn't), but along Tverskaya there is something almost silly about the insistence on giving everything trimmings, like the almost Gothic little bay window that creeps out at one corner of an overgrown Tuscan palazzo. At the centres of most of the housing blocks are huge archways. You spot several of these, walking up Tverskaya. You might also spot all the plaques here to famous residents, the great and the good of Soviet power, many of them artists in grace and favour flats: the novelist Ilya Ehrenburg, 'proletarian poet' Demyan Bedny, film director Sergei Bondarchuk, and Lenin himself, for a few months in 1918 (but not in these later, opulent buildings) – all are represented in individually designed sculptural plaques, which compete with the shop signs, window displays and giant adverts for the pedestrian's attention.

To the north as the street slopes upwards is a mini-skyscraper, the Hotel Peking, enclosing Triumfalnaya Square, originally Mayakovsky Square, after the Futurist poet. It is a good place to stop, stretch your legs, sit on a bench, and admire the late-1950s statue of the great man, with his baggy-trousered legs caught mid-stride and his stylishly quiffed hair. When she first sees it Agata demands a photo, and so I have one of her underneath him copying his confident stance, staring towards the future. This has often been a symbolic spot – the short-lived Russian protest movement of winter 2011 began here, with a spontaneous demonstration

The Mayakovsky statue, Moscow (1960s postcard)

against rigged elections.[6] Looking out from here you can see Moscow at its most despotic, where the Boulevard Ring charges forward, choked with traffic that is channelled below the square into an underpass, with the silhouette of a Gothic skyscraper in the distance. Its shape is mirrored by the Hotel Peking's deliberately oriental spire, a cousin of the Stalinist 'high buildings', which we will turn to later. To the south is a series of ever-more monumental apartment buildings, all with those great central archways, along both sides of the widened street. The little remnants of pre-Stalin Soviet architecture, like the Central Post Office, a combination of stark glass volumes, factory-style repetition and Art Deco ironwork, or the stern little block of the former Lenin Institute, the first constructed after his death in 1924, are completely dwarfed by the likes of the Mossovet building, a red-coloured structure that looks like a classical palazzo hoisted three storeys into the air by a rogue basement extension. It looks like that because that's what it is – originally of three storeys, it was designed in 1782 by Matvei Kazakov as the residence of Moscow's governor-general; in the revolutionary period, it became the headquarters of the Moscow Soviet of Workers' and Soldiers' Deputies. In 1937–8 it

The stretched classicism of Mossovet (1955 postcard)

was moved back from the street 14 metres and given a new extension; then in 1946 the architect Dmitry Chechulin added two storeys below the portico, which was raised into the air. It isn't the only building to have been warped and transformed in the change from Tverskaya to Gorky Street – an early-1930s Modernist block of flats by Nikolai Ladovsky was consumed in a few years into a block by Mordvinov, the main designer of the street.

Mordvinov's (re)designs are full of details which are intended to catch the eye of the pedestrian – arches and pediments on the ninth storey frame little balconies, reliefs of sheaves of wheat decorate the top floors, and those rugged rusticated ground floors are there to give an impression of immensity. But what happens when you walk through one of those archways? Pick the one leading to Bryusa Pereulok (Bryusa Lane), and you find that those giant blocks of flats are extremely thin, and past them the giant scale completely disappears. From this side, they look like fragments of a different city altogether. Next to the arch is the crooked spire of a small Orthodox chapel, next to that some more one-storey classical houses, rendered in pastel blues and oranges, and opposite a four-storey, vaguely Modernist apartment block of the 1920s, housing the former living quarters of the great theatre director Vsevolod Meyerhold (now an expensive, mildly disappointing house-museum). Adolf Loos called the original *Ringstrasse* in Vienna a 'Potemkinstadt', and one wonders what he would have made of this.

Keep going south and Tverskaya curves towards Red Square and the hulking buildings fail to follow the curve with any great skill; but the transition is heralded by several particularly authoritarian buildings of the Stalin era. The Gosplan HQ, a squat, truncated skyscraper like an Art Deco building without the glitz, and Alexey Shchusev's similarly wide, symmetrical and pompous 1935 Hotel Moskva, famous from the Stolichnaya bottles – or, rather, a reconstructed 2010 version of the Hotel Moskva, the original of which was demolished allegedly so that a new car park could be constructed underneath, a reminder of the Byzantine levels of corruption and wastefulness in the latter-day Russian capital. The reconstruction took off the Soviet symbols but retained the most notorious thing about the Hotel Moskva – the two differently decorated side façades, which were supposedly produced by Stalin carelessly signing off both when he was presented with two possible blueprints. Fork left at

'Potemkin city': Bryusa Lane, Moscow

this point, rather than continuing towards the Kremlin, and you find 1960s monuments to Marx and Engels – angular, granite, slightly cubistic – facing the Bolshoi Theatre, and the Art Nouveau Hotel Metropol, whose decorative display was an obvious source for the new Tverskaya (though perhaps not its light scent of opiated, fin-de-siècle decadence). In the ground floor, another plaque, this time to the hotel's pivotal role in Moscow's part in the October Revolution. Classical Socialist Realism in miniature, a relief of striving workers, guns in hand, waving red flags. A few yards after that, the Lubyanka.

Like many of the buildings along Tverskaya itself, the Lubyanka is a drastic remodelling of an existing building, doubled in height and increased in length; the redesign, as old photographs make clear, involved changing a commercial Baroque building, with naughtily lacy ornament, into a Renaissance one, classical but 'tasteful'. The result is chilling. Even if you didn't know what it was, or know about the nearly countless people who were held, tortured and 'liquidated' here, or if you didn't read the small (and rare) monument to its victims in front of it, the building's fearsome nature is expressed amply. Like the Hotel Moskva it was (re)designed in the early 1950s by Soviet architecture's great chameleon, Alexey Shchusev, who we will find several times along this journey. All the devices used along Tverskaya – the rusticated bases, the tiered organization, the decorative details borrowed from the Italian Cinquecento – are made much tighter, arranged into a composition rather than just a vague mass of motifs. The details are highlighted in deep, resonant and unusual colours – a warm pink, a burnished yellow. A wide square gives you plenty of space to contemplate it. The eye is drawn to the windowless top floor, leading to the small but unmistakable sword-and-shield insignia of the secret police at the top. The building is, incidentally, still used by its current incarnation, the FSB. In front, there is a tiny monument which you can easily miss, dedicated to the inmates of the Gulag – a stone from the Solovetsky Islands.[7]

Leave Tverskaya Metro station in the other direction, away from Red Square, and the street eventually becomes the even wider and more monumental Leningradsky Boulevard, the main approach from Sheremetyevo airport. Its traffic is fittingly monolithic, so if you're travelling by car, you will get a *lot* of time to look at it. The blocks are bigger and bigger, topped by spires and more spires, iced with neo-Renaissance detail, to the point where it eventually becomes quite numbing. But much as the 1930s show the relative informality of the 1920s being bashed around and stiffened up, this stretch of the boulevard shows the opposite, with neo-Baroque order dissolving into the informal groupings of late

Modernism. What you learn here is that, even in the Soviet Union, the urge to provide a singular, unbroken image of linear power could not last – another urge, to break it up and provide counterpoints and contradictions, came in instead. Two blocks almost facing each other here make clear how people struggled to find ways out. Rather than walking all the way up this interminable magistrale, which by this point is broken up with flyovers and impassable to pedestrians, it is best reached from Dynamo Metro station, where those with an interest both in football and 1920s avant-garde architecture could once enjoy the laconic Constructivism of the original Dynamo Moscow stadium.[8]

One of these two break-out structures is a block of flats from the late 1930s by Andrey Burov. The architect had been a Modernist, a collaborator of Sergei Eisenstein, an epigone and guide in Moscow to Le Corbusier. You wouldn't know from the ornament draped on this building. But look closely, and you'll notice something new. Rather than being 'applied' by plasterer or sculptor, these ornaments – trees with intertwining branches, small architectural emblems of Renaissance derivation in

The New Brutalist 'Centipede', Moscow

'marble' – are visibly mass-produced. They were in fact prefabricated, panels of precast concrete assembled in a factory. This is the first prefab housing block in Moscow, the first of very, very many, a new approach which would create a very different symbolic space to city centre neoclassical boulevards. Opposite is a residential complex, by a team of architects led by A. Meerson. It is, conversely, one of a kind – the only actual 'New Brutalist' building in a city habitually described as Brutalist and brutalizing. Completed in 1978, it borrows forms from late Le Corbusier and from Japanese architects like Kenzo Tange, to create an image of repetition, physicality and collectivity. A long block of raw, poured, board-marked concrete has its considerable weight supported on multiple thin, twisted limbs, which garnered the building the nickname 'the Centipede'. Bulging, heavy tubes of lift towers are placed rhythmically along the façade. It stands at an angle to the long street, as if to avoid it, wanting to define its own space rather than being swept up into someone else's. It must have looked peculiar during the parades.

'EUROPE'S LAST GREAT STREETS'

Tverskaya, and even more its northward extension, is exhausting. The expanse of space created by land nationalization and glorified for the purpose of military display feels dusty, worn, tiring, even claustrophobic in its gridlocked traffic. Not all magistrale are like this, it must be noted – least of all the street which is perhaps the most impressive of all the Stalinist boulevards I have come across in person or in history, one which the Italian architect and historian Aldo Rossi called 'Europe's last great street'.[9] This is Karl-Marx-Allee, or, as it was originally known, Stalinallee, in East Berlin. Politically, this exceptionally loaded place was where the proletariat as image and as reality suffered its greatest disjunction.

A little history will be useful; history which the street, and not only by its information boards in English and German, will be able to tell you itself. This was originally Frankfurter Allee, Berlin's main east–west thoroughfare, running through the inner-city working class district of Friedrichshain, and the route by which the Red Army fought its way into the city in 1945. After the war, it became part of what (then still unified) Berlin's avant-garde city planner Hans Scharoun called the 'Friedrichshain

Living Cell'.[10] Small, undemonstrative four-storey deck-access apartment blocks were built in the interstices of the destroyed city, spaced out widely between strips of parkland; some of them faced Frankfurter Allee itself, which soon, on the occasion of the despot's birthday, was renamed 'Stalinallee'. Scharoun was dismissed, and the new Stalinallee was reimagined as a magistrale – and if the magistrale had always had the look of an imperial 'Via Triumphalis', then here there was a very actual triumph to be commemorated: the defeat of Nazi Germany, largely at the hands of the Red Army. Just next to the 'Living Cell', a prototype was built, a small housing estate built around a tower block, the Hochhaus an der Weberwiese, designed by a Modernist who had recently executed the requisite self-criticism, Hermann Henselmann. These blocks were harder up against the street, onto which looked balconies and clear, obvious front doors; corner features were picked out as towers and copulas. Sculptural reliefs, some in ceramic tile, showed frolicking children and marching workers, framed by the Brandenburg Gate and the bulbous towers of the Gendarmenmarkt. The tower itself was symmetrical, and tricked out in Meissen tiles, with stern black columns to the entrance.

Workers and domes: detail on the estate on Weberwiese, Berlin

This new style would be taken up completely just round the corner at Frankfurter Allee/Stalinallee. The street was widened, and widened far further than the relatively modest dimensions of Tverskaya; and it was divided into several immense blocks, most of them given to repentant Modernists to design, such as the former Bauhaus student Richard Paulick. Specially designed lampposts, where fluted, winged concrete poles carried twin bulbs, were planted all along the triumphal route, inescapably compared unkindly to suspiciously similar ones designed by Albert Speer for Hitler's own Via Triumphalis, the would-be centre of the imperial capital Germania. Yet while Germania was to be in a pure, reduced form of classicism, supposedly devoid of kitsch, Stalinallee was kitsch run riot: decorations scattered everywhere, as if the result of a ram-raid on a Prussian builders' yard, draped across blocks of surreal proportions – a typical chunk of Stalinallee is a single block of eight storeys and fifty bays, broken up via projecting wings. At each end of the magistrale are ceremonial gateway twin towers, both by Henselmann – one pair in a striking classical-Futurist idiom recalling the famous Soviet pavilion in the

The twin towers of the Frankfurter Tor, Berlin

1937 Paris Expo, with stone volumes progressively rising and projecting forward – and the other pair basically a stretching out of the eighteenth-century Baroque domes of the Gendarmenmarkt. Welcome to Berlin, 'Capital of World Communism'.

Except there was another half of Berlin under the joint control of the British, French and American armies, and they had their own building projects, whose informality and modernity more closely resembled Hans Scharoun's original Living Cells. A Dutch historian has recently slightly fancifully claimed that the West's ridicule of the grandiosity of the magistrale came from fear – not fear at the totalitarian dystopia it represented, but fear of its possible success. 'They feared Socialist Realism because of what it was: a very rich popular style that symbolised the successful emancipation of the common man.'[11] That's as may be, but the common man in East Berlin had other things on his mind in 1953, as the Stalinallee neared completion. As in many Stalinist projects, 'Stakhanovism' and 'shock-work' were enforced, by which workers were encouraged, pressured, cajoled and given wage scales to encourage them to overfulfil their norms, and to work ever harder and longer hours. This evidently didn't have the desired effect, as on 17 June 1953 the workers on Stalinallee had their minimum norms suddenly raised. They responded with strikes, then with riots, then with a generalized, uncoordinated uprising, suppressed by Soviet tanks. This was the first (and last) major workers' protest of the new German Democratic Republic. In Bertolt Brecht's famous lines, not of course published in the GDR, this created the absurd situation where the East German Party declared that it had lost confidence in the German working class. The striking workers were looked down on throughout their protest by reliefs, sculptures and mosaics of themselves, joyously relishing the heroic building work that they were now rebelling against. The Stalinallee, quietly renamed Karl-Marx-Allee a few years later, is by its very existence an indictment of the vainglory, hypocrisy and dubious claims to 'socialism' of the Soviet-backed state.

But I will not even attempt to deny that every time I have visited it I've found it hugely exhilarating. The width of the tree-lined pavements, the quality of the materials (all of it, typically for Berlin, is listed, preserved and scrupulously restored), the generosity of the public spaces, the bizarre, eye-catching, sometimes moving details on the buildings, the general sense of ease, openness and metropolitan grandeur – it doesn't seem at all hyperbolic to call it 'Europe's last great street', at least not if Marszałkowska in Warsaw and the Kreschatyk in Kiev are included in the same bracket. That's partly because of the embrace of all the functions of the grand capital-city boulevard that it borrows from Paris – with the shade of trees, the cafés, bookshops and benches, managing to turn what is really a six-lane highway into what feels like a single public square, extruded out and plunging towards the heart of the city. Everything in it is designed to catch the eye, whether of driver or, more probably, of pedestrian. The shops in the ground floors have neon signs (many of them salvaged from the GDR, and not always describing what is inside – the Karl-Marx-Bookshop was recently turned into the offices of a hipster art publisher, who kept the sign), sculptures and plaques (whether the original monuments to Marx and the East German leader Wilhelm Pieck, or the new information boards that tell the street's story) . . . all turn it into a sort of open-air exhibition, albeit one which never feels like a museum, either – it remains a living piece of public space, co-ordinated by those two pairs of framing towers. I don't know to what extent it was a real propaganda success in divided Berlin – the Wall built a year after its completion in 1960 would suggest the effect was not spectacular – but, today, it speaks of a socialism with real generosity and grandeur, all its hierarchical features subordinated to the rule of the public's footsteps. I can't imagine Jane Jacobs and her disciples approving entirely – it is too wide to be a 'real' traditional street or boulevard, with crossing the street never an easy task – but it does reclaim the idea of the street at a time when it was in major abeyance at the hands of Modernism, and does so in a surprisingly convincing way.

It continues to do this, curiously, after its architects junk neoclassical detail and traditional street plans cleaving to the street line, and return to Modernist verities. After 1960, the (now renamed) Karl-Marx-Allee was continued all the way to the showpiece public square of Alexanderplatz,[12] in the form of unornamented blocks of flats, spaced well back behind trees and gardens, which continued behind them – classic Modernist 'blocks in space' urbanism. Yet its planners and architects were smart enough to realize the value of the street structure they had been left by the Stalinists. Their new structures are 'street' buildings, while not being at all classical. One of them, the Kosmos cinema, actually replaced Richard Paulick's neoclassicist Sports Hall, built as part of the original Stalinallee

The Modernist Karl-Marx-Allee, Berlin (1969 postcard)

barely a decade earlier – an astonishing rate of replacement, dictated here perhaps by the unambiguously Nazi appearance of this stripped classical edifice. In its place is a rotunda with a low cubic volume projecting from it, clad in multicoloured tiles framing large glass walls, with a square in front, onto which tables and chairs spill out – an open, delicately detailed piece of architecture. More dramatic is the same architects' Kino International, the façades of its vaulting windowless concrete auditorium decorated in what are this time slightly less domineering images of progress and labour. Opposite that, meanwhile, is the Cafe Moskau, a striking, witty and clever architectural tribute to East Germany's liberator-oppressor. Like the rest of the complex, it recognizes the importance for the street of looking and loitering, giving the eye a lot to do. It is another long glass box, its façade giving way at the corner entrance to a patterned concrete screen, giving a view of the restaurant courtyard inside; next to that is a mosaic, showing the various Soviet peoples and their then-familiar achievements in agriculture, industry, universal brotherhood and outer space. A model sputnik acts as spire. Scattered elsewhere along the street are several small glass boxes, the new,

Modernist boulevard's shops, no longer included on the ground floor of the apartments. It all gives the impression of a continuous space that just happens to be broken up into two competing stylistic camps – both of them a matter of no-expense-spared public space and public housing. There is not really a better case to be made for the German Democratic Republic than the fact it built this. It did so, though, in the awareness that here it was being watched, especially after the crushing of the workers' protests. Not all of East Berlin, needless to say, was of the same quality.

A MAGISTRALE IN REVOLUTION

Another boulevard that feels 'successful' today, that is a viable public space rather than just a despotic folly, is the Kreschatyk in Kiev. This, like the Stalinallee, is another 'Via Triumphalis', a complete redesign of the Ukrainian capital's main artery after it was destroyed during the Great Patriotic War (largely, in this case, by the Red Army mining its buildings after they were forced to withdraw in 1941). As architecture, it remains an almost complete showcase of Stalinist aesthetics and its paradoxical preference for 'street' life. It would be possible to argue that the street life of the average magistrale is a side effect, an unintended by-product of the intention to create an awe-inspiring parade path for tanks and such; but if so, it'd be hard to explain all the wide pavements, trees, benches and archways, which give the Kreschatyk much of its appeal. Yet while Berlin's magistrale is conspicuously non-commercial, with little on sale in those ground floor shops but sundries for its mixed population of hipsters and ageing Party diehards, the Kreschatyk spent the 1990s and 2000s awash with New Money – reclaimed by the nomenklatura in their new function as private capitalists. However, it has often been taken over for by other, more unruly, uses. It was exactly this area – the Kreschatyk, the nearby government buildings on Hrushevsky Street and Maidan Nezalezhnosti (Independence Square, usually shortened to just 'Maidan'), all of them grand projects of the Stalin era – where the violent insurrection that overthrew president Viktor Yanukovych in early 2014 occurred. This is of course ironic, given that this sort of planning originated in Haussmann's means of deterring revolution.

Beginning at the early-twentieth-century Besarabsky Market, Kreschatyk sweeps through Kiev's historic centre with a prickly skyline of spires and obelisks, with façades coated in decorative tiles, to a 1949 design by the architect Anatoly Dobrovolsky. It was created as the showpiece of a capital city – at the time Stalin was trying to get a UN seat for Soviet Ukraine.[13] In the plans, the boulevard led to a two-level square, one side ringed by a circus of neo-Baroque office buildings, the other marked by a skyscraping luxury hotel – the centrifugal arrangement similar to one of the clearest of Haussmann's free-fire zones, the Place de la République. Under Khrushchev, the square was left half finished and some buildings were completed on the cheap – the mega-hotel, now the Hotel Ukraina, was built without the planned pinnacles and spires, and the circus wasn't finished until the early 1980s, when it was accompanied by a Lenin Museum and the Trade Union House, both in a sharper, modernized version of classicism. The square's main monument, as ever, was a massive granite Lenin, flanked by revolutionaries, as a memorial to the October 1917 insurrection. If Haussmann wanted to stop revolution, Stalin and his successors constantly appealed to its memory. At Maidan Nezalezh-

The Kreschatyk meets October Revolution Square in Kiev (1979 postcard)

nosti Metro station, there are bronze plaques on the walls dedicated to 1917, a remnant from when it was October Revolution Square station. When we made our way out of the station on our third visit to the city, in March 2014, half of the exits were still blocked by barricades made from tyres, sandbags, paving stones and furniture. Outside was the aftermath of a real urban insurrection.

The renamed 'Maidan' had already lost its Lenin in 1991, and was redeveloped in 2001 under the regime of Leonid Kuchma with kitsch new statues and decorations which evoke equally the high-Stalinist era and eighteenth-century Ukrainian Baroque; the gesture to the twenty-first century was the Globus shopping mall underneath, whose glass domes pop out at random over the square, products of when this became Ukraine's Regent Street, its thoroughfare of expensive chains. In 2004 it became the centre of the smaller, controlled 'Orange Revolution' against electoral fraud, when a tent city was set up on Maidan. We hadn't visited Kiev between March 2011 and March 2014, so it was astonishing how different Maidan looked a month after the insurrection. Pedestrian

The transformed Maidan seen from Kreschatyk, Kiev, spring 2014

pathways ran through encampments and barricades four feet high. The ground was charred, with the paving stones unreplaced, armoured cars blared out rousing songs, a stage was taken by an Orthodox priest. A tall frame around one of the kitsch monuments installed in 2001 had become a frame for posters, banners, slogans and information; and, most obvious of all, the Trade Union House, occupied by the revolutionaries and set on fire, very likely by the police, was a charred husk, the greater number of its windows blown out. McDonald's, which became a makeshift mental hospital at the close of the protests, had become a McDonald's again, our friends noted with regret. The Globus mall, we were told, had stayed open throughout.

Coming in, as we did, from the Kreschatyk, the change from the ordinary city to this was more subtle. Walking down the nineteenth-century Taras Shevchenko Boulevard, the turn into the Kreschatyk is clear when you find the plinth of the Lenin statue toppled by members of the far-right Svoboda party in December 2013, sprayed with graffiti either in cryptic, esoteric far-right symbols or with the more obvious 'glory to Ukraine'. The Kreschatyk is interrupted after one street block by tents and surviving barricades in front of towering Stalinist castles. These are astonishing structures, among the most flamboyant of their kind. Half-way along the street is one of two skyscrapers placed in strategic places, but unlike the Hotel Ukraina this one was completed to its original plan, with twenty or so storeys and a rising profile reminiscent of the dystopian cities of pre-war comic books. It is flanked by two bloated Beaux Arts mini-towers (in the corner, a luxury Modernist tower of the 2000s has been discreetly squeezed). Grand flights of steps march their way up to them. The bulk of the buildings are residential, with a post office and Kiev's City Hall among them, and they're not greatly dissimilar to those of Tverskaya. However, the architects have had a great deal more fun, if that's the word, within the parameters of bureaucrat's Baroque. There are rusticated bases again, along the long, columned apartment complexes, and there is even more detail in strange, eye-craning places than usual. Unlike the High Renaissance itself, Baroque was not generally acceptable under the architectural strictures of the 1930s–1950s, representing an era of decadence and reaction, the aesthetics of the Counter-Reformation. Never mind that, though, as this is a purely Baroque space, in detail and in plan. On those upper storeys you find applied columns twisted into weird, scaled shapes, ending in little spikes; in the lofts of some of the flats are thick, ceremonial, sculptural leaves, which look, in the manner of Rococo architectural follies, almost edible; on the top of the skyscraper is a pediment, with another pediment in relief inside that.

Under these are the obligatory grand archways leading to the less

Barricades and the Stalinist Baroque in Kiev, spring 2014

impressive sidestreets. On our first visits to Kiev in 2010 and 2011, these had become typically ultra-capitalist spaces; one of the arches, three storeys high, was decorated by an LG advertisement, arranged to follow the curve of the arch, reading 'Life's Good', in English. Other ads and new signs found their way onto the boulevard, many of them working with the ceremonial spaces, using them as an appropriately eye-catching place to hang their slogans and logos. This was one of the peculiar aspects of the insurrection's first phase in late 2013, as a 'Euromaidan' – when the young protesters demanded to become a 'normal' part of Europe, they were marching down a street bedecked in giant canvas ads for West European companies, to a degree unthinkable in any West European street. Regardless, by March 2014 these grand archways were blocked with tyres rather than bedecked with billboards, Kiev City Hall was caked in graffiti, and occupying a travel agent next to a branch of Oggi was the far-right paramilitary alliance Pravy Sektor. Souvenir sellers were taking up what space wasn't taken by barricades and tents; they were selling postcard sets of scenes from the insurrection, national flags, magnets of some rather

A blocked archway in Kiev, spring 2014

dubious historical figures. A man in a pink bunny suit went round selling similar trinkets, walking casually past the men in fatigues with their hair made up in Cossack style (shaved with a long flick of fringe, a rather New Romantic look). The overall effect was of a slightly farcical nationalist carnival, a reclamation of the space of one 'totalitarianism', Stalinism, for another, fascism – which, due to the straitened circumstances of the participants, looked more like a desperate encampment than a unified, choreographed rally. This was partly also dictated by their use of the space, in which they actually resisted rather than embraced its urban authoritarianism, at the same time that they used its arches, steps and passageways as useful means for barricading and defending.

The movement itself is usually called 'Maidan', and its opponents were known as the 'Anti-Maidan'. One could argue that this reflected the importance of the reclaimed public space to the protesters, all of whom, whether in Kiev or in the counter-protests in south-eastern Ukrainian cities like Donetsk, Kharkiv or Odessa, favoured large Soviet squares. It also marks an absence of political content other than a (surely justified) hatred of eastern Ukrainian oligarchs and Vladimir Putin. The far right proved highly adept at filling that vacuum. This was blindingly obvious when we visited Maidan, and although it might be unfair to judge 'Maidan' as a movement on its aftermath, when Russia's annexation of Crimea had exacerbated tension, the political content of what we saw was not pretty. There were some posters calling for peace, many of the national poet and revolutionary Taras Shevchenko, a few anarchist symbols and one image of Mayakovsky, with the speech bubble 'Comrade *Moskal* [a derogatory term for Russian], leave Ukraine alone!' – but they were overwhelmingly outnumbered by the symbols of the extreme right. At Maidan, next to the stage, a banner displayed the visage of Stepan Bandera, whose Organization of Ukrainian Nationalists (OUN(B)) and Ukrainian Insurgent Army (UPA) were an openly fascist partisan force during and after the Second World War; their red and black colours were ubiquitous.[14] The effect, with all these tents in the shadow of massive ultra-urban buildings, was as if the protesters were replicating the wartime partisan camps in rural western Ukraine, from where most of them had come, in the metropolitan streets and squares of Kiev.

Yet according to our friends here – admittedly a bunch of intelligentsia: an unemployed architect, a journalist and architectural historian, an art student and a documentary film-maker, all of them participants in Maidan, all of the left – what we saw was one of many Maidans, which shifted from a middle-class revolt to a mass popular uprising – 'at first it was all these people who wanted to be in the EU, and then it was like the Middle Ages.' When we were there, the air of menace created by the armed presence of the far right contrasted with a memorial, even festive spirit – at the weekend, countless ordinary people were casually walking around Kreschatyk and Maidan, squeezing through the barricades either to leave flowers at the memorial to the hundred protesters killed by snipers, or just to look at this transformation.

Looking out at Maidan from the Kreschatyk, you can see where the luxurious magistrale ran out of money, building by building. The boulevard curves, and is lined by five individual tower-like structures, all topped by an advertising billboard. As your eye travels along the row, you'll notice less ornament in each, until they have been entirely stripped, and eventually become something more rectilinear and modern. Keep turning round, and you find the Hotel Ukraina, from where many of the snipers were firing. Fulsome with imperial trimmings in the original drawings, it was trimmed of almost all ornament under Khrushchev, who wanted to use materials and labour for less whimsical purposes than grand hotels in a ruined city with a housing crisis. Yet while East German architects responded to this change by returning to their spurned Modernist roots, and created sparkling, light spaces, here the heaviness remained, as if architects had forgotten there was any other way of designing. Stripped of the eye-fascinating proliferation of details, sculptures, mosaics and applied columns, all there was left was a reductive, thuggish power and scale.[15]

At the end of Kreschatyk, the Hotel Dnipro, another of these stripped Stalinist buildings, faces the later Ukrainian House, the former Lenin Museum. This, our friends here told us, was always the best part of the revolution, the place where the Maidan Left organized, its rotunda enclosing a shelter, a library, a university and a cinema – with spectacular stained-glass images of revolution above, and a real revolt below. 'I'd always hoped to see it like that', the architect Oleksandr Burlaka told us.[16] While he did so, it was full of armed, armband-wearing men. 'It's gone very Stanford Experiment in there, they're setting up their own little totalitarian state.' Opposite in the Hotel Dnipro, until they were forcibly evicted by police on Monday night, after a shooting spree in which they had shot and injured Kiev's deputy mayor, was another encampment of Pravy Sektor. Next to that was a pile of paving stones ready to replace those removed. The graffiti – the *Wolfsangel*, or numerical symbols referring to Hitler's date of birth – told its own story.

At this point, the steep Hrushevsky Street begins, leading to the sinister, ultra-Stalinist Ministry of Foreign Affairs and the parliament, both scenes of heavy fighting. The colonnade leading to the Dynamo Kiev stadium was surrounded by the heaviest of the barricades and men in fatigues staring at fires. Opposite them, the week we visited, the Doric, austere Museum of Art had opened its doors for the first time since the battles caused it to close. The permanent collection features some spectacular work by the revolutionary avant-garde artists who supported the revolution of 1917, and a fair bit of Socialist Realism. In one epic painting of the Russian Civil War, Fedir Krychevskyi's 1935 canvas *Victors Over Wrangel*, the three unshaven, rough, ordinary-looking Red Army soldiers, one of them unassumingly rolling a cigarette, looked a lot like the Pravy Sektor members loitering just outside. At the entrance to the museum was the following message, in English and Ukrainian: 'We have fully realized the meaning of life and creativity as the transformation of the world and the human being through art, which was proclaimed by modern artists and which could have been observed during the last months in Kiev.' That is, what is happening outside is what they, the artists, had dreamed of. The architecture and planning may have had a similar effect – but the spectral, unreal masses imagined filling these spaces have, in reality, filled it with a very different content. The symbols of a social revolution nearly a century ago are now supplemented with those of a 'national revolution', the only sort that is acceptable in post-socialist countries. On the empty plinth of that toppled Lenin in Kiev, surrounded as it is by Stalinist spectacle and Ukrainian insurgent camps, is a quote from the Bolshevik leader: 'a free Ukraine is impossible without the unity of Russian and Ukrainian workers'. It's almost obscured by the scrawl, but it's there.

A HIPSTER MAGISTRALE

It is inconceivable that they wanted or expected them to be used for urban insurrection, but an important part of the rhetorical appeal made by the magistrale was the reclamation of the city centre for the working class. The large 1954 commemorative volume produced for the Marszałkowska-MDM scheme in Warsaw begins with a poem by Adam Ważyk, 'The People Return to the City Centre'. It is anachronistic to assume this means that 'The People' are returning from their exile in the towers and semis of the suburbs, although this would become an issue later on, in Warsaw as with most European cities. They are returning to the city centre because the city centre – most of the city, in fact – was burned to the ground by its Nazi German occupiers after the suppression of the Warsaw Rising in 1944, so, until the early 1950s, there wasn't a city centre to return to. For that, within a decade or so this element of Socialist Realist practice would become something quite unusual – the use or transformation of high-rent, prestigious or otherwise important inner-urban space as ordinary, low-rent housing. In their avoidance of this, later socialist regimes in Poland were not unusual, building their large estates mostly on the periphery.

So rather than just another boulevard, MDM was also a deliberately residential space – its full name in Polish, Marszałkowska Dzielnica Mieszkaniowa, means the Marszałkowska Residential District. It is built along the line of another devastated pre-war street, and again it blows its scale apart, to create the requisite space for parading and/or marching. But it embraces in the same scheme many of the surrounding streets, pulling them into a unified, axial composition. Although it is not 'officially' part of MDM, instructive contrasts are provided by the start of the street Plac Unii Lubelskiej, the only entirely surviving pre-war part of Marszałkowska. It is a roundabout overlooked by turn-of-the-century tenements, built around the time that Warsaw reached a million residents, becoming the third-largest city in the Tsarist Empire after St Petersburg and Moscow. These reach nine storeys, and are commanding, though also eclectic and confused in their details, as if they're trying to disguise their bulk. Behind them are dense courtyards, following the typical nineteenth-century model, maximizing the space that could be let.

Their scale is impressive, either way, but in a different fashion from a magistrale – there has obviously been no co-ordination between them. They follow the contours of an already created space, they do not create it.

Another notable feature of the MDM propaganda volume is a figure-ground plan of Warsaw's city centre in 1939, and the same city centre as it 'will be' in 1965. 'The new Warsaw will not repeat the old', reads the slogan, and in this there is an obvious intent to make something more than just a cosmetic change in the look of the city, instead to transform the exploitation visible in the 1939 plan, where the map is almost black through the density of the buildings outlined therein, to something more airy and open, where the streets are still outlined but the space behind is left blank and clear, ready to be filled with parks and gardens. Short shrift is given to the 'capitalist city' in the book. Facing pages show the street as a typical piece of turn-of-the-century East European big city urbanism, lined with eclectic buildings, and then they show you the dilapidated, collapsing, quasi-rural buildings that still existed next to them – 'the great artery of the capitalist city of contrasts'. On the facing page is an image of Plac Unii Lubelskiej itself, described as 'the cheapness of the ugly, cosmopolitan street'. The lack of planning is obvious, as a strange collection of buildings, from one-storey classical gatehouses to ten-storey tenements, fail to command the roundabout; the force of the argument is reinforced with a big quote from Bolesław Bierut, general secretary, local 'little Stalin' and official author of the *Six-Year Plan for the Rebuilding of Warsaw*. Other possible alternatives that were around after the war are subjected to ridicule – under a photograph of a model for the area entered into a 1948 competition, showing four cylindrical towers and long, open, mid-rise Modernist blocks in open space, we are told that these 'house-machines' are intrinsically capitalist – rather inexplicably, as they 'waste' a lot of lettable space. 'No, this is not how we will build Marszałkowska!'

How they did build Marszałkowska can be found slightly further on, as blocks that are not familiar begin their march along the boulevard. Here, they are still slightly interspersed with earlier apartment buildings, either in eclectic or in Modernist dress, so the total sweep has not occurred – unsurprisingly, given the extent of the wartime damage, there is some retention of what survived, so that there is actually quite a bit of patched nineteenth-century fabric to be found behind the grand façades. The architectural team at MDM, led by Józef Sigalin, didn't break much with the magistrale model in their architectural vocabulary. This is plaster and a thin layer of marble or granite applied to brick and concrete, with the tiered order of classicism (bases, attics and so forth) stretched out to an overscaled degree. There are differences – the spikiness of the specially designed streetlights is a deliberate reference to the local Baroque tradition, for instance. At one point it becomes a bridge, as a highway runs underneath, and a curved corner tower defines the change in space. The street is not massively wide at this point, and some of the buildings

Baroque lamps on Constitution Square, Warsaw (1955 postcard)

compensate for this by setting themselves back behind large pavements, with steps leading up to the flats, creating the requisite sense of pride and importance. After a while of this, you get to another roundabout, and a big and pretty wild nineteenth-century Baroque church, tall, with twisted copper spires, typically 'Slavic' in its eldritch presence. It had mostly survived the war, battered but intact, and there are various myths about the preservation of this church, principal among them the claim that Marszałkowska was realigned when it was rebuilt into MDM to remove the terminating role of the church, shifting it out of sight to the pedestrian or driver going up the boulevard. Actually, the streetplan of this part of MDM is of completely the same dimensions as the pre-war one, but the story's existence shows some of the low esteem the plan is held in, and for what potential reasons. St Saviour's Church is the main monument of Plac Zbawiciela, or Saviour Square – the name was also not changed.

Agata met me here when she first took me to the city, knowing I'd be impressed. Plac Zbawiciela became one of the first places I got to know in Warsaw, as I suspect it has been for many other Western visitors and expats – students and hipsters started reclaiming this space a good while ago, with bars and clubs like the noted Plan B having been here for a while; its uneasy status as the centre of young, open, tolerant Poland can be garnered by the frequent arson attacks on the large rainbow sculpture at its heart, which represents the (unusual, in Poland) tolerance here for LGBT people. Over the last few years I've watched this square gradually follow the usual pattern of hipster urbanism – first a neglected area is taken over via rough, noisy clubs and suchlike, and then money is attracted to the point where it starts forcing the artists, musicians and their ilk out of the area. The most obvious battleground is also the most obvious change in the square from its unplanned pre-war form to its Socialist Realist incarnation – its grandly scaled colonnades. This Italian Renaissance feature is used all over MDM. At Plac Konstytucji (Constitution Square), there are large, airy arcades on both sides, with coffering and heroic mosaics above, at the southern end of Marszałkowska they form slimmer spaces demarcated by free-style columns and monumental sculptures of workers, and here at Plac Zbawiciela they are more informal, neo-Renaissance spaces. In all cases they're lovely things, making total sense in the often inhospitable Warsaw climate – shelter both from hot summers and cold winters. Here, as intended, café and restaurant terraces spill out, and streetlife occurs in the requisite manner.

The circle that they were intended to form is incomplete – as in Kiev, the death of Stalin meant a scaling down, and two pre-war eclectic

Colonnades at MDM, Warsaw

Singed Gay Pride rainbow at Saviour Square, MDM, Warsaw

buildings were retained, one of them on the massive scale of Plac Unii Lubelskiej, one with the same four-storey scale as the Socialist Realist blocks. You can walk from one to another easily enough, and there is the rub – there is no obvious divide between the various commercial premises. At first, this was fairly informally marked out with thin little screens, but the recently arrived luxurious bars for the older, more genuinely moneyed part of the Warsaw middle class have started to glaze off their parts of the colonnades, putting glass walls between the wine bars and expensive restaurants and the shabbier spaces of Vietnamese restaurants and studenty cafés. Places where the non-customer could wander, linger and take shelter are privatized by these guardians of bourgeois civilization in the most blunt, barbaric way – a planned continuous space is bisected out of snobbery and greed. Bolesław Bierut would not have approved, and on this point it is hard not to agree with him.

That's not to forget the role of this place, as with Karl-Marx-Allee, in the displacement of actual workers' power with the image of powerful workers. It's even more the case here than in East Berlin, in fact, because the southern colonnades of Marszałkowska are lined with giant workers – miner, construction worker, textile worker, steelworker and more, all with the tools of their trade. They're enormous, displaying the peculiarly angular, reductive approach to anatomy and facial features typical of the time – giant, rugged faces made out of straight unbroken planes, granite cheekbones you could cut yourself on. The units within these colonnades are now luxury shops, their clientèle unperturbed by their inanimate proletarian neighbours. Follow this cyclopean sculpture gallery and you come to the real showpiece of MDM – Plac Konstytucji, Constitution Square, which commemorates the proclamation not of the first Polish Constitution in 1791 – an Enlightenment-inspired radical programme, only the second in the world after the USA – but of the Constitution of the Polish People's Republic. If the scale up till now has uneasily combined huge buildings and a street with a mere, piddling four lanes, now it suddenly opens into a wide, symmetrical plaza, framed by particularly huge neoclassical flats, and given, as with Karl-Marx-Allee, special gateway buildings to the street beyond. In fact, there isn't much beyond them to justify the gesture – Marszałkowska continues, but after two blocks the Stalinist overabundance of sgraffito, sculptures and mosaics is replaced with a more prosaic Modernist urbanism, here equally uneventful in both pre- and post-1989 form.

The gateway buildings are worth lingering over, because they depict Marszałkowska itself – its creation imaginatively, by architects, and its construction, by workers. You can't always see the sculptural reliefs, as this has become another space of giant canvas ads, that ubiquitous plague of contemporary East European urbanism: in over five years of regularly walking through and looking at this place, I have only once seen the Hotel MDM not covered by a giant canvas ad of some sort, usually for a car, sometimes for an item of clothing, sometimes for a mobile-phone company. But if you can get a look at the gateway unencumbered, you can admire the pointless features of 'Socialist' 'Classicism' (usually ignoring any previous notion of either), with its columns that hold up nothing, fluted and decorated according to the architects' own whims, rather than following historical precedent. Turn around here and survey the square and its colonnades, and there's something from a later era of socialist urbanism worth seeing – the proliferation of neon signs.

Affixed usually to the tops and the sides of buildings, these were produced en masse from the late 1950s on under Władysław Gomułka's post-Stalinist regime, all of them by the same body, the Reklama advertising company.[17] They are usually dismissed as a simulation of commerce in a country that had, at that point, no real 'consumerism' to speak of, but their individuality, imagination, flair and wit mark them out from the globalized canvas banners that are rolled out across this square, usually with only the Polish translation to distinguish them from the same ads on a billboard in any other city (though only east of the Oder–Neisse Line are they rolled out across hotels, offices and people's flats, blocking their windows). Trace your eye around the square at night, and the two you'll spot most are those at the tourist-oriented family restaurant U Szwejk (as in *The Good Soldier*), where appropriately heavy and hearty fare is signified by flashing puffs of smoke, billowing their way up the side of the building; or the Volleyball Player, a neon sign that once drew attention to a sports shop but now sits on its own as an artwork, the woman's red and yellow neon outline paid for via a project by the painter Paulina Ołowska. Rather than seeing these (plausibly enough) as a form of longing for the joys of capitalist advertisement, their neighbouring the banality of real capitalist imagery suggests that they pointed to something more interesting, the use of urban space – even urban space as heavy and weighty as this – as the canvas for experiments in kinetic art, in writing and drawing in light. In Warsaw, designers after Stalinism found their own way to modernity, on their own terms; the comprador capitalism of contemporary Poland is evidently unable to do so. That doesn't mean that they're dead, however – the newer bars in Plac Zbawiciela have taken to commissioning their own retro-Modernist neon signs, although it stays at the level of nostalgia, dwarfed by the contributions of Volvo and T-Mobile.

MDM is more than just the magistrale of Marszałkowska – several streets, like Waryńskiego, Mokotowska, Wyzwolenia, are pulled into it, and they initially spread out from Plac Zbawiciela and Plac Konstytucji in the same style. In the last-built parts, the monumentality is becoming homelier, with Eleonora Sekrecka's 'MDM 3' drawing closer to eighteenth-century French classicism, featuring mansard roofs, light colours and pretty, spreading trees with benches underneath. There are sculptures to be found here also. On Waryńskiego there's a group showing an actual march on the magistrale, the people of Warsaw heralding the building of MDM with flags and flowers, unveiled on the date in 1952 that the first buildings here were completed – depicting an event that had not actually happened at the time the relief was sculpted. Evidently they were sure there would be no surprises. Peer around the back of these places, look round the corners of the non-boulevard parts of MDM, and you find that the open promise of 'City Centre in 1965' was not kept, and that many older tenement blocks survive, sometimes cut off by war or redevelopment from the grander frontages they were originally connected to. These survived because they were given early on to secret policemen and other especially privileged groups, especially in the cluster of 1930s Modernist flats down a cul-de-sac in Ulica Jaworzyńska. Actual workers, labourers, did get housed in MDM – those who performed especially impressive feats of socialist labour, those who overfulfilled the norm, would see the state fulfil its side of the bargain, giving them flats in which they could daily take in the splendour they themselves had created. Some of 'The People', though, were clearly more important.

BOULEVARDS AGAINST THE BAROQUE

As planning and architecture after Stalin got further and further away from these spectacular Potemkin cities, did it also abandon the embrace of the grand street as the privileged place of power and city life? Not entirely. There are scattered magistrale that were executed in an entirely Modernist idiom – and at least one which uses Modernism's taste for repetition to create abstracted vistas every bit as powerful and authoritarian. Modernists of the interwar period have, as we've noticed, become pejorative for their hostility to the street. For Jonathan Raban, in his justly classic account of Southampton, London and Boston, *Soft City*, the totalitarian aspirations of Le Corbusier are encapsulated in the slogan from *The Radiant City*, 'We must kill the street.' Kill the street, Raban writes, 'and one cuts out the heart of cities as they are actually used and lived in'.[18] The magistrale, and its many less enormous cousins in Eastern Bloc cities, make it clear enough that states with more than just totalitarian aspirations were actually deeply attracted to the street's propensity for spectacle and display. The street is to be killed for various reasons. Raban suggests that it's because of its unpredictability, its tendency to riot and riotousness; Le Corbusier himself would have argued that the street had to be killed because it was noisy, dangerous (think of how many children living on MDM or Karl-Marx-Allee must have been killed wandering onto those multi-lane highways so close to their doorsteps), and it produced a dubious typology, the front-and-back tenement, where the deeper inside you went, the more grim and cheap the flats, and the less light or air there was. The fatwah on the street was extreme, even among Le Corbusier's contemporaries – Erich Mendelsohn in particular produced superb street architecture, all dramatic corners and neon lights – but another, slightly earlier version of his credo was commonly accepted: 'we must kill the corridor street', the street in its narrowest, murkiest form.

Boulevard planners could get behind that – 'slum clearance' was always their rationale. But before the war, there were a few quasi-modernist boulevards, spaces that took over the form inherited from the nineteenth century, applying the new abstracted style to it. One of these was a tabula rasa produced under Piłsudski's dictatorship in interwar Poland – Ulica 10 Lutego (10 February Street) in the newly created port of Gdynia. Close to the then Free City of Danzig, it was aimed at creating a politically reliable entrepôt in the thin 'Polish corridor' carved out of East Prussia for that purpose by the Treaty of Versailles. Hence, it was ideologically loaded, although in a lighter, more optimistic way than was common either under Stalinism or under Piłsudski's interwar police state. All it needed to signify was that Poland was modern, and was capable of building a port. It does these two things in some style. Now it's a boulevard one part 1930s and one part 1960s, and the differences between the two are very apparent – though, unusually, here of equal quality. The street starts near the railway station with several offices which make obvious reference to the town's status as port – continuous ribbon windows, generous curves in white-painted concrete. This is Modernism in Erich Mendelsohn's version, defining the street via features stressing its linearity and sharp corner turns. It's luxury of a different kind from the post-war magistrale, something much more deliberately contemporary and bourgeois, the comfort and raffish modernity of a 1930s ocean liner rather than the bloated historical mishmash that apparently defined 'proletarian' luxury. Post-Stalinist Poland continued the boulevard in the 1960s, at the point where it actually forms a short, thin peninsula, jutting out into the Baltic.

The difference is marked where the street reaches a fountain-as-abstract-sculpture, and then becomes a plunge straight into the sea. The sense of space is breathtaking – the openness, the sea air. The buildings flanking either side of the pedestrianized boulevard are Modernist also, though in a later, more expressive manner – a club/boathouse, a museum/aquarium, both using concrete forms to create singular objects in space – sharp angles, or continuous sweeps of glass, with curved concrete stairways leading up to observation points. At the end, looked over by a twin tower of dramatic if confused-looking asymmetrical luxury flats, are two monuments, one a concrete sail containing a figure of the novelist and Polish seafarer Joseph Conrad, the other a series of interlinked crosses dedicated to the strikers who fought with the government in the wildcat strikes of 1970 that helped create the foundations for Solidarity. As many as forty workers were shot dead by police. Even with this harsh reminder as its terminus, though, 10 Lutego is a space that feels unusually optimistic, a non-despotic vision of modernity and planning.

The major post-Stalinist boulevard in Moscow is not so imaginative,

Ulica 10 Lutego pointing to the sea, Gdynia

although not without interest for that. New Arbat (after The Arbat, the much more restrained Tsarist street that runs parallel, a tourist draw that is one of Moscow's nearest things to 'normal' 'European' urbanism), as most call it, or Kalinin Prospekt, as it was officially named, is a magistrale on the most demented scale. Tourist guides will tell you that it was created to imitate the skyscraper-lined streets that Khrushchev had seen on a visit to Havana, although one should be sceptical of this, as Khrushchev was no fan of that particular typology – 'if you've seen one skyscraper, you've seen them all', he dictated in his memoirs. Or maybe this was the reason why Kalinin Prospekt, laid out in 1963 by Mikhail Posokhin, consists of a series of identical skyscrapers, repeated, resonant notes in a continuous, minimalist composition. On one side, identical office towers are wide, splayed, spreading out in a tilted V-shape – on the other, they are I-shaped residential point blocks, and at the end the curved curtain wall of the Comecon building, the headquarters of the 'socialist camp's economic co-ordination council, where materials were symbolically taken from brother/subject republics.

There are, especially after the 1960s, a lot of wide roads lined with

Kalinin Prospekt, Moscow (1980 postcard)

towers in the USSR and its satellites, and most of them have little in the way of defined streetspace – the street has usually been quite definitively killed. This is not the case at Kalinin Prospekt, where several glass pavilions have been laid along the length of it, with wide pavements, even by magistrale standards, laid out in front of them. Walking and enjoying the space rather than just driving through is obviously encouraged, and it appears to have been successful: especially at night, this is one of Moscow's brightest, busiest areas, where ridiculously priced department stores and restaurants still advertise their wares via neon lights, pulsing green, blue and red. Here as well there's an ideological supplement, in the form of the Oktyabr cinema, with its façade defined by a double-height mosaic depicting heroic deeds in 1917. Again, the point is made here that neither classicism, nor even representational buildings with a definite front and back, are needed for the creation of streets of the most dramatic kind. Like any magistrale, it looks as if it has emerged all at once, as the creation of a single plan – and it has.

The Socialist Federal Republic of Yugoslavia did things differently. Having been expelled by Stalin from the Cominform for nationalist deviations in 1948, the Tito regime did not build anything remotely of the grandiose order of MDM or Karl-Marx-Allee. Ideologically and representationally, it tried to emphasize other qualities. Planning was usually a matter not of fixed Five-Year Plans but of outlines to be followed by the self-managed factories that were the basis of the economy. Accordingly, its spaces are often a matter of strongly defined pieces of town planning that have then been gradually filled in a visibly incremental fashion. This sense of accretion is particularly visible in the nearest thing the SFRY had to a magistrale (as they had parades, too) in the Croatian capital, Zagreb. Not that outsiders aren't just as liable to find this an equally dystopian space.

In one scene in Orson Welles's 1962 film adaptation of Kafka's *The Trial*, a character leaves a room in a studio set to walk through a Paris railway station out into Zagreb. When I first visited Zagreb in 2009, I was most excited when the people who had invited me said we were driving through the very street where Josef K, played by Anthony Perkins, tries to ask an old woman if he can carry her incredibly heavy suitcase, as she drags it through a landscape of open space and overpowering slabs. I made sure to have a walk along this street the next day. What is unique about Zagreb is that it's incredibly precise in terms of the periods of its architecture – one era succeeds the previous, usually without one spilling into the other. The part that is Hapsburg is very, very Hapsburg, lushly crumbling, a stage set of bourgeois decay. The part of the city where I was staying was south of this, in a district of 1930s tenements; then you hit a similarly uninterrupted swathe of post-war Modernism, a seemingly no-expense-spared showpiece of spatial planning. Running throughout is an expansive eight-lane highway, lined by large buildings which are fronted by, and lead to, pedestrianized green spaces. There's little of the partial infill or tying together of the loose and messy that marks many East/Central European capitals. If you don't drive it can be a tad intimidating, but it all seems to work on its own terms, if one ignores the amount of carbon being belched into the clouds by the horrendous traffic. That's not always easy: when I returned here two years later, the city was bathed in the thickest smog I've ever seen.

At the centre of the ensemble the road turns towards a gigantic square, which looks like it exists purely for the purposes of military commemorations – green, lined by Croatian flags, with a pyramid instead commemorating victims of the war. That is, the war that happened in the 1990s. This road (well, 'road' is a slightly paltry description for this canyon) has at various points been called Moscow Avenue and Avenue of the Proletarian Brigades, and is currently Ulica Grada Vukovara (City of Vukovar Street), after the town that was destroyed in the Yugoslav wars. Nonetheless, most of what there is to see here was built when it was the Avenue of the Proletarian Brigades. Coming from the city centre, it begins with the city's tallest tower, the delightfully named 'Zagreb Lady', designed by Slavko Jelinek and Berislav Vinković in the early 1970s. It echoes the Brazilian Modernism of Oscar Niemeyer in its balance between the curtain wall's repetition and the wilful curving and enveloping it is subjected to – but it is more restless, less hedonistic, than Niemeyer, the product of a cooler climate. Near it are perpendicular slab blocks, running the length of the boulevard.

The first, and architecturally the finest, was designed in 1953 by Drago Galić, a student of Le Corbusier, for army officers. It is in raw, shuttered concrete with a peculiar green tint to it, with thick, anthropomorphic pilotis surmounted by a regular grid, created by its exposed structural frame. It is collective housing as envisaged in Le Corbusier's Unité

Back side of the apartments for army officers, Zagreb

d'habitation – well-appointed, proud and also singular, not to be repeated. It doesn't define the street as Kalinin Prospekt does, but sets itself back behind a strip of parkland, so that the inhabitants can enjoy nature with their traffic. Walk under those pilotis, though, and turn towards the building's non-back side (remember, no front-and-back in Modernism, though this hasn't stopped some dodgy residents' additions, glazing off their balconies), and you realize that the Avenue of Proletarian Brigades was also a Potemkinstadt, as battered little dwellings sit hard against the confident Corbusian slabs. Yet at the bottom of most of the blocks in and around the boulevard, there are shops and well-used cafés, something which would not always be part of the Modernist programme; while the tenants of the flats look affluent, suggesting that the buildings' general dilapidation is deceptive.

In among the blocks of flats are similarly huge offices, many of which turn the regular notes of Modernism into something more discordant, playing with angles, walkways and Brutalist hieratic vents and extrusions, as at the Ministry of Agriculture, where structural features, clad in fair-faced concrete, are treated as sculptural towers. Some of these buildings are used by the University of Zagreb, which when I first visited had just ended an occupation, one which was apparently considered the first major political action since Croatian independence – i.e. for over fifteen years. Its protagonists got on the national news, rotating their speakers so that the media could not make figureheads out of any of them; their stencils and graffiti were still to be found here and there on the buildings, indicting the boredom of work, the grimness of neoliberal capitalism, the constant imprecation to sell or be sold. Election posters on the same street, coincidentally enough, showed the usual shiny-faced careerists. Opposite the university is a slick glass tower of interlocking cubes, the only new building of any consequence in this part of Zagreb – typically, it is called the Eurotower, expressive of Croatia's hope – granted in 2013 – of joining the European Union. Leave the boulevard for a little and walk around here, where there are more slick, late-modern offices to be found, and you'll notice that often something earlier and less modern pokes out. It's fairly shocking when it does so, especially given the general homogeneity of the place – shacks in among the Corbusian slabs and the would-rather-be-in-Frankfurt towers.

The far end of the Avenue of the Proletarian Brigades, where Josef K lives, is much as you would expect – slabs and open space, lots of good, albeit scrubby and windswept, examples of what architects today insist on calling 'public realm', and with plenty of facilities on the ground floors, including a smoky bar where I got a very 'you're not from round here' look. The presence of such a bar, though, and the trees and schools in the in-between spaces, suggests this was not quite as grim as Orson Welles's depiction suggested. Surrounding low blocks and towers, their strongly modelled concrete frames filled with red or green brick, is that 'realm' at its most basic: a large playing field with rusty goalposts, where on one of the school buildings is a peculiar and faintly chilling piece of graffiti – a marching crowd holding up an entirely blank banner, the press-ganged crowd of the magistrale visualized. As the boulevard basically stops here and becomes a motorway, you might walk deeper into Josef K's estate, which now starts to come closer to a more familiar East European (sub) urbanism – repeated towers in green space, surmounted by the signs for a drive-in McDonald's. Buffoonish imperial pundit Thomas Friedman once claimed that no two countries with McDonald's had ever had a war with

Josef K's housing estate, Zagreb

each other, obviously unaware that McDonald's had in fact co-existed in Yugoslavia in the 1990s alongside brutally fought nationalist wars. But architecture in Zagreb, surprisingly, still cleaves to the International Style – a new development near to Josef K's pad is in almost the same concrete-framed grid as the architecture of the 1960s, as if Zagreb has ended its peculiar progressive succession of styles, and decided instead on a sober, neat International Style of Modernism definitively, as if this really were the architectural end of history after all.

THE CONDUCTATOR'S GRANDS BOULEVARDS

There is one ex-'real socialist' city where you can directly follow the progression of the magistrale from its Parisian ancestry through its Stalinist form and into the Postmodern era, and that's Bucharest. The Romanian capital has had a boulevard-mania ever since the middle of the nineteenth

A flower seller on the Boulevard of the Victory of Socialism, Bucharest (late-1980s postcard)

century, regularly slicing wide arteries and grand buildings through a messy, chaotic medieval agglomeration, practically uninterrupted until the most preposterous and violent of Haussmannian surgeries was embarked on in the 1980s, by its most famous leader, the sceptre-wielding 'Conductator', Nicolae Ceauşescu. This helped provide one of the most notorious images of Stalinist urbanism, broadcast around the world in the aftermath of Ceauşescu's overthrow and execution – the overwhelming and half-finished 'Boulevard of the Victory of Socialism', leading to 'Ceauşescu's Palace', a building so outrageously overscaled and pompous that it was (and is) the second-largest building in the world, after the Pentagon. In my own hazy memory of Christmas 1989 and the wall-to-wall broadcasts of the events, I learnt the expression 'firing squad' and saw the image of this enormous palace, which was, I thought, only for the use of this one man and his similarly executed wife. This eight-year-old's mangled view of the events is probably roughly that held by most non-Romanians.

Bucharest, founded in the late-medieval era, was the capital of the

Ottoman vassal of Wallachia and, later, of the independent Romanian state. In the nineteenth century Paris was an exceptionally seductive urban model, the very definition both of sophisticated bourgeois lifestyle and of sophisticated mob control, and its example was followed from Cairo to Szczecin; but perhaps nowhere was quite so enthusiastic as Bucharest. Every big East European city thinks it is or was (until the commies) 'the Paris of the East', but here you can see why. The boulevards start out fairly irregular, without the hard Haussmann right-angle being wielded – the first, and probably the most easy and pleasant of them, Calea Victoriei (Victory Avenue), has a gentle curve and slope, which the buildings, no matter how pompous – and some are as ludicrously ornament-encrusted and bulkily outsized as anything built in the late nineteenth century – manage to accommodate, pushing the street closer to picturesque townscape than a clear path for the troops to fire down. The boulevards that came after it, like Regina Elisabeta Boulevard, are straighter and stiffer. Built right up until the 1940s, these new boulevards had much of the paraphernalia of Parisian urban life – ground-floor cafés, bookshops, banks, museums, elegant iron and glass arcades.[19] What makes them odd, and unlike Paris, is, first, the aggression of the architecture. It often seems as if Bucharest's architects (as often French as Romanian) had been inspired most of all by the genocidal Belgian king Leopold II's Palace of Justice in Brussels, a nightmare pile-up of Baroque masonry, its hulking, dynastic forms welded together with a thuggish power and decorated with a tasteless trowel. There are several elegant Art Deco apartment buildings and office blocks, but as late as the end of the 1930s, official buildings – such as the National Art Museum – were being erected that resembled in every detail the architecture of fifty years previously, right down to the mansard roofs. Others, such as the 'Belvedere' blocks facing the Dâmbovița river, piled up needless ornamental details onto a bulgy, bulky silhouette, with the result feeling creepy and uneasy. It was all capped off in 1936 by a part Paris, part Germania Triumphal Arch to symbolize the military victories of Greater Romania, which at that point encompassed much of what is now Moldova, along with parts of Ukraine and Bulgaria.

More to the point, it was one of the most unequal cities in Europe. As one historian points out, 'the (still undoubtedly true) statistics often used by communist rhetoric after the war show that in Bucharest 45% of dwellings had been constructed using inadequate materials, and 80% had no sewerage, 72% no running water, 52% no electricity.'[20] The 'Parisian' boulevards slashed through an unplanned cluster of tight medieval lanes, which would then have contained horrific poverty. These little streets are now the most picturesque (and touristic) parts of the centre, with their pompous ambitions foiled by the chaotic tangle of the streets, leading to an intriguing combination of grandeur and jaggedness – political distance so often helps with architectural appreciation. But whatever point there might have been in a 'dictatorship of the proletariat' in this overwhelmingly peasant country, a socialist government's first priority should have been to even out the absurd and horrible inequality of a city that was one part Paris in the 1930s, another part Paris in the 1390s. Typically for Stalinism, the response was instead to convey a huge amount of resources into a giant and not particularly useful grand project.

Bucharest has no Stalinallee, but it does have Casa Scânteii, a mini-skyscraper built for the printworks and offices of the communist press (*Scânteii – The Spark* – was the Party paper). It is placed as the

The termination of the grand boulevard: Casa Scânteii, Bucharest

terminus of one of the 'Paris' boulevards of the pre-war dictatorship, Kiseleff Street, a Champs Elysées-like wide, tree-lined parkway with embassies behind the dense tree cover. Casa Scânteii is in fact directly aligned with the Arcul de Triumf, acting as its culmination. As a building, it makes an interesting contrast with the many big structures of Romania's previous, hard-right regime: compared with the blank, glowering, stripped classicism of the Victoria Palace, a government headquarters finished in 1944, it has a lot more wit about it, and far more pleasant public spaces, with mock-medieval colonnades and a big public square, and reasonably public cafés to be found inside, all capped by a goofily futuristic tower, breaking yet more rules of classical composition. The concessions to Romanian 'national form' are present and as cosmetic as always, with neo-Byzantine arches over the stone mullions of its central tower and hammer and sickles rendered with Greek Orthodox decorative motifs. The eventual building, designed by the city architect Horia Maicu, was chosen after proposals that resembled the 'correct' classicism which dominated before 1945 were rejected, apparently because of a 'heaviness and lack of flight toward the future'.[21] What exactly was that future?

After 1956, when Casa Scânteii was finished, as almost everywhere else in the Bloc, the historic centre was left alone to picturesquely crumble, and energies and resources were conveyed into clearing slums and shanty towns and replacing them with workers' districts on the outskirts of mammoth size, such as the aptly named Titan, eventually home to 450,000 people. This typical post-Stalinist pragmatism was combined with increasing independence from the USSR – Romania, under its new leader, Nicolae Ceauşescu, was the only Warsaw Pact country to refuse to take part in the suppression of the Prague Spring, which was in fact publicly condemned by Ceauşescu at an impromptu speech outside the Central Committee building on Calea Victoriei. Anti-Sovietism did not mean 'liberalism', however, and in 1971, after returning, impressed, from a visit to North Korea, Ceauşescu began to impose the most Stalinist regime seen in Europe since 1953, and this time he would do it with abundant Western assistance, via credit lines from Western banks. Stephen Kotkin and Jan Tomasz Gross argue that under Ceauşescu neo-Stalinism became, paradoxically, a means of asserting independence from Moscow. 'All East Bloc countries were national communist, to a greater or lesser degree', they write, but 'what set Romania apart was not the nationalism per se but the absence of a reform wing within the Leninist structures, which placed Bucharest closer to Pyongyang . . . nationalism, rather than reinforcing a reform inclination as elsewhere in Eastern Europe, nourished resistance to reform, since reforms came from Moscow (first under Khrushchev, then under Gorbachev).'[22] The appeal of North Korea was its state philosophy of *Juche*, or self-reliance, which rapidly supplanted even a rhetorical commitment to Marxism. Some of the first results of the Conductator's 'I've seen the future, and it works' encounter with North Korea were in architecture and city planning.

In 1971, the year of his 'July Theses' that set Romania on its neo-Stalinist course, Ceauşescu gave a speech to the Union of Architects. It would be highly critical of the planning of areas like Titan, and has an extremely familiar ring to it. 'The apartment buildings are dispersed randomly, they do not create streets and boulevards, in a clear urban idea', and, moreover, 'architects have quite often neglected the rich traditional values of Romanian architecture, our national specificity.'[23] This was Stalinist rhetoric, familiar from the screeds against the anti-street 'packing cases' condemned in the 1940s; but it was rhetoric that was issued during an era when Modernist ideas in architecture were, under the influence of such as Jane Jacobs and Robert Venturi, being replaced with Postmodernist ones, stressing 'real streets', historical continuity and traditional reference. The most immediate effect of this new architectural direction – enshrined in official government policy, in the 'Streets Law' of 1975 – is that the new high-rise districts grew a 'wall' in front of them of Modernist apartments, hard onto the street, something you can see at Nicolae Titulescu Boulevard, near Kiseleff Road, or in the area of Titan immediately around its Metro station. Proper streets with cafés and shops on the ground floor and streets above. The stylistic change came soon after, in response to an earthquake in 1977. An entire swathe of the city centre was to be levelled and replaced with a Centrul Civic ('civic centre') of grand tree-lined boulevards and civic buildings, sweeping away the last remnants of the irregular city that survived behind the 'Parisian' streets of the old regime. The Little Stalin of Little Paris now became a Big Haussmann.

This just happened to coincide with the IMF calling in its debts, as it did in Mexico, Yugoslavia and nearly everywhere else in the poorer parts of the world, in response to the higher price of borrowing created by the oil crisis and the sudden raising of interest rates by the US Federal Reserve (known to economists as the 'Volcker shock').[24] The result was an awful combination of a crisis caused ultimately by Romania's integration into the world capitalist system, and a flagrantly oppressive ruling style that was deeply specific to Stalinism. Ceaușescu, by now ruling by decree, insisted that every last penny of Romania's debt was paid back, ushering in an austerity regime that led to blackouts, food shortages (almost everything produced had to be exported) and a sudden collapse right back into the dire poverty from which Romanians had only recently emerged. And all through this, workers constructed the Centrul Civic, at the cost of 40,000 displaced people, of dozens of historic churches and monasteries, and, eventually, of a violent revolution.[25] The buildings were made entirely out of Romanian materials and were mostly, if not entirely, finished by December 1989. Looking at the Centrul Civic today, it is hard not to wonder how on earth this all managed to happen. It is, as intended, quite coherent – the architects were instructed by the leader to borrow from the 'Belvedere' blocks nearby, and the result is indeed close to the city's

Wide empty space: the Centrul Civic, Bucharest

unlovely, domineering interwar classicism. Yet the results are coherent enough to form a specific and identifiable 'style'.

That style was Postmodernism. Although the approach was Stalinist in the extreme, the built heritage of Romanian Stalinism was rejected under Ceaușescu. Casa Scânteii was described in the 1980s as a 'shame for Romania's architects', so glaringly had it borrowed from Soviet precedent. The blocks that we found in the Centrul Civic, and in associated projects like the rebuilding of Victory Square, share the Stalinist love of impure form, extraneous decoration (nearly everything seems to have a colonnade on the roof), bay windows and monumental symmetry, but the details have no similarity at all. In fact, they resemble very closely the work of the Spanish Postmodernist Ricardo Bofill, whose housing projects, such as the Espaces d'Abraxas in the Parisian suburb of Marne-la-Vallée, were used by Terry Gilliam as the set for his totalitarian burlesque 1986 film, *Brazil*, where their sinister, bulging forms and classical borrowings fit rather neatly a story of bureaucratic mania. If only Gilliam had taken his crew to Bucharest, he'd have had an actual 'totalitarianism' to work with.[26] Along and around the Stalinallee of this new development, the Boulevard of the Victory of Socialism (now Boulevard Unirii), the apartment blocks are tall, heavy and on a strict traditional streetplan, but there's something about the heavy concrete eyebrows over big glass windows that specifically suggests real local precedent, the overpowered and overpowering architecture of Little Paris. This really was, maybe more than any other Stalinist project outside Russia, wholly in tune with the genius loci. It was also the ultimate Potemkinstadt. Many of the Byzantine churches that were not demolished were simply encased by the back walls of the Centrul Civic's blocks of flats, meaning that, sometimes, historical architecture and entire blocks of the nineteenth-century city can be found, pickled, in the most peculiar places. The boulevard itself is straight, banal, and seemingly endless – it is the only one in this chapter that we did not walk all the way down, because it was just too hot and too tiring. Despite the city's extreme climate, the boulevard has a notable lack of cafés or bars, with the retail units rather tellingly taken up by ultra-expensive boutiques.

There are actually some attractive details to be found in the Boulevard of the Victory of Socialism – it is wide enough for each street to have two tree-lined pedestrian paths, and the architects had a lot more fun with the fruity cyber-Baroque lamp standards and illuminated fountains than they did with the aggressively banal buildings themselves. Mid-way it meets Unirii Square, the city's Piccadilly Circus or Times Square, where the Conductator's hulking blocks are today draped in adverts. From here, you get a straight view down towards the Palace, framed by the trees, and the trick is ruthlessly obvious, the most obnoxiously channelled image of power we managed to find anywhere in the 'socialist camp', all space sucked towards a ziggurat. Built as the House of the People, and designed in 1983 by the competition-winning 28-year-old architect Anca Petrescu, it was closely directed by Ceauşescu from the very start. Since the early 1990s, it has housed the Romanian parliament, giving it the official name of the Palace of the Parliament. It now has the dubious honour of being the city's tourist attraction – how can it not be, as the largest building in Europe and the second-largest in the world?

Inevitably, we walked to it, through Constitution Square, a vast and empty crescent of government offices. However, we found to our amazement that there is simply no direct public access to the building from its front façade. Instead, it faces the street with a defensive escarpment, dense with trees, something that you would hope the 'democratic' use of the building would have led to being changed, but which is more likely the reason for its retention. The only access from the front is through sloping roads intended solely for cars, guarded by security. You can, as a tourist, get a tour if you book in advance, but the only way to see any of it from the street is via the back end, converted into a contemporary art gallery in 2004. Just how anti-public the building is becomes obvious here, with it all screened by high stone walls, as if it were Buck House. On the way past these, you can see just how much of the Centrul Civic there is – boulevard after boulevard, massive wide symmetrical government office after massive wide symmetrical government office. The day we visited, one of the Centrul Civic's yawning plazas was housing a music festival, and the MC made booming declarations about 'Count Dracula' – one sinister Romanian stereotype against another. By the time we got to the entrance of the gallery, we were exhausted, and unprepared.

The gallery itself was nearly empty and much like any other gallery of its sort, enlivened by a brave and pointless attempt to place Modernist forms against the neoclassical bulk, with chic glazed lifts running up the façade for no reason in particular. Up close, the Palace of the Parliament

House of the People, Bucharest: No Entry for the Public

is remarkably 'tasteful' for a building of its genre, just like the buildings of Romania's interwar monarchy. Unlike the architecture of high Stalinism, there is no 'flight to the future', but a scrupulous copying of historical details – the only difference is the flamboyance and fearlessly demented scale with which Petrescu organized the building, which gives that unforgettable pyramidal silhouette, the aspect of the building that makes it compellingly alien and sinister. Without that, there wouldn't be much here worth remarking on other than sheer quantity. The details are both well made and dispiritingly . . . normal. Near the entrance to the art gallery is a Corinthian portico, strewn with bottles, binbags and trade papers, as if in the aftermath of a bout of corporate binge drinking. From here, you can survey the unrepaired damage done to the city by the Centrul Civic – a wasteland almost as wide as the Palace itself, one corner of which is being given over to a reconstruction of one of the many demolished churches, the rest of it a steppe of wisteria and scrub.

At the end of all of this Agata and I both found, somewhat to our surprise, that we hated the damn thing. Worried by our uncharacteristic

Inspecting the Palace of the Parliament, Bucharest

disgust towards the monuments of a Stalinist regime, we tried to work out why we found it so horrible, why it was that we could not only tolerate but enjoy the Stalinallee, but not the Boulevard of the Victory of Socialism and its People's Palace. Was it because it was too new, or too Postmodernist – were we just being heritage snobs? It can't have been a moral matter, as however awful Ceauşescu may have been, he was no Stalin; and it can't have been a matter of taste, as it was no more or less tasteless than the Kreschatyk, although the banal 'correctness' of the Palace's ornament was rather depressing. It did have a lot to do with the anti-public planning of it all. Most likely, it was because if Stalinism was the 'first time as tragedy', this was the second time as farce, with any of the original emancipatory ideals that were buried in the Stalinist monumental pile-up more distant than ever. Or maybe it was because it was someone else's story, from which we were too geographically distant. Or because we now realized the truth. This was the magistrale with all the shiny red granite, sparkling mosaics and statues of workers, peasants and students stripped away, revealing itself only as a brutal and banal safeguard against revolution. And a failed one, as its builder would find out.

2
Microrayon

Here too are dreaming landscapes,
lunar, derelict.
Here too are the masses
tillers of the soil.
And cells, fighters
who lay down their lives
for a song.

Here too are cemeteries
fame and snow.
And I hear murmuring,
the revolt of immense estates.

Miroslav Holub, 'In the Microscope'[1]

Here, by all accounts, is the worst. The immense estates. In the touristic view, they are the first sight of the legacy left by 'communism', and as such a stunning, numbing indictment – the sheer barbarity, the intellectual, visual and human vacancy of surrounding such diverse, picturesque and richly decorative cities as Budapest, Prague, St Petersburg, Kraków, Vilnius, Tallinn, with a cordon sanitaire of monolithic, univocal and reductive concrete slabs. You must trudge in a coach or cab through communism to arrive at the gorgeous past, and the contrast is not kind. In the view of locals, it's unsurprisingly a little more complex – you can come across everything from extreme hostility to a slightly rueful but warm nostalgia, but few would disagree with the notion that something went seriously wrong when these places were made. They are so relentless, so different from what went before, and so inescapable, that they demand a response.

It is ironic that these 'inhuman' structures, barely even recognizable as 'architecture', are usually the result of what was one of the Soviet empire's most humane policies – the provision of decent housing at such a subsidy that it was virtually free – rents for this (publicly or co-operatively owned) housing was usually pegged at between 3 and 5 per cent of income.[2] They begin to be built en masse in the second half of the 1950s, and are a reaction to the Potemkin cities of high Stalinism. Rather than building grand archways that lead to slums, boulevards fit for not much more than tanks, and bureaucrats' castles of faïence and granite, reformers like Khrushchev or Gomułka promised they would create – for literally the first time in nearly all of these cities – decent housing for all workers, where they wouldn't have to share rooms or flats with other families, where they would have central heating, electricity, warm water and other then-unusual mod cons. This needed to be done, and fast, as both the war and a breakneck industrial revolution had caused massive urban overpopulation. As they would have known from *Capital*, or from Engels' *Condition of the Working Class in England*, the first industrial revolution led to terrible housing conditions, with hundreds of thousands of people crammed into cellars and courts. They promised to use exactly the industrial forces that had created this to provide the solution – mass-produced housing, made in factories just like cars or anything else. By the 1970s, there was more factory-made housing being built in the USSR than anywhere else in the world.[3]

So what went wrong? In his poem quoted above, the Czech scientist Miroslav Holub is making an ironic allusion to his own work, where he is required to look intensely at microscopic life, finding that it too contains within it the history of class struggles; but it serves, partly intentionally, as a poem about the planner's-eye view that was always present in the rhetoric (and reality) of 'real socialism'. The projects always look magnificent from the model, and superb from above: there, the patterns of the blocks are clear, the parkland and the lakes look genuinely verdant – abstract images of modern luxury. But the ground, invisible to the microscope, is – at least in the conventional view – illegible. Instead, slabs are surrounded by scrubland, without viable public space or coherence. This is how the council estates of the West have often been seen, too – a top-down imposition from architects and planners upon the unknowing workers and peasants, who lost their baby (community life in a place with a distinctive identity) with the (surely undeniably filthy) bathwater. For the likes of Jane Jacobs, the

The centre of Lazdynai, Vilnius (1986 postcard)

'slums' should have been left alone to 'unslum' themselves[4] – though this was hardly likely in the teeming conditions that created the several-families-to-a-flat kommunalka. In the Soviet-controlled countries, the problem was huge, and so was the solution – neither incremental rebuilding nor a gradual reform were even plausible, even if they had been seriously considered (which they weren't). What was needed were not 'estates', but entire new districts, and thousands of them. What eventually resulted was called in Soviet jargon the 'microrayon' – literally 'micro-region', which gives some sense of the scale we're dealing with. Regions. 'Estates' that had populations larger than most cities. Their names are often notorious. Marzahn. Halle-Neustadt. Petržalka. Nowa Huta. Lazdynai. Mustamäe. Ursynów. Belyayevo. Urban ungentrifiables. These are the sort of places this chapter will cover: districts at the edge of cities, that were supposed to have all the facilities of a real city district – schools, shops, sports halls, cinemas, etc. They all still exist, none have been demolished, although some have been trimmed at the edges and some have actually been densified. Some have been renovated, usually with EU money, others are practically falling to pieces. Are they as awful as they (apparently) look?

Before we venture into them, it's worth remembering that factory-made housing was once specifically rejected under 'real socialism', especially during its darkest, most Stalinist years. The forefathers of these places, like so many of the twentieth century's more contentious inventions, can be found in the built legacy of the Weimar Republic. Red Vienna's inner-city interventions were not followed in Germany itself, in the 1920s and early 1930s; rather than compulsorily seizing urban land, Social Democracy there favoured the purchase of lower-priced sites outside the city, building what were in effect garden suburbs. City councils, co-operatives and trade union building societies in Frankfurt-am-Main, Hamburg and Berlin all built several Modernist housing estates on virginal sites on their outskirts. Interspersed with lots and lots of greenery, after the English model of Hampstead Garden Suburb, Welwyn or Letchworth, were far from English houses – cubic, regular, brightly coloured, arranged along winding paths or semi-abstract geometric patterns rather than grid-planned streets. Something similar was being attempted in the 1930s in Warsaw by WSM, the Warszawska Spółdzielnia Mieszkaniowa (Warsaw Housing Co-operative), a co-op run by members of the Polish Socialist Party, which had a precarious but popular life while Poland was under the dictatorship of its former leader, Józef Piłsudski. The same models were used in WSM estates, mostly in Żoliborz, a new district being created on the site of a former Tsarist fort, at what was then the northern edge of the Polish capital. These too were simple, modern, bright, angular and low-rise, planned around well-planted public spaces.

Sometimes, especially in Frankfurt, building these estates entailed the use of factory-made components – precast concrete panels, making the construction of housing much quicker and cheaper for these usually cash-strapped public bodies. And in an era when machines and machine production were fetishized by politicians and architects alike, this was turned to out of enthusiasm as much as desperation. But partly because they're low-rise, partly because of their bright colours, pleasing curves and angles, and partly because of a generalized longing for the supposedly more glamorous life that existed between the wars, these are now popular places, much more so than their successors. Capitalism has often been good for them – the WSM estates in Żoliborz are by now an enclave of the intelligentsia, a Polish Hampstead, the unambiguous socialism of their builders invisible but for the plaques. Some of them, though, are more obviously the fathers of the microrayon. Those who aren't intimately familiar with the historiography of modern architecture might mistake Törten, on the outskirts of the East German town of Dessau, for a product of the 1960s not the 1920s.

Dessau-Törten was designed in 1926, by Walter Gropius, then the director of the Bauhaus, and the designer of its new headquarters, which had just been built when Törten was being started. The Bauhaus buildings are not too far from the centre of this post-industrial town, which in its mix of nineteenth-century pomp, dereliction and prefab Modernism is basically the East German equivalent of a small, depressed industrial town in the West Midlands. The fame of the Bauhaus brings architectural tourism, though, something which the GDR recognized when it restored this genuinely 'iconic' concrete-and-glass school in the 1970s. Next to it are houses for the Bauhaus's 'masters' – Gropius, Kandinsky, Moholy-Nagy – also designed by Gropius, all one-off, bespoke cubic villas. Originally Dessau council wanted to build its workers' estate just next to these, but land prices were too high, so instead you have to take a tram further out to Törten, and when you do, it is a bit of a shock. No 1920s glamour here.

Prefab Prairie, Dessau

Row upon parallel row of rectilinear terraces end at a flat prairie, whose electricity pylons reach into the estate, as if, like Stephen Spender, Gropius considered the pylons to be potential monuments. This was probably the largest-scale experiment in industrialized building in the Weimar Republic, commissioned by the local Social Democratic council as council housing, and roundly attacked by the Nazis, who seized power in the city in 1932 (one of the first things they did was expel the Bauhaus). Gropius once said his ambition was to be 'the Ford of housing', creating an object as useful, durable, interchangeable and eventually disposable as a Model T. Evidently here he succeeded, at least to some degree. The long lines of terraces suggest the semi-industrialized building of nineteenth-century England or Belgium, with its grids of houses near factories – but here the pattern is because they were actually made on a real production line, a conveyor belt which ran along the building site. The houses are made out of concrete panels. Dig around a little and you'll find one house, of different but even more severe design made of steel (basically uninhabitable, and now used as a Bauhaus information centre), designed by the future Stalinallee architect, Richard Paulick. Gropius's houses aren't horrible – in another circumstance they could be rather attractive, as contemporary houses are in Berlin, Warsaw or Frankfurt. They're crisp, sharp and bright, and each has a front door and a garden. A cold wind blasts through them nonetheless. They feel as if they're at the edge of the

Traktornaya housing scheme, Leningrad

world, a factory whose roof and walls have been taken off, leaving the production line lost and exposed on the endless north German plains. Something is missing here, something which stops the place from feeling like even a real suburb, let alone a town.

In the same year, the city council of Leningrad was building something quite different for its tenants. It isn't wholly fair to compare a minor industrial town with that million-plus metropolis, the 'cradle of three revolutions', but the difference in practice is interesting nonetheless. The Traktornaya housing scheme is closer to the centre of the city today, but at the time it neighboured the Narva Gate and the Putilov engineering works – the ceremonial entry to the city and the crucible of its industrial power. Designed by a team headed by Alexander Gegello, it's a series of low-rise blocks of flats, designed around open courtyards, with plenty of trees. The first things you notice are the colours – pink and orange, providing accents in what is already a brightly painted city – and the half-arches which punctuate the buildings, or the mouldings around the doors and windows. The scheme creates a rupture with St Petersburg's neoclassical architecture, but through subtle gestures – strange geometries, the lack of a divide between front and back, broken forms – rather than by rudely dominating it.

This engagement with classical tradition would be briefly superseded by Modernism. A year or so later, Moscow built Usachevka, three- to five-storey blocks of flats, unornamented, with the kind of angular balconies and ornament-free smooth surfaces favoured in Weimar Germany – but Moscow's authorities would soon reject these 'house-machines', in favour of (a much more domineering version of) quasi-classical one-offs like Traktornaya. Although the old towns had a major housing crisis, new towns were built in their dozens under Stalin and his satraps, usually in a manner which extended the principles of the magistrale to entire cities, always serving a specific factory – most famously, the new town of Magnitogorsk, built around a steelworks to a town plan by the architect of the 'New Frankfurt', Ernst May. Central and Eastern Europe of the 1950s has some of these discrete towns – Stalinstadt (now Eisenhüttenstadt) in Germany, Sztálinváros (now Dunaújváros) in Hungary, et al. – but what it also has are Stalinist microrayons, i.e. entire new city districts in the Stalinist Empire style, also usually built around, and for, new factories and their workers. They were built as a deliberate critique of the results of industrialized building, as

Stalinist ideology saw it. Impersonal, mechanistic, inhumane, boring, ahistorical . . . epithets that may sound familiar to those who are familiar with the architectural views of Charles Windsor. The Stalinist alternative to Modernist practice shadows its Modernist successors, often literally. Nonetheless, we ought to begin with the lowest common denominator.

There are certain aspects of Soviet practice that always invited the monolithic repetition of the microrayon, particularly the limits of the planned, or more accurately 'command', economy. On the one hand, there was an opposition to the very idea of individual districts, as represented by the 'quarter'. Writing approvingly in 1932 about Soviet utopian planning, Berthold Lubetkin argued that 'urban quarters are simply the obsolete survivals of capitalistic principles of planning. They represent class and caste prejudices (ghettoes, international concessions, west and east ends, brothel districts) or the now-superannuated ideas of strategic defence, etc.'[5] Because of this, the only aspect of a given area that could influence any individuality in its architecture or layout was the demands of the site. When this hostility was combined with the results of command economics, the results were drastic. 'It would be to the greatest advantage of a centrally directed system of production', wrote Havel in the 1980s, 'if only one type of prefabricated panel were constructed, from which one type of apartment building would be constructed; these buildings in turn would be fitted with a single kind of door, door handle, window, toilet, washbasin and so on, and together this would create a single type of housing development constructed according to one standardized urban development plan, with minor adjustments for landscape, given the regrettable irregularity of the earth's surface.'[6] He was talking about something quite specific, housing estates that he knew well. What is this kind of almost militaristic regularity and repetition like to live in?

THE STANDARD

'Let us look at what is happening in modern architecture,' implored Roy Medvedev of his Soviet samizdat audience in the 1970s. It is 'a field where enormous transformations are taking place, thanks to the use of new materials and construction methods, resulting in a fresh international style'. All well and good. But 'this, however, is no excuse for building new and completely impersonal residential areas with standardised houses of identical design in Moscow, Baku and Tashkent. What is appropriate for an industrial city may be out of place in the capital of a national republic. And what suits one capital may not necessarily suit another.'[7] Notoriously, this was seldom taken into account, and one of the famous – if inadvertent – results of Khrushchev's 1954 decree on 'Industrialized Building' and 'Against Architectural Excesses' was that an International Style truly took hold in a way that those who coined that term couldn't have imagined – precisely the same style, aesthetic and often constructional approach for a transcontinental territory that stretches from the borders of Scandinavia to the edge of Afghanistan to a sea border with Japan. However grim these developments may appear, they were often highly prized at the time. A contemporary account of the Lazdynai microrayon in Vilnius, which became something close to the state of the art, with its approach often replicated, gives a pure blast of the ideology of the microrayon. 'Every bend in the street has been thought out. If you go along Architectas Street by car, new vistas and compositions continually open up before you, flashing by at kaleidoscopic speed like sequences of a film. Skilled town-builders of yore perfectly mastered the art of creating this visual effect and their traditions are now being continued by the architects of today.'[8] So it is both fragmented – like a film – and complete, a series of vistas. It is planned, really, really planned. The writer continues: 'Lazdynai was built all at once, to a single design, and single set of principles, and the builders of Vilnius's Order of Lenin Housing-Construction Works accurately and conscientiously fulfilled the architects' talented design.'[9] Is it totalitarian, this insistence on total designs by total designers built totally? Oh no. 'Lazdynai's architecture does not overshadow man, on the contrary, it uplifts him.'[10]

Our example for the standard, the most straightforward and symptomatic microrayon, is in Kiev, but it could be anywhere – this one suffices because, well, we had the privilege of staying there and got to explore. It wasn't *totally* typical, though – the Hotel Slavutych is the only building in the microdistrict of Rusanivka that isn't based solely on right angles. The entirety of the left bank of the wide, overgrown and winding River Dnieper is, essentially, one microrayon of a million-plus people. In the even more damning parlance, these places are known locally as 'sleeping districts', and here that is especially obvious, given that in Kiev practically everything else is on the right bank, in a particularly extreme version of the riverside divides that mark out so many cities. The direct left bank gets a good view of this, too – the golden domes of the Kievsko-Pecherska Lavra, the monastery that is the main survivor of the city's days as the capital of Kievan Rus, are visible from much of it, as is the steel statue of Victory that we will discuss in more detail later in this book. Further on are all the main shopping streets, museums, the central railway station, and much of the city's surviving industry. All there is here is housing, thousands upon thousands of units of it, with, admittedly, some ancillary buildings such as shops, civic offices, a hospital and, after a long journey, the city's main international airport. The divide is stylistic even more than functional. While the right bank has, at least in the centre, a density of successive styles – Byzantine, Baroque, neoclassical, Constructivist, Stalinist, Modernist – on the left bank there is only the attenuated Modernism of the 1960s–1980s, relieved only recently, and in a somewhat depressing fashion. Accordingly, it serves as a good example of what the general standard was – a place where you can see a city-sized area that has been built over entirely with blocks of flats using industrialized prefabrication methods. And as well as the architectural context on the other side of the Dnieper, which it entirely ignores, it also has, around the Hotel Slavutych, a rich natural landscape that it doesn't entirely ignore. Nature, unlike historical architecture, was to be accommodated in the microrayon.

The area that we got to walk around most is Rusanivka, an island formed by a canal that veers off from the Dnieper, lazily curving round to define a very particular zone, where the proximity of water was originally intended to have a role in the architectural and spatial design of the area – riverbuses were supposed to serve as transport along the canal. On the basis of this, a 1980s book proclaimed that 'the white-stoned Rusanivka district with its wide canals is often called "the Venice of Kiev"', and although this vision never came to pass, it did mean that the area has a particularly large amount of open space, without highways driving through it. The canal itself has been landscaped nicely, albeit without much fanfare – granite steps lead down to it, and trees have been either retained or planted all along. The blocks, though, are exactly the same as those on the outskirts of any other Soviet city – I've seen an identical model just in my own relatively meagre experience in Kharkiv, Vilnius, Riga, St Petersburg, Tallinn, Tbilisi, Moscow.

'The Venice of Kiev' (1980s postcard)

They come mostly in two types, slab and tower; the slabs are sometimes incredibly long, particularly along the shopping street facing the Dnieper. They're all of either seven or nine storeys, and architecturally, if that's the word, there has been an attempt to give them visual qualities of some kind – along with the prefabricated panels used to construct them, similarly factory-made tiles and balconies run along their length. Near the ceiling, the tiles change colour, creating a red and cream pattern above an expanse of beige. These external features have not weathered well, and their grids are sagging, becoming irregular; in response, or perhaps just because they can, residents have reacted by affixing balcony extensions, some of them the size of entire rooms. These are then interspersed with the towers, which look quite thin and sprightly by comparison with these long, looming monoliths, but use exactly the same materials and exactly the same devices. The hotel also uses the same materials, but is the only building to acknowledge the curve of the canal, opening out to it as it is channelled from the Dnieper; evidently the factories could cope with doing something other than right-angles if it was for a good enough client. This extends eastwards along the maybe not aptly named Enthusiasts Street, for about four miles, without much in the way of change and development – aside from newer blocks right on the river for a better class of Ukrainian, which are basically the same but for crowning rooftop 'features' and a lack of the earlier blocks' public space. The hatred that these places have often inspired does not, from here, seem particularly extravagant.

Walk around the back of the blocks into the aforementioned public space, and you find that, irrespective of the lack of private gardens, there is actually a lot of green here, and it is being used quite intensively. It didn't look spectacularly attractive in March 2011, with the tall trees bereft of leaves or much in the way of colours other than grey and a dun green, but there is a lot of it, thickly planted and dense, overshadowing and sometimes seemingly growing out of the garages and primary schools that take up part of this space. Another usage appeared to be allotment gardens, as there's enough space here for it – something that, judging by the emergency look of the little huts scattered through the green, happened in response to the economic crisis of the 1990s, when Ukraine's economy suffered the same drastic collapse as Russia's – growing your own food would have been a sensible solution. Along the canal, the slabs and towers form a long linear pathway, one that might have been rather attractive before the buildings' cladding started to discolour and wilt (after all, as you can see, it once appeared on a postcard). The flats have access to the canal, with nice views, and form a sharply modern visual counterpoint to the (currently frozen) water, even given that they haven't been specifically designed for that purpose, being merely predetermined building blocks put in place with only an ex-post-facto attempt at compromise with their site.

The road to Boryspil, Kiev

That's about as impressive as it gets, and on a site like this – opposite one of Eastern Europe's most famous architectural ensembles, surrounded by what in Britain gets called 'Outstanding Natural Beauty' – it's obviously not a great achievement, although that may not have bothered the people who moved here from a kommunalka. It seems positively human-scaled, though, compared with what happens further east, where there aren't rivers, canals or golden domes for contrast. The highway that goes out towards Boryspil airport sees the blocks grow ever bigger and more assertive as you get further away from the city centre. There is more ornament here, prefabricated concrete patterns representing Ukrainian national motifs; the Soviet buildings are set back a little from the motorway, although new, circular tower blocks have no such compunction. Billboards and supermarkets take up some of the slack, and many of the towers reach up to forty storeys – you could be in a poorer version of a modern East Asian metropolis. You can, if you look closely here, see some buildings that aren't harshly modern under construction – Orthodox churches, constructed out of breezeblocks and bricks and then painted over, with little domes no different in form from those of Kievan Rus, over a thousand years ago. If modernity looks like this, then . . .

AGAINST THE STANDARD, FOR SOCIALIST REALISM!

Khrushchev's precursors were keen to denounce the possible results of 'decadent', 'formalist', 'Western' 'house-machines' on the face of the Soviet landscape, and though they can be convicted of a far more negligent and brutal approach to the population's basic needs, it could be that they were right to do so. Or, as neo-Stalinists might have more bluntly put it – compare the grandeur of the Kreschatyk, built under Stalin, with the shabbiness of Rusanivka, built under Khrushchev and Brezhnev. The neo-Stalinist's argument falls apart when it's pointed out that the former was offices and luxury flats for bureaucrats and the latter housing for workers and clerks, but is it possible that the repugnant regime that held power from the late 1920s till the mid-1950s might have created better, more beautiful microrayons, workers' districts that instilled the sort of sense of identity, history, pride and place that is so stunningly absent on the left bank of Kiev? 'Palaces for the people' was, after all, one of its slogans.

The most famous surviving Stalinist extension to an existing European city is probably Nowa Huta, on the outskirts of Kraków, and hence fully on the stag party trail. Its name, best translated as 'New Steelmill', says what it is – a new town joined to the old one, built around a very large steelworks, which would at the time have been practically the sole employer. It is commonly assumed, without much in the way of evidence, that Nowa Huta was foisted upon Kraków as some sort of revenge for its status as historic capital and cradle of the Catholic intelligentsia; but as Kraków has (or rather had) an uncomplicated railway connection to the raw materials it would be using (iron ore, from Kryvyi Rih in Ukraine) and is right next to the large Silesian coalfield, it may have been built there for rather more pragmatic reasons. Either way, it was certainly treated as a propaganda project, an attempt to turn Poles into good communists, a project Uncle Joe once compared to 'fitting a saddle onto a cow'. Its original plan consists of three mini-magistrales, five-storey neoclassical blocks lined with specially designed, rather Art Deco-like lamp standards, ending in colonnades, which meet in a triangular square, which currently lumbers under the name of 'Plac Ronalda Reagana', although mercifully without a statue of the great man. It is all obviously meant to instill some sort of sense of pride and order, a feeling that in these small flats were the heroic builders of the new society, but the choice of materials – grey cement, grey granite – means that the frequently used appellation of 'Orwellian' to describe Nowa Huta doesn't seem far off. Like the magistrales, it can perhaps be praised for being accommodating to street life (especially as the roads are not as wide as they are in Warsaw, Berlin or Moscow), but it hardly seems much more like a vision of human emancipation.

There are places where you can actually see Socialist Realism taking over from Modernism and its machine aesthetic in the space of a single building, gradually eating it up and consuming it, literally turning it to stone. Two examples are in peripheral estates built by ZOR, the new state housing body – ZOR Koło East and ZOR Praga 1, in the suburbs of Warsaw, semi-virgin territories that provided the first new housing estates to be built there, in theory and sometimes in practice, for the people who were rebuilding the city centre from (still uninhabitable) ruins. Both were designed initially by the architects Helena and Szymon

Syrkus, Modernists and committed socialist intellectuals who had designed some of the (far less contentious) Modernist estates in the inter-war city; Szymon Syrkus had survived Auschwitz, before returning to build what can sometimes seem like some stunningly optimistic places, given the context in which they were made. ZOR Koło is the more famous and the better of the two. It was the first major housing scheme in Poland to use prefabricated materials, but the regimentation of Dessau-Törten is nowhere emulated. The modular, prefabricated parts – cement blocks, or repeated features like doorways and balconies – do not result in something rectilinear, since factories are entirely capable of producing things that do not run in straight lines. Rather, ZOR Koło *begins* as a series of gently waving, subtle, colourful blocks of flats, which gradually straighten, harden and turn grey.

When Agata and I took our excursion to Koło, she got a shock on getting out of the tram. In stark black capitals over the cultural centre that marks the entry to the estate are the words 'OSIEDLE ROBOTNICZE IMIENA STEFANA ŻEROMSKIEGO' – 'WORKERS' ESTATE IN THE NAME OF STEFAN ŻEROMSKI'. All the rest of the similar signs in Warsaw have been dismantled, whether because after privatization people didn't want their estates to be officially designated as working class, or because their names had changed. This wasn't the case here, as Żeromski (1864–1925), author and Polish nationalist of slightly centre-left sympathies, was not a controversial figure either in People's Poland or today. An identifiably Soviet memorial of the man, his bust atop an asymmetric grey granite plinth with beaten copper lettering, sits next to the entrance; as does a 1958 memorial plaque to the heroic deeds 'for freedom and socialism' of the local branch of the People's Army, the communist resistance movement during the war – whose importance was then inflated at the expense of the far larger Home Army, but which is now mostly forgotten or denigrated. So already there's a charged atmosphere on entering this place – one which actually entirely dissipates on getting inside.

The blocks of flats are of three storeys, and run in long terraces, their length subtly broken up via the wavy curves of the ground plan; these are more obvious on the back of the blocks, where concrete access balconies whip around the usual green, tree-filled space. They are broken up at regular intervals by pilotis, thin, red-painted Le Corbusier-issue pillars, which mean you can walk through the entire place with much freedom of

Helena and Szymon Syrkus's Swiss cheese balconies, Koło, Warsaw

movement, as yet unencumbered by private gating. The first details you notice about the Syrkuses' flats are the entrances – triangular walls with a curved roof on top, with holes punched in them at random, giving them the appearance of a cartoon drawing of Swiss cheese; the balconies subdivided in a similarly strange, witty way with precast waffle-shaped partitions. Not all of the flats wave around picturesquely, as some are more rectangular, with square bay windows and curved, glazed stair towers round the back; all are clad in bright, reasonably well-kept cream tiles.

'*Kocham cie Gosiu*', 'I love you, Gosia', reads a piece of graffiti scribbled everywhere. In the middle is a hill (formed out of rubble) and a lake, and there are the usual schools, Domy Kultury and suchlike. It is a straightforward continuation of the Modernist project that the architects began here in the 1930s, now become more playful, rolled out on a much larger scale – the house-machine humanized.

So, though it would have been understandable if somewhere like Rusanivka had been the reason for a sudden shift into neoclassicism, what actually happened in Koło, at least, was a dour, authoritarian reaction to a style which was subtle, clever and humane. From 1948 onwards the Polish state issued official anathemas on modern architecture, and even projects – like ZOR Koło – that were already under construction had to conform – as they did, with the architects themselves issuing the requested public self-criticisms. Due to the haste involved, they started to classicize (or Stalinize) their buildings mid-way through the process. In some of the Koło blocks you can see pilotis change into Doric columns, and the deliberately light ceramic tiles start to thicken up and imitate stone; parapets appear on the roofs. The continuous glazed stair towers are the same shape, but now have little windows instead. The floorplan, though, is identical. For the next phase, that last-minute adjustment is replaced with outright stodgy Stalinism – square, symmetrical blocks, with the Swiss cheese entrances replaced with stern neoclassical doorways, the iron balconies cast in vaguely Polish-Renaissance fashion. Looking at this newest part of the complex, facing the main road for the tram back, we notice the street is still named after Vladimir Mayakovsky, that lifetime enemy of pomposity and passé-ism.

The other of the two ZOR housing estates is several miles east in Praga, on the left bank of the River Vistula. If in Kiev right bank is history and left concrete modernity, it's the opposite here. This is where the Red Army were notoriously camped as the rest of Warsaw was razed to the ground by the Wehrmacht in 1944, which had the unintended side effect of leaving this the most preserved district of the city. It was also always one of the poorest, and still is – Praga is full of tall tenements whose flaking plaster ornament forms accidental patterns with revealed sheer brick walls, enclosing sunless, sullen courtyards, usually enlivened by little shrines to the Holy Mother of God; and, more occasionally, street art, as this has been Warsaw's aspiring Shoreditch for the last few years. Hipsters and artists moved here for the cheap rents, but the continuous presence of an unloved, seldom (until recently) visited, jerry-built, murky and dilapidated nineteenth-century district hasn't affected nostalgia for the nineteenth-century city much. It did exercise the city's rebuilders. Although they obviously weren't crazy enough to demolish the one habitable area left in the city, they did do something different when extending it into open country in the late 1940s. The first part of it, ZOR Praga 1, is again by Szymon and Helena Syrkus, and is based on the non-wavy parts of their work at Koło, a little toned down, without the affectionate little details, and given an odd vertical feature – a small, seven-storey tower block, basically devoid of ornament but so thin-lipped and unnerving with its small windows and marble-clad austerity as to look quite authentically Stalinist. A year or so after that, however, the city embarked upon New Praga. Designed by Jerzy Gieysztor and Jerzy Kumelowski in 1949 and eventually completed in 1960, during de-Stalinization, it closely resembles Nowa Huta, or a peripheral relation to MDM, only with a lot of the 'obvious' propagandistic elements removed – no mosaics, no sculptures, no Mannerist verdigris lamps. It is the Stalinist empire style stripped down to its essentials, a grid of flats for 25,000 people in six eight-storey blocks around squares and boulevards. While apartments in MDM were offered to Stakhanovites and the nomenklatura, these were occupied from the start by ordinary Warsaw workers, freshly arrived from the countryside to repopulate and rebuild the devastated capital; accordingly, it had a bad rep, even in this allegedly classless society – a recent book describes it as a 'rarely renovated and consistently devastated settlement . . . a neglected zone'.[11]

Sculptures and mosaics or not, it is still a highly impressive space. In a comparison which makes pretty clear exactly where things stood in People's Poland, its relation to MDM is essentially that of an eastern Parisian arrondissement – Belleville, say – to the Champs-Elysées. Recognizably of the same typology, taking a similar approach to spatial planning using basically similar materials, obviously part of the same general project, but equally obviously intended for the lower orders, with the factories where most of the inhabitants worked in convenient walking distance. It is as nineteenth century in its layout and plan as that, and it is also nineteenth century in the way it accommodates fairly easy street life – shops and bars (not too salubrious) on most of the ground floors, Hapsburg-style green strips in between the tenements; but its aesthetic, however classical it might appear, is a great deal more imposing. The removal of the usual heraldic fol-de-rol of the era means that the blocks appear much more monumental, their mass unbroken. The ancillary blocks, along Ulica Bertolta Brechta (Bertolt Brecht Street, surprisingly not renamed), have what look distinctly like penthouses, marked out by strange stripped

Monumentality at Praga 2, Warsaw

classical pavilions on the roof, like little temples; while grandiose symmetries demarcate the main showpiece, Plac Hallera (as it is now, named after Józef Haller, a nationalist interwar general, but originally named after the interwar communist leader Julian Lenski, who was murdered on Stalin's orders). At Koło, you can see the Stalinist style consuming Modernism, and here, barely ten years later, you can see the opposite, with the ideology of 'nothing superfluous' imposed on the blocks at the last minute, making their underlying structural grid more important than the imposition of borrowed details. But there is no modernist 'truth to materials' here either – one of the main parts of the original programme is retained, the use of would-be-luxurious facing materials, so all of these tenements, erected with concrete or brick, are faced with a veneer of stone; rusticated to the ground floor just like in Tverskaya, and, above, polished marble, which catches the light – grey, brown and a deep, dark red.

If there is one suburb, workers' district, sleeping district or microrayon that we came across where Socialist Realism produced something genuinely staggering, something harder to resist, it was Poruba, on the outskirts of the Czech industrial city of Ostrava. This, the Czech Republic's third-largest city, lies in the Silesian industrial conurbation that is a sort of trans-border equivalent to the Ruhr or South Yorkshire, i.e. a coalfield liberally covered with steelworks; the pollution in the area is still notorious, although improved somewhat by the economic collapse and mass unemployment of the 1990s. As such, it is the sort of place that was always communism's bastion, in terms both of its self-representation and, here at least, of its popular support. In Czechoslovakia, the Communist Party, which had been a mass party before the war and had led the resistance, won a plurality without much need for ballot-stuffing, 'salami tactics' and intimidation at the last free elections in 1946, and the subsequent coup in 1948 had a lot of popular support. Although they may not have chosen *this* communism, the majority of Czechs and a lesser but still large percentage of Slovaks definitely – unlike the Poles, Hungarians or Romanians – chose some sort of communism. The communists were a mass party in Ostrava from early on, and they won a sizeable share of the vote here in the elections of 2013. Perhaps some of the support that the Stalinists had here is reflected in the relative flamboyance and richness of the new town they built on Ostrava's outskirts.

Built to serve the mines and steelworks (then) nearby, Poruba is a motorway journey by bus from the city itself, at a far enough distance to make it appear as a new settlement entirely, rather than just a suburb, estate or 'sleeping district'. It makes its ambitions clear from the very start, where it opens itself out through a crescent, a sweep of crazily over-encrusted Baroque around parkland, with a triumphal arch in the middle through which the bus has to travel. Unlike the MDM–New Praga/elite–proletariat divide, evidently here no expense has been spared. Like most Stalin-era projects the marble and stone are a visibly fairly thin veneer on more mundane constructional materials, but the intensity of their application here is on the level of central Moscow. At the end of the crescent is a clock tower, with a central loggia for one very lucky flat, with an octagonal tower on top of that, and a red metal spire rising above it, ending in a long, thin spike surmounted by a sheaf of wheat. The triumphal arch, designed by Vladimir Meduna in 1951, is corbelled and decorated by double colonnades of thick Doric columns, which probably aren't holding anything up, but look very imposing. At the top of the arch are sculptures of the heroic builders, doing the usual Socialist Realist things – heroic workers and their children greeting each other around two

The sights of Ostrava-Poruba (1960s postcard)

crossed hammers. Already this is seriously opulent, muscular classicism, driven by the overload of detail and the embrace of shameless spatial melodrama right into kitsch. It is hard at first to work out exactly where the historical references are coming from and what exactly that signifies – a liking for Michelangelo and Tsarist Baroque, largely. But mostly what this grand crescent-archway is is an overwhelming statement of entrance – welcome here, we have built this for you, where you, Czech miner and steelworker, can live like the doges and Medicis.

Through the arch, and you find something much less pompous – the small houses and low-rise blocks that came first, since – as always – Socialist Realism was imposed a few years after 1945, onto an architectural profession that was still almost entirely Modernist, irrespective of whether it had communist sympathies or not. Stalinism in Czechoslovakia was brief, but of a terrifying brutality, with the Slánský trial of 1952 particularly notorious for its barbarism and thinly disguised anti-Semitism; the popular support the communists enjoyed did not prevent them from importing full Stalinism in all its horror, something which is worth remembering given the excuses that were made for it at the time. Even in the twisted omelette-making logic of the 1940s and 1950s, it is hard to see how forcibly turning an industrialized country with a mass Communist Party and extremely widespread socialist sympathies into a carbon copy of the USSR's despotic developmental state was at all *necessary*. That automatism of Stalinism, its favouring of its one conceivable solution forged in conditions of scarcity and barbarity, regardless of what different conditions might have led to, is one of its most enduringly horrible aspects. What we have here is, it must be remembered, that regime's self-glorification, and its colonial nature is obvious from that amazing triumphal archway, when you realize what it is actually directly based on – the General Staff building in St Petersburg. In a country that had never been part of the Tsarist Empire it's a structure that mimics its forms, a blaring propaganda instrument aimed at what would otherwise have been a sympathetic population; and above all else, it's an import, with absolutely no 'roots' in this place, architecturally or socially, at all. The embrace of the 'national tradition' that Socialist Realism called for usually meant the embrace of someone else's (mutated, at least half-imaginary) national tradition.[12]

Yet the forms of the buildings could be given applied detail that made 'reference' to local tradition, or rather the local architecture of the sixteenth and seventeenth centuries a couple of hours' train journey away in Prague. After those little, undemonstrative blocks of flats, painted yellow with glazed stairways and pitched roofs, the neoclassical bombast starts up again; but the massive forms go weird and florid at the top, with sgraffito cherubs playing in the attics, pointing to a legend extolling the virtues of steelmaking, education and world peace. There are little obelisks at the corners. It's an amalgamated conjunction of the 'officially' acceptable aesthetics of the Hussites, the radical early-Protestant sect that seized control of the Czech lands from the Hapsburg Empire in the fifteenth century; the stepped towers come from their fortresses; and the surely less acceptable styles of the empire itself, i.e. the style of the Counter-Reformation, provide the model for the rest. All that is applied to what is essentially Tverskaya, right down to the grand archways. But it isn't remotely like a magistrale in plan, but rather like an extremely grandiose suburb.

That pleasantly slightly suburban feeling is enforced by the relatively narrow street, of an entirely normal two lanes, and the huge amount of trees everywhere. The street curves around towards a much larger street, but before we get there, it's worth going through one of those grand Muscovite archways, because what you find there, as in Moscow, is something much more informal and small-scale. But what's different is that rather than a scattered older city through the archway, you find that this estate also got rid of most of the nineteenth-century typologies that had hitherto dominated workers' housing. There are lots of neoclassical blocks, for sure, but they're informally organized, with a lot of trees and a lot of space, so that it never feels like a descent into a sunless courtyard; a lot of the trees are so thick and wide that they must have been taken over from the open country that was here before, rather than planted especially; and there are shallow hills rolling between, so it is hardly featureless. The effect is weird, because the buildings are not at all 'suburban' or 'radiant' in their looks or their scale; but it does make it unexpectedly enjoyable to walk around and inside the blocks.

So, oddly, the embrace of the nineteenth-century city is skin-deep, with behind it something a great deal less inhumane – a deeply unusual example of Stalinist planning being more humane than it looks. As a suburb – since that is what it is – the main flaw seems to be the distance from any kind of centre. Like any suburb, it has its facilities – a 1950s

Inside the courtyards of Ostrava-Poruba

House of Culture still in use, where giant sculpted miners look down on dance classes and language courses, schools, colleges, some surviving light industry, parks, shopping malls – but it is quiet, though a flyer glued to a lamppost bearing the face of Bootsy Collins suggests that there is nightlife of some description. The mini-magistrale that runs through Poruba, Hlavní Třída (originally Leninka), which leads back to Ostrava proper, is a full multi-lane monster, lined with cafés and shops, although again without much in the way of actual traffic, and with a wide pedestrian path interspersed with lawns and flowers in the middle, so that you can walk through it and appreciate the symmetry. The seeming central point is a square where, again, the architecture has wormed its way from one style into another, back out of this strange mania of imported opulence, melodrama and pomposity into a more sober and somewhat less historically charged Modernism – at one point, you can see one of the Tverskaya-esque arches, its pilasters picked out in a warm pink and a buttery yellow, exactly frame a tower block built a few years later. At the pedestrian square at the heart of Poruba, neoclassical wings frame a Modernist tower, where modern volumes are decorated with sculptures again – and this time the imagery of the figures is more up to date, at least temporally, with space exploration being the general theme. Right across a Greek restaurant is a continuous frieze depicting semi-nude male and female figures flying through the air, fists aloft, while diodes, drills and sputniks float in the void in between and around them. Here you can see the space age heralded via imagery that looks like a combination of Victoriana and Marvel Comics. Opposite is a statue of a steelworker in overalls. The unemployment rate in Ostrava is 15 per cent, roughly the communist share of the vote.

AGAINST THE STANDARD, FOR A BETTER KIND OF MODERNISM!

In Kiev, Ostrava, Warsaw or Kraków, we have seen Stalinist 'palaces for the people' be replaced with standardized housing estates of striking banality and interchangeability, where, seemingly, all the fears of the Stalinist architectural commissars came true, and identity and urban legibility were overwhelmed by a production line of concrete panels. This is not the whole of the story – there isn't, in fact, any real reason why these sorts of techniques should result in something so monolithically bland and obvious; as Helena and Szymon Syrkus made clear in ZOR Koło, you could use factory-made components to create architecture that was distinctive and original. What it would take is some sort of intervention into the production line process itself, to get the factories to produce different kinds of prefabricated parts – as indeed they were doing in the car industry, which by the 1950s in the West had moved on considerably from 'any colour as long as it's black' into the mass production of individuality – contra Havel, there is no good reason why a planned economy cannot follow suit, as this aspect of capitalist economies is also tightly planned. It does present the problem of economies of scale, however; in an economy of scarcity, it would only be considered a useful approach to housing construction if it could be deployed on a large enough number of units – i.e. if it were done for thousands of flats. We visited three (of many) microrayons where the requisite scale seems to have met with the appropriate manufactures – and you start to see giant homogeneous housing estates which are trying, architecturally, to not be homogeneous.

Sometimes this attempt is defeated from the off simply by the fact that a peripheral estate is a peripheral estate, and a ghetto is a ghetto, no matter how cleverly planned it might be. One such example is Fužine, on the outskirts of Ljubljana, then the capital of the Socialist Republic of Slovenia, the richest part of the Socialist Federal Republic of Yugoslavia. The extreme combined and uneven development of that country meant that the wealthier areas, such as this alpine Art Nouveau city, had massive rates of in-migration from the poorer areas in the south like Bosnia or Macedonia; and although draconian immigration policies meant that this didn't become as apocalyptic as it could have been in the 1990s, it still feels like a place apart. The richness of the historical architecture in the city centre is accompanied by a rich modern architecture, which derives from some eclectic influences – Hapsburg imperial Modernist Otto Wagner, interwar Slovenia's unorthodox neoclassicist Jože Plečnik, and Le Corbusier, through whose atelier some of its architects briefly passed. Designers like Edvard Ravnikar favoured a decorative form of Modernism, where brick and marble cladding was fastidiously applied to asymmetric towers and ziggurats, placed cleverly among Ljubljana's boulevards and winding streets; exemplary examples of 'critical regionalism', the adaptation of modern architecture to historical context without going for the pat references and borrowings of Socialist Realism. This didn't quite extend to building new areas.

In Fužine, the new migrants could find a few of the careful little details that Slovenian architects excelled at, in a gigantic estate that tried to use

The concrete outskirts of Hapsburg Ljubljana

shapes to avoid the usual sense of serried ranks of prefabricated monoliths. Every block here is visibly constructed from grey concrete panels, with strongly modelled balconies and a top floor of painted coloured metal; the entrances to the blocks are marked by cantilevered entryways and clinker-brick stairwells. These are then put into various combinations – the plans are here V-shaped, there W-shaped, here a row of three-storey flats one after the other with hedges and tight gardens, there a random scattering with green space flowing between. Parking is provided in specially designed multistoreys with concrete pitched roofs, but by now there are so many cars that the public space is fairly dominated by them. You can see how much effort has been expended to create some kind of diversity and surprise, without opting for obviously decorative or retro devices – no 'streets', no 'houses'. It's the extremity of the contrast with the affluent centre that makes it uncomfortable; when, so nearby, you have something so rich and distinctive, it is hard for it not to feel vague and somewhat disconsolate. It feels like a decent, greying, down-at-heel estate in Western Europe, more than anywhere else we visited for this chapter;

for all the gestures at irregularity, it does not look like its own place, but like the dormitory of somewhere else.

Like most microrayons, Fužine has no obvious 'centre', and does not try to provide one; but some of its contemporaries did. One is in Šeškinė, a peripheral estate in Vilnius, then part of the USSR, capital of the Lithuanian Soviet Republic. Vilnius is fringed with hills, which stop it from growing 'organically'; this problem was solved by throwing motorways across them to new peripheral settlements. These were something of a local speciality; Lithuanian architects, while using much the same prefabricated methods as those in the rest of the Union, often created more clearly distinctive, more obviously 'designed' environments, something often put down to the proximity of, and ideas borrowed from, Scandinavia. These estates were then held up as models elsewhere – particularly the large microrayon of Lazdynai, which won its architects the Lenin Prize in 1974. That these places were once considered prestigious is hard to fathom on first glance, as they're usually as dilapidated as those in Kiev. The European Union has a fund for Infrastructure and Development, which is often used for the renovation of Soviet-era microdistricts, which, as we'll see, has been applied in Poland with mixed results. Either the money has not reached Šeškinė yet, or they've decided to spend it elsewhere, because the state of it is not encouraging, something that initially obscures the fact that here we're dealing with an exceptionally late attempt to save the system of standardization from itself.

Constructed between 1977 and 1983 to the designs of B. Krūminis and D. Ruseckas, Šeškinė is the northern entry point to Vilnius, something which is stressed by the northernmost of its towers, which carry the large sign 'VILNIUS' to inform you that you've arrived, serving the function of a heraldic 'city gate' – even the most abstracted Modernism becomes here an *architecture parlante*, something representational, speaking as a grand entryway to a modern city. If your car or bus is going in this direction, the road soon plunges down the hill, and the more familiar Baroque (and, now, high-tech/slick Modernist) skyline of the city reveals itself. From the city centre itself, the first buildings you spot after getting off the bus are the towers, of which there about fifteen, scattered across a sprawling site bisected by the motorway. At first, you might think you're looking at a tower that has stapled the ocean liner corners of 1930s villas onto itself at random. Forty or so sweeping, curved bay windows protrude from the façade, their concrete structure obviously prefabricated, as is the rest of the building, with the joins between the panels still clear. The white concrete is discoloured by random brown patches in some, or is recently painted in others. These semi-circular modules are distributed in irregular fashion all the way down the tower – four here in a row pointing east, two in a row pointing north, and so on to the bottom of their twelve storeys, with the reverse on each of its four corners. The dashing, dramatic quality of 1930s luxury architecture is here snatched out of its original context and made into a component of public housing.

The human-scale city centre, Šeškine, Vilnius (1989 postcard)

But look more closely, and you'll notice that each of these deep bay windows has a different frame – some of wood, some of metal, some of uPVC. We spotted that a quarter or so of the buildings have wide curved balconies the same shape as the bay windows, and we realized that almost all the balconies have been changed into rooms – something necessitated by families outgrowing the flats they were allocated twenty-five years ago by a very different social system, or, we're told, in some cases to provide an electricity-free fridge in winter.

Prefabrication and adaptive reuse are held in an uneasy tension; which is an interesting irony, given that these towers were obviously designed to avoid the sense of regularity and interchangeability of so much Soviet housing, replacing blocks on blocks with this asymmetric pattern of swooping curves. That designed irregularity becomes the accidental irregularity of everyone paying a different (and, from the looks of it, usually dodgy) contractor to transform their streamlined balconies into rooms. The result, when combined with the rotting state of the concrete, is extremely jarring, resembling some sort of Heath Robinson Constructivism. Looking up at a

The prefab futurist fridge, Šeškinė, Vilnius

particularly distressed example of these towers, where the ovals of the balconies lead up to a castellated skyline of cylindrical concrete pipes, Agata says 'They're very steampunk, aren't they?' Temporalities that don't make sense – buildings from the 1980s that suggest a cut-up collage version of the 1930s, made using the technologies of the 1960s, given gimcrack additions in the 1990s and left to rot in the 2010s.

Around the deliberately 'unique' towers are the more usual rectilinear units common to any microrayon, albeit here a little more carefully planned than Kiev, with the social spaces between seeming rather less like afterthoughts. Winding paths run through the overgrown lawns and trees, and steel climbing frames are scattered around, many of them done in space-age style – planets, rockets, weird irregular grids that imply children playing in three-dimensional minimalist sculptures. The surrounding blocks are standard issue, exactly the same as those in Rusanivka, each of them given an individual number, written out in robotic, right-angled lines, so you have to squint a little to read them. Yet they have a much less dogmatic plan – rather than running in linear parallel lines, they enclose space, forming

Block 206, Šeškinė, Vilnius

certain half-squares, where children play and old ladies sit on benches and chat to each other. There don't seem to be many people between those ages. These in-between spaces are enduringly controversial here as they are in the West – their obvious freedom, their lack of prescribed use, oddly appears not to endear them to people in their newfound 'free' societies and free economies. They're hardly completely useless, though, with an obvious function for those who want to use them, or are familiar with them.[13]

The centre of Šeškinė is, again, something else entirely. Usually these places have shopping centres as strung out, long and linear as the buildings they serve. Šeškinė has what looks like an attempt to create some kind of agora, a central public space which is much more focused and much more clearly 'urban', without replicating the old system of streets, 'active frontages' and so forth revived in the magistrale and the Socialist Realist housing estates. The least successful aspect of it is the approach from the flats and towers; clear pedestrian paths lead there, but what you see are the back ends of buildings, their service areas, with sheer walls, bins and lorries as your welcome. If you were driving, you could loop round this to the even more car-centric spaces of the exurban retail parks and entertainment parks that drift out from Vilnius to the countryside. Walk, on foot, into the complex itself, and you can see what the designers were up to.

The architects were awarded a prize for this centre in 1987, and it does seem to have some relation to the then-contemporary ideas of glasnost and perestroika: an attempt to move from monolithic abstraction to something more clearly 'close to the people'. Five two-level short 'streets', with shops mostly on the ground floor and public facilities (local government office, kindergarten, advice bureau and such) lead to a square, where a sculptural tower serves as a decorative beacon. The buildings are all of red brick in a poured-concrete frame, in what looks like a combination of prefabrication and more straightforward on-site methods, since unlike the towers these components were surely too complex to be mass-produced in Soviet factories. However they were made, they're in an appalling state for buildings that are not even thirty years old – the aggregate has come off a lot of the steps, leaving the steel reinforcement bare, so you find yourself walking up stairs that are one third a bare, spindly metal frame; surely evidence that under Gorbachev the base was not managing to keep up with the superstructure.

This is a shame, as from here you can see what a clever and successful piece of planning it is: genuinely bustling, full of people and activity, albeit not always of the most heartwarming sort, with large quantities of cheap and questionable goods being sold. The architecture, constructional dodginess aside, is strong and distinctive, with the upper levels especially managing to make this sprawling estate legible – from here you can see all of those bizarre collaged towers at once, and can place them and yourself in some kind of order. Concrete awnings provide some shelter from the weather (sunny, on the day of our visit), and the buildings are richly articulated, with arcading, peculiar angles and sudden curves, with their brick cladding a materiality that offers a more richly coloured contrast with the concrete all around. At one end, it turns into a street market, where we eat some excellent and exceptionally cheap *Chłodnik* – a cold Lithuanian borscht, exactly the sort of thing required as we slump ourselves, weary and sweaty from hours of walking, onto the plastic seats. The tiny, packed café isn't in one of the original buildings, but in a little prefab, of the sort you find in markets anywhere in Europe – the automatic architecture of Postmodern 'informal' commerce meeting that of Soviet high modernity.

The ideas in Šeškinė are brave, and at least partly successful in their attempt to provide some kind of coherence and distinctiveness to the straggling form of the Modernist microrayon, without turning towards the certainties of an imaginary past; but the huge difficulties that building technologies had in erecting it are equally conspicuous. What might it look like, then, if it was actually maintained, if the EU infrastructure budget had been lavished on it? A clue is provided by the Thousandth Anniversary Estate (Osiedle Tysiąclecia), a microrayon on the edge of the Polish Silesian city of Katowice. A long time before the 'Gherkin' and its ilk became the semi-official nomenclature for appropriately shaped skyscrapers, Katowice knew this estate as 'the corns'. When, from the centre of Katowice, we bought our tram tickets to visit, Agata asked first how much it would be to the Thousandth Anniversary Estate, she got a blank look; but on asking for 'the corns', got a seemingly overpriced ticket. Upon challenging them – 'this is more than tram tickets cost in Warsaw!' – the man in the kiosk told us: 'Look, we're all miners here. And of course it's more expensive, we're a bigger city than Warsaw!' Which, at least in terms of its conurbation, is true – Katowice is at the centre of an urban area that encompasses a dozen or so large towns, from Gliwice to Bielsko-Biała, with a population of 2.7 million, with most of the population growth coming in Poland's post-war industrialization, when this became the heartland of coal and steel, and the power base of the modernizing leader Edward Gierek, still surprisingly well-regarded in these parts. Those towns all sprouted peripheral estates like 'the corns', which make it a practically continuous industrial metropolis, mostly made up of Modernist housing estates. In order for it not to seem homogeneous, some sporadic attempt was made to move away from blocks on blocks on blocks; shapes and patterns came in instead.

The tram runs through the typical Silesian landscape of abandoned or dilapidated steelworks and their shopping mall and retail park replacements, which are as interchangeable and homogeneous as, if not more so, the blocks of old. Certainly there's no doubt in the arrival – the estate is still heralded by a 'Os. Tysiąclecia' sign. The thousandth anniversary of what, you may ask? The name refers to the millennial anniversary of the conversion of the Poles to Christianity in AD 966, a strange thing for an avowedly atheist government to be celebrating. This isn't because of contorted claims that monotheism was more progressive historically than paganism, but because the Polish Catholic Church had launched a campaign for 1966 to celebrate this anniversary, drawing enormous crowds in the process, meaning that the Party would look foolish or unpopular if it were to officially oppose it; it was merely slightly rephrased as the anniversary of Polish statehood. They tried to co-opt it, just as they did Polish nationalism and even anti-Semitism in the same decade. The state-owned co-operative that built the Thousandth Anniversary Estate was called 'Piast', after the medieval Polish dynasty whose empire stretched into much of what is now eastern Germany and the Czech Republic; this being the historical justification for Poland's annexation of almost entirely German-populated areas like Pomerania and Lower Silesia after 1945. The place is mostly named after Piast kings or those of the later Jagiellonian dynasty, and their symbols are everywhere. All this deeply odd, contradictory and uncomfortable history would, in the late 1940s and early 1950s, have resulted in some twisted Stalino-Baroque fantasy where all those contradictions were fully on view, where 'identity' was stressed in the most drastic way. Here, unless you knew a bit of Polish and a bit of the history, you'd never know – everything you can see is abstract and nearly everything you can see is delightful.

The estate, designed incrementally between the early 1960s and late 1970s, stretches into rolling open country, with the dips and meadows

The Thousandth Anniversary Estate, Katowice

retained as much as possible, in the manner recommended in Le Corbusier's Ville Radieuse. In countries that do not have a Mediterranean coastline, the beauty of these places can be very dependent on the weather. We were there in August, and it looked stunning. Around the entrance sign are the usual semi-representational 'gates', two ribbon-windowed rectangles linked by glass skyways; opposite is the Silesian Park of Culture and Leisure, and the zoo. Deeper in, you find that the more complicated land has often got the less complicated blocks on it, those which are crisp little slabs dotted down the hills, with schools and pavilions selling groceries, flowers and such in between. Each of the square towers has a big, cartoonish painted sign – clearly recently renovated, and equally clearly not a recent piece of design – which bears the Piast logo in space-age bubble writing, a silhouetted cartoon of a castle or a Piast king, and the road and street number. The buildings are obviously in the late stages of a renovation programme, with a little bit of scaffolding around the fringes but mostly spotless new white, purple, blue and black render across the concrete façades. Polish cities have mostly fully availed themselves of EU money, and the process usually involves putting a layer of styrofoam on the building to insulate it and protect the sometimes expanding joints between the prefabricated parts. As we'll see elsewhere, for all its welcome effects in keeping the buildings together and making people's homes habitable, this doesn't always have the most encouraging aesthetic effects – but here, the renderers have been subtle, respecting the buildings. It probably looks better here now than it ever has, especially with the landscape growing up around it, and the pathways and playgrounds mostly renovated alongside. Having often lived in actual Western European council estates myself, I felt a little jealous.

As for 'the corns' themselves, the things that make this place (locally) famous, they do look a little like cobs of corn if you squint. They give the impression of being six or eight tubes bunched together around a central core, their heights going from ten to thirty storeys, with cantilevered square pods housing shops, banks and communal services sticking out above the ground floors over raised public squares which disguise built-in car parks. They are not irregular like those of Šeškinė, not asymmetrical or random, but obviously they're trying to do something similar – commissioning different parts from the factory, so that the product does not scream its production line origin. Architecturally, at least, it really works – they look like they were built yesterday. They don't encourage individuality in the same way, though – there are satellite dishes and washing lines, but anyone who turned their balcony into a room seems to have (forcibly?) had it removed, making them look like single works of

'The corns' through the trees, Katowice

architecture rather than the scene of the decomposition of the public sphere. Much more than in Fužine or Šeškinė, the spaces between have some sort of flow and ease to them; winding, narrow roads lined with ferns, with small shops dotted around, and benches to the street. The same prefab system of interlocking circles is used for a church (more of which later) and a shopping centre, which has typically unexciting but useful suburban contents – bar, supermarket (Biedronka, basically the Polish Lidl), fitness centre, pharmacist. As suburbs go, it seems really quite lovely, the usual fixation on private space exchanged for an abundance of public virtues – coherence, flow, collectivity. Like any suburb, it's not for hipsters, but it compares well with the best of the era in Scandinavia or elsewhere. Osiedle Tysiąclecia ends with a lake, looked over by those square, ribbon-windowed blocks. You could be in an American campus university, not a Polish coal and steel town.

A fair comparison with this obvious success is an estate where the design is not so easily adaptable to the addition of styrofoam insulation, and which sits on a rather more valuable site. One of the most extravagant housing estates in post-war Poland is Plac Grunwaldzki, just outside the centre of the Lower Silesian city of Wrocław, cleared of its overwhelmingly German population after the defeat of its earlier incarnation, 'Fortress Breslau', in 1945. It is named after another famed victory over the Germans, the 1410 Battle of Grunwald, in which a Polish–Lithuanian alliance destroyed for good the Teutonic Knights, an event much recalled in 'People's Poland'. Plac Grunwaldzki, aside from the similar historic associations of its name, is also an ambitious effort in three-dimensional city planning akin to the Thousandth Anniversary Estate, equally sculptural and imaginative. Designed in 1967 by Jadwiga Grabowska-Hawrylak, it consists of six large tower blocks on a raised podium with shops and the usual social facilities on the podium floor. It's an architectural triumph, marking a sucessful transition from the historic city of Breslau into the modern metropolis of Wrocław, with a sense of visual interest that microrayons usually lack, right down to the hieratic 'crowns' on top of each tower, lined with porthole windows.

What makes this rather tricky is that the prefabricated components of the façades are complex, an overlay of concave and convex chunks, with a heavily tactile, thought-out choice of materials – shuttered concrete and red tile, whose rippling moulding makes the towers vibrate like kinetic

Too complex for styrofoam: Plac Grunwaldzki, Wrocław

sculptures. This means that their architectural integrity would be fatally compromised by a layer of yellow-painted insulation, and that – plus perhaps the potentially very lucrative inner-urban site – means they lurk worn out and unrenovated, the prefab joints filled in messily where they've started to give. The street life below, on that raised podium, is a curious combination of rather yuppiesque bars, kebab shops and cheap supermarkets, that vibrant mix which property developers like so much. However, this is a chapter about what were, by and large, banal developments, not special, spectacular monuments like these in Katowice and Wrocław. To those we must return.

THE STANDARD DISINTEGRATES

At this point, I ought to tell you about where I've been living while writing this book. When Warsaw started building peripheral districts en masse in the 1970s, it concentrated them in the south of the city, in three huge housing estates, almost impossible to tell apart – Stegny, Służew nad Dolinką and Ursynów, much of which makes up the Ursynów district of Warsaw city council, the Polish capital's largest and most populous. It begins where the mostly 1930s tenement and villa district of Mokotów ends; suddenly, the 'streets' stop, the towers start, and they don't let up until you eventually reach the secluded, gated villa estates of elites past and present. We live in exactly that place, just before the borough of Mokotów ends and Ursynów begins; a place where the affluent and the poor, the planned and the anarchically capitalistic, meet in some very unexpected ways, as strange historical forms shake themselves out in a peculiar order and eras collapse into each other; where the era of standardization ends, not by any deliberate effort, but by a combination of inertia and rapid development. Look at the two pictures opposite.

The lower of the two is the view from the window of the newly built flat Agata moved into in 2008. The flat is single aspect, so this is the only view you can get from the room itself, of the new towers – the other is taken near the communal stairwell, and shows the old ones. The earlier towers are prefab, these are concrete-framed, too irregular to find appropriate components. The earlier shows the usual block/space block/space arrangement of Corbusian town planning; the latter, an arrangement whereby a grand façade encloses another block, which encloses another block. Polish capitalism has managed to reinvent the 'rental barrack' and sell it as middle-class housing. For all that, I've quite enjoyed having these flats curve around me every day, watching the lights on the emergency stairs switch on and off at night. We never got round to fitting curtains in the unfurnished flat, so we spend, or at least I do, a lot of time gazing out of the window. Visitors often comment on how intimidating it looks, having a hundred or more flats loom down on you all the time, but the result has a certain bleak big-city frisson to it, the feeling that you are in some Varsovian remake of Wong Kar-Wai's Hong Kong, with a frontline seat for people-watching en bloc.

With 'socialism' long gone, there's no need for the blocks to assume an egalitarian appearance – generally, the more extraneous things they have on their façades, the more expensive the flats therein. The reaction against prefab, panel-built Modernism doesn't take the form here of the tacked-on bits of wood or barcode façades as in the UK, but seems more metropolitan, more unashamed about its pretensions to luxury. The model appears

Two views of Ulica Bukowińska, Warsaw

to be Art Deco, some sort of *Scarface* version of Miami, with all of the appliqué pastels and polished stone-effect surfaces. The biggest and visibly richest of the blocks has a triumphal column at its entrance, here, a monument to nothing but itself – an eagle on a plinth, in a peculiar Postmodernist-via-fascist composite. Just behind the eagle is a fitness centre on the block's ground floor, with large glass walls so you can watch the straining and heaving. It's not gated, however, and you can walk around the spaces (mostly car parks) without anyone telling you not to take photographs, except for one gated outpost right at the back. Here you find a far more traditional piece of high Modernism – regardless of its lack of orientation to the sun, the aesthetics are strictly Bauhaus, with white walls and strip windows. Inside are glass walkways crossing the CCTV cameras.

We soon realized on a walk round the estate why the block's owners might just be keen on stressing the security aspect. Not because they're worried about the tenants of the 1970s towers that still make up half of the estate – in fact, given the vagaries of the housing market in a city with a long-standing housing shortage, with many tenants exercising the Polish equivalent of right-to-buy, they may not even be that much poorer. The paranoia seems to have much more to do with the large swathe of indeterminate space round the back. One spring day in 2010 we went on a walk into it, not knowing exactly what to expect. Definitely neither of us had expected farmland, but that's what we found. First you come across hedges and trees that have obviously grown up at random, weeds and wisteria with a path between, where rubbish is usually strewn around. If you walk down the path and then turn around, you can see two kinds of Modernist estate – on the right are the serried blocks of the 1970s, on the left the ostensibly less regular new towers. But both of them have behind them the same stretch of wasteland, with little more than a track of mud leading out to the next estate. In this stretch are a succession of small houses, some with attached smallholdings which are visibly being tilled. The houses are guarded by some very unfriendly dogs, and are way more dilapidated than the recently renovated, pastel-rendered 1970s blocks. Yet these crumbling little farmhouses have the same Warsaw City street signs you see on the massive, ultra-urban boulevards of MDM, this time appended to the fences of a one-storey *dom* or a tumbledown shed. In every other available space, the new blocks of flats were springing up, completely unconcerned about their incongruousness. Contemporary Warsaw is not a city shy of its own modernity, which makes this vertiginous fall into the peasant society it only emerged from in the 1960s particularly alarming.

Further on from here, we found ourselves back in a fairly normal suburbia, rather than that extraordinary Modernist/rustic zone behind the tower blocks. Property adverts are placed along a row of 1990s houses, among the first to market themselves to the new private buyer. A few days before, I'd heard the sound of church bells, always redolent of my grandparents' house, across the high-rises, and was pleased to finally find their source – a steel bell-tower, which is in front of a red-brick church school that resembles a Lancashire factory, and a Modernist church, raw and bulky, in Hanseatic brick. By this point we were hanging round places where Agata had grown up, although she wasn't exactly overcome by nostalgia. At least not until we got to the Settlement of Służew nad Dolinka, where she lived until she was eight and her parents, members of what under 'socialism' would have been called the 'technical intelligentsia', got themselves a private house. That actual egalitarianism which had them living in the same towers as the local steelworkers has long gone, but the towers have all been given a similar coloured render like the new blocks a quarter of a mile away, and have the open spaces and orientation that the new ones lack. I defer to Agata's judgement: it was incredibly depressing living here and she would never do so again under any circumstances. There's definitely a lack of stuff to do, only a couple of shops and a hairdresser. They have all been given red or yellow or green render, and some of them have been painted as grey as the concrete underneath, but the prefabrication is now masked – you can't see the joins any more, which is probably a relief to the inhabitants, as many of the expansion joints on the panels were at risk of causing structural failure. We're in an estate as standardized as the one in Kiev where we began this chapter, but recent efforts have managed to obscure this, in the look of the buildings themselves, if not in the repetitious, unimaginative way they've been strung out across the landscape.

This was my first proper experience of a prefabricated microrayon, however, so I had no major point of comparison but for the much smaller equivalents in Western Europe. So what I noticed as different from a British council estate, aside from the (recent) upkeep, is, first, the sheer *quantity*. As a space it's dull if not unpleasant – lots of trees and landscaping, a mediocre but not especially obnoxious design which encompasses low rises as well as high, shops on the ground floor, schools and such – but it goes on for ever, as far as the eye can see, never changing, never developing, at least until another era barges it out of the way. As we talked about the place while wandering through it, I said I'd far rather live here than in a crumbling, damp-ridden nineteenth-century tenement in Praga – although there's no doubt that you see more people there in a few minutes there than in half an hour here – but if the comparison is with the newer blocks, I'm not so sure. Certainly the developers of the Warsaw flat where we reside would never pay for the frankly rather lush riverside park that curves round the entire estate – too much 'empty' space which could be better filled by profit-making development. From there, we descended into the Metro and went back home to capitalism.

After four years of living here on and off, certain aspects started to change, though not those you would expect; the little irritants of the area persist. After seven years, most of the area still had no real streets, neither in a Jane Jacobs or a Le Corbusier sense – the pedestrian (as we both are) has to stumble over mud tracks, over stones scattered to create makeshift paths, crossing roads littered with potholes; then this was suddenly solved by building a massive road, a dual carriageway where residents now have to wait a few extra minutes to get to and from the Metro. Still no 'street'. In the other direction from the farmland, towards Wilanowska Metro station, there were until recently several other dilapidated small rural houses, this time without cultivable land in front of them but rather a wide and barren semi-public space. Across the wide roads that lead out of the city and towards the airport, the 1970s towers take over again; so this indeterminate expanse around the Metro station serves as a sort of transit point between the two. People sell homegrown fruit and veg or second-hand books, kebab stalls occupy the unplanned alleys of space between developments, and a full-scale market selling cheap knock-off goods is right in front of a tower of luxury flats; it's caught in between speculative building, prefab Modernism and remnants of a not-so-distant rural past, and naturally the speculative development is gradually winning. Neither developers nor city council have managed to build pavements, but they are at the time of writing mid-way through building a new road with lots of parking space. The houses without their own land to grow stuff on are being bought out and demolished.

Round the back end, however, where they still have their fields and their scary dogs, the farmhouses survive. We had another long walk through them in October 2013, on the way to the polling station in the Stegny district. There was a city-wide referendum calling for the resignation of Hanna Gronkiewicz-Waltz, the capital's conservative mayor. The referendum was caused by a public petition, decrying her administration's well-above-inflation hikes in public transport fares, vanity projects (i.e. unusable stadia) and failure to provide basic services. The absence of pedestrian paths even in this partly affluent district we've already noticed, but the main indictment was the refusal to build a hospital in the borough of Ursynów, which covers the three huge housing estates to the south of the city; around 250,000 people have no access to a public general hospital nearby. This has been a problem for some time; although her parents lived in the area Agata was born in early-1980s Praga, on the other side of the river, as it was easier for the ambulance to get there. So while the area

Lean-to behind Bukowińska, Warsaw

might be subject to a rash of new development, the facilities it was promised when built have still not actually been provided. However, it's had certain other knock-on effects. When walking through the farmland we found most of the houses as they were three and a half years earlier, only sinking a little more into dilapidation; there's what could be a shed, a chicken coop or an aviary turned into a piece of avant-garde architecture, a cantilevered roof held up by planks and a strategically placed ladder. A little further along the same path, one corner has been fenced off, presumably successfully sold; 'exclusive houses, apartments, penthouses', at 'Potoki Residence Mokotów', following the English practice of placing a property in an area of bad repute in the adjacent one with a better rep. The ad shows an image of small cubic flats.

Through one of Warsaw's several depressing interzones of wasteland, wide arterial roads and billboards, Stegny comes to seem relatively attractive; and the renovations embarked upon in recent years must have done a favour to the public perception of prefab architecture in People's Poland – the older towers ranged around basketball courts, schools (one of which is the polling station), a swimming pool, florists and greengrocers don't look all that different, here, from the new ones being built in their interstices, but for the clarity of their design. Like most microrayons, Stegny is a matter of towers and slabs, and the slabs are usually the worst, at least visually – long, unbroken masses, sullen and repetitive; another Expressionist church next to them displays its individuality to surely successful counter-propagandist effect. Possibly mindful of this bleakness, the styrofoam and render job done on these is particularly excessive in its application of pastels – that rather 1930s deco green again, looking incongruous and vague. The towers and the mid-rise blocks got done over in reds and dark yellows, which on this autumn afternoon fit perfectly the colours of the trees that have grown up around them; it could be Sweden. Compared with the unfinished clash between socialism and speculation that we'd walked from, it looked really quite idyllic. In front of one cluster of towers is a new pond, with little pavilions alongside; a sharp, humane design in, surprise surprise, unrelieved grey concrete. There are lots of people around, almost entirely young families with children. This pond, decorated by concrete fountains, adjoins both the old towers and the newer, slightly smaller luxury flats adjacent, as if as an offering of peace between these two forces. Privatization with a

A new pond in Stegny, Warsaw

human face, through the incorporation, and even expansion, of the once-despised public spaces of 'socialism'. Here something unexpected seems to be happening – the slow gentrification of a microrayon, a gradual claiming and infill by the affluent of the most pejoratively horrible and inhumane spaces of the old system – a vote of confidence in its prefab Modernism from those with 'wherewithal'. Still no hospital, though – the mayor of Warsaw lost the referendum, with over 90 per cent voting against her, but the turnout was so low that the vote was declared invalid.

MODEL WORKERS OF THE MODEL MOTORDISTRICT

It is often unclear where a microrayon ends and a company town begins, given how many of them were arranged around a specific factory. Company towns and company districts were not rare in the 1930s, but few of them were so ambitious, or so freighted with ideology and cross-cultural exchanges and misunderstandings, as the Avtozavod district of the central Russian city of Nizhny Novgorod. An entire district of over 100,000 people, all of whom were working in or around a vast automobile plant built by an American company with American technology, housed – at least at first – in an experiment in collective living. Workers flocked there, not solely from the Soviet Union, and labour leaders visited to find out what this 'workers' paradise' was actually like, and to discover in what ways a district built for Ford factory workers in the USSR differed from one built for Ford factory workers in the UK or US, like Becontree or Dearborn. Most of the Socialist City or 'Sotsgorod' still stands today, and though altered and relatively depopulated, it is still a three-dimensional showcase of what a Soviet socialist company district was meant to be.

From the centre of Nizhny Novgorod the Avtozavod district is best reached by the city's one-and-a-bit-line Metro, built between 1977 and 1985. Simply in terms of infrastructure, the new industrial district is considerably better served than comparable British examples – comparing like with like, you might note the fact that in 2014 the 1930s workers' garden suburb of Wythenshawe on the outskirts of Manchester, a similarly sized city to Nizhny, is only now being connected with the rest of the city by a tram, and never had a rail connection. By contrast, somewhat rickety trams go through Avtozavod every minute or so, and the more infrequent but certainly more impressive Metro serves it with five stops. But once you get out at the other end, you notice some other differences with British practice. One, that the factory is still working, albeit at massively reduced capacity and with a far smaller workforce; two, that the factory is still adorned with a whole series of various ideological artworks and decorations; and three, that even now, the best workers and citizens of the district are still immortalized on billboards, hoisted up on the lampposts. 'Model Workers', 'People of Avtozavod', both can get their name and a photo on a billboard.

The permanent monuments include a faintly cheap-looking plastery Lenin, the first truck produced here mounted on a plinth made up of the number '1932' in concrete numerals, and, most impressive of all, two large mosaic panels produced in 1982 for the factory's fiftieth anniversary, depicting lone figures waving banners in the foreground, with smaller workers behind, in overalls and protective masks building the automobiles on one panel, making and driving tanks on the other, all pieced together with glittering blue, red and orange stones. The fact that the factory has long been a totally capitalist proposition – owned by the oligarch and friend of Peter Mandelson, Oleg Deripaska – hasn't led to any 'de-communization' of the visual rhetoric and street furniture around the red granite factory gates. Far from it: recent printed photo-panels tell the story of the factory, with due attention to the role of iron-fisted bosses such as Stalin's Minister of Industry Sergo Ordzhonikidze, the efficacy of its tanks built by women during the Great Patriotic War, and a fleet of black Volgas on Westminster Bridge. You don't get things like this outside the Ford factory in Dagenham. Clearly, here, being able to put together a car on a production line had an ideological meaning somewhat different from the American one as signifier of freedom and individuality.

That's ironic, given that this was a Soviet–American co-operation from the very start. The factory was a project of the Ford Motor Company, and for a time early on the Ford logo even accompanied the medallion of Lenin on the factory gates. The factory was closely modelled on Ford's structures in Detroit and elsewhere, only with the difference that this time it wouldn't be owned by them – the Great Depression meant the famously union-bashing, right-wing Ford assented to building nationalized factories for communists. The construction of the city itself was managed by the Austin Company, an engineering firm based in Cleveland, Ohio (not to be confused with the English motor company). Richard Stites, in his compendium of early-Soviet utopias, *Revolutionary Dreams*, disparagingly refers to it as one of the partial, unsuccessful, botched attempts to realize the various new collective environments envisaged in the first post-revolutionary years. 'The workers' city of the Nizhny Novgorod Plant was designed by Americans and approved by the Soviets, with centralized schooling, clubs, hospitals, bakeries, kitchens, laundries and other services for its 18,000 employees in communal blocks of 300 residents each – a symmetrical phalanstery on a modern industrial site. An entire village of 3000 people was moved to make way for its construction. Yet as late as 1932 there were not enough beds and the premises had no water. These sites were parodies of the bright dreams of the clean, rational, community building homes envisioned by the architects and planners of the 1920s.'

The utopian dream here came up against the messy reality of a rural, 'backward' country undergoing forced, rapid industrialization. In this particular case we have a document which makes it clear how complex the interactions between the American industrialists and Soviet architects actually were, and how far from inevitable this decline into Potemkin Modernism actually was. The Sotsgorod's history has been told by Richard Cartwright Austin, the son of the head of the Austin company, in his book *Building Utopia*. He points out how the design was based on an architectural competition at the 'Soviet Bauhaus', VKhUTEMAS, the winner of which constituted several collective blocks in a parallel arrangement, with open space between, an interconnecting walkway between each, and all of them fully equipped with collective facilities. This was then adapted by the Austin Company's engineers, who recognized that all this concrete and glass was way beyond the Russian building industry's capabilities, replacing it with subtly detailed brick and smaller windows, but with no changes, at first, to the programme. In fact, it seems to have elicited some enthusiasm from the Methodist engineering firm. The head of the project, Allen Austin, wrote in 1931 for the *New York Times Magazine* of the communalization planned for the new city – 'the fourth floor of each building is composed of larger rooms, the size of a double and single room combined. These are intended to be occupied by "Communes" – groups of three or four young men or women who study, live or work together'.[14] When this failed to be actualized, it was not because of the direct importation of American morality and conformism, nor a 'totalitarian' insistence on collectivity, but the demographic tumult created by the Five-Year Plan itself, specifically by its massive underestimation of the population shift to the cities and industrial centres.

Cartwright Austin quotes a contemporary report by an American journalist, Milly Bennett, in terms which, aside from the exoticizing tone, immediately evoke the peri-urban 'maelstrom' of breakneck industrialization: 'the Russian workers come to the plant from the villages, husky peasant men and women with packs on their backs. They live in long, rude barracks. And, impatiently, they move into the unfinished model houses of the Workers City, 300 families strong, and camp there.' This occurred, she points out, before electrical and other services were finished in the flats. Cartwright Austin notes the unpopularity of the communal flats, but it seems unlikely that ideology had much to do with this – in fact, 'some of the scheduled communal facilities were never provided.' A comparative image in the book of the Workers' City over the course of the 1930s shows the aesthetic becoming more conservative after the design passed out of the Austin engineers' hands, with pitched roofs added to the new blocks and the experiment with communal walkways not repeated. The end of this Soviet–American ideal industrial settlement came the same year the first car was produced – 'the utopian city of 1930 was overtaken by economic necessity. It was finally abandoned in 1932 . . . workers in the new automobile factory would live very much as industrial workers in other parts of the world.'[15] As a place to live, he was probably right. The writer and scion of the Avtozavod Kirill Kobrin writes in his short story *The Last European* of how an encounter with Dublin nightlife immediately 'tipped him back, into the Soviet proletarian 1970s', and a memory of 'women chipped with alcohol, their eyes full of yearning. Sharp-nosed urchins, shiveringly wrapping themselves in cheap jackets. Lads always ready for drinking and fighting. On Mondays, the irrepressible stink of puke in the streets. Gorky. Avtozavod.'[16]

The several streetblocks that make up that first part of the Avtozavod are still lined with those short rows of tenements, their brick façades sometimes in their original state, sometimes with cheap corrugated metal balconies, and sometimes with rather alarming red roofs with built-in attic floors which look very recent indeed. As architecture, their heritage in Constructivism is invisible, but as space you can spot it – this is a collective city in a garden, with easy, rather informal tree-lined boulevards running through it, without much obvious activity save some vague strolling. It's quiet, and quite pretty, not a garden suburb but a suburb in a park. The difference with Becontree or Wythenshawe is most obvious in the collectivity of the housing. There, as in the US, the single-family house with a big front and back garden, and lots of domestic space inside, was the model; here, the green space is all exterior, public. Bar a tiny colony built for the American engineers, there are no single-family houses at all.

The mass unemployment of the Great Depression coinciding with the full employment in the Soviet Union meant that the Avtozavod district was, for a time, a magnet for workers and socialist activists, both trade union leaders and their rank-and-file. Among the latter were the brothers Victor and Walter Reuther, who didn't find conditions there to be

Utopia: Sotsgorod, Nizhny Novgorod

particularly different from those in the USA. They were both blacklisted after leading a strike at Avtozavod, and on their return to the USA would be prominent in the then-militant United Automobile Workers, and became the best-known leaders of the General Motors strike of 1936. As in Nizhny – renamed Gorky in 1933 – they suffered a blacklist in the USA, not to mention beatings and assassination attempts, but here at least they won, helping to unionize the auto industry for the first time. The brothers later wound up Khrushchev during a meeting with American labour leaders as part of his visit to America in 1959, by asking him – in Russian: 'Is the Gorky Automobile Works still named after Molotov?', soon after the former Foreign Minister's purging. 'Can you give us one single example', asked Walter Reuther, getting the chance to ask the questions he couldn't in Gorky, 'in which one of your unions ever disagreed with government policy?' 'Why poke your nose into our business?' retorted Khrushchev.[17]

But another observer, from the other side of the trade union movement, gave more attention to the living conditions of the Avtozavod workers. The then-leader of the British TUC, Sir Walter Citrine, was keen to contrast the conditions of the recently uprooted peasant workforce of the Soviet city with the council houses, large rooms, gardens and municipal facilities enjoyed by many workers in the UK, due to the lobbying of the trade union movement. He called his travelogue of a 1935 trip round the USSR *I Search for Truth in Russia*, and found the truth in the Sotsgorod to be muddy. 'We visited the Socialist City', he writes, 'and found it to be exceptionally well-planned, with good, wide streets, which some day, I hope, will be concreted. At present, they are a mass of slush, and I could not help wondering whether they will ever be anything different. These people rush to put up buildings but never seem to finish them. They never seem to have time.' He is puzzled that the streets are not paved but trees have been carefully planted, obviously not considering that asphalt and concrete were far more scarce at the time than seeds. With marvellously English discomfort, he notes: 'I did not like to think we were going to visit apartments with our boots simply ankle-deep in mud. We did so, however.' He found in them flats of 5.5 square metres a head, admittedly in advance of 3.5 in the rest of Gorky – and families of four taking up two rooms, with the kitchen shared with the neighbours, a version of collective life somewhat less well-serviced than that which had been planned in the ateliers of VKhUTEMAS. He doesn't say so much about the facilities themselves, largely because they weren't finished at the time of writing, but it's here that the difference is most obvious.

At Wythenshawe, for instance, the main architectural interest for those not so fascinated by pretty Arts and Crafts houses is Expressionist churches and streamlined modern cinemas and shopping parades. Obviously there were none of the former in this deliberately godless city, but cinema and consumption had a role. The main department store, or Univermag, designed in 1935 by L. M. Nappelbaum, is in the style called in Russia 'Post-Constructivism', i.e. with Modernist simplified, glazed volumes given a slightly classical dressing. The grandly curved central glass stairwell is still very impressive, with its neatly crafted balustrade unaffected by its dividing up into the usual tacky, chaotic Russian mini-mall. There are no small shops but for impromptu recent kiosks, but then big Co-ops were equally dominant in the company towns and giant estates of 1930s England. They had super-cinemas too, but there are no Odeons quite like the Gorky Avtozavod's Kinoteatr Mir, another 1935 building, this one by A. Z. Grinberg. A square, coffered portal dressed in dark granite forms the entrance, and a wing with restaurants and other facilities is topped by a row of finely detailed Socialist Realist figures, athletic men and curvaceous women, both detailed with a fine, sinuous plasticity.

Opposite is the Palace of Culture, one of those comprehensive centres for theatre, music and general improving activity that were as important here as they were in a paternalist garden suburb like Bourneville, although here on a much greater scale. It's a banal piece of Stalinist architecture, a massive block whose linear mass is detailed with randomly applied classical detail. Inside, however, past a grand neoclassical central atrium that has been subject to some rather unsympathetic renovation, is a series of murals of the Thaw era. A central mosaic of Lenin is flanked by two panels where all the heaviness of the building disappears, replaced with vivid, light, colourful images of revolution, construction, science, football and general leaping about and frolicking. All the images are of activity, activity, activity. Panels are being hoisted to make buildings. Smoke swirls from chimneys. Men row in long dinghies. Youths sit around campfires. Female

Scientists on the walls of the Avtozavod Palace of Culture, Nizhny Novgorod

scientists peruse test-tubes. At the head of it all, at the top of the stairwell's ceiling, is a drawing of Vera Mukhina's 'iconic' sculpture *Worker and Kolkhoz Woman*, the Soviet Union's nearest thing to a Statue of Liberty. Together the murals are a society's idealized self-presentation, in three distinct styles – the 'sports' murals are realist but bright and stark, the ceiling mural has a similar simplified, cartoonish, modern line to the work of an American post-war illustrator like Saul Steinberg, and the Lenin is a great deal more lumbering and staid. Opposite the murals were realist paintings of the nearby Volga river, a subject on which contemporary and Soviet aesthetics could agree.

After gazing at these for a while, we sat down in the small café here, had some herring salad, and took out our cameras to get souvenirs of the murals. At which point two security guards emerged to sternly tell us we couldn't photograph it, though they wouldn't say why. We snatched the photograph here when we thought they weren't looking, although we were wrong, as they noticed, and came and reprimanded us again a minute later, although at least our cameras were left alone. The only explanation we could think of, sitting in the almost empty cafeteria of a provincial Palace of Culture on a weekday afternoon, was guilt at the fact that the main foyer had been redecorated in a weird 1980s restaurant style, with plastic yuccas, flowery wallpaper and shiny metal in random places, to the extent that its grand coffered hall looked rather diminished. Maybe they were about to do the same to the upstairs, with its murals, and were annoyed by our enthusiasm for the things they were about to destroy.

Some of the activities depicted in the murals can still be enjoyed today at the mini-Gorky Park adjacent, a typical piece of 'amenity', perhaps not too different from the parks spread across the company towns and council estates of the interwar years in the West, although with a little more heroic sculpture and a bit more tolerance for kitsch, one part municipal park and one part funfair. Surrounding this Park Kultury are later, neoclassical blocks of flats, the hierarchical, monumental architecture that succeeded the collective ambitions of Constructivism – some of it designed by former Constructivists, like a gigantic crescent of flats with curved balconies, an unexpected product of the Vesnin brothers. Running linear to the park are crumbly prefab 'Khrushchevki', a ruined power station and a series of identical red-brick-clad point blocks. Dilapidation is ubiquitous. Yet, for all the unemployment, inequality, decay and decline, one of the most obvious things about the Avtozavod district is not discontinuity, but the way certain things have endured. Not necessarily the more attractive aspects of the Soviet past such as rent at 5 per cent of income or full employment, but still some of those aspects most alien to the Fordist towns in the West. Of course there are those banners of the good citizens of Nizhny, hung up all the way down the boulevard. But at the end of the Park Kultury, there's something that is more continuation than survival.

Opposite the park's edge is an impromptu beach, around a lake carved out of an old industrial pit. On a sunny day in May, it was strewn with litter, but also full of people enthusiastically using the beach, flirting, sunbathing topless, sitting around, drinking, perhaps much as they would if there were a beach in Dagenham. We sat down on the benches provided, at least until it (inevitably) started to rain. Framing the beach is an immense development of repeated tower blocks, visibly system-built, in a linear structure like a wall surrounding the other side of the water to the beach. They look like they were built in 1980, but were erected 'just a few

Sunbathing in the the Avtozavod district, Nizhny Novgorod

years ago', we were told – no longer given away nearly free to industrial workers, but following almost identical architectural and spatial precepts to those blocks that were. It's a twenty-first-century microrayon. All the 'social' aspects of socialism are abandoned except as a residuum, but its aesthetics have, evidently, proven surprisingly useful. Maybe some of the new tenants of these hulking towers will be lucky enough to have their faces on a poster, as Model Workers of Avtozavod.

3
Social Condenser

When everything was ready for the opening, he went up to the platform, and ashen-pale, took his place. His knees trembled under him. His throat was choked. And with a voice as rasping as the sawing of heavy, oak boards, he announced:

'Comrades! The Holy Ark is a worker's Ark because I'm a worker! And I carved it with my own carpenter's hands, so it's a proletarian's Ark!' And Berl the carpenter, filled to overflowing with inexplicable sorrow and pride, continued. 'I spent a year and a half carving it. I carved it beautifully, as if I carved it for . . .'

Berl caught himself and swallowed the word that was on the tip of his tongue. 'And now, Comrades, let it stay as part of the club. It'll be a place for books and newspapers. Workers' newspapers. Because it's a workers' Ark.'

And, for the first time, the Workers' Club, named in honour of Comrade Rosa Luxemburg, was filled with loud, jubilant shouts, and the wooden clapping of strong workers' hands.

Peretz Markish, 'The Workers' Club' (1928)[1]

THE WORKERS' ARK

In his 1933 tract *The Mass Psychology of Fascism*, Wilhelm Reich, disappointed communist and psychoanalyst, pointed to the Soviet fetish for construction projects as evidence of the regime's failure to promise a psychologically different form of society. 'It has been a typical and basic error on the part of socialists and communists', he wrote, 'to extol an apartment building, a public transportation system, or a new school as "socialistic" achievements. Apartment houses, public transport and schools', he continues, 'tell us something about the technical development of a society. They do not tell us whether the members of that society are suppressed subjects or free workers, whether they are rational or irrational men and women.'[2] Indeed they don't, as such. However, a Constructivist architect in the year Reich wrote his book could have had an answer to that complaint – a typology designed to instil a specifically communal way of life and of thinking, which was called the 'social condenser'.

In the aftermath of October 1917, and even of November 1918, architects' drawing boards were filled with miscellaneous 'houses of the people', designs for what would replace the transcended places of assembly common under bourgeois society – particularly, the theatre and the church – with something less alienated, something which did not rely either upon the spectacle of actorly performance or on that of religious transcendence. A new collective life was supposed to be coming into being, and new structures were needed for it; otherwise, those new lives would have to be lived in old structures, which were not fit for the purpose. In the Russian Empire in the first few years after the revolution 'workers' clubs' sprang up everywhere, in order to provide social facilities, education, games, films and plays in a deliberately vodka-free environment. There isn't much doubt that these were as much a bottom-up as a top-down phenomenon, drawing on the social spaces that workers had carved out before the revolution; and their early expression was appropriately ad hoc. Churches themselves or, as in the anecdote repeated in Peretz Markish's short story, synagogues, were often transformed via ingenious redesigns into modern buildings for communist self-education. These acts of literal desecration also make clear how these buildings were meant to replace something central, something deeply important, in everyday life. In short, they had the difficult, loaded role of replacing religious assembly and collective religious experience with something which was equally fulfilling, while abandoning all the aesthetic and spiritual props that its rituals had relied upon.

That public buildings were loaded in a society which elevated the public good and considered the private irrelevant or dangerous is unsurprising. But paradoxically these are often great spaces of non-standardization, where individual expression was to some degree encouraged. Most of the buildings in this chapter are unique works of art, unrepeatable designs utterly specific to their place and their function. They point to a great tension at the heart of how the Soviet and Soviet-influenced economies worked, in that they sidestepped completely the usual primacy of the production line. There were of course 'types', to some degree: cinemas, swimming pools and houses of culture were, in the USSR and even outside it, sometimes reproduced from city to city – the same cinema in Minsk and Moscow, the same 'song festival' concert hall in Riga and Tallinn; even, in one instance, substantially the same swimming pool in Gdańsk and Vilnius. Even then, though, the standardized buildings were often decorated by different artists and given some obvious signs of their own individuality. It is maybe a measure of the Soviet economy's eventual failure in building cities that these are often by a long way the most attractive buildings of the era – surprising, vivid and sometimes eccentric structures, where standard components weren't needed and institutions and their designers had the budgets to commission one-offs. This was not supposed to be an economy of great one-offs, but of the mass production of durable goods whose individuality or 'specialness' was irrelevant. That conflicts here with the need to provide a 'special' space for collective or ritual experience, providing some of the richest 'pure' architecture in Eastern Europe, of any era.

There was some pre-revolutionary tradition to draw on here. The House of the People in Brussels, designed by the 'inventor' of Art Nouveau, Victor Horta, was one of the largest-scale building projects of the Second International, the worldwide umbrella organization from which the future communists split at the Zimmerwald conference of 1915 (after, it should be remembered, the International's mainstream had disgraced itself by voting for the First World War). It was actually at the House of the People that the retrospectively famous split between Bolsheviks and Mensheviks occurred in the Russian Social Democratic Labour Party. Horta did not provide what would later have been called a 'proletarian' architecture, with ostentatiously physical and muscular features; rather, he designed a steel-and-glass construction which was, for the time, extremely technically advanced, wrapping around the street with the confident self-display of a turn-of-the-century department store. Inside was a library, meeting halls, all the possible spaces of an organization dedicated to the immense project of working-class self-emancipation. The piling of function upon function recalls the architectural plans of the French Utopian Socialist Charles Fourier, who proposed in early-nineteenth-century France the 'phalanstery', which combined housing and social facilities in one structure, some of which were built and turned out to be socially successful.[3] Linked by glass walkways across large central spaces, these would be a combination of living quarters, theatre, library, factory and communal eatery; a collective life would be lived therein where each inhabitant would find at their disposal the preconditions for their individual self-realization. It is hard not to imagine that Soviet architects were thinking of Fourier in the early 1920s when they devised the 'social condenser', the model building for a new public life.

The Soviet architect Moisei Ginzburg argued in 1928 that the 'essential goal' of Constructivist architects was 'the definition and creation of the SOCIAL CONDENSERS of our age', which would, as he put it when describing a specific social condenser he had designed, have 'certain features that would stimulate the transition to a socially superior mode of life – stimulate, but not dictate' – through the inclusion, for instance, of corridors wide and comfortable enough to act as public forums, through the mixing up of private and public space, and through connecting public facilities to homes as closely as possible.[4] As a notion it is, among other things, the negation of one of the most common ideas of twentieth-century planning, that of rigid zoning.

From the Beaux Arts to Le Corbusier, the dominant notion by the 1920s was of the separation of urban functions, with, at its most extreme, a division of cities into eating zones, theatrical zones, working zones, living zones, administrative zones and shopping zones, all of them at a low density, and provided with lots of green and open space in between; usually this arose as a reaction against the chaotic, insanitary results of nineteenth-century building speculation, although the belief that concentration encouraged sedition must surely have been a factor as well. As the name implies, the 'social condenser' was not low density, was not zoned, but threw together functions with great abandon. The nearest Ginzburg got to his 'social condenser' was the series of public buildings he designed in Moscow, Sverdlovsk and Alma-Ata, where offices, flats ('communized', 'transitional' and private), canteens, restaurants, libraries and gymnasia (and, in the unbuilt schemes, cinemas and theatres) are arranged around small parks, with public roof gardens on top. Two Dom Kommuny, or Communal Houses, of this type survive in Moscow, though neither,

The Communal House of the Textile Institute, Moscow, mid-renovation

unsurprisingly, are fulfilling their original typology. Ginzburg's Narkomfin is a famous ruin, and another, Ivan Nikolaev's Communal House of the Textile Institute, is being restored at the time of writing to more or less its original function as a student hostel, albeit with all the ideological ballast attached to its function basically abandoned.

After architects began reading Jane Jacobs in the 1970s, the disdain for 'zoning' became an orthodoxy in Western, capitalist architecture. Instead of zoning, we had 'mixed-use development', and the circle turned right round again to speculation. The social condenser did not mix functions together for the sake of speculation or even convenience, but because it was thought that such an arrangement would encourage collective life. People would meet, and meet often, and make friends. They wouldn't eat alone, but in the canteen. They would read in the library or go and see a film in the workers' club after work, rather than getting blasted on *samogon*. This is, curiously enough, exactly what the hardly socialist Jacobs thought that urban planning should do, and it was picked up by American architect-speculators early on – the multifunctional pile-up of New York's Rockefeller Centre, and especially Radio City Music Hall, was directly inspired by this Soviet practice.[5]

Not all public or ritual buildings built under 'real socialism' are social condensers in the wholesale sense of the Dom Kommuny – the smaller type of the 'worker's club' usually sufficed. The connection between this and the earlier, 'cultic' social space was stressed in 1929 by El Lissitzky, who places the 'Club' and the 'Palace' in opposition as possible types. 'Buildings designed to serve all of society have always acted as a repository of the sum total of all creative energies. Depending on the prevalent social order, these have usually been of either a religious or a governmental character: the Church and the Palace. These were the power sources of the old order. Their power can only be transcended by establishing new power sources belonging to our new order. Some years ago it was thought that Palaces would serve this purpose, except that now they were to be called "Palaces of Labour". This created the danger of introducing a foreign and superficial pathos into our lives.' Instead, the simpler 'Club' would display 'new spatial volumes and construction methods . . . capable of providing all the age groups of the working masses with facilities for recreation and relaxation after a day's work, i.e. a place to store up new sources of energy'.[6]

These buildings, which stress at every point the importance of collective and social space, often – though a Modernist like Lissitzky wouldn't have approved – try to 'speak' of this, in an *architecture parlante* that actually continues the slightly Pavlovian aspects of the 'social condenser': planning and buildings that are intended to make people do certain things, think in a certain way, perform certain rituals. These are buildings where socialism happens, where, in Stephen Kotkin's ironic phrase, people would 'perform' socialism, and where socialists were supposed to be created – all of this via the particular means of architectural expression. This could easily be accused of being authoritarian, and certainly there are several occasions when the accusation is fair: the Communal House of the Textile Institute originally had a Taylorist daily itinerary for the student residents – physical jerks at 6 a.m. and the like.

There are plenty of others, though, that show an impressive level of freedom, both in their design and in their possible uses. Even those that are more standardized frequently display a joy and extravagance in their surfaces and fittings that can contrast very sharply indeed with the usually more sullen buildings for the mundane needs of working and sleeping. This relationship of foreground (public building) and background (private building) is normal in most bourgeois societies, especially our own, with its 'icons' designed by 'signature architects', which act as little punctuations in the dross of speculative housing. At least most of the time, 'real socialism' didn't so much abandon the dichotomies of the bourgeois city as amplify them, blow them out of all proportion.

Perhaps the best place to find 'the social condenser in one city' at its most impressive is Vilnius, where a dozen or so theatres, clubs, ritual buildings and similar facilities were built as infill in this relatively small Baroque city, from 1945 onwards, to give it the functions of a republican capital.[7] Within a mile or so there is the Trade Union House of Culture, on a hill overlooking the town, with ostentatious pride of place – the Stalinist version of the Palace of Culture, one of several sub-Parthenons built at that point, now dilapidated and subdivided into various things – currently it is derelict, with a junk market outside. Architecturally it was scraped of all ornament, a victim of the post-Stalin war against fol-de-rol, and hence is far more impressive from a distance than up close. Just further on along the same hill is the Palace of Weddings, which was to administer marriage ceremonies without recourse to the Sight of God; it was built in 1974 to designs by Gediminas Baravykas as a sort of concrete wave, linking the openness of the park and the curvatures of the trees to the more formal structure of the street.[8] It provides a gateway to that park; facing a semi-abstract sculpture of a couple scooped up into a single being, it features a ceremonial stairway leading upwards, just as in a

The Palace of Weddings, Vilnius

classical building, to provide the required sense of occasion. It looks open, even rather sensual in its rippling white concrete curves. Inside is a nearly floor-to-ceiling glass chandelier – glassware was a speciality of Lithuanian designers in the Soviet period, treated as a form of crystalline abstract sculpture. The opulence of Catholic ceremony is transferred to the new-old ceremony – something that was consciously planned.[9]

Not too far from here in one direction is Cafe Neringa, a bizarre, beautifully made mid-century-modern fantasy on aquatic themes, detailed in exquisite treated wood; in the other, a cinema, the Lietuva, derelict and graffiti-covered, but a flash, zippy piece of modern architecture; and going south, an art gallery opposite an especially crazed Baroque church, made up of fragmented forms along the street, deferring to but not copying the Counter-Reformation swagger all around. Going back down the hill from the Trade Union Club is the fabulous Opera and Ballet Theatre, built in 1974 to the designs of Elena Nijolė Bučiūtė. Here, clearly, no expense was spared. Hoisted up on a platform of steps, discrete plazas and ponds, it shows how much Soviet Modernism was often already 'Postmodern',

State Opera and Ballet Theatre, Vilnius (1986 postcard)

incorporating huge amounts of pre-modern materials and details. In its huge glazed foyers there are black marble surfaces dotted with what look like nineteenth-century street lanterns, Scando-modern tables and chairs, terrazzo floors and, once again, stunning pieces of glassware, usually as chandeliers, hanging from the ceiling, designed specially by Yuri Markyov. And just over the river, in one direction there is the three-dimensional Malevich of the former Lenin Museum, now extensively redesigned inside as a Museum of Modern Art; in the other, a Brutalist Concert and Sports Hall, a great concrete hulk, its weight rearing up into a bull-horn profile, with another glass sculpture inside.

Proletarian culture, atheist marriage, sport, high and low arts, all the schizophrenic revolutionary-conservative aspects of Soviet public life appear one after the other, all of the buildings designed with imagination, wit and urban specificity, all of them full of large circulation spaces filled with visual content and rich, tactile surfaces; almost all of them commanding public squares filled with sculptures and benches. The architectural interest almost always comes from the ingenuity involved in fitting the buildings into the sites, and from the craftsmanship of the interiors – never from standardized virtues like precision, economy or order. And all of them, peculiarly enough, manage to exist in the in-between spaces of a pre-existing 'bourgeois' city, providing contrasts to it, for sure, but seldom breaking with it altogether. Lithuania was annexed after the war by the USSR, in a straightforwardly colonial act, so it did not – perhaps but for the brief 'Lit-Bel Soviet Republic' of 1919 – partake in the revolutionary period, or of the avant-garde ideas of someone like Moisei Ginzburg. Few of the architects who designed these buildings would even have been aware of his theories. But even – maybe especially – this peripheral, semi-colonial outpost shows a proliferation in public buildings that would have been unusual at that time in the West. Something different seems to be happening here.

FROM WORKERS' CLUBS TO PALACES OF CULTURE

Almost all these Vilnius buildings are in some way 'contextual'; they respond to what is around them, architecturally or topographically, shaping and interacting with their space. In this, they are inadvertent successors to the practice of the Moscow architect Konstantin Melnikov – not to his theory, as he didn't have one. Melnikov, a protean architect from a working-class background, became famous after designing the Soviet pavilion at the Paris Expo in 1925. He would design several workers' clubs in Moscow between 1926 and 1929; another was designed by his occasional collaborator, Ilya Golosov. All of them were commissioned by the trade unions. In recent years those historians who have had access to the archives – such as Kevin Murphy, in his *Revolution and Counter-Revolution: Class Struggle in a Moscow Metal Factory* – have stressed how independent the trade unions were in that decade, genuinely capable of defending their members, calling strikes, and cutting favourable deals with management. According to Murphy, the great majority of labour disputes in 1920s Moscow went in the workers' favour. This is usually taken as a surprise, because Bolshevik practice is notoriously hostile to 'trade union consciousness', pejoratively regarded as a mere instrument of defence within the system, incapable of pointing to what could be possible outside it; and at least for a decade, that's the role that they performed in the new system. But already in 1921, towards the end of the civil war, Trotsky actually proposed incorporating the unions into the state, which was eventually achieved by Stalin in 1929–30 by the purging of the 'Right Opposition', led by the trade union leader Mikhail Tomsky. So these are, among other things, the inadvertent architectural expression of trade unionism's last two or three years of freedom, monuments to a success which would soon be forcibly curtailed. Melnikov's architecture could, a little fancifully, be regarded as the architectural expression of this 'consciousness'. It does not break the existing city, by creating its own space; it joins onto it, on to its corners and streets, bending what exists to its will, rather than changing what exists.

To get some idea of what this means, take Melnikov's most famous workers' club, the Rusakov, designed in 1927 for employees of Moscow's municipal tram company. It commands a wide street in the sort of mixed industrial/residential area produced by nineteenth-century speculators when it fell to them to provide places for the working classes to live; not all of that survives now, but enough of it does to give the impression of a

Melnikov's Rusakov Workers' Club, Moscow

smoky, congested district. The main façade faces one of Moscow's wide arterial roads, with the usual procession of Ladas and sudden, speeding black limos; it seems to animate the street, to work as a sort of monumental traffic inspector, pointing in three directions at once. The directions are articulated through three cantilevered volumes, giant polygons punching the air; between them are strips of plate glass. It all erupts from a triangular site, thrusting outwards from a point, which can only be found round the back. To the main street, it is a surge of released tension. Everything is forced outwards – it embraces the street, pulls it right into it, via two walkways which spur out from either side of the symmetrical façade, bringing the pedestrian up off the pavement and onto skyways and viewing platforms and a second entrance to the building. It is breathtaking and utterly, spectacularly unique. It isn't an 'icon' in the contemporary sense, however, something dropped onto an area from afar; go round to the back and you find an almost mundane façade in the same red brick as the factory district it serves and was built for.

The Rusakov Workers' Club's fame precedes it, though. It is listed as a historic monument, with a plaque to prove it, but that doesn't mean much in Moscow. Both times I visited, a year apart, a sign in the doorway read 'STOP!' in Latin script and then proceeded, in Russian, to point out that the theatre inside is closed for renovation. The door was open, though, so we tried to blag it, only to be told off by a policeman inside. The windows of the side wings are stopped up, and have been for decades; more recent is the Azerbaijani restaurant stuffed into one corner, serving delicious Caucasian specialities and bearing no visible relation to the building it latches on to whatsoever. It is hard not to despair at finding a building this astonishing being treated so carelessly – if its users can't notice why *this* building is special, which can they?[10] – but it also fulfils the original programme probably more than it would if turned into an oligarch-owned centre of contemporary art. It was meant to be mundane, and it was meant to have strange and unexpected and multiple things happening inside it. It picks the area up, with its consent, and propels it into the future.

This is the most dramatic of Melnikov's clubs, but others show a similar sense of urban context. The Kauchuk Factory Club, for instance, designed in 1926 for the workers of a rubber factory, is on a corner site opposite the Red Army HQ, a mid-1930s monolith which screams 'totalitarianism!!!' better than most Moscow buildings; but it is also an area that still has nearby a pocket park, a Constructivist housing scheme and an Orthodox church, a typically twisted little collection of domes and spires crammed into a tiny space; it is their small scale, rather than the shockingly domineering mass of the military buildings opposite, that dictated the club's form when built. It is a semicircular rotunda, its curve ending in angular little towers. Like the Rusakov, a system of cantilevered walkways protrudes from the glass-and-concrete façade, as if suspended in air. Inside, as a big sign tells you, there is a 'KARAOKE KLUB'. Again, an ambiguous victory of the mundane – Melnikov's Bakhmatevsky Bus Garage in the north of the city is now an arts centre run by Roman Abramovich's partner, Dasha Zhukova; it is impeccably restored, for sure, but a worse insult to the building's original ideas is hard to imagine. Better karaoke than oligarchy. The Orthodox church nearby is a reminder that you can, if you want, find precedents for what Melnikov was doing in the way early-Russian architecture gloried in differing forms pulled together, and in sharp, sudden cantilevers; the (reconstructed) medieval Golden Gates in Kiev, for instance, are especially Melnikovian in their sense of angular forward motion. You don't have to dig around in tradition for precedent to understand it, though – the effect is produced by a keen sense of urban space, of ways in which already built-up spaces can be supplemented and charged with energy.

Equally charged is the Zuev Workers' Club, this time for workers in a particular district rather than one factory, also designed in 1927, and also placed in a built-up, industrial area. Like the Rusakov club, it's one of the famous 'icons' of the Constructivist 1920s, a corner building where tense, unstable geometries of glass and concrete culminate in an all-glass cylindrical stair tower, placed exactly at the corner, a model for all manner of imitators from the 1920s to the 2000s. Exactly next door to it is a long redbrick engineering works, one of several along Ulica Lesnaya, next to the Belarus railway station. Like the club, it is defined by a contrast between glass and masonry, though it doesn't do much with it, pointlessly castellating a long factory shed; but the club picks up its scale, rationalizing the chaos of nineteenth-century industry into an image of charging progress which, unusually for later years, does not dominate, but adopts the small scale of everything around it. This didn't stop Moscow's planners from dumping two nondescript blocks of flats on either side of it, completely changing that scale, but you can at least get a sense of it retrospectively. And although this place too is in a much worse state than its listed status and its shiny plaque might imply, at least those who run the place – still as a local club – know how special it is, welcoming visitors and providing information boards on its history. You can just walk round Moscow and stumble on these places, sometimes – entirely by accident, at one point, I found the Club of the Association of Political Prisoners, a strange cubic structure designed by the Vesnin brothers in 1928, stuck round the back of a street corner.

These small-scale pieces of avant-garde architecture are a remarkable achievement, especially given that they were usually the projects of the trade unions and not the state itself. They are also not wholly exclusive to Moscow – in Kiev, there is a superb example with similar principles, the Club of Workers in the Food Industry, a 1932 design by N. A. Shakhanin, made up of gently overlapping curved volumes, with a top-lit interior. It is placed next to the elegant, pretty Doric of the early-nineteenth-century Contracts House, which it complements subtly while refusing to make

The Club of Workers in the Food Industry, Kiev

any stylistic compromise whatsoever, and similarly serves as a focal point for the pedestrian, a piece of humane, non-domineering street architecture. But, at some point, the clubs expanded in scale with the economy that they were supposed to serve. Around the same time and for the same reason the trade unions lost their independence, a country that was only industrial in pockets (Moscow being one of the largest of those pockets) underwent the most violent industrial revolution in history; and one obvious result of this was that factories became huge, gigantic enterprises employing tens of thousands of workers. One of Moscow's biggest was the ZiL motor works, sometimes called the Likhachev works after its Stalinist boss, a massive complex in Moscow's Proletarskii district. For the workers of this place (*for*, rather than *by*, at this point) a 'workers' club' was obviously too small, not sufficiently glorious. Instead, the workers would have a Palace of Culture. For this purpose, the Simonov Monastery, a medieval complex that would surely have been preserved anywhere else, was partly demolished (some towers do still stand) and a large enough site was cleared for an appropriately magnificent workers' palace.

Commenced in 1931, the ZiL Palace of Culture is still Modernist; it is a 'palace' in ethos, not in aesthetic. The designers, the Vesnin brothers, had fingers in every one of the various pies of the 1920s – abstract painting, stage design, heavy engineering and, as we've seen, workers' clubs. Their Palace of Culture is probably the largest-scale deployment of the early ideas of the avant-garde, ironically completed as late as 1938, when such ideas were practically illegal. It belongs entirely to the previous era. Its scale, though large, is not emphasized, it is never domineering. Placed in a small park, it is asymmetrical, informal, friendly, even – of all of these buildings, it is the only one we managed to explore properly, both inside and out. It was housing a baffling amount of things that day – theatrical performances, a planetarium, dance classes, café, restaurant, library, bar (not dry), car boot sale and what looked like a kids' birthday party – all the sorts of things a social condenser was intended to condense. To the street, the Palace is defined by a curved glass wall, the foyer of the theatre; the elevation then creates an L-shape, with strip windows, some flat, some curved, with the planetarium placed in the corner where the wings meet. While Melnikov's Rusakov club is a vision of solidity, three hard volumes being thrown at you, the Palace of Culture constantly breaks up its mass with glass, recessions, roof gardens, pilotis; while it is not a building which is interested in its architectural surroundings, as Melnikov's was, it is also more obviously welcoming, providing lots of greenery, shelter and seclusion; as much as it doesn't try to be solid or aggressive, it doesn't accommodate to the space it is put in; rather, it creates its own space. Despite the name, and the large scale, it is not at all grandiose.

This sense of openness and welcome extends to the way it relates not so much to the street (there isn't really one) but to the pedestrian who might want to wander inside. We found most workers' clubs not especially keen on letting us in, even given Agata's ability to speak Russian in such a way that they didn't twig she wasn't; but here, we just wandered in off the street and nosed around. It was rewarding. Space here is treated in the sort of flowing, open way that visitors to the Royal Festival Hall might be familiar with; rooms flow into each other, different floors are visible at once, double-height rooms and mezzanines seem part of the same space. There are a lot of closed net curtains, which no doubt reduces the glare those great ribbon windows might produce, but it does lessen the effect a little of airiness and openness; as does the comprehensive redesign that the place has received. According to one of the Vesnins' former partners, writing in the 1960s, the interior was renovated 'during the period of excessive embellishment', but what we saw there, aside from the double-height café designed in the modern nondescript they call over here 'Euro-Remont', was something quite weird: a combination of the clean lines, thin columns, glazed surfaces and parquet floors of 1930s Modernism, and the clunkier decorative Modernism of the 1970s; what is there is ornamental and decorative, but not obviously classical. Very comfortable-looking green sofas are placed for you to laze on by pilotis encased in white marble; there are blue polished marble steps, there are glass ornaments like those you find everywhere in Vilnius, and on the mezzanine a bust of Lenin on a plinth, backed by the quote, in white capitals set into the marble: 'Learn, Learn and once again Learn!' *Gemütlichkeit* may have overtaken the Vesnins' Modernism a little, but the message the architects wanted to convey is put here a lot more bluntly. Still, any learning that occurs here does so in a building which is both comfortable and strongly Modernist, sometimes strikingly so. From that mezzanine floor, a wonderful cast-concrete staircase whirls you up into the planetarium on the roof, a miniature prefiguring of Frank Lloyd

УЧИТЬСЯ,
УЧИТЬСЯ,
И ЕЩЕ РАЗ УЧИТЬСЯ ...
В.И. ЛЕНИН

Lenin insists you learn, at the ZiL Palace of Culture, Moscow

Wright's Guggenheim Museum, placed like a toy in the corner of what is basically a workers' social club in an industrial suburb. We will find a Palace of Culture that justified the name in the next chapter, somewhere that was genuinely, almost psychotically, palatial; but here, we'll remain at the

On the way into the ZiL Palace of Culture, Moscow

smaller, less demented scale of the 1920s and 1970s, and consider another major human activity which was to be 'condensed'.

LET'S PIONEER THE PROVISION OF COMMUNAL EATING FACILITIES!

In *Archaeologies of the Future*, his heavy volume on science fiction and Utopia, Fredric Jameson argues that collective, social eating facilities are an essential part of any socialist Utopia. Why? Mainly because they immediately abolish in their very existence one of the main aspects of domestic drudgery, and of unpaid housework, liberating women to (alternately) 'govern the state' (as Lenin once put it) or at least to participate in the labour process. It goes without saying that works canteens are not in themselves utopian, so this is an ambiguous process – is cooking (and eating) at home being abolished because this is a precondition of freedom, enabling women to free themselves from what dozens of 1920s propaganda posters called 'kitchen slavery', or is it being abolished so that their alienated labour (now in factories) can be supplemented by the alienated labour of professional cooks? Was this another way of making sure that even the basic functions of consuming and excreting were necessarily part of the public sphere and could be appropriately surveilled? Either way, collective eating was always claimed to be a central plank of urban provision under 'real socialism' – cheap, inexpensive, functional food that would be served outside the home, near to the workplace, so that in the rest of your time you could either 'fish, hunt and philosophize' (Marx) or 'learn, learn and once again learn' (Lenin). Like many progressive policies this was often honoured more in the breach; but three survivors that we managed to discover suggest that some legacy has been left; in one case, a surprisingly healthy legacy, except perhaps for the food.

The Narva, or Kirov district, in St Petersburg, the heartland of the revolution and home to the Bolsheviks' main base of support, the Putilov engineering works, has particularly rich pickings of such structures. The building currently called the Kirovsky Univermag was one of many in Leningrad named after the assassinated local party boss, who had proved to be considerably more popular than Stalin in the elections to the 1934 Party Congress – if he did do it the chutzpah of immortalizing someone you have had killed is impressive.[11] It was designed, however, in 1928, as the Narvskaya Factory Kitchen, by a team of architects from the 'psychotechnic' architectural collective ASNOVA, and completed in 1932. The team included Iosif Meerzon, who was one of the four designers (along with Tatlin himself) of the Monument to the Third International. The building is a remarkably dramatic piece of street architecture, divided into several distinct volumes: a series of double-height, all-glazed, cubic bays right on the street, a big glass front pointing towards the Metro station, and a long first floor that, in the manner of many early-Soviet avant-garde buildings, appears to drag the street along with it, animating its dynamism; a curved restaurant wing leads on to a small park.

It has long since ceased to be a factory kitchen as such, though it still contains various peculiar things – a bootleg DVD stall, various cheap clothes emporia, and the like. However, to eat, you have two choices. One is a fairly normal Russian eatery where you can get reasonably priced shashlik in a Euro-Remont environment, but the other is McDonald's. I was not keen on the idea of visiting, but Agata, pointing out Nikita Khrushchev's alleged enthusiasm for the unpretentious mass-produced ease of the hamburger, convinced me. We went in and admired the remarkable universalism and egalitarianism of McDonald's – our Chicken McNuggets tasted exactly the same and were priced nearly the same as any other Chicken McNuggets anywhere on the planet. We can be fairly certain that Moisei Ginzburg would have regarded organic burgers and sourdough bakeries as petit-bourgeois sentimentality of the rankest kind, so on that level we felt no post-socialist guilt. A life of burger-flipping, however, is nobody's idea of liberated labour.

The Narvskaya Factory Kitchen was a place I went looking for specifically, trying to find a (semi-)famous architectural monument, a social condenser designed by a team which included one of Tatlin's collaborators, a place of Modernist and socialist pilgrimage. The more interesting places are, as usual, the ones you stumble upon on the way to somewhere else, and so it was with the eating facilities of the Bratislava Trade Union Headquarters, a major building in (what was then) Czechoslovakia. This couldn't, at least in terms of the amount of historical water under the bridge, be much further from Constructivism, social condensers, and the world-transforming experimental zest of early post-revolutionary Russia; it was one of the largest building projects in the Slovak capital during the period of 'normalization', after the human face the Czechs and Slovaks had tried to give socialism was smashed in. It is a building built for trade unions that had no de facto and very little de jure independence, that did not have the right to strike, but which basically served as a sort of compulsory social infrastructure that was called upon to sort out holidays and sick pay, rather than defend workers at the point of production. All that said, something quite fascinating happens inside here, something that is heavily amplified by the current geopolitical status of Bratislava itself, something that could probably not have been found when this was a working building under 'real socialism'. Bratislava is less than an hour's journey away from Vienna, but feels considerably less 'socialist' – public transport, food and above all taxis are considerably more expensive than in the Austrian capital, there is a lot more in the way of chain stores and (usually giant) adverts, and a hell of a lot less in the way of good, well-kept social housing. As Pyzik points out in *Poor but Sexy*, it's the distressing spectacle of how, after winning the Cold War, the West even managed to retain more remnants of socialism for itself than were permitted in the East. That's certainly what the close proximity of Vienna and Bratislava heavily implies. Walking round Bratislava, on the first of our visits there, Agata found the contrast profoundly depressing, and my attempts to cheer her up via the contemplation of its (fairly extensive) socialist Modernism were not greatly appreciated. It is also quite hard to find a cheap place to eat.

The Bratislava Trade Union Headquarters was completed in 1981 to designs by Ferdinand Končeк, Il'ja Skoček and L'ubomír Titl, as a plaque handily informs you; it is a showpiece on a large site just north of the city centre. It commands a triangular plaza, defined by steel lamps which open out at the top as interconnected semicircles, another bit of *architecture parlante* – look at them from a distance, and they look like a crowd of raised, clenched fists. The exterior consists of sharply angled low-rise wings, clad in more of those peculiarly Soviet-1970s bluish white marble panels, which arch around a tall tower, a glass curtain wall fringed at the

Lamps as fists at the Bratislava Trade Union Headquarters

corners by that strange Marblette. It is quite open – you can wander in, and the green courtyard, with a big abstract sculpture of some sort of exploding sputnik, is also easily accessible to the public, which is pleasantly surprising, as it's still a functioning office building for the (by now, of course, independent) Slovak Confederation of Trade Unions. It's probably because of the subdivision of the lower-rise parts of this (always multifunctional) building.

There are a concert hall, a theatre and a restaurant, as there always were, and various odd little commercial concessions doing hard-to-define things – EFL, travel agents, indeterminate stuff. But what we both got very excited about indeed was that restaurant. We'd been wandering around the foyers, just to look at the (specially designed, typically craft-based) furnishings – aluminium-clad columns, one of which has an indentation where it looks like someone's kicked it, lots of curved and treated wood, an aesthetic somewhere between 1970s airport lounge and spacecraft, all very elegant but completely empty. The restaurant, however, was full of people, all of whom were availing themselves of enormous three-course meals for around three euros, in a city where mostly you would be lucky to buy a bag of chips for that. Nearly every table full, broth from a vat, dark beer. Here was a part of the city which had somehow managed to preserve that sense of filling, slightly stodgy comfort which features so often in the memories of those who remember 'real socialism'. It's a pleasure of its own, and probably more so now that it's quite beleaguered.

In Poland, there is legislation that actually protects these spaces. Milk bars, an innovation of the 1960s, are still given public subsidy, although governments constantly threaten to withdraw it, and when one goes out of business it is never replaced; a similar experience can be found at the *stolovayas* of Russia and Ukraine.[12] They're seldom architectural objects in and of themselves; only a few retain their original furnishings, and most are just in the ground floors of perfectly normal buildings, though sometimes in surprising locations. Agata swears by these places and so has an encyclopedic knowledge of where you can find them, even in the most unlikely spots, from tourist thoroughfares in Kraków to side streets in Łódź. At Bar Familjny, you can get a filling meal for the equivalent of a quid on Nowy Świat, essentially Warsaw's Regent Street; Bar Bambino on Ulica Krucza is similarly odd and welcome in its provision of fresh

The milk bar of the Sady Żoliborskie estate, Warsaw

budget foodstuffs in a well-heeled part of town. There are a few which were specially designed, usually placed in prominent places in a microrayon. In Warsaw, there is Praga's Bar Alpejski, with a multicoloured mosaic outlining the shape of the Alps; there is a particularly bleak one in Universam Grochów, a department store complex surrounded by high-rises; or, conversely, there is Bar Sady, a bright piece of Pop architecture in the once-award-winning Żoliborskie housing estate, a series of neat, almost prim low-rise blocks placed in between the retained trees of what was previously an orchard, an internationally renowned 1959 scheme by the architect Halina Skibniewska. Bar Sady has not obviously changed since the era of the Thaw, and is just a big, column-free cranked-steel roof, enclosing an airy little bar to eat your klopsy in, light, easy and convenient.

The clientèle for these *Bar Mleczny* is a mix of those who lost out in the 'transition' – the elderly, the ill, the homeless – and a lot of students, and sometimes young people enjoying them for their downbeat, slightly kitschy 'PRL' vibe and the very 1950s notions of service and convenience. Sometimes people in there are very poor indeed, and the uneasy social mix can get uncomfortable; also there are almost never toilets, something presumably dictated by the fact that these are intended just as places to stop briefly to eat next to your place of work; but it can be a problem if, like the author, you suffer from Crohn's disease; it can't be easy on the elderly diners either. The food is good, solid fare – *barszcz, pierogi, surówka i inne jedzenie*, with 'kompot', a drink made from crushed berries, offered for around tuppence, and extremely cheap even if you take relative cost of living and wages into account.

You queue up (obviously), you ask for what you want (or what is available) on the menu, you're given a ticket, and then you line up by a niche for the food to be dispensed straight from the kitchen. You eat it, you go home. The entire process is actually, even when there's a long queue, very fast, and the food is heavy, fresh and very filling. There are no airs and graces, nobody ever tries to elicit tips (nor could you give one if you wanted to), there is not even any 'service' as such, nobody 'waits' on your table – you are obliged to leave your plate at another niche. For Agata, and who am I to argue with her, the milk bar is the most convincing remnant in Poland of 'real socialism' – you get from here exactly what you need, and you can even enjoy it (not too much, mind!); you could just eat in these every day and nowhere else and have an entirely balanced and healthy diet, something which could not be said of McDonald's. It's quick and reliable, and there is no obvious class relation within the space of eating – nobody has to act servilely for the sake of a tip, and if you get a smile out of someone it is because you have made them smile. It's obviously lacking in luxury, in the cheaper examples lacking even comfort, but there is something here that is completely inaccessible anywhere else under capitalism, something which genuinely seems to be part of an entirely different economic system. It's this that people are defending when they argue for the preservation of the milk bar; but look around for symbols in the average bar and you'll find a cross, not a star.

LEARN, LEARN AND ONCE AGAIN LEARN

Socialism was, of course, to rest on higher things than the belly, and, as the speech bubble behind the bust of Lenin implies, education was of paramount importance in Soviet-era building programmes. Schools were built much as schools were built en masse, but a more specific typology is the 'Palace of Pioneers', which were built for the younger of the two communist youth organizations – if the well-known Komsomol (acronym for 'Communist League of Youth') corresponded to the Scouts, the Pioneers roughly corresponded to the Cubs. Their buildings had a certain significance in Soviet architectural history, in that the Moscow and Kiev Palaces of Pioneers were the first really confident, truly Modernist buildings in the USSR after the end of Stalinist architecture. The Kiev Palace of Pioneers, finished in 1965 to earlier designs by Abraham Miletskiy, sits at the edge of the city centre, before it steps down with an overgrown ravine towards the Dnieper. Currently surrounded by hideous luxury flats, it is still clean and relatively well-treated, and is still used as a youth centre. It is a social condenser on the smallest scale, which nonetheless pulls in all kinds of architectural devices – a long glazed block, an obelisk, a pool with mosaics, and a flowing, circular interior lined with some particularly fine woodwork. At the focus of this foyer is a relief mural showing the friendship of the peoples, with children of various races holding hands and grinning. Aimed as it is at seven-year-olds, it is one occasion when Soviet iconography cannot be accused of being too patronizing. But in this case,

The friendship of nations at the Kiev Palace of Pioneers

at least, architecture for adults was often fittingly complex and multifaceted.

Public libraries are among the most unusual and original buildings of the era, the places where the astonishing rise in literacy between the 1910s and 1960s occurred – a situation where, as the Romanian-Hungarian ex-dissident and Marxist G. M. Tamás puts it,

> everywhere in the Soviet bloc there existed a strange combination of high Modernism and – looked at from today, or from the West – an incredible and tradition-laden cult of Letters, of the Arts, of Science and Philosophy. 'Socialist' modernization, apart from putting an end to illiteracy, epidemics and abject poverty, by introducing hygiene and indoor plumbing, heating, old-age pensions, paid holidays, free health care and free education, cheap public transport, numeracy and so on, also opened lending libraries in every district and all the larger firms. It introduced – for the first time – scholarly and critical editions, and an enormous volume of high-quality mass publishing, social sciences, serious literary and art criticism; dozens of new theatres and museums were opened, hundreds of new cinemas – art film flourished; all extremely high-minded. Millions of people learned to read music and sang in choirs. Philosophy had never been regarded as part of the national culture before 1945. National classics were properly edited and published for the first time. Hundreds of scholars worked on translations. These were extremely bookish nations. At the same time, as this was a system of state capitalism, tempered and limited by planning both production and redistribution – and steered by very complex mathematics – politics was disproportionately rational or, rather, rationalistic. As a system still based on commodity production, wage labour, money and the separation of the producers from the means of production, class differences and inequality persisted. In this, the Party represented a kind of collective *tribunus plebis*, always adjusting consumption levels, life quality and cultural participation towards equality and maintaining – in a largely, but not exclusively, symbolic fashion – the primacy of the working class. Social mobility was swift and advantages were offered to working-class kids in access to higher education and cadre promotion. Statistics show that even in the 1980s, a crushing majority of leading officials and managers came from proletarian families.

This, he argues, is one of the aspects of the regime most detested by today's elites. ' "Actually existing socialism", although it was not socialist, was unique in operating a terrific moral switch by asserting the superiority of manual labour and putting the worker at the pinnacle of the moral hierarchy. It is seldom understood what a tremendous cultural *coupure* this was. It earned the regime more hatred than anything else; the post-1989 eastern European press is still joking about it, in their sincere contempt (good old class hatred) for grease-smeared yahoos in cloth caps – called here, characteristically, "Lenin hats". The very existence of workers reading Brecht and listening to Bartók is denied.' Although the number of people using them may now be considerably lower, the spaces where this happened are often among the most declarative of buildings, the theatres and libraries where knowledge was instantly available, either for free or for a token charge. Some of them are as obvious and as bluntly didactic as the Victorian civic buildings they so closely resemble. The Lenin Library in Moscow, close by the Kremlin, is a neoclassical redesign of a Modernist scheme by Vladimir Shchuko, where you can still sense the Modernist approach to space in its thin pillars and its asymmetric, informal layout, wings enclosing a square with a large, repetitious bookstack behind. When we visited, the bookstack was decorated with a giant Samsung advert, but the wings still featured their top-floor frieze of workers and peasants striving for knowledge and the busts in niches of Copernicus, 'Darvin' and an especially pugnacious Pavlov, chin jutting right out of the niche. Since the early 1990s, the presiding sculpture at the entrance has been Dostoevsky, rather than Lenin. The halls inside are still known for their airy luxuriousness, and for the notorious difficulty of obtaining certain materials. That procession of busts is mostly scientific, of course; the Sciences, even during the era of Lysenko, were generally more reliable than the humanities, in a situation where, as Francis Spufford put it, 'nothing was dumbed down except the Marxism'.[13] I've not worked at all in the Lenin Library, but I have spent time in the main library of People's Poland.

Biblioteka Narodowa, the National Library, was constructed on Pole Mokotowskie, a park just south of the centre of Warsaw; as a project, it lasted nearly as long as the protracted battle over Colin St John Wilson's British Library. The first design, by its head architect, Stanisław Fijałkowski, was of 1976, and it was finally completed as late as 1990. I have also written much of this book in the British Library, and the contrasts between these two buildings, so close in time, complexity, craftsmanship and symbolic import, are interesting. Wilson's building is a deliberately compromised Modernism, with strong Brutalist volumes leavened by redbrick, travertine and a lot of oak; it is a ridiculously English building in its air of mild-mannered compromise, trying to plough a path between the Scylla of the Prince Charles tendency and the Charybdis of an extremist, history-is-bunk Modernism. For all its crafted and sculpted masonry, it aspires to lightness – white walls, placidity, a sense of metaphorical and literal 'enlightenment'. Fijałkowski's building, by contrast, is sombre, murky, deliberately maze-like – knowledge as a puzzle to solve, not as an open book.

You can't gather that entirely from the façade, which is a clipped and sprawling, stretched-out piece of late Modernism; it is more than a little bit like the Vesnin brothers' rejected original design for the Lenin Library in fact, and like their ZiL Palace it spreads its volumes out across the park – a long curtain-walled glass-and-marble façade to the street, another at the back of the park, unassumingly grouped around a windowless bookstack; canopies provide good places to smoke round the back and in the corners, with intersecting walkways enclosing a quadrangle. The difference between this and the Vesnin brothers can be spotted in the panels to the entrance, where a three-dimensional stone relief, unveiled in 1982 to designs by Jan Kucz, of alternately gaseous and fleshy abstract forms is captioned with 'Biblioteka Narodowa' in cursive lettering that has crept in from a Surrealist painting. There is going to be something other than mere reason at work in this library.

Go inside, and the dominant colours are not Wilson's red and white, but black and gold. The floors are of black and yellow terrazzo, with black benches; the columns are in an exotic yellow stone which looks like marble veined with nicotine stains. That strange yellowish colour is everywhere: in the wood of the boxes for the card indexes and the desks in the reading rooms, in the bronze handles of the doors to the toilets, with 'BN' carved onto them. The yellowy columns of the reading rooms lead to a suspended ceiling that is divided into a faceted grid, where wood panels are followed by clusters of egg-shaped bulbs, bisected by dark-yellow strip lighting. The Surrealism continues downstairs, where there is a small cinema, and the walls alternate between black, white-veined marble and corrugated concrete, with splay-legged settees underneath. The restaurant is where it tips over into near-horror, as diners are accompanied by a

The restaurant of Warsaw's National Library

continuous panel of beaten metal, showing similar eerie organic forms to those at the entrance, except here emphasized by the dim and murky light. It is not an illegitimate vision of knowledge and its achievement, this; nor is it entirely an image of the various monsters created by the sleep of reason. It is education transmuted as a difficult, strange and endlessly surprising quest, a hall of mirrors, something you can find especially in the almost deliberately sinister, narrow yellow-and-black corridors – an endless search which can take you to where you never knew you wanted to be. It's also a social condenser, at least of sorts – films and exhibitions run here, and unlike in the British Library you can wander into the reading rooms without fear of security guards. One exhibition there entailed a series of unusually seditious slogans from Bernard Shaw, Toni Negri and others embossed on the wall, in blue letters. If you were going to found a clandestine organization anywhere . . .

As a monument in space, a piece of city, the most intriguing of Soviet-era libraries is another National Library, a repository of knowledge that symbolizes the intellectual life of a specific country, Estonia, and like Warsaw's national library it was finished just after the collapse of 'communism', in 1992, having been begun in 1984, at the fag end of the 'era of stagnation'. Because of that, understandably, there have been attempts to claim it as an example of 'national' architecture, some act of subversion that somehow managed to con Brezhnev out of tens of millions of roubles and raw materials. This does not seem likely; and in fact it adheres closely to Soviet doctrine by following the old 1930s model of 'national in form, socialist in content'. Unlike most buildings like that, its 'national form' is not appliquéd ornament, but an elemental reworking of historical architecture from the ground up.

The architect of Tallinn's National Library, Raine Karp, might just be (he is still alive, and would probably not appreciate the description) the most original of Soviet architects, at least after Melnikov; an architect who took the intuitive sense of form and scrupulousness towards context visible in that Moscow designer's work and amplified it into buildings that practically became landscape, that did not complement topography but became topography. Karp's best-known building is Linnahall, on a

Architecture as landscape: Linnahall, Tallinn

promontory leading out into the Baltic Sea. It's hard to know exactly where the 'building' starts and ends at Linnahall; it's really a series of platforms, giving you a magnificent view of Tallinn's Hanseatic skyline and the sea, with ships sailing off to Finland and Russia; and appropriately enough, given that Cold War theorists considered the USSR a modern reincarnation of 'Oriental Despotism', it elicits comparisons with the pyramids, the ziggurat of Ur, the temples of the Aztecs . . . a symmetrical cross-shape from above, it has underneath it a concert hall and the usual foyers and cafés. From below, on the platforms themselves, all you feel is the series of steps and multiple levels, detailed in crumbling limestone and concrete, with grass growing between it. Currently derelict, it's where Tallinn teenagers assemble of an evening, and the floor is littered with their bottles of cheap booze. Watching them chat, argue and swig, with the sunset and the sea behind them, they've got something much better here than they probably think they have. There is nothing else like it on earth.

The National Library is not quite as insane, which is one reason (of many) why Linnahall is derelict and the Library is well-kept; while the youth of Tallinn were drinking dubious-looking plonk in the former, they (or at least a group of art students) were sketching and painting the monumental lines of the building in the latter. Like Linnahall, it is practically geological, an eruption of elemental form. A symmetrical stone entrance, with a circular stained-glass window, somewhere between the Romanesque and Brutalism, is the nearest thing to conventional architecture – a 'normal' façade, with a square to the rest of the city. It has steps either side. Walk up these and you're on more of Raine Karp's platforms, which steer themselves around stepped reading rooms, creating another monumental pyramid/temple/ziggurat, again in an utterly original language which appears to fuse the most experimental mid-twentieth-century architecture with something entirely ancient. Look down, along those walkways, and you'll see a series of vaults like some kind of Renaissance prison, catacombs of books. All of it encourages exploration – you keep finding new corners and spaces where you can wander, new views of the building and the city around it, which the platforms encourage you to look out towards. These two are the most prominent, and by far the best, twentieth-century buildings in Tallinn, and it's enduringly puzzling that it was the Brezhnevian dotage of the USSR that funded them. This is

National Library of Estonia, Tallinn

usually explained by the concept of 'regional' architecture, allegedly emerging as a covert protest against Soviet systematization.

Late-socialist 'regional' architecture often involved an intensification of the old 'national in form, socialist in content' idea, removing the socialist content; a typical example is Hungarian Organic Architecture, which entailed learning from the yurts of ancient nomadic Magyars, i.e. from a form of housing actual Magyars had not lived in for over a thousand years. It was fascinating architecturally, but otherwise a combination of fanciful history and ugly politics, particularly in the case of its greatest exponent, the late Imre Makovecz, who began as an anti-totalitarian dissident architect banned from designing much more than private houses and interiors, and ended as an openly anti-Semitic supporter of Viktor Orbán's managed democracy. In the Baltic republics of the USSR, with such elaborate conceptions less plausible, regionalism meant, more simply, an interest in and adaptation of the modern architecture of nearby Scandinavia. Raine Karp's buildings do neither. However elemental, they make no reference to any historic form of dwelling; and there is no attempt to emulate, imitate or have a dialogue with Sweden or Finland, there is no Aalto-like restraint, although there is perhaps a Finnish eye for tactile materials. They come instead from an intense architectural intellect, drawing on forms that are personal, historical, geological, but which most of all appear as structures that try to help the visitor to make sense of other architectures and landscapes. As much as they are regional, they are literally internationalist: buildings as monumental viewing platforms looking seaward, containing within them, as if almost by side effect, repositories of culture like theatres and libraries.

Another, less obvious means of building for 'culture' and instruction was the mass production of cinemas across the Soviet Bloc. This would not be particularly unlike Western practice in the interwar years, but while cinema design declined massively in the UK, say, after 1945, affected both by a change in architectural patronage and the rise of television, it would remain exceptionally important in Central and Eastern Europe. Cinemas are, in fact, often a lot more conspicuous and attractive than branch libraries, which are frequently just built into blocks of flats or shopping parades. Either way, they are part of the same dual educational-propagandist project. The fare in them would vary enormously according to country and level of censorship – in Poland after 1956 the great majority of major Western films were shown, while the GDR's or the USSR's repertoire was rather more restricted. All of the following are now more or less arthouse cinemas, and none of them are multiplexes – their small scale and unpretentious placing largely in inner-city residential areas lend themselves to the genre. I have seen films in all of them, usually of the bleakly mid-European variety.

One of the most interesting surviving examples, Kino Muranów in Warsaw, gives a clue as to why cinema buildings were given such importance. It takes up the ground floor of a deeply weird Socialist Realist complex built on the levelled site of the former Warsaw Ghetto, where steps upon steps lead up to a high, Boullée-esque free classicist archway which serves as the entrance to an informal, green and dilapidated council estate. Under the raised plaza that frames the archway is the cinema. Immediately upon stepping inside, you find a lavishness of materials – a recent gazetteer lists its use of 'several marble varieties on the floor (including brown Bolechowice and black Dębnik), wrought gates and sconces'; the effect is both funereal and anticipatory, as if you're about to enter a space of ritual, the 'cultic' effect that Constructivists tried so hard to avoid. This, as much as any 1920s Picture Palace, is intended to be a space of dreams, a shrouded space where you sleep and let someone else's story take over – as useful to Stalinism (it was built in the early 1950s) as to Hollywood. There are stars on the capitals of the columns, and as two flights of stairs lead down from the box office to a café, you find above you the words, in gold lettering, 'FOR US CINEMA IS THE MOST IMPORTANT ART'. Of course, it doesn't tell you that this is a quote from Lenin – it would probably have been removed had it done so – but it explains why it is all so luxurious, a plush comfort that extends to the auditoriums, which you reach through shadowy colonnades. Others in this Stalin Picture Palace idiom are dotted around Warsaw, to a standard design – the best-preserved is Kino Iluzjon, in the well-heeled Mokotów district, which is a kind of unofficial National Film Theatre, reliant on People's Republic-era prints – copies of *Serpico* dubbed into Italian then subtitled into Polish, and similar delights.

These are mild, however, compared to Tallinn's Kino Sõprus. The only Soviet building in the UNESCO-listed Hanseatic centre of the city, its attempts to 'blend in' via the very slightly Scandinavian classical details of its concave portico aren't fooling anybody, with the particular form of warped, strongly symmetrical, faintly Gothicized classicism instantly recognizable as a product of high Stalinism. Inside, though, the original auditorium's Stalin-style fittings are alongside the pointillism and scrawl of the post-1956 era, speaking of a less obviously palatial approach to the dreamworlds of cinema. In Poland, in particular, cinemas became outright Surrealist in their imagery and decoration. Kino Wisła at Plac Wilsona is on the ground floor of a heavy, unlikeable Stalinist housing block, but after you descend the steps to its underground screens, the usual contemporary tat is surrounded by bizarre aquatic imagery, in reference to the cinema's name (translatable as the (River) Vistula Cinema). On a polychrome mosaic surface of yellow and blue stones, the early-1960s design by the artist Wiktoria Iljin traced three humanoid sea-creatures out of simple white lines, cryptic, alien and rather cute.

Similar undersea imagery can be found, albeit of a much more abstract kind, at the larger Kino Kijów (Kiev Cinema) in Kraków, this time

Dream Factory: Kino *Sõ*prus, Tallinn

without any obvious connection to the thing the cinema is named after. Inside this light, swooping concrete pavilion is a full-height ceramic artwork, created in 1967 by Krystyna Zgud-Strachowska, depicting never-before-seen sea creatures, of the sort you might expect in the Surrealist animations of the time. The surface is thickly tactile: you can run your fingers along its blobs and outgrowths, the ferns and undersea plants. On the reverse façade, a red mosaic sun pulsates. The various different kinds of dream life to be found in these cinemas, aside from pointing to the formal exuberance possible in the era, suggest that wakeful instruction often took a back seat to the creation of fantasy – either in the respect-instilling classical devices used at the Sõprus or Muranów, or in these much stranger, more inexplicable artworks, where coherent reference has crept off elsewhere and a free play of the imagination serves as the entranceway to the (surely often comparatively prosaic) awaiting films themselves.

SUN, SEA AND SOCIALISM ON THE BLACK SEA

Another of the putatively socialist environments I had enjoyed under capitalism was something called the Militant Labour Summer Camp. My parents were members of the clandestine, Trotskyist Militant Tendency in the British Labour Party, an organization once considered, when it controlled one council and had three MPs, to be the fourth-largest political party in the country. When they were expelled from Labour en masse in the late 1980s, most of the 'Millies' formed an independent Militant Labour party, eventually morphing into the Socialist Party of England and Wales, under which name it still endures, with its one or two councillors in Coventry. My mother took me and my brother and sister to the Militant summer camp just the once, in 1995; it promised 'sun, sea and socialism', and took place in Mersea Island, Essex. A minibus picked up comrades from around the south-east – as soon as I saw the bearded man clad in nothing but a leather jacket and a pair of tight shorts waiting by Colchester bus station, I somehow knew he was coming with us – and took us across a thin causeway to a grey, desolate island in the North Sea. There would prove to be no sun, though there was sea – my siblings spent their time on the wide muddy beach, poking sticks at dying jellyfish, and I sulked in my tent with headphones on – but was there socialism? Sort of. The meetings made up for the obligatory Chumbawamba-playing disco, giving a programme of lectures and talks that were actually very interesting if you're a curious and bored fourteen-year-old, and there was a good film programme, of which I extensively availed myself until Mum physically dragged me out of a screening of *Romper Stomper.*

In some 'socialist countries' there was both sun and sea, usually the Adriatic, the Baltic and the Black Sea. The latter in particular worked very well as a sort of Stalinist Med from the 1930s onwards. Seaside resorts were built particularly extensively from the 1960s on in Crimea and Bulgaria, on what would seem on the face of it to be a very similar model to that which fascist juntas in Spain and Greece specialized in marketing to the newly enfranchised, newly holiday-enjoying workers of Britain and West Germany. The Bulgarian coast provided much the same service for workers from Poland, Czechoslovakia, Hungary and East

Germany (and often West Germany too, where it was a budget trip). I suspect that most comrades at the Militant Labour Summer Camp would have considered the existence of these resorts to be yet more evidence that not much really divided the 'deformed workers' states' of 'Stalinism' from those of post-war capitalism, with both equally alienated and technocratic, with similar tower block hotels along big yellow beaches. When Agata and I went to one of those Black Sea resorts, however, we found somewhere which explained better than most what sort of human environment 'real socialism' really wanted, a heavily planned, controlled, homogeneous and egalitarian space.

We picked – largely because we'd found some intriguing postcards of it in second-hand bookshops in Warsaw, of concrete step-pyramids stretching floor by descending floor to the sands – a resort called Albena, around twenty miles from Varna. This turned out to be a very good choice. We found later in a publication on the seaside resorts of Bulgaria and Croatia that Albena was the only one of the big Bulgarian resorts to have avoided the wholesale, chaotic privatization that was the norm elsewhere along the coast, when the ultra-high-density Spanish model was followed assiduously, filling every available space with cheap hotels and aiming the lot at the stag party market. On the road out from Varna to Albena you can see these places – Sunny Day and Golden Sands, monstrously kitsch, overdeveloped agglomerations of Trespa and pink-painted concrete, all big pitched roofs, decorative balconies and fibreglass columns. Most of these

Albena while still under construction (late-1960s postcard)

are 1960s hotels reclad and rebuilt with extra floors and new wings, spreading out into the original open spaces. Albena, however, is all but untouched. This is because, rather than the 'mafia privatization' that took place in the other resorts, where the usual competing vested interests and gangsters fought over every available space, it was privatized *in toto* as a joint-stock company, owned by the resort's employees. The Albena joint-stock company still owns the entire resort including all its hotels and restaurants, and cleans its streets and maintains its spaces.[14] As a result, it is a place that is obviously 'other' in the context of Bulgaria's chaotic capitalism – still controlled by an evidently single architectural and spatial idea.

In their book *Holidays after the Fall*, the historians Elke Beyer, Anke Hagemann and Michael Zinganel argue that it was Albena's distinctive architecture that gave its employees confidence in their 'tourist product'. It was built between the late 1960s and the early 1980s to the designs of the architect Nikolay Nenov, with extensive use of prefabricated concrete panels, as an experimental project of the Bulgarian Research Institute on Standardization and Industrialization in Architecture, a sort of prototype

Albena's Hotel Dobrudja from the beach

for putative prefab housing estates. Actually the results are a lot more joyful and playful than is typical in microrayons, perhaps because they didn't need to be particularly robust. Albena's hotels are full of Pop Art *brises soleil* of thin, curved louvres and eaves, and the modular construction enables the mid-rise hotels to form themselves into deliberately irregular pyramids, each step of which features a large balcony. The public toilets liberally placed along the beach are bulbous concrete shell domes, sculpted into the shape of a pair of upturned buttocks. It's Pop Brutalism, high Modernism on the razzle, and it's very enjoyable. The public spaces too are extremely extensive, and almost all pedestrianized, with most of the resort made up of parkland, into which the pyramids and the single high-rise, the twenty-storey Hotel Dobrudja, are placed; each has an outdoor swimming pool, and the grounds around them are well landscaped; the beach has parasols laid on, though you have to pay extra for a plastic chaise longue. Specialized public transport – a minibus in the shape of a train – loops around the beach, the hotels and the bus station.

Despite all this spatial egalitarianism and deliberate avoidance of hierarchy – nowhere has a worse view than anywhere else – we spotted a few differences from one part to another. We stayed in the Hotel Dobrudja, where the rooms hadn't been visibly updated since the 1980s, although the lack of change meant that original features we would expect to have been wiped out survived – lots of typical late-socialist murals still decorate the foyer and the dramatic, Corbusian swimming pool. Breakfast was grim and gristly, served in a huge hall with a high-tech ceramic abstract relief. The pyramids on the beach, on the other hand, were a great deal more swish, with inoffensively bland Euro interiors and much better food, eaten by richer-looking Germans. Food was expensive throughout the entire place. But more than in any microrayon, this felt like a real social condenser – every space is public, and you can wander from the grounds of one hotel to another with great ease, each garden and swimming pool flowing into another, across, below and above the decorative concrete buildings. In summer, it is more like an Ideal City than any of the actual cities, although in January it probably looks like the most desolate of microrayons. But drinks prices aside, it appears to have salvaged more genuine egalitarianism than almost everywhere else we would encounter. It is unpretentious – lots of muscular Bulgarian beach bums and elderly German couples lazing around, playing volleyball and listening to terrible music – and in its architectural conception it is avant-garde, a real, working 'ville radieuse', with no trace of any form of urbanism predating 1960, lined with ambitious, discordant architecture more commonly seen in elite university campuses than seaside resorts. It was only later, when we took the bus up the road to Varna, that we realized that, like all the great European Utopias, this City of the Sun had left something out. There were no poor people. No beggars, no old women selling all their possessions, no drunks, none of the construction workers sweating away at renovating nineteenth-century commercial palaces. They could all be found, in abundance, just twenty miles away, and they never penetrate the gates of Albena. But at least Albena doesn't have a church.

LEISURE AND RECUPERATION: THE BALTIC SEA

One of the many Things That Are Not There Any More which would otherwise be in this book is an outdoor swimming pool in Moscow with an interesting backstory. Its site was formerly that of the pompous neo-Orthodox Cathedral of Christ the Saviour, which was dynamited around 1932 – a 'grotesque' nineteenth-century pile, 'no great loss' according to historian of Russian architecture Catherine Cooke[15] – in favour of the putative Palace of the Soviets, subject of a notorious architectural competition which elicited entries from virtually every practising architect on the globe, almost all of whom were defeated in favour of the Italian-trained Russian Boris Iofan and Hector Hamilton, an Anglo-American architect whose oeuvre is otherwise represented by a small parade of shops in Woolwich and a luxury apartment block in Bournemouth; we will encounter the spectre of their winning tower in the next chapter. When their ludicrous Woolworth-Building-with-Lenin-on-top was finally cancelled in the 1960s, the building's deep foundations were filled in to create the heated, open-air pool that sat in the centre of the city for decades before it was eventually replaced with a facsimile of the cathedral in the 1990s. Facilities for sports and leisure are often the most original buildings of the Soviet era; the steroidal concrete hulks erected for the 1980 Olympics are a particular feature of the coffee-table books of *Totally Awesome Ruined Soviet Architecture*, something which chimes with the liking for synchronized mass ornaments in Soviet parades and in their gigantist stadia; a social condenser of some sort, perhaps. Yet mass sport, for all its pharmaceutical excess in the Soviet Bloc, is not necessarily a feature intrinsic to 'real socialism' – if it were, Midwestern America would be a hotbed of tankies – so we will mostly ignore it in this book. What *might* have been more of a distinctive feature is sports and leisure – holidays especially – treated in a different way, made more of an everyday pursuit, put into unlikely places and experienced in distinctive ways.

In Tallinn, for instance, the (ex-)industrial port quite quickly becomes a beach when you walk along the main road by the Baltic. On our way there one summer as a respite from the constant tramping of the Hansa-Soviet landscape, we found that its sulphurous smell didn't seem at all to bother the Estonian-Russian populace lazing around in briefs and bikinis. This beach, running along a main road with a vast microrayon not far away, eventually becomes a full-blown resort, Pirita. The major buildings of Pirita are all from the 1970s and 1980s, and are mostly projects for the 1980 Olympics, where Tallinn had a major cameo in Moscow's show. Walking along the sand, you come after a while to the Pirita Top Spa Hotel, a typical example of how mainstream Soviet architecture continued to churn out ultramodern gigantism by the time that most of the rest of Europe and Asia had moved on aesthetically to an embrace of the passé and the cosy. If this was in Japan, France or Germany, you wouldn't date it later than 1972; *definitely* pre-oil crisis.

Towards the old town, concrete terraces – the hotel rooms – descend in steps from a central, steel-clad polygon; more ziggurats, albeit detailed in smooth concrete, without any of Raine Karp's eye for historical fantasy. They eventually culminate in the front entrance, where a long glass volume is suspended for almost its entire length on concrete supports, cantilevered out as far as they'll go, Melnikov-style. Opposite, there's (even more belated, aesthetically) a Socialist Realist sculpture of a naked man, waving his hands in the air. Given the water all around and the swimming pools and marinas, he's obviously supposed to be a diver; but looked at from behind, it seems as if he's trying to draw the recklessly cantilevered building's attention – 'Look out or you'll fall!' From there, a much wider beach, one that looks like a relatively normal seaside resort, lined by an arc of hotels and restaurants, ends in a glazed viewing platform – the buildings mostly, it transpires, late Soviet, though so over-restored that they look like typical examples of contemporary Tallinn's slightly cold white-walled neo-Modernism. A forest stretches behind, and on the day we visit, there's an impromptu music festival, with a female-fronted Eesti grunge band called Amor Veneris being especially apt, given all the scantily clad people flirting with each other on the sand. It's obviously a planned space, designed to give the precise amount of mass-produced leisure and nature in conjunction, with fast bus services back to the microrayons.

The beach described above was supposed to be a break, and so it's a bit odd to put it in this book, its being a holiday from the dogged collection of the urban environments of the Bloc; but we came across some traces which are evidently not holidays as they are usually currently practised. Agata was keen to take me to Jastrzębia Góra, a resort on Poland's Baltic coast, where she'd had her holidays in the 1980s – 'You'll love it. It's the Polish Bournemouth.' In preparation, I'd found a fold-out book of postcards of the place in the 1970s, showing several concrete-framed hotels dotted around, all of them built by a particular (state-controlled, pre-Solidarity) trade union for its workers' exclusive use as holiday homes or, sometimes, sanatoria; inter alia, there are hotels solely for workers of a Warsaw power station, for miners from Bytom and for a cement factory in Wejherowo, as well as a concrete lift tower to take holidaymakers down the steep cliffs to the beach. By September 2013, almost all of this – right down to the lift tower – had disappeared, which was probably fortunate as it meant we had an actual holiday, lying on the beaches (lush, sandy, at the foot of forested ravines) rather than spending our time tramping around looking at communist architecture. This was helped by the kind of town it is – there is no 'there' here, no obvious high street, not much in the way of streets at all, just a lot of ad hoc souvenir shops and restaurants in huts strung along a long road, with villas and two-storey pensions behind, and some communist-era megahotels further back towards the woods, reclad and renovated to a different society's idea of luxury. It was as if they'd deliberately tried to make sure nothing would distract you from the beach.

We were both still keen to find at least some traces of the place where she'd had her childhood holidays, though, and equipped with the fold-out book of trade union resort hotels we had a look. One survived, the one for Bytom miners, a clinker-brick hostel lying derelict in a garden behind a strip of sheds and prefabs selling souvenirs and kebabs; and one particularly impressive block not in the book endured, 'Hutnik', or 'steelworker', which was obviously for more Silesian holidaymakers; it is big, and has a slightly op-art concrete frame which juts out for shading. It's big maybe more to offer views, rather than to pack people in – there's not much else around it – and it's the only tall building of any kind. Our own hostel was another survivor; made up of a big Pomo thing like one of the dubious-looking houses built on the outskirts of cities everywhere after 1989, it also had cheap rooms – which we availed ourselves of – in a two-storey concrete building prettily painted, with the structure in white and the balconies in alternating blue, green and pink. The nearest obvious trace of these places' former use as workers' resorts was visible in the large group of burly holidaymakers dancing in a wooden hut to disco polo, Poland's Europop; 'They're from Silesia,' the receptionist told us, and so were those who came there to stay at the hotels of the 1970s, only now in the new system they can also have the excitement of staying with peripatetic intellectuals who don't talk to them.

All around are forests, and after a walk down one of the (somewhat

Holiday home for Bytom miners in Jastrzębia Góra (1980 postcard)

terrifyingly, unlit) forest roads you arrive at the larger resort of Władysławowo, which is much more like a normal seaside town, with amenities, a funfair, streets and streetlights. It was built as a resort and port in interwar Poland, as part of the 'Polish corridor', but almost nothing of that earlier incarnation survived the war. The beach aside, there are several interesting things: twisted sculptures in rusty steel; a small, rather lush low-rise housing estate set among pines, evidently for workers at the port rather than holidaymakers; a central 'House of the Fisherman', culminating in a Venetian-style clock tower, visible from the beaches several miles away. With its arcades, Gothic clock and steel globe on a spike, we assume it is 1920s or 1930s but it turns out to be Socialist Realist, designed in 1953 and finished a couple of years later. Presumably it was 'national in form' for the historic constructions of the Kashubians and not a reference to Venice at all. It houses a museum of butterflies. Most remarkable of all is the church, designed in 1961 by the architects Baum and Kulesza – a great unashamed concrete-framed shed with prismatic, abstract stained glass set into its high triangular windows, giddy with colour and personality. In People's Poland it was often the churches which best expressed the possibilities of the unusual amalgam of Modernism, Expressionism and *architecture parlante* that dominated post-Stalinist design, and it is to these that we must now turn, to ask how, under an avowedly atheist regime that controlled all building permits and owned the means of production, they managed to get away with it.

THE POLISH CATHOLIC CHURCH, INHERITOR OF COMMUNIST ARCHITECTURE?

That's the question it's hard not to ask on confronting something like the Church of Our Lady Queen of the World, in the industrial town of Radom. We found it on our way back from a wedding party, hungover, seen in the distance from a bridge. Agata doesn't remember it, but I've found pictures online and it really did exist – three steel orchids exploding out of a central core, placed in the middle of a drab microrayon, like the Sydney Opera House centralized and opened outwards. If you didn't spot the cross at the top, you would probably date it to the 1970s and assume it to be a strange socialist public building of some kind, rather than a Catholic church completed as recently as 2002 (albeit to designs from 1982, by the architect Wojciech Gęsiak). Long before his religious conversion, in his erstwhile role as the human face of People's Poland, the Radom-born philosopher and Polish United Workers' Party activist Leszek Kołakowski reflected on the problem of the widespread and enduring popularity of the Catholic church. 'We are not only immune to the benefits of religious consolation, but deeply convinced, besides, that the continuing influence of religious institutions upon public life is damaging.' Yet, 'our people have no intention of listening to our arguments on the subject . . . [the church's] influence undoubtedly manifests itself in accordance with the will of the people.'[16]

That's one way of looking at it – that the church was tolerated because the regime, in its humanitarianism and/or helplessness, would not turn its extensive apparatus of repression upon such a popular institution, in contrast to the Soviet Party's acts in the 1920s and 1930s. This conflicts with the popular view that the church was always an intransigently oppositional force, which was instrumental in supporting Solidarity and bringing down 'communism'; and it supports another argument, made by the left-wing political essayist Peter Gowan among others at the time, that the government was fairly content with the church as its loyal opposition – as was the church itself.[17] This is supported by claims made by some that after martial law was declared against Solidarity, those activists who could get references from the church were allowed to apply for asylum and receive aid, but those who could not cite a connection with the mother church – Trotskyists, anarchists – faced the full brunt of the repression.[18]

From the 1950s, Pax, an official Catholic party (an 'astroturf' party, as it'd be called now), sat in the parliament, controlled its own press and publishing house, educated children, and built a lot of churches. Among its leaders was Bolesław Piasecki, a prominent fascist leader in pre-war Poland. After 1956, Pax was replaced with the somewhat less circumscribed Znak movement, which also sat as a party in the Sejm and from which many later Oppositionists – such as the first post-communist president, Tadeusz Mazowiecki – emerged. In many ways, the system tolerated them, and they tolerated it. This would seem to be borne out by the fact that Cardinal Wyszyński, the head of the Polish church, refused to publicly back Solidarity, calling instead for calm in the midst of the 1980 strike wave. But because the papacy itself appeared to back Solidarity, the more familiar story is generally accepted. The Pope and Wałęsa brought down the bad people. 'I love to see workers on their knees,' as Harold Macmillan commented on the images of workers at mass in the Gdańsk shipyards.[19]

That's all as may be, but what is undeniable is that in the 1960s, 1970s, and most of all the 1980s, the Catholic church was allowed to embark upon huge construction projects, building churches, chapels, seminaries and sanctuaries on a larger scale than had been seen in Poland since the eighteenth century. Of course, they were funded by the church itself, and boosted by a great many donations from working-class Poles; but they were tolerated, given access to rich materials (in a time of shortage) and granted countless planning permissions by the avowedly atheist state. In a 1980 special issue of the magazine *Architektura*, an editorial pondered the fact that 'during the whole period of Modernism in Poland the only architectural objects in relation to which no architect proposed the standardization of function and site prefabrication were ecclesiastical objects'. Within the issue were countless images of grand, enormously scaled churches, many of which were surely implicitly criticized by the writer Janusz Kazubiński, who talks about how 'when he lays hands on a subject he can do anything in, a designer, frustrated with the "large panel", loses restraint. He would like to put everything he could not include in a prefabricated estate into a small church, and he puts it up. The tragedy is deepened by his skills.'[20] This is indeed a tragedy for fans of architectural purity and elegance, but the resultant overwrought pile-up leaves much to enjoy for the rest of us.

These were not retrograde designs, not 'reactionary' visually or architecturally at any rate, and they continue, fairly unchanged in their approach, right up to the present day – designs of the 1980s are still being brought to completion. This is also a mainly Polish phenomenon, with little correspondence in its neighbours. There are one or two neatly modern post-1991 Lutheran churches in Estonia, a couple of concrete Expressionist Catholic chapels in Lithuania, but in Russia and Ukraine the Orthodox church (and also, in cities like Kazan, the local Muslim hierarchy) favours outright replicas of their medieval structures, albeit without the delicacy of medieval technique. A few new Polish churches are similarly uninspired and historicist, but in travelling around the country I've found them to be a minority. The experience of opposition might be what led to the wonderful confidence, flamboyance and physical heft of Polish churches; or, conversely, it might be the experience of toleration, or *collaboration*, even, that made the requisite expense and scale possible. In any case, the church has become the unexpected inheritor of the Soviet tradition of unusual and extreme public buildings. Many of the churches built in Poland since 1956 would fit easily in the likes of Frédéric Chaubin's *CCCP* or Roman Bezjak's *Socialist Modernism*. Their expressed structure, monumental scale, and their placing, by accident or for contrast, in areas dominated by repetitious and featureless prefabricated blocks make them close cousins to the various Palaces of Weddings, Palaces of Pioneers, Palaces of Sport and their ilk.

The one whose story is most often reiterated makes clear the genuinely close link between the church and the new Polish proletariat. The Arka Pana was built in Nowa Huta, a town originally intended to be entirely without a church, just as there was no need for a church in Nizhny Novgorod's Avtozavod district. Workers were eventually promised a church in the 1950s, and agitation for one had even culminated in violent clashes with the police over the corner site, marked with a cross, which had been allotted for that purpose. The building was opened by Karol Wojtyła, archbishop of Kraków, soon to become Pope John Paul II. This was, quite literally, the answer to the workers' prayers. And ironically, given how places like Nowa Huta have so often been blamed on Le Corbusier, it is the most Le Corbusier-influenced building in the area, obviously a successor of his 'ark' in Ronchamp, where the atheist architect aimed to produce the effects – of light, of sanctuary, of succour and comfort – provided by a traditional church, without using any of the established props and devices that were usually called upon to do this. 'I don't care about your church, I didn't ask you to do it. And if I do it, I'll do it my way. It interests me because it's a plastic work. It's difficult', the architect claimed.[21] Like Ronchamp, the billowing walls are detailed in a rough, peasant-like concrete, studded with an aggregate made up of tens of thousands of smooth pebbles, which are formed and sculpted into organic contours

Wojciech Pietrzyk's design is, like any church, an *architecture parlante*, and it takes the notion of an 'ark' very literally – something that gathers

The masses assemble at Arka Pana, Nowa Huta (1970s postcard)

up and shelters. As in Le Corbusier's building, a heavy, bulky roof caps the whole thing, its concrete shaped into something resembling woodchip or scales. This lurching concrete creature is hoisted up on a ceremonial swirl of steps, and, inside, is a showcase of Modernist sacred art – a colossal, roughly modelled bronze Christ is nailed to the gallery with great steel tubes, his chest stretched out as he convulses in agony. The usual – and convincing – explanation for the church's post-war popularity is the need for consolation after the horrors that Poland went through during the war – 20 per cent of the pre-war population were killed; only the churchless Belarus suffered worse – and this image of screaming agony would suggest so. What, then, to make of the murals nearby? The sufferings of Christ are depicted in a creepy, cartoonish-realist way, and a few of those who are mocking him boast the sort of exaggeratedly Semitic features you'd otherwise expect in *Der Stürmer*. The particular group of Polish citizens who suffered most during the war might well feel more than normally uncomfortable here.

I've dragged Agata to numerous Catholic churches, usually against her will. She did not appreciate it when I cajoled her to come with me to the church where she had her first communion, feels no particular affection for an institution she considers herself lucky to have escaped from, and regards my interest in Polish sacral architecture as pure tourism, the disconnected aesthetic response of someone who had no religious upbringing, so has the privilege of an uninvolved distance. But at Arka Pana she was hugely impressed by the building, and surprised and depressed by the incongruity of the openness and imagination of the structure and this banal old anti-Semitic imagery. 'The people who built this were progressive people,' she insists. This is a hard case, though, and its extreme grandeur and sombre mass contrast with earlier efforts, in less politically charged circumstances. The Church of the Sacred Heart of Jesus in Gdynia, for instance, is much lighter in its effects, sweet and almost cute in its approach, rather than going for the overwhelming, painful emotional experience of the Arka Pana. Its twisted, spiky spire is deliberately perverse, as are its concrete-framed vaults, culminating in a squat tower open to the sky, which, when you're inside it, provides an experience that is both delightful and kitschy. The mosaic Christ here has escaped from post-war Latin America, as has the purple abstract stained glass. There are other churches with a similar lightness of touch, which reflect maybe the other currents in post-Vatican II church architecture, the decentralized, white-concrete-framed churches of Oscar Niemeyer in particular: the Sanctuary of Saint Andrew Bobola in Mokotów, an enormous

Latinate Modernist edifice in concrete and glass, for instance – are in this bright, outgoing tradition.

Much more common, especially in Warsaw, is a 1980s style that seems to derive from the rich, sheer red brickwork of the Hanseatic League, curved and bent into centralized structures with tall bell towers, taking from Gothic rather than the more easily encountered Polish Baroque – rough, industrial, humble, quasi-proletarian, contrasting with the bland concrete (and now coloured render) surfaces of mass-produced Modernism. These are 'familiar' designs, for all their aggression; vaults and spires, in 'medieval' materials, the sort of thing that a priest called upon to comment on churches in the aforementioned 1980 issue of *Architektura* meant when he said 'one should respect stereotypes of thought on the part of future users. So one should operate with elements of forms from the past, on an equal footing with new proposals . . . [church-goers] do not want a new church to open their wounds, they want a place of mental rest.'[22] Mother of God in Stegny, the main public building in that huge estate, is a case in point – a vaulted structure, it is topped with copper and decorated with the deepest, darkest red bricks, each one cut and pointed with deliberate imprecision, as a gesture towards the Gothic love of irregularity and the stonemason's self-expression. At the corner is a beacon-like tower made up of three unornamented concrete walls curving towards each other, enclosing the bell. There is a very similar design with a less expressive tower at the Church of the Conversion of the Apostle Paul in Grochów, on the other side of the Vistula, and there are several of their kin across the capital, all with immense halls lined in brick, the sobriety and sombreness of their materials fighting with the applied kitsch so necessary to the Catholic church, whose tokens of piety are every bit as mass-produced as the apartment blocks outside.

In the more intelligently designed estates, though, the architects have tried to complement the blocks, to make the church and the residential area into a unity, when the more common effect is the pathetic contrast of the church's richness and individuality against the state's poverty and interchangeability. There is a church at the furthest edge of the Tysiąclecia estate in Katowice to the designs of the same architects as the rest of it, which picks up the curves of 'the corns' to transformative effect, with every surface made up of delicately balanced intersecting rings, either clad in

The Thousandth Anniversary Church, Katowice

that lush brick or left in brown concrete, ignoring any obvious Christian referent and borrowing from eclectic sources like the Great Mosque of Samarra in Iraq. In Warsaw, the alternative-posing nature of this modern Gothic reaches its height in Marek Budzyński's emblematic 'ark' in

Ursynów, where the architect of that nondescript prefab expanse offered penance by designing something conversely warm, tactile and crafted – the effect of elevating the provisions of the church at the expense of those from the state is so striking it's hard to imagine the architect did not plan it. Not to say that this richness of surface didn't preclude a sometimes startling formal rigour, as in the Church of the Blessed Virgin in Mokotów, finished in 1989. No matter whether they drape massive canvas pictures of the former Pope across it or not, this is a structure completely without external ornament: two vaulted wings and a blocky tower, all in stark red and purple brick, unrelieved by anything other than a few slit-like windows. Although far more well-made, it is as harsh in its way as anything being built by the state itself; going inside, you find that the Lourdes style has won out over Hansa Brutalism; the church too was perhaps unable to give people what they *really wanted*, albeit less so than the authorities.

Newer designs often turn to compromise. At the Church of St Thomas in Ursynów, completed in 2007 to a 1980s design by Andrzej Fabierkiewicz and Stanisław Stefanowicz, the hard brick style is not only

Catholic Constructivism: St Thomas's, Ursynów, Warsaw

recapitulated but extended – the jagged brick vaults step down tier by tier along the back, producing a skyline of sharp buttresses, in asymmetric balance with the two tall bell towers of the front façade. The design is as tensed and compacted with suppressed energy as anything by Melnikov – not a fanciful reference, as a cheap little book on Melnikov was published in Poland in the late 1970s, when these churches were being designed. St Thomas's also shares Melnikov's occasional tendency to kitsch, with the two rectangular towers enclosing a cross and a representational sculpture of its dedicatee. But here you can see clearly that much as birds are the unexpected but actual successors of the dinosaurs, the churches are the most complete successors of socialist architecture. Rather than the socialist movement assimilating, desacralizing and transforming the forms of the church, in Poland the church itself took the forms that reaction took, and bent them to its own ends, proving much more resilient than could ever have been hoped when workers started turning half-empty churches and synagogues into workers' clubs.

4
High Buildings

> Communist life will not be formed blindly, like coral islands, but will be built consciously, will be tested by thought, will be directed and corrected. Life will cease to be elemental, and for this reason stagnant. Man, who will learn how to move rivers and mountains, how to build peoples' palaces on the peaks of Mont Blanc and at the bottom of the Atlantic, will not only be able to add to his own life richness, brilliancy and intensity, but also a dynamic quality of the highest degree. The shell of life will hardly have time to form before it will burst open again under the pressure of new technical and cultural inventions and achievements. Life in the future will not be monotonous.
>
> *Leon Trotsky,* Literature and Revolution *(1924)*[1]

SCULPTING MOUNTAINS

In an atypically lyrical passage in his book *Literature and Revolution*, Leon Trotsky tries to see into the future, breaking that cardinal rule among Marxists that to imagine the outlines of a new society is to erect a commodified Utopia. In the future, instead of contending political groups, there will be contending artistic ones, arguing for different ways of reshaping the world; and an entirely new art form will arise from the human being's complete mastery over nature – both their own and that outside them. We will be able to bend mountains to our will, and transform them into three-dimensional sculpture: hence, forty years later, the Ještěd telecommunications tower, a structure that would give any lover of nature a heart attack. Just outside the industrial town of Liberec in the north of Bohemia, in what was then Czechoslovakia, this tower, designed by Karel Hubáček with interiors by Otakar Binar and constructed between 1966 and 1969, is built into the peak of a mountain, which previously ended in a 'flat' top, without a spire-like peak. The tower 'completes' the mountain, by rising from a wide base right at the mountain's centre, taking what nature had only half designed and finishing it off, doing it better. As built, it was (and is) open to the public, with a restaurant and hotel rooms, from which you can contemplate the vanquishing of our natural limits.

Czechoslovakia has a major Surrealist tradition, and the Ještěd Tower is as ambiguously poised with disparate curios as the best Surrealist paintings. At first, it seems utopian, a dreamlike monument to the conquest of nature, with views that extend into three different countries – the Czech Republic, Germany and Poland. In the interior, glass meteorites slam into a billowing concrete core, and a hotel-restaurant serves rich, stodgy Czech food, as if to counteract the effect of weightlessness.[2] Its continuous strip windows are set at an angle, offering a view above the clouds. Up the stairs, towards the hotel rooms, foetal seats coated in shagpile are hung from the ceiling by chains. All this peculiar display fails to obscure a certain undercurrent of unease. Partly I felt this unease because of the reason I was here – as part of a press junket, elicited by the fact the building's original model was a major part of a V&A exhibition on the 'Cold War Modern'. We, the English journalists, were entertained by hosts hoping that our pieces would get the building the UNESCO listing (and funding) they were hoping for (they didn't). We were each given a free room for the night and an amazing quantity of Ještěd memorabilia, from little plastic mazes to unbuildable paper models. At night, when the other hacks had gone to bed, I wandered around the interiors taking awful, unprintable pictures of all these extraordinary objects, of the empty dining room with its planets-as-light-fittings, of those hanging shagpile seats, of the concrete constellations of the lift tower, of the almost medieval wrought-iron gates at the entrance to the hotel rooms, all of them lit by the unearthly mountain light, and all in surprisingly fine condition, suggesting the owners knew exactly what they had here. At the same time it was hard not to think in Cold War clichés about the possible uses this place could have been turned to, were things to have gone horribly wrong. You could imagine it as the ideal place to be when the bomb drops, above the clouds, above the fallout – there was even a large Soviet nuclear base nearby, ready for massive retaliation. The local bureaucrats might have sheltered in here, surviving on tinned food until the distant cities below became inhabitable again.

The Ještěd Tower, despite the relatively obscure corner of Central Europe it is placed in, is one of the strangest and most exciting exemplars of the state socialist tendency to create skylines in the most unlikely places, something which was intrinsic from the start, something caused perhaps by the fact that the post-First World War revolutions coincided with the golden age of the American skyscraper, but also by a certain ambition to, in Marx's phrase, 'storm heaven'. This aspect of the resultant states never really disappeared until their collapse, going through various metamorphoses. First, a rash of unbuilt skyscraper proposals emerged across the post-revolutionary states of Europe in 1917–23, then gradually a neo-Gothic high-rise style emerged in the USSR in the early 1930s. After 1956, the horizontal, non-hierarchical skylines of the microrayons were accompanied by an entirely different form of urban punctuation – a rash of telecommunications towers, often placed at or near the centres of cities, which became the unavoidable central pivots in cities that were otherwise planned to avoid (visual) hierarchy. Late on, some cities – East Berlin, Warsaw, Zagreb, Belgrade, suburban Prague – gradually pieced together a 'normal' capitalist skyline of Mies van der Rohe-influenced glass office blocks, which expanded with great speed after 1991, meaning that many former 'real socialist' cities have the most dramatic of capitalist skylines – and here, especially, we should be able to discover the differences between the capitalist and 'non-capitalist' approach to the idea of an urban skyline. There's a lot of choice – for most of the last half-century, the tallest building in Europe has been in the former Bloc, and for a time, with the Ostankino TV tower in Moscow, the tallest man-made structure (TV towers are not officially classed as 'buildings' in the rankings) in the world was in its capital.

SKYSCRAPERS, SKYHOOKS, SKYCITIES

In 2013, the Mercury City Tower in Moscow overtook the Shard to become the tallest skyscraper in Europe. This angular, off-red tower is not the first Moscow building to have had this accolade; bar the years 1990–2005, when it was elbowed out for a time by Frankfurt, and a two-year interval when the Shard inched above the Mercury Tower, a Moscow building of some kind has been the tallest in Europe for over sixty years. Those towers are an unusual bunch, and few of them resemble the post-war glass volumes that dominate the City of London, Brussels, Paris's La Défense or Frankfurt am Main. There are Dmitry Chechulin's Kotelnicheskaya Embankment, the first Russian title-holder in 1952, an assembly of Renaissance details pulled into a Gothic skyline; then Lev Rudnev's tower for Moscow State University, which held the title for longest, from 1953 to 1990, an even more chilling neo-Gothic Stalinist tower. In 2005, they were actually imitated in the design of the Triumph Palace, on the northern outskirts of Moscow, which inched above Frankfurt's Commerzbank. And from 2007 a cluster of ever-taller record-holders in the 'Moscow City' complex have emerged. Successively, the 'tallest' title has been held by: the sub-Norman Foster glass curves of Rogers, Taliaferro, Kostritsky and Lamb's Naberezhnaya Tower; the twin towers of 'City of Capitals', by Naramore, Bain, Brady and Johanson, whose staggered cubes are by far the most visually arresting of this cluster; and now the current tallest, designed by Frank Williams with Mikhail Posokhin Jr, scion of a Soviet architectural dynasty. It's an unresolved design, zigzagging its way down its seventy-five storeys as if unsure about what form to take. These last are the only towers that resemble those in Western financial districts; accordingly, they attempt to make large-scale contemporary Russian corporate architecture look 'normal'. This, in a city which has seen more – usually unbuilt – innovative, avant-garde skyscrapers than any other.

The most famous of Soviet skyscrapers was planned for Petrograd – Vladimir Tatlin's 1919 Monument to the Third International. Its delicate, open, iron-and-glass form implied Parisian rather than American inspiration, though this was not true of its symbolic import. Tatlin's Eiffel-style steel skeleton was to support revolving glass volumes – a cube, a cylinder, a pyramid – housing the Communist International, which would revolve at different speeds in a suitably dialectical fashion. But, soon after, the new/old capital of the 1920s saw dozens of proposed high-rises. Some were quite obviously unbuildable, such as the entries for the competition, in 1922, to house Vesenkha, the new USSR's Supreme Economic Council. Two of the proposals, both from architects associated with the 'psychotechnic' architectural group ASNOVA, were startlingly prophetic of advanced architecture half a century hence. One skyscraper design by the VKhUTEMAS student Lopatin, with its interlocking rectangular volumes rising in a stepped section, like an extremely rationalized, futuristic response to the New York zoning code, has a more than passing resemblance to Skidmore, Owings and Merrill's Sears Tower in Chicago, which had its own short reign as America's tallest. More radical was Vladimir Krinsky's entry. Its clash of structural systems, left open and unadorned and organized into a tall tower, suggested a building that would never be entirely finished – a perpetual skyscraper-in-becoming, something later proposed by the late Lebbeus Woods for the World Trade Centre competition in 2002. Krinsky's photomontage image of the tower placed into Lubyanka Square stressed its disjointed, deliberately cranky relationship to the existing city.

The early Soviet Union was hardly unique in this – the Weimar Republic was rife with skyscraper proposals. Bruno Taut's proposals for the *Stadtkrone*, or city-crown, were to sit at the heart of the ideal socialist community, literal beacons of light, sculpted from coloured glass, a uniting point, like – again! – the cathedral spire. Other proposals, even though they came out of the post-revolutionary atmosphere, were more a matter of making obvious the latent possibilities of a capitalist skyline – Mies van der Rohe's Friedrichstrasse glass skyscraper proposal of 1919, for instance, which would eventually be built as part of a real capitalist cityscape. Few of them ever saw the light of day; the Weimar Republic raised a few ten- to fifteen-storey rationalist towers and factory office blocks, while in the USSR the Derzhprom/Gosprom complex in Kharkiv came much closer to the socialist-skyscraper ideal. Constructed as the headquarters of the Ukrainian government, it is a set of towers of eight to twelve storeys, of staggered heights, interconnected with high-level concrete and glass walkways, on a semicircular plan which pulls the buildings constantly into different alignments. Walking under these walkways, or

The instant Constructivist skyline of Derzhprom, Kharkiv

viewing the complex from across the huge square in front of it, adds up to one of the most unique and vertiginous experiences of twentieth-century architecture in Europe.[3] Even this, however, is hardly a skyscraper. It doesn't really pass the test of being visible for miles; in fact, it barely surpasses the height of the city's main Orthodox cathedral. For the most part, even in the skyscraper-mad USSR of the 1920s, European skyscrapers between the wars were a matter of 'paper architecture'.

If these towers were extreme as individual buildings, others suggested a different approach to the city itself. Skyscrapers were a strange thing for communists to be enthusing over, given that the skyscraper was and is such a consummately capitalist creation: the product, essentially, of maximizing ground rent in grid-planned American cities, with its structural innovations – the steel frame, non-load-bearing walls – originally a way of keeping skilled, unionized workers out of the production process. The scuffle of the New York skyline, with its competing buildings-as-advertisements, both horrified and excited Soviet designers and ideologists – as did the way that the New York zoning code turned the skyscraper into a Babylonian ziggurat as a way of preventing streets from being completely and constantly overshadowed. How to adapt the idea of the skyscraper and plan it to enrich a city in a rational, reasoned manner rather than this unplanned chaos created by the needs and egos of competing corporations? In 1926 El Lissitzky advocated T-shaped towers that would be 'skyhooks', not skyscrapers, leaving the ground floor open for pedestrians, placed in a co-ordinated fashion around the Garden Ring, using Moscow's concentric plan rather than the New York grid. It was a great example of Vladimir Paperny's 'Culture One', in that it took the skyscraper and tried to make it horizontal, non-hierarchical, something in principle rather perverse. Again, this had eventual influence elsewhere, albeit with a Soviet mediator – the astonishing, out-of-nowhere Ministry of Highways in Tbilisi, built in 1974 but seeming to owe more to a topographically specific adaptation of the ideas of El Lissitzky to a city which is never flat for more than a few yards, rather than to anything happening to Soviet architecture in the 1970s. From the 'front entrance' at the top of a ravine – the only real public access – this is two long concrete fingers which balance upon two seventeen-storey towers, with subsidiary fingers firing off at angles before the tower meets the ground. It's an incredible performance, a re-imagining of the skyscraper as anything but hierarchical and grid-planned, though sharing its ingenious approach to fitting architectural forms into confined spaces. In a recent interview, one of its architects, George Chakhava, criticizes the 'imposed steppe architecture'[4] inflicted on the newly annexed Eurasian city of Tbilisi by the St Petersburg authorities in the early nineteenth century – the ironing out of an uneven surface to create long, wide and straight spaces. Inspired by the 'patio houses'of Tbilisi's crowded hills, where each house spills out into the one below, the Ministry of Highways exploits its placing in a steep ravine; as the co-architect Zurab Jalanshania put it, 'we occupied the minimum amount of land and developed the building above it – in the air',[5] where the tower's horizontal subsidiary blocks surge sideways and forwards into the empty space. The success of the ministry inside may be measured by the fact there is no pedestrian access to the lowest level of the building. These forms later recur, adapted to the steppe, in the Chinese buildings of Rem Koolhaas and the Office for Metropolitan

Neo-Constructivism: the Ministry of Highways, Tbilisi

Architecture, like the CCTV building in Beijing or the Shenzhen stock exchange, both of which borrow these egalitarian devices for the purpose of iconic emblems of a distinctly capitalistic 'socialism with Chinese characteristics'.

It was Lissitzky's planning rather than his architectural ideas that would come to affect the skyline of Moscow after the Second World War. Before then, Moscow was the centre of two of the most macabre architectural competitions in history – the Palace of the Soviets, in 1932, and the lesser-known Commissariat of Heavy Industry, in 1934, both for sites near the Kremlin. They elicited dozens of bizarre, impressive and oppressive entries, but ended in victories for schemes that basically resurrected what was then actually an obsolete type – the American skyscraper of the 1900s and 1910s, where a steel frame was clad in historicist ornament, whether Gothic or Baroque. Alternatives, like Ivan Leonidov's remarkable contextual Constructivist design for the Commissariat, were peremptorily dismissed. The new Stalinist Moscow was to resemble pre-war New York. It would not be unplanned like New York – but that didn't mean it wouldn't be indebted to Americans. In the early 1930s, a Russian translation appeared of the American architectural draughtsman Hugh Ferriss's book *The Metropolis of Tomorrow*. Ferriss proposed a city where spreading, ziggurat-like, hierarchical skyscrapers would be placed strategically on axial boulevards, each a city within itself; universities, hospitals, ministries, with smaller ziggurats as housing lining the wide, wide roads. After 1945, this is what happened to Moscow, when seven 'high buildings' ('skyscrapers' were too American a term for Cold War usage) were built that closely resembled Ferriss' proposals. These would form the most complete skyscraper skyline of any European city. Other 'high buildings' were in turn exported to the satellite states, which despite having exactly the same silhouettes as those in Moscow, were given appliqué cladding in approximate reference to the architectural culture of each given country: Riga's Academy of Sciences, the Hotel International in Prague, Casa Scânteii in Bucharest, and, perhaps most remarkable of all, and the only true public building among them, the Palace of Culture and Science in Warsaw.

When Moscow built the tallest in Europe again, in 2005, it was as a sad attempt at evoking these Stalinist 'glories' – the Triumph Palace, elite apartments (again), given an approximation of the spires and the cladding of Stalin's NKVD skycities. The new towers of the Moscow City complex are visually different, their relative sobriety a seeming attempt to avoid a stereotypically 'New Russian' thuggish kitsch. The development itself is designed to lure Eastern Europe-oriented financial institutions away from the competing financial centre of Warsaw.[6] Like Warsaw's towers, they are slick, anonymous corporate architecture, mostly designed by US-based multinational firms – now, instead of imitating or interpreting the Americans, they're merely imported. But the way the towers crowd into each other, on a very small post-industrial site, abandons the idea of planning and co-ordinating a high-rise city, whether Lissitzky's non-hierarchical city or the neo-Assyrian despotic metropolis created by Stalin. The Mercury City Tower caps a real capitalist skyline, presumably to accompany a 'real' capitalism, one where the violence and rapacity of primitive accumulation can be as distant and forgotten about as it is in Frankfurt. Moscow City is smooth, immaculate, glazed, anonymous, guiltless. Previous Moscow skyscrapers were not quite so shy about their underlying evil.

AN ARCHITECTURAL CHEKA

Looking at something like the Ministry of Foreign Affairs in Moscow one may recall a crass but apposite comedy sketch where two SS officers look at their uniforms – death's heads and all – and nervously wonder: 'Are we the bad guys?' It is not a building that is subtle in its assertion of authority. Clad in dark-brown stone, it rises to thirty storeys, with a discoloured dun spire on top; two subsidiary towers of a mere twenty storeys are pulled into the design on each side. Thick mullions between the paired windows, of the sort used to give a neo-Gothic upward momentum in interwar American skyscrapers like the Chicago Tribune Tower or the Empire State Building, run all the way up the thirty storeys; but while skyscrapers had begun in the 1930s to look less obviously 'hierarchical', the Ministry of Foreign Affairs, designed in 1948 by Gelfreikh and Minkus, has a strict Beaux Arts division of its continuous mass into component parts, each of them expressed to give the sort of visual hierarchy that was spatially necessary in cathedrals or palaces. There are miniature skylines at each of the terminating points of the ministry, a dozen or so little obelisks at the end of each component tower. Like the New York skyscrapers of the 1920s, it is stepped, with the tower using 'setbacks', giving a ziggurat-like effect. At the tower's crown is the state insignia, a hammer and sickle with laurel leaves – still very much in place – and above that a spire, which is blindingly obviously cribbed directly from the Kremlin, albeit here in harsh sandstone rather than red brick, but using exactly the same Byzantine-Gothic architectural forms. The overall effect, which must surely have been intended, is fear; in here is something very powerful and very sinister which you would not want to tangle with. Of course, this is hardly surprising, given that it formed part of one of Stalin's personal pet building projects, to the degree that he actually intervened in the design. That spire was his idea.

Moscow's density of Orthodox churches – whose 'bulbosities', strange bunched towers and deliberately irregular silhouettes have always provided a distinctly foreign ambience to the Western visitor – led Walter Benjamin to describe the effect as being 'followed around by an architectural *Okhrana*'.[7] Although huge quantities of these churches were destroyed between the 1920s and the 1960s (some were later reconstructed), their effect was emulated in the creation of the post-war Moscow skyline. The aim to fill Moscow with skyscrapers, as we've seen, begins with the never-built Palace of the Soviets in 1932, where Boris Iofan and his team

Orthodox spires, Stalinist spires, Moscow

successfully proposed a tiered, cylindrical tower topped with an arm-waving Lenin, designed to be as tall as the Empire State – a bizarre thing in a city which, at the time, was still dominated by one- and two-storey houses. The ideology behind this became more clear after the war, when a series of skyscrapers were planned to encircle the Palace of the Soviets itself – which was not significantly resumed, but which was always part of the city's post-war plans, until its abandonment and replacement with a swimming pool. Six of the towers were placed either directly upon, or just adjacent to, the Garden Ring, the historic ringroad replanned since the late 1920s as a boulevard of office blocks and ministries, initially in Constructivist style, which makes a direct one-to-one comparison of Cultures One and Two very easy. Another, Moscow State University, was planned for the Sparrow Hills (then the 'Lenin Hills') outside the city centre; another, never built, was to rise just behind the famous multi-coloured onion domes of St Basil's Cathedral on Red Square. Even though the plan was not entirely executed, given that the two towers intended to be within the Ring were never put up, the effect is still instantly recognizable to any visitor to Moscow, for whom these are usually the first things to be noticed as strange and memorable (as indeed they are). The city centre is literally encircled by six advancing skyscrapers, each with a towering, scraping spire, all of which bear down on you, paranoid and threatening, like an Inquisition; try to escape, and another is waiting for you, wings outstretched, at the Lenin Hills. And yet, the planning idea is exactly that of El Lissitzky in 1926, for his anti-hierarchical, non-religious-reminiscent Cloud Iron – the placement of 'gateway' buildings all the way along the Garden Ring.[8] And this planning of a ring of skyscrapers is not the only break with capitalist urban practice.

In his *Metropolis of Tomorrow*, Ferriss imagines the *planning* of the skyscraper. The Beaux Arts designs of the New York golden age could only do this in individual structures – for instance, the Municipal Building in Lower Manhattan (an obvious stylistic source for Stalin's 'seven') is as ornamental, hiearchical and symmetrical as any European public building, but gives out not onto a square or a boulevard but onto random, overbuilt commercial streets. However, Ferriss was inspired by the way that New York had, by the 1920s, insisted on the stepping of towers to avoid the effect of entire streets being shadowed for much of the day by sheer cliffs of offices; the pyramidal results sparked off in his febrile imagination the prospect of hotels, offices, residences and hospitals designed as ziggurats, connected in their lower levels to progressively larger/smaller towers, placed as focal points across the entire city, giving the modern urban silhouette the same 'representational' function as that of the medieval city. Much as the skyline of, say, Bruges declared the power of the church and the guilds (and the actual New York skyline the power of big business), the Metropolis of Tomorrow would proclaim the great public bodies and their functions, using the most spectacular means available – a mutated version of the boulevards, axes and vistas of Beaux Arts planning, blown up to an extreme. Apart from the absence of a high-rise hospital, this is exactly what happened in post-war Moscow. Despite the book being translated in the 1930s, there's no reason to think the planners were directly inspired by it, as it concurred with their existing inclinations.

The *skyscraper*, stepped or otherwise, is individualist, which incidentally makes it unlike the European and/or Modernist *high-rise*. Thousands of square plots are individually filled with towers, usually designed by different architects, to go as far as it is possible to go (the businessman who commissioned the Empire State, meeting his prospective architect, stood a pencil on the table and said: 'How high can you make this without it falling over?'). So the visual effect is of a crowd of different individuals jostling each other, held together only by their common steel frames and their forced adherence to the grid. Moscow, not a grid-planned city anyway, did not have to do this. The state decided where plots could go, it had the power to clear away entire city blocks at will, and it had the power and inclination to co-ordinate the actions of architects. Accordingly, none of the 'Moscow Seven' is just 'a tower', as a skyscraper is; it is an assemblage of usually at least an entire city block (in one case less, in some cases more) into one singular-willed assemblage, culminating in a multistoreyed tower, topped in every case with a spire. It is indisputable that the thing that made the Moscow Seven possible was land nationalization, but, as ever, land nationalization does not equal socialism; there is very little that is egalitarian or democratic about these structures, and in almost all cases they were for the purposes of a (by this point surely self-conscious) elite. And, for once, the attribution of the design to Stalin – by this point described as 'The Great Architect of Communism' – is indisputable, with each of the Kremlin spires on top decreed by the despot himself. It is as if,

The Barrikadnaya Apartments,
Moscow (1955 postcard)

The Ministry of Foreign Affairs,
Moscow (1956 postcard)

The Hotel Ukraina, Moscow
(1966 postcard)

Moscow State University on the
Lenin Hills (1959 postcard)

in responding to the accusations from his opponents of Oriental Despotism ('he is the new Genghis Khan' – Bukharin; 'primitive accumulation via the methods of Tamerlane' – the Menshevik Valentinov[9]), Stalin decided to evoke the aesthetics of old Muscovy, that state founded by tax collectors for the Golden Horde. He decreed it be done, at least partly via the labour of German prisoners-of-war, with the most modern building technology of the time – the steel frame, which was always hidden with fake load-bearing stone walls. These buildings are the most obvious and clear built legacy of Stalin's despotism, their roots unambiguous, their purpose (inside and out) easy to spot, the psychoses that created them easy to read. That may make it a little surprising that they have been, in recent years, consciously emulated – but we must not get ahead of ourselves.

There are reasons for these towers' strange popularity other than a general imperial-nostalgic neo-Stalinism, local mostly, if not entirely, to the Russian Federation. The Seven are, within their common Stalin-set limits, a disparate bunch, and after a couple of days in the city you learn which is which – more than that, you *use* them, and find yourself treating them as actual beacons, as the points by which you orientate yourself around the city – if you find the Ministry of Foreign Affairs or the Barrikadnaya Apartments looming up before you, you're on your way to the Arbat; if it's the Hotel Ukraina or the 'high building' on Kotelnicheskaya Embankment, you're about to cross the Moskva to the south of the city; if it's the Ministry of Heavy Industry on Krasnye Vorota or the Hotel Leningradskaya you're going due north; if it's the shadow of Moscow State University on the horizon, you're heading for the south-western suburbs.

Each has its own distinct silhouette, and some are more dominant than others; the Hotel Leningradskaya, for instance, is the mildest, with the smallest footprint, and only two small wings to its (relatively) thin twenty storeys, something necessitated by its placing in one of the city's most built-up areas, just next to several major railway stations, the Moscow equivalent of Euston Road, with the succession of the Kazan, Leningrad and Yaroslavl stations. It also has the most amusingly obvious knock-off Kremlin on top, borrowing the original's red-and-white colour scheme, with the succession of spires clearly a neo-Orthodox gesture. Krasnye Vorota is also relatively thin. On the north of the Garden Ring, the white-tile-clad structure, largely designed by Alexey Dushkin, whose

Hotel Leningradskaya and Kazan station, Moscow

work elsewhere (not here) makes clear he was among the architects of real genius produced by the USSR, culminates in a single, tall black spire in weird proportion to the rest of the building, which, like many of them, seems deliberately to be totally out of scale, breaking elementary rules of balance and composition, while insisting on a strict classical system of articulation in order to avoid any 'American', 'capitalist' repetitiousness ('skyscrapers' being both too interchangeable *and* too individualist, as Stalinist dialecticians could easily prove). The towers that really spread out, like Arkady Mordvinov's Hotel Ukraina (which piles ornament upon ornament, helping it adapt imperceptibly from Stalinist kitsch to New Russian capitalist kitsch) or the sprawling, scraping blocks of luxury flats at Barrikadnaya and Kotelnicheskaya, are like cities in themselves, whole streets culminating in a symmetrical system of ever-rising towers. They are all of them different from whichever angle you look at them, albeit almost always symmetrical; the Barrikadnaya block could be another building when looked at from its immense wings, which would dominate anywhere else on their own. All of this, however obviously insane, intimidating, monstrous and excessive, encourages looking; there are so many weird things going on, visually, that you can't tear your eyes away. The spires, and the strategic placing along the city's main artery, encourage identification, even affection.

If the latter sounds a bit of a stretch, a visit to Moscow State University may be in order. Designed by Lev Rudnev, completed in 1953 and the tallest building in Europe until 1990, this complex is, for Vladimir Paperny,

Worker-scholars at Moscow State University

'the creation of a culture that was able to force professionals to create folklore'. He continues: 'Moscow State University has nothing in common with professional architecture; it should instead be examined together with the *Iliad*, the *Mahabharata*, the Finnish *Kalevala*, or *Beowulf* – or at least together with the building folklore of India, Egypt, or Babylon.'[10] That is, exactly the same myth-driven, apparently intuitive, oral-tradition-derived style of those poems and buildings is here repeated in what was then the world's second-largest industrial economy and second-greatest world power – one which within a couple of years of the building's completion was firing rockets, dogs and then people into outer space. It is in the project that the absurdity lies, not in Paperny's assertions about it. As the tallest, most opulent and most *parlante* of the Seven, it is suffused with deliberate meaning. Unlike most of them it has a non-governmental, non-luxury-residence public function (though swipe cards for students meant we couldn't get in ourselves to have a proper look around), and it is the richest in its decoration. The white tile and red brick applied to the steel frame are supplemented with clocks, crowns, lanterns, corbels, scrolls, polychrome panels, reliefs, swags, Michelangelesque sculptures of heavy-set male and female worker-students, and, as with a few others of the Seven, a red star and a wreath at the very top of the spire, following Stalin's addition of a red star to the top of the Kremlin's Spasskaya Tower. The wings stretch out to such an extent that the university didn't even add subsidiary buildings until the 1990s, most of its functions easily taken care of in Rudnev's megastructure.

Like most Stalinist buildings, Moscow State University is not Gothic in detail – there is not a pointed arch, a Venetian gallery or a rose window to be seen, and the columns, arches and spires are a sort of free improvisation on Renaissance themes – but it is completely Gothic in effect, in the most violent, burning-of-heretics sense. It's possible maybe to compare the folkloric aspect of the Seven to the way that high-Victorian architects like Augustus Welby Pugin really thought that by designing in the medieval way, they could reclaim the medieval spirit – Pugin, of course, ate, and dressed himself and his family, accordingly. In something like William Butterfield's Margaret Street church in London, the architect palpably wanted to blast himself, through the pulsating, polychromatic force of his spatial will, right back into an allegedly superior past. Aside from the fact that, as Paperny makes clear, the architects were not manifesto-making fanatics or enthusiasts but sober-minded professionals (who did not design anything so bizarre before Stalin, and would not do so after him), the difference – and it is also the difference with the almost neo-Georgian tastefulness of Nazi architecture – is that there is no purity in the Moscow Seven. They are a wildly unstable, furiously kitsch assemblage of disparate elements, some of which were not even to be admitted on pain of denunciation or death, such as the blindingly obvious resemblance in visual and structural (if not planning) terms to pre-New Deal ultracapitalist American skyscrapers. But it bears repeating that none of this seemed to even remotely affect the extremely advanced work that went on here. From the space programme to the ANS synthesizer, extraordinarily enlightened things were devised and executed in this extraordinarily despotic structure. Function did not follow form; or rather, it could even be argued – although not by me – that the fantasy embodied in this bizarre structure actually *encouraged* the sort of mental exploration needed for really experimental work in the sciences and the arts, better perhaps than a thin-lipped glass tower might have done. It is a structure determined by dreams; but the fact that these were at least partly the dreams of one of the most terrifying despots in history cannot but colour it. All the contradictions inherent in the Stalinist 'high building' come out even more in another Lev Rudnev design, this one now in the European Union.

Although there are borderline cases in Prague, Riga, Kiev and Bucharest, and in several smaller Soviet cities, the only fully fledged equal to the Seven in terms of scale, expense, opulence, urban centrality and effect is Warsaw's Palace of Culture and Science, designed by Rudnev in 1952 and finished to the original specifications in 1955, after Stalin's death. I was once sternly told by an English architect with Polish connections that the 'Palace of Culture and Science in the Name of Josef Stalin'[11] – as it was originally named – was so universally loathed that it never features on the city's mental map of itself. If you ask a cab driver to take you to the Palace, I was assured, he will pretend not to know where or what it is. I was minded to produce a card in my possession from a Warsaw cab driver which actually has the Palace on it, lit by floodlights, with a little taxi in front of it. I don't doubt his assertion, but I do date it. A generational shift has happened in the appreciation of the tower, which now appears on mugs, on the city's promotional literature, on hipster T-shirts, on

The attractions of the Palace of Culture and Science, Warsaw (1977 postcard)

adverts, on election campaign posters, as ubiquitous as St Paul's or the Eiffel Tower. When the Polish foreign secretary and Bullingdon Club alumnus Radek Sikorski recently pledged his hope to one day demolish the (listed) building, he may not have been aware his views were vehemently not shared by young Varsovians. Moreover, Agata's support of the building is unyielding. In fact, upon seeing the Moscow Seven, she pronounced them to be inferior to their Russo-Polish sibling.

Yet the hostility is real among the older generation, and with good reason. The Palace of Culture and Science was an obviously colonial project, an 'offer you can't refuse' from Stalin to Bolesław Bierut, constructed by Russian workers and designed by a Russian architect in the largest of what the US State Department used to call the 'captive nations'. The shock of this may not be quite so spectacular now, in a city with ten or so American-designed glass towers, but it was real. The main Polish engagement with the project was in insisting it be a public building rather than a university, a ministry or luxury flats, and it is this which probably saved it, guaranteeing its eventual (overwhelmingly young, often grudging, typically semi-ironic, almost always double-edged) popularity. In a few decades it will be as uncontroversial as the neo-Gothic English-designed railway stations of India.

Probably the aspect of the building that has the least effect in that popularity, save perhaps for the extra kitsch value it adds, is that which was most emphasized in the propaganda of the time – the reference to Polish tradition. The flat roofs at the top of each sub-tower – there are six in total, four in the wings, two in the main tower itself – are each topped with a 'Polish attic', an ornamental form developed during the Polish Renaissance of the sixteenth century, the surviving monuments of which were visited by Rudnev and his team. Not having any Roman ruins to copy nearby, this eastern outpost of the new Italian architecture had to improvise, and developed what resembles a series of small spiky gables, without Gothic detail, but with peculiar swags and obelisks, something which can be seen in situ across eastern Polish towns like Lublin. Here, they just look like another instance of the Stalinist craze for random spiky ornament. More likely, the Palace endures partly due to the flattering effect of the new Warsaw skyline, an overdevelopment of towering glass offices which have been busily transforming the city centre into Eastern Europe's own answer to Frankfurt am Main; by comparison with these prosaic emblems of capitalist 'normalization', the freakish, granite-clad, ornamental gusto of the Palace of Culture and Science cannot but look utterly extraordinary, something which its 'specialness' (i.e. the lack of any similar towers elsewhere in the city, or indeed in Poland) can only assist. I have often heard – occasionally, from my mouth – the words 'Gotham City' used to describe 'PKiN' (Pałac Kultury i Nauki, in Polish). It does resemble more than a little the sort of pre-modernist American skyscraper that punctuates superhero films; one of the many pleasures available here is in watching blockbuster films at Kinoteka, the multiplex that occupies one part of the wings (not some capitalist intrusion – there was always a cinema in the building), and then walking out into your own personal apocalyptic spectacular.

Kinoteka is only one of the Palace's many public attractions. Follow it from here westwards and (at the time of writing, in March 2015) you come first to the Museum of Technology, an almost unchanged didactic exhibit of industrial know-how, with dioramas and miniature cutaway models of mines and steelworks. Next to that is the Congress Hall, now a concert venue; keep going and you come to the Museum of Evolution (with dinosaurs), then the Palace of Youth, with various sports and other facilities for children; then the Studio Theatre (now with a Socialist Realist yuppie bar attached); then opposite, across part of Plac Defilad, the vast, uneasy, semi-derelict square-cum-car-park the building commands,

Insect chandelier at PKiN, Warsaw

is the Dramatic Theatre, which has inside it an art gallery and the Cafe Kulturalna, which keeps most of its original fittings as haunting colour for its daily programme of DJs and (relatively) overpriced vodka. Inside the main entrance, under a frieze showing a ceremonial meeting of workers and peasants, are numerous offices, a swimming pool, a viewing platform with an unrivalled view of the city, another café . . . Then there are the furnishings themselves, so various and odd that entire books can be (and have been) filled with photographs just of them. In this book I can only single out a handful – the chandeliers round the back of the cloakrooms of the Dramatic Theatre, the lamps of which look like giant magnified insects' eyes, multiplied and shaped into gold; the Yuri Gagarin Hall, where a circle of smooth Doric columns surround a tinselly chandelier; the red-veined marble floor by the lifts . . .

All this is in turn enclosed on two sides by parks, with the entrances (most reached by very non-'accessible' flights of steps) guarded by more Michelangelesque colossi – Polish heroes like Copernicus and Mickiewicz, symbolic figures of knowledge, work, education, science, painting, sculpture . . . their powerful bodies look out at the giant adverts around, a rather different, if not necessarily more liberating model of male and female beauty, based around stern physical strength (of men – not so much has changed there) or an unusual combination of work-worthy heft and vigorous child-bearing healthiness (of women, where much more has changed since). But, some of the offices aside, the various uses all follow an intended original function. The building was supposed to be like this: it was intended as a social condenser and it functions as such; it is vastly more complex and labyrinthine than it appears, and it stands as something now exceptionally unusual – a *public building* as the main icon on a capital city's skyline. As weird, authoritarian, excessive and absurd as it is, only the most dogmatic Modernist or most devoted anti-communist could possibly prefer the adjacent office towers that were built to break its emphasis from the 1960s onwards. The total dominance of the Palace on the skyline only seems to increase with every new skyscraper, each of them shamed and shown up by its demented flamboyance. It *should* be possible to design something that is as all-encompassing and magnificently, terrifyingly dreamlike as this without recourse to myths and lies, but if that's the case, nobody has done so yet.

Much of the Palace of Culture and Science's appeal can be explained by the fact that it is – unlike, for instance, Bucharest's Palace of the Parliament – a real, living public building rather than a combination of government office and tourist horrorshow. While you can barely even enter the Palace of the Parliament, the Palace of Culture and Science is actually remarkably permeable, an only *superficially* forbidding piece of architecture. But all of this enthusiasm, I should make clear, comes from having used and explored the building for several years, with someone who knows where its secrets are; if I were to just see it from a distance, particularly during the years when it stood unopposed in an otherwise low-rise city, its original symbolic intent as an emblem of brute colonial power would be much less easy to forget.

If it can be possible to 'hide' a building so tall and so dominant, then the Czech city planners of the Stalinist period managed to hide their own clone of the Moscow Seven. The Hotel International in Prague was not, unlike the Palace of Culture and Science, a 'gift from the Soviet people', or from Stalin; as with so much else in Czech Stalinism, the wound was self-inflicted, or at best a display of coerced fealty. At least the exile to the suburbs means that – rather amazingly – this fifteen-storey tower on a hill does not feature in any of the possible city centre views of the Prague skyline, unless you're particularly high up; a concession to heritage and urban good manners which, as we will see, was not maintained by the Czechoslovak capital's post-Stalinist planners. Designed in 1951 by František Jeřábek, it is a lot less tall than the Seven or than the Warsaw Palace, but is large by most other measures. The typology is identical, as is the silhouette – wide wings rising step by step into a tall tower with a crown, topped by a spire. There is a grand, projecting entrance hall much as in any in the Moscow–Warsaw 7+1, and there is representational art integrated into the exterior architecture, here in the form of sgraffito work in red and white, much like that we've seen in Ostrava–Poruba, and a heroic frieze over the doorway. Apart from that, the exterior is relatively bare, without the flashy granite or tile cladding of its relatives; as befits the semi-public function, much of the interest is inside, where we wandered in unharassed one summer evening and admired the showcase of Socialist Realism on the main stairway, where murals of celebratory folk in traditional costume accompany what must even then have been a comfortable, unfolky clientèle. The 'national form' is always in there somewhere. Details are also sometimes staggering in their excess of

Door handles of the Hotel International, Prague

opulence and craftsmanship – banisters of marble, wood and sculpted gold leaves. In the restaurant, a tapestry depicts a very different Prague from the one Westerners flock to, with its Gothic and Baroque spires crowded out by dozens of smoking factory chimneys, a statement of industrial pride. On glass doors, gold-plated handles bear a relief of the building you're in, an example of that peculiar Stalinist habit of celebrating things that either haven't happened yet or have just occurred.

Riga's Academy of Sciences, another 'gift', this time to the capital of a country that was not even nominally independent, reveals perhaps better than any other the absurdity of the entire project. It is a central part of the Riga skyline, but, in a city whose dire poverty reveals itself extremely abruptly as soon as you get out of the tourist-centred Old Town, it is very much off the beaten track. It is in the Maskavas District, a working-class area of early-nineteenth-century painted wooden houses, whose sometimes extreme dilapidation hides often exquisite decorative touches; it's not, despite appearances, some unplanned peasant agglomeration, but a genuinely planned, urban space, arranged around an elegant neoclassical church, also in wood. This shabby small scale is suddenly, inexplicably broken with, and at only one point. This effect evaporates if you look at the city centre skyline from a distance, or from the other side of the Daugava river, where the Academy of Sciences is a complementary, not a discordant, note in a series of spires, a component, non-dominant part of

The Academy of Sciences, Riga, in its context

what is one of the greatest northern skylines, with spire after spire in different but harmonic styles. The fact that (by Moscow–Warsaw standards) it is not that high is something you would only notice from a distance. If it is carefully planned for the observer from a distance, in the Maskavas ('Moscow', ironically) District itself it is crazily domineering, approximately twenty times taller than nearly everything else in sight. This makes a little more sense if you know that it was supposed to be part of a wider rebuilding of the area. Riga's city architect Nikolajs Rendels wrote in 1951 that the tower was 'the start and point of departure for rebuilding the entire Moscow District; this shabby, working-class outskirt will turn into a well-arranged, green district of Riga'; in the second decade of the twenty-first century, this still hadn't occurred, and the effect, as Pyzik points out, 'could be the set for a ghost town in a low-budget western',[12] only a Wild West that has had a carny version of a New York skyscraper rammed right into the heart of it. We stayed in the district while we were in Riga, in what is in many ways an equally bizarre presence – a new and very clean budget hotel aimed at the more cash-strapped traveller, capitalizing on the closeness to the stag-party central of the Old Town. Close only in physical proximity.

Unlike those in Prague or Warsaw, the Riga 'high building' makes no attempt at any concessions to 'national form', and since those gestures were always comically cosmetic, that's not a terrible loss; but it must surely signify the even more directly colonial status of Latvia after its wartime annexation by the USSR. More kindly, it could be argued that since Riga's existing 'vernacular' is an international, cosmopolitan succession of Gothic, Baroque, Art Nouveau, it doesn't matter – it had no existing homogeneity to pay lip service to. And, unlike in Warsaw, the architect, Osvalds Tīlmanis, was local. It was originally planned as the House of the Collective Farmer, a social building like the Warsaw Palace, with educational facilities for the kolkhoz workers, a theatre and a hotel for when they wanted to stay in the city; it was taken over by the Academy of Sciences late in construction, in 1958. So this university building was mostly built with the proceeds of the collectivization of Latvian peasantry, which cannot have endeared it to people.

It is, however, open to the public, and has a breathtaking rooftop viewing platform – where the Warsaw platform is partly enclosed, this view of Riga's magnificent 'city-picture' is open to the air, as you walk along the obelisks and the other random functionless 'features' that are as always placed at the top, with the ceramic hammer and sickles (amazingly unmolested) just below you. As for the tower itself, it is the usual typology, with city-block-sized flanking wings and twenty-storey tower rising into crown and spire, the only real difference being that this time the granite and marble disguise a concrete rather than a steel frame. The architect, Tīlmanis, has allowed himself some licence – the unusual, Baroque-inspired, wave-like sculpting of the mullions gives an especially sharp vertical emphasis, and the spire is supported on two tiers of open columns, as in a seventeenth-century church tower. Abandon what would at the time have been good taste and even sanity, and it's clear that in the 1950s you could do new things with the venerable language of the Baroque. Not perhaps what the Soviet avant-garde of the 1920s, which included among it expats from Riga like Sergei Eisenstein or Gustav Klutsis, had hoped of socialist architecture, but there it is. While they dreamt of cities that were as responsive and useful as the best machines, what the Academy of Sciences displays is a profoundly, dubiously pictorial conception of architecture – wonderful seen from a distance, but bafflingly overscaled to the street itself.

Whatever its virtues and flaws, it is deeply peculiar that the largest complete bells-and-whistles 'Stalin skyscraper' in the USSR outside Moscow should be in Riga, not in any of its other great cities, neither Leningrad nor Kharkiv, Stalingrad nor Baku, Sverdlovsk nor Gorky. Like that of Warsaw, the Riga 'high building' serves as a reminder of outside power, a little Moscow-not-in-Moscow. But there was, as we've already seen, in the Kreschatyk in Kiev, an already half-built skyscraper that was stripped of its ornament, stripped of its crown and stripped of its spire, much as the architects of the Hotel Leningradskaya were stripped of their Stalin Prize by Khrushchev in 1954, as the most heinous offenders in the culture of 'architectural excess'. That there would now be 'nothing superfluous' meant that dreamlike/nightmarish cities of hierarchical spires were out, and egalitarian cities of towers of near-identical height were in. That didn't preclude at least one form of structure from continuing the old role of the 'high buildings' as the carrier of symbolic value. It's just that different things were now being symbolized.

THE BATTLE FOR THE TV TOWER

The first major structure of any kind built after the October Revolution, and the years of shortage, blockade, civil war and famine that followed it, was the Shabolovka Radio Tower in Moscow, designed by the engineer Vladimir Shukhov, and occasionally called the Third International Radio Tower, for its (somewhat hopeful) role in disseminating socialist propaganda westwards. In his account of a later visit to Russia, Ernst Toller, the playwright and brief leader of the Bavarian Soviet Republic, expressed his joy at finally seeing the tower that had conveyed radio messages from the Russian Soviets to their German comrades. In fact it's unlikely to have been this tower, which wasn't completed until 1922, three years after the Bavarian communists were crushed, but it is a beautiful story, a reminder of an uncoerced revolutionary brotherhood that would vanish within a decade. It is today better remembered as a piece of revolutionary engineering than as an example of revolutionary telecommunications – recent proposals to alter or demolish the tower led to a public statement in its defence by none other than Norman Foster, whose work is clearly in Shukhov's tradition of lightweight steel structures, formed out of subtle interconnected rings; Foster's ubiquitous diagrid has a forebear in the crossed cylindrical forms of this tall, tapering tower, and the 'tensegral' geodesic domes of Buckminster Fuller are another relative. Of the various radio towers built in the 1920s (in Prague and Berlin, for instance), few are as original in their structure as this, favouring instead an Eiffel Tower arrangement of straight steel members. Shukhov's design takes the form of concentric circles, which were lifted into place one above the other, rather than built from the ground up, making it look much lighter, and with the (surely unintended) visual effect of looking like stylized radio waves billowing from the bottom upwards into the sky – something which helped it feature in tens, maybe hundreds, of Bolshevik propaganda posters and films in the 1920s, before the iconography shifted into something with a more blood-and-soil tone.

Happily, and unusually for Moscow, people seem to know this one is special. Leave Shabolovka Metro station and there is a hoarding showing the Shabolovka tower's compatriots around the world, from a minaret in Mecca, through the Eiffel Tower to the Seattle Space Needle and the

Shabolovka Radio Tower, Moscow

Berlin TV tower. But although the tower is tall, it does not dominate the Moscow skyline like most of these do; it is too thin, too light and too suburban in its site to be a *Stadtkrone*, no matter how much it was propagandized. It does not become *the* building of Moscow in the way those above are in their respective cities, though it may have been so for a time in the 1920s. Yet from the 1960s on, when the Cold War took on its definitive, technophile aesthetic form, telecommunications towers would emerge all over Central and Eastern Europe, on both sides of the Curtain. A northern NATO outpost like Britain did not have a good showing here (the Post Office Towers of London and Birmingham or St John's Beacon in Liverpool are too staid and well-mannered, lacking the slightly villainous technocratic gusto that makes a real TV tower), but Western German-speaking countries certainly did, with inner-city space needles erected from Hamburg through Cologne to Vienna in close enough proximity to channel TV and Radio Free Europe broadcasts to the enemy; and the density of TV towers on the other side, likewise, was in part intended to block these signals, eventually unsuccessfully.[13]

Towers like these were not, however, directly instruments of Cold War, as the many in the USA make clear; and our concern here is not how the towers were specifically used as telecommunications technology, but what they were like as urban monuments. At least one, for instance, is designed to signify entry into a country – the TV tower in Ruse, in the far north of Bulgaria, on its Danube border with Romania. From the bridge that crosses the Danube – pretty much the main way to get between the two countries – Bulgaria is heralded through a seductive, ultra-modern skyline of high-rises and hotels, with a tall and elegant TV tower rising above them; their shabbiness is only really clear when you're up close. The Ruse TV tower is on the outskirts of the city, but placed in a careful alignment; when you're walking around the city centre, just next to the Brutalist City Hall, you can unexpectedly find it in the middle of a tree-lined boulevard, right on an axis – high tech and Beaux Arts.

This sort of symbolism is intrinsic to many TV towers, and this is how the most definitive 'real socialist' telecommunications tower was justified by the architect who devised it. Like most of the really interesting urban things in East Berlin, the Berlin Fernsehturm was the brainchild of that prolific architectural chameleon, Hermann Henselmann, who was initially ridiculed when he proposed the tallest telecommunications tower in

A boulevard route to the Ruse TV tower

Europe for a site just next to Alexanderplatz. When architectural fashions shifted and the Wall was up, the idea was executed to the designs of Fritz Dieter and Günter Franke. Actually, their design is a lot more unusual than Henselmann's, and although it is surely (over)familiar to any visitor

Two spires in East Berlin (1972 postcard)

to Berlin, as intended, it is worth describing just how strange it is. Most of its relatives are concrete poles with an office and revolving restaurant in the top, all in sweeps of concrete with convex shapes towards the top, from which thin satellite-dish-laden 'spires' extrude. The Berlin

Fernsehturm, as befits its position in the centre of the city, makes some effort to produce an architecture for the pedestrian, in the form of concrete legs that splay out onto the ground, tall enough for you to walk beneath them and shelter therein from Berlin's often drastic weather. The lifts go here, and the concrete pole shoots up leading to a globe, detailed with dozens of little faceted steel panels, with ribbon windows of tinted red glass for the restaurant inside. The design is instantly, in contemporary parlance, 'iconic', memorable and available in model form in tourist outlets all over the city. But as Berlin never went in for either skyscrapers or Stalinist 'high buildings', on either side of the Wall (despite proposals for both), it is the unquestioned monument of the city of Berlin, visible for miles and miles, and instantly redolent of the divided, now 'healed' city that it was between 1961 and 1989 – straight away, it says: 'Here be spies and slightly scary, seedy modernity.' It was intended to say: 'Here is the capital of the German Democratic Republic, a modern industrial economy, the eighth-largest in the world.' It could say that to the other part of Berlin, too, but it's doubtful they were impressed.

Due to the general right-angled sternness of Prussian architecture and planning and the relentless bombing the city suffered, Berlin's TV tower is not, except by the occasional heritage zealot, considered to be a destructive force on an otherwise lovely skyline. The same could not be said about an even more startling and original design, the Žižkov TV tower in Prague. While, as we've seen, the Hotel International had the urban good manners to take its Stalinist city-defining to an obscure site in the suburbs (though this good sense was compromised somewhat by the gigantic Stalin statue set on a hilltop at the same time), the regime of post-1968 'normalization' had no such qualms, building the obligatory TV tower in the mostly untouched, undamaged nineteenth-century Žižkov district, close enough to the centre to elicit the horrified appreciation of a generation of tourists. There are angles where it makes a little more sense. See it from the wide Olšanská Street, for instance, and it appears at the centre of a socialist–modern axis, between equally rusty, cranky structures, to which it shows its only symmetrical elevation, and the three concrete supports that hold up the curved blobs where the restaurant and offices are placed seem to rise up out of the tram lines, part of some other grimy, dilapidated, Modernist-industrial Prague to the one most of us are visiting.

The fact that very few people consider Olšanská a street of Prague worth visiting means that, for most, this is a bafflingly tall and aggressive building inserted violently into a well-mannered district of Biedermeier tenements, where the only other tall accents are Baroque churches. If you want the preservation of historic architecture to consist of a kind of cognitive trick, whereby you can pretend, but for the cars, that you're walking around the given area in 1860, then the tower is offensive. If not, it's quite fabulous, a structure whose designer, Václav Aulický, and engineer, Jiří Kozák, were fully aware that something this tall needed some visual drama, some sense that it was worthy of being looked at all the time, qualities that a more 'normal' TV tower would have lacked. So looked at from Vítkov Hill, say, you can apprehend the Žižkov Tower as a minor masterpiece of 1980s high tech, a genre otherwise limited to the capitalist world. It is a visible cousin to the likes of the Lloyd's Building: dark, twisted, both quasi-organic and ruthlessly metallic, Gothic, physical and shamelessly phallic. As we've seen in Liberec, these sorts of structures were a bit of a speciality of the Czechoslovak Socialist Republic, both before and after the spring of 1968, which seems to have had no effect whatsoever on the fearless power and unambiguously central, always-visible placing of them.

The Kamzík TV tower, also engineered by Jiří Kozák and built in 1967 on the northern outskirts of Bratislava, completely dominates the skyline of this hilly city. It is designed as an irregular diamond, rising outwards from its base to support the various functional things inside, then changing course towards its eventual spire. Like the Shabolovka Tower, it is unclear to the untrained eye how the thing is actually supported, looking improbable in its precarious balance on the ground. It's the opposite of the Žižkov Tower, showing the amount of leeway the basic form made possible – light, not heavy, with its offices and restaurants enclosed in its structure rather than cantilevered from it. Again, some historical distance is probably necessary to appreciate these towers, at a point when they're no longer actively involved in trying to stop you from watching uncensored telly. The Žižkov Tower had, at the time we were photographing it in 2011, a sculptural intervention by David Černý, in the form of a group of sinister giant babies climbing up its penile trunks. Usually these domestications are an attempt to 'normalize' a 'real socialist' structure, to make it nice, to make it into a straightforward advert – I was aghast in 2006 to

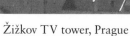

Žižkov TV tower, Prague

Kamzík TV tower, Bratislava

find the Berlin Fernsehturm transformed into a giant T-Mobile-sponsored pink football for the European Championship. Černý's work on the Žižkov tower emphasizes its Surrealism rather than trying shamefacedly to cover it up, playing instead with its underlying perversity.

The Soviet Union was as enthusiastic for the form as the Czechs and

Slovaks, and in the 1960s to 1980s a dozen or more large-scale towers were built in provincial cities and the capitals of nearly all the union's republics – usually, it should be noted, on the outskirts rather than occupying the historical centre, as in westerly outposts like Berlin or Prague. The largest of all, until overtaken in the 1970s by Toronto's CN Tower, was the Ostankino Tower, a fine structure in its own right which we will come to presently. Most of them adhere to the usual flying-saucer-on-a-stick typology, though there are significant exceptions, and many are clearly deliberately planned as accents in a skyline. The Riga TV tower is one of the best, especially when seen from the motorway bridge on the way into the city, where it forms yet another part of that incredible skyline, a Futurist-Hanseatic-Soviet melange coordinated by a mixture of geographical felicity and the need to define this port city to seafarers. It forms the first in a series of punctuating urban accents, defining the space along the wide river before the Academy of Sciences, followed by the Baroque and Gothic spires of the centre, leading on to the Baltic Sea. The effect can hardly have been accidental. The building itself, built in 1980 to the designs of Gunārs Asaris, is entirely unlike the top-heavy norm. The supports appear caught in the act of swinging into each other, enclosing a triangular volume into which the functions are carried up; this part is in red, the frame in yellow – an outré design by any standard. It is far enough from the centre to be fairly uncontroversial, though it is not always architecture as such that has made Soviet TV towers notorious.

At least two of them were at the centre of the stagnant Soviet Union's collapse and its supplanting by an exceptionally ruthless, neoliberal 'managed democracy'. Both were at the centre of a 'battle for the TV tower', and their respective fame is instructive. One is the Vilnius TV tower, a generic, attractive 1980 hat-on-a-spike design by V. Obydovas in the microrayon of Lazdynai, which can easily be avoided when walking round the Baroque centre but which is immediately obvious when you reach the River Neris, where it demarcates the city's edge. It was battled over in January 1991, when pro-independence activists tried to defend it from the Red Army, who were then attempting to reoccupy the Lithuanian capital, which had declared independence some weeks earlier. Several protesters were killed, a major stain on Gorbachev's saintly reputation, although by this point events were slipping out of his or anyone's control.

As the most violent event in the generally peaceful disintegration of the USSR – at least until the Caucasus descended into vicious post-imperial warfare soon after – it is very well remembered, a heroic narrative of struggle centring on a seemingly unlikely architectural form, as if in accidental remembrance of the fact that the seizing of the telephone exchange was probably more important than the storming of the Winter Palace in October 1917. There is a memorial, with cross and plaque, to the victims outside the TV tower, but maybe more indicative, we thought, was an exhibit we found in the summer of 2013 outside the contentiously named Museum of Genocide Victims in central Vilnius (more of which later). Here the events are represented in children's drawings, where they appear as the major event of Lithuanian history – the invasion of the Red Army and the deportations of the NKVD in 1940 are followed by the Red Army's 'defeat' in 1991. Each is represented by (obviously) inept and bloody drawings. One of the more skilled children has drawn a shadowy mass of Lithuanians gathered around the concrete tower, with one

Child's drawing of the Battle for the TV Tower at the Museum of Genocide Victims, Vilnius

waving a Lithuanian flag towards the fallen Red Army men, who are tied by barbed wire to crosses. The symbolism is outlandish and unnerving, but at least here popular action is commemorated, albeit in a creepily nationalistic way.

There is no such commemoration at the Ostankino Tower in Moscow. Erected in 1967 to the designs of Nikolai Nikitin to coincide with the fiftieth anniversary of the October Revolution, this is another faintly organic design, intersecting trunks and rings pulled into a skyscraping tower which, despite its prodigious height, does not feel at all dominating – you can see here what made these things popular during the Thaw, in that they expressed both power and technology in a way that was much more subtle than the thuggishly Chekist display of the Moscow Seven. It was at the centre of the events of October 1993, when the elected parliament refused to ratify the shock therapy measures insisted upon by Boris Yeltsin and his group of unelected 'young reformers' and attempted to remove them from power.[14] To stop this 'communist–Fascist coup', parliament was bombarded by tanks – according to government statistics 187 people were killed, in opposition estimates around 2,000; either way, far more than the thirteen victims of January 1991 in Vilnius, or indeed in the more famous failed neo-Stalinist coup in Moscow in August the same year, where three people died. In 1993, parliamentary supporters tried to take the TV tower, a sensible decision given that the media was controlled by Yeltsin and his incipient 'family' of oligarchs, not by parliament. They failed in their objectives, and a presidential republic with systematic ballot-rigging was set up which endures at the time of writing. You won't find the struggle being commemorated here, or in many other places, given that Yeltsin had full support from the 'international community' in his actions against a 'red–brown' coalition out to defeat his daring reforms. Ilya Budraitskis, a curator at Moscow's Historical Museum, resigned from his job in October 2013 after an exhibition he had put together on the events' twentieth anniversary was abruptly pulled.[15] It is not to be remembered. The TV tower goes on disseminating the voice of power.

Ostankino TV tower, Moscow (1973 postcard)

THE (POST-)COMMUNIST CORPORATE SKYLINE

After 1945, a new skyscraper style emerged in the United States, which essentially involved hiring European architects to design the things for which there was neither the technology nor the gumption in interwar Europe. The United Nations building, in New York – Wallace K. Harrison's tweaking of a Le Corbusier proposal – and the Lake Shore Drive apartments in Chicago by Mies van der Rohe pioneered this International Style of clean, expensive surfaces, laconic detailing and an almost classical serenity. Regardless of the fact that Moscow had played host to some of its precursors, this style was anathematized in the USSR and its satellites, only to be quickly and brusquely adopted after 1956. The style is the skyscraper with the romanticism purged out of it – the direct opposite of the Stalinist 'high buildings', which must have seemed to Americans like their own recent past breaking out and overtaking their official enemy.

The contrast between the pinnacles, statuary and ornament of Moscow State University and the purified steel and glass structural Expressionism of Mies's Seagram Building did not escape comment from either side in the 1950s. What was not mentioned at the time was the fact that this was a reversal of the relative aesthetic differences of the 1920s, though some at least spotted the provenance.[16] In 1922, the *Chicago Tribune*, which had launched an architectural competition for its new HQ, ignored several designs by continental Modernists for stark, bared-structure technocratic skyscrapers, and built a neo-Gothic skyscraper instead; one of the unsuccessful European entries became the model for the Izvestia building off Tverskaya. By 1952, the order had completely reversed; but ten years later, various Eastern European capitals were experimenting with the International Style, building what would now be considered 'normal' flat-roofed glass skyscrapers, sometimes to crowd out the Stalinist towers completed less than a decade earlier. This is the area of architecture that has probably changed least after 1989, and these 'real socialist' mini-Manhattans have been supplemented with the very similar EU style, derived from Skidmore, Owings and Merrill and Norman Foster, of sheer glass façades, occasionally in 'iconic' shapes, crowded into the space of 'central business districts'.

As with much else, they vary sharply according to where they're placed. Of all the capitals and big cities, Bratislava is subject to the most obviously chaotic form of neoliberal nonplanning – from the hills around the centre, you can see glass and steel towers thrown up at random, with thirty-storey blocks rammed into low-rise districts so that any sense of place or coherence is lost, either a deliberate gesture against uniformity or as an example of a total negligence of urban responsibility. In Ljubljana, the new towers are often indistinguishable from the scrupulously detailed, neatly arranged office blocks of the 1970s, where market socialism brought about a more 'normal' corporate skyline some years before the collapse. But elsewhere you can often find outright neoliberal skylines being managed and tamed by some vestige of 'real socialist' town planning. In Tallinn, speculative skyscrapers are exiled to a slightly suburban site around the 1980 Hotel Olympia. In Vilnius, the left bank of the River Neris was planned under Brezhnev as the showcase for a new town of office blocks, hotels and the like; the few that were designed, like a rusty Miesian tower now inhabited by a company called 'Molesta' and the thoroughly restored Hotel Lietuva, are accompanied by a busy squeeze of coloured and tinted glass, erected over the last decade during the financial boom that hit the Baltic states especially hard. They run the gamut of recent corporate style – the Vilnius City Hall, rather strikingly, is housed in a barcode façade tower that could be in contemporary Manchester; the SwedBank tower, a sprawling and imaginative pair of red metal-clad wings enclosing a glass core, suggests the more imaginative architectural culture of Sweden, though Ambrasas, its architects, are a Lithuanian firm;[17] and the other towers, usually for Scandinavian banks, are tubes and shoeboxes in the Frankfurt style, impossible to really praise or blame.

These ultra-modern corporate skylines in Tallinn and Vilnius are among the principal evidence for the oft-made and ideologically loaded claim that these are 'Nordic' rather than 'Eastern European' countries, which is certainly true insofar as their economies are owned almost entirely by Nordic banks and corporations. But in a second-hand bookshop in Vilnius's Old Town I found a definition that you wouldn't find in SwedBank, in an old textbook on Scandinavian town planning, no doubt owned by a planner in the 1980s, pining for Olof Palme over Brezhnev. A 'Nordic' economy, it contends, involves the following:

1. Every individual shall be given all possibilities for personal development and self-realization in proportion to abilities.

2. Society, as a collective whole, should be so developed as to promote good social relations and to control damaging social obstacles to such a society.

3. Society should make secure both individual and collective welfare, giving thought to maintaining a balance between them.

4. Every person must be given 'full citizenship' status.

5. Equality is an important value that needs to be planned and secured by law.

6. Economic planning and control are essential.

7. The social security system is an integral part of the welfare system.[18]

The Nordic model also, now, involves the economic colonization of countries that have no hope or prospect of any of the social benefits and social cohesion listed therein, but whether or not the Baltic countries ever were or are Nordic is a moot point. The USSR obviously broke points 1 and 3; the Baltic countries today all break with 1, 2, 3, 5, 6 and 7 – in fact, if a mainstream party there proposed any of them, they'd be accused of communism. That said, Lithuania is alone in the Baltic countries for not breaking 4 – unlike Latvia and Estonia, which maintain citizenship laws that effectively bar a large (and Russian-speaking) percentage of the population from voting. But perhaps this is all missing the point – what 'Nordic' means now is educated, modern, stylish, tall, blonde and pale-skinned – and certainly many Lithuanians, Latvians and Estonians fit these categories.

The record should show that Warsaw was first to turn to a seemingly capitalist, corporate aesthetic, in the early 1960s. For the 'Eastern Wall' opposite the Palace of Culture and Science a Stalinist masterplan was scrapped and replaced with a shopping centre and three towers of flats; the shops were in the Mies style, although it was too expensive for the high-rises, detailed in concrete. On a site opposite the central railway station, two towers were built a few years later: two clear, stark glass-and-granite rectangles connected by overhead walkways. These were supplemented in the 1970s and 1980s with towers by outside architects, as at the Warsaw Novotel, a frankly hideous silo with tiny windows, courtesy of Swedish designers, or the 'Blue Skyscraper', by Yugoslav contractors.

The obvious intention, from the very beginning, was to gradually crowd out the dominance of the Palace, which would otherwise have been twenty times taller than everything else in the city, a constant reminder of Stalin and his gift to the Polish people. The way to get rid of this was to build a version of downtown Frankfurt am Main, whose two dozen or so competing towers of finance appear to have held a frankly surprising fascination for the city planners of Central and Eastern Europe. The dominance of the Frankfurt style over the Palace of Culture, at least to the degree that the Palace cannot be seen without also seeing its neighbours, was only achieved in the last few years, through the building of several skyscrapers just behind it. As architecture, they are a mixed bunch, ranging from Daniel Libeskind's shamefully inept and poorly detailed contribution to less flashy, more restrained towers by Skidmore, Owings and Merrill and other large American corporate firms, which have mostly revived the tradition of leaving the skyline of the Polish capital to non-Polish architects – not, on the evidence of the handful they did design, that Poles would propose anything significantly different.

Miesian Modernism: the Marriott Hotel, Warsaw

Like most skyscraper skylines, they're best seen from a distance, from where you can most enjoy their exhibitionist and unabashed embrace of neon lights and a faintly dystopian electronic modernity. At night the

Marriott, a slight 1989 remodelling of a tower originally designed in the 1970s for the Polish national airline, LOT, constantly flashes LED messages about its rooms, the time of day and the temperature, and suchlike; but given the futuristic context and the 2-million-strong emigration from Poland it may as well be beaming out 'a new life awaits you in the off-world colonies!' During the day or during the weekend, walk around the same tower on the ground, and you can find it eerily empty, like most central business districts when the office workers aren't home. We once wandered around the walkways that connect the Marriott and the neighbouring Sharp tower, designed to the same height and to similar dimensions in 1976 by the same architect, Jerzy Skrzypczak. We found nobody there bar a couple of skateboarders and a bored security guard. The late-1960s planners who conceived this place tried to ensure some sort of coherent urbanism for pedestrians, not just a motorcity – there's a long podium to the busy Aleje Jerozolimskie, where an arcade of aluminium pilotis leads into various (even then) upper-crust establishments; but go round the corner, up onto the stone-clad concrete walkways, and the desolation is marvellously complete.

Most skyscraper districts have this extreme night–day contrast; but many of Warsaw's other corporate office blocks have a new kind of juxtaposition, slammed as they are right into the uniform skylines created by post-war tower blocks. This is dramatic in the inner-city microrayon of the 'Iron Gate', the green interstices of which are occupied in every available spot by glass-and-Trespa towers for banks and for accommodating wealthier Varsovians, in turn putting unsurprising pressure on the older buildings and their rents. The conflict there is no longer the smooth Miesian office block versus the Stalinist neo-Gothic palace – two models of urban hierarchy against each other – but the individualism of demonstrative, speculative office and apartment blocks against the massive uniformity of around eighteen identical blocks of 1960s flats, rolled out one after the other across a square mile. The contrast between the urban practice of the Modernist Thaw and of neoliberalism seems larger than between Stalinism and neoliberalism – something you can see much more clearly in Moscow.

Central Moscow has only one 'Modernist' high-rise office block of note, and it stretches the definition of modern architecture to the brink of Pomo – the Academy of Sciences, designed in the early 1980s by Yuri

Surreal monumentalism: the Academy of Sciences, Moscow

Platonov. It features regularly in the volumes of *Totally Awesome Ruined Soviet Architecture*, which may have made us a little sniffy about it, and we did not explore the place on earlier visits despite spending much time at the adjacent monument to Yuri Gagarin. This was partly dictated by the fact that it is incredibly hard to get to as a pedestrian, as like the Warsaw Marriott and Sharp towers it lifts itself up on a system of walkways and raised plazas, but unlike them the means of getting up to them is fiendishly complex, involving a few road bridges over a horrendous motorway, which we found unexpectedly emerging from the courtyards of Stalinist apartment buildings. On Agata's insistence we made our way up these, and found ourselves on an airy car-free plateau – a rare thing indeed in Moscow – from where we could survey the city, and see the way that the new capitalist skyline was crammed into a tiny little space, and could see just how much it had broken with decades of state planning, replacing it only with a chaotic mulch unified solely by height. The Academy of Sciences itself, though, is an impure high of absurd pop Futurism, a symmetrically planned tower-with-wings whose roof is topped by anodized gold panels, some of which were intended to generate power, which apparently seldom if ever worked, but is formally far more odd than 'green' gestures tend to be – not merely opulent in their choice of metal but also strangely constructed, bristly and organic, as if – fittingly – the project of a cracked scientist.

However, Moscow has relatively few 'normal' office blocks, which are mostly concentrated along the glassy rush of Kalinin Prospekt. Not far from there are two dour concrete-framed blocks which, from a distance, reveal themselves to be symmetrically placed around the Ministry of Foreign Affairs, thus deliberately emphasizing the earlier Stalinist style. At night, today, they are transformed into a continuous neon artwork, pulsating imperial symbols – the Russian flag, the Tsarist eagle. Moscow was already using modern architecture as a frame, a backdrop, to the sky-scraping eclecticism it's better known for. But this is a subtle thing, in a city which does not generally do subtle. Before Moscow City and its belated turn to 'normal' corporate architecture, Yeltsin and Putin's capital was subject to a sudden revival of the aesthetics of Stalinism itself; like much else here, it is coloured with the darkest, most malevolent humour. The direct revival of Stalinist architecture did not begin in the 1990s, it should be noted; in the 1970s project for what is now the Duma, the parliament, just off the culmination of Kalinin Prospekt, there was no attempt at creating a 'new' building – the Moscow authorities simply dug out a competition entry by Lev Rudnev for the 1934 Commissariat of Heavy Industry competition and built it, as an architectural confirmation of the neo-Stalinist trend that Medvedev saw at work in that decade. Completed in 1980, it forms a looming, lumpen culmination to Khrushchev's Modernist boulevard, and gained what fame it has from its bombardment in 1993; after he had retaken the building, Yeltsin commissioned a new wall around it. According to Boris Kagarlitsky, the cost of this fence exceeded the purchase price of all but three of the countless state enterprises that were subject to a countrywide fire sale at that point.[19] These sorts of faintly sick ironies were soon incorporated into the buildings themselves.

Take the 'Patriarch Building', near Red Square, designed in the early 2000s by Sergey Tkachenko and SPAT architects. Not a full-blown skyscraper, it is definitely a tower of some kind, designed to complement the Hotel Moskva and the towers of the Kremlin itself; it weaves together two blocks of luxury residences, both detailed with the full Stalinist armoury

Neo-Stalinist tower outside Kursk station, Moscow

of columns, spires, 'superfluous' detail and statuary, although the structural fakery is now even more obvious, this time deliberately. It is full of torn-off fragments of other buildings, held aloft like trophies – at the top of one of its two spires is a model of Tatlin's Monument to the Third International, some sort of symbol of the victory over Modernism and world revolution. But look at those statues: they're not heroic workers and peasants this time, but – and I'm not joking here – they're heroic statues of the property developers who commissioned the thing in the first place.[20] Similar, taller towers without quite the same excesses can be found in the centre at the Administrative Buildings on Paveletskaya Square, outside Kursk station, or at the Riverside Towers, opposite the reconstructed Cathedral of Christ the Saviour; there is even that 'Eighth Sister' of the Moscow Seven, the luxury apartment complex known as the Triumph Palace, finished in 2005 and still by some way the largest residential building in Europe, a pantomime, wax-museum version of the Moscow State University's horrifying original. Like the Stalinist towers themselves, these are an expression of sheer, naked power, this time financial *and* political; and, this time, they come with a knowingly cynical, end-of-history wink. They abandon all of the town-planning ideas that were actually present in 'real socialism', instead popping up wherever a developer has a suitable site – they were a particular favourite of the outgoing mayor, Yuri Luzhkov, whose wife was Moscow's biggest property developer. Put bluntly, like the 1950s towers they imitate, they are built on blood.

So why did we feel a slight sense of disappointment when we found this style dying out, as the city reverted to the Frankfurt style for its crowded, glassy 'CBD' at Moscow City? Nagging at both Agata and me in Moscow was the – surely, I admit, touristic – feeling that here we'd finally found a place which didn't give a damn, which didn't have the overwhelming feeling of loss and shame over not being 'civilized', 'normal' or 'Western', and which would find the prospect of remodelling itself to resemble a Rhineland financial capital deeply depressing. Its new buildings, horrible as they are, reflect a capitalism of (actual) criminals, not a capitalism of compradors, and hence they have a certain gusto lacking in those cities where planners and architects are constantly looking over their shoulders. Good taste is their enemy. Looking at proposals for new Moscow buildings offered him by the Baron of Thames Bank, the repellent Luzhkov once opined: 'But Mr Foster, this is not Moscow.' Here, a sense of pride and place when building in the sky seems inextricably tied to blood and soil.

5
Metro

When we are victorious on a world scale I think we shall use gold for the purpose of building public lavatories in the streets of some of the largest cities of the world. This would be the most 'just' and most educational way of utilising gold for the benefit of those generations which have not forgotten how, for the sake of gold, ten million men were killed and thirty millions maimed in the 'great war for freedom', the war of 1914–1918.

V. I. Lenin, 'The Importance of Gold Now and after the Complete Victory of Socialism' (1921)[1]

THE WORLD'S MOST ADVANCED TWENTY-FIRST-CENTURY ECONOMY

When writing a book like this, it is difficult not to worry that you're going to sound like an apologist, an omelette-maker – a 'tankie', as the rest of the left used to call those who defended the Soviets over East Germany in 1953, Hungary in 1956, Czechoslovakia in 1968, Poland in 1981. That's why it's worth stressing how often what happened was unnecessary, that it was not logical or inevitable; that no matter how difficult the circumstances, choices were made, and those choices were, more often than not, made by power against its subjects. I knew when I got round to writing this book that there would be only one chapter where I would definitely be accused of outright apologism, of cheerleading for the aesthetics of something repugnant. That is, the chapter on urban rapid transit systems, or, as they're usually known, metros – the one area where I genuinely do believe that the practice of the Soviet Union was vastly superior to that of the West, and where I genuinely will contend that mayors, city councils, university occupiers, strikers, whoever, should study their example and learn from it as much as possible. The urban underground railways that were built between the early 1930s and the early 1990s were and are a magnificent achievement, and one which many people are still, rightly, proud of. What makes this pride difficult is that here as elsewhere is a story of brutality followed by negligence – the difference is that in this case, there were real, spectacular results. Here, there was really was an omelette.

Why Metro systems? It's unclear exactly how this became such a Soviet specialism, to the point where it exported its experts around the world, well outside the 'socialist camp', as the Russian Federation still does. Conceivably, the Soviet economies' very success in the creation of public transport infrastructure may be an indication of their failure elsewhere; for much of the twentieth century, the efficiency and scale of an advanced economy were always measured by the quantity and quality of cars it produced. Anyone born in the UK before around 1985 will recall the ridicule that that Eastern European cars induced: the Dacia (Romania), the Lada (USSR), the Trabant (GDR), the Škoda (Czechoslovakia) – these were not objects of consumer desire. I can attest that 'Your dad drives a Škoda' or 'I saw your mum pick you up in her Lada' were commonly thrown insults in Southampton comprehensive school playgrounds in the 1980s. The car industry that existed was often an importation anyway – the Volgas made in the Gorky Avtozavod were closely modelled on Fords, the Lada was produced in Togliatti, a new town outside Samara, in factories basically replicated from Fiat, and the iconic car of People's Poland, still occasionally visible on the streets, was the 'Little Fiat', a small Polonized version produced in Polish factories in the 1970s, for the Polish consumer, not for export. Even then, after the likes of the Trabant went into mass production, car ownership lagged well behind Western Europe. Acting on that weakness meant that the USSR and its empire had to develop public transport instead.[2] That didn't mean there wasn't interesting infrastructure for private transport as such – early Stalinism occasionally favoured road bridges with heroic statuary, as at the Green Bridge in Vilnius. There are some daringly engineered road bridges here and there, but mostly they are glorious, crazed exceptions, such as the Slovak National Uprising Bridge in Bratislava, an outrageous design that merges a suspension bridge with the sort of space-age tower-restaurant usually found in telecommunications towers. Counter-intuitive as it might sound, given the Soviet propensity for pointlessly widening urban arteries and the hell that crossing a road in Moscow entails, in terms of architecture and design pedestrians got the better deal.

And, like much else here, the result is that, from today's perspective, the Soviet economy looks quite a lot more impressive than it would have looked to observers, here at least partly by accident. All countries are agreed on, and most Western European and East Asian ones to some degree act upon, the idea that the car is a problem, for its profligate carbon emissions, for the suburbanization it creates, for the amount of people it kills; and hence since the late 1990s there's been an expansion of Metro and tram networks, both of which were seen in, say, the 1960s, 1970s and 1980s as dated, obsolete forms of transport. In the same decades that the UK was abandoning urban rapid transport – closing and demolishing the Liverpool Overhead Railway, abolishing trams everywhere but Blackpool, neglecting the tube, cancelling a mooted Manchester Metro, and ploughing everything into the motorways – the USSR was extending tram and trolleybus networks into its new microrayons and building Metros at a rate paralleled only by China in the last decade.

Then, this was proof that it was, to quote one well-known dismissal, 'the world's most advanced nineteenth-century economy', stuck in the fin-de-siècle era of the Paris Metro, incapable of propelling itself into the future via the motorway, the private car and the internal combustion engine; now, it looks much more advanced than we were, building for a future of public transport conveyed through the grandest, best designed of public spaces. Here, historical accident stops and deliberate act comes in. The USSR may have preferred to have had a 'real' car economy in its cities, but the tram-and-Metro economy it did have meant, of necessity, the development of public, collective spaces for people to travel through. The results were often truly astonishing, the ennobling of mundane tasks and everyday life via 'palaces of the people', not the aggrandizing and housing of an elite via the same. In the case of the underground railway, the achievement was astounding – and also, at least at first, horrifying.

THE EPIC OF THE MOSCOW METRO

In 1921, Lenin wrote a short text, quoted above, on the uses of gold before and after the worldwide triumph of socialism. The rhetoric was as dramatic as the actual content was deeply pragmatic – the piece attempts to convince the Bolshevik Party that it needs to learn trade, and needs to create a 'state capitalism' upon which it *may*, later, with the assistance of the rest of the world, be able to build socialism. In so doing it will need to store, trade and generally accumulate capital and, accordingly, gold. As if in order to remind the rank and file that this, like so many later lapses, is considered strictly temporary, he imagines that this now-worthless metal will be used for the furnishing of public toilets, as a symbolic gesture – in short, after the revolution we will shit on gold. Nikita Khrushchev later cited this on his visit to the United States: 'one old man, who was quite decrepit, but who was very wealthy and influential, as I was told, kept asking how much gold we produced and why we didn't trade with America for gold . . . I said: "Mr. So-and-So (I don't remember his name), I will answer your question about gold. Are you familiar with the statement made at one time by our leader Vladimir Ilyich Lenin, that we should hold on to our gold for the time being? At a certain stage of development of human society (Lenin said) gold will lose its value, and therefore gold should be kept in reserve, to make public toilets out of. That's what we're keeping our gold for, and when the time comes and communist society has been established, gold will lose its value as a means of exchange, and then, to carry out Lenin's testament, we will use gold to decorate the public toilets under communist society. That's why we're holding on to our gold."'[3]

Khrushchev seems to have missed the point somewhere. He did not appear to agree with the notion that gold was pointless and worthless in a communist society, but was arguing instead that gold would be used to furnish the most basic, straightforward, essential and plebeian functions because it is beautiful. If nothing is too good for the working man, as the communist architect Berthold Lubetkin once opined, then the working man will have gold latrines. That Khrushchev would have argued for this is not so surprising if we consider his prominent role in the construction of the Moscow Metro – a subway system rather than a sewer system, but nonetheless a succession of pragmatic underground tunnels for a seemingly banal purpose. The comparison makes even more sense if we remember how the tiling, smell and upkeep of so many Western Metro systems can be rather lavatorial. But the Moscow Metro has several stations which feature large quantities of gold in their underground fittings, details and dressings. At Komsomolskaya Koltsevaya, opened in 1952 to the designs of Alexey Shchusev, there are gold chandeliers and gold mosaics; in Novoslobodskaya there are niches with stained glass ringed by gilded leaves and swags; in Aviamotornaya, the ceiling of the hall is dressed with golden triangles arranged in an abstract pattern, with the electric lights set into them. 'More marble,' noted one historian, 'went into the stations of the first line than into all the palaces of the Tsar in the fifty years before the revolution.'[4] And unlike most public toilets, it was all kept exceptionally clean.

There weren't so many signs in the Moscow Metro's first line that it would reach these levels of opulence in overdrive. Finished in 1935, these are definitely products of the aesthetic change that occurred after Stalin gained absolute power, but here Modernism and its laconic, anti-rhetorical use of materials and love for space has been adapted as much as abolished. It peacefully coexists with a very non-Modernist love for natural textured surfaces, traditional materials and representational art. Even so, there is nothing here that compares with anything previously done at an underground railway. If you start at the first station to be opened, Sokolniki, you'll notice first the entrance building. Often the more conservative aspect of a Moscow Metro station, this one is a Modernist pavilion with classical details, featuring a black frieze of the Metro's builders, a raw, roughly modelled relief of workers toiling half-naked in the rock. Descend, and you'll be struck by the tall pylons that hold up the underground hall, sheathed in an intense light-blue marble, with a coffered ceiling and yellow tiles to the walls. These have forebears of some sort in the double-height columns of some of Alfred Grenander's stations for the Berlin U-Bahn, but are much more demonstrative and commanding, and on a larger scale. Carry on along the same line and you will soon arrive at Krasnye Vorota, or 'Red Gates', named after a Rococo triumphal arch that used to stand on the site, demolished in the widening (and de-greening) of the Garden Ring. The surface station here is actually still modern, probably the last entirely modern building to be built in

Moscow for twenty years, designed by Nikolai Ladovsky as a dreamlike grand gateway, a scallop shell of descending arches, which creates the requisite sense of entry and dreaminess without using any obviously retro details.

The station halls below, though, are always the places of real interest in the Moscow Metro, by contrast with London or Paris. In almost all cases they are extremely simple arched hallways with arcades on either side, through which you pass to catch the train. They immediately (and expensively) eliminate all the petty inconveniences of tube travel – no cramped little stations with people squeezed in, no marching up and down stairs to find the other platform, which is in nearly all cases on the other side of the hall. North goes north, south goes south. It makes sense, given the impressive convenience and scale of these halls, that it's here that the architectural experiments began. The underground vestibule at Red Gates was designed as a tribute to the Red Gate that was destroyed, by the unorthodox neo-classicist Ivan Fomin. Thick red marble pillars with niches, a palatial ceiling, and a red-and-white-checked ballroom floor. The intense red of the place is overwhelming, as if its red marble has become a gaseous miasma. This neo-Tsarist dungeon gives some hint of what would come later, but other stations on the first line are still very light and airy; Komsomolskaya features a two-level arcade, suspended by double-height columns in a strange pinkish-gold marble with gold capitals featuring Soviet symbols, and a majolica mural of communist youth building the Metro, whose freely drawn figures have yet to acquire the exaggerated musculature and iron-set expressions characteristic of the Stalinist body; the Lenin Library, a sweeping cofferred ceiling; and at Kropotkinskaya, originally Palace of the Soviets (for the never-built edifice) the young designer Alexey Dushkin created a space almost without any architectural precedent whatsoever, where fluted, upturned columns contained lights within their outstretched tops that lit the hall above, creating a wide enfilade of plant-like moulded concrete pillars.

As architecture, this first line is already a colossal achievement, made perhaps more so by its relative subtlety in comparison with what would come next. But it is equally a political achievement, which the tourist of the revolution Bertolt Brecht was referring to in his poem, 'The Moscow Workers Take Possession of the Great Metro on April 27, 1935', about the first line's opening. It is worth citing in large chunks:

Entering Red Gates station, Moscow

Inside Red Gates

The owners came to view it and
To ride on it, they were the selfsame people
Who had built it.
Thousands of them were there, walking about,
Examining the great halls, while in the trains
Great multitudes were riding past, their faces –
Men, women and children, greybeards as well –
Turned to the stations, beaming as if at the theatre, for the stations
Were all built differently, of different stone
In different styles; the light also
Came each time from a different source.
[. . .] as often as possible
The travellers rushed out and inspected
With eager, flashing eyes the finished job.
They felt the pillars
And appraised their gloss.
They tested the wall surfaces and fingered the glass.
When we saw them riding in their trains
The work of their own hands, we knew:
This is the grand picture that once upon a time
Rocked the classic writers who foresaw it.

Now Brecht was unusual for a communist-aligned writer of his period in that he seldom wrote outright apologetics; even his poem about Stalin composed after the despot's death praises him for the fear he instilled in the West, rather than mentioning any 'positive achievements'. Here, however, he spills over into total, outright, uncompromising and agape praise. Why? Perhaps because the Metro's achievement was so undeniable that even the most sceptical fellow travellers dropped their reservations and fell into applause. And what he is praising is also the architecture, and more particularly an architecture that would not (then) have been possible under Modernism, so focused was it on the surface quality of materials and the craftsmanship of details.

Modern architecture, at least until it was transformed from the late 1930s on by the craft fixation of Scandinavians like Arne Jacobsen and Alvar Aalto, was not an architecture of surfaces but of spaces; the detailing of the concrete, steel and glass was to be precise and machine-like, rather than to be admired for any more specific qualities. The modelling of concrete into something raw and tactile came much later, in post-war Japan, Brazil and Britain. So the workers who are walking along here, 'testing the surfaces', 'fingering the glass', 'feeling the pillars', admiring the 'different stone' and 'different styles', would simply not have been able to do this if the stations had all been designed by Moisei Ginzburg or the Vesnin brothers. For the first time since William Morris and the Arts and Crafts movement, the workers' movement was displaying in its structures a showcase of *workmanship*, and the many diverse, rich and strange surfaces and shapes it can create, rather than a celebration of machine work and its concomitant promise to alleviate hard physical labour. But what of the poem's other contention, that the Metro's builders were its owners? Here, things become considerably more murky, to say the least.

From much else in this book, the impression may be given of Nikita Khrushchev as a brave reformer, a leader who had steered the Soviet Union away from despotism, autarchy and massive inequality towards a more genuine attempt at achieving some kind of socialism. I hope not, because as one of the main driving forces of the Moscow Metro he did things that would have landed him in prison practically anywhere else. The story of the Metro, as told by the historian Benson Bobrick, is one of staggering negligence towards the lives and livelihoods of its constructors and 'owners'. Work began in 1931, at the height of Stalin's first Five-Year Plan, under the command of Lazar Kaganovich and his deputy, Khrushchev. It employed a force which had not taken part in any similar work before – textile workers, workers from chemical plants, municipal employees, metalworkers from the Urals, miners from Donbass, labourers from the newly, violently established collective farms; its chief engineer was Pavel Rottert, who had experience in Germany and the USA and had been responsible a few years earlier for the immense Gosprom complex in Kharkiv. But in Bobrick's – and in Khrushchev's – own account the Metro was the future leader's baby, enforced with the utmost brutality. Here, 'negligence was sometimes perversely portrayed as heroic' – in one speech, Khrushchev responded to worries that buildings would collapse when their foundations were undermined with the remark: 'What, are you afraid of a building?' He would push the advance of a shift to four times what was safe, and 'whole shifts were sometimes crushed to death in cave-ins or drowned by inundations in the shafts'.[5] Delays in completing the line on schedule, even then, led to the addition of *subbotniks*, voluntary labourers from Komsomol, the communist youth league – 80,000 of them. From then on it was two to three times quicker than any comparable work. The Metro was constructed via a combination of shocking brutality and uncoerced enthusiasm.

Not that sticks were not occasionally waved at volunteers as well; Kaganovich used his speeches to threaten workers thus: 'We must detect the unconscientious workers and catch them red-handed . . . we will check up from day to day. The organs of authority will take all measures necessary. I hope we will not have to use these measures.'[6] Readers of Solzhenitsyn will be aware that an 'organ' is a division of the Cheka.[7] Workers were not the only problem, of course – Kaganovich also complained of 'old-regime geology' as a factor, in a situation where drastic climatic conditions meant that an experimental technique of hardening topsoil had to be used. A 1938 guide pointed out that the Metro's builders had to contend with every one of the problems faced by previous Metros – 'crooked streets, a dense network of underground installations, remnants of the ancient town, a surface intersected with hills and valleys, and treacherous water-bearing strata. A hard and treacherous struggle with nature awaited the builders.'[8] Or, in Kaganovich's words, 'geology proved to be a pre-revolutionary part of the old regime, incompatible with the Bolsheviks, working against us.'[9] For his pains, the Metro was initially officially called the Metropoliten in the Name of Lazar Kaganovich, only to be renamed later after Lenin, as was practically everything else. After the completion of the first line, prisoners were conscripted into the building of the subsequent ones; in effect, the Metro became a branch of the Gulag. Solzhenitsyn excoriated *Belomor*, the collectively written book 'in praise of slave labour' that was produced on the White Sea Canal, and no doubt he would have felt the same about commemoration of the Metro, too; except unlike that useless pharaonic construction, the Metro was evidently useful and beautiful, and was seen as such by Muscovites. Nobody has ever had to be coerced to sing its praises. But, bearing this in mind, it should not be forgotten that Metro lines and stations built from the mid-1930s to the mid-1950s used prison labour extensively, and surely had high casualties, though figures are hard to come by. As a work of infrastructure and architecture, it now shifts from something still relatively sane, if startlingly opulent, into an entire dreamworld, a continuous artwork. A friend from Kiev, the historian and activist Oleksiy Radynski, once casually called the Metro 'the greatest work of art of the twentieth century'. He is unsqueamish enough to admit it.

Khrushchev recalled in his memoirs that 'we were very unsophisticated. We thought of a subway as something almost supernatural.'[10] From 1938 on, the stations begin to reflect that new Stalinist mysticism. They remained a collective effort, even down to the design, achieved by a team ranging from veterans like Shchusev and Fomin, former Modernists like the Vesnin brothers, Nikolai Kolli and Nikolai Ladovsky, ubiquitous Stalinist designers like Boris Iofan and Dimitri Chechulin, and dozens of unsung architects like Sergei Serafimov, Samuil Kravets and Nadezhda Bykova; and an even larger team of craftsmen, sculptors, stained-glass artists, letterers, mosaic artists, makers of majolica panels and much else, all the way down to the frequently brutally treated 'owners' digging away at the bottom. But if there was a designer whose spirit presided over it all – as it were, a genius of the Moscow Metro, whose stations are in almost all cases the most complete, elegant and exhilarating – it was the Ukrainian architect Alexey Dushkin. Only twenty-nine when brought in to design the Palace of the Soviets station, Dushkin was responsible for such bizarre and remarkable stations as Kropotkinskaya, Mayakovskaya, Ploshchad Revolutsii, Avtozavodskaya and Novoslobodskaya, which seem to come from a place both futuristic and unnervingly, imposingly eternal, a negation of the binaries of Paperny's 'Culture Two' into an utterly unique architecture that owes equal amounts to both – heavy and light, high speed and eternal. The most famous of these is Mayakovskaya, a stop on every Moscow tourist's itinerary since 1938. It was named after the Futurist poet who had committed suicide in 1930. After initially being regarded as a non-person, a rehabilitation campaign led by Louis Aragon's partner, Elsa Triolet, led to a pronouncement, by Stalin himself, that 'ignorance of Mayakovsky's memory is a crime'. These were not words to be taken lightly, and so the most prominent Futurist of post-revolutionary Russia is immortalized in countless neoclassical memorials – this a writer who declaimed, in one of his last poems:

Mayakovskaya, Moscow

The hell I care
for bronze's weight memorial,
the hell I care
for marble's frozen slime!

Here his ideas are frozen in that very slime.

Dushkin created something that combined lashings of opulent materials with a futuristic sheen and dash appropriate to its subject. The station hall is long and high, on a greater scale than any built before, and very few since. The arches are scored underneath in fluted chrome, and looked at in enfilade ripple in a pattern of white and silver until the tube of space reaches the escalator (which, from 1938 on, became long passageways to a station-cum-bomb-shelter, on which you can stand for several minutes before you end up at the station hall). There are cupolas above, and therein are mosaics, lit by little lamps underneath. These mosaics, created by I. L. Lubennikov after designs by the painter Aleksandr Deineka, depict a *Twenty-Four-Hour Soviet Sky*, from dawn to dusk; images, seen from below, of the Soviet conquest of the air, the perspectives cleverly and vertiginously tilted by Deineka so that you can look at the heavens while deep in the bowels of the earth. The mosaics tell a familiar propagandistic story – Soviet aviators! Blast furnaces! Divers! Parachutists! Pylons! Sturdy collective farm women! – but they do so in a startlingly unfamiliar way, showing the amount of space for expressiveness an artist could have if he didn't challenge the basic tenets of Socialist Realism of compulsory hurrah-optimism; they are constantly surprising, intriguing images, ranging from the rumbling industrial drama of the furnaces (at 'night') to the image of a woman holding up her baby to see the aviators (during the 'day'). It marks the development of something that would become ever-present in later Metro stations – the transformation of infrastructure into narrative.

At Ploshchad Revolutsii (just by Red Square), the same year, Dushkin created a somewhat heavier hall, with red marble arches in a white-painted vestibule, lit by dozens of suspended lamps; yet it is as simple and memorable as Mayakovskaya. As in that station, there is a total integration of architecture and art, this time in the form of monumental bronze statues by Matvey Manizer, like so much Soviet sculpture in the muscular style of Michelangelo. Dushkin has squeezed them into the archways leading to the tracks, so each of them – male on one side of the arch, female on the other – has to crouch. Given that this was Revolution Square, and that these were symbolic figures of the October Revolution in Moscow, and given that 1938 was one of the years of the Great Terror, this was potentially a risky move – one of the many Metro stories with the slight tone of urban myth about them tells of the designers being terrified that the design would be interpreted as showing the Soviet people 'on their knees'. If so, what saved them was the realism of the monumental sculptures of revolutionaries, workers, peasants, sportsmen and sportswomen. Stalin spent some time at the opening looking at and caressing Manizer's statues, murmuring: 'They look alive, almost alive.'[11] The labourers who built this station, close to the Kremlin, uncovered a torture chamber used by Ivan the Terrible. The German historian Karl Schlögel notes of Dushkin that he 'acknowledged that he had studied the architecture of Egyptian tombs as an aid to solving the problems of metro building', and imagines that his use of expressed structure, his severity of style, was intended as a mark of 'respect' to the Metro builders, rather than effacing it completely under layers of ornament. That's as may be, but it is remarkably neat, historically, that these popular dungeons were built using methods directly taken from the pharaonic architecture of death. There's no reason to doubt this, but, equally, Dushkin's stations are obviously some of Moscow's most loved, as can be garnered from the amount of stories and habits that have built up around them; one of the bronze men at Ploshchad Revolutsii carries a German shepherd, whose nose has been rubbed shiny by millions of Metro travellers for good luck; at Mayakovskaya, it's known that you can spin a kopeck all the way up the fluted chrome arches.

The building of stations at the height of the Terror is quite unnerving enough, but several were constructed during the Great Patriotic War itself. A 1980 English-language guide to the Metro claims that they 'mirror the Soviet people's gallant fight against fascism and that spirit of unity which made of the entire country one armed camp'.[12] And indeed they do. At Novokuznetskaya, there are more ceiling mosaics by Aleksandr Deineka, executed by V. A. Frolov, who was caught in Leningrad during its 900-day siege. They were pieced together there – exquisite, sparkling and vertiginous, showing women workers alternately making munitions, tractors and tanks, or laying flowers – and after its artist had succumbed to the siege's privations in 1942, they were transported from the blockaded and starving city, at immense risk, over Lake Ladoga. As with so much here, it's hard to say which is stronger: an awe of admiration or an awe of horror. There are several other stations showing wartime labour and war itself at the very moment it is happening – Avtozavodskaya, the station for the ZiL Palace of Culture, where a version of Kropotkinskaya with even taller, thinner, stranger tapered columns has at near-ceiling height a mural showing the rolling out of tanks, planes and supplies, interspersed with a sculptural frieze of presumably grateful workers and peasants. The decorative detail of the wartime stations coexists with a remarkably free approach to architectural borrowing, an impure eclecticism that can throw up something like Elektrozavodskaya station, where meticulously, obsessively detailed figures of a mostly female workforce fill large metopes above the columns, while the ceiling is decorated with dozens of round, inset electric lights. This was designed by Vladimir Shchuko and Vladimir Gelfreikh, who had designed both in a Constructivist and a neo-Renaissance idiom, and here managed to

Zoya Kosmodemyanskaya guards Partizanskaya, Moscow

produce the most convincing fusion of the two. Meanwhile, at Partizanskaya, the highest of station halls features colossal figures, again by Manizer, of the famous partisan-martyrs Zoya Kosmodemyanskaya and Matvey Kuzmin. Both of them stand in front of tall columns, as if hiding

Overkill at Novokuznetskaya, Moscow

behind trees. Sometimes, in the wartime stations, the excess starts to become too much – at Novokuznetskaya, the combination of mosaics, intricate plaster coffering, friezes of sculpture and large, man-sized bronze lamps set into the marble floor is too much for the eye to take in at once – you would have to wait an hour here to work out what exactly is going on, and the trains leave every minute.

The palaces of excess are most overwhelming, spectacular and indigestible on the Ring Line, Moscow's Circle Line, which links all the major railway stations. It is always very crowded, so here even the prodigious size of the stations cannot entirely relieve congestion – and the architecture generally serves to add to it. On evenings when visiting Moscow, Agata and I spent our time doing Metro tourism until the stations started to close after midnight; and the place to do this if you're really after an experience is the Ring, where you easily get your kopeck's worth. The use of narrative in the 1938 and 1943 stations has here become an obsession – every single one of these stations, built between 1950 and 1954, tells a story, some of them consecutively, eventually building up an entire Metro line that is one continuous epic, an awesome and terrifying propaganda blockbuster, dripping with heroism, stupidity and kitsch.

The stops serve specific overground stations, which of course lead to specific places, and so those places are evoked. At Kievskaya Koltsevaya, the station for the railway terminal that leads to the Ukrainian capital, Khrushchev personally oversaw a competition for a design that would 'express the Ukraine'. The winning design, by a Ukrainian team under E. I. Katonin, does this via a series of mosaic panels, framed with sculpted wheatsheaves, which stretch uneasily along the curve of the arched hall. They depict, in full-on musclebound, bosom-heaving Socialist Realist style, pivotal events in that country's history (this time, captioned, so there's no ambiguity). The alliance between Russia and Ukraine signed by the Cossacks after their successful rebellion against the Polish empire in the seventeenth century. The October Revolution, or rather the Arsenal rising that was Kiev's equivalent. The completion of the Dnieper Dam, overseen by Mikhail Kalinin and Sergo Ordzhonikidze (still there, though Stalin was removed). Obviously 'socialist' history of strikes and risings is slotted into official, Tsarist, imperial history with the two becoming completely indistinguishable, the ideology of the Great Patriotic War encapsulated.

Komsomolskaya Koltsevaya is similar. The last built work of Alexey Shchusev, and after Mayakovskaya probably the most photographed, as it was intended to be, it is adjacent to three major railway stations (Leningrad, Kazan and Yaroslavl), so is a deliberate 'gateway to Moscow'. It takes the form of a Rococo ballroom that very closely resembles (as do many Moscow Metro stations) the style and proportions of the Georgievsky Hall in the Grand Kremlin Palace, built in the early nineteenth century – much as Shchusev's own late-Romanov Kazan station, designed nearly half a century earlier, was modelled on the Kremlin itself. Here the mosaics are again on the ceilings – this time, illustrating a wartime speech by Stalin, which placed the Great Patriotic War in a lineage of Russian imperial wars. On the mosaics themselves, by Pavel Korin, the eye-craning perspectives indulged in by Deineka have been abandoned in favour of flat images of medieval Russian warlords, Lenin speaking to the Red Army in Red Square, a stylized goddess of peace waving a hammer, a sickle and a laurel leaf in front of his mausoleum, and the like. At Belorusskaya, the ceiling panels are flat, stylized folk-images of

Komsomolskaya Koltsevaya, Moscow

Belarusians both in their peculiarly Polish-looking national dress and in the more up-to-date socialist garb of sportsmen and soldiers. At the end of the station is a statue of heavy, hairy partisans, unveiled after Stalin's death – the struggle and suffering of those who fought the Nazis in the forests behind the lines were often denigrated during his rule, in favour of those who moved their offices out to Siberia.

The Ring Line's combination of grandeur, opulence and mental illness reaches its surreal height (or should that be depth?) at Novoslobodskaya, the last station to be designed by Dushkin. The arches are framed with stained-glass panels, which of course being underground have to be backlit. This outright religious gesture, according to Metro historians Egor Larichev and Anastasia Uglik, was not entirely received as Christian – stained glass not being a feature of Orthodox churches – but the effect is such. It is obviously a mystical space, a 'supernatural' space, devoted to magic and irrationalism, something abetted by the 'dematerialized' light of the backlit stained glass.[13] The stained-glass panels (again by a team led by Pavel Korin) don't depict anyone actually doing anything

Stained glass and gold at Novoslobodskaya, Moscow

obviously 'mystical': men work at turbines, peruse journals in libraries, work at drawing boards, and generally act in an impeccably scientific fashion. The figures are in circular niches, with the panels around them decorated with flowers, in a proliferation of wild colours – sky blues, bright greens, deep oranges, sharply artificial yellows – which are in turn framed with gold leaf, with little acorns cast in gold. At the end of it is the goddess of peace again, in gilded mosaic, holding a baby aloft. The stained glass was taken from the cathedral in the newly occupied Latvian capital of Riga. From the colonies to the capital, an act of imperial plunder.

NATIONAL IN METRO, SOCIALIST IN CONTENT

While we were in Belorusskaya Koltsevaya, Agata wondered out loud: 'Did they have a patronizing station for each one of the nationalities?' From the off, this project of nationalist, imperial display was also intended to express the entirety of the USSR. In the 1939 guide to the Moscow Metro designed for Western tourists, E. Abakumov observes that 'thirteen different kinds of marble were used in the six stations of the Gorky Street [i.e. 1938] line alone . . . these marbles come from the Urals and Armenia, the Far East and Georgia, Uzbekistan and Siberia.'[14] Reeling off the names of the materials stresses their exoticism – Ufalei, Biryuk-Yankoy, Gazgan, Nizhny Tagil, onyx, porphyry. It can be a shock, if you've spent more time in the Metro than in the Hermitage, to find that parts of the tsars' art gallery closely resemble a Metro station – the classical sculpture galleries of the New Hermitage use similar exotic marbles to those that you can lean against while waiting for your train to the suburbs; even the way the sculptures are balanced along the pillars and pylons feels oddly familiar. As we've seen, materials were shipped from blockaded Leningrad and from recently annexed Latvia; to adapt a phrase from the Stalinist era in Poland, 'the whole nation built its Metro'. Inevitably, even in a state as ferociously centralized and uneven as Stalin's USSR, Metros would be built in other large cities as well; and at least in Stalin's era they would be built to the same specifications and on the same demented scale. By the end of the 1940s, Metros were under way in Leningrad and in Kiev, the start of a rapid extension of these systems across the USSR – by the time of its collapse forty years later they had been completed or nearly competed in (in order) Leningrad, Kiev, Tbilisi, Baku, Kharkiv, Tashkent, Yerevan, Minsk, Nizhny Novgorod (then Gorky), Novosibirsk, Samara (then Kuibyshev), Ekaterinburg (then Sverdlovsk) and Dnepropetrovsk, while semi-underground 'Metrotrams' with a few opulent subterranean stations each were built in Volgograd and Krivyi Rih. This is a staggering urban infrastructure programme for a state that was by all accounts becoming 'stagnant', in its extent comparable only with the rash of Metro building in China during the last fifteen years. As architecture, rather than what would be expected – a slow decline of the bizarre palatial grandeur of the 1930s and 1940s into a more modern and utilitarian style – the Metro shows a constant, unresolved back-and-forth between Modernism and surreal eclecticism.

The first line to be built in Leningrad, opened in 1955 and now Line 1 of the St Petersburg Metro, is on a fully Muscovite scale. It was designed almost entirely by Leningrad-based architects, which is peculiar, as they were at the time managing to fight a partly successful rearguard action against the pressures to introduce Stalinist planning and the wilful tastelessness of Stalinist architecture to the chilly grandeur of the northern capital – this was mainly confined to that aptly named Moscow Prospekt which leads from the historical centre to the airport. There is no restraint to be found in the first line of the Leningradsky Metropoliten, and as a Metro tourist I don't think I found any of the Metro systems quite so unnerving as this. Perhaps this is because the friend I was staying with when I was first in town, an American adoptive Petersburgian, was keen to inform me that I might get arrested if I took photographs (due to their doubling as bomb shelters, Metro stations are still officially classed as military installations), and that young people don't take the Metro so that policemen won't forcibly conscript them. This reminder of the place's vicious realities perhaps stopped me from just wandering around agog, as in Moscow. The extreme coldness of the architecture's grandeur, though, was also a factor, intimidating one into silence and awe. On returning a few years later with a camera, Agata and I were unmolested, and even found that the St Petersburg Metro featured that exceptionally rare thing, signage in Latin script; but the effect remains.

The average depth of the Metro in the centre of St Petersburg is *80 metres*,[15] for reasons of the boggy geology as much as the need for shelters. Trips on escalators are leisurely, giving you much time to look at the Art Deco fittings of the uplighters and handrails. In the stations on the surface in the city centre, only the looming darkness of the materials – lots of granite – makes you notice the contrast with the neoclassical context all around, a gesture of Petersburgian urban good manners; the station underground, with its revolutionary motifs in bronze, is often more Muscovite, though you never find the horror vacui of the Moscow Ring. Line 1 runs north to south, from the city centre to the industrial districts of the south, those bastions of the October Revolution – the Narvskaya district and the Putilov (by then Kirov) engineering works. In the centre there are things to see – Ploshchad Vosstaniya ('Uprising Square'), where relief sculptures provide one of the most 'lives of the saints' depictions of Lenin, with his seclusion in Finland on the eve of October presented as an overcoated, flat-capped version of the forty days and forty nights in the wilderness. Yet it is at the three stations in the southern suburbs where the surviving remnants of old metropolitan good taste are thrown overboard, and the results are dense with detail. At

Workers holding up a model of Narvskaya station, Leningrad

Narvskaya, as you mount the escalator, a full-scale relief sculpture of Lenin speaking to the Petrograd masses is above your head, with the spire of the Admiralty (or is it Moscow State University?) behind him; anachronism is courted by the worker carrying a flag reading 'GLORY

TO WORK', rather than 'PEACE, LAND, BREAD' or 'ALL POWER TO THE SOVIETS'. Beneath, after your long descent, are strips of electric light treated as if they were heraldic wreaths which are connected to the pillars with golden clasps. At eye level are hammer-and-sickle grilles, and in niches above each pillar, metopes crowded with figures. These are full of detail, full of activity – architects perusing the blueprints of the station, engineers, schoolchildren with their schoolbooks, handsome vest-wearing male workers, women workers in overalls and high heels.

If these relief sculptures show the 'humanist' side of Stalinist aesthetics, with its images of peaceful labour and mildly progressive gender roles, then the Kirov Works station is martial and militaristic. It is of particularly huge proportions, the hulking blue marble columns demarcating great spaces for the waiting pedestrian, in this case most likely because of the tens of thousands of people who would have used this to get to and from the famous factory. There are no images of workers, only small metal medallions as capitals to the pillars, which feature electricity pylons, hooks, chains, smelters, wheels, derricks. If you're going station-by-station through the suburbs of St Petersburg, you will by this point already be quite overwhelmed. What nothing can prepare you for is Avtovo, the original terminus, designed by Evgeny Levinson and opened in 1955. This enormous rectangular hall is lined with gigantic columns, all of which bar the last four (where the materials ran out) are clad in glass, which has been sculpted so that it is covered, coated, in Soviet symbols – stars, laurels, the usual. What is so unbelievable is how this most obviously light of materials has been treated in such a way that it is every bit as thick, heavy and imposing as marble or granite. The bizarre feeling of an underground chamber supported on columns of mere glass is only half of the paradox. If, as you recall, Vladimir Paperny argued in 1980s Moscow that the Modernist 'Culture One' favoured the lightness, thinness and transparency of glass and the Stalinist 'Culture Two' preferred the heavy, eternal nature of stone, here is the ultimate victory over Constructivism. At the start of the Moscow Metro, in 1935, at Sokolniki, blue marble was treated as a light, Modernist material. But at Avtovo, in 1955, glass has been turned to stone, literally petrified. Aptly, the rest of the station's fittings – bronze uplighters and chandeliers in a spiky neoclassical style, the coffered ceiling of a Tsar's palace – are outright funereal.

As with the stripping down of the former 'high building' of the Hotel

Glass columns at Avtovo, Leningrad (1959 postcard)

Ukrainia, Kiev was the testing bed for a new pared-down form of Metro decoration and, as with that, the first examples just look like Stalinist stations that have been denuded of some of their fancy dress, rather than any kind of distinctive new style. Larichev and Uglik argue that this was a rather conspiratorial decision by Khrushchev. After he had overseen the most opulent of all stations at Kievskaya Koltsevaya, completed in 1954, his strictures on architectural 'excess' ensured that no further stations

Waiting at Vokzalna, Kiev

would or could rival it. So in Metro histories Kiev, where the first line was completed in 1960 (partly to designs submitted in 1949), is where sanity or boredom takes over, according to your taste or your politics.[16] This may be its place in the history, but it wasn't how it seemed to us as tourists/'culture workers' on our first visit to the city, where Agata was assigned to take part in an NGO's art conference. This was her first experience of any Soviet city, and arrival from bus to Metro station was a major shock to her – everything, even by Warsaw standards, on a terrifyingly imperial scale. Vokzal (Central station), opened in 1960, was the station in question. It is actually one of the milder examples, Stalin Baroque on manners. The entrance hall is massive, and below there are medallions with revolutionary scenes, less detailed than they would have been ten years earlier, and light fittings where electric tubes are collected into little Baroque chandeliers, but mostly otherness is expressed through the crypt-like marble pylons and the seemingly endless escalator journey.

Where we came out, however, was even more startling – Teatralna station, designed much later, in 1987. It was originally named 'Lenina', and aside from the fact that illumination is provided by concealed electric uplighting rather than Rococo chandeliers, you could be in a Moscow station of the late 1930s. When we first visited, we found dark-red marble pylons enclosing niches filled with crumpled bronze flags, onto which are emblazoned quotes from Lenin. The sainted leader himself takes the form of an oversized, disembodied bust emerging from another quote-draped flag, his square, goateed jaw jutting out. Although it seems Stalinoid, it isn't quite – actual quotes from Lenin (as opposed to Stalin) are nonexistent in the early Metro stations, most likely because it was often hard to find one entirely 'on message'; as Tamara Deutscher pointed out, one thing that happened after the Thaw was a brief transformation of Lenin from deity to human being, one who said and did (often complex) things rather than presiding over them as a sort of coffee-house demigod.[17] Regardless of the sophistication of the quotations, the effect is of a giant head staring at you and your doings, keeping a very sharp eye on you (or at least he did until he was removed for fear of vandalism at the start of 2014). Up at the top of the escalator is a relief sculpture where classic

Lenin, always watching, at Teatralna, Kiev

Stalinist subjects – heroic revolutionary deeds, the building of the Dnieper Dam, etc. – are rendered in a new, more fragmented style, with great shards of stucco holding low-relief figures doing the requisite struggling and striving. The sculpture begins around the lamp at the top of the escalator, proceeding to swirl around an entire anteroom.

Most of the special qualities of the Kiev Metro come from its geological extremity. Arsenalna station has the world's deepest escalators – after standing on one for nearly ten minutes you get to another, which eventually leads to the most brutally truncated of the first-line stations, with a hall of almost Londonesque cramped dimensions; but the same line then takes you out at Dnipro, where you're suddenly on an elevated concrete bridge over the Dnieper, framed by two colossal statues (woman releasing doves, man holding sputnik aloft). But mainly what we would learn in the Kiev Metro is that the initial Metro style, though mostly absent in its original form, remained popular enough to be revived extensively from the mid-1970s onwards. That said, there are more than a few traces of Stalinist grandeur along the original 1949/1960 stations – Universitet, for instance, with its various academicians in niches, retains its planned statuary, zigzag marble flooring and sculptural embellishments, and none of the surface stations suffered much in the way of stripping, so even

Universitet, Kiev (1962 postcard)

Arsenalna, with its memorial to the workers of 1918, is grand in scale. They also have a distinctive feature dictated by the profundity of their placing – between those two double sets of escalators are domed halls where you can sit on a bench if the journey is wearing you out, something that makes them particularly appealing for buskers. Like the rest of the Kiev Metro, they are an engineering feat. According to one historian, 'Geological surveys had proved the presence of a large amount of quicksand in the area, so traditional mining methods were either unsuitable or would prolong the construction for several years. The decision was therefore made to erect the entire structure of the intermediate landing on the surface, and sink it into position inside a temporary shaft . . . passers-by remarked on the structure gradually sinking lower and lower until, to their surprise, it disappeared all together.'[18]

The first two stations built after the Khrushchev 'embellishments decree' are actually very attractive examples of 1960s sci-fi aesthetics, redolent of the new optimism and lightness, and the workers are cartoonish rather than superheroic. In one of these, Shuliavska (originally Zavod Bilshovyk, 'Bolshevik Factory'), two mosaic men hold up the atom. Running along the railings at the top of the pylons we found the repeated legend 'Peace, Work, Freedom', in Ukrainian, with the preceding word, 'Communism', visibly erased, with only the 'K' left ('But how can you have the one without the other?' mused Agata not entirely facetiously). After that are several stations in a style that would be impressive anywhere else, but are in the context of the earlier work strikingly ordinary – everything is still marble-clad, but they are otherwise unornamented, with tall, spindly stone-sheathed columns, a style also popular in 1960s Moscow and dubbed the 'centipede', after the dozens of 'legs'. Normal.

Somehow, perhaps because of the 'neo-Stalinist' trend noted in the early 1970s by Roy Medvedev, this goes out of the window at exactly this point. The stations built for or just after the 1980 Olympics are the 'Futurist' side of this, as they manage to use much the same constructional spaces, techniques and materials – the wide underground vaults with trains leaving from tunnels on either side, the niches, the marble, the mosaic – while dropping historical reminiscences. Palats Ukrainia (originally Red Army) station, designed, like Teatralnaya by the team of Anatoliy Krushynskyi, Tamara Chelikovska and Mykola Alyoshkin,

Suprematist ballroom: Palats Ukrainia, Kiev

dresses its heavy columns in a glittering coating of red, gold and black stone, and ring-shaped silver space-age chandeliers lead to a mosaic featuring a Red Guard, his trenchcoat lined with gold, representing the Kiev Bolshevik rising of January 1918. Behind the guard is a vivid representation of abstract revolutionary space, with a red globe and grey triangles, as if in tribute to the avant-garde painting of the Kiev-born Kazimir Malevich. At Republic Stadium are vaults lined in blue marble and a sculpture where the Olympic rings are set into an organic mass of twisted red flags, at Taras Shevchenko a dreamlike imagining of the work of the national poet, and at Heroes of the Dnieper, the terminus, there are heavy, angular red-marble columns whose capitals have the light fittings inside them, working both as columns and lanterns, with a hammer and sickle at the top of each.

Somehow, by the end of the 1980s, this promise of futurity is reversed completely. Two stations in particular show a sudden embrace of an outright neo-Byzantine aesthetic as alarming in its sense of time-slip despotism as much of the Moscow Ring Line. Druzhby Narodiv ('Friendship

Golden Gate of the Kievan Rus Metro, Kiev

of Nations') has brick-clad columns, as if you're in the crypt of an Orthodox cathedral; and at Zoloti Vorota ('Golden Gate'), opened in 1989, the underground vault, designed by Boris and Vadim Zhezherin, has become a tribute to Kievan Rus, with the ceiling lined in Byzantine mosaic patterns and an actual Orthodox mosaic of St Michael, with wings, sword and shield; yet the innovations of the Moscow Metro can still be seen, in the dazzling, Dushkin-like effect of a buttressed ceiling rippling off towards the escalators, their weight held up here by stubby little marble columns. It all comes full circle, and all the 'socialist' and 'modern' trappings attached to this creepily future-past aesthetic are stripped away, leaving just neo-Byzantinism. Two years before the collapse of the USSR and the independence of Ukraine, the 'socialist content' disappears, leaving only the 'national form'.

While an opposition can be – and has been – set up between the building of opulent Metro systems and the construction of housing infrastructure, under Brezhnev they managed to do both without much trouble, although the (bespoke, crafted) Metro stations appear to be mostly of a far higher quality than the (standardized, factory-made) housing. The Soviets were now designing in the styles of both Cultures One and Two, but were evidently vastly more skilled at the latter. Yet when we spoke to some (if not all – we met a few enthusiasts) of the people we met in Kiev about the Metro, they would usually shrug and say: 'Have you been to Moscow?' The comparatively low esteem the system is held in, or perhaps the extreme oligarchical capitalism of contemporary Ukraine, may have contributed to a rather shocking phenomenon we saw there on all of our visits, in 2010, 2011 and 2014 – the sheathing of marble columns with giant adverts, and the placing in several stations of TVs, suspended from the ceiling, serving a continuous diet of adverts, with the original grandeur being eaten away by tat. In 'normal' countries Metro architecture is just a backdrop to advertising, so why not here?

FUTURISM AND STAGNATION UNDERGROUND

Kiev's Metro history, and its shift towards increasingly nationalistic imagery, is paralleled by its immediate successor, the Tbilisi Metro, whose two lines were opened in 1965 and 1979 respectively. It can be hard to discover the original intentions here, as a campaign under Georgia's ruler in the late 2000s, Mikheil Saakashvili, alternately modernized and vandalized the stations with great ineptitude, replacing finely wrought works of art with cheap murals, placing trespa and tacky metal cladding over marble – but half-heartedly, so that the Metro is in a prolonged state of half-renovation; even more than elsewhere, Agata and I got some very funny looks for getting our cameras out – walking towards the bust of the eponymous leftist theatre director at the end of (Kote) Marjanishvili station, we were helpfully told 'the exit's the other way'. However, more than half of the stations are only partly butchered, so you can see how in the 1960s the 'national form' was applied to sparse halls, with giant busts of great Georgian poets and relief friezes of medieval scenes, sometimes combined with paradoxical Modernist gestures, as at Isani station, where a light concrete shell structure above protects the heroic deeds of ancient kings inside. Most of the inner-city stations are dedicated to Georgian writers, theatre directors and poets. At Rustaveli station, the dark-red

The vital south: Technical University station, Tbilisi

columns are inset with golden panthers, in reference to the twelfth-century poet Shota Rustaveli's *Knight in the Panther's Skin*, continued in a concrete relief above the entrance. References to Russians are nowhere to be found, and – unlike revolutionary motifs – would not have been before the renovation either, the inescapable Lenin aside. That doesn't mean that there isn't still a certain note of folk kitsch, and often a certain knowing revelling in the sort of joyous southern, sun-kissed imagery seldom to be found on the steppe. The peak of this can be found in the two mosaic friezes inside the vaulted niches of Technical University station.[19] Designed in 1979 by Radish Tordia, Iden Tabidze and Apolon Kharebava, it is a lush and shamelessly vitalist display of frolicking, dancing, gyrating and discovering, with scientists, satellites and sputniks proving the Soviet provenance. These plaster figures are surrounded and caressed with swirls of shimmering mosaic. It's both thrilling and a bit much.

It is strange perhaps that the Kiev and Tbilisi Metros moved gradually towards a new national style, as one of the most widely publicized and technically innovative systems, built in 1975, was strongly modern in its aesthetic, while still being visibly in the tradition begun in 1935. But, again, that's not the first thing we noticed about the Kharkiv Metro. Like the earlier systems, the portals on the street lead down to short passageways with kiosks selling essentials, themselves clad in so much marble that they look richer than most actual stations in other countries. In Kharkiv, once a powerful industrial-scientific city and still Ukraine's second largest, the results of the collapse of the economy in the 1990s are not easy to avoid. Old women spread out their goods to sell in the passageways, and we we descended we (and a hundred or so Kharkivians) watched a clock tell us exactly how long we had been waiting for a tube – the clocks that count up how long you've been waiting rather than counting down to tell you when the next one is coming are a mark of confidence in Moscow, where you seldom have more than ninety seconds to wait; here they are something more despondent. Maybe aptly, as the aesthetic of the Kharkiv Metro is perhaps best described as a Futurism of the era of stagnation.

Radianska (in Russian, 'Sovietskaya'), the station where we spent some time waiting, is lit by light fittings made up of X-shaped lamps bunched together, like functional op-art sculptures. The Historical Museum station, opened in 1984 to designs by V. A. Spivachuk, P. G. Chechalnitsky and I. T. Karpenko, is made up of heavy, greyish-yellow marble columns, which seem subject to some sort of ingress (Kharkiv Metro is the only one we've found in anything less than tip-top upkeep). These are classic Soviet Metro style gone quasi-Expressionist, their weight now expressed rather than hidden, via an almost Cubist system of tapering, giving the sense of being somewhere that is at once dungeon, castle, palace and space station. The latter is not an idle cliché, but a precise comparison – a design analogue between one windowless, enclosed, high-tech space into which oxygen must be pumped to make it habitable and another. Along the platforms for the trains are steel medallions with the usual Soviet heraldry, but above you are not 'chandeliers'; instead suspended sculptures are made up of lights in little boxes, linked by twisted, tangled steel antennae – rich, surreal and, on our visit, only half being used, adding to the grotto-like feel, but also the evident poverty of the city and its decaying infrastructure.

Trainspotters designate a particular kind of wide-vaulted, columnless station found all over the world as the 'Kharkiv type', due to the

Historical Museum station, Kharkiv

innovations in construction that were brought in here. These then-experimental stations, like Sportivna, resemble the basic Moscow type without the supporting arches, giving them an even greater vastness of space, with the vault coffered in a non-classical pattern of stucco diamonds, in which the light is hidden. But as this is a book on architecture rather than engineering, we will note the regular stations which manage more than any in Moscow or elsewhere to play perverse games with the fact that you're deep underground with tens of metres and tons of earth on top of you. Universitet, for instance, designed by the same architects as Historical Museum, is in a paradoxical style which could be described as stripped Rococo,[20] or Vostok Baroque. Marble pilotis enclose the vault and upper-level galleries, and wide, repeated copulas feature Futurist chandeliers, where some sputnik-like globe has affixed to it several cylindrical lamp standards, all pulled together into an interconnected wheel. They look like satellites, placed one after another along the long hall, no doubt as a reference to the scientific work that goes on in the University nearby – but they do not replicate anything, they are not explicitly representational. Nearby, the Derzhprom station – serving the complex usually known in English by its Russian name, Gosprom, and finished (to a 1980s design by Spivachuk and Karpenko) in 1995 – shows the aesthetic still healthy; bent blue-marble pylons creating a continuous, polygonal space, with the directional signs in bubble-shaped blue plastic, the space station style still in place in the decade of the *Mir* disaster. Presumably nobody believed in it by then, but it seems the architects didn't agree. The next station along, Architekt Beketova, combines the stuck-in-a-dilapidated-space-station feel with something that once seemed so nakedly mystical at Novoslobodskaya – stained glass, here depicting Beketov, a local architect, his bearded bust framed by motifs one part Byzantine, one part Kandinsky. At Moskovsky Prospekt, a wide single vault features more satellites-cum-fittings; and at Gagarinska, there is stained glass of the man himself, unfortunately not backlit the month we visited.

In the all-important propaganda pamphlet, it is noted that 'the stations are characterized by their free space, colourful design of the interior, abundance of light and air . . . the ideological and artistic decoration

Chandelier at Universitet station, Kharkiv

reflect the great revolutionary and fighting traditions of the city and its present day labour rhythm . . . the level of comfort of the Metro influences not only the passengers' mood, but their process of production and social activity.'[21] It's a strangely Pavlovian boast, but it draws attention to the

Half-lit chandeliers at Pushkinskaya, Kharkiv

particular intensity of the Kharkiv stations. Every one of the various systems appears to have some specific speciality or quirk, and in Kharkiv it's the lighting. The lamps and chandeliers of the Kharkiv Metro are a magnificent and historically puzzling thing, examples of something which shouldn't exist, according to the tenets of architectural history. They are obviously not neoclassical or neo-Baroque, and they confidently go off to explore new worlds as much as any Modernist spatial experiment; yet their decorative extravagance and exquisite, if worn craftsmanship, in marbles and metals, are outside any otherwise known architectural canon, comparable only to the Futurist Baroque of the 1970s public buildings we found in Vilnius. The lot of them could form the basis of an exhibition at the V&A, 'the baffling lamps of the Soviet 1970s', or suchlike. Even here, though, this confidence and freakish individuality eventually go neoclassical – at the mid-1980s Pushkinskaya station, designed by E. V. Nezim, E. A. Perepelitsa and V. A. Spivachuk, there are still the wonderfully flamboyant Expressionist angular pylons found in other stations on the network, but elsewhere there are gold cursive lettering and ceramic panels showing the great poet going about his business in nineteenth-century Petersburg, and the chandeliers have gone straight Rococo, and not all of them are lit. The last construction of note in the Kharkiv Metro was not courtesy of any state body: a 2009 statue made from waste materials by Metro workers themselves, called *Exhausting Night of an Underground Labourer*. With its twisted steel and unheroic slumping posture, it was hardly Socialist Realist. It was removed in 2010.

So how was it that the underground labourers' nights remained so exhausting? One explanation can be found in the depths of the Leningrad Metro. The response there to the 'embellishments decree' was to concentrate on technology rather than decoration. Most stations of the 1960s expansion of the line have a system known as 'horizontal lift', which Londoners who use the Jubilee Line will know via the more cynical term 'suicide doors'. If you wait at a station like Gostiny Dvor, Moskovskaya or Mayakovskaya, you have the same vaulted halls, but the arcades are blocked, so you feel as if you're in a tunnel rather than a ballroom, unable to see the tracks. The walls 'open' along the arcades, offering entry to the trains. This entailed a high level of automation for the Soviet 1960s, involving an impressive precision to get all the various components to line up, and the doors to meet the openings, quite apart from the darker

'1958 – opening of the first Soviet automated factory', Technological Institute station, Leningrad

function of stopping the line from slowing down because of people killing themselves. There are still a few decorative details on these stations, fittingly of a more peppy, Modernist form. One suspects that Mayakovsky would have been less disturbed by the jagged, glinting red mosaics of 'his' outpost in Leningrad than the splendour of 'his' Moscow station. The bigger clue is in Technological Institute 2 station, an interchange with one of the Line 1 palaces. Each pillar is decorated with an inscription in chic 1960s letters recalling some particular Soviet technological triumph, and one of the most prominent reads: '1958 – OPENING OF THE FIRST SOVIET AUTOMATED FACTORY'. Automation takes command, as it does in the promise of Oscar Wilde's *Soul of Man under Socialism* – 'let the machines do it.'

The propaganda literature of the Thaw is full of this rhetoric. One 1958 book, *Automation Serves Man*, lists such advances as remote-controlled mines and the introduction of driverless trains on the Moscow Metro (this in the late 1950s!). The reasons given are telling. On the one hand, it is necessary because machines do things better, as 'an automaton is always in the same "mood"', while 'the human brain is so arranged that it needs time to comprehend an event and take a correct decision'.[22] So 'automatic drivers drive trains with a great degree of accuracy, correcting all violations of the time-table'. The workers of the Metro will merely 'tune' the line for a couple of hours and then, in the words of the planner Strumlin, 'engage in their leisure time in technical inventions or swell the ranks of public figures, scientists and writers, inspired musicians and painters . . . and all these huge replenishments from among the workers will take the place of the one-sided workmen of the old system of labour division and make up the new society which we will call communism'.[23] The banner of which no longer reads 'GLORY TO WORK'.

These promises of communism through technical 'acceleration' fell into abeyance somewhat during the Brezhnev years, but were revived by Gorbachev. Several Metro systems were either completed or begun during his tenure, one of them being that of Nizhny Novgorod, opened at the end of 1985. However, the new press freedom meant that working conditions could now be openly discussed. One report is a long way from the promise thirty years earlier of automatic mines and drastically shortened working days, and fulfilled to some degree with automatic doors and driverless trains. Ernest Mandel relates that 'in *Pravda* of 1st March 1986, A. S. Suchanov, a member of the workers' brigade building the extension to the Moscow underground . . . revealed that the proportion of purely manual labour on the site was exactly what it had been half a century earlier, just about 40%. They used pneumatic drills similar to those produced in 1935, but of inferior quality.' Another Metro worker's complaint was published a year later in *Moscow News*: 'We are without working tools. We have no means of transporting them to the site where the new station will soon be established. We have to put up the frames by hand. We carry cement in shovels. We still use the pickaxe. This is not modern work, this work is from the stone age.'[24] The gap between ideology, promise and the miserable working reality was now yawning, and workers could finally say so publicly.

The result of this was not improvement so much as collapse. At the Gorky Metro (as it then was), it is notable how the planning of the system was oriented completely around the needs of industrial workers rather than, as today, those of white-collar workers and tourists; as it was a 'closed city' until 1991, the latter were pretty unlikely anyway. The first, and more or less only, line goes from the factories in the 'lower' city to the microrayons, and did not, at first, enter the administrative and touristic historic 'upper' city on the other side of the Oka river at all. Until a station opened there in 2012, the Metro existed only in the city's working-class areas, closely integrated with a comprehensive tram and bus system – far more public-transport provision than any working-class district or factory zone in the West would have received. However, you soon notice that the stations are not examples of the full-scale splendour that was the norm in Moscow, Leningrad or even Kiev. They are almost all either 'Kharkiv' or 'centipede' type, and rather murky in their design, with dark marble columns and laconic concealed lights. They are also exceptionally shallow – presumably, Gorky was far enough away from any possible frontline for stations-as-bomb-shelters not to be considered necessary. An average station involves a descent down steps rather than escalators, through entrances where granite panels lead to cheap, corrugated iron and red-brick pavilions, making clear exactly where the money ran out, or signifying that beauty underground was more important than beauty on the surface.

At the ticket halls, you find that the artistic budget has often been spent here precisely. In the Kirovskaya station, a bust of the assassinated leader sits surrounded by a sparkling red, black and blue abstract mosaic; at Leninskaya the man himself appears in stained glass; and elsewhere you have flying stars and busts of model workers. Much of the interest is in the panels above your head as you descend the stairs onto the platform, where you can find rather hauntingly pretty images of Chekhovian dacha life (in Park Kultury), images of Moscow State University or *Worker and Kolkhoz Woman* (at Moskovskaya, the interchange for the railway station) or abstracted images of free-floating revolutionary symbols. At the Avtozavodskaya station itself, a continuous mural frieze all the way along each side shows the building, assembly and enjoyment of the factory's products. There is, by any normal standard, a lot to admire and a lot to take in, but if you've been to any of the Metro systems of republican capitals, you know you're in one of the 'second tier' cities here.

What remains in this strictly proletarian Metro, even with the endless ceremonial descent and the huge budgets removed, is a sense of specialness, a feeling that you are in something that matters, that is removed from everyday life, with a certain dream logic – and, most importantly, that munificence of scale, which means that even this tightly budgeted Metro feels far more comfortable, open and pleasant than anything on the London Underground, the New York Subway or the Paris Metro. The 'Kharkiv' stations are especially memorable in this regard, particularly because, as in Kharkiv itself, you may have to wait rather a while for your tube train, given that the maintenance of this facility for taking those workers who still work in the factory to their place of employment has evidently not been treated as a priority. It is quite probable that something like the Leninskaya station, with its simple sculpted concrete vault, has been hewn in the most basic way from the subterranean mud and rock, using the most basic materials, even if it was no longer the case that slaves rather than proletarians did the most dangerous labour. The 'Futurism' of it may be entirely formal, a question of aesthetic preference rather than technical reality. But if you're waiting there for fifteen minutes that's not what you think about, instead being rather thankful that you can be bored in so splendid and generous an environment.

Waiting at Leninskaya station, Nizhny Novgorod

METROS AS DIPLOMACY

The Moscow Metro has many potential thematic routes that you can enjoy if you have a free evening and not a lot of money. You can, if you're so inclined, glide around it as if it were an international routeway, stopping off at various 'nations' and cities, which have usually been designed in tribute to sister cities and fraternal countries. One Moscow evening, tiring of spending the equivalent of five quid on a coffee and the similar delights of urban life in the Russian capital, we decided to go out in search of these fragments of and tributes to other cities, most of them dating from the turn of the 1980s, when stations adrift in the endless panel-built sprawl needed some distinctive identification. We stopped off in 'Sebastopol', where little mosaics showed the seaside obelisks, ships and other landmarks of this wartime 'Hero City' in the Crimea. This was a couple of months after it was annexed by Russia, and mercifully this recent triumph is uncelebrated in the station's iconography at the time of writing. At 'Prague' we found ourselves in a dark piece of 1970s high tech, with crepuscular strip lighting and subtly curved, golden-red columns formed from some light metal alloy. There was no reference to the historic architectural glories of the Czechoslovak capital itself, which was not the case in 'Warsaw', where repeated silver engravings show the Baroque skyline of the old town, the Modernist churches and hotels of the 1970s city and, of course, the Palace of Culture and Science; we stopped here to photograph ourselves in this underground home-from-home. After that, we moved on to 'Washington', the only unofficial example here, actually called 'Red Guard' station but closely based on the Brutalism of the American capital's Metro, with its sweeping vaults of concrete coffers. We ended our journey in a more recent station, opened in 2013 and named after Kazakhstan's largest city Alma-Ata. Tall, bent red uplighters made their way down the hall, whose symbolic import was unknown to us. By this time, having spent several hours underground, we began to feel deeply unhealthy, tired of the shuddering roar of the trains, our fingers grimy and our mouths dusty, and made our way back to the centre. Anyway, irrespective of the places you can go to under Moscow, the internationalism of the Metro was not limited to its own stylistic borrowings and tributes.

'Warsaw', Moscow Metro

Given that the Moscow Metro and its descendants were one of the most obviously successful aspects of the Soviet environment, guaranteed to awe all but the most hostile guests, it is not altogether surprising that their technology and expertise would be exported to the 'socialist camp'. In fact, the first attempt at replicating the Moscow Metro's dimensions and design did not occur in Eastern Europe, but in 1940s London – the twin platforms divided by a wide coffered vault in Gants Hill tube station were specifically modelled on Moscow's example, albeit with a rather subtler use of facing materials. It did not catch on. Several cities were proposed for Soviet-style Metro systems in the Stalinist period, especially Warsaw and Bucharest; and the former went some distance in constructing the tunnels, in extremely unsympathetic geological conditions, before the Metro was cancelled by Gomułka, suspicious of grandiose and apparently useless grand projects.[25] Several of the architecture–propaganda books of the late 1940s and early 1950s feature prospective images of the Warsaw Metro, all of them with Moscow scale and materials – great vaults with marble floors, Rococo chandeliers, stuccoed ceilings, heroic figures and murals. As it is, perhaps the only full Stalinist station built outside the USSR, at least until the mid-1960s, was actually a remodelling of an existing East Berlin station, then named (after the communist leader and Nazi victim) Ernst Thälmann, now known as Mohrenstrasse. Retaining exactly the airy, if relatively modest, proportions of the U-Bahn, it is coated entirely with the heavily veined deep red marble that is ubiquitous in Moscow or Kiev – in different shades, on the benches, on the walls, on the columns. The marble was not from the Urals this time, but plundered from Speer's demolished Reich Chancellery.

When Metros were finally built in the capitals of the Eastern Bloc, it was still as a partly imperial act, but no longer as an example of sheer imitation. The first is actually an extension of the world's second full underground line – in Budapest, which had already built a system in 1890 along the line of the main artery of Pest, Andrássy út. With the assistance of Soviet advisers and engineers, this was then extended with one, then two new lines of wide-vaulted marble-lined halls, reached by the usual endless escalators. The Second Line, built in the 1960s and opened in 1970, was, like Tbilisi but with less outright vandalism, recently 'de-Sovietized' via cladding and adverts, so that its provenance is obvious more in the proportions (and the checked black and grey granite floors and the heavy, beige marble columns) rather than the style; and perhaps in its contrast with the original line, where entrances to different directions are found on different sides of the street and the iron-columned spaces are on what gets called a 'human scale'. Fittingly, the most 'Muscovite' station, Széll Kálmán tér, was originally called 'Moszkva tér'

'Moscow' station, Budapest

('Moscow Square') and is, on the surface, a unique Brutalist concrete and glass vestibule, described in one Budapest gazetteer as 'an expressionistic building which is as much public sculpture as architecture'.[26] True enough, but it also closely resembles a larger, more confident re-creation of Ryazansky Prospekt station in Moscow itself, built a few years earlier in 1966, which has an identical jagged roof line.

The Third Line, built slightly later, is also visibly Soviet-inspired, largely by dint of its expansive use of space and atmospheric lighting. Stylistically, it is as slightly clunkily Modernist as the contemporary systems in Brussels or Stockholm, with fabulous hot-orange moulded plastic seats and chrome-plated columns, and a murky light cast by square lamps against black marble. In one of the films set in Soviet-era Metros – more of a subgenre than you may assume – it takes its place as a particularly seedy mise-en-scène. Nimród E. Antal's 2003 film *Kontroll* is shot entirely in the Third Line, most likely because it is the only line sufficiently dilapidated, spacious, labyrinthine, lavatorial and unusual enough to serve the purpose of the plot, where a set of depressed Metro workers constantly chase a clientèle that constantly refuses to pay the already nominal fee of their public transport, which could, at a stretch, be seen as a cinematic metaphor for the declining esteem held towards public space. The place comes across in the film as unloved but essential, the artery of a dour underground city where modernity has gone to die, with all the investment ploughed into the fin-de-siècle capital above. In this, it closely recalls the slightly later Metro built in the Romanian capital. Fitting its tendencies towards nationalism and autarchy, Bucharest under Ceauşescu was the only capital to plan and execute a Metro system without any Soviet assistance, and the only one where you will not, in the twenty-first century, find old Russian tube trains shunting their way between the stations; it is also the only one with levels of squalor that Londoners or New Yorkers will find familiar, with surfaces mostly filthy. For all that, it was the most extensive 'socialist Metro' built outside the USSR, with thirty-nine stations on three lines by 1989, largely in order to connect factories to microrayons, and it shares the conviction that underground architecture should be special and atmospheric.

Like the Boulevard of the Victory of Socialism and the Centrul Civic – whose late-1970s to late-1980s time period it was contemporary with – the Bucharest Metro is recognizably Soviet-inspired while avoiding any non-architectural rhetoric, with absolutely no statues, mosaics or obvious exhortations, merely a spatial power. Unlike the Boulevard, though, the architecture is clever, imaginative, and devoid of heaviness and authoritarianism. With its mix of clashing materials (plastic and marble, steel and brick) it is Postmodernist, but Postmodernism as pop architecture rather than reactionary revanche. Columns are wrapped in braids of blue marble at Politehnica, and even the most mundane stations have handrails and benches clad in imperial travertine. The stations are all different, but certain principles are followed. None are particularly deep; there are escalators but you can walk down their multiple levels, which are the main architectural attraction – some decades before Michael Hopkins tried the same trick at Westminster station in London, they leave enough space around the circulation that you can always sense the different levels, with staircases, escalators and floors ascending and descending in Piranesian fashion. Many stations are double height, with arcades on the second level, and the platforms entered from wide circuses, as at Universitate and Victory Square. The generous spaces of the latter were

Universitate station, Bucharest

opened in December 1989, but were surely less inflammatory, less revolution-provoking, than the Palace of the Parliament going up at the same time.

Aside from Titan station, a massive concrete hall of 'Kharkiv type', the ideas and problems of the Bucharest Metro are those of Romanian engineers and architects – save for the notion that Metros should be big, spacious and treated as national propaganda projects, it has a tangential relation to the Soviet model, and that was a matter of autarchic pride for Romanian 'National Communism'. Elsewhere, the link between Metro building and imperial geopolitics was extremely direct. It may be coincidental that the Soviet investment in Hungary that got the Metro's later lines built came soon after the suppression of the 1956 revolution. It certainly wasn't when the Prague Metro was built a couple of years later.

The Prague Metro was begun in 1966, and then intended as a combined 'metrotram' that would run both in streets and in tunnels; after construction had already started, it was upgraded to a full Metro a year later. But the Metro as we know it today, the first line of which was opened in 1974, was funded to the hilt by the USSR as some sort of sop, some sort of evidence of the occupier's munificence, after the suppression of the Prague Spring by Warsaw Pact tanks in 1968. Or, put delicately, 'In view of the important technical assistance rendered by the Soviet Union, the underground railway is marked as a structure of Czechoslovak–Soviet co-operation.'[27] The first, originally planned line is as dull and unexciting as the systems being built around the same time in, say, Cologne or Rotterdam, and aside from being typically spatially profligate, has little to distinguish itself from them in its mildly Futurist fittings, aside from the use of wide halls with trains leaving on either side. It is with the Second Line, opened in 1978, that Prague started to create something equal in its dreaminess to that of its occupier/backer. The stations are all very precisely in the Soviet style of deep escalators leading to long, wide-arched vaults with platforms on either side, but the rejection of neoclassicism and the embrace of a weird, intense form of late Futurism has gone here even further than in Kharkiv. And unlike the Ukrainian city, where each station is still deliberately designed in a different idiom, there is also an embrace of a certain measure of standardization, even of branding.

Several stations in the city centre, along what is now 'Line A' – Muzeum, Hradčanská, Jiřího z Poděbrad, Flora, Malostranská, Náměstí Míru, Můstek and Staroměstská, to a design by Jan Reiterman and Jaroslav Otruba – follow a similar model of vaulted halls bedecked in various unusual kinds of fruitily coloured marble – grey-green, silver. The ceilings are covered with green and blue panels, slightly bulbous, like an animal's hide; but unlike in Soviet stations, it is on the waiting platforms that the designers have concentrated their energies. Each of the arched waiting rooms is covered in hundreds of little concave and convex lenses, all in various vividly artificial shades of blue, gold, scarlet and purple – the photographs here cannot do the slightest justice to them – which have the names of the stations set into them, not a strong point in Moscow, where design frequently triumphs over orientation.

Across this common aesthetic, there is still room for some frequently very experimental work. At Karlovo Náměstí, opened in 1985, the arches that divide the vaults from the platforms are dressed with inset bands of glassware by František Vizner, ribbed so that they give off a shimmering light, rather than turned into heavy neoclassical columns as in Leningrad. These then reappear all the way through the subsidiary tunnels to the

Muzeum station, Prague

'Moscow' station, Prague

exits. Elsewhere, there are deliberate 'tributes' to the original inspiration, from which the Czechs had veered so far in details. The Anděl (originally Moskevská, or 'Moscow') station of 1985 was co-designed by the Czechs Marie Davidová and Eva Břuschová with a Moscow architect, Lev Popov – as part of an exchange, whereby Czech Metro designers got to do that coldly metallic 'Prague' station in Moscow. Anděl resembles very closely the layout of Rimskaya station in Moscow, which was actually built later, a white-grey marble hall with little 'skylights' set in niches and sculptural reliefs in the tunnels. Unlike the 'high buildings' of an earlier era this doesn't feel like an import, just a spin on the Metro's existing style. The colonial aspect is in the iconography.

The 'space station' style is in Prague taken to a thrilling extreme, a series of spaces immediately evoking extreme modernity set down unobtrusively under castles, palaces and cathedrals. It is a neat modern/traditional divide that for once does little violence to either. The Prague Metro appears to have all of this without any obvious ideological trappings, but appearances are deceptive. For sure, the main interest of the designs was always in the abstract, non-representational surfaces of the underground halls, but that didn't mean there wasn't propaganda scattered around strategically as well. The colours of seemingly abstract stations were, according to the Metro historian Radomira Sedláková, chosen for lightly symbolic reasons – the patterns were in gold at Hradčanská for the castle, green at Malostranská for the gardens, and red at Staroměstská for the history of revolutionary activity in the area.[28] Anděl, as we've seen, was originally named after Moscow, and still has the legend 'MOSKVA–PRAHA' in the vestibule and a few revolutionary reliefs. The Metro map once featured a Leninova and a Gottwaldova, named after the repellent Czech Stalinist leader – which originally featured a mosaic on the communist seizure of power in 1948, now covered up. Želivského features some revolutionary heritage in the form of rough, evocative mosaics of Hussites, sufficiently historically distant in their millenarian fanaticism to be uncontroversial. The system as a whole was subject after 1989 to a selective act of (actual) iconoclasm, which leaves it looking much more ideologically neutral today than was originally intended. Even so, all the major design decisions taken by the Czech and Slovak designers of the Prague Metro were towards abstraction rather than a literal *architecture parlante*. As you can attest if you visit the later – perfectly functional, entirely forgettable – Metro stations in the Czech capital, the difference is in the way that the designers were obviously given a blank cheque to realize their dreams, to produce spaces as wilfully dramatic and chromatically wild as these. Aside from a confidence in the future and a deeply anti-traditionalist love of artificial surface, there is little that you could pinpoint as specifically 'real socialist' in this, other than the mere fact that it exists – Metros in Germany or the Netherlands or Belgium do not have this sort of scale or flamboyance. The Czech engineers and architects and their Soviet advisers obviously did the city proud; but one suspects that if asked whether they wanted an end to censorship or a really fantastic Metro system, most Czechs in 1968 would have opted for the former; the tragedy is that neither they, or anyone else, ever had the option of both.

So too with Warsaw, when it came to construct its Metro. The full Stalinist system was cancelled by Gomułka largely, one suspects, because, brought to power on a wave of popular demonstrations, he must have felt secure enough in his popular support without having to resort to bread and circuses. The same is not necessarily true of the man who actually got the Warsaw Metro built, General Wojciech Jaruzelski. Literally only a month after his coup d'état to suppress Solidarity in December 1981, the new leader announced that the Warsaw Metro would finally be built – with, of course, great and munificent Soviet assistance. Once again, a Metro in exchange for sovereignty. The Warsaw Metro began on site a year later, and was fully opened in 1995; there have been expansions since and a second line is under construction at the time of writing, but compared to even a smaller, seemingly less important city like Kharkiv it is still fairly paltry today, albeit very clean, very fast and very nice. Only the first section of the line is now as it was designed in 1983, all of the stations serving the sprawling microrayons in the Ursynów borough. A team headed by the architect Jasna Strzałkowska-Ryszka[29] introduced a common abstract aesthetic, as in Prague, and also one which to this day precludes any space for advertisements on many of the stations. These are shallow compared to the Soviet norm, but the sense of descending into the bowels of the earth is given the *architecture parlante* treatment, by heavy, rusticated stone panels at all of the stairwells from the street, as if you were entering a crypt. The halls are mostly held up with columns, and are decorated along each platform with a continuous abstract

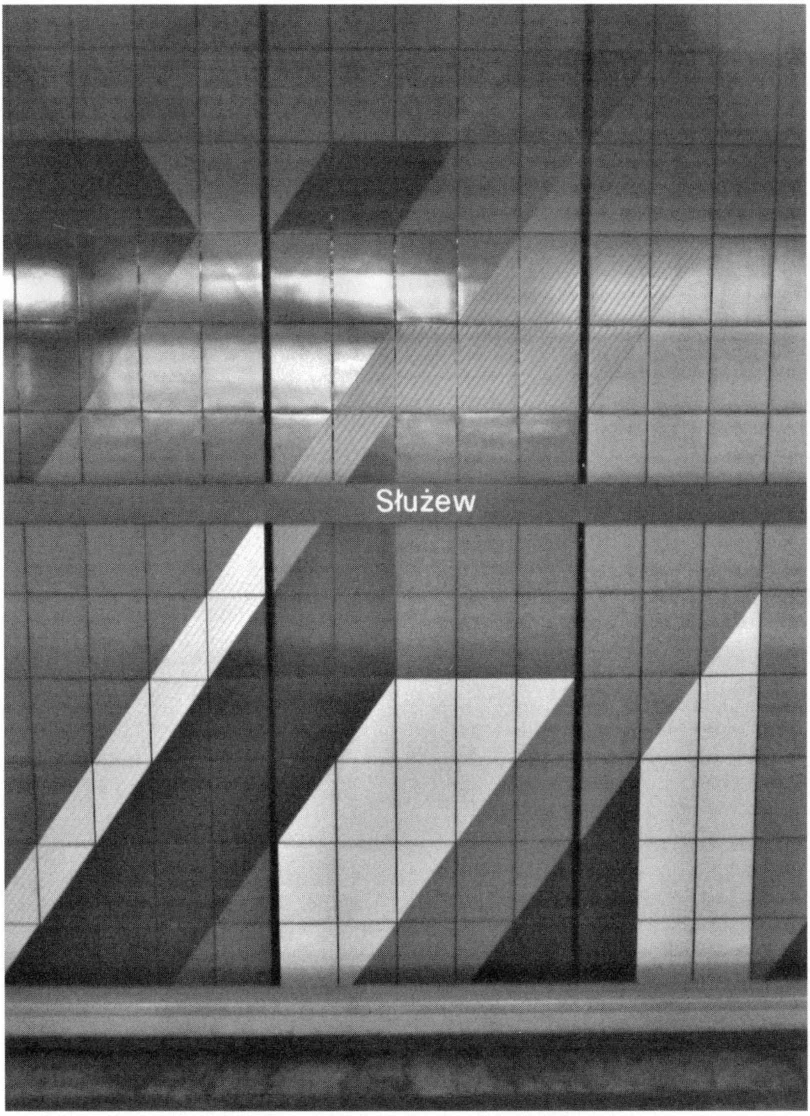

Modernist murals at Służew station, Warsaw

ceramic mural, not visibly 'referring' to anything but partaking in a tradition of abstraction derived from Malevich and De Stijl, one which was unbroken in the Polish capital. The typically murky, atmospheric light is offset by the vivid brightness of the continuous artwork.

After that initial run, the Warsaw Metro built several stations of the 'Kharkiv type' – Wierzbno, Racławicka, Pole Mokotowskie – still with Russian assistance; these show just what would happen if the Soviet-style Metro was really 'normalized', with the same dimensions and none of the aesthetic fripperies. There are some cute Modernist light fittings, but marble is out, bare concrete is in. The large vaulted space is still rather exciting, but the sense of otherness has completely disappeared, the dreamworld has ended, and the result is just a very good piece of transport infrastructure. Even then, at least one station suggests a precedent was set that there should at least be something a little bit special about the Metro – the 2002 Plac Wilsona station in Żoliborz once won a 'most beautiful Metro station in the world' award, which – as hopefully this chapter proves – is a little extravagant, but it is still a superb piece of design, where a (rather low-ceilinged) platform roofed with what looks like bubbled plastic opens out by the exit to a wide rotunda whose lights change colour with the weather. But having lived in Warsaw, I've been able to notice certain things that I wouldn't be able to spot in Moscow, Kiev or Prague.

The original planned line that was eventually finished completely in 2002 was built to connect two large microrayons in the south and the north to the centre, with massive factories such as the Huta Warszawa in Bielany connected to it so that workers could get to work and to town quickly and comfortably. This, as in the Nizhny Novgorod Metro, is worth noting, because (for instance) the huge London County Council estates of the 1960s, which were sometimes nearly as populous as those in Warsaw – the Alton Estate, Thamesmead – were never connected to the tube, and certainly connecting manual workers to their factories was never a major priority either. On that basis, it's obvious that the actual layout of the Metro was 'different', serving completely separate priorities from those of a capitalist metropolis. Getting from Ursynów to the city centre was supposed to be, and now is, extremely quick and easy. When land is no longer publicly owned and property speculation runs free, a Metro has other purposes. Any land near a Metro station necessarily rises in value, as Londoners or Parisians well know; so Warsaw's stations in the peripheral housing estates are often ringed with new speculative developments, one of which we live in. Accordingly, Warsaw has been recentred on a north–south axis, now the richest strip of the city, despite the harsh poverty that is still in evidence in much of Ursynów. The areas that aren't part of the Metro – such as Praga or Wola – are more dilapidated and more neglected. The Warsaw Metro was designed to serve a self-described 'socialist city' and ended up helping to create the capitalist one.

The saddest outpost of the International Soviet Metro is strictly post-socialist. Vukov Spomenik is the single underground station on Belgrade's suburban railway, opened in 1995, and it appears to have absconded from 1980s Moscow or Kiev. Descending from the city centre near the university, passing through what was evidently an attempt at a Western shopping mall decorated with Serbian nationalist relief sculpture, which has turned into a series of dingy spaces for youth to play video games and use cheap internet access, you arrive at a long, high, vaulted hall, with (heavy, non-Metro) trains leaving from either side. From the golden ornamental coursing to the hidden uplighters, to the Orthodox Church-referencing relief sculpture at the far end of the platform, this is 'Soviet, Soviet, Soviet'. That's peculiar, given that between 1948 and 1991 there were few political and fewer aesthetic links

Non-socialist Sovietism runs under Belgrade

between the Yugoslav and Soviet governments. The station was built by the engineering firm Energoprojekt, and designed by its lead architect, Zoran Bojović.[30] You can see their advertisements opposite the platforms, unaltered since 1995 – the Serbian economy has been essentially in freefall ever since, preserving this museum of early 1990s design. Most advertise the newly privatized, formerly self-managed institutions of socialist Yugoslavia, a few are more touristic – displaying Belgrade's newly constructed Orthodox cathedral as if it were Hagia Sophia – and one is for home computing. The biggest advert, for Energoprojekt itself, has a map of the world showing locations of all the projects it has worked on, from dams to power stations and housing estates, where you can clearly see projects in Eastern Europe massively outnumbered by those in Africa, South-East Asia and Latin America – there's even one in Scotland. One thing capitalism did in post-socialist Serbia is ally itself closely with the new capitalist Russia, as if to reopen the old Orthodox bonds severed in 1917. The most Stalinist building in Belgrade, Vukov Spomenik is a monument to the anti-socialist reaction, fixed in that unheroic moment.

Regardless of this peculiar geopolitical freak, the death knell of the Soviet Metro – or so it must have seemed at the time – happened not in one of the 'satellites', but in a country that was then part of the Soviet Union itself. The rule, as we've seen, was that once a city reached one million inhabitants, it was eligible to be granted a Metro. By the end of the 1970s, Riga was getting ever closer to that mark – largely through the still hugely controversial migration of Russians to work in its factories – and was promised the requisite funding in 1977, with the first stations set to open between 1990 and 1997. The geographical and geological conditions, even more hostile than those in Leningrad and Moscow, would have made this the most expensive Metro system built in the USSR, at an estimated 25 million roubles per kilometre; although it should be remembered that such projects were often effectively given a blank cheque, and, at the time of commissioning, around half a dozen Metros were under construction in provincial industrial cities. The designs for stations were completed in 1983, well in advance of their construction (as in Warsaw), and they can easily be found, for instance, on the Metro's Wikipedia page.[31] They are beautiful monochrome drawings, showing something quite similar to some of the very late-Soviet Metros such as Sverdlovsk or Dnepropetrovsk, a sleeker, more streamlined version of the stripped Rococo/marble

Futurism found in the Kharkiv stations. The Metro was eventually defeated for a variety of reasons, most of them tied up with the independence movement growing in the Baltic republic – environmentalists didn't like the amount of demolition it would require in the historical centre, nationalists felt that it would only encourage even more Russian migration to Riga, which even now is around 50 per cent Russian-speaking. With independence in 1991 the Metro was quietly shelved. Alfreds Rubiks, then mayor of the city – a hardliner jailed in the 1990s, whose party now forms part of the city's governing post-communist coalition 'Harmony Centre' – has commented that the project was plausible when Moscow was ready to shovel huge quantities of money and resources at it, which implies that the independent republic has no such chance; even, presumably, given its EU membership. But the population of Riga has declined so heavily since 1991, first when Russians were encouraged to leave, and more recently when it faced the deepest recession in all of Europe, that it is well below the million citizens that would have secured it the Moscow funding in the first place.

THE UNDEATH OF THE SOVIET METRO

It would be convenient to end the story there, with the inescapably imperial project of the Soviet Metro finally upended by a peripheral republic refusing to be treated as a colony to be compensated by great public works. A story of hubris eventually defeated, and of a legacy that exists entirely in the past. That would be neat, but it would not be accurate. After a fallow period under Yeltsin, when a 'light Metro' paralleled the Khrushchev era in the relative restraint of its design, the Moscow Metro has, in recent years, opened several new stations that are, very clearly, Moscow Metro stations. Regardless of the need or otherwise for nuclear shelters, they're still buried deep in the ground; ubiquitous still is the expensive, laborious, but highly legible and architecturally breathtaking practice of providing high-ceilinged vaults, with the trains leaving from either side. Given that many of the new stations and the extensions under construction were planned under the USSR it is in the applied art, rather than in the architecture, that you find the differences with Soviet practice. Park Pobedy, in 2003, was the Metro's equivalent of the neo-Stalinist trend in architecture, with red marble and Zurab Tsereteli murals of the victories over Napoleon and Hitler – a vacuous version of the USSR's more architecturally imaginative hurrah-patriotism. Other 1990s stations seem to sit half-way between optimistic late-Soviet Futurism and something more ambiguous. Rimskaya, for instance, is in its main hall another science-fiction hangar, but examine its sculptures and you find babies atop collapsed columns, allegedly a reference to Romulus and Remus, but with an obvious pertinence to a more recently collapsed empire.

Much more coherent is something like the Dostoevskaya station, finished in 2010 – here we have a narrative station again, with macabre little illustrations of scenes from Dostoevsky's novels, executed in a creepy, cartoonish style far from Tsereteli's clumsy heroics. As if to poke fun at the authoritarianism behind the Metro, a looming portrait of the author himself stares out at the commuter at the end of one of the vaults. That's only mentioning Moscow. In Nizhny Novgorod, when the system finally crossed to the centre of the city in 2012, the resultant station was actually more grand than those built in the 1980s, and equally explicit in its Soviet

Ceramic mural at Gorkovskaya station, Nizhny Novgorod

visual rhetoric, with murals of the city's Lenin statue and plenty of images of the writer the city was once named after – you could imagine that this was a design of the 1980s executed thirty years later but in fact is near contemporary with the station's opening. In Kiev, meanwhile, twenty-first-century stations like Akademmistechko are distinguishable from those of the 1980s only in their slightly cheaper, albeit shinier materials. Their iconography shows continuity too, although more in the sense of technocracy than the figures of Lenin or Gorky. A Metro historian describes Akademmistechko's chandeliers as forming 'a pattern suggestive of organic molecules, the lamps representing atoms'. The head architects, Tamara Chelikovska and Anatoliy Krushinsky, had designed many of those grand Metro stations like Teatralna, and had clearly not come up with many new ideas in the thirty years since then. No doubt some would see this as evidence of dead post-Soviet weight, but then, in this particular case, why fix something that is in no way broken? And this is just extensions; in the last decade entire new lines have been built in strictly Moscow Metro style, in Kazan in the Russian Federation and in the former capital of Kazakhstan, Alma-Ata. All of these new Metro stations do not look like thin, deliberately parodic imitations of the originals, as do the new 'high buildings' in Moscow. They look like a tradition being continued, proudly. Why?

It is too easy to say that this is just because they're Potemkin villages underground, as even intelligent anti-Stalinist communists once did. Victor Serge once claimed, inaccurately, that the Moscow Metro had no benches for tired workers to sit on, and Trotsky saw them as pretentious examples of the warped priorities of Stalinism. There is truth in the argument that Metros, however 'useful', were bread and circuses, designed to dazzle, while basic human needs remained unmet; the economic historian Alec Nove notes that in the years when 'Stalin seemed more concerned with prestige projects, such as the lavishly decorated Moscow underground railway, than with ordinary housebuilding or the maintenance and repair of existing houses', a full 5 per cent of Muscovites lived in kitchens and corridors, while 25.6 per cent occupied only part of a room.[32] Yet in the 1970s and 1980s, opulent Metros were built at the same time as one of the biggest housebuilding projects in history. There must, at some level, be a question of pride and utility at work in this persistence.

Or perhaps this is the subject's genuflection towards the munificence of the great leader. In Khrushchev's memoirs, his admiration of Stalin comes out most in the section on the building of the Metro, where he waved away the objections of more experienced engineers like Pavel Rottert, who wanted shallow, Berlin-style stations, in favour of a more experimental, high-tech, deep-level design, suggested by one Makovsky, using the precedent of London's Piccadilly Circus. 'At one point Rottert said "what you're proposing is much too expensive." But Stalin cut him off sharply. "Comrade Rottert, the question of what is expensive and what is inexpensive will be left up to the Government to decide. Now, tell us, is the proposal of the young engineer Makovsky technically feasible?" "Yes, but it will be much too expensive." "I just told you, Comrade Rottert, the Government will decide that. We will go ahead and accept Comrade Makovsky's plan for deep tunnelling"'[33] – the great despot waving away the objections of those who would point to the costs. It is easy, in this context, to understand, if not condone, the recent re-inscribing of Stalin's name, previously erased, onto the neoclassical vestibule of Kurskaya station. It also helps explain the counter-reaction – in early 2014, the giant Lenin head and quotes were removed by the Metro authorities from Teatralna station in Kiev, out of fear that the insurgents on the Maidan would do the job themselves.

However, rather than mere spaces of spectacle, the Metros are also exemplary spaces of the transformation of the everyday, taking two kinds of rituals – those of religion, with the sacred vaulted spaces, created atmospheres and representational icons that implies, and the mundane daily rituals of waiting for trains, of getting to work and meeting friends. People think differently about space because of them; on an early date, Agata and I arranged to meet at a London tube station. She assumed we would be meeting on the platform itself, because, well, isn't that what you do, when the platform halls are grand public showcases? After half an hour or more of her waiting in a grim, cramped little tunnel and me in the ticket office above, we realized our mistake. The rituals and acts the Metro inspires are many: at Ploshchad Revolutsii, the dog's nose is rubbed for good luck in exams, the feet of one of the girls when rubbed is supposed to offer help with unhappy love affairs. Lenin would have been disgusted to have seen the workers of Moscow resort to such superstition decades after the revolution, but this is what Khrushchev meant when he talked of the Metro being 'supernatural' – somewhere between the ordinary and the extraordinary.

The most basic explanation for the Metro's endurance is given in a recent English-language guide to the system, which cites a famous story about the Metro and its finest architect, on the subject of what is now Kropotkinskaya station. 'When the project was presented to the commission, Kaganovich objected that they had paraphrased the house of the Pharaohs, i.e. the Great Temple of Ammon at Karnak. But Dushkin denied the charge with words that have become a household phrase: "Their palaces are for Pharaohs, but ours are for the people." '[34] Surely he would have said that, if challenged, about his palatial, skyscraping castle of evil for bureaucrats at Krasnye Vorota as well. But here, it is true. These palaces really are for the people. They were then and they are now. At worst, they are a cheap holiday in someone else's luxury; at best, a glimpse of the practice of everyday life being completely transformed and transcended, with mundane tasks transfigured into a dream of egalitarian space. The Metro systems of the Soviet Union and its satellites are its most convincing microcosms of a communist future you can walk through, smell and touch.

'Our Palaces are for the People': the Temple of Karnak, Kropotkinskaya station, Moscow

6
Reconstruction

When I got off the train at Warsaw
I saw through the whole act
This was not Warsaw at all
(just like the train was not a train)
but one big phantom
one monumental con-machine
cheap elaborate joke
at my expense
at every turn I discover
the phoniness
time and again I see
the hardboard showing through fake façades
. . . cartoon cut-out profiles
proletariat stuffed with sawdust
all flash but no flesh
everything old hat
makes you laugh
except at night
through the window
it haunts you
the Phantom Warsaw

Andrzej Bursa, 'Phantom Warsaw' (1956)[1]

LIKE IT NEVER WENT AWAY

There is a curious and largely unexplored backstory behind the enormous visual contrast between the delightful old town left behind by pre-communism and the concrete misery created by communism – the fact that the delightful old town was also, in many cases, created by communism. This is not quite as counterintuitive as it sounds if you bear in mind exactly what the Second World War did in this part of Europe. Yugoslavia, Poland, the western republics and provinces of what was then the Soviet Union and, understandably, Germany were devastated on a scale way beyond the (huge in any other circumstances) war damage in France, the UK, Italy or the Low Countries. Although there are some old towns that were lucky enough to have escaped near-total destruction, like Budapest, Kraków or Prague, a great many historic centres which now have a tourist-pleasing level of completeness are either entirely or extensively a post-war product. Tsarist St Petersburg and Riga, Dutch Baroque Gdańsk, Saxon Baroque Dresden, Prussian imperial Berlin, and most famously the apparently meticulous piecing back together of the royal centre of Warsaw – these are all the projects in one way or another of post-war communist governments, and sweeping, complete rebuilding on this scale was not attempted or even contemplated west of the Elbe. For some reason, the ideology of 'real socialism' – or rather, at this point (1945–55, roughly), of Stalinism.

The reason why the communists could do this apparently populist thing was the complete absence in Stalinist discourse of Modernism, at least in its limited, architecture-and-town-planning sense, what was called at the time 'the modern movement'. Under Stalin this movement had been decisively suppressed in the early 1930s, and a similar suppression would happen in the late 1940s across countries where Modernism had been strong and built widely before 1939, like Latvia, Estonia, Hungary, Poland and especially Czechoslovakia – in Germany, of course, Hitler had already done the job. The modern movement, reflecting its grounding in the Arts and Crafts movement, with its notions of 'honesty' and 'truth to materials', derived at a remove or two from John Ruskin and William Morris or from the anti-scenographic urban theories of Adolf Loos, did not regard reconstruction in this sense – as replicas of the old – as desirable or even

Historic Gdańsk, built in the 1950s (1964 postcard)

possible. Morris had argued that it was always better to leave a medieval church or guildhall as a ruin rather than add our workmanship to that of the original masons. To do so was fakery, was anti-historical, was obscuring the imprint of the real craftsmen of an earlier age, and was always bound, even with the best scholarship, to be fundamentally inaccurate, our very particular version of what might or might not have existed in the past. What nineteenth-century church and cathedral restorers like Viollet-le-Duc or George Gilbert Scott did was as gross as completing an unfinished Renaissance painting. However, the sheer amount of ruins in 1945 meant that the only conceivable choices in reconstruction were either starting anew or creating replicas. Some places in the West did a bit of both – in London, the bombed-out remains of Wren's churches or the Houses of Parliament were pieced back together fairly faithfully. In Cologne, an otherwise completely rebuilt Modernist city centre was complemented and punctuated by reconstructions of its destroyed Romanesque churches.

Mostly, however, new cities that had suffered from blitzkriegs or from Bomber Harris – Hamburg, Frankfurt, Coventry, Plymouth, Southampton, Rotterdam, Liège, Le Havre – looked new. In many of these, most famously Coventry and Rotterdam, reconstruction was radical, and was actually seen as an opportunity to finally deploy urban theories that had been largely untried before the war – pedestrian cities of austere, often tall buildings, with spatial class relations dissolved, usually with fearsome ringroads to keep the traffic out of the centre itself. In the first ten years of reconstruction in the Soviet-occupied zone there was none of this. Why should there have been, when the architectural theories of 'Socialist Realism', with their deliberate unreality, their façade-deep ornamentalism, were the complete rejection of the theories of Loos or Ruskin?

Partly this was the result of the way that, in the 1930s, the Soviet regime repositioned itself as the defender of 'humanism' and the Enlightenment heritage. Although this draws on the way in which the early-Soviet regime was, for all its Modernism, a major sponsor of the architectural heritage – Soviet-era guidebooks liked to cite the fact that one of Lenin's first acts when the Bolshevik government moved to Moscow was to begin plans for the conservation of the Kremlin. This 'humanism' is more unexpected in the mid-1930s, given that the apparently quasi-medieval insanity of the Show Trials and purges seemed like a regression to the Spanish Inquisition, but it is a fact nonetheless, with various Congresses to defend 'culture' from the barbarians (from Nazis or from Modernists or both, depending on the Line) a major component of Stalinism, along with, as we've seen, a rehabilitation of patriotism and national culture – Russian first and foremost, to be sure, but with other nations getting their relative due as well. When this discourse began to become part of the Cold War, the West's disdain for the humanist heritage was abundantly displayed by the inhuman 'packing-case architecture' of Mies van der Rohe or Le Corbusier. In Budapest, Prague and Warsaw this took time to take hold, with several Modernist buildings being instigated or even completed before the total imposition of the Soviet system began in 1948. And on some level, of course, what happened here was an act of populism: a regime which was popularly rejected everywhere but Czechoslovakia, Bulgaria and Yugoslavia keeping the people quiet by giving them what they 'really want', the pretty, the familiar and the historic – the 'national', even. The fact that they had no qualms about 'fakes' derived from an explicitly rejected theory on what architects can and can't do with the past, which was under Stalinism exceptionally mutable at the best of times.

The result is that precisely what Western traditionalists have been calling for over the last few decades (and occasionally doing, as with the rash of replicas, especially in the UK, during the 1980s and 1990s) was fulfilled by regimes which owed their existence and their ideas largely to J. V. Stalin. This might have made the traditionalists ask some questions about these ideas, about whether or not it really is as humane and democratic as they think it is to assume that architectural change should have been frozen in 1914, and whether it really is 'traditionalist' to break with the centuries-old convention that each generation builds in its own style (think of Wren, importing his funny modern continental ideas in St Paul's, when he could have just rebuilt the Gothic cathedral like the people wanted). They might reflect on the political provenance of treating the city as scenery, as a picture that must not be altered. They probably won't, of course, although some of them – veteran British commentator Simon Jenkins, for one – have long advocated the Stalinist approach to urban rebuilding regardless. In fact, Jenkins went one better by praising the urban planning of Moscow's former mayor Yuri Luzhkov, the husband of the city's leading property developer, who created hundreds of what critics call 'sham replicas' at a rapid pace after the collapse of the old system.[2] The somewhat less terrifying example of Dresden is also invoked, where a reconstruction programme that began under Walter Ulbricht is culminating in the final recompletion of the skyline incinerated by the RAF. What is seldom mentioned here is that reconstruction actually returned long before the collapse in 1989 – *like it never went away*, in fact.

The only eras of state socialism that rejected the creation of historical replicas were the immediate post-revolutionary decade and later the Thaw, the (at a stretch) twenty years or so from the mid-1950s to the mid-1970s when 'Eastern' practice in architectural terms was at its closest to that of the West. Except when reconstruction returned in the mid-1970s, it was also in train with Western cities attempting the same thing, in reaction to the apparent failures of Modernism. London went in for neo-neo-Georgian and built replicas of Victorian offices in Piccadilly and Trafalgar Square; Frankfurt complemented its skyscrapers with a replica old town. This is often dated to the influence of Postmodernism, where suddenly 'honesty' and 'truth' were less important than affect, familiarity and complexity. According to Fredric Jameson, Postmodernism was 'the cultural logic of late capitalism', and yet very similar movements appeared in the 1970s at the hands of architects in East Germany, People's Poland and the USSR. The neo-Stalinist trend in Eastern Europe is only partly to blame here, as architects often used Western precedent to justify their return to the practice of 1948 and the era of the Cominform. The upshot? In the historical centres of socialist cities, little is what it seems. The most convincing skylines are often fictional, and the areas where the air of the past can, it would seem, be smelled are in some cases not even reconstructions but free improvisations on historical themes, with no more relation to how people lived 'then' than Tesco's Organic range relates to pre-industrial agriculture. It also brings another conundrum. Not only is it hard to spot the fake, but it is hard to tell yourself that fakes are bad and hence cannot be beautiful when you're wandering around the centres of Dresden or Warsaw. At the same time, it is here that the influence of capital upon building is perhaps least palpable. It is the cycle of rents and obsolescence that dictates the constant replacement of housing and the urban tissue; it is, more arguably, the need to constantly resell the same product that dictates the periodic changes in architectural style – or fashion. If fashion and rent are irrelevant, and to varying degrees they were, then not only do we have an explanation for the striking preservation of such largely unbombed old towns as Prague or Kraków, but we find that another encumbrance on replicas and reconstruction disappears. 'It isn't communism that's radical,' said Bertolt Brecht, 'it's capitalism.'[3]

SIMULACRA, SIMULATION AND SOCIALISM: THE RECONSTRUCTION OF WARSAW

Several cities reconstructed immediately after the war present themselves as if nothing much had happened – unless you knew it, or ventured round the corners where the ornament on the gabled tenements is conspicuously flimsy, you wouldn't know that the red-brick Gothic and Baroque of Gdańsk was largely a product of the 1950s; similarly, it's only by comparing images of St Petersburg today with photographs of the city pockmarked with bombsites from the appalling siege of Leningrad that you could realize how extensive and thorough its reconstruction was. These are less famous examples, but one city presents itself both as a reconstruction and as something entirely authentic – Warsaw. The thing about Warsaw that almost everyone knows is that 85 per cent of it was destroyed in 1944 as collective punishment for the Warsaw Rising, and that it was then reconstructed to the letter after 1945. Strangely, this coexists with another idea of Warsaw as a centre of wide streets, towers and general Warsaw Pact monolithism, with the peculiar consequence that the city is alternately hailed and excoriated by architectural traditionalists. Accordingly, for a certain type of architectural critic or historian, Warsaw is irresistible. It is the road not travelled (at least in the West) – a city where, instead of Modernism, we got a dignified reconstruction of the old world.

In fact, neither of the famous statements – total destruction, total rebuilding – is exactly true. Recent research makes clear that the 85 per cent figure includes a great deal that was severely damaged but not irretrievably destroyed, and reconstructors were selective. Astonishingly, late-nineteenth-century buildings that had survived were actually being *demolished* in the early 1950s. It is also clear that the reconstructed city frequently took huge liberties with the historical fabric – given what had happened, how could they possibly not have done? And having spent a lot of time in this oddly almost neglected part of the Polish capital, it's clear that the Modernist objection to the place – as a Disneyfied simulacrum of interest only to tourists – isn't quite right either. New-Old Warsaw is above all a place of paradox. A project of the Communist Party,[4] it is loved by nationalists; the only 'authentically Polish' part of Warsaw, it is anything but authentic. An architectural historian, Marta Leśniakowska, caused something of a stir in her authoritative *Architecture of Warsaw* for the dismissive tone with which she described the rebuilt city; buildings are 'vaguely inspired by' particular historic buildings (while plaques affixed to them assure you that this *is* that building); one of the most ostensibly successful parts of it, the rebuilt neoclassical 'Royal Route', has 'façades loosely reminiscent of the buildings destroyed in 1944'.[5]

Moreover, it is a particularly strong piece of evidence against the proposition that Postmodernism was a product specifically of capitalism, of the 'End of History', as here you can see a government that by all accounts saw itself as fulfilling *the will of History*, utilizing every one of the four orders of simulation described by the philosopher and occasional architectural commentator Jean Baudrillard in 1981, in his *Simulacra and Simulation*, a pivotal text in defining the suddenly ahistorical, retro-oriented culture that followed the oil crisis in 1974. Baudrillard defined these as the 'first order of simulacra', where you have a faithful copy which claims to reflect something entirely actual and real, although it admits that it is not the 'original' of that real thing; a 'second order', which is an inaccurate copy, where we are aware of some foul play, some distortion; a 'third order', where you have a 'copy without an original', although this completely decoupled copy still claims to be something in some way faithful and real; and a 'fourth order', where there is no longer any adherence to any kind of fidelity or veracity, but only a 'sign', something which makes references to 'real' stuff but has become completely free-floating, unashamedly artificial.

It is this sheer inauthenticity, and the propagandistic trimmings that are visible only slightly below the surface that are part of what makes the Old Town interesting. But we're already conflating several different things when talking about the 'Old Town'. It represents a spin on three distinct phases in the actual development of the real Warsaw once upon a time. There is the Stare Miasto, the Old Town, the original walled city, largely from the sixteenth century, enclosed by rebuilt walls; there's Nowe Miasto, the New Town, built in the Baroque era as an extension to the original;

and the Trakt Królewski, the 'Royal Route', a largely eighteenth-century neoclassical artery that reaches from the edge of the Old Town for a couple of miles before dissolving into an indistinct district of villas and embassies. Seen that way, the rebuilding ends at the exact point that Polish statehood does, with the swallowing of Poland by its neighbours in the 1790s – but at the edges of that a couple of neo-Renaissance streets of the middle of the nineteenth century were also rebuilt, so in practice the rebuilding stops at the point where what in Britain we'd call 'Victorian' architecture begins, with its façadery and eclecticism – ironically enough, given that the practice of Socialist Realist architects so often resembles Victorianism itself. This also had the consequence that the area of Warsaw most completely destroyed – the northern districts turned into the 'Warsaw Ghetto' by the Nazi occupiers, which were levelled in their entirety in the aftermath of the Ghetto Uprising in 1943 – is not even slightly reconstructed, being instead replaced by a Socialist Realist showpiece, a slightly cut-price equivalent to MDM; only one extremely short street of brick tenements survives as a tangible remnant of what was once the biggest Jewish city in the world, and the memorials that have been built there since – beginning in the 1940s with Nathan Rapoport's moving Socialist Realist Monument to the Ghetto Fighters – are surrounded by buildings that have no pretension to 'speak' of what happened here. To be fair, how could they possibly – though evidently the choosiness about what parts of the city should be preserved could be interpreted as being about more than just architectural discrimination.

What was rebuilt is intensely scenographic, as it should be given that it was notoriously based as much on the eighteenth-century paintings of Bernardo Bellotto, one of the painters who used the brandname 'Canaletto' – who took a fair amount of historical liberties even then – rather than on documentary record. It is all based on the 'correct' way to see the various ensembles of spires, columns and gables – but for our purposes in this book the best way to reach the Stare Miasto is via the Trasa W–Z, a west–east promenade that was very much part of the project, and was later lined with tower blocks. Its sandwiching function gives its name to a still-produced local cake. Even before the edges of it started being filled with high-rises in the 1960s, it was a project far from the traditional notion of historically scrupulous reconstruction, where if you must do it, you must use as much as possible of the original fabric and

Trasa W–Z, the motorway under Warsaw Old Town

street plan. Instead, in order to make the whole apparition of the destroyed city's re-emergence into something functionally viable, a road was cut under and across it. The city's 1950s Victory monument, a standard piece of Stalinoid angry-yet-maternal womanhood, was moved here in the 1990s from its former position in front of the National Theatre (rather than being demolished), to the point where she now seems to guard the reconstruction.

Then, if you're in a car or on a tram, you get to a glowing, tile-lined underpass, as modern as can be inside but clad to the exterior – to the scenic view – in heavy masonry, as surely the Polish–Lithuanian Commonwealth would have done had it built motorways. There is, however, a pedestrian route to enter the Old Town from ground level as well, and it is equally unexpected: an underpass with a connecting escalator, which is, rather amazingly given the non-building of the much-trumpeted Warsaw Metro in the 1950s, a directly transposed piece of the Moscow Metro in Warsaw. Literally so – the project was partly designed and built by employees of Moskva Metrostroi, and there are inscriptions in Russian if

'Moscow Metro', Warsaw Old Town

you know where to look. The lamps are Soviet in derivation, showing that peculiar heaven-in-the-bowels-of-the-earth style that was fundamental to Soviet underground systems. The statues, too, are of, first, the People's Army, and, second, the builders, who are always also the Builders of Communism. Both sets of statues are under glass panels, very probably to stop them from being vandalized – this protection is also very unexpected in a country which prides itself on anti-communism. Entering the Old Town via this route you emerge from 1950s Moscow into seventeenth-century Warsaw.

The vestibule for the 'Metro' is a reconstruction of the florid Baroque 'John House', visible in one of the most famous of the 'Canaletto' paintings of Warsaw, and it doesn't seem particularly affected by its posthumous transformation – reincarnation? – into an escalator leading to a motorway, with a public toilet attached. As we know, the Warsaw Metro was cancelled when the relatively reformist Gomułka regime took power, Gomułka considering it an expensive vanity project. He was keen on building a lot of housing, fast: hence those towers along the Trasa

The 'Metro' vestibule at the 'John House', Warsaw

W–Z. The General Secretary wasn't particularly keen on historical reconstructions either, allegedly declaring that the Royal Castle – left out of the original reconstruction, as a matter either of expense or residual fidelity to socialist ideas about monarchs and their palaces – would be rebuilt over his dead body. Its rebuilding was completed a couple of years after he died. It is hard to imagine the Old Town without it, with its strangely flat pink front façade and soaring, distinctively Slavic verdigris spire. It was built in 1976, although unlike many of the other reconstructed buildings, it doesn't declare the year of (re)construction on it, and it appears as a much more obviously historicist venture, scrupulous and sober – the first order of simulacra, as if confidence in the illusion had lessened somewhat, so that the little visual clues as to the real date had to be toned down. There was little of that in the 1940s and 1950s. What is most striking is that the reconstructions from the Stalinist era are just a lot more fun.

When the reconstructed Warsaw is praised, it's usually the Old Town Square which is meant – a giant cobbled expanse, surrounded by a jagged skyline of sweetly marzipan-like Mitteleuropean buildings, with a market inside. This impressive visual effect, like a real civic hub, a real town centre, means that for the neophyte it is easy to mistake it for the Polish capital's agora, its heart, and to extend this to the Old Town itself. It didn't take long staying here and living with a Varsovian to realize that it is no such thing. The Old Town has no Metro station, no tram stop save for the one at the other end of the Moscow Metro. It has no facilities other than museums, antique shops, (relatively) expensive restaurants and stalls with knick-knacks – though there is one solitary milk bar to be found if you look hard enough. The centre of Warsaw, in terms of where Varsovians go to work, go to bars and nightclubs, shop and promenade is defined by the Modernist geometry of the Eastern Wall, Stalin's 'gift' of the Palace of Culture and Science and the Futurist Central station – all nearly a mile away – and aside from the Royal Route little of the reconstructed city is regularly used by people who live here. This place is an adjunct, an oddity, divorced from the city's everyday experience, and hence is surely the 'Disneyland' city centre that it is often accused of being. But, again, appearances are deceptive. The reason why this place is so quiet is that these tenements were built as public housing. The often elderly residents don't like noise, and so block any attempt to bring the din that usually signifies 'liveliness' into the old city walls. It is quiet not because it isn't a 'real', lived place, but because it is.

Returning to Baudrillard's inadvertent description of New-Old Warsaw, it is worth noting that the reconstructed eighteenth-century classical buildings along the Royal Route are usually from the First Order of Simulacra. They were 'high architecture' when built, and so some of them actually have blueprints, named architects, or details that must be reproduced in order for the buildings to really convince as reconstructions. They are more often the remaking of something that already exists, as faithfully as the technology allows. The earlier, sixteenth- and seventeenth-century buildings didn't really have an original, or at least not in the sense of something unchangeable – these tall, dreamy tenements, with their fairy-tale skylines of attics teetering in tiers to provide extra storeys, had been constantly added to and remade over the centuries, so the 1950s could, while remaking them, feel free to do much the same. These are the second order of Stare Miasto Simulacra, where the designers have had some fun in adding completely mid-twentieth-century rooflines, mosaics, sgraffito, reliefs, murals, signs and other extraneous things which don't pretend to be from some earlier age – except perhaps for the more universal one of childhood. The buildings are vividly coloured in a panoply of blues, purples, oranges, yellows, with scuffed, worn bits that look as if they've been deliberately beaten about to look older. The applied art is strongly reminiscent of the animation of the era, the cut-out and montage films by the likes of Jan Lenica and Walerian Borowczyk, or the illustrations common then in children's books. These cute, angular forms are hardly comparable with the heroic workers of Socialist Realism. Elsewhere, they're straightforward abstraction of various kinds, either slightly disturbing dismembered bodies, bits of neoclassical sculpture arranged at random, or, on some tenements, a move into lush, shimmering abstraction, with mosaic patterns in flying polygons forming a continuous frieze midway up a neoclassical house.

These cute fantasies of builders, maidens, fairies, mermaids and suchlike are charming, but it is a mistake to think that they are entirely separate from the ideology. Look at the two sgraffito pieces adjacent, and you realize that they are propaganda of a sotto voce kind. Both are flaking away, but one much more than the other. The one in better condition bears the Latin title 'Varsovia', and shows the city of the seventeenth century, with the Vistula filled with ships just behind it. The other, flaking at so rapid a rate that it may be illegible by the time you read this, depicts the Stakhanovite bricklayers who were reconstructing that city, and at record speeds. They're in the same cartoonish style as all the Little Mermaids and sprites, but much less well-restored, as if the socialist provenance – or even the fact it was built, in the twentieth century, by workers – were best forgotten. Step into the courtyards of some of these blocks and you find that they have the paraphernalia of mid-century mass housing – there is even a long deck-access block of flats at the Old Town's southern corner, where the dressing as a Renaissance arcade is fooling nobody.

The third order of simulacra in the Warsaw Old Town is Mariensztat, a place which really didn't exist before, but which is aesthetically completely of a piece with the earlier orders of simulacra that make up most of it. There were houses here, on this steep hill that curves down to the Vistula, but they bore no resemblance to what is there now, which was completely replanned on a new pattern by the communist authorities. This, not the blaring Stalinism of MDM or PKiN, became their first showpiece housing estate, built, as Marta Leśniakowska points out,

Before, 'Varsovia'

'using socialist competition methods', i.e. via an ideologized, pseudo-socialist version of payment by results (but what results!). The approach, visually, is exactly the same as the Old Town itself. The paint, now worn enough to almost look convincingly historic; the winding streets; the

After, 'Warsaw'

cobbles; and the sgraffito, which here too is surely the cutest thing ever implemented by the Six-Year Plan of an iron-fisted Stalinist regime. Mariensztat opens out to a large public square, with another very pretty bit of trimming (this time a mosaic clock, to designs by Zofia

Czarnocka-Kowalska, responsible for some of the most charming artworks in the Old Town) at the corner. If being unkind, one could point out that this is not a style massively unlike that of Nazi architecture at its more vernacular and *völkisch*. What makes it most unlike the Nazi aesthetic is that strange, out-of-place ultramodern cutesiness. Not the cutesiness of the carefully worn, and higgledy-piggledy, but of the very 1950s, wholly-of-their-time clocks, paintings and drawings. The inspiration seems to come a little from Warsaw's one-time Prussian *Gauleiter* E. T. A. Hoffmann, with inanimate but harmless things coming to life. It is surely the most unlikely response to mass murder in the corpus of public art and city planning. Warsaw had, and still builds, gigantic monuments to its heroism, self-sacrifice and fortitude, but here everything is Lilliputian and pretty. The impulse seems to be comparable to that of post-war Modernism – the urge to shake off all of that horrible weight of history and instead create something light, joyous and dreamlike. But that modernity is applied; the casual visitor would still assume that he's in a real old town which happened to have been subject to a very progressive public art programme.

The satellite dishes that line the houses might imply that those within the Old Town simulacra have other fantasies and simulations to think about, and that the fourth order can be found there, on their TV screens – but, actually, you can find it in a large housing estate just round the back of the Royal Route, off the lovely Nowy Świat ('New World') Street, built, like the Modernist and Socialist Realist estates of the same era, by the public housing body ZOR. The houses along the main arteries, Nowy Świat and Krakowskie Przedmieście, are the first order, claiming (if not always accurately) to reproduce an original, which is often signposted by plaques. Historians have shown how this tasteful reconstruction, with its uniform roofline, actually replaced a much more chaotic, capitalistic street of mixed heights, blanketed with ads and signs; and the way that it joins onto the more standard Stalinist boulevard of Aleje Jerozolimskie shows again that consciousness that a 'scene' is being created; on one side, the 'new', in the form of the domineering headquarters of the Polish United Workers' Party, a starkly authoritarian edifice; and on the other, the heritage, whose artifice is here signposted for the only time along the Royal Route, via a Modernist mosaic of communist guerrillas and the legend 'THE WHOLE COUNTRY BUILDS ITS CAPITAL'. It tells you just at the entrance that what you're seeing is a construct, and then leaves you to it. But this development, the central street of which is rather tellingly named after Winnie-the-Pooh (or *Kubusia Puchatka*, as he's known in Polish), is completely fictional, and unlike at Mariensztat the sleight of hand is far more obvious. While quite happy to reproduce a facsimile of the grand curving street of the Royal Route, the planners of

Old World aesthetics in the New World estate, Warsaw (1960 postcard)

post-war Warsaw were less keen on reproducing the typical cramped courtyards behind – they shared the aversion to these spaces, with their unflattering contrast of handsome front and miserable back, with the ideologists of the modern movement. Behind the frontages are low-rise tenements with pocket parks in between.

Many of the details have, like much of reconstructed Warsaw, a small-town feel that sits strangely in this metropolis of nearly 2 million people. There is a little tower with a smiley sun on it that drags us almost into Poundbury territory, so cloying is the reference to provincial *Gemütlichkeit*, without the hints of Surrealism that you find in the Old Town. The arcades that run through the blocks feel Socialist Realist in their incongruity, rather than being derived from some kind of indigenous tradition; at one end of it all is the Ministry of Finance, a Sovietized Art Deco block with reliefs of heroic workers charged with the task of electrification, and at the other a symmetrical, stepped eight-storey block with historicist details. What makes it feel particularly peculiar is the way that the blocks of flats straddle the roads that lead out towards the 'real'

Historico-socialist tenements on Winnie-the-Pooh Street, Warsaw

centre, with (at the time) its mix of ruins and Socialist Realism or (now) its glass office blocks. The roads that take you out of the simulacra run underneath. This doesn't happen once, but twice, so when looking out towards the rest of the city you see instead a series of grand arches giving way to nothing. There is only one real precedent for this, and it is the Stalinist Potemkin city at Tverskaya; and the architects are quite clearly drawing attention to this fact. And as a place to live or to grow up in, this was and is quite something, combining all the virtues of centrality, urbanity, greenery and streetlife, plus those archways are now often closed to the public on the Royal Route, which gives it something of the air of a gated community, one of Warsaw's many – a sad but apt fate for an estate designed for the top level of apparatchiks, Stakhanovites and court writers. It is as lovely as it is unreal.

The other question is whether or not there is a difference between the 'unreal' old towns of Gdańsk or Warsaw and the 'real' old town of a city that avoided total destruction. If you compare the Stare and Nowe Miasto of Warsaw with the old town of Lublin, an eastern Polish city near the borders with Belarus and Ukraine, one of the most important cities of the Polish–Lithuanian Commonwealth, you can find several aspects that contrast sharply. For one, perhaps unsurprisingly, you find that a real old town is also often an exceptionally poor town. The squares, gateways and streets of Old Lublin are exceptionally pretty, and also exceptionally strange. More than in Warsaw, there are several traces of the unusual forms the Renaissance took when it was adopted in Poland, the free hand that designers had in the absence of actual Roman precedent nearby to draw from; there is, in short, a lot less in the way of good taste. There are many of the ornamented attics that Lev Rudnev transplanted onto the tops of his towers in the Palace of Culture and Science, and there is ornamentation and statuary of a deeply weird order, chubby little figures that are no longer Gothic but very far from the realistic forms of their Italian inspiration; there are sgraffito patterns that give way to bare brick when the plaster flakes off. Historically and architecturally it is fascinating, but many of the houses and tenements are in a state of advanced disrepair, to the point where some would by now surely have to be replaced rather than renovated. Enter one of the courtyards and you don't find thinly disguised mid-century public housing, but an age-old squalor.[6] The best view of the Lublin skyline is from a dodgy street market in a derelict

The poverty of the real: Lublin Old Town

interzone. How strange, when the simulation is scrupulously maintained and the 'real' left to rot.

CREATIVE DESTRUCTION

The great counter-example to Warsaw is the city of Kołobrzeg, in Pomerania, western Poland. This Hanseatic port city was given a drastically reduced form of reconstruction much closer to the then-current Western model. The result is deeply strange but, in its peculiar way, rather instructive. Although it was founded as part of Piast Poland in the early Middle Ages, for most of its history Kołobrzeg, or rather Kolberg, was a German port. Like most port cities on the Baltic coast it had, by the time of the Second World War, a great many brick Gothic buildings, such as a remarkably blunt, brutal cathedral and the usual clutch of towering warehouses, ornamental customs houses and merchants' tenements. It even had a town hall designed by the great Prussian neoclassicist Schinkel, although designed in a neo-Gothic idiom. These coexisted with the infrastructure of a resort town, with hotels, pensions and villas, and a linear park screening a sandy beach from the city itself. It was the site of the March 1945 Battle of Kolberg between the Wehrmacht and the combined forces of the Red Army and the Polish First Army, which caused a nearly Warsaw level of devastation, with 80 per cent of the city destroyed. Unlike in Warsaw, even the untrained eye would spot very easily indeed that there was no serious attempt to reconstruct the destroyed city, which was instead the site of an extremely brusque form of town replanning.

Around 1930, during the most radical era of Soviet planning, it was proposed by some that central Moscow should be transformed into a park of monuments, with practically everything else demolished for its lack of historical or aesthetic worth. The city centre would be an expanse of trees and green space, in which you would be able to find such picturesque things as the Kremlin or St Basil's Cathedral, while the real life of the city went on somewhere else entirely, in a series of 'disurbanized' collective settlements. It's very unlikely that the Polish planners who administered post-war Kołobrzeg were specifically thinking of this when they started to rebuild the city, as it passed into their hands when the Polish borders were shifted sharply westwards, but their practice closely resembles this apparently absurd theory from the high utopian moment of Constructivism. A clutch of buildings that were accepted as of truly historic value were indeed rebuilt, as they were in nearby Gdańsk – the town hall, a couple of Hanseatic remnants, and the unromantic, pugilistic hard-man Gothic of the cathedral – and everything else was abandoned. Many of the northern, formerly Prussian cities that Poland had obtained via the Yalta Conference were ransacked for bricks to be used in the reconstruction of Warsaw, and Kołobrzeg was no exception. Not much new was built to fill in the huge gaps left by urban warfare, until in the 1960s the city was subject to a two-pronged redesign. Along the coast, the German bourgeoisie's villas and grand hotels were replaced with a series of Modernist pensions and sanatoriums, just as in Jastrzębia Góra, aimed at particular groups of workers and administered by their state-run trade unions – and a surprising number of these are in good condition today. Inland, around the centre of the historic city, panel housing was built on an enormous scale, giving much of it the appearance of being a microrayon with a cathedral in the middle.

We found this out, as most non-residents must, when taking a holiday in the first part of the 1960s reconstruction, in one of the many large and architecturally dramatic hotels built around what is by any standard an exceptionally nice beach, its sand so white and soft it looks almost like snow. Around here, there are several signs of the ideological underpinnings of this project of erasure. One of these multistorey hotels, now the Hotel Baltic but built as the House of Combatants, was previously a sanatorium for Polish army veterans, though you wouldn't know from its attractive, if generic, form of Costa del Sol Modernism, all rippling concrete façades and deep balconies. There are various little pointers to the hotel's former function in the statues scattered around the gardens, a sort of historic 'ascent of the Polish soldier', from fourteenth-century knights through to Soviet allies, although in all cases with an unnerving robotic cast to their features. Further along the beach a little is a monument by the sculptor Wiktor Tołkin, commemorating the 'marriage to the sea' that Poland's First Army enacted upon victory in spring 1945, in the suitably unsubtle symbolic form of a phallic sweep upwards with a deep

House of Combatants, Kołobrzeg (1984 postcard)

arched hole below, framing the sea. In a similar pebbly sculpted concrete to Arka Pana, it also features a strange alignment of historic medieval soldiers (from the last, distant time that this was Polish territory) and the Red Army, in a set of inscriptions in the concrete that resemble the brushstrokes of cave painting, plus the usual set of robotic Soviet warriors.

Coming in conjunction with the city's main museum, an almost untouched early-1980s showcase dealing mainly with the Polish and Soviet armies, their weaponry and their battle to seize this place in 1945, the entire reconstructed town can often feel like one large and triumphalist war memorial to the historic struggle between the Slavs and the Teutons, coexisting strangely with a resort whose cheapness and proximity to Germany, Denmark and Sweden ensures a lot of Teutonic tourists. It doesn't seem to deter anybody, and merely survives as a bit of curious and largely ignored monumental colour. What it does is make clear that here, a certain purgative act had to take place before the city could be remade, an act claiming it not only for a new regime, but for a different nation

Dom Handlowy and cathedral, Kołobrzeg

entirely from that to which it (and its ethnically cleansed population) had hitherto belonged. However, the 'old town' is the most weird and fascinating part of this project, and, given that, Agata and I boggled at one of the most interesting components mid-demolition in summer 2014. In front of the cathedral, a glass shopping pavilion, whose exposed, tapering structural concrete columns have some logical relation to the Gothic principles of the original building. There is some architectural intelligence at work in the way its horizontal rectangle relates to the vertical rectangle of the cathedral itself, but the avoidance of any stylistic resemblance and the undignified cheap and cheesy pop-Modernist design of the signage are an obvious obstacle to any attempt at making reconstructed Kołobrzeg feel like a 'real' old town.

A much bigger and far more obvious obstacle is the fact that the tiny reconstructed fragment is surrounded by immensely long prefabricated slabs, which unusually for Poland have yet to be renovated – although if they're given the brightly coloured styrofoam cladding common elsewhere they'll be even less 'in keeping' with the cathedral and the town hall, whereas today their grimy grey has at least the chromatic virtue of staying in the background. In Poland, flats like this are seldom demolished – in the UK, they'd be the first target of the 'regenerators' – so this will remain, very probably, the defining feature of the city centre, keeping a working-class population close to the mixed population of tourists that settle here in the summer. However, if they couldn't demolish it, subsequent architectural and political regimes have tried their utmost to make sure new development – first public, and more recently private – has doffed its cap to the city that was wiped from the map in 1945. A reasonably coherent grid of streets was built in the interstices between the heritage and the slabs, with a 'vernacular' aesthetic of fake half-timbering and neo-Hansa brickwork. Parts of it are quite pleasant, with cafés, a library and open courtyards which make for a pleasant if slightly parochial townscape. But given the way that the city was indelibly defined by the construction of ten or so gigantic concrete slabs around a medieval cathedral, it is worth asking why they bothered – short of an equally sweeping demolition programme, this is one reconstruction that will always be defined by a bullishly unromantic, anti-historical approach, which no matter how hard the city tries can never be screened from the eyes of tourists. It does pose the question of whether there was a possible

A view of Kołobrzeg 'old town'

alternative between the straining for historical delicacy and tributes to national endurance that you can find in Warsaw, and the ferocious disdain for someone else's history so conspicuously on display in Kołobrzeg. That is, was it ever possible to rebuild a historic city in a modern, socialist and historically respectful way?

CREATIVE RECONSTRUCTION

Like Socialist Realism itself, reconstruction in Central and Eastern Europe was as brief as it was intense, and was similarly succeeded by Modernism, with all that entailed; the argument of this book is that the way prefab estates seem more dominant here than in the West, where they began, is by and large the consequence of industrialization and a massive wave of urbanization more than anything expressly ideological. That noted, what is conspicuous about later communist regimes like those of Edward Gierek or Erich Honecker is a simultaneous love of grand projects which displayed the apparent efficiency of their economies and a concurrent lack of ideology with regard to aesthetics. Gierek, unlike Gomułka, was fine about both building castles and building concrete panel blocks of flats; and Honecker would be the sponsor both of one of the largest, if most debased, Modernist public-housing projects in history, and of one of the first attempts to return (again) to 'national heritage' in architecture. East Berlin, especially, saw a wave of reconstruction and outright simulacra in the 1980s, and architects and theorists in the USSR and Poland were among the first to start reversing the effects of the Modernism they'd (re-)introduced barely twenty years earlier. This is seemingly a puzzle, another paradox, especially if we cling to the view that the actions of these states were myopically determined by ideology. They were quite content to build thousands of towers from panels and to reconstruct sandstone and stucco edifices at once, and without seeing any apparent contradiction. In fact, in the case of East Berlin, they began to reconstruct those sandstone and stucco edifices out of the very same concrete panels they were otherwise using to make starkly reductive workers' housing.

As so often between 1945 and 1989, the first theoretical advances here were made in Poland, which in the 1970s was much more open to influences from the West – the main architectural journal, *Architektura*, even published parallel texts in English during that decade, when the norm was to be bilingual in Polish and Russian. The Western reaction against monolithic, bleak Modernism – via such writers as Jane Jacobs, Kevin Lynch and Aldo Rossi – was a regular feature; and, perhaps oddly, Polish architects were not making the point that they had anticipated these theories several decades earlier under Stalinism. The generally de-ideologized context of these discussions is striking for anyone expecting *diamat* and dogma. The absence of much consideration of Poland's very recent experience of urban traditionalism is also explained by the fact that this time, the question was often one of rehabilitation rather than rebuilding. In a special issue on 'The Revaluation of Historic Cities', mainly consisting of short case studies on the renovation of various historic towns, Zygmunt M. Stępiński advocated reconstruction and rehabilitation rather than destruction or newbuild, for reasons psychological (the encouragement of identification), patriotic (the national heritage, again) and for the preservation of the historic record. But he was aware that another human factor existed, too. 'The revaluation problems of historic cities become also problems of their inhabitants. Attempts at reconstruction of historic buildings as apartment houses of high standard, undertaken in some European countries, undoubtedly wrong this part of the poor population which, attached to their place of living, would like to remain in the quarter. Such attempts lead also to social monoculture, to selectivity. Nevertheless, certain social melioration of revalued districts is necessary in principle; in particular it concerns removal of a-social individuals who often devastate the buildings thoughtlessly.'[7] What is being advocated here, in 1978, in a 'socialist country', is what would later be known as gentrification – the revaluation, in late-European and American capitalism, of a historic area often achieved by the removal of its unpicturesque current inhabitants. A guest essay by Pier Luigi Cervellati, of that PCI bastion Bologna, 'Innovation or Conservation?', which asks: 'Why the towns of the past?' and answers, rather oddly: 'The whole town belonged to the residents and constituted the common property, governed and utilised as a whole . . . the town was never divided by class and hierarchy, as today it is.'[8] Bear in mind, again, that this is a writer in a 'socialist' magazine claiming that cities were more equal under feudalism or early capitalism than in the late twentieth century. Moreover, 'the contemporary town, whether we like it or not, does not express the population, which resides in it, any more: it is the mechanical realization of a few more or less successful designs carried out by economic, bureaucratic and administrative authorities . . . citizens do not want the contemporary town, and they flee from it.'[9] He argues that they flee not to the old towns, but to the suburbs, though the implications of this are not pursued. Elsewhere, the Polish architect Jan Maciej Chmielewski suggested throwing out functionalist dogma entirely, at the time in which system-built estates like Ursynów were under construction. 'Prefabricated elements make it impossible – to a considerable degree – to imitate the old forms', and to this the architect should respond by ignoring the notion of 'truth to materials' altogether – 'use of traditional materials in the perimeter walls in historic developments should be obligatory, even if it means insincerity toward the building construction. Only in this way can the local colour be preserved.'[10]

This continues in another special issue, this time on 'The Scope of Rehabilitation', where the project has even extended to undoing the mistakes of the Modernist planning that wasn't even in the past at this point, featuring among its examples several projects to increase legibility and colourfulness in concrete panel estates, alongside the more expected images of pretty gables and cobbles. This time the enemy is not just building new, but especially building new next to the old, something which became popular after 1956. In a dialogue that takes up much of the issue, Jerzy Kuźmienko criticizes the glazed extension to the neo-Gothic Warsaw market hall Hala Mirowska – much admired in its day, and admired now by Warsaw's Modernism aficionados – 'a sound building from the Tsarist era which even bombs were not able to destroy was absolutely destroyed artistically', and the editors reply: 'That's how it was in the sixties. In those days the rule of contrast between the old and new architecture promoted the neglect of any rules of continuity in architecture'; a continuity that now begins to sound particularly Prince Charles-like. What is different here, in the year that disgust with the inequalities of state socialism helped spawn Solidarity – the foreign-currency shops, privileges and grace-and-favour housing enjoyed by the nomenklatura were particular targets – is an emphasis on at least some attempt to explain why things might be different in the East. An editorial comment points out that the continuous changing of the built landscape may be Modernist, but is not necessarily communist – 'allowing a house to be downgraded when the originally planned exploitation period has passed is contrary to socialist principles'.[11] Somewhat more darkly, Adam Andrzejewski points out, in reference to the already raised issue of gentrification, that '[in the West] modernization is usually connected with the exchange of residents. Our way is different – we provide the residents with temporary lodgings and later – the apartment the modernization of which was very expensive, for free.'[12] That is: we in Poland can't do this, because we can't afford to embark on something so complex and prohibitively priced as a total renovation of historic cities according to the socialist system of massively subsidized housing. Yet this all comes to pass in its richer neighbour, the German Democratic Republic. Except here they did it their own way, creating in the process one of the least influential, if most peculiar, urban experiments in the era.

Right in Mitte, the centre of Berlin, just round the back of the giant 1960s Modernist showpiece of Alexanderplatz, on the banks of the Spree, is a place called the Nikolaiviertel. It is not an obscure part of the city, although much here depends on age – it is popular with older tourists, but

Prefab townscape, Nikolaiviertel, Berlin

has a conspicuous absence of the picturesquely dishevelled youth culture that otherwise dominates the eastern districts of Berlin. You approach it from the 'Red Rathaus', the nineteenth-century town hall, which like a lot of Berlin's Wilhelmine public buildings suggests the confident, throw-taste-to-the-wind civic architecture of northern England. From here there is a wall to the street of prefabricated concrete panels – a familiar sight in East Berlin even now, where what Rudolf Bahro scornfully called the 'hallowed' panel[13] still has a ubiquitous presence. There is something else afoot, however – an almost Gothic arcade to the ground floor, which is visibly also made from precast concrete. Walk under the pillars of the arcade, noting the historicist lamp-fittings, go round the corner, and you find this concrete wall now has balconies inside – so it's public housing, OK, not so surprising – though the amount of restaurants on the ground floor is certainly unusual, as is their völkisch tone, with a smell of dark beer, sausage and sauerkraut. From here, you may be much more surprised to find you turn off onto a cobbled street. The cobbles are accompanied by ironwork street signs with Gothic script and wrought-iron shop signs, but the buildings themselves remain as concretey as concrete can be – the concrete panels are decoratively 'ribbed' with rough vertical strips, something which will be familiar to most people who've ever lived in or visited a late-1960s housing estate. But on top of each of the blocks now is a 'feature', in the form of either hipped roofs with red tiles or, most bafflingly of all, full-scale stepped gables, constructed from exactly the same bare, ribbed concrete panels as the rest of the scheme, albeit with little crowns and motifs on top.

Walk around these little streets and you find that they're arranged around a stark Gothic church, with all the streets aligned to create picturesque partial views of its two sharp twin towers in Hanseatic style. But go into the Nikolaikirche and you're in an art gallery rather than a religious building, with various sculptures and reliefs left around as if at random, in a Soane Museum-like pile-up. Leave the church and wander round through the arcades and you'll note they're filled with souvenir shops, traditional German eateries with remarkably convincing 'historical' interiors, and attractions, such as the Zille Museum, which showcases the work of Heinrich Zille, the left-wing cartoonist, photographer, pornographer and chronicler of proletarian life in the early-twentieth-century capital. The cafés and *Kneipen* all have terraces, and this is one of the only places in Berlin that really uses the River Spree, its calm thin flow neighboured by tables, chairs and gabled concrete. There are even a few 'real' historical buildings in here too, neoclassical tenements and Biedermeier houses.

By now you've obviously worked out that what is happening here is a construction, that it isn't a 'real' part of the historical city or even a 'real' part of the Modernist GDR capital. Instead even the most obtuse tourist is surely aware that this can't have borne any resemblance to some actual development of the past, even though the little brochures on sale in the souvenir shops describe the Nikolaiviertel as the 'oldest', or 'first', part of Berlin. Go into any of the courtyards of the blocks of flats and, aside from the relative tightness of enclosure, you could be in a peripheral estate like Marzahn, a grid of concrete panels filled with playgrounds and trees. There are even parts of it that are expressly Modernist. Go full circle back to the entrance from the main road to the cobbled alleyway and look around. In front of you is a restaurant whose façade is cast in black metal, with bulbous glass windows. Behind you, above the restaurant-filled arcade, is a continuous cast-concrete sculptural frieze. Look at these figures in low relief and you can see some familiar historical scenes – the workers of Berlin in the nineteenth century and, more expectedly from the GDR, revolutionary scenes from the socialist uprisings in 1918, 1919 and 1923. It doesn't stop there, though, but carries on through the Battle of Berlin, with the Red Army waving the red (well, here, grey) flag over the ruined city, with planes overhead and the Brandenburg Gate in the distance; the words 'KPD' and 'ROTE KAPELLE' (the communist spy ring under Nazism) are cast into the scene. A fleeing mother carries a

Panel heroics at the Nikolaiviertel, Berlin

baby with her. But soon after that there are rallies, the building of a new city (the TV tower looms over the masses), even waving cosmonauts; and, of course, a worker hauling a concrete panel into its place in a new apartment block. Practically the only aspect of East Berlin's history not featured in here somewhere is the construction of the 'Anti-Fascist Protection Rampart'. At the end of it demonstrators crowd around an emblem emblazoned with the years '1237–1987'. So what on earth is this place? An Old Berlin theme park constructed from the only viable material, the precast panel? An experiment in socialist Postmodernism? An elaborate joke?

Nikolaiviertel was the most extensive and certainly the most extreme example of a city-wide return to familiar urban virtues to coincide with Berlin's 750th anniversary in 1987. On both sides of the Wall (albeit more famously in the West) left-wing movements began to revalue and defend the demonized Berlin *Mietskaserne*, and large areas where they had survived – Kreuzberg in the West, Prenzlauer Berg in the East – were eventually subject, after much lobbying and protest, to what was called 'careful urban renewal'; and this *Altbau* movement soon inspired a *Neubau* one to fill the divided city's many holes, which would conserve the character of the city rather than replace it with serried blocks in space, as had happened in the 1950s and 1960s. The Western version of this *Neubau* movement was very well known in its day, in architectural circles – Interbau 1987. Under the direction of the architect Josef Paul Kleihues, a remarkable quantity of famous world architects – Aldo Rossi, Álvaro Siza, John Hejduk, OMA/Rem Koolhaas, Rob Krier, Peter Eisenman and, in her first built project, Zaha Hadid – were set to work building council housing. The results are justly renowned for the way in which they used the same scale as the historic city – four- to five-storey tenements on infill (i.e. bomb) sites, usually with shops on the ground floor – without ever feeling the need for the patronizing 'references', smug historical jokes and the general fear of modernity or social advance that marked Postmodernism in, for instance, the US and UK. There, in the form of the both pompous and bumptious work of Terry Farrell or Michael Graves, it was the cancellation of social democracy and its future-oriented town planning; but, in West Berlin, Postmodernist housing was the result of public pressure, of social movements, and perhaps this is part of the reason why the architecture feels 'progressive' rather than fearful.

Kleihues called this approach 'critical reconstruction', and exactly the 'critical' aspect was lost after 1990, when his ideas were adapted into the neo-Prussian building programme of Hans Stimmann, where the same concern with filling gaps and urban context was combined with an imposed architectural order and palette, with the legislated imposition of thin veneers of stone onto everything. In an amusing but surely completely inadvertent historical irony, the best of the built results, such as Hans Kolhoff's haunting Walter-Benjamin-Platz, resembled not so much united, historic nineteenth-century Berlin as a more luxurious, less crude and unsophisticated version of the town planning of 1950s East Berlin. By contrast, the 1980s redevelopment of Kreuzberg in particular left one of the most clever and unpretentious concentrations of public housing and architectural experiment to be found anywhere in such a small area. Nikolaiviertel and its related developments along Friedrichstrasse or in the 'Spandauer Vorstadt' on the other side of Alexanderplatz are quite clearly and consciously the East Berlin spin on all this, and maybe in this they are not flattering – goofy, ingenuous, kitsch, and much

Neo-Stalinist United Berlin: Walter-Benjamin-Platz

more obviously Postmodernist than the Interbau in their use of obvious 'references' to old Berlin, extending to Gothic signs, beer halls and cobblestones. However, closer attention suggests the architects knew exactly what they were doing here – the creation of a dream space, a part of the city that was deliberately set at a remove from reality.

The architectural historian Florian Urban argues that these old-Berlin-in-panels projects were designed to illustrate, not contrast with, a vulgar Marxist 'progressive' view of history. The bourgeois heritage was there to be reclaimed and placed in a lineage with the apparent coming to power of the proletariat. There was a prehistory to this – in the Stalinist era Berlin, like Warsaw and Leningrad, was to some degree rebuilt, particularly along Unter den Linden, where what Urban, like Leśniakowska, regards as 'loose' and 'interpretive' approximations of its classical apartments were erected along the processional artery. Here, as in Warsaw, you wouldn't know the fakery unless you were expressly looking for it. Not everything was retained, particularly if it strongly evoked imperial Prussian power – the old imperial palace, the Schloss, was salvageable but nevertheless demolished, and the statue of Frederick the Great was removed in 1950. It was put back exactly thirty years later. This may have been the fruit of a 1976 state resolution to 'preserve or recreate the architecturally valuable of the past', in consequence of the successful tenement rehab projects in Prenzlauer Berg a couple of years earlier – though an early-1980s article in the design magazine *Form und Zweck*, Urban notes, was officially censured for stressing the role of public action in the reclaiming of the area – only the state was apparently allowed to take action. And, arguably, the state-sponsored rebuilding projects stand in contrast to the informality of the public rehabilitation of old areas – lumbering, kitschy, still insisting on that bloody concrete panel.

Smaller concentrations of this can be found particularly near Friedrichstrasse station, the main crossing point of Western tourists into East Berlin, and their combination of rigid traditional urbanism and concrete panels is not particularly lovely. Neither is the infill of large holes in Spandauer Vorstadt, a series of affluent streets west of Alexanderplatz and south of the Volksbühne, with concrete tenement blocks, by a large team of architects including Iris Grund, Manfred Hartung and Martin Navratil. These are not pretty, but they are imaginative, disproving the Polish theorists by showing that you can do all sorts of things with a concrete

Hipster *Plattenbau* at Spandauer Vorstadt, Berlin

panel, including negotiating the irregular corners of an unplanned urban area. To the ground floor these tenements are not 'Old Berlin' but residually pop-Futurist, with their shop windows emphasized by angular, colourful decorative surrounds, and in some cases there are gables with decorative motifs.[14] They show an aesthetic wanting to have its cake and eat it, with both a return to traditional urban verities and a relentless insistence on form following function. The Poles recommended hiding the real construction materials with contextual masonry or stucco, if you had to – the East Germans evidently considered that a step too far.

Irony, though, could be pushed quite far in the architecture of the late GDR. These gable details, Urban notes, were chosen according to the place the work teams had come from to work in Berlin – entire firms of building workers from all over the GDR were hired to reconstruct the capital in the 1980s. So the gables of those tenements whose concrete panels were assembled by workers from the north had neo-Hanseatic details, and so forth. Here, at least, it's hard not to think that the designers and their sponsors were pushing their luck, or, more bluntly, taking the piss. Some architects of the 1980s certainly were, and pushed their luck even further – one team of young designers were actually imprisoned for proposing a 'watchtower' in an architectural competition for a playground in Bersarinplatz, from which the children could be 'shot' if they tried to 'escape'.

Nikolaiviertel is the place where all these ironies – in Postmodernist parlance, these 'complexities and contradictions' – were put fully on display. It was, unusually for the GDR, the project of a single architect, Günter Stahn, who liked it so much that he moved in immediately. He consistently denied any connection with Postmodernism, with its opposition to 'Grand Narratives', and did not seem at all bothered by the fact that the area was loomed over by an immense Futurist TV tower. Reconstruction – and some of the Nikolaiviertel's buildings, such as the classical Knoblauchhaus and the Nikolaikirche were once 'real', and were re-created in such a way that the illusion was not immediately obvious – was acceptable, according to Stahn, if buildings were 'alive as *pictorial memories* in the consciousness of the people' (my emphasis).[15] Memory, as Stahn was fully aware, is not the same as history or archaeology – it is not a discipline or a science, but it is selective, distorting, and heavily influenced by the present context in which you are recalling the past. To create a more precise duplicate, Stahn wrote, would be 'dubious nostalgia' for a 'seemingly unambiguous' past – and the Nikolaiviertel is certainly not unambiguous. It presents all at once medieval Berlin, classical Berlin, imperial Berlin (not those of the rulers, but those of Zille's lusty proletariat) and socialist Berlin, all of them distinct and visible. It respects the intelligence of the visitor by mixing both obvious artifice with careful archaeological reconstruction, production-line modernity with craftsmanship, nostalgia with 'progress'. What seems at first like a Fordist mania, an almost psychotic insistence on the panel, even when remaking a historic district, becomes instead an experiment in historical perception.

It is also today rather notably the most obviously 'normal' part of central Berlin, with a near-total absence of the international creative class, strikingly so given the process that they began in the rest of the Mitte district, where artists followed by the really wealthy took the area over block by block. But what was an architect doing moving into a concrete-panel estate anyway? Florian Urban claims, and it would tally with what the Polish theorists had already advocated, that the gentrification of East Berlin began with the movement of rehabilitation and reconstruction. He argues that the appreciation of Old Berlin – as opposed to the new high-rise periphery – was 'a mark of distinction' among the city's left-wing intelligentsia. If the high-rise suburbs were a universal project, then this was much more selective, as 'in the 1980s, East Germany increasingly blatantly allocated new comfortable apartments to selected citizens' in the city centre. This should not be overstated – the rent controls were still so strict in East Berlin that the phenomenon of rising rents pushing out working-class residents was still inconceivable, and the new periphery had a much greater social mix than its Western equivalents – but it does suggest that when the Eastern Bloc turned to a less 'universal' approach to architecture, it also did so socially. The movement towards reconstruction and rehabilitation was still fresh at the time of the 1989–91 collapse, so there are few other obvious examples of it – but it certainly had a presence in the capital of the Latvian Soviet Socialist Republic.

Riga is one of those cities, like Budapest or Glasgow, which appears to have been forcibly stopped in 1914 – then one of Europe's most advanced industrial metropoles, but relatively neglected over the century since. The result is that it has a certain steampunk aspect, the feeling of what was once extreme modernity kept for ever at the point of possibility. Streets of grand tenements are left only half-way completed, with their wooden one-storey precursors giving them the look of gap-filled teeth; industrial areas are cutting edge for 1910, with factories designed by the most important architects of the day, like Robert Maillart or Peter Behrens. Some – albeit hardly all – of this would have been swept away as part of the urban renewal accompanying the unbuilt Riga Metro, but today only cars, a couple of microrayons, the odd bit of Modernist infill, a couple of bland Postmodernist office complexes, a far higher unemployment rate, and a layer of dirt and dust conceivably separate much of the city in 2013 from that of a century earlier. As most of its development happened before the advent both of the Soviet industrial revolution and of Modernist urban planning, what it presents to the walker is some absolutely superb street architecture, all of it designed to catch the eye of the pedestrian, all of it designed according to strict street lines in order to maximize profit. The majority of this is in that international Belle Époque idiom called alternately Art Nouveau, Secession or (in Russia and Spain)

'Modernism'. And much of that is like Art Nouveau anywhere else, with the same flowery surrounds, the same howling masks, the same lovely ladies draping themselves across the stucco façades. The leading architect of this style in Riga was Mikhail Eisenstein, father of the great film director, and Sergei's scorn for the kitsch façadery of this work is mostly rather justified. It is all surface, 'decorated sheds', as the Postmodernists would call it, with little interest in the defining of space, inside or out, or in the texture or tactility of material. It's fun to look at but forgettable. It was immediately succeeded, though, by two very similar styles which local historians call 'Perpendicular Art Nouveau' and 'National Romanticism', which are far more original and vigorous.

Because of this, Riga is a fabulous city for walking and for getting deliberately lost in, although you'll seldom find anything of interest in the 'active frontages' of those ground-floor shops. We spent hours in Riga wandering through its grand boulevards, trying not to think about how much they've gone to seed, or about how many of them house branches of the charity shop Humana (sometimes including the original stucco details, with portals leading to racks of old shirts), and stopping at the odd vaguely hipster café (one of which was graced with a collection, in English, of L. Ron Hubbard's fictional works). The most interesting of its architects, like Eižens Laube, Ernests Pole and Aleksandrs Vanags, were masters of creating street space – corner towers, turrets, bays, archways, arcades, all of which serve to give character and direction to the arteries and sidestreets. As these architects were 'National Romantics' one might assume a hoary conservatism here, but, as with the baronial borrowings of Charles Rennie Mackintosh, they seem to have used the medieval architecture of a peripheral country as a springboard into modernity – something which usually happened in the flamboyant treatment of corners. At Pole's apartment block and photographer's studio on Aleksandra Čaka iela, the corner is formed of three tall cubic towers with similarly square bay windows, in grey stucco; the ground floor and part of the second are overtaken by raw, mock-medieval caveman rustication. In Vanags' apartments on Blaumaņa iela, the corner has morphed into a stretched, phallic dome, held up with a single Egyptian column to the street. Or in Laube's apartment complex on Brīvības iela, an assemblage of gables and deep pointed roofs is pulled into weird asymmetries, with the windows alternately stretched into the sort of vertical strips found in skyscrapers, or emphasized in peculiar miniature bays. You can follow these sorts of experiments into the German Expressionism of the early 1920s, with its wildly morphing forms, and into its adaptation into the streamlined Modernism of Erich Mendelsohn – and there are a few worthwhile Mendelsohn tributes in the sparse interwar additions to the boulevards. It also shares certain values with the Socialist Realism which takes over from it in the city's northern edges, albeit with a much less felicitous use of ornament. But was there any way that the more staid, production-line aesthetics of Soviet Modernism could have accommodated it?

The surprising answer was yes. As with anywhere else, the aspect which even apologists had to concede was not terribly pleasant in capitalist urbanism was the divide between grand façade and miserable courtyard. In one redevelopment scheme in Grīziņkalns, a working-class suburb, the courtyard of an Art Nouveau apartment block has been erased, and undemonstratively replaced with a series of Modernist blocks of flats, with more considered public spaces, large windows and right angles. Neither part is anything special on its own, but it was very surprising indeed to find the two coexisting, bolted onto each other, rather than being placed in intractable opposition. There are also places – particularly the Royal Hotel in the Old Town, built between 1987 and 1992 – where the inspiration seems to have been the prefab historicism of late-1980s East Berlin, a slightly ungainly Modernist contextualism. Elsewhere, though, it appears more like West Berlin was the example, a deployment of 'critical reconstruction' that mostly avoided the obvious, and that generally had little interest in the evocation of memory. The huge Agroprojekts office building in the Maskavas District, to 1979 designs by Juris Skalbergs, is a case in point – it follows historical street lines, but is otherwise confident, almost Brutalist, with a rigorous grid of curved concrete window-frames, an industrialized Gothic. Surrounded by dereliction as it is, it appears as part of a doomed attempt to modernize this area of dilapidated wooden houses and lost tenements – unusually via street architecture rather than blocks in space. The Aeroflot offices on Brīvības iela, a 1986 design by Modris Ģelzis, is in the Art Nouveau heart of the city, and adopts the approach set in the 1910s, hard onto the street with a demonstrative corner. Dolomite-clad volumes surge towards a bulging turret, culminating in a glazed cube. No nostalgic reference to be seen, nothing

National romantic apartments in
Aleksandra Čaka iela, Riga

National romantic apartments in
Blaumaņa iela, Riga

Soviet contextual offices in the
Maskavas district, Riga

Soviet contextual offices in
Brīvības iela, Riga

'in keeping', but nonetheless part of the street, following all of its unwritten rules. This could be contrasted with the Latvian Arts Theatre, constructed from 1959 on to designs by the architect Marta Stana. Like the 'social condensers' in Vilnius it is an original, elegant Modernist building, but it steps back very deliberately from the street into green space. A little further up the same long boulevard, you get to a tenement complex in red brick and tile, made up of three sawtooth-roofed towers, all of them with concrete balconies into which reliefs (of fighting lions, of all things) have been set – from the emulation of urban Art Nouveau into full Postmodernism, albeit of a particularly vigorous and strange variety. The swiftness and comprehensiveness of the reaction is surprising, as if the quality of the existing urban architecture were obvious to younger designers.

As an architectural project, the informal 'critical reconstruction' of early-twentieth-century Riga is a striking, unusual success. As a social project, the results are a little more predictable. There are several apartment complexes of the 1980s which return to 'the street', often in brick rather than stone or stucco, making a similar use of well-defined urbanism and faintly heraldic towers. The effect, curiously, is closer to that of Red Vienna than Belle Époque Riga, a simpler, more monumental approach to street architecture; on Krišjāņa Valdemāra iela there is a 1980 complex whose grand, if stark, volumes were built to house 'high-ranking communist Party members'.[16] There's a similar 1986 complex on Miera iela, one of a couple of mini Karl-Marx-Hofs built as part of the reconstruction of an incomplete pre-First World War district. Here the tall corner tower is much more obviously emulating the likes of Laube and Vanags, and contains among other things 'exclusive two-level apartments'[17] on the top floor – the spaces were classed, much as the old tenements were. It is depressing to learn, in all this, that West Berlin was actually more capable of providing city centre public housing than East Berlin or Soviet Riga, although even then it's worth remembering the rents would have been much less of a portion of a tenant's income. Something about the return to the bourgeois past in city planning made it accompany the return to class forms of urbanism, more a sign of a loss of ideological and political conviction and control than a sign of the adaptability of the system. The only real difference, maybe, between these schemes and their successors – like the dull neo-Prussian tenements of reunited Berlin, or the thin, tacky commercial Pomo of independent Riga – is their relative architectural quality.

ENDLESS RECONSTRUCTION

This would be borne out by the way in which several cities just can't stop reconstructing. Riga itself contains one of the more distressing examples of this, in the form of what was originally the Riflemen Square, at the heart of the old town. The only building here which really attempted to express the present at the time it was built was the Museum of the Red Riflemen, dedicated to the (many) Latvian soldiers of the first war who joined the Bolshevik side in the 'Russian' Civil War, but now the Museum of the Occupation. A monument to the Riflemen still stands at the heart of the square. We'll consider the ideological contents of this place in a later chapter, but as an urban object, it is strange, stark, almost windowless, made up of dozens of copper panels, as murky and dramatic as the events it (originally) described. It was surely deliberately ascetic and hermetic in its context, looked over by Riga's panoply of spires; that has been severely redressed since 1991, as the entire square has become the showcase for a very uncritical reconstruction. First, in 1995, the 'Blackhead's House', a seventeenth-century Dutch-style confection of richly ornamented red brick gables destroyed in 1941, was rebuilt; then another war casualty, the eighteenth-century Town Hall, was rebuilt in 2000; and this was accompanied by 'Kamarin's House', a small office block very loosely based on a bombed mid-nineteenth-century townhouse. This ensemble makes for a very eerie space indeed. It can't just be the fakery, since we've seen various kinds of subterfuge resulting in enthralling or at least intriguing urban spaces – it's more the total failure of imagination. The Blackhead's House is the best of the three, largely because it was obviously such a spectacular building to begin with, an example of the most over-the-top northern Baroque; look closely and you can see how cheap it is, with thin stucco details, but as with Warsaw it doesn't matter greatly. This one really is a reconstruction – someone has just copied out the older details and reproduced a facsimile as best they could. The Town Hall is vaguer, more Disney-like, and it draws attention to its illusion with a visibly glazed roof; the materials are so thin they resemble plastic.

Uncritical reconstruction in Riga: capitalist to Stalinist from left to right

Kamarin's House, though, is the pits, a tacky Pomo office block that would disgrace a provincial town. The argument is clear – after the Soviet Occupation Riga once again becomes a Great Historical City.

Where all the skill and wit its architects displayed in the 1980s and early 1990s disappeared to is one question, and its unthought-out relation to the real architecture of the Occupation is another. Look around the square for a moment, and you find two gabled apartment blocks of the early 1950s by Stalinist skyscraper designer Osvalds Tīlmanis, and on the other side of the Riflemen, the Riga Polytechnic by the same architect. Neither bears any resemblance to any previous structure on the site, but their bouncily inaccurate evocation of Hanseatic Old Riga is considerably less witless than the contemporary version. It may be the slight hint of dishonesty in the appeal – we know and the architects know that the Soviet Occupation was not the unmitigated disaster for the city they claim it is, and we know that its heritage was not always badly treated. But Josef Paul Kleihues or Günter Stahn could have fingered the real culprit – the appeal is not to the particular qualities of a city's structure, its housing, even its memory, but to the alleged authenticity of a 'real', uncomplicated past, to the Good Old Days – a move which is always, in all circumstances, reactionary.

Although it ostensibly had no 'Occupation' to react against, Moscow, to the cheers of Simon Jenkins, has been furiously indulging in something similar, in tandem with the revaluation of its Stalinist, if not Modernist, heritage – hence the reconstruction of the Cathedral of Christ the Saviour, that bland, pompous Victorian hippo; and hence also the remaking of Red Square, closing up the tanks' old entrance and rebuilding the diminutive, complex Kazan Cathedral that was cleared out of their way in the 1930s. Meanwhile, the Stalinist practice of taking an extremely interventionist approach to conservation continues – much as a department store was transformed into the Lubyanka and old buildings on Tverskaya were hoisted into the air, so contemporary Moscow is full of 'sham replicas', where two- to four-storey palazzos become components in massive oligarchic streetblocks, which ape their style and detail.[18] The depressing sense of reaction taking over a city can be found all over the former Soviet sphere; the generous can say it's a reaction to the twentieth century's traumas, the ungenerous that it's a handmaiden to the often extreme nationalism that came with independence. Either way, like much nationalism it is based on fantasy more than history. The Macedonian capital of Skopje, for instance, a city rebuilt in high-Modernist style in the 1960s after an earthquake, has been building the historic capital that never actually existed here, filling it with various faux-Hellenic architectural knick-knacks; attempts to conserve the reconstructed city, an internationally significant project by the Japanese architect Kenzo Tange, are meanwhile neglected or ridiculed.

One city, though, is permanently under reconstruction, an endless project to restore what once really existed. Dresden is a permanent historicist building site. The first to be remade was the Zwinger. This joyously perverse palace of the arts, with its provocative figures, fountains for frolicking and trompe l'oeil effects, was surely the most erotically charged piece of architecture ever (re)built in the GDR; by the 1980s, with the completion of the Opera House's replica apparently ending the East German authorities' thirty-year reconstruction effort, around a mile or so of Baroque along the Elbe had been put back together, often in a dark, blackened stone – enough to make it once again a tourist destination.

When we visited at the end of 2013 I sat and waited in a café as Agata perused the branches of Humana, and got into a conversation with an elderly German gentleman. From the windows of the café we could see two very large public buildings; one of them, the Palace of Culture, designed by Wolfgang Hänsch, Herbert Löschau, Heinz Zimmermann, Dieter Schölzel and Leopold Weil and built in 1962, and the other, the Frauenkirche, designed by George Bähr in 1743 and rebuilt in its entirety in the early 2000s. Contrast aside, I wasn't surprised he wanted to talk about the church – 'When do you think it was made?' His was quite a typical story of eastern Germany – born in 1943, he left Silesia with his family when it was annexed by Poland. Since retiring, he had started visiting the now-Polish city where they had lived, and on the way regularly stopped to see the progress of the restoration. By now, long complete, it was a part of the landscape, an inextricable part of the skyline. I wanted to talk about how things were different in Coventry, but when he assumed I wanted to tell him off for what happened there ('I was born in 1943, you know'), we changed the subject.

Palace of Culture, Dresden

Frauenkirche, Dresden

What happened in Coventry, when it was subject to what Goebbels called 'Coventrieren', was not only that its cathedral was destroyed, but that it was left as a ruin, and a new cathedral built next door in alignment to it. Similarly, bombed churches were left as ruins, as permanent memorials, in bombed towns like Plymouth, Woolwich or my hometown, Southampton. I've always admired this gesture, not just for its display of the consequences of barbarism (i.e. its showcase of the now-fragmentary beauty of what was destroyed) but for the way it is based on a refusal to forget – something which does not preclude other reactions, as with the legend 'Father Forgive' in the ruins of the old Coventry Cathedral. Dresden's post-war planners evidently thought the same of the Frauenkirche, leaving it as a vast fragment, until reconstruction – planned already in the mid-1980s, under the GDR – began. Partly, it is noted, it benefited from the financial assistance of the Queen . . .

There are many things to admire here, if you want to. The Frauenkirche was a spectacular structure, a great bulbous Baroque dome, and it clearly adds to Dresden's skyline. The designers of the reconstruction left in as many fragments of the ruin as they could and made them highly visible, so that the church rises from a charred sandstone base, and is pockmarked with salvaged 'original' stones. It is not, then, as total a nothing-ever-happened-ever gesture as the Cathedral of Christ the Saviour in Moscow. I can't help preferring what Coventry did, though, and that may have more to do with the context it is in than the church itself. The area surrounding the Neumarkt is in that reductive, neo-Prussian style so beloved of contemporary German architects, bloodless and thin-lipped. But it's the Palace of Culture next to it that spurred the bad thoughts. This enormous glass concert venue, as open, optimistic and confident in the possibilities of industrial society as the Royal Festival Hall, is also being restored. Among the things they're touching up is the mural that takes up a large part of the façade – another succession of scenes from the German labour movement, with Marx and Engels, Luxemburg and Liebknecht, insurgents of 1848 and Spartacists of 1919, all picked out in red and brown tiles. Red stars and hammer and sickles abound. Elsewhere – Riga, for one – things of this kind would be ruthlessly erased, but in Germany, as we've found, the survival of a residual socialist tradition in West Germany paradoxically means they're usually better treated – even restored. Socialist architecture too is of historical value, in some cases. A lot was demolished in Dresden after the Wall came down, but the basic structure of the GDR centre was left in place.

It begins near the railway station with the mini-magistrale of Prager Strasse, with its serried blocks of hotels (the Baroque tourists could get

Reconstructed Dresden mark II: Prager Strasse (1973 postcard)

a good view from up here), many of which still have their original pop-Futurist concrete patterns and ground floor mosaics, though many of the department stores and ancillary buildings (with their murals) have been removed. Everything is relentlessly clean and tidy – if I may be so Basil Fawlty about it, the comparison with the bird-shit-encrusted neglect of remade post-war Coventry could make you ask who exactly won the war. After Prager Strasse, you come to the Altmarkt, which is made up of two immense Socialist Realist blocks – one extremely long, one only very long. A relief panel at the start of them places the labour movement in the lineage of the city, with an inscription telling of its history, achievements, uprisings and myths, culminating in 1955 with the completion of the first Five-Year Plan of the German Democratic Republic. The relief sculptures that are interspersed with the inscription combine the sauciness of the Zwinger (the bare-breasted woman in chains, poking her tongue out – what is her role?) with the monumental heroics of Soviet workerism. It's heady, all this.

The stated opposition of Socialist Realism to the 'decadent' Baroque of the likes of the Zwinger (and in this case, for once, the word was well used) was ignored, and Saxon Baroque details pervade the arcades, balconies and attics of these blocks. Especially with the intensity of the 'old-new' all around, you could easily mistake these for 'real' Baroque apartment buildings, as the narrowness of the street prevents you from seeing their Socialist Realist bloatedness of scale. Restoration is heavy here too, but of a strange new sort, as careless of the 'real' original buildings as was the Nikolaiviertel. All the plaques are still there, including the ones which tell you about how great the GDR leadership was for rebuilding the city, but walk into any of these apartment blocks, past their relief panels of heroic gender-balanced workers and peasants, and you find that this whole complex has become the façade for a steel and glass shopping mall – something especially shocking in Cafe Prag, a lovely

Reconstructed Dresden mark I: Altmarkt (1966 postcard)

Socialist-Modern-via-Socialist-Realist creation whose central staircase reveals a vertiginous view of the mall inside. That's not all – what looked, earlier on Prager Strasse, like a typical abstract-façade GDR department store is actually entirely new, with its steel ornaments merely a tribute to the old East German *Kaufhäuser*. The endless historicism, the incessant proliferation of simulacra, reaches here its extreme, swallowing Socialist Realism and GDR Futurism into its maw. All of it, practically, is one gigantic shopping mall. The same happened in Coventry, of course, but there the results are squalid. Here, everything is shiny – the bizarre insistence that everything be at once historical and at the same time incredibly, gleamingly clean.

The fastidiousness of all this is more than a little unnerving – this need to always clear away the ruins, to make it clear that nothing bad ever happened here (and that we never did anything bad). There are war memorials aplenty, but the scars that war leaves on a city are more quickly erased in this part of Europe than any other, as if the relatively extreme destruction evoked a relatively extreme reconstruction.

Ruins of the Ministry of Defence, Belgrade

The cataloguers of the Ruins of Socialism or the Ruins of the Future are usually being wistful about post-war buildings, well outside anywhere that tourists might be looking. The result is that it can be a shock when you stumble upon the actual results of war in the heart of a historic city – suddenly, it isn't so picturesque. At the heart of Belgrade is a Modernist building by the veteran architect Nikola Dobrović, designed in 1963 for the Socialist Federal Republic of Yugoslavia's Ministry of Defence – two twin blocks, stepped downwards like ziggurats, working as a ceremonial entrance to the city from the main railway station, well detailed, red tiles alternating with bands of white concrete. Regardless of the fact it might have won some architectural awards in some no-longer-extant country or other, this was the heart of 'Milošević's War Machine', so was an obvious target in the bombing campaign of 1999. Belgrade's poverty, and the building's listing, means that there has been no attempt to repair it in the fifteen years since then, so it lurks there as a bombed-out wreck, perhaps again serving a ceremonial role – welcome to Belgrade, where we have actual ruins!

There is, in post-war and particularly post-1989 Eastern and Central Europe only one reconstruction scheme which follows the precepts for conservation set up by John Ruskin, William Morris and the Society for the Protection of Ancient Buildings; and without wanting to be chauvinist, it is very telling that it is the project of a British architect, the classical-Modernist David Chipperfield, along with the conservation architect Julian Harrap. During the GDR, Berlin's Neues Museum, a late part of the strongly neoclassical 'Museum Island' built up in the Prussian capital, sat as a war-ravaged wreck waiting for restoration. By 1989, plans were already under way to restore it as closely as possible to its original appearance. Unusually, the 1990s saw a rethink in favour of experimentation rather than the continuance on a bigger budget of East Germany's crude historical literalism that so characterizes Dresden. That isn't to say that this was unpopular – in fact, there was a major 'traditionalist' campaign waged against the new proposals. What Chipperfield and Harrap advocated was building around the ruin, rather than building the ruin out of existence – stabilizing the structure, adding new sections that did not ape the old, restoring but not filling the holes in the building's embedded artworks, and rehousing the museum's collection of Egyptian, Greek and Roman sculpture and miscellaneous ancient artefacts in a series of redesigned rooms and vitrines. This was too radical for many, and it is in many ways surprising that Chipperfield won the battle over his redesign of the Neues, so sharply does it contrast with almost all contemporary practice. Finally, here is an engagement with the past that is devoid of literalism, sentimentality and kitsch, and that respects the visitor's intelligence – though it's certainly not devoid of romanticism.

The exterior of the building, with its colonnades and its not particularly wonderful neoclassical façade, has been filled in at various points with a thin, rough brick, to roughly the same colour as the surviving sandstone, but easily identifiable as newly built and separate, while continuing its outline. Inside, the museum's original fittings had a touchingly literal imperial and Victorian penchant for illustration – every room had frescoes which depicted the era that the artefacts came from, so as to fill in the gaps in the imagination left by the fragmentary nature of these statues and remnants. This is completely reversed in Chipperfield's building, as the frescoes are themselves left as fragments – restored, to be

The Rise and Fall of the Great City of Berlin, Neues Museum

sure, but with massive gaps left by bomb damage. In fact, this rather fits their melodramatic visual rhetoric, their depiction of fallen civilizations at their bygone apogee; it is hard not to remember the fate of the Thousand-Year Reich and its 'theory of ruin value', although the building predates the Nazis by several decades. A hostile observer could argue that the ruin-romanticism of this approach consecrates the nineteenth-century approach to the depiction of historic civilizations, making it more affecting and poignant than it might be if restored to full kitsch detail. However, Chipperfield's other interventions, like the thin glass vitrines, the complex, atmospheric lighting and the insistence on showing how everything has been made, on revealing the nineteenth-century brick coursing behind the mock-Byzantine arcades, are harshly at variance with Nazi and Victorian practice – everywhere you can see the joins, and you are supposed to. In that it is a Brechtian building, baring the monumental device and revelling instead in transience, change and the unheralded skills of the working mason rather than the classical artist. It speaks of more socialist values than any reconstruction effected by the German Democratic Republic. It is, however, alone.

The Neues Museum reconstruction is in every way exceptional. Elsewhere, the story is more mixed. As we've already implied, a return took place to certain very laudable virtues of the past – varieties of style and surface, a city which invites exploration, a conception of a city as an emotional rather than merely functional thing – but, in practice, it often led to an uncritical embrace of the past, a shrinking away from modernity, and eventually, solace in local chauvinisms. Maybe in different political circumstances, this could have had different results, as it did to some degree in Berlin and in Riga. What can't be escaped is that the second wave of reconstruction (after the 1940s and 1950s) from the 1980s onwards happened to accompany a real restoration. In most Eastern and Central European countries, the land nationalizations of the 1940s were repealed after 1989, with the result that property owners were allowed their sites back. All over, schools have been closed to make way for speculative office blocks, tenants have been thrown out of their apartments – in an unusually considerate move, there were even special blocks built by the Tallinn municipality for victims of restitution[19] – and in extreme cases, those who have fought back, such as the Warsaw tenants' rights campaigner Jolanta

Brzeska, have been the victims of assassination.[20] Depressingly, in cities that once had a large Jewish population, 'the Jews' have sometimes been blamed for the results – anti-Semitism, as ever, being the socialism of idiots – but this other reconstruction has not gone unopposed. As it is, in ownership as much as in architecture, the tradition of all the dead generations weighs especially heavily here – 'like a nightmare on the brain of the living'.[21]

7
Improvisation

I want a left-wing city, a constructively destructive, diffusely coherent dialogue about the perils of being human; a brazenly contemporary afterworld that is not only thought but also thinking itself; where city planning is a war of liberation fought against dumb, featureless squares, where city dwellers transmit their secret wishes to their possessions, line their bodies with memories, have jurisdiction over their organs, wrest from space new possibilities, and immerse themselves in their culture. The fragile structures of the city are regularly repeated messages from a misshapen void, aimed at our incorporeal mother who in the hall of possibilities plays a cheap little ditty about time and space. Over precarious and crumbling heaps I want unexpected, slender shapes, whose ever-growing possibilities question their own viability – a city that its citizens use to debate and make love in. Through the language of objects they can communicate with the dead, and on their door-knobs shake hands with vanished forebears. I want a city where only what joy guards remains, and where the traffic of innovations is never choked off. I want streets where the eyes of passers-by reveal that something happened to them: they twitched in a spasm of existence and stretched out in lukewarm death.

György Konrád, The City Builder *(1977)*[1]

THINGS THAT AREN'T THERE

Take a train between any large Russian cities, and stare out of the window at that notoriously flat and 'spiritual' countryside, and you'll find something rather unexpected. If you didn't know better, you'd assume that the 'disurbanist' city advocated by the Constructivists in 1930 had actually come to pass. A surprisingly large amount of land is given over to a carpet of tiny, prefabricated villas, which seem almost to cling to the railway line, offering a clear view, revealing how many of them derive from a handful of standard designs – a folksy wooden house, a more modern, monopitch-roofed villa – spread out in irregular sets of streets, never rising above the population of a village, but also obviously *not* a village. These are dacha colonies, which proliferated especially after they were encouraged by Khrushchev, and they form the flipside of the 'Khrushchevka' prefab apartment blocks. Inside the city, the state provided high-density and, gradually, high-rise housing; outside it, it provided nationalized land essentially for free and a prefab kit to build your own house. Like many Soviet ideas, it is so obviously right and so obviously botched. The dacha settlements did have an absolutely pivotal role in keeping a lot of city dwellers alive in the 1990s, as a place where they could grow food, but as an idea they suggest that a planned economy could be an enabler of freedom, encouraging on a massive scale the sort of unplanned 'plotlands' celebrated by anarchists in the UK. This sort of space is not generally considered part of the 'communist landscape', but ideas like this have always been part of 'communism' as conceived by many communists.

The places described in this book so far were the result of 'the powers that build'. The power in question is sometimes outright personal, the despotic power to reshape cities of individuals such as Josef Stalin or Nicolae Ceauşescu. More often it is oligarchic, the power of ruling parties or more often politburos; and the only forces which it has described that aren't dictatorial or oligarchic are in no way democratic – the Catholic church, more recently the vested interests of property. So given that this book describes the cities built and rebuilt as a direct result of the October Revolution there is obviously something missing – the 'self-activity' of the proletariat described by Marx, which for him differentiated his socialism from that of sundry utopian paternalists; or the direct democracy of the Soviets of Workers' and Soldiers' Deputies, in whose name power was seized in 1917, and which Lenin described – perhaps accurately, at the time – as the highest form of democracy. There is a school of thought which argues that the 'masses' of 1917 were not conscious actors in history, that 'the poor chaps had no idea what was happening to them',[2] that most people don't particularly want to 'participate in history' but would like to be left alone; that, contra Lenin, the cook doesn't want to govern, so should be left to cook. This isn't borne out by the completely autonomous, spontaneous formation of workers' councils and other organizations set up by everyone from the workers of Petrograd in 1917, through to the partisans of Yugoslavia or Belarus in the 1940s, the councils of Budapest in 1956, and the autonomous unions of Gdańsk in 1980. These people, whatever they might have thought they were doing, were practising, in their egalitarianism, democracy, creativity and the restraint of their actions (no wild jacqueries, these), a form of communism, one considerably more admirable than the lip-service ideological automatism of the states that took its name. This isn't a catechism, but a fact – the question, however, is what happened next to this direct, democratic power.

Every act of destruction is succeeded by a period of construction, and it's there, it would seem, that the power of vested interests wrests back control. Accordingly, as we're talking here about construction, we can find extremely little that has directly – instead of residually – stemmed from that 'self-activity of the working class', although of course they are always the ones who have been doing the actual construction. The buildings and cityscapes this book describes are almost all bureaucratically marshalled, built using various forms of labour discipline, from the glorified piece rates of Stakhanovism to the unthinking, mechanized labour of the Soviet spin on Fordism. When we find something different, it's the work of craftsmen, of exceptionally skilled labourers – and, ironically enough, we find much more of that in the most oppressive era, Stalinism, which with its labour passports and punitive factory discipline was hardly kinder to workers. But are there things here that were made by democratic socialist organs, by co-operatives, 'artels', amateurs? Moreover, did the moment of 'freedom' – the apparent release from bureaucratic power and control in 1987–91 – lead to any proliferation of popular creativity, of instant, non-bureaucratic urbanism, or was all that momentum and effervescence quickly absorbed into the new capitalism? In this chapter, we'll try to find out.

The problem with anything like this is its necessarily temporary nature – something which generations of political and architectural revolutionaries have seen as a virtue. This would begin with the 'street art of the revolution' that was so vivid in the aftermath of October 1917. The reinvention by abstract artists of squares and public spaces from Petrograd to Vitebsk, the homemade decorations carried on banners in demonstrations, all of these were as architecturally important as actual buildings, and they often prefigured them – there is a photograph of marching workers carrying a homemade model of Tatlin's Monument to the Third International, and another from the mid-1920s of Moscow workers carrying a model on a placard of Modernist housing. Unlike most architecture, these are in some way forms of self-activity, in which in most cases non-'artists' directly participated in creating space, albeit in a less immediate way than they transformed it in the revolution itself. Something similar happened with the instant spectacles of 1956, 1968, 1980 and 1989 – not only the tearing down of statues, but also the emergence of architects and designers whose work called for public participation: not because they thought it'd be a nice idea, but because the public had moved into the political arena and they wanted to create a form of architecture they could use. Examples of this range from the instant kinetic environments of the Movement group in the USSR to the participatory planning advocated by the Polish architect Oskar Hansen.[3] What almost all of these things have in common is that they were impermanent – although this was necessarily because of the lack of materials, infrastructure and power that would enable them to be made permanent. As always, though, twentieth-century communists have had a tendency to make a virtue of necessity, so to fix them in space would apparently be to commodify or cheapen the pure communist idea.

Imagining what this might look like if made permanent is difficult, because it usually involves a reaction against a particular state of oppression, and hence can disappear if that particular oppression is taken away. One of the most suggestive arguments for permanent improvised working-class creativity comes in the Hungarian Maoist-turned-liberal Miklós Haraszti's account of piece-rate labour in a Hungarian engineering works, in the early 1970s. Haraszti, then still a Maoist, saw the potential for communism not in the Communist Party but in something called 'homers', the products made on the sly by workers for their own enjoyment, or as gifts. Similar things have been noted on production lines in capitalism, of course – I once listened to a former worker at Ford Halewood in Liverpool describe something almost identical – but it's worth following Haraszti's argument in detail. In the context of sweated, uncreative labour, 'for us,' he writes, 'the potential of milling machines, lathes and borers stimulates and at the same time limits our imaginations. The raw material is chiefly metal. The objects that can be made are key-holders, bases for flower-pots, ashtrays, pencil boxes, rulers and set squares, little boxes to bring salt to the factory for the morning break, bath mats, counters to teach children simple arithmetic, pendants made from broken milling-teeth, wheels for roulette-type games, dice, magnetised soap-holders, TV aerials, locks and bolts, coat-holders, knives, daggers, knuckle-dusters and so on.'

This sounds like petty capitalism, making stuff to sell on the sly, but Haraszti disagrees. First, he points out, this is an example of real, spontaneous creative labour, because the decision is always made by the worker himself. 'In place of the order "you make that" comes a question, "what can I make?" But if this work is an end in itself, it is not thereby without a purpose . . . the worker who makes a "homer" uses his head and keeps his eyes open . . . it is the only form possible of free and creative work. The tiny gaps which the factory allows us become natural islands where, like free men, we can mine hidden riches, gather fruits, and pick up treasures at our feet.'[4] The 'homer' also has its own distinctive aesthetic. 'They are created out of junk, from useless scraps of iron, from leftovers, and this ensures that their beauty comes first and foremost from the labour itself . . . were it not that "homers" have to be made in a few snatched minutes, then one could claim that there were two schools: the first "functionalist", the second "secessionist"' – that is, some display their skill via an economy of form suggestive of Modernism, others do so via their decorative detail. The significance is that this all occurs in a factory where 'altruism is rare' and, perhaps more tellingly, the product is never sold. 'Black labour after factory hours' making things for the 'informal' market (as we call it nowadays) is a different, paid thing, which workers do not discuss and aren't particularly proud of – 'homers', on the other hand, are achievements that the workers talk about and ask other workers for help with. Finally, for Haraszti, 'these two steps towards the senseless – producing useless things and renouncing payment – in fact turn out to be two steps in the direction of freedom', the 'Great Homer' that he imagines taking place in a future without alienated labour. We are a long way from the Great Homer – further away, for all the advances in automation, than Haraszti was – but there are flashes of it, including among the places mentioned already in this book. The Monument to the Sleepless Metro Worker in Universitet station on the Kharkiv Metro is an exemplary homer, albeit perhaps a sardonic one, made out of waste by workers when they could snatch the time.

We will not find many Homers in this chapter, but we will go in search at least for the improvised and informal. We will tread carefully, as the cult of the informal is a pernicious part of architectural ideology – as if crazed by having to spend their day jobs designing luxury flats, trading floors and wonky art galleries, contemporary architects have an obsession with squats, shanty towns and 'informal' commerce, whether it's Rem Koolhaas marvelling at the non-state (but certainly not non-mafia) networks that make up the infrastructure of Lagos,[5] and everyone else marvelling that in India's enormous shanty cities like Dharavi in Mumbai, as the Dead Kennedys sneered in 'Holiday in Cambodia', 'the slum's got so much soul!' The poverty of much of Central and Eastern Europe, especially the former USSR, means that there is a lot of 'informal' urbanism to goggle at and marvel at the creativity of. Whether this 'informality' constitutes political activity or just a straightforward, understandable and wholly unromantic means of survival is an open question, although you will by now have worked out where I stand on it. First, then, we'll turn to the more banal versions of improvisation – the stuff people have done in the aftermath of crisis to create some space, to make a living, when the state and the Party have abdicated.

ANARCHIC ARCHITECTURES OF INSTANT CAPITALISM

Łódź, Poland's second city until it was recently denied the accolade by the haemorrhage of population caused by its de-industrialization, is dominated by two distinct kinds of nineteenth-century architecture: the sort of cake-decoration stucco eclecticism which looks rich and opulent if regularly maintained, which means that in Łódź it looks both dreamy and grim, with the various cherubs and angels subsiding into a goo of bare brick and petrol-smeared plaster; and a castellated red-brick

K67 kiosk as corner shop, Łódź

industrialism which evokes the north of England, as well it might, given that the machinery powering the hulking cotton mills of the late-Tsarist Empire's primary factory town was imported directly from Cottonopolis. The twentieth-century architecture that dominates the centre, bar a small complex of weary-looking Miesian office towers near the closed Łódź Fabryczna railway station, is much more small-scale than either. Dozens and dozens of tiny structures, roughly seven feet by two by four, are placed around the city seemingly at random – sometimes in rows, as if to form a 'street', and often in ones and twos at street corners and junctions. The basic type appears to be prefabricated out of curved plastic. The pieces are riveted together so that you have protruding little bays, with one, two or three curved-bordered windows to serve the customers, which at night are covered with grilles or metal shutters: all this varies, as the standard type is rejigged – you can combine them to create double-fronted kiosks.

As design, they reveal themselves to be products made some time between the mid-1960s and early 1970s, from that *Barbarella* period of pop Futurism where everything was curved, brightly coloured and made of wipe-clean surfaces. They are as standard as the panels the apartment blocks are made of, clearly put together on a production line, and hence partake of the 1960s dream of nomadic architecture, easily transportable, easily demountable, disposable, bright and modern; but – in contrast to most of that architecture – they exist. Unlike the standard apartment blocks, they encourage customization, something which comes with the fact that each of them, however mass-produced, is an individual object. This in itself is not necessarily non-socialist – it recalls, in fact, the pod housing recommended by 'disurbanists' in the late 1920s in the Soviet Union for a mobile, self-directing proletariat. These, though, appear at first to be the response to a sudden injection of capitalism – similar to the wooden 'jaws' that street traders carried around and erected in cities all over the ex-Bloc. They're not, quite.

A little digging revealed that these are actually examples of the K67 kiosk, first created in Yugoslavia in 1966, to the designs of the Slovenian architect Saša J. Mächtig, and produced until the 1990s in a factory in Slovenia, whose clients were largely in the SFRY and in the countries of the Eastern economic bloc, Comecon, although a few were bought in the West.[6] They appear, according to those I've spoken to, to have emerged in Poland en masse shortly before the 'transition' at the end of the 1980s, as a basic form of kiosk in a shortage economy trying to introduce 'market socialism'; they then proliferated in the 1990s. We've found a few in scattered cities around the former Bloc, but mostly they've been replaced by more formal commerce – except in Łódź, where they remain completely ubiquitous. Here, they still have printed on the side the name of the company that provides them to putative traders – 'Lucas Box, Łódź Zelwerowicza 59', with a phone number should you want to order your own – in attractive, late-Modernist bubble-typography.

Given that you'd have to turn them upside down to be able to sleep inside them, these are not for living in – not even in Łódź – but for selling stuff in. Accordingly they're subject to a wide range of different treatments, and are painted up and decorated in a variety of styles. The most basic we found is a kebab shop, where the module is painted red and a sign above the window reads 'Stambul Kebap'; but they come in all sorts. One (derelict) kiosk advertises itself via writing down the sides and a placard on top as selling drinks, cigarettes, drinks, hamburgers and articles, with a little 'Zapraszamy' (in this context roughly: 'At your service') curving upwards at the bottom; this one is painted blue and yellow. Another version, oddly with right angles rather than curves – so the module itself eventually achieved variety – sells lottery tickets; another is 'Bar Saigon', selling Vietnamese fast food (Vietnamese guest workers and their descendants, invited over in the 1970s, are contemporary Poland's only remotely sizeable minority); this one has dragons and a satellite dish. All this you expect to find being sold in small, temporary street and roadside pavilions and kiosks, at least in Poland, where there's a lot of it – the current dominant version, especially in wealthier areas, is a steel-and-glass box branded with the name of the Ruch company. The K67 kiosk, though, which is obviously considerably cheaper, also accommodates less obvious uses – such as a record shop, which is so permanent and rooted to a permanent pitch that it even features its address (Kilińskiego 141, if you're wondering) on its bright-blue façade. It can be dated by the fact that it advertises itself as selling mainly 'kasety'.

As always it's a mistake to see all of this as a 'popular capitalism', the work of the little guy/the 'petit-bourgeois' (according to your politics), separate from the monopolistic monoculture of large corporations – as the transformation of one K67 kiosk into a mobile-phone stand painted

K67 kiosk as record shop, Łódź

orange with a big Orange sign on top amply demonstrates. If they are 'popular' and 'free', it is as always at the point of consumption rather than of production, given that these are almost every time mass-produced goods that are being sold. They do carry a little bit of that promise, though, and there's something quite charming about them, a small-scale unity of Modernist design and customization; and K67s come cheap, cheaper than an actual shop in an actual building, while the module stops them from looking as squalid as the market stalls set up in various interstices from the 1980s onwards. Not that they don't evoke poverty for some, and they're not always terribly popular with city authorities, who are either gradually forcing them out or replacing them with the recent, un-customizable Ruch kiosks. As Poland, for one, becomes more like a 'normal European country' these sorts of spaces are in decline, or at least being forced further out of the city centres. A good/alarming example of this dispersal can still be found outside the department store Universam Grochów, in Warsaw, surrounded with a seemingly endless street market, which, seen from the store's upper windows, resembles a sprawling shanty town spiralling out around the space between high-rises. As pieces of design, the K67 kiosks suggested some possible ways around the dichotomy of desperate vs corporate.

The standard modules of public housing did not exactly encourage improvisation, addition or customization, though, as we've already seen in Vilnius and Warsaw, this hasn't precluded the widespread glazing in of balconies. It's a mistake to see this as solely a reaction to the crushing austerity of system-built housing – it can take hold of any architectural style, any era, any form of housing. It does not discriminate. An exploration of central Kiev, for instance, makes this abundantly clear.

Kiev's incarnation as a turn-of-the-century boomtown has left it with several streets of Art Nouveau and neoclassical tenements – nothing so original as Riga, but interesting and pretty nonetheless. Walk around the centre for a little while, and you start to notice the way that these tenements have often been subject to very radical intervention. In the next photograph you can see a very typical example – a four-storey corner building, its ornamental façade picked out with orange stucco. You can see the original balconies in some places, simple ironwork balustrades from which you could presumably enjoy the balmy summers (when they come) or more probably hang your washing out. A few of these have had their balustrades filled in, so that the space inside feels more 'private' – but there are a total of six balconies that have stopped being balconies, and become rooms instead. All of them have different treatments, from floor-to-ceiling glazing to half-and-half with wood, and some of them already look pretty distressed, their wood in an increasingly manky state. But all it would take is a couple more new room-balconies on the corner, and a remarkable transformation will have occurred – an elegant Art Nouveau tenement will have become a particularly shabbily constructed block of Modernist flats.

Multiple balcony pile-up in Kiev

The balcony constructors are relentless in their inattention. You can see blocks where a giant glass box balcony is pushed hard right up against the usual Secessionist swags, masks and Rapunzels; where the new cantilevered cube is next to an existing Art Nouveau cantilevered bay; you can find one almost funny example of a mammoth new room shoved into the

Balcony surgery, Kiev

front façade of a three-storey neo-Byzantine block, completely transforming it into the sort of architectural joke that gets circulated around the internet. In some, you can find the complete transformation of eclecticism into emergency Modernism – the three bays of one corner building

Extra rooms in Rusanivka, Kiev

have all sprouted boxes, all of different shapes and different treatments, one with curved white-metal mullions, the other two in the usual wood – one eating the iron balustrade, one balanced precariously on top of it. Then there are the more obvious examples – the blank façades of 1920s Modernism don't cause too many problems (though the brick Expressionist Apartment Building for Red Doctors has balconies too angular and complex to be boxed in, and is among the few unrenovated buildings in the centre not to have been consumed by them), the rectilinear tiles applied to Socialist Realist façades accommodate mega-balconies a little bit less horrendously, and of course there are hundreds, probably thousands, of giant room-sized balconies stuck onto the brick-built 'Khrushchevkas' and their concrete successors.

For a certain kind of urbanist, these are all very exciting things – people doing things for themselves! The irregular, chaotic, downright nasty excitement of people taking control of their city! And as the account above probably makes obvious, they are genuinely fascinating in their breaking of all possible architectural rules; and when they're absent, or cleared away, as on the handful of renovated, painted-up Art Nouveau tenements in the centre of Kiev, it's usually part of a land grab, a transformation of space in favour of those who can afford a clean and shiny place to live – i.e. Kiev's population of oligarchs, who are, even more than in Russia, beyond the rule of law and of taxation. But then exactly the same shock capitalism that created the oligarchs (or, rather, that was created by them) gave rise to these super-balconies in the first place – a housing shortage due to the abolition of public housing, overcrowding resulting from same and from the grim legacy of the old Soviet kommunalka, plus the existence, in a totally unregulated housing market, of various dubious, quasi-mafioso bodies that can do the job.

If the balcony surgery in Kiev (or Vilnius) seems purely a matter of anarchic and random individual intervention, the most extreme example of post-Soviet self-built extensions can actually be demonstrated to be the direct result of straining at the limits of the Soviet planned economy. In the USSR, Georgia had something of a reputation for graft – it had the highest standard of living in the Union with one of the lowest levels of economic growth, something sometimes put down to widespread participation in the black market. That's as may be, but in 1985 the Georgian Soviet Republic's construction bureau hit on an exceptionally daring and innovative means of fulfilling the increased mass housing targets introduced by Gorbachev. As one historian explains, 'it was decided to allow and encourage the inhabitants of housing blocks to join together and construct multi-storey additions to their building at their own expense.'[7] This was then added to the announced results of the plan, as official state-sponsored constructed living space. Corruption or libertarian improvisation, as you like.

In any Georgian city, but especially shockingly in Tbilisi, you can see the results. Slab blocks and even towers have all received an extra layer of flats, poking out at odd angles but in an obvious grid. Rather than being total chaos, the extension occurs first when a steel frame is attached to and cantilevered out from the original prefab panel surface, and then, as per the dreams of 1960s 'plug-in' paper architects, residents or 'informal' mediators have constructed into the frame individual units out of whatever random materials are to hand – brick, concrete, sheet metal, corrugated iron. From the polluted, traffic-clogged streets you only see this at corners, but behind almost every block, half to all of the surface

An extra layer of flats eats a slab block, Tbilisi

has been covered with an instant favela, in an improbable, parasitic alliance between Modernist mass housing and shanty self-build. This is, again, the sort of thing radical contemporary architects get very excited about, but it is important to be clear precisely why this happened, and what it means. With the election of former dissidents on a 'Georgia for

Extruding a block of flats, Tbilisi

the Georgians' ticket at the turn of the 1990s, Georgia descended into a ferocious war with separatists in the autonomous provinces of Abkhazia and South Ossetia – something reprised with major Russian assistance fifteen years later in 2008. The result was the total collapse of the Georgian economy and a wave of refugees from ethnic cleansing in the de facto independent provinces. Tbilisi faced a huge housing crisis, alleviated only by these emergency additions to housing blocks, which of course were no longer even slightly regulated, meaning regular collapses and fatalities. Picturesque and bizarre as it may be, the 'kamikaze loggia' cantilevered out from a mundane housing block is an image of human disaster more than of emancipation.

It isn't pretty, in any case, and the traces Kiev and Tbilisi contain of an anarchistic urbanism is not completely complementary to anarchism. It's anarchic in the way that neoliberalism is anarchic – relations of power are blurred, the state and democratic bodies both leave the scene, money is all that has any import whatsoever. But then there are actual, conscious anarchists in this part of Europe, and have been since the days of Bakunin. After 1917, a statist mock-socialism emerged, at a remove or several from Marx's theories, as they always said it would. Did its collapse give them room to create new architectures, new urban spaces?

THE ANARCHIST INTERNATIONAL STYLE

The revolutions of 1989 are perhaps unique in that they did not give rise to anything 'new', only a restoration of what was on rather spurious grounds considered to be *normality*. Because of this, to expect the results to involve some sort of new space is missing the point – what everyone allegedly wanted was to live in California, or Frankfurt am Main, or at least Stockholm, and in some cases they got it, although more frequently some combination of Essex, Iowa and Stalin's Moscow resulted instead. But there was a gap between one system collapsing and another absorbing it, and in that time there were much more ambitious groups of people ready to fill that gap. There are large squats and squatters' movements which can trace their roots back to this moment in (among others) Poznań, Warsaw, Ljubljana and, of course, Berlin. The social movements that came out of 1968 in West Germany (and West Berlin) were often keen to claim and reclaim urban space, and in that they were joined by the tenement rehabilitators of 1970s East Berlin, and to some degree its revolutionaries in autumn 1989, with their banners quoting Rosa Luxemburg, were their disavowed comrades. There were a lot of buildings in central locations whose ownership was indeterminate, as the GDR's assets were gradually sold off piece by piece. Accordingly, East Berlin in the 1990s was famously full of impromptu spaces – nightclubs in the old Wall 'death-strip', disused bunkers and factories, housing co-ops and ubiquitous squats, which had special legal status in West Berlin already. A history remains to be written of their rise and decline. By the time I started visiting the city in the 2000s this was already beginning to peter out, with the gaps being filled, and the Friedrichshain tenements being renovated. At the time of writing, only a handful survive, usually somewhat beleaguered, as the (Social Democratic–Green Party–Left Party coalition) city government has reacted to bankruptcy with a wave of sell-offs.

One of the in-between sites where they manage to survive is in Köpenicker Strasse, a still very uneasy interzone that straddles the former 'death strip' (remember, there were two Walls, and the space in between was patrolled and kept under surveillance by guards but otherwise left to rot). Part of it is blocks, GDR *Plattenbau* at its most naïve and austere, some of which have been turned into hostels for young tourists; there are a few Wilhelmine warehouses and factories, most of them given over to the usual regenerative uses (such as the Deutsches Architektur Zentrum); and there are swanky office buildings; at the end, there are the tenements of Kreuzberg; there are apartments on the river, which we'll come to; and then there are the gaps. In one of these gaps is a lonely squat, a mess of warehouses, caravans and overgrown vegetation, surrounded by a fence which has been flyposted sheer with gig posters. They know they're on the way to being forced out, and the messages posted on the gate outside plead politely for the tourists to leave them alone – there are people living here, please don't photograph us. A graffitied rat on a background of the red and black flag of libertarian communism declares: 'We don't want no yuppie flats – we are happy with our rats'. Every May Day there are riots nearby, in the squares of Kreuzberg, and although there's always a certain amount of macho acting-out going on, the city is gradually closing off the option of other ways of living – there are a lot of Berliners who want to live in other ways than in individual apartments in purpose-built buildings. Even with rent control. However, just round the corner on the Spree is another, rather cleaner example – a small new scheme of *Baugruppe* housing, where a co-operative is formed of residents, with co-operative ownership and a non-profit structure written into the legal deeds of the scheme and the place organized as a live–work environment rather than a mere block of flats.[8] Like most schemes of this sort it has the problem of scale and of the electiveness of the model: i.e. that it needs members with a lot of time and wherewithal – it does not solve the problems of this sort of urban politics, but makes it a lot more seductive, a grown-up, more serious version of the politics of the squats on the other side of Köpenicker Strasse, only this time barely distinguishable on the outside from any other block of Berlin luxury apartments.

There is one mega-squat that was always on every tourist's itinerary from the 1990s right up until it closed in 2012: Tacheles. Taking up around a block or so of city in the Oranienburger Strasse area of Mitte, it was built in 1907 as Friedrichstadtpassagen, a department store, an early piece of concrete construction, very advanced in its day. Left derelict, half-destroyed, slated for demolition and seemingly ownerless after 1989, it was transformed by an artists' collective into an enormous, fundamentally free live–work space, entirely open to the public; the building ended up in the ownership of Nordbank, who according to some sources paid the artists to leave, though the metal workshop still exists at the time of writing. Artists lived here and exhibited their sculptures and canvases, there were bars, gigs, clubs and events, and you could just wander in off the street and explore without anyone asking what you were up to, a wonderful luxury in any European capital. As a space, it was at first incredibly exciting, with its wild chaos of graffiti, monsters lurking in scrawl, and its vertiginous spaces, full of holes, views and bizarre fragments of the original building, whose austere stone lines were taking the damage nobly – and the repairs to the derelict store by the collective were the punk version of adaptive reuse, abrupt, unsentimental and chaotic. The concrete walkway that spans part of it capped the comic-book sense of crumbling, gimcrack modernity. As a form of 'critical reconstruction' of the existing city it was a standing reproach both to the stone-clad tedium inflicted upon the city by Hans Stimmann and to the egoistic geometries of more spectacular architecture. For all that, when it finally went in 2012, there were quite a few shrugged shoulders.

Everything was caked in tags at all times, something which is completely ubiquitous in the city, a continuous layer of meaningless calligraphy and scrawl going up to about the height of the average person and then stopping. It was only on the fourth or fifth visit that it started to become obvious that the paintings were usually awful, the music terrible and the standards of hygiene not fantastic. None of that was ever the point: if this was a reservation, knowingly out of step and in its own world, then of course that didn't matter. If it was, in the jingle that some in the milieu like to quote, *the change they wanted to see in the world*, then that became another question. Could you grow up in this, have children in it, grow old? Would you ever be able to, say, sit at home and read a book? Would you want to live – as opposed to visit – here if you had to work at something grim and repetitive the rest of the time?

After a while, it all starts to become, well, boring. One squatted place looks much like another, their individual 'creativity' not much more individuated than the façade of an average Modernist block of flats. The visual language of squatting and of anarchism is strikingly conformist – the only difference is the degree of participation in the most banal sense – i.e. that you've tagged the place you live in. This may sound harsh and unfair given how beleaguered these people currently are, and given how much their activism often contributes to a genuine civic culture, so let me give a better example. Six or so miles west of Tacheles is a former CIA listening outpost called Teufelsberg, on one of the many mounds on the edge of the city made up of wartime rubble. It's an interesting spot, an overgrown green landscape with strange objects (e.g. an actual Le Corbusier Unité d'habitation) popping up out over the bushes. Go through the frequently cut security fences and you get to a building made up of cubes and geodesic domes, one of them on a tower, from which the Americans had an unrivalled vantage point to listen to what the Soviets were up to, given that West Berlin was deep in East German territory. Again, nobody particularly knows who owns or controls it, so it has been squatted for the last few years. On visiting it, you find that people are living there, and they'll mutter 'tourists' under their breath, like some disgruntled inhabitants of the Boul' Mich'. The rooms where spies did their business have been completely stripped and covered with graffiti, mostly tags as always but with the odd passive-aggressive slogan (nearly always in English, naturally), saying such things as 'Gate to hell', 'Hate capitalism' or 'Please! Don't crucified places like this!' There's buckled and twisted metal from where the gates have been destroyed, and the panels on the walls have been torn away, leaving bare steel frames and their asbestos insulation floating freely. What an astonishingly stupid thing, to risk your life for the sake of an interesting bit of apocalypse chic. Teufelsberg got a mention as a hip destination in the easyJet in-flight magazine in 2013.[9]

It all has a certain sublimity, these emptied rooms and half-torn-apart buckyballs, but what is sad is that they've managed to take a CIA spy base and turn it into a near carbon copy of Tacheles, an act surely of astounding pointlessness. The graffiti is (almost exactly) the same, the come/don't come attitude towards outsiders is the same, the sense of a continuous artwork transcending the divide between art and life is the same. Like a GDR panel builder, they descend upon the most amazingly dissimilar places and make them all look identical. A nineteenth-century tenement, the wasteland where the Wall used to be, a department store, a former spy base; what the hell, get the cans out. Politically, I can't help but admire the confidence of their reclamation of space and their wresting it away from capital, but I wish in the process they weren't so bullishly insistent on their not particularly interesting choices in aesthetics and lifestyle.

That isn't to say that these places are not worth defending against the vested interests that are constantly threatening them. Take for instance Metelkova, the social centre which still occupies the scattered, small buildings of a former Hapsburg barracks in Ljubljana. After being vacated when the Yugoslavian army dissolved, it was seized and squatted in 1993 by activists and members of the Slovene punk scene, who immediately made it a public space, with a programme of gigs, events and exhibitions, which continue in some form at the time of writing.[10] I first went there some years ago to take part in an institution called the Workers' and Punks' University (its name, I later realized, was a reference to the 'Workers' Universities' of the old Socialist Federal Republic). Looking around, then or now, you would see several small pitched-roofed buildings coated in a blaring spraypaint noise of tags, with various additions bolted on, wooden-framed extensions cantilevered like lean-tos with thin rods of steel, the results then coated in some more of the indeterminate spraypaint gloop; or yurt-like structures with great pointed tent roofs supported by thick wooden posts, or walls transformed by mosaics made

The autonomous zone of Metelkova, Ljubljana

of waste. The courtyards between have benches in a circular pattern, so you can sit around and have a good argument. Tagging and monsters aside, the 'artworks' have some range, as with the various brightly painted pictureless picture frames affixed to one wall. And then there's the aforementioned Workers' and Punks' University, where classes with various international Marxist luminaries were, until recently, offered for free. Wondering how all of this was financially possible – they paid speakers and put them up in hotels, even – I was told by one University organizer that they relied on money from George Soros's Open Society Foundations, but were expecting it to be cancelled sooner rather than later (as it was). The problem was that the money was geared towards ensuring the development of liberal democracy. There may be the occasional pogrom against Roma, but unlike, say, Russia, Ukraine, Hungary, Poland, Latvia or Serbia, Slovenia looks very unlikely to ever go hardline nationalist, let alone fascist. They'd created 'civil society' by now, so could be left to fend for themselves.

Metelkova certainly feels a lot more organized and less pointless than Tacheles – the 'art' is still not much cop and it is still visibly part of the

Anarchist International Style, but there is a sense that, in a phrase they won't appreciate, *things get done here*. Like Berlin (but unlike most Eastern and Central European capitals), Ljubljana has an active, lively and young far left of communists and anarchists, both of which groups were involved in the massive anti-austerity protest movement that spread across Slovenia in 2013, the biggest social manifestation there since the 1940s. In the aftermath of the protests, in its new, post-Soros guise as the Centre for Labour Studies, the Workers' and Punks' University became part of an electoral coalition, the Slovenian United Left. This is the only former communist country with a significant radical (i.e. not 'post-socialist' or 'post-communist', but socialist, communist) left, and since its launch at the elections of spring 2014, the United Left sits in parliament as the third-largest party, despite having been formed barely a year earlier.

In this context it was strange to discover that funding from avowedly capitalist financiers lay behind much of Metelkova, but as long as it remains a cultural rather than directly political body, there's no urgent contradiction. The city council has moments of hostility towards it, as when it insisted on demolishing some ancillary buildings in 2006; but, on the whole, the centre has managed to survive impressively, albeit via some curious alliances. Just on its periphery, the central location and perhaps its status as a tourist attraction have spurred the creation of some classic spaces of regeneration – luxury flats and an art gallery, all of decent quality but perhaps unsurprisingly very different in aesthetic, with clean glazed lines and neat brickwork. Anything 'successful' and 'creative' always brings this in its train, but as a collective, non-money-making social space, Metelkova still endures.

In those improvisations where Soros isn't the direct source of funding you can find a strange political conformity which contrasts curiously with all the general edginess. In Poland, street art – that more visually acceptable, less obviously atomized and egotistical version of graffiti – is given some degree of public funding by local authorities and ministries of culture, via the annual 'Street Art Doping' festival, where gable-ends all over Warsaw are given a going over by local artists. There are similar initiatives in Lublin, Łódź and elsewhere, and they're not quite as unprecedented as they look. Something resembling it took place on gable-ends under the People's Republic, particularly when their bare forms were uncovered by

People's Republic street art in Łódź

clearance, war damage or botched renovation projects. Łódź, which has several bare gable ends in the centre, boasts a lot of them, often untouched since 1989. A classic abstract pattern straight from a Constructivist painting advertises the textiles of the East German city 'Karl-Marx-Stadt' (now Chemnitz again); another, in a pixellated corona of pastelly orange and green, informs you of the wares of the People's Army factory. There are several of these too in the Praga district of Warsaw, advertising clocks and cameras. They're a much shabbier painted analogue to the sexier neon signs of the same period, but maybe it's a stretch to put them in the same lineage as street art just because they both paint the ends of walls. Perhaps, insofar as street art can actually be *more* didactic than the People's Republic's unideological ads-on-the-cheap.

They're not always directly representational – the murals in Lublin are so strictly geometrical and abstract that it's a surprise to find they're recent and not of socialist vintage. A favourite, recently destroyed in Warsaw, showed a panorama of a cityscape, traversed by biplanes, across a large concrete garden wall. Others are more directly communicative, and that isn't entirely a bad thing, as sometimes they're a welcome reminder of the histories this history-obsessed city prefers not to tell. A klezmer group is stencilled onto a Praga tenement, a Muranów courtyard features the Bundist socialist and Ghetto insurgent Marek Edelman with fist aloft, and a lost pre-war building in the wasteland by Wilanowska Metro station features on one side a swag-bag-carrying banker with the (English) legend 'Bailout Folks!', and on the other, 'Syn Ulicy', 'son of the street', a really quite lovely stylized painting of the Dachau survivor and Warsaw dialect singer Stanisław Grzesiuk, banjo in hand. Others are more obvious. In Łódź there are a few bouncy murals of the city's pre-war inhabitants on the sides of tenements, painted as if they're waving out of the window, and in Warsaw there's one mural commemorating the pre-war dictator Marshal Józef Piłsudski, riding an iron horse, no less. This is as official as a mural of Lenin would have been thirty years ago – probably more so, in fact. There's no reason why it shouldn't be – why should 'alternative' art not reflect dominant values? You occasionally find street art stencils of Piłsudski's rival, the pre-war far-right leader Roman Dmowski, so why not funky images of the Marshal, who was the lesser of those two evils?

As interventions in space, though, Warsaw street art can still be radical, actually for how conscious they are in a city where often everything seems to happen by accident. One of the best post-communist improvisations in Warsaw is not on the railways, but as part of Trasa Łazienkowska, a motorway-underpass-overpass-bridge built in the 1970s. At one point along its route there is a straggling space where the flyover lifts itself across the ground-level roads, on several hulking concrete pillars. Over the last few years, graffiti artists, some based in the local Rozbrat squat, have used these as canvases. Not by tagging them, by adding their own ad hoc logos to the collection of giant logos that plague this advertising-choked city, but by using them as panels, open to public view. The resultant artworks veer from an angrily proletarian Homer Simpson to Russian dolls, from vivid, flowing abstractions to comic horrors, anti-televisual rants to anarchist agitprop, defaced by far-right scrawl on the day in 2010 these pictures were taken. It runs for quarter of a mile, until it ends in Legia insignia and a bizarre, extended, scrawled anti-art diatribe. If 1950s Warsaw was promised and denied the kind of representational infrastructures that narrate the commuter through St Petersburg and Moscow, it has a similar *architecture parlante* here, a place that is both gallery and road – but, given its site in an indeterminate wasteland rather than a 'vibrant' cultural district, it becomes an unconscious demonstration of the possibilities of public infrastructure. Could a flyover be a public artwork?

A Socialist Realist pillar of Trasa 'Ł', Warsaw

A defaced anarchist pillar of Trasa 'Ł', Warsaw

Could it become one without becoming cutesy or sanitized? This place answers both questions in the affirmative, with a multivocal maze of colour and form.

All the above are or aspire to be permanent. Because of this they tend not to have architects, or 'architecture', involved, as this is, as we know, exceptionally capital-intensive. Because of that capital-intensiveness, two things happen to architecture in a financial crisis – one, it stops getting built, and two, architects, or the best of them, start to think about something a little more interesting to do instead. The result has at worst been the proliferation of 'pop-ups', where, in London especially, the holes left by the crash were briefly filled with more or less whimsical temporary uses. A 'pop-up' restaurant in a closed-down Asian women's refuge. One project which shares the form, if not the politics, of the pop-up and which I got to visit was something called 'The Knot'. Rather than a mere exercise in 'Hey, wouldn't it be fun to do the show right here?', The Knot was expressly, if mildly, political. To describe it in terms of what it actually was, as architecture, is ridiculously simple – three giant, table-shaped inflatables of green and purple, which are blown up and then used as the focus of instant public spaces. These inflatables were transported for stays in the three largest cities of Eastern-Central Europe – three spots in Berlin, three in Warsaw and one stop-off in Bucharest. In the couple of

Inflatable agora: The Knot in situ at the Kulturforum, Berlin

weeks or so they were in each location they had a rolling programme of concerts, artworks, discussions and activities, embarked upon by the large Polish–German–Romanian team, like some instant-city version of the underground 'flying universities' during the Polish People's Republic. In addition to the inflatables, they had in their van a sound system, a screen, cooking implements and all manner of other delights. The pitches they picked in each city were disparate – in Bucharest they took the central Carol Park, in Warsaw they used alternately a derelict palace in Praga, the Pole Mokotowskie park and a green space among the blocks of Ursynów. In Berlin, they occupied the disused Tempelhof airport, Mariannenplatz in Kreuzberg, and the Kulturforum, near the former East–West border at Potsdamer Platz.

I only visited the latter, so I can't vouch for how successful it was elsewhere – certainly the book they produced out of it suggests that in Mariannenplatz and in Praga, especially, they had a lot of visitors,[11] and in Praga locals tried to maintain the momentum by founding an arts centre in the vicinity. At the Kulturforum, The Knot entailed some talks, some very good food and a large group of educated international people hanging around and wondering why nobody was coming in off the street, something which was surely a comment in some way on the sterility of the space, revealing it as an afterthought between grand cultural buildings. How different it might have been in Alexanderplatz is a tantalizing thought. This was part of an investigation into different kinds of urban space, and they had to gain express permission for their week or so of occupation in each, which was unsurprisingly more difficult in Poland and Romania than in the capital of world hipsterdom. Yet for the organizers, the entire project was aimed at trying to drag an uncommodified space for thought and experiment into cities which are relentlessly neoliberal, bent on the eradication of any remnants of the public sphere in the city, from housing to schools – so success in Warsaw or Bucharest must surely have been more important to them.

By the end of the evening at the Kulturforum, a heated night-time discussion had developed between Croatian, Polish and Romanian thinkers about the legacy of communism and what could be salvaged from it (opinions, needless to say, differed). This, though an 'official' part of the programme, could easily be mistaken by passers-by for a group of friends having a good argument over drinks, which to a degree it was, and you don't just butt in and involve yourself in such things if you don't know the people in question. What The Knot, and other temporary spaces like it, really entailed was some attempt, in a context where permanent public spaces are endangered, to create them momentarily, which is without doubt better than not creating them at all. If it came across solely as a series of discussions in Globish on leftist art then it would have failed in its aims, but the organizers would have a right to argue that they were doing all that they possibly could. If The Knot had set itself up as some sort of activist roadshow, turning up and throwing itself into proletarian struggles (i.e. those over housing, schools, hospitals, wages, pensions, all of which have been fought over in these three cities in the last few years), it would no doubt have been regarded with some suspicion; but, perhaps more importantly, it would not have been able to obtain funding from various cultural institutes, which, even in something as light-on-the-earth as this, is logistically essential.

This is rather more of a dilemma in what seemed at first to be the most exciting of the various temporary spaces we had come across. Nowy Wspaniały Świat ('Brave New World') was a centre run for a time on Nowy Świat, Warsaw, by the NGO Krytyka Polityczna ('Political Critique'). Set up as a magazine in 2002, Krytyka Polityczna branched out into publishing, causing a stir by picking for their first book the 1917 writings of Lenin, a bold gesture indeed in Poland, even when given an evasive, extremely dialectical introduction and gloss by Slavoj Žižek. Given that propagating communism is (literally) illegal in Poland, this was brave, and successful – no court actions ensued, and they branched out to translate and publish most of the current left-philosophical canon, from Jacques Rancière to Judith Butler. At the same time, they set up a series of discussion clubs across Poland, of which this was the largest and by far the most prominent. The reconstructed neoclassical curve of Nowy Świat, the central part of the Royal Route, is the nearest thing Warsaw has to a Regent Street – despite a couple of surviving dives and one milk bar it is a strip of high-end boutiques, bars and restaurants. Accordingly, Nowy Wspaniały Świat was shockingly clean and neat-looking for a left-wing space. Housed in one of those remade eighteenth-century houses, with a renovated interior full of elegant fittings and decorations, it couldn't possibly have been further from Metelkova or Tacheles, with graffiti limited strictly to the toilets. The talks were upstairs, a kiosk selling their beautifully designed books was in the lobby, and a bar took up most of the space. The bar was a little too overpriced, but otherwise this seemed a fabulous and surprising thing to find in a country that barely has an organized left – the space of some new designer social democracy, not interested in politics for matters of lifestyle, or even 'creativity', but interested in providing a neutral, smart, even rather chic space for discussion and organization. If only, I said to a sceptical Agata, we could have this in London (or insert Western capital as appropriate). A leftist space in the heart of the city without lifestyle politics, sulky sectarianism or white people in dreadlocks!

It was widely expected that Krytyka Polityczna would eventually become a political party, capable of replacing the decrepit left organized around the former communist apparatchiks of the Democratic Left Alliance, in terminal decline since its last government was toppled by a corruption scandal in 2004–5. Krytyka Polityczna never did enter politics, and to some degree their potential thunder was stolen by the Palikot Movement, a breakaway from the ruling Civic Platform which had a programme much more normal for the politics of post-communist youth: legalize drugs, introduce a flat tax, and so forth. Krytyka Polityczna produced in what they did do – the programme of talks, discussions, books, here and in other cities – an uneasy combination of appeals to the old anti-communist opposition and attempts to build an internationalist left that had nothing to do with who was on what side in 1981. They branched out into Ukraine, and translated an increasingly eclectic selection of texts that went from the neo-Maoism of Alain Badiou to the anti-communist polemics of Tony Judt. Any organization that publishes both V. I. Lenin and Václav Havel is trying very hard to be friends with some potentially very unfriendly groups, and this balancing act was upended in November 2012, during the now-annual nationalist riot on Polish Independence Day. Anti-fascist counter-marchers sheltered in Nowy Wspaniały Świat, and many were beaten. No matter how much they tried to be neutral, for others they were unambiguously on the far left – 'commies'. Their lease on the building on Nowy Świat was not renewed, and they moved into a far less publicly accessible office on the upper storeys of a pre-war tenement nearby.

Why so much effort to be all things to all people? I wondered. My more conspiratorial friends claimed that this was because they were an astroturf left. Much as the Kremlin manufactures opposition parties, such as the 'social democratic' party A Just Russia, so, they told me, the old oppositionists like Adam Michnik, now usually business magnates, 'created' a cosy, unthreatening left, both to absorb the energies of young people and maybe in some nostalgic gesture towards the socialist politics of their youth. Their sources of funding include obvious donors such as Soros's Open Society Foundations and the Polish Ministry of Culture, but also Swiss banks, Siemens, the European Union; their English-language promotional brochure even includes Poland's right-wing president, Bronisław Komorowski, taking part in one of their events. If they became a political party, and hence quite possibly a danger to the cosy post-communist carve-up between oppositionists, apparatchiks and the church, all that funding might suddenly evaporate. So places that would never exist in somewhere like London are allowed to occupy quite prominent parts of the city, so long as they don't pose any sort of threat.

THE SELF-MANAGED CITY?

In the current circumstances – it probably couldn't be otherwise – everything is stacked against the people behind Metelkova, The Knot or Krytyka Polityczna. So long as they're a 'civil society' that is largely the preserve of the educated middle class, they're allowed to exist – are even, at times, embraced by the establishment. Otherwise, all they would have is impotence, clean hands and a feeling of righteous self-satisfaction that they didn't touch any dirty money, and there's far, far too much of that in the European left. Either way, it's a matter of enclaves. Although Krytyka Polityczna managed to have for a time probably the most prominent left-wing enclave in Europe, it is hard to believe it seriously pushed Poland's two-right-wing-parties system to the left; its 'leader', Sławomir Sierakowski, has claimed this is because 'real politics' doesn't happen in parliaments,[12] something the designer social democrat and the anarchist can agree on. Let's say that a social movement somewhere in Europe, rather than at a safe distance in Latin America, did come to power, and did embark on a campaign to remake cities. Is there anything in the former 'socialist camp' that could suggest ways such a thing might develop, and mistakes it ought to avoid? If there is, it's far from the Soros-funded enclaves, but in the enormous dormitory suburb of New Belgrade, on the other side of the River Sava from the current Serbian capital.

The 'Yugoslav experiment', as it was once called, made the Socialist Federal Republic of Yugoslavia one of the most admired countries in the world, in its heyday. From the 1950s to the 1980s, it was often pointed to on the left as a possible 'third way' between 'real socialism' and capitalism, as if it were a sort of Leninist Sweden. Its collapse into war and the resultant coinage of the phrase *ethnic cleansing* meant that this experiment was forgotten almost overnight. If it ended like this, then surely it must have failed, and failed utterly. Yet between 1948 and 1990 it had seemed by far the most hopeful, open and democratic of the various countries founded by communists in the aftermath of the Second World War. The experiment and its aftermath are well discussed in academia, but before we can work out what sort of a place New Belgrade was, we need to know what Yugoslavia was. Founded after the first war as a 'Kingdom of Serbs, Croats and Slovenes', it was dominated by the political power of Serbia and the economic power of the two more developed ex-Hapsburg nations, with other groups – Bosnian Muslims, Macedonians, Montenegrins, Kosovar Albanians – suppressed. During the second war, it was dismembered by Nazi Germany and Italy and shared between themselves, with the assistance of a psychopathically violent independent Croatian state, ruled by the fascist Ustaše. Ten per cent of the population of Yugoslavia were killed.

Though it doesn't feature in Timothy Snyder's *Bloodlands*, perhaps because Yugoslavs happened to be massacred en masse by fascists alone rather than fascists *and* communists, it was one of the countries most destroyed by the war. The only movement that transcended the borders of the dismembered Yugoslavia was the communist-dominated Partisan movement, which was equally strong in most of the Yugoslav territories, and resurrected Yugoslavia after the war as a federation. The Yugoslav communists' independence in gaining power meant that they were suspicious to Moscow from the off, and the Soviets excommunicated them in 1948 on technicalities. They were forced then to balance between East and West, accepting American aid and becoming instrumental in forming the 'Non-Aligned Movement' with former colonial countries like India, Egypt and Indonesia in the 1950s. The 'experiment', though, was what was called Self-Management Socialism. Now everyone from the Slovene neo-Leninist Slavoj Žižek to the late social democrat Tony Judt are agreed it was always a 'myth', but observers at the time were not so sure.

Though it may have resulted from grass roots pressure, the policy was decided at the top. According to the account of Milovan Djilas, a Partisan leader, later a prominent dissident, but at this point part of the ruling group in the Yugoslav Party, self-management was decided upon rather ad hoc. In 1950, he wrote: 'It occurred to me that we Yugoslav communists were now in a position to start creating Marx's free association of producers.' The factories would be left in their hands, with the sole proviso that they should pay a tax for military and other state needs 'that remained essential'. He then put this to the other leaders, Boris Kidrič, Edvard Kardelj and Josip Broz Tito, who 'paced up and down, as though completely wrapped up in his own thoughts. Suddenly he stopped and exclaimed "factories belonging to their workers – something that has never yet been achieved!"' A few months later, Tito himself put the bill to the National Assembly. After Djilas was purged, for arguing in a series of articles on 'the new class' that the next step should be the destruction of the party elite itself, self-management still continued – genuinely fulfilling the aim of 'the withering away of the state' promised by Marx and Lenin was taken surprisingly seriously by Yugoslav leaders.

The system was largely devised by the Slovene leader, Edvard Kardelj, who regarded it as a way of building 'socialist democracy' without a multi-party system, since anything outside the Party (regrouped even as it was into a decentralized League of Communists) would 'inescapably become the rallying point' for any counter-revolutionary forces. So a system was set up based on workers' councils, where delegates of 'workers qua workers' alongside 'workers qua consumers' would make the decisions in the economy. This might seem like a strange form of workers' self-activity, decreed from the top, and deliberately done to preclude multi-party democracy – 'manage yourselves!' – but it can equally be considered a way of maintaining the popular momentum of the Partisan movement, rather than subsuming it into the usual bureaucratic monolith – though a pervasive personality cult of Tito himself was created at the same time, with the leader's birthday a national holiday.

What Kardelj introduced that was especially novel, though, was the idea that self-management would be a principle outside the factory. He insisted that the 'hierarchy of supreme workers' councils should be extended to the republican and federal levels'.[13] This meant that decentralization was extended to the governance of the Yugoslav Republics (Slovenia, Croatia, Serbia, Bosnia-Herzegovina, Macedonia and Montenegro) and its Autonomous Provinces (Vojvodina, Kosovo), which were given a large degree of independence; this principle extended down to the cities, run by self-managed 'communes'. The main decision-making bodies in the economy itself were, in theory and to a large degree in practice, the 'BOALs', the Basic Organizations of Associated Labour, the self-management councils in every workplace. From the mid-1960s on, when residual Stalinists were expelled (they'd been tapping Tito's phone), there were competitive elections supervised by a (at least nominally) non-party Socialist Alliance, a consumer culture with lots of Western imports, and a largely free press. During this time the self-managed economy registered among the highest growth rates in the world, a startling demonstration that workers' control and decentralization could coincide with – could help in – the building of a modern, industrial state. Yet this was hardly the entire story.

In 1965, it was decided to decentralize even further, introducing a system which was called by its opponents 'laissez-faire socialism', where self-managed enterprises were left to fend for themselves, acting competitively. Foreign investment was encouraged by a law that enabled foreign capital to own up to 49 per cent of an enterprise. The results were ambiguous. Yugoslavia always involved bringing together a relatively industrialized, educated ex-Hapsburg north and a less developed south, and unsurprisingly market socialism widened the divide between them. In a Fabian Society study on self-management, the British trade unionist Roy Moore charted the disparities that came as a result. Income differentials within the federation rose from 4:1 in 1959 to 8:1 in 1969.[14] He found that this extended into the way workers managed their enterprises: 'research into the agendas of workers' councils showed that in the less developed republics questions of canteen, toilet and working conditions predominated, whilst in the more advanced republics general plant policy, issues such as expansion and prices, formed the agenda items.' Meanwhile, the economy as a whole showed a 'general preference for external finance as opposed to any distribution of Yugoslav funds'.[15] What this all meant in practice was that the self-management system worked much better for those already doing well than for those who were not, while the socialist system as a whole was being pushed ever closer towards the world economy. But the system still had its admirers – a detailed explanation of the system was published in English in 1978, with a glowing introduction by none other than Tony Benn.[16]

Within a few years, though, this complex, decentralized edifice began to collapse under the weight of its inner contradictions and its immense external debt. It was subject to IMF structural-adjustment programmes from 1981 onwards. In 1985, Branka Magaš, writing of a country in economic turmoil, argued that 'Yugoslavia's economic problems have, no doubt, been aggravated by the high cost of money characteristic of the international finance markets since the oil crisis in 1976. Yet their roots are structural: they are to be found in the great imbalance created over the past two decades between an extractive industry which has been systematically neglected (along with other infrastructural investments like agriculture, transport, energy and health), and a bloated processing industry, mostly financed by foreign loans, dependent on imported raw materials, primary industrial goods and machine spares – all of which have to be purchased in hard Western currency.'

That is, the integration into the world system and the orientation to it had become Yugoslavia's weakness. An IMF austerity programme did all the usual things austerity programmes do, slashing social spending, causing hyperinflation and mass unemployment. By the mid-1980s, the IMF had already helped destroy self-management – 'it is instructive,' wrote Magaš, 'that it was the West rather than the East that struck the final blow' – but it also insisted on greater centralization, something which fed a rising nationalism.[17] An explosion of Croatian nationalism in the early 1970s had been clamped down upon by Tito; a year after his death, in 1981, the Yugoslav army shot at protesting Albanians in Kosovo, and in the 1980s the rise of the Serbian nationalists grouped around Slobodan Milošević dealt the final blow. The IMF's strictures led to several long-drawn-out strikes, where 'the workers almost everywhere marched with Tito's portraits, shouted "Tito-Partija", and sang old revolutionary songs that maintain the man's cult ("Comrade Tito, we swear to you that we will follow your road, etc.").'[18] The Party did not support them, and collapsed into (soon to be literally) warring pro-capitalist factions. We all know what happened next, with massacres, mass rapes and 'ethnic cleansing' perpetuated by Serbian and Croatian armies and 'auxiliaries'. Rosa

Luxemburg's choice between 'socialism or barbarism' had been answered in favour of the latter.

That is (an extremely simplified version of) the history, but any attempt to give a synopsis is doomed to failure. During its existence, the SFRY was a fiendishly complex thing: a one-party state embarking on an experiment in radical democracy; a hugely decentralized country with a collective leadership and a widespread (and enduring) personality cult around Marshal Tito, its extent in post-Stalin communist Europe rivalled only by Ceauşescu; a state where the economy rested on the decisions of workers and where bureaucrats had much the same privileges as in any other 'real socialist' country; a socialist country that refused to intervene in the economy to prevent unemployment, and which maintained its growth rates by exporting gastarbeiter; an extraordinary attempt at laissez-faire Leninism. Its collapse meant that all that was suddenly forgotten or dismissed as an unworkable Utopia. New Belgrade, however, was its most representational space, its greatest pride and showcase. If we want to find out what sort of a city self-management socialism wanted to build, and did build, it seems an obvious place to start. It was always planned as a representative space. Just west of the Serbian capital, it was until the 1950s marshland, which had for hundreds of years been the border between the former Ottoman and Hapsburg empires. It was, as young ex-Yugoslav historians write, 'intended to serve as a symbol of Yugoslav unity'; its 'symbolic charge greatly outweighed its practical necessity' at a time of a great housing crisis after the war. The first, Modernist plan by Nikola Dobrović in 1947 imagined a north–south 'civic axis', which was never really built; 'as the Yugoslav state decentralised, the city's role as the seat of a massive federal administration dwindled and was increasingly replaced by housing'.[19] As a result, it became 'a curious hybrid of a political poster board and a mass dormitory', pitched somewhere between Brasilia and Ursynów. It also became the home of large informal settlements – shanty towns, essentially – and accordingly an urban measure of the failure of self-management socialism. But what sort of a place is it?

You get an immediate impression of New Belgrade if you enter the city, as we did, from the air. Belgrade Nikola Tesla Airport – itself a remarkable combination of lightweight concrete-and-glass structures, figurative murals and abstract Brutalism – is itself in New Belgrade. The axis from here to the city centre passes through a huge 'gateway' skyscraper, two twin towers in raw, organic concrete, linked together and surmounted by a spacecraft-shaped lookout. You pass immense quantities of high-rises in green space, collections and clusters of towers sometimes neat and prim, sometimes gruffly Brutalist, all of them grouped into distinct skylines, occasionally complemented by the odd cheap-looking Postmodernist block of flats or offices. Finally, you glide past a large, symmetrical office complex, so cold and austere it surely has to be governmental; then you cross the River Sava into Belgrade proper. It makes an unforgettable first impression. It may be a dormitory, but there aren't a lot of dormitories like this – dramatic, strongly modelled and urban, each part of it seemingly 'planned' but not necessarily in conjunction with each other; the only unifying thing is the system of wide, deeply pedestrian-unfriendly highways that bisects each one of the housing complexes, turning them into islands. It is clearly fragmented, yet dense with tight clusters of striking buildings. If this is the self-managed city – or rather, the remnants of the self-managed city – it is maybe appropriately a combination of dirigisme and chaos.

That governmental-looking building was originally built for the Yugoslav presidency, and then became the Federal Executive. The axial

Across the Sava to New Belgrade (1978 postcard)

symmetry is a vestige of the brief Stalinist era, when Tito was still intent on following the Soviet model – he had asked the designers for 'the eternal beauty of Greek columns', but after the split with Stalin got instead, after an extensive redesign by the architect Mihailo Janković, a long, sprawling office block, with two tall wings balanced by a glazed congress hall. The result is clear and crisp, but still bears traces of its original authoritarianism.

On a later journey to Belgrade, I got to go inside and find out what the self-managed parliament was like to visit. Readers of William Morris's Utopia of Arts and Crafts communism, *News From Nowhere*, will remember that the Houses of Parliament are converted therein into a shed for storing manure. This came to mind in October 2014 when I and fifty or so others were given a guided tour of the Federal Executive Council of the Socialist Federal Republic of Yugoslavia, in Belgrade. This was this long-dead state's equivalent in symbolic importance to the Houses of Parliament, and while it hasn't quite been filled with dung, the disrespect in which it was held by its owners was conspicuous. The tour of the building – now called the 'Palace of Serbia' – was advertised by the organizers as part of a symposium on 'Disappearing Architecture'. The current owners, the Serbian government, who use it occasionally for meetings and ministries, did not give permission until literally the night before. Still, the big turnout suggested a lot of people wanted to see inside.

As much as the art and design of the United Nations in New York or UNESCO in Paris embodied the post-war spirit with the unusual bonus of a massive budget, so too did this building exemplify what socialist Yugoslavia liked to think about itself. Through the main hall that housed the council, flanked by two long, wide wings of offices, an anteroom leads to a panoramic, Picasso-esque mural, depicting a crucial battle of the Partisan war. Placed by the entrance to the council, it would be seen by everyone that entered the building, and its reminder of pan-Balkan unity and equality obviously didn't help much when the state collapsed into war in the early 1990s. Yet the only gestures against it are two flanking 1998 busts of Serbian national heroes, including the Croatian-born Nikola Tesla. The space around the mural is more opulent than was the norm in this or any other era – intense rose-coloured marble, a top-lit ceiling with a Mondrian-esque pattern in yellow and violet. This then leads to the council's main hall, which is flanked by subsidiary halls for each republic.

And here, really, is where the image of the Houses of Parliament as dung-heap came in. 'Palace of Serbia' as it may now be, in the building's original design Serbia is but one of six republics given its own office. The building's guide and official curator, a strikingly dodgy-looking geezer, gave descriptions so dismissive that, I was told, the English interpreter began adding extra things that he hadn't bothered to mention. The first republican office we came to was that of Macedonia – 'There's a lot of red, because Macedonia is very hot'; the next was Montenegro's – 'That lion on the carpet is there because that's how Montenegrins like to see themselves.' Or he'd point to an abstract by a Kosovan artist and call it 'a typical Albanian landscape', or to another painting and describe it as being by 'a Croatian Jew'. However, he did take care to point out his own contributions, copies of Byzantine icons or photographs of Tesla.

To give him credit, however, he must have had some role in preserving much of the building's original design, which is in the absolute first rank of its era, as important and fascinating as the Royal Festival Hall or Oscar Niemeyer's Communist Party Headquarters in Paris, the two buildings which it most resembles. The furniture is both comfortable and sharply modern, the carpets, with their motifs plundered as much from Abstract Expressionism as from local historic motifs, are completely unique, and the light fittings – chandeliers in a variety of twisted and warped repeated forms, different in every room – are in a genre all of their own. However, the Festival Hall, or Niemeyer's public buildings, are still used by their original owners. Here, nearly every fitting, nearly every artwork, has a political meaning – with dozens of paintings, abstracts, reliefs and sculptures referring to the Partisans, plenty of others referring to socialism, and, most of all, with the entire design and layout of all but one room designed to evoke the history, climate and values of countries that are not Serbia. It was obvious why our host's paintings on national themes were thrown in, as a sort of inoculating charm against the values of the building.

The most obvious criticism that could be made of the building was its occasional gestures to national kitsch, particularly in the cosy warmth of the Macedonian office. The central Hall of Yugoslavia, however, is truly something. An Abstract Expressionist painting in rich oranges and reds by the painter Petar Lubarda takes up one wall, a bright, naïf/abstract

The Hall of Yugoslavia, New Belgrade

representation by Lazar Vujaklija of Yugoslavia and its role in the world occupies another, and a mosaic of the Partisans frames the doors, all under a convex circular light-well, its glass faceted and patterned, arranged into the shape of a star. One of the initial functions of this room on its completion in 1961 was to host the first meeting of the Non-Aligned Movement, founded by Yugoslavia and newly independent countries like India and Ghana and intended as a counterweight to the imperialism of America and Russia, a support network of countries committing themselves to an agenda of modernization and equality. 'We're as distant from this now as modern Greeks are from ancient Greeks,' comments one of the symposium's Serbian participants.

This would remain the only major representational building of state in the whole of New Belgrade, but the fact it very quickly stopped being considered the official capital of the Socialist Federal Republic didn't mean that it wasn't exceptionally loaded. The next public buildings to be built were a Party headquarters for the Serbian wing of the League of Communists, and – of all things – a Museum of Modern Art. These are just over the river from the centre of Belgrade, highly visible from the medieval fortress of Kalemegdan, and on our first day in the current capital of Serbia on a crisp spring day (which helped) the two of us walked across to have a wander round them.

The Sava on the New Belgrade side is lined with restaurants on boats, giving an air of ease and festivity; but the Museum of Modern Art is completely derelict, which we hadn't expected. Designed in 1959 by Ivan Antić and Ivanka Raspopović, its concrete frame is filled with six top-lit galleries clad in pale, well-cut stone, which are linked by glass cubes. The galleries are an elliptical shape, irregular polygons canted at the sides over a wide, completely neglected public park; though symmetrical, the building proclaims its decentralization, with no obvious centrifugal gestures, and the entrances are simply picked out with long concrete porches, reaching out like bridges over the uncut grass. Sculptures – usually rather vitalistic, slightly abstracted figures of striving and stretching bodies, with several wholly abstract works among them – are scattered through the disused park. Remarkably, none of them have been pinched or vandalized. The museum is an unusual public building, even for the 1960s: evidently chosen as a project to demonstrate the enlightened nature of Yugoslav Leninism's artistic policies – no campaigns against 'decadent formalism' here – it has a certain repose, and is in remarkably good condition for a building which, we later learned, had been left derelict for some years.

The other public building, the Party HQ, less surprisingly does not survive in its original form. A Mies-aping glass tower, it had its own role in the personality cult, flashing 'TITO-PARTIJA' in neon for miles around. Bombed in 1999, it was reconstructed as a Euro-remont blue-glass office block with a shopping mall. It still looks ethereal from a distance, looming over the derelict Museum. The urbanism here is still totally disjointed, however – the large park and a flyover cut the museum off from New Belgrade proper, so it doesn't feel like the centre of anything, more an unexpected, lonely, if lush, Modernist adjunct to Belgrade's historic centre. The day after, we got a lift round New Belgrade proper from a friend of ours, a local architect and historian, who explained to us the way in which New Belgrade (and, by association, the other self-managed city extensions, housing estates and new towns) came into being; here, it's best if I quote from her book rather than from memory.

Scrub and sculpture at the Museum of Modern Art, New Belgrade

'Among the numerous new human rights that self-management, and socialist Yugoslavia, established', she writes, 'the right to housing was one of the more important.' In 1953, the 'permanent right to use an apartment' was legislatively 'prescribed as a principle', and as late as 1985 the law on planning stated that 'Spatial Planning and Development is based on the rights and duties of workers and all working people to handle space, preserve nature and the values created by labour, prevent and eliminate any adverse affects that are jeopardising those values, and to ensure and advance social and economic development, providing the permanent right to use an apartment.'[20] Fine words, but how was this 'right' to be achieved in practice? Housing and city planning happened via the BOALs, the Basic Organizations of Associated Labour, i.e the workers' councils, in the workplace itself. They were legally required to provide housing and to plan it – to that end a monthly sum was deducted from salaries. At New Belgrade, she notes, 'apartments were distributed according to the "Right to Housing" scheme. An enterprise would purchase a number of apartments in the same building and distribute them to employees, thereby creating a diverse social structure within the blocks.' So far, so impressive, and she makes clear the housing that resulted was the best, on almost any measure, that most Yugoslavs had before or since. Much the same can be said of any 1960s housing, though. And the absence, in 'laissez-faire socialism', of much state intervention meant that a lot of people fell through the cracks of the system, particularly given the widespread unemployment provoked first by the market and then even more so by the IMF.

As the self-managed firm distributed flats, a lot depended on the success of the self-managed company itself – first, how successfully the workers controlled it,[21] and second, how much of the profits the company was able to redistribute. The international construction firm Energoprojekt, one of the most successful firms in the SFRY, was notorious for not housing its workers properly. Migrant workers and especially the unemployed were not subject to the system at all. This was exacerbated by the endemic unemployment after the market reforms of 1965 – 'unemployment and insufficient housing were interconnected . . . the idea of hiring new workers was always juxtaposed with the number of new flats to be acquired'; unlike in the Eastern Bloc, the state did not step in, or rather it did so to a relatively small degree.[22] The resulting export of labour, both in the form of guest workers in West Germany and in the international firms that constructed buildings, cities and factories everywhere from Estonia to Kuwait, had its own knock-on effects.

That is, shanty towns emerged. 'Gastarbeiters became important investors in "wild construction"' to meet the need that wasn't being met by workplaces or the state. On the edge of Belgrade on the other side of the Sava, the instant suburb Kaluđerica emerged, 'the largest informal settlement in the Balkans', essentially a favela, albeit with some villas for the wealthy taking advantage of its legal grey status. Some of the houses were large, and like New Belgrade itself, it also had a mix of social groups – migrant workers and returning gastarbeiter, but many skilled workers in construction companies too, most of whom had come back from working abroad on the building programmes of the Non-Aligned Movement. And already before the civil war began, it absorbed migrants fleeing from ethnic tension in Croatia. The result is an accidental district larger than all of the 'official' ones, a capitalist underside to self-management – it actually looks fairly normal, a sprawl of pitched-roofed houses, more suburb in appearance than favela – but with no infrastructure, 'no running water, sewers, or streets'.[23] This was finally exacerbated to crisis point in 1990, when the federal government abolished the right to housing, with the law changed to make it the 'responsibility' of 'working people and citizens' as individuals. With war and privatization, the result was a massive expansion of the informal, with more 'wild construction', this time encompassing roof extensions often larger than the original buildings they're built on to, a chaos that continues to this day.

Unless you're inclined to the advocacy of shanty towns, there is little actually surviving of self-managed practice; but the shell of it is easy to find. Dubravka drove us first to the 1961 New Belgrade Town Hall, which encapsulates some of the puzzling things about the new city. Within its patch of grid, it feels exceptionally civic. Typically for New Belgrade, but atypically for other 'socialist countries', it is Brutalist in the strict sense – concrete Expressionism based on a scrupulous truth to materials, with a confident approach to form – there are low offices enclosing a lush courtyard filled with abstract sculpture, and shade is provided by a sharply cantilevered flying concrete creature, which makes the design, by the architects Stojan Maksimović and Branislav Jovin, instantly memorable. Surrounding it are offices, some equally vivid and Brutalist, others showing a sudden descent into the cheapest Enterprise Zone Pomo, with steel pitched roofs over mirror glass. Tower blocks are everywhere, sheltered by the mature trees retained from the old marshlands, and the results are very handsome, on the Ville Radieuse model; but everything is sliced apart by enormous roads. The SFRY's aforementioned lack of investment in transport infrastructure means that Belgrade is the biggest post-socialist city without a Metro – there isn't much in the way of buses or trams, either, compared with Warsaw or Prague. New Belgrade is a city of the car, and if you're indulgent you could argue that's because in self-management you could self-manage your own transport.

After this, we drove off to see our first piece of self-managed housing – the Genex Tower, that remarkable gateway from the airport to the city.

Self-managed skyscraper: the Genex Tower, New Belgrade

Designed by Mihailo Mitrović in 1970, it is a very powerful piece of architecture, caught agreeably between Brutalist grandeur and space-age kitsch. The twin towers' structure is simple and clear – offices on one side, flats on the other, held up with immense cylindrical buttresses, the Modernist fetish for grain silos deployed for the purposes of a skyscraper. The units go inside, and it is all linked together by an enclosed double-level walkway and that flying saucer on top – to which, unfortunately, we did not manage to blag access. It's bravura architecture, a Brutalist-Baroque balancing act, Ernő Goldfinger's Trellick Tower gone Gagarin, and we were content to just wander round it, amazed, for some time. We were probably equally amazed when Dubravka told us there was no hierarchy to who got the flats. If you worked for Generalexport, a foreign trade conglomerate based in Belgrade, whether as cleaner or manager, you were eligible for a flat here, and chances were you got one. This place, at least, is quite a vindication of the system. Yet, like the others, it's an object tightly packed into a motorway grid, without clear connections to anything much else. On the ground floor of the Genex Tower there are a pizzeria, some murals by children, and some beaten-up but impressive amphitheatre-like landscaping, but it still feels a little lost.

There are parts of New Belgrade, we would learn, where there was some space to stretch out and create a more viable community life, though their names do not always imply this was high up in the self-managed planners' priorities. Blok 23 and Blok 19A would each be regarded elsewhere as two discrete housing estates facing each other across another one of those multi-lane highways – thousands of flats in system-built towers, with schools, shops and such spread out in the green space in between. Visually, they're very different. Blok 23, built between 1968 and 1978, is the more immediately impressive, a wildly confident Brutalist mini-city. Car parked, it presents a classic Modernist combination of slab blocks and point blocks, but the concrete modules are as richly articulated as Gothic cathedrals, with recesses and protrusions breaking out all over their elevations; the services of the blocks are shaped into harsh, stubby, asymmetrical spires. As at the Genex Tower, it's exciting architecture – fearless, wild, unforgettable. As a social space, it comes across as rather more successful. The shops, bars and cafés form a coherent street running along the estate, where there were a lot of people hanging around enjoying the weather; signage, for typography enthusi-

'Blok 23 is best, fuck all the rest'. New Belgrade

asts, is original and impressive, white on red with neat arrows. Walk under the rectangular pilotis of the slab blocks (graffiti, in English – 'Eazy E, RIP, Compton', 'Blok 23 is best, fuck all the rest') and you get, first, to something rather shocking – a tight, cubic concrete courtyard, an almost

A school and playground inside Blok 23, New Belgrade

dystopian image of futuristic urbanity. At this point you might wonder if the architects, Božidar Janković, Branislav Karadžić and Aleksandar Stepanović, weren't going a little too far – though they were, it should be noted, selected by a BOAL, and though the workers hadn't abolished the division of labour between labourer and architect, they did have power of commissioning. But just past that square yard is a park-like space, with playgrounds and a pretty red-brick and concrete school with big windows and a stepped section to emphasize the greenery. Suddenly, it's all quite idyllic.

Blok 19A, though, is consciously attempting the homely. Belgrade architects were very good at doing interesting things with concrete panels, and here the designers, Milan Lojanica, Predrag Cagić and Borivoje Jovanović, banded the components together in a way which makes them look almost mock-Tudor, with a strong brown grid that looks from a distance like wood. They're grouped here into mid-rise blocks of irregular heights, with pitched roofs – equally distinctive, but with less of the deafening roar of the heroic socialist future about them. If Blok 23 and the

Genex Tower display a dangerous, thrilling tightrope act between monumental form and easy public space, Blok 19A shows, like a lot of late-1970s architecture, a shift towards an accommodation between tradition and technology. Both Bloks apparently constitute some of the most popular parts of New Belgrade, and as much as this seems linked to their relative proximity to central Belgrade, it also must have a lot to do with how much they seem to form a very coherent community, clear and strongly centralized, if surrounded with a wider city space of straggle and detritus. They suggest an analogue to a political situation where the individual workplace (and the space it plans for itself) might be highly democratic, but the space around is correspondingly messy. Some argue this is New Belgrade's strength – that already by the 1970s it took on 'the appearance of an unplanned concrescence of diversified leftovers made by interrupted attempts to achieve comprehensive urbanity'. After this extreme, vertiginous landscape of planned and unplanned, held in constant and unresolved tension, 'the city was possessed by one-off buildings radiating images of fake globalized luxury'.[24] Banalization, both informal and formal, was the result.

Opposite Blok 23 and Blok 19A is the major public building in this part of the new city – the Sava Centre, a congress hall/conference centre/shopping centre/concert hall, designed by Stojan Maksimović in 1976 and completed three years later. In 1978, it became obvious to Yugoslavia's leaders that they were about to enter an economic crisis, as the debts were called in; in 1980, Tito died. The Sava Centre was intended as a design to create a 'self-contained world', and it does. It's an example of a sadly brief architectural trend of the 1970s known as 'Zoom', and within a laconic, long, tilted sweep of mirrorglass are brightly coloured metallic fittings, all the surfaces buffed to a sheen – dangling lights like robot arms, bristles of red air vents, a web of tubular bulbs, and all the pipework exposed and painted in garish colours – this is only just after the Pompidou Centre in Paris, and has a similar kids'-playground approach to Futurism, everything asking for exploration and enthusiastic boggling. As urbanism, it is hopeless – the problem with New Belgrade was that it was becoming a dormitory rather than an independent settlement, and building a big car-centred hangar for moneyed guests already suggested the bankruptcy of self-management socialism in terms of making a coherent city out of its capital. As an architectural representation of self-management socialism's internationalist, open ideology, however, it is rivalled only by the Federal Executive Council at the other side of New Belgrade. What began there was ended here.

Among the many intriguing fittings of the building is a world map behind the reception area made up of blue triangular panels, and some desultory luxury shops for the international conference guests. The first of these was the International Monetary Fund, just after the construction was completed, ready to thump down the tablets of the structural-adjustment programmes that did perhaps more than anything else to tear Yugoslavia apart. It is precisely here that the efforts to create the 'free association of producers', meshing in often hostile fashion with the attempt of a Leninist movement to open itself up to a mostly capitalist world, ended in a crushing, bloody defeat. They were not, in the end, more successful than those regimes which banned foreign travel and created petty despots out of bosses and managers; the end was capitalism and nationalism too, only the means of getting there was even nastier. The designers of the Sava Centre can have known none of this; they merely wanted to present the face of one of the twentieth century's greatest success stories to the world.

8
Memorial

> Every dictatorship, whether of man or of party, leads to the forms that schizophrenia loves most: the monologue and the mausoleum. Moscow [is] full of gagged people and monuments to the revolution.
>
> *Octavio Paz*[1]

MONUMENTS WITHOUT BEARDS

Not long after the nationalization of land, the publication of all secret treaties and other more obviously contentious moves, the new communist government in the former Russian Empire decreed a 'call for monumental propaganda'. This was not the action of a government confident of its longevity. Lenin, famously and uncharacteristically, broke into a little dance on the day that the Petrograd Commune of 1917 outlasted the couple of months or so that was allowed to the Paris Commune in 1871; each subsequent day was counted as 'Commune plus one', 'Commune plus two', and so forth, until it began to run into months and years. The Commune, with its close participation from aesthetes like Gustave Courbet and Arthur Rimbaud, may have had some ideas about constructing monuments of its own, but it is much better known for toppling them – the Vendôme Column, most notoriously, as a monument to imperialism and absolute power – for which crime Courbet was held personally responsible. The idea of 'monumental propaganda' was an attempt at leaving something ostensibly permanent, at least more so than the temporary 'street art of the revolution' – albeit in the awareness that counter-revolution would remove the results as soon as it could.

The approach they took was perhaps more prosaic than the actual ideas themselves – busts and small statues of various bearded men, usually made from plaster due to the shortage of materials caused by civil war and international blockade; but the choice was impressively eclectic. Marx and Engels, of course, but also Robespierre, the anarchist Mikhail Bakunin, the Ukrainian poet Taras Shevchenko, part of a list that combined practically every possible revolutionary hero, whether they were politician or poet, follower of the current General Line or not. As for the aesthetic, most were pretty traditional, though a Cubo-Futurist bust of Bakunin was part of the programme. Needless to say, none were of living leaders – no Lenins, no Trotskys, certainly no Stalins. The only sculptural survivor of this immediate post-revolutionary euphoria doesn't feature a human visage at all: it's a rock on the Field of Mars in St Petersburg, with an inscription commemorating the very few who died in the seizure of power.

'Monument' and 'memorial' are generally synonymous, denoting objects that try to speak of the past, whether in a heroic or mournful register. In this sense, they're a matter of memory. But if this 1918 programme for monumental propaganda is remembered at all, it is for its most implausible proposal, which unlike the others never spent a year or two decorating a Petrograd or Moscow street – Vladimir Tatlin's Monument to the Third International. We've encountered this already, this most famous unbuilt project of revolutionary communism. It was, strictly speaking, a building rather than a piece of monumental sculpture, but Tatlin so loaded it with symbolic content that it was intended to serve as a more true monument and embodiment of the revolution than the various ossified figures of Great Men, this new form of socialist idolatry. It would be socialist in its content, by housing the Communist International in their daily business of setting the world aflame; it would also be socialist in its form, riven with symbols that had reference only to the political movement to which it was dedicated, given that the rotating glass volumes inside the spiralling steel structure were intended to 'literally' embody revolution and the dialectic. Tatlin knew all of this was impossible – notoriously, there wasn't enough steel in Russia to construct it; nor was there even enough in Petrograd at that point to build a steel model, so it was pieced together in wood, instead, before being exhibited at the House of Trade Unions. What it was, was a statement about memorials themselves, and about their architectural form. It is iconoclasm, in the original sense. In the new society, it demands, we should not go on creating statues of great men – to do so would be ill-fitting for the egalitarian society we want to create. Instead we will build structures that will be both abstract and symbolic, high tech and dreamlike, revolutionary and playful – as was noticed, Tatlin's tower closely resembled a helter-skelter. They will encapsulate a new kind of city. Nothing built hitherto even approached the spatial extravagance, the wild revolutionary spectacle, of this monument; if it had been built where intended, on the Neva in the centre of St Petersburg, the entire city would have been refocused on and transformed by it. It was not static, either, not a fixed piece of architecture made from heavy masonry: it rotated, it moved, it broadcast calls to revolution across Europe from the radio mast at its peak. Mayakovsky caught it best when he called it 'the first monument without a beard'.[2]

It is some measure of the failure of these early revolutionary hopes that thousands upon thousands of monuments with beards (and moustaches) were constructed across the 'socialist countries'. Were it not for Mao's clean-shaven visage, we could talk about tens of thousands. Yet of all the constructions left by the self-described communist regimes, few are so obvious (or so intriguing) to the foreign visitor, or so enduringly controversial in those countries themselves, as the memorials and monuments that communism erected to itself. They face a difficult, ambiguous fate. First of all, those which have survived in their original place are few and far between in the former Eastern Bloc, and have been pared down in the former USSR as well. What endures is a strange ragbag, and it doesn't always endure for the reasons one might expect. Stalins were the first to go, in the 1960s, except, notoriously, for a few in Georgia, particularly, as we shall see, in his hometown of Gori; there have even been occasional new Stalins erected at the hands of the reactionary Communist Parties of Russia or Ukraine – one was built in 2010 in the Ukrainian industrial city of Zaporizhia. In all of the countries that are now part of the European Union, the once ubiquitous Lenins have disappeared, as have the various local communist leaders who were once immortalized, from the Latvian

Pēteris Stučka to the Hungarian Béla Kun or the Pole Julian Marchlewski; communists who were victims of Stalin were removed along with loyal Stalinists like Klement Gottwald. Communists survive better, in fact, in the former GDR, as a partial consequence of its annexation by a Western country with a Marxist tradition – so in (East) Berlin, Leipzig or Chemnitz (the former 'Karl-Marx-Stadt') the Marxes and Engelses are inviolate. Counterintuitively, some of the most common survivals in terms of monumental propaganda are the most 'Stalinist' complexes in form – the numerous Monuments to the Red Army which were left in liberated cities after 1945, many of which still have inscriptions from Stalin himself. These largely survive as part of an informal agreement with Gorbachev when pulling the Red Army out in 1990, that these large-scale ensembles, often on the site of mass graves, would be retained as a mark of respect to the more than 20 million Soviet citizens who were killed. Which is more than fair, although their strikingly authoritarian, often Socialist Realist form is a reminder of why that liberation was not universally welcomed.

The monuments that do survive, and can be visited – and which are frequently far from ruined, often even having fresh flowers left on them – are usually on the most ruthless, domineering scale, deliberately despotic. Huge soldier-supermen gesticulate and lunge, skyscraping mothers wave swords aloft, concrete escarpments become ritual ziggurats and temples, and eternal flames burn (or, in many cases, don't burn) at the heart of them. Their scale, with their large plazas, steps and other ceremonial spaces, is not conducive to all the things a capitalist city should have – movement, shopping, adverts, *footfall*, as they call it. As a result, some are unexpectedly cherished. The Bulgarian historian Maria Todorova writes that 'while the monumental evidence from the communist period is clearly diminishing, it is more noticeable now when its presence is not mandated. It is acquiring the status of the formerly cherished pre-communist monuments.' Those pre-revolutionary monuments, like the Freedom Monument in Riga, were loved because they were a reminder that something other than Soviet domination was possible. Do Soviet monuments, conversely, contain within them some suggestion that – muscles, beards, guns and all – something other than capitalism is possible?

EMBALMING THE REVOLUTION: THREE MAUSOLEA

Rather than spaces of possibility, the most intense ritual spaces of 'real socialism' are closed off, literally deathly. They form perhaps the best architectural argument for the hackneyed thesis that the USSR was a strange industrial spin on 'oriental despotism', where leaders of revolutions that were intended to do away with all hierarchy, all cults of personal power, were treated as if they were pharaohs. Typically, the magic was achieved via advanced technology. Lenin was embalmed, not mummified. This way, a ritual was created, whereby people would queue outside the mausoleum, then file around the sacred body – placed, incidentally, in a polygonal glass coffin designed by Konstantin Melnikov – then leave, having 'seen' Lenin. This happened against the will of Lenin's family – his widow, Nadezhda Krupskaya, and his sister, Maria Ulyanova – and of many in the Party, including Trotsky. The process by which the decision was made is murky, but it appears to have been an improvised reaction by the Soviet leadership around Grigori Zinoviev to the unexpected mass outpouring of grief at Lenin's death. Suddenly, an insecure government realized that they were popular.

Also popular was the graveside speech by Stalin, whose position, 'General Secretary', at that point meant basically *treasurer* rather than *despot*, but who had nonetheless been a major subject of Lenin's 'testament', which urged that he be removed from his position lest he abuse his power. Stalin's speech was steeped in religious cadences, a series of pledges to the deceased leader – 'We vow to thee, comrade Lenin', and so forth. To get some measure of how much this would have alarmed and disgusted Lenin, it's worth recalling his reaction to his colleagues who intended to create a 'religion of socialism'. 'An agitator or a person addressing the workers [may] speak of "socialism as my religion" in order to make himself better understood . . . while in this case censure would be mere carping, or even inappropriate restriction of the freedom of the agitator, of his freedom in choosing "pedagogical" methods, when a writer begins to preach "god-building", or god-building socialism, party censure is necessary and essential. For some the statement "socialism is a religion" is a form of transition from religion to socialism; for others, it is a form of transition *from* socialism to religion.' And so it occurred. The opinions of the man who once inhabited that embalmed body inside are one thing – and, anyway, it is claimed by some that, even embalmed, Lenin's corpse has started to decompose, and is partly a reconstruction – but the mausoleum that contains him is something else entirely.

Lenin's mausoleum has been claimed by some – cartographer of Constructivism Richard Pare, for instance – as the foundational building of Stalinist architecture, and by others as one of the last works of the avant-garde. The first, temporary mausoleum was erected hastily in winter, in early 1924, to the designs of Alexey Shchusev, the eclectic architect then best known for his neo-Orthodox Kazan station. Shchusev's sources are obscure, but he may have been inspired both by ancient, despotic ritual architecture – Mexican temples, Assyrian ziggurats, the pyramids of the pharaohs – and by the elemental forms of avant-garde painting, the abstract, 'non-objective' shapes floating in space that featured in the work of Kazimir Malevich and his disciples. The mausoleum was placed on the outer wall of the Kremlin, facing not the governmental inner sanctum but the public space of Red Square. The first version was made of a light wood, as the building (and the embalming) was intended to be temporary; it was soon followed by a semi-permanent version, as the Politburo became appreciative of the devotional effect of the corpse-in-state; what sits on Red Square now was redesigned in stone by Shchusev in 1930. By this time, the chameleonic Shchusev had become important as a derivative but skilled Constructivist architect, with elegantly mechanized, streamlined buildings like the Ministry of Agriculture on the Garden Ring; and this new experience informed the re-formed mausoleum. Any mouldings, ornaments or protrusions in the first versions were eliminated, in favour of smooth planes of marble. In a move that would come to dominate the prestige architecture of the 'socialist countries', from the Moscow Metro to the Warsaw Biblioteka Narodowa, he selected rich, unusual stones – veiny black-and-red porphyry, bulky and cubic, but deftly giving way at the corner to create a niche for stairs. These stepped upwards to a temple at the top. In the middle was a speaker's platform – this last was included as a gesture to the ubiquitous parades, forming part of an ensemble with the new Tverskaya/Gorky Street. The tanks and gymnasts and dancers would arrive here to be saluted by the leadership.

This is the mausoleum as it exists today, although it was redesigned for

Red Square, with the Lenin Mausoleum in the foreground
(1961 postcard)

a time to house an embalmed Stalin alongside Lenin, before Khrushchev expelled him from his sarcophagus. Some minor additions have been made, usually farcical – the ill, ineffectual, one-time second-most powerful man in the world Konstantin Chernenko allegedly had an escalator installed in 1984 so that he could wave to parades without having to climb the stairs. Since 1991, both anti-communists and Lenin's family, who would otherwise have little in common, have demanded his reburial with his mother, as he had specifically requested, but the ensemble is too useful to Russian imperial power, even in its current, deeply attenuated form. As a project, Lenin's mausoleum is indefensible on every possible level – political, moral, personal; but not, unfortunately, architectural. Both as an object on its own and as part of the gradual, incremental design of Red Square, Shchusev's building is a masterpiece. Though considerably smaller than most of the other buildings around the ancient Tsarist set-piece of Red Square, from the iron-and-glass Russian Harrods of GUM to the neo-Russian pinnacles of the former Historical Museum, it feels integral, much less of an imposition than the Hotel Moskva nearby. It doesn't follow the materials of the red-brick, spikily turreted Kremlin wall, but its red stone complements it; the way it steps down from its position, aligned with one of the Kremlin towers, to the long, flat square is masterful; and its presence and power for such a tiny structure is awesome and unforgettable. Even then, the first time we visited Red Square, I couldn't bring myself to go in, despite Agata's protestations – she couldn't see why I had any problem with it, and assumed, correctly, that it was connected with some sentimentality about Lenin himself. In 2014 she convinced me, and we finally waited in line for our encounter with the great man.

The queues are not as long as they used to be, when visitors from all over the USSR and the socialist camp had this as an integral part of their itineraries, and the apparatus of fences around the mausoleum designed to hold them usually looks mostly empty; given also that it was raining heavily when we visited, we waited for a mere two minutes before beginning our entry, or, rather, our descent. You enter the mausoleum through a small black-marble door, and then walk down a flight of marble steps into a dark, black crypt. Guards stand upright on either side; Agata whispers a question to me and is immediately silenced by a soldier imposingly, if wordlessly, putting a finger to his lips. Then you get to the room where the sarcophagus lies. It is small, hoisted on a plinth, around which you are to slowly file – travelogues often mention the line being pushed around it at great speed to keep the queue going, but we're given a good few minutes and left unharassed, unless anyone makes the mistake of turning around, breaking the orderly progression around the body. Under the ceiling are stylized red flags in a Constructivist zigzag, but this room is not a Constructivist space, and Melnikov's glass coffin was long replaced with an equally strange, if more ornate, glazed sarcophagus by the sculptor Nikolai Tomsky. The room is deathly, unearthly, and strongly ritualistic – 'spiritual'. The corpse or waxwork or composite of the two is backlit, revealing a pale, slightly ginger head and a frail, tiny body, approximately one tenth the size of the average Lenin statue. The backlighting makes the head glow, making it appear especially waxy. Then you're out, and the guards chaperone you around the memorials of communist worthies between the mausoleum and the Kremlin Wall, where Stalin's grave has been predictably and depressingly furnished with fresh bouquets. It was raining so heavily by this point that I attempted to just walk across the square and get shelter in GUM, but a blast on a guard's whistle put paid to any ideas like that. I couldn't connect the experience remotely with the revolutionary whose body I had just encountered. It was the first and only corpse I have ever seen, given that the secular funerals of my grandparents didn't encourage contemplation of their bodies. If they'd been much more important communists, some decades earlier, in another country . . .

What the Lenin Mausoleum does – still – is drill into the mind the power of a minutely choreographed intersection of architecture and ritual. It is hugely effective, every part of the process – when you enter the door and begin your descent down those black steps it is hard not to gasp. The success of the Lenin ritual was not lost on other communist leaders, at least not when their own big men started to die off. Lenin's embalming team came into high demand from the late 1940s onwards. The first to be embalmed was the Bulgarian premier and Comintern leader Georgi Dimitrov, renowned in his day for defending himself against Göring in the Reichstag trial; persistent rumour has it that he was poisoned on Stalin's orders for being potentially too close to Tito. True or not, Sofia got a temple devoted to his corpse, again of a severe, rectilinear, reduced form; alone of all of them, it was demolished in 1999, to widespread protest. Undemolished is the mausoleum for the Czechoslovak Stalinist Klement Gottwald, a vile figure who instituted the most bloody of all the purges outside the USSR, sending many close friends and comrades to their graves while fully aware of their innocence; and outside Europe Mao and Ho Chi Minh also got their own temple-mausolea, in both cases against their clearly expressed wishes.[3] Tito, though not embalmed, also received a mausoleum. Two of these can be fairly easily visited, so we did so.

The mausoleum of Klement Gottwald still exists, but the body of Gottwald himself no longer occupies it, and has not done since quite soon after his embalming – mistakes were made, and he started rotting, so was placed into a closed sarcophagus instead. One reason why the mausoleum survives is that it forms only one part of a larger complex, rather than being dedicated just to the high-tech showcasing of one man's dead body – the Czech National Memorial, a museum complex on Vítkov Hill in Prague. It is one of the former Czechoslovak capital's many vertical features built onto hilltop sites, and was begun in 1925, to the designs of Jan Zázvorka. As architecture, it is the functionalism dominant in interwar Czechoslovakia classicized and stone-clad in order to serve convincingly as an eternal monument rather than as a transient thing like a department store or workers' housing – a marble cube on a plinth, essentially. Only the front façade was completed, complemented after the war by an equestrian statue of the Hussite leader Jan Žižka. The Gottwald Mausoleum is at the back of the mostly Socialist Realist complex that this was rebuilt into after the war, to revised designs by Zázvorka, and which received an annexe for the dead leader after his demise in 1953. As the mausoleum forms the culmination of a processional route, the rest of the museum needs to be described first. The spaces of the National Memorial, which entail congress halls, war memorials, the mausoleum and a relatively new permanent exhibition on communist Czechoslovakia, are a spectacular reminder of just how little there was to choose between official monumental architecture, even in a liberal democracy like interwar Czechoslovakia, and Socialist Realism; you can walk through it even having some familiarity with architectural styles and not know what is from before the war and what is from after it.

This can be seen in the spaces of memory that occupy the high, columned space that now includes the permanent exhibition. The surfaces everywhere here are familiar to any visitor to the Lenin Mausoleum or the Moscow Metro – shiny, rich, intense marble everywhere, in red, black and grey. At the side of this is the Chapel to Soldiers Killed in the War. In the original design, this was dedicated to executed Czech legionnaires who fought in the First World War against their Austrian masters. The mosaic decoration of this murky alcove was executed by Max Švabinský, and in terms of form, it isn't far from the Moscow Metro – realistic figures, fretted with enamel and gold. The elongated, unproletarian bodies and use of symbolic nudity (a floating nymph with breast bared and head covered, raising a finger to her lips) are the giveaway. On the doors, a very late Art Nouveau candelabra of two nude figures in mourning is neighboured by reliefs of workmen's hands carrying hammers and sickles; verses by the former Surrealist communist poet Vítězslav Nezval are embossed in gold on marble. On the other side is the Tomb of the Unknown Soldier, three black marble sarcophagi capped by golden lamps, with what appear to be demounted flags as their bases. In between, there are the recent spaces of memory, a series of objects tracing the peculiar history of Czech Communism – resistance, electoral victory, coup, terror, 'socialism with a human face', Warsaw Pact-imposed 'normalization' and eventual defeat. Bar a more sympathetic portrayal of Václav Havel than would be accepted by many Czechs, it is informative and uncontroversial, and contains at the end a room where you can write your own political slogans, demands or ideas on the wall. There are scrawled hammer and sickles and, among others, the slogans 'No! I want communism!' (in Czech), 'Poland remembers too' (in Polish) and 'I heart democracy, even if it doesn't work' (in English), which is a quite apt summation of common Czech, Polish and Anglo-American sentiments.

What does it mean to want to write that you want communism after walking round a place like this? Providing this is what you think communism is, what is it exactly that you want? The meeting hall here is one of the most memorable, and terrifying, spaces created by Stalinism anywhere in Europe. Its cyclopean scale and use of so much red marble that you're practically irradiated as you walk around is comparable to very few buildings, and Albert Speer's Reich Chancellery is one of them. The triple-height space is suspended with fluted columns that are almost purple, and the third tier is deep red. A non-structural frame of red marble appears to hold it all together, leading to a partly glazed ceiling, though it all feels impervious to natural light or fresh air. At the head of the hall is a huge bronze wreath fit to be placed on the head of a giant. Such an imposing, intense and (vain)glorious space is undeniably impressive and affecting, although you could be forgiven for reacting the other way, by refusing to be intimidated and seeing it just as overblown and pompous. There is a another mosaic at the entrance to the Hall of Czech

The Memorial Hall at Vitkov Hill, Prague

Peasants, and compared to those in the chapel these men and women here are rather sturdier, people who work with their hands, although also people of remarkable rosy-cheeked beauty. Here, communism means an imperial level of glory, grandeur, opulence and display, one which is perhaps attractive in a context of pragmatic, unromantic capitalist 'normalization' but not of great value in itself.

Finally, after all this, you reach the mausoleum. It is in a semi-circular extension at the furthest end of the National Memorial, symmetrical with that cubic front façade. At one point, you could have entered from this direction, through some curious doors decorated with high bas-reliefs of Red Army soldiers liberating Czechs. The figures are like little toys in their scrupulously detailed beards and trenchcoats, gesticulating, playing accordion, stretching their arms out to point the way forward to the future. Inside, you reach Gottwald as the terminus, as the official culmination of the national history of the Socialist Republic of Czechoslovakia. Through doors lined in more black marble you come first to a sarcophagus in white marble containing the despot (formerly – he was cremated in 1962). In front of you are several mosaic figures in Socialist Realist style depicting Czech soldiers, parachutists, generals; in between each is an uplighter straight out of the Moscow Metro design guide. Above is a mosaic blue sky full of stars, and the lion, the Czech national emblem.

Soviet–Czech friendship on the doors of the National Memorial, Prague

Even here, we are national in form, socialist in content. This is a typical Stalinist space, then, with not much to distinguish it but the extremely high level of craftsmanship and the intense crepuscular creepiness. The only thing the new owners of the space did after 1989 was open a passageway underneath, directly aligned with the sarcophagus. Walk down its stairs and you're at a control room in blue teak and black plastic, where various dials and knobs would regulate the temperature of the mausoleum in order to ensure that Gottwald stayed inviolate. Opposite those controls are busts of Lenin, Stalin and Gottwald himself, darkly lit in horror film fashion. It is a clever, theatrical revelation of the subterfuge, of the technology behind the magic, an ironic cry of 'Pay no attention to the man behind the curtain!' A member of staff tells us that this too is a fake – the control panels are not authentic but are 'put there for the tourists'. But what the National Memorial does is mostly rather subtle. Rather than whacking you over the head and telling you that Communism Was Very Bad, it preserves its ceremonial space as much as possible, only making little interventions to highlight some of the greater absurdities; it fits closely with the ironical, ambiguous view that many Czechs have of the regime, rather than the absolute moral certainty sometimes common elsewhere.

Though Klement Gottwald and Josip Broz Tito were both, in 1945, ardent Stalinists, the sort of fanatical local chieftains that terrified their opponents, the places where each was buried are most unalike, reflecting their particular trajectories. Tito's mausoleum is easily found from the centre of Belgrade, a walk down a steep hill from the Serbian capital's largest building, a neo-Byzantine Orthodox cathedral, handsome from a distance, tacky up close, begun in the 1930s, left well alone under the communists and then expensively completed under Milošević. The memorial space to Tito is really three buildings, two of them completed during his lifetime, the other after his death; all them are in a small park, reached via winding paths from a concrete amphitheatre, with a pool and defunct fountains, and steps upwards; there is a view of the Belgrade skyline and loitering youth. Here there's one of the Marshal's several villas, a typical bit of mid-century contemporary, of interest in showcasing the tastes of Tito – he shocked more ascetic foreign communists with his taste for cigars, yachts and Adriatic villas, forming friendships with Liz Taylor, Richard Burton and their ilk. The Praxis group philosopher Svetozar

Stojanović explained these lapses in terms of class. 'Communists who have grown up in an impoverished and envious environment, like Tito, are most often inclined to enjoy material privileges and a high lifestyle. Communists from well-off families usually endeavour to "redeem" themselves by despising high comforts and benefits.' It was only the revolutionaries from bourgeois backgrounds (like Lenin, presumably) who followed its principles in their actual lives.[4] One historian has claimed that this wasn't so much a breach of Leninist decency as an extreme example of the highly developed consumer culture in the Socialist Federal Republic. That's as may be, but the building housing his body is neither austere nor, in fact, particularly showy or luxurious. The actual mausoleum is known as the 'House of Flowers', and is relatively simple – rather than the darkly lit funereal pomp of Stalinism, we have a small greenhouse, filled with constantly renewed flowers, with Tito underneath an undemonstrative gravestone. It's one of the few communist memorial spaces that is in no way frightening.

In fact, the personality cult of Tito is more extensively expressed in the 25 May Museum, a museum, mark you, devoted to the annual

The House of Flowers, Belgrade (1980s postcard)

celebrations of Tito's birthday, built in his honour as a public gallery of the esteem in which he was held. It is now officially the Museum of Yugoslav History, though it doesn't seem to serve this purpose much.[5] If you didn't know anything about the numerous paradoxes and hypocrisies of self-management socialism you would assume that such a thing would only be devoted to a Ceauşescu or a Kim Il-sung. So it is a monument to a personality cult, and personality cults are by definition a bad thing, but there is quite a lot to like about the Tito's Birthday Museum. Placed at an incline up the hill from the disused fountains, it rests lightly on a ridge between dense trees, a symmetrical glass building held up on thin, tapered pilotis. Its wings are wing-shaped, and in between is a black and grey mosaic in Archaic Greek style showing, on one side, Partisans, on the other, what appear to be ancient warriors with pikes, an unexpectedly atavistic image in the usually Modernist vocabulary of socialist Yugoslavia, with its anti-nationalist ideology of 'brotherhood and unity'. Partisan leader and Warrior, then. Inside, a spiral staircase and Yugoslav ships in vitrines; on the counter, various kinds of Yugo-tat are for sale, examples of the popular form of Ostalgia over here. Rather than seeing this as a longing for socialism, some in the former Yugoslavia see it as another form of its suppression; as the young Slovene critic Primož Krašovec writes, 'it is not a coincidence that this form of (collective) popular memory is named after a term from the repertoire of individual psychology. The term "(Yugo)nostalgia" is very precise and telling, since (Yugo)nostalgia is a result of a process whereby collective (and thus political) memory becomes reduced to a sum of personal experiences and individual memories. Yugonostalgia is what remains after the process of depoliticization of the collective memory of socialism – it is a form of popular memory that has been washed clean of all traces of political demands for social equality, workers' participation in the production process, and internationalism as well as for the anti-fascism, anti-imperialism, and anti-chauvinism that constituted the core of the revolutionary politics of socialism.' Most fundamentally, it's based on buying stuff, whether actual 'vintage' or the contemporary Titoist trinkets available here. We followed suit, our rectitude compromised by amazement at seeing a still-extant public and publicly-funded institution completely and unambiguously celebrating the leader of a socialist revolution, the leader of a Communist Party.

But does that mean the 25 May Museum celebrates socialism and communism? Unsurprisingly, not really. Along with the permanent collection of gifts for Tito – tapestries, cigar cases, etc. – there is a very good collection of Yugoslav modern art, and the original fittings of the Museum's first incarnation. Principal among these is a golden map, onto which the various places that Marshal Tito visited are highlighted, with the year. Walter Benjamin spotted one much like this in Moscow, in 1926, soon after Lenin's death; he wrote that on it, 'Lenin's life resembles a campaign of colonial conquest across Europe'.[6] The Tito version is the same bar the absence of flashing lights. If there is anything interesting in the map, it's the internationalist trajectory it highlights. Great Britain, France, Poland, Hungary and Czechoslovakia were given a mere one visit each by the Marshal – Egypt (the 'United Arab Republic' when the map was made), though, was visited five times, India and the USSR three times each, plus visits to Ghana, Indonesia, Algeria . . . the reason for this is of course Yugoslavia's position in the Non-Aligned Movement – i.e. its international alignment with countries that had successfully resisted

The Non-Aligned Map at the 25 May Museum, Belgrade

colonialism, and that were taking a path of developmentalism and independence from either of the imperial blocs. The 25 May Museum is of dubious significance for any kind of socialism, but it has this one little moment that points elsewhere. Since 1989, everywhere in the former Soviet empire has desperately wanted to be a Normal European Country and begged its way into NATO and the EU, leaping from one imperial bloc into another; each has rewritten its history so that it becomes, as Dubravka Ugrešić puts it, a bulwark against something, usually something from the East.[7] For Europeans striving not to be colonies of Russia or America, making common cause with those in Africa or Asia striving not to be colonies of Britain or France is a distant but oddly inspiring moment. In a context where spaces are so full of death that they appear permanently – and, often, mercifully – closed, it is a rare flash of possibility.

THE MISSING MEMORIALS OF THE REVOLUTION

Krašovec's argument that iconography from the socialist era can be assimilated so long as it doesn't actually suggest socialist politics is amply supported by the striking absence in the post-communist space of something that was once exceptionally common – memorials to, and museums of, revolution. You are considerably more likely to find a war memorial with an extended, gilded inscription from a speech of Josef Stalin than you are to find a memorial to the October Revolution still surviving. The fate of two statues in prominent places in Ukraine's second city, Kharkiv, makes this very clear. One of them is a Monument to the Establishment of Soviet Power in Ukraine, the other is one of the survivors of the vast quantity of Lenin monuments scattered in their tens of thousands from Erfurt to Ulan Bator. The Monument to the Establishment of Soviet Power needs some history to be fully explained. The 'Russian' Civil War was at its most complex and multifaceted in Ukraine, where the Red Army, first with and then against a large anarchist force led by Nestor Makhno, faced off against not only the Tsarist revanche and foreign armies of intervention (here, largely German) that they faced everywhere else, but also against various Ukrainian nationalist armies under the nominal control of Ukrainian governments – whose face could be social democratic, like the historian Mihailo Hrushevsky, or fiercely nationalistic, as with Symon Petliura, whose forces were notorious for pogroms on a scale unprecedented even here, estimated to have killed 60,000 Jewish

The Monument to the Establishment of Soviet Power in Ukraine, Kharkiv

civilians.[8] The rising of the workers at the Kiev Arsenal in 1918 failed to secure the city for the Bolsheviks, so a Ukrainian Soviet Republic was set up in the much more pro-Bolshevik industrial city of Kharkiv instead – which became, after the Reds' victory in 1921, the centre of the largest expansion of Ukrainian-language education and culture that had been seen to that date, so fulfilling many of the Ukrainian nationalists' demands.[9]

So the monument is not wholly a monument to Russian domination, but it does, obviously, take a side. The working men and women and Red Army soldiers who seized the city in 1918 are depicted as chiselled-cheekboned behemoths, pieced together out of great cubic chunks of red sandstone, so large that you can see cement-seeping gaps between them that revealed them to be cladding on concrete. The design is original, but conforms to a standard type of the later Soviet era, with the five giants ranged around a central, semi-abstract plinth, so that the monument could be admired from all sides. Look at photographs, when they survive, of the people who were the revolution and they do not look like this: they were awkward, with strange Edwardian facial hair, spindly and ill-fed, and their heroism was in their actions rather than their appearance. The monument was a spectacularization of the revolution, its travesty into superheroics.

This is unlikely to be the reason why the monument was demolished in 2012.[10] It stood in the relatively picturesque part of Kharkiv, where socialist neo-Baroque, Art Nouveau and some Orthodox domes in pretty green squares connected by steps form a non-concrete enclave. Accordingly, it was in the bit of the city that tourists were likely to see when they visited to watch football games there in the Poland/Ukraine-hosted European Championship. But in the vast asphalt plain of the former Dzerzhinsky Square, Lenin remained on his red granite plinth, pointing proudly to the Gosprom/Derzhprom building behind him. In fact, in one of the pre-tournament ads shown in Ukraine the square, in some accounts the largest in Europe, was proudly shown – without Lenin. A press release was sent out by city authorities to reassure people that actually this was just a bit of creative retouching on the part of the advertiser and Lenin was staying put. A Soviet statue depicting a collective action is unacceptable. That's *communist*. One that shows a heroic leader is just fine. Lenin, in Putinist ideology (and the ideas of Ukraine's Party of the Regions were

Lenin, Freedom/Dzerzhinsky Square, Kharkiv (1987 postcard)

not dissimilar), is remembered along with Ivan the Terrible, Peter, Catherine, Nicholas II, Stalin, Brezhnev, and whoever else had a sufficiently iron fist, as one of the people that made Russia 'great'. Lenin's repeated denunciations of 'Great Russian chauvinism' and reprimands for those colleagues (like Dzerzhinsky and Stalin) who made concessions to it are, naturally, forgotten, in the event that they were ever known in the first place.

It is possible that Lenin survives as a 'hero' not because he's seen as a socialist, but because he's seen – albeit on the most fraudulent historical grounds – as a nationalist. He was certainly a state-builder; and in the statue in Dzerzhinsky Square, it would seem he was a body-builder. However, to object to these statues on the basis of their bad taste or their travesty of history is to miss the role they play in maintaining Soviet memory for a significant part of the population, for those who refuse to recall their youth as an endless Gulag, but as something of which they are, at times justly, quite proud. In the aftermath of the overthrow of Yanukovych and the Party of Regions in early 2014, Lenin statues were toppled all over Ukraine. This was explained to us by young Ukrainian leftists as something that the celebratory people not in Kiev could do, an act they could commit to show their support for the rising and relief after Yanukovych's flight; 'the monuments were devoid of real political meaning from the moment they were put up', Oleksandr Burlaka told Agata and me. We weren't totally convinced – why else were they a target other than through an ideology they were seen to encapsulate, and why did far-rightists from the Svoboda party so often take the lead in removing them? And why, in many cities in eastern and southern Ukraine, did groups of citizens form to defend them? It seems too easy to say, as did Slavoj Žižek among others,[11] that the defenders of Lenin, just like the topplers of the statues, saw him as a symbol of Russian nationalism (here seen positively). One of the statues which citizens assembled to defend was exactly this Lenin-colossus in Kharkiv. By April 2014, the local Maidan (here, as in Kiev, with many left-wingers among them) had apparently agreed with this 'Anti-Maidan' to leave Lenin alone, but it was eventually pulled down to the acclaim of world liberals in a small demonstration that September, led by the openly neo-Nazi Azov Batallion, stationed here for the war with the Russian-backed 'republics' in nearby Donbass. The mayor of Kharkiv immediately pledged to rebuild it.[12]

What the Leninoclasm of Ukraine in early 2014 revealed was partly a certain weakness for cliché, a belated replay of 1989 for those who wanted one: there's nothing like a toppled communist statue to cry 'Democracy!' and 'Freedom!' to liberals and Western journalists, even if its removal was hugely unpopular (a massive majority in a Kiev opinion poll saw the statue's removal as mere vandalism), and even if it was torn down by neo-fascists and then daubed in anti-Semitic graffiti. Yet it also revealed just how many Lenins were left. Maps appeared, showing dozens of toppled (or soon-to-be-toppled) statues across central and eastern Ukraine. This was a reminder that Lenins were, quite literally, an industry. A samizdat photograph taken in the 1970s showed the yard of one of the factories that created Lenins[13] – twenty or so identical Vladimir Ilyiches, seated and bent imposingly forward, a common Lenin pose, along with the more famous outstretched arm (there are no photographs of him in either position, of course). They first became an institution only a couple of years after Lenin's death. The earliest surviving – the earliest of all – was designed for the square in front of Leningrad's newly renamed Finland Station, and erected in 1926. As anyone who's read *Ten Days*

That Shook the World or seen *October* knows, it is here that Lenin arrived from exile in April 1917, jumped onto an armoured car, and announced to the assembled crowd that the workers' and soldiers' Soviets should prepare to seize power from the Provisional Government – to the alarm and horror of most Bolsheviks.[14] How to represent such an event, where there was a such a link between the leader and the masses, rather than a lone bearded gent in a square?

Later statues, such as that in Freedom/Dzerzhinsky Square in Kharkiv, would get around this in a typically Stalinist way, by featuring an assembled flag-waving crowd in low-relief in the bottom tiers of a stepped plinth, with Lenin himself, giant-size, at the top. The designer of the Finland Station Lenin, the architect Vladimir Schukuo, must have thought the option of Lenin on top of an armoured car a little bit literal. What he designed for the leader was an abstract sculpture in bronze, where the car would be suggested by an avant-garde assemblage of cubes and cylinders, as if in motion, in the process of formation; but on top of that, a strict realist bronze of the man pointing forward and looking more healthy and musclebound than ascetic, itinerant intellectuals tend to. Like the Lenin Mausoleum itself, it's caught between early-Soviet Modernism and the traditionalist-eclectic domination that would follow. It was recently repaired, having been shot at by an oligarch, passing in his chauffered car. He blasted the backside of Lenin with a bazooka, and perhaps deserves credit for knowing fully what Lenin actually stood for, i.e. the destruction of people like him.

Other Lenins survive, albeit mostly limited to the East Slavic nations. In the EU, there are a couple in Bulgaria or the Russian-speaking districts of Estonia, but there's at least one prominent Lenin in almost every large-sized Russian, Belarusian and eastern/southern Ukrainian city. The standard didn't leave much room for artistic development – the plinths are often more interesting, though they always have a frisson. Take the various Lenins in Nizhny Novgorod. We found at least five in situ during a week in the city, and as our friend Kirill Kobrin pointed out, they have a 'life of Jesus' quality, showing the various possible ways you could identify with Vladimir Ilyich – baby Lenin (a plaque in high relief showing the Ulyanov family), youthful insurgent Lenin (attending the 'Nizhny Novgorod Marxist group' in 1900, outside the heavy, sandstone KGB building), or fatherly leader Lenin (a three-foot-high bust outside the entrance to an apartment block on the river). Addressing the Oka river, commanding a vast square, is one of the USSR's largest, not much smaller than the tower blocks and hotels that frame it – again, a gigantic Lenin figure with square jaw and sweeping, beckoning gesture, this time flanked by subsidiary figures – woman with flag, workers rising from the ground to fly the banner aloft, etc. They are as repetitive and as specifically meaningful as icons, depicting a man who declared at the start of the 1920s 'we will sell everything except icons and vodka'.

The Holy Ulyanov family, Nizhny Novgorod

For both Agata and me, coming across a Lenin at the helm of a square was always a sign that we'd left Normal European Countries behind, which was no doubt part of the reason why they were toppled in Ukraine's 'Euromaidan'. Even when Lenins do endure, the Lenin Museums generally do not, with a couple of exceptions in the Russian Federation.[15] Lenin Museums and Museums of the Revolution were sometimes synonymous as spaces of Soviet ritual, but there was the necessary difference in content – the revolutionary museum had to emphasize mass struggle, maybe, even, accidentally, spontaneous action. They had a strange performative role, one which could, without doing it too much injustice, be called 'magical'. In his short book on Soviet Marxism, Herbert Marcuse wrote of Soviet phraseology that it was meant 'to be performed like a ritual, which accompanies the realizing action. They are to recall and sustain the required practice. Taken by themselves they are no more committed to the truth than are orders or advertisements: their "truth" is in their effect. *Magical* elements gain ascendancy over comprehending thought and action.' Does that mean that this is more evidence of some primeval atavism, some eternal Slavic soul longing for the irrational? On the contrary, Marcuse argued that it was actually very modern, and linked closely with the failure of the revolution to realize its promises.

'The contemporary reactivation of magical elements is far from primitive. The irrational elements enter into the system of scientifically planned and practised administration – they become part of the scientific management of society. Moreover, the magical features of Soviet theory are turned into an instrument for rescuing the truth. While the ritual formulas, severed from their original cognitive context, thus serve to provide unquestioned directives for unquestioned mass behaviour, they retain, in a hypostatized form, their historical substance. The rigidity with which they are celebrated is to preserve the purity of their substance in the face of an apparently contradicting reality and to enforce verification in the face of apparently conflicting facts which make the pre-established truth into a paradox. It defies reason; it seems absurd. But the absurdity of Soviet Marxism has an objective ground: it reflects the absurdity of a historical situation in which the realisation of the Marxian promises appeared – only to be delayed again – and in which the new productive forces are again used as instruments for productive repression'.[16]

What this apparently cryptic Hegelian language is pointing to is that the magic in the Soviet ritual 'works': it brings something into being. The evidence of the revolution's betrayal, of the total contradiction of the actual politics of Lenin himself, the absence of real solidarity, is in its turn contradicted by the performance of the revolution's commemoration, the public pledging of fealty, the transformation of Lenin into a god, and the ritualization of solidarity in the form of the parade. In architecture, this had a particular spatial kick – spaces that stressed the history of the workers' movement were ways of both reviving in the memory the hopes

Great Patriotic waxworks, the Central Museum of the Revolution, Moscow

and dreams of that movement, and making sure that their realization was impossible.

Take Moscow's Museum of the Revolution, one of the few survivors. Renamed the Museum of Contemporary History after 1991, it is spread across several sites – a panorama in the Krasnopresnaya district, the preserved houses of revolutionaries, and a Central Museum of the Revolution in the former English Club, a pretty red-painted Doric revival building, the only major survivor of the street's steroidal Stalinist rebuilding. We visited in 2014 expecting a triumphalist post-socialist redesign, and the entrance hall, with its great framed photographs of V. V. Putin, seemed to confirm this; but after we entered, the only major concessions to the new narratives since the 1990s were occasionally puzzlingly conflicting captions to exhibits – while the exhibits you were looking at would denounce the Tsarist secret police, a caption would tell you what a good job they had done to hold the country together; a celebratory proclamation of the Bolshevik seizure of power would feature a little bilingual text about the Socialist Revolutionary Party, the largest part of the non-Bolshevik left who Trotsky had thrown into the 'dustbin of history'; and Trotsky himself was a little more present among the photographs and ephemera than he can possibly have been before glasnost. But for these cosmetic changes, this is a Museum of the Revolution, full of exhibits which can't possibly make any sense to anyone not familiar with that history, as it was drilled into every young brain until 1991. The museum consists of artefacts on display inside and outside glass cases, with what would today maybe be called 'interactive' rooms where waxwork people sit permanently in a historic environment of some sort, which goes chronologically from the 1900s to the 1980s. These are fascinating constructions, saying a lot about the era's values.

The earliest of these environments is a Tsarist prison that you can peek into through the slit in a ragged wooden door, at the end of a corridor. Inside, a waxwork worker suffering *katorga* sits by a lamp, ill and unshaven. On the adjacent wall, above a samovar and a chamber pot, is a painting of a prison revolt. Nearby is the room of a bourgeois, with ornate furniture and a microscope. These smaller rooms are reached from a vestibule where old magazines, leaflets, paintings and other ephemera are organized round a sculpture of a worker picking up a hammer, as if to wield it imminently, in the revolution of 1905. All the rooms are arranged like this – a central sculpture, exhibits around it, and 'rooms' from consecutive political periods. For the 1920s, a model of the Shabolovka Tower is the central sculpture, while a flapper-hairstyled woman sits looking cool in an NEP café, in front of a cake and a pineapple, as if to signify the slightly suspicious semi-capitalist abundance of the era. For the 1930s, the 'sculpture' is a tractor, the room is a mock-up of the office of the Stalinist Commissar of Industry, Sergo Ordzhonikidze. In the section on the Russian Civil War, the room features a kulak hoarding grain in a grim wooden house; for the post-war high-Stalinist era, a teenage girl sits at her study in front of an image of Moscow State University; and for the Khrushchev era, the sculpture is of course a Vostok space module. This masquerade coexists happily with 'real' exhibits, just as it does in, say, London's Imperial War Museum: real handwritten banners from the revolution, real mimeographed leaflets from red Petrograd, real shells, real scraggy uniforms. Objects from which the real messy unplanned revolution seeps through are placed on the wall alongside monumental realist canvases of the exact same events, to enforce their meaning. The authentic and the constructed, priceless works of art and 1980s kitsch, align together in a historical fantasy which is both obviously a construction while being scrupulously naturalistic. You become

GDR Council of Ministers Building, Berlin, with Liebknecht's sacred balcony (1969 postcard)

'closer to history' through these immersive spaces, but it is not a history open to interpretation.

Yet in museums you are aware you're seeing something curated, something pieced together, no matter how apparently immersive or interactive its artefacts. Another way that the magic was conveyed was through a 'real' space which had endured through the years, and hence could become a sort of sacred relic. Sometimes the cultic historic buildings actually existed, but often these relics were salvaged from ruins; in some cases, they actually had to be re-created, as when the planners of post-war Minsk, projecting the Belarusian capital anew as a Stalinist showcase, rebuilt only a small wooden house, simply because it had hosted the first conference of the Russian Social Democratic Labour Party, best known for its later warring factions, the Mensheviks and Bolsheviks. The former Council of Ministers Building in East Berlin is one of the GDR's more immediately odd structures, as it doesn't appear to conform to either the Socialist Realist or Modernist versions of East German aesthetics. There is a block facing the street with wide windows, dressed with red mullions – good contemporary architecture, maybe with a little classicizing hint in the delicate mouldings. But there in the middle for some reason is a fragment of granite eighteenth-century Baroque.

This atypical linking of classical and modern in one structure, rather than being placed apart and in contrast, is the consequence of the decision to preserve just one part of a largely bomb-destroyed building – the central wing with its balcony, because from here the communist Karl Liebknecht, leader with Rosa Luxemburg of the far-left, anti-war Spartacus movement, had proclaimed a Socialist Republic in the chaos of the German Revolution of November 1918. The official proclamation of the Republic the same day by the Social Democrats was not a sign of their confidence – some were still holding out for a constitutional monarchy – but a way of neutralizing any Spartacist claim to the revolution. This would be confirmed, it must be said, by the elections soon after, where (amid considerable anti-Spartacist violence) the official Social Democrats won a clear victory, with the anti-war Independent Social Democrats coming second. But though a majority of Germans may have rejected communism at the polls, keeping the balcony was a means of keeping the claim of the German Socialist Republic alive, a constant, three-dimensional proof of legitimacy. Though libertarian socialists like Liebknecht and Luxemburg had little in common politically with Walther Ulbricht or Erich Honecker, keeping their memory alive was essential for the GDR, a way of proving the existence of a popular mandate. The cult of the popular murdered pre-1933 communist leader Ernst Thälmann served a similar purpose, hence his gigantist – and preserved – memorial complex in Prenzlauer Berg. But it wasn't enough just to point to the historical record – no, the actual balcony itself had to be retained. This way of regarding historic buildings is not limited to 'real socialism': note, for instance, that during the clearance of a huge swathe of terraced housing near the centre of Liverpool, campaigners successfully won the concession that the street where Ringo Starr used to live would be saved – but their distinctive combination of militant materialism and magical thinking meant that they had a particular taste for it.

One pivotal building for the Russian socialist movement that didn't have to be put back together or replicated is the house of Matilda Kshesinskaya, in the Petrogradsky district of St Petersburg, on the north side of the Neva. It was eventually purchased by the state and turned in 1957 into the Museum of the Revolution, and more recently became, with some considerable tweaking, the Museum of Russian Political History. Rather than a revolutionary, Kshesinskaya was a ballerina and favourite of Tsar Nicholas II, and she was wealthy enough to commission a house, a typical piece of decadent Art Nouveau built in 1906. After Nicholas's abdication, but before their seizure of power, the Bolsheviks expropriated it and used it as an office. Hounded out after the riots of July 1917, their more famous base of operations was similarly unlikely – a neoclassical girls' school, the Smolny Institute, which still has a Lenin in front of it, but otherwise serves a non-commemorative role as the governor of St Petersburg's office. So perhaps the only space left that strictly commemorates the 'Great October Socialist Revolution' in the city where it occurred just happens to be a very pretty Jugendstil villa built for a ballerina. As architecture, it's quite delightful, an asymmetrical design with turrets, neatly cut yellow glazed bricks, stained glass and lots of iron and glass, including a large, beautifully detailed curved-glass bay window, from which Kshesinskaya could watch the world go by in the street outside. It's Art Nouveau at its more modern edge, spreading out with an informal, de-centred plan which suggests the influence of Frank Lloyd Wright's Prairie Houses, rather than Art Nouveau as a form of appliqué onto the usual tenement or house. It's a house which people might conceivably visit for its own sake, though peculiarly ill-suited for its later purpose. Poets of the revolution were aware of the incongruity: Mayakovsky wrote of how:

> Kshesinskaya's palace,
> earned by twiddling toes
> today's invaded
> by boots steel-heeled

In the museum itself, we do not learn what the assembled revolutionaries may have thought about this piece of bourgeois decadence – and remember, Art Nouveau was the lowest of the low in their architectural ideology – but rather it is treated with the same reverence as the city's neoclassical relics. It would be interesting to know whether these railings of flowers and leaves, these big glass bays, were of interest to the ragged-arsed proletariat that expropriated it. But then, the proletariat isn't supposed to look like that, and in one of the building's surviving furnishings from its former incarnation, they don't. You do get the full

The Pantheon of National Revival Heroes, Ruse

intimidating treatment from the staff – special prices for foreigners, plastic bags for your feet so you don't stomp around getting it muddy (imagine the same stricture in 1917!), and strictly no photography. Murals on the walls show heroic workers and peasants doing their heroic-workers-and-peasants thing, and in the vitrines documents which take an ambiguous view, but generally a negative one, of the Bolsheviks, the revolution and its consequences, although Lenin's room is still preserved. A room which used to have revolutionary porcelain now has exhibits on Putin and Medvedev, something which saddened even those formidable women on the staff. Why it was preserved for this purpose is still enduringly strange. When walking round you were supposed to think about what happened in this building, but are presumed not to be interested in the building itself; to feel the air of revolution, to get its whiff, to touch the same walls that Lenin touched (if the guards will let you). That doesn't mean the building itself is neutral – how can it be when it has to be closely preserved and re-created?

If 1917 is still far too controversial for most of its memorials to be left as they were, the same is not necessarily true of other revolutions. In Ruse, in northern Bulgaria, there is an unusual Pantheon to the revolutionary heroes that helped the country throw off the 'Ottoman Yoke' in the late nineteenth century. Since national oppression was perpetrated by Turks rather than Russians – in fact, the Tsarist Empire actively supported the Bulgarian revolutionaries – it was quite acceptable to celebrate a national revolution here, with no likelihood that this could, as commemorations of anti-Tsarist risings did, spill over into the public expression of anti-Soviet sentiments.[17] The first sight of the Pantheon, just outside Ruse's attractive, recently renovated fin-de-siècle centre, reveals a very unexpected steal: although the building you are looking at from the other side of a sweeping and overgrown square is a 1970s memorial and ossuary to the heroic figures of a revolutionary movement of the 1870s, you are in fact looking at a rebuilding of the 1890s Secession building in Vienna, which was a deliberately decadent, opulent showcase for various naughty, aestheticist kinds of art. The heavy, neo-Assyrian stone pylons and the gold-plated cupola are not only similar in superficial appearance; they also have similar relations of proportion. The major difference is the relative lack of ornament and fol-de-rol in that cupola, and the fact that a cross has been placed on top of it – recently, as an act of 're-Christianization'.

As with many of the 'social condensers', this memorial has the clear aim of replacing a religious experience, and not only because it replaced a church, to much enduring controversy. The 'National Revival' of the 1870s may have been in some ways a secular revolution, although aided by the Orthodox big brother next door against a Muslim empire, but the building has attempted the creation of the sense of hushed awe and uncanniness found in a church. The architect, Nikola Nikolov, had to avoid obvious Christian (or, here, Byzantine) references, and the gilded dome is not unique to any particular faith; and like Shchusev in the Lenin Mausoleum, many of the other architectural gestures are borrowed from the heavy, elemental style of the antique Near East. Inside, the place is haunting, with a gauzy light coming from the slits under the cupola, ethereal marble ladies in mourning built sheer into the walls, coffins along the floor, and a remarkable wooden frieze of nineteenth-century insurgents. In the centre, under the dome, is an exhibition. Agata whispers to me, so as not to be heard by a Bulgarian tour group: 'They have icons painted *last year.*' Again, religion has reclaimed the attempt to build a space of secular revolutionary ritual.

However, this building, no matter how derivative, is still deeply peculiar and unique – most revolutionary memorials aimed at a more generic quality. It's surprising at first to find that even in cities that are keen to erase any traces of the commemoration of the October Revolution, the monuments to its 'rehearsal', the revolution of 1905, are generally preserved, even in countries that pride themselves on anti-communism. 1905 was remarkably similar in its trajectory to 1917. As a result of military defeat (here at the hands of Japan, in the Russo-Japanese war), poverty, poor working conditions and imperial oppression, risings broke out all over the Russian Empire. At first they were peaceful and even monarchist – as in the infamous 'Bloody Sunday', where priest and police spy Father Gapon led a devout crowd to be massacred in St Petersburg's Palace Square; then, they became much more radical and explicitly socialist, with workers forming, for the first time, 'Soviets', directly elected councils, to organize their affairs; in St Petersburg, Trotsky, then a Menshevik, was elected as the Soviet's leader. Though the Tsar neutralized the protests by allowing relatively free elections, protests and strikes raged on until 1906, before repression had its effect. The main difference with 1917, other than defeat, was the fact it encompassed the whole Russian Empire, without a large chunk of it being occupied by Germany, as it was twelve years later – which means that the revolution also took place in Poland, Finland, Lithuania, Latvia and Estonia, all of which had lock-outs, strikes, risings and Soviets.

There are monuments, then, in the centres of Tallinn and Riga; these are not full-on quasi-architectural ensembles but the more regular bronzes on plinths, though their survival in cities that have otherwise cleansed themselves almost entirely of heroic monuments is notable enough. As they are monuments to a defeated revolution, their heroism has to be in some way combined with pathos, a mix of emotions that made it a trickier job for sculptors than most. The Tallinn monument is made up of three figures – a man, a woman and a child, on top of the usual red-granite steps, which are simply decorated with the bronze year '1905'. The man, a bare-chested worker, is prone, and covering part of his chest with a cloth, implying that he has been shot; he lies on collapsed flags. The woman, with the small child clinging to her skirts, waves her hand in the air as if to beg the soldiers to hold their fire. This is Socialist Realism in its high-Stalinist version, so rather than the heroes being abstracted and slightly cubic, the example is still the Renaissance: the three figures are held in a perfectly balanced tension, with the curve of the woman's arm matching the curled-in leg of the injured worker. Her face is carefully rendered, her look one of mingled concern and anger. The Riga monument, too, captures the moment of defeat in strictly realist fashion, with one worker fallen, and another, above him, striving forward, flag in hand; its arcing forms harmonize rather well with the recently completed late-1980s National Library on the other side of the Daugava. The largest surviving memorial complex that we managed to find was in Łódź, which was, along with St Petersburg, one of the most militant cities in the revolution, with its largely female workforce conducting long, bitter strikes, aided – or not – by actions from the paramilitary organizations of the Polish Socialist Party, led then by one Józef Piłsudski.

We found out that the Łódź 1905 memorial survived through pure accident, rather than through research – there were photographs of it in a 1970s book, and notes in a tourist booklet suggested that a 'hideously ugly' monument to 1905 survived in Józef Piłsudski Park. We put two and two together, and after walking for nearly an hour through the interminable parks planted on the edges of the city centre after the war to give the dense industrial city some relief, we managed to find somebody who

Monument of the Revolutionary Deed, Łódź

could tell us where it was – an elderly couple who seemed as pleased as they were surprised that anybody was interested. When we found it, the structure was unmistakable. It is officially known as the 'Monument of the Revolutionary Deed', and was designed for the sixtieth anniversary in

1975 by the sculptor Kazimierz Karpiński. It consists of six billowing, twisted obelisks and a low relief of sculptures and inscriptions, all of it in glorious grey granite and reinforced concrete. No red sandstone, bronze or Michelangelesque balance here. The square in front is set on a slope, with pathways and steps leading off back into the park on either side, something which makes it prime skateboarding territory. These wavy semi-obelisks have been modelled as organic abstract sculpture, the concrete riddled with fleshy indentations, with them all being joined at the top by concrete arms. Each bears a year between 1905 and 1909 (after which Łódź was fully 'pacified'), with of course 1905 itself at the front.

Originally, however, as our 1970s book proved,[18] one of the arms featured the year '1948', when Polish communists took full power; this was removed and replaced with just another '1905'. This is fair enough, as 1905 was a popular revolution, and 1948 was a coup courtesy of elections rigged at its eastern neighbour's behest; the problem is not its excision, but its being read backwards so that one determines the other. Regardless, the relief sculpture is Soviet as Soviet can be, in the 'severe style' that directly succeeded Socialist Realism – workers in concrete so stark that they're Easter Island-esque, with no details, just all face and force – the granite cladding is set in an overlaying pattern, broken only by jaws, fists, noses, forearms, breasts. But as a secluded spot, with a slope and lots of places to sit, it's a major congregation point for Łódź's youth; each of these twisted obelisks, stelae, tentacles or whatever they are is coated on the lower levels by dozens of inscriptions saying who loves whom. So the memorial is domesticated, and it is probably better than the authoritarian rituals of stomping parades and worthy speeches. Can its domestication coexist with a revolutionary charge? It seems unlikely. But compared with the state of public sculpture in Łódź – its main streets filled with a hundred or so recent bronzes of local characters – it is at least evidence of a revolution in aesthetics, in favour of sculpture that is dramatic, large-scale, raw and filled with contentious political content.

The fact that this is now in a park named after Józef Piłsudski is the clue as to why the 1905 Revolution memorials survive when others do not. Unlike 1917, where the only narrative available is either revolutionary socialism or Russian dominance (as we've noted, on dubious historical grounds), 1905 can be spun, not wholly inaccurately, as a 'springtime of the peoples'. The westernmost peoples in the Russian Empire – Poles and

Latvians especially – were among the most revolutionary, the most determined to destroy Tsarism. Although national *independence* was seldom raised as a slogan, many of those involved – most obviously, Piłsudski himself – would become after 1917 the organizers of actual independence from Russia. wAnd in the other countries (if not Poland) there wasn't much in the way of nationalist agitation before 1917, and forebears have to be found. So although this was in fact a revolution in which Poles, Russians, Ukrainians, Latvians and Lithuanians all fought on the same side against a common enemy – and a revolution in which class, with worker set against boss, was paramount – it can be remembered as a revolution against Russian imperialism and absolute monarchy, which it was too. In short, it can be remembered as a national revolution, which is the only acceptable kind, and we can forget about the possibility that national oppression was once linked with class exploitation. Safe in people's knowledge that revolutionary monuments do not induce revolutionary attitudes by osmosis, they are left alone despite being fundamentally identical to monuments to the revolution that happened twelve years later; and they

Kutaisi's Monument to Socialist Labour

could be just any other monuments to striving nations, to heroic patriots. As we shall see, they often used the same sculptors anyway.

SOVIET JINGOISM

It is not easy to find monuments that glorify the present possibilities and enjoyments of socialist existence, bar perhaps the various monuments to the space programme. What there is can be particularly unconvincing. In a secluded square just off the central park of Kutaisi, the second-largest city in Georgia, is a Monument to Socialist Labour. Kutaisi is a town where, aside from a few restored central streets and a bizarrely incongruous ultra-modern government headquarters on its outskirts, modernity seems to have stopped in the 1990s, leaving in its absence a strange, jagged chaos of wi-fi-equipped self-built shacks, fences within fences, crumbling apartment buildings and half-finished pavements. It is thus a strange place to find the glorification of Soviet work, or rather the perfect place, depending on your politics. Sitting in between a Stalinist office block and a piquant Art Nouveau cinema, *Glory to Work* consists of several stepped plinths with figures on top, each of them representing a 'Hero of Socialist Labour of Our City'. By the time the monument was built in 1985, the official Hero of Socialist Labour award didn't mean much more in ideological terms than an MBE, so the actual figures on top of each plinth just represent (rather lithe) dancers and suchlike rather than hulking proletarians. In fact, it is only the spatial extravagance of the monument, with its plinths framed by semi-circular stone frames, arranged around each other to form oblique compositions, that suggests it is Soviet at all – it resembles more the post-socialist monuments of the bizarrely successful post-Soviet sculptor Zurab Tsereteli, purveyor of outrageous vitalist kitsch from Cannon Street to the Kremlin, but who began as a bright, talented mosaic artist in Soviet Georgia. This curious, if rather diverting, failure to represent the socialist present convincingly is a reminder that the regime legitimized itself largely on the basis of past victories, more than present achievements. Of those bygone triumphs, none were greater than 1945.

The Great Patriotic War of 1941–5 – as opposed to the Second World War of 1939–45 – was, after the revolution itself, the Soviet regime's greatest legitimation. It is not always remembered as such outside Russia or Belarus (and, to a degree, Ukraine), something which is largely to do with two things: the Cold War, which by now we really ought to have grown out of; and, more understandably, the Molotov–Ribbentrop pact, which we will come to. The facts are that the Red Army and the citizens of the Soviet Union suffered more than any other country at the hands of Nazi Germany, and the facts are that they did more than any other country to defeat it, with the overwhelming majority of the fighting in Europe being done by the Soviets. The oft-quoted figure of 20 million Soviet citizens killed is considered by many to be an understatement. And contrary to the stereotype that the killing and the victory were caused by the Russians' cavalier attitude to human life, with soldiers just being thrown at the Germans and victory resulting from sheer numbers, the greater number of that 20 million were, in most estimates, civilians.[19] It is, then, an indisputable fact that the world was saved from what, in 1940, could have looked like certain Nazi hegemony, almost solely by the actions of the Soviet Union and its people. This sounds like the most absurd propaganda, but it is corroborated by all but the most hostile historians. For all the (understandable) focus on the sacrifices of, say, Poland, the USSR's contribution was vastly greater. It is impossible to understand anything of what happened next without bearing this in mind.

In addition, the Holocaust began here, when the *Einsatzgruppen* followed in the rear of the Wehrmacht, capturing Soviet Jews and shooting them en masse in pits, as at Babi Yar in Kiev. In the argument of Arno J. Mayer, the Holocaust and the war against the Soviets were almost inextricably linked as part of what was called 'Judeo-Bolshevism' – as some still call it in Poland, unironically, *Żydokomuna*. Irrespective of current, usually geopolitically motivated claims otherwise, there is no serious doubt that Nazi rule was vastly worse than Stalinist rule. The Baltic states, western Ukraine and Poland had communist governments imposed against the popular will, and all faced large-scale deportations of citizens to the Gulag; but Generalplan Ost envisaged these countries' wholesale clearance, depopulation, deindustrialization and extermination so that they could serve as agricultural German colonies. In Poland, Belarus, Ukraine and western Russia they had already got quite far in the attempt. As Richard J. Evans has put it, 'the Red Army may not have liberated these countries in 1945, but it certainly rescued them.'[20] In this context, the least that Europe could have done after the USSR's collapse was to leave their memorials alone.

However, it isn't just their Stalinist form that makes this controversial. Partly, it's the forty-four years of (mostly) imposed communist rule; but, partly, it's the memory of the Molotov–Ribbentrop pact, when in 1939 the Nazis and Soviets carved up Eastern Europe between themselves, with the latter taking the Baltic states, eastern Poland, and the strip of Romania that is now Bukovina in western Ukraine and the Republic of Moldova. This gave the USSR most of the territory of the Russian Empire, with only the heart of Poland and nearly all of Finland outside its jurisdiction. Although it could be, and has been, justified as necessary to form a strategic 'glacis' against the Nazis – and nobody was under any delusion that war with them would come soon enough – it is obviously and justly seen in those countries as an imperialist act, especially as all of this – with the tiny exception of a sliver of Poland around Białystok, which was returned to Poland – remained part of the USSR after 1945. The problem is that when one side starts calling hypocrisy, other facts might be recalled. It is sincerely believed by otherwise intelligent Poles that the war would not have happened without the Molotov–Ribbentrop pact, as if the remilitarization of the Rhineland, the *Anschluss* with Austria, and the occupation and invasion of the Czech lands (not to mention the Spanish Civil War, the Italian invasion of Ethiopia, the Japanese war on China) were all mere minor scuffles. Poland may have reason to forget this, given that it used the Nazi annexation of the Czech lands in 1938 as an opportunity to carve off a Polish-speaking area of Moravia, much as a year later the Soviets would use the Nazi invasion of Poland to carve off its mainly Ukrainian and Belarusian-speaking eastern territories. Countries that ritually denounce the pact often directly benefited from it – the reason why Vilnius is part of Lithuania and Lviv part of Ukraine is their having been carved off from Poland by the Soviets and the Soviet-imposed ethnic cleansing of their largely Polish population. As remembering all of this is extremely uncomfortable, the entire debate can be stopped by the claim, 'Yeah, but the communists killed more than the Nazis anyway.'[21] Despite the talk of 'two totalitarianisms', anti-communism very frequently spills over into rehabilitation or excuse-making for fascism; it is rare indeed to find a place that can commemorate both truths without any travesty. The nearest thing is in the centre of Kiev, where an obelisk to the Great

Patriotic War on a hill above the Dnieper was supplemented recently with a minaret-like sculpture commemorating the great famine of 1932–3, though, even here, both memorials overstep – the war memorial cannot speak of what the Red Army and the NKVD were doing in 1939 and 1940, and the famine memorial throws together the dissimilar Civil War-created famine of 1921 with the undoubtedly exceptional hecatombs of 1933.[22] These two hilltop obelisks are as close as anywhere comes to a democratic, unhysterical memorial space acknowledging both sides of the Soviet experience.

Regardless: what is undoubtedly true is that the war was horrifically complex on its Eastern Front, and however much the Soviets were preferable to the Nazis, it is asking too much to expect Poles or Balts to hail them as heroes – which is precisely what these monuments all do. The least morally complicated are those in German territory, at least in ethos if not content. The largest of all war memorials outside the Soviet Union, the combined cemetery and memorial at Treptower Park, in south-eastern Berlin near the River Spree, was the first of these I ever visited, and it is as shocking in its way as the first sight of the Stalinallee. The enormous bronze soldier, baby in hand, foot on a swastika, flanked by red-marble flags (that marble from the Reich Chancellery again) may seem a simple-minded way of commemorating mass death, compared to, say, the laconic, austere First World War memorials of Edwin Lutyens such as the Cenotaph in London or the Thiepval Memorial in northern France. To his immense credit, Lutyens rejected all the attempts to impose Christian or national symbols on these quasi-architectural structures, which instead have about them the sense of almost dumb shock that contemplation of this pointless slaughter induces. They may be massive, imposing and built of stone, they may be beloved of Colonel Blimps, but they do not glorify. Treptower Park shouts its glory from the skies. It could be argued that this was because, unlike the Battle of the Somme, the Battle of Berlin did indeed have a purpose. The counter-argument, though, is that the incessant glorification turns all that achievement and sacrifice into a cartoon, a giant three-dimensional war comic.

Look, for instance, at two typical superheroic memorials in Varna, Bulgaria: the Monument to the Anti-Fascist Fighters features two mammoth granite men over a funereal mound, hewn from hulking great stones, robotic-jawed, and incomparable to any imaginable human being. At first

A Soviet kurgan, Varna

you might feel utterly repelled, and refuse to allow yourself to be intimidated or awed by something so melodramatic; circle round it, and you'll find smaller, narrative reliefs to both the fight against Nazism and the earlier Bulgarian communist uprising of 1923, with the names of the dead on stelae around the memorial's perimeter – you may also find, as we did, several bouquets of flowers laid at the gate to the mound. These mounds are a regular feature, borrowed from the *kurgans*, or burial mounds, of the ancient Scythians,[23] and hence religious but not specifically Christian; the most famous Soviet interpretation is Mamayev Kurgan, the centrepiece of the Stalingrad Memorial Complex in Volgograd. Varna has another on a much larger scale, a monument both to the Red Army and to the Russian armies that helped liberate Bulgaria from the Ottomans, on the city's outskirts, towards the Black Sea resorts, a piled-up overgrown mound featuring more razor-faced supermen, their pupil-less eyes looking out over the sea. The figures are integrated into an abstract concrete sculpture in the form of a partially folded wing. Like the burial sites of a long-abandoned religion, these may be intriguing works of art, but it can be hard to find any emotional or historical connection in them.

Elsewhere, the Socialist Realist memorials to the Red Army built in the cities it liberated can be very moving, and sometimes that's because of their sheer unexpectedness among comfortable European plenty. Some places liberated by the Soviets ended up in Western hands due to prior agreements with the Allies. Chancing upon the Red Army memorial in the Tiergarten, in the affluent part of West Berlin, is a surprise – it was built quickly, before the borders of the four-power control of the defeated capital were drawn. Another capital taken by the Red Army is that shadow socialist city, Vienna, where there is a colossal monument right in the city centre; this one is even a piece of contextual design, with its circus of colonnades rather cleverly placed on the Ringstrasse; the reminder here is how much the shiny affluence of post-war Europe owed to the sacrifices of those men always represented (particularly in contemporary war films like *Róża* or *Joy Division*) as bestial, grunting Mongols.

Every Eastern and Central European capital has one in or near its

The Red Army taking Budapest in relief

centre. Sometimes, as in the obelisk in the centre of Budapest near the Hungarian parliament (and a statue of Ronald Reagan), they are so Victorian as to directly depict the battle, with the parliament's Gothic dome visible in the background of the relief sculpture. As the agreement with Gorbachev about their retention was informal, they can be altered – the largest of the Soviet war memorials in Budapest, for instance, had its Red Army soldier removed, leaving only a towering Art Deco female figure holding aloft a laurel; it has also been rhetorically de-Sovietized via the story that the sculptor originally designed the statue for the apparently so much more humane Hungarian leader and Nazi collaborator Admiral Horthy. In Tallinn, the central memorial, a single bronze soldier with bowed head, was removed and taken to a cemetery on the outskirts, sparking riots by Russian-Estonian youth, in a city where they make up nearly half of the population.[24] There are three examples worth looking at here, from the various eras of the Red Army monolithic memorial – one, 1950s and Stalinist, in Bratislava; one, 1960s and Modernist, in outer Tallinn; and one, 1980s and neo-Stalinist, in Riga.

Bratislava was taken by the Red Army in April 1945, after a failed anti-Nazi uprising in the city the previous August. The memorial on Slavin Hill was completed in 1960 to mid-1950s designs by the Slovak architect Jan Světlík, and placed at the city's highest point – but the design in all its fundamentals was actually conceived by the same designer in 1951 to commemorate the rising itself.[25] The bulk of the Slovak capital is fairly flat, but at its edges it suddenly lifts itself upwards, forming three acropoli, one with a castle, one with a TV tower, and one which can be spotted from a distance owing to the great obelisk with a man on top at the heart of it. The walk up there takes you through the affluent part of Bratislava, with large villas spreading across winding suburban streets, like a Central European Hollywood Hills; turn around and you have a magnificent view of the chaotic skyline, with sub-Norman Foster blue glass Eurotowers interspersed with Futurist oddities such as the steel-framed upturned pyramid of the Slovak Radio building, with the apparently endless flat slabs of Petržalka behind. The monument itself begins in a clearing between bushes, with twin sets of stairs flanking a relief of Red Army soldiers, one carrying a flag, one of them limping. At this point you can see what is on top of the long, thin obelisk – a soldier waving a flag aloft, with a golden star at its handle.

Slavin Hill Memorial Complex, Bratislava

The building underneath him fuses, in very expensive-looking, high-quality granite (none of that shabby granite cladding you get in the 1970s), two noted authoritarian architectures – the rectangular open columns of stripped classicism and the obelisks of ancient Egypt, with the latter built onto the former, integrated together into a whole. On either side of you are large bronzes of women carrying offerings to the soldiers. Although hardly Modernist, the temple-obelisk has a quality of stern abstraction, a funereal lack of fussiness, that might please an Adolf Loos. Flanking it, reached as always by several flights of polished steps, are soldiers carrying their wounded; on the temple, the names of the battles the Soviets fought in Slovakia, and, on its doors, tiny high-relief figures peculiarly similar to the jolly accordion-playing Russians and Czechs on the National Memorial in Prague, only, this time, showing worn and weary soldiers, public hangings, crying mothers. Bouquets, on the summer afternoon in 2012 we visited, had been laid in front of the doors, and individual flowers were laid on top of some of these figures on the door. Down the hill a little, for those whose consolatory needs are not met by red stars and hammer and sickles, a wooden Orthodox cross has been erected. It's a great deal more mournful than the vainglorious thunder of Treptower Park and Vienna – almost sensitive, by the standards of Stalinism. Around it, as in all of them, is a mass grave, with only the officers being individually named in the places they were buried – and though there is elsewhere a list of all the dead, this segregation does not appear to be a particularly communist gesture. As Gavin Stamp points out, the Imperial War Graves Commission after 1918 insisted on 'the crucial principle of equality of treatment, that there was no distinction between the officers and men'.[26] With the single exception of the anti-fascist memorial in Varna, you would not find a 'communist' memorial that paid the common soldier the same courtesy.

Architecturally speaking, there is a similar relative gracefulness about the memorial on the outskirts of Tallinn, although it is formally completely different. The Red Army memorial at Tallinn-Maarjamäe is on the road which leads along the beach on the Baltic Sea from the Hanseatic centre to the bizarre Olympic architecture of Pirita. It is again in two parts, one of them an obelisk, but this time they serve separate purposes. The

The War Memorial at Tallinn-Maarjamäe

obelisk was built to commemorate Red Army soldiers who died here in 1918, during the battles over Estonia between Germany and the Soviets that formed one of the many parts of the Civil War; it was built from local limestone in a much freer style than that in Bratislava, with no neoclassical fluting, but as a sharp, expressionistic limestone spike. The complex around it commemorates the Red Army soldiers that fought over Tallinn in 1941 and 1944, but it doesn't have any obvious iconography, with nary even a Red Star. It isn't quite an example of Lutyens-style non-representational sculpture, though. To describe it is more complex than most of these memorials, as it presents different shapes and angles at every point, with no obvious parade route that you're supposed to take. Carved into artificial hills are triangular limestone stelae, broken in half, with long granite pathways between them. Separating some of these land sculptures are sculptural interventions – an indefinable bronze creature is squeezed, its body torn and twisted, between two of them; on two of them are giant impressed hands. The parades and rituals that have to go here somewhere are provided on each side with steps, which are by now heavily overgrown with grass and weeds. Pushing it even closer to a 'normal', non-judgemental, non-side-taking war memorial is a grave for German soldiers, with crosses, just around the corner. The ensemble was designed in 1965 by a large team of architects (Allan Murdmaa, Peep Jänes, Rein Kersten, Henno Sepmann and Valve Pormeister), with the obelisk to 1918 by Mart Port and Lembit Tolli, from 1960. It's remarkable that designers had such freedom to interpret so hallowed a subject as the Great Patriotic War. This relative freedom in Baltic Soviet design enabled them not just to create a design that pleased them aesthetically, but to try and express the war without throwing heroism or suffering in anyone's face, something that might be rather crucial given the very different memories.

If the 1960s allowed freedom on this subject, the 1980s certainly did not. Many of the biggest, most seemingly Stalinoid war memorials in the USSR were projects of the late-Brezhnev era, or even from Andropov or Gorbachev's reforming tenure – products, in short, of a time when that elusive legitimation was desperately needed, with the ideology ever more residual and the economy no longer delivering rising living standards. The main results of this that you can find within the confines of the European Union is the Monument to the Liberators of Riga, completed to the designs of a team led by Ermens Balins in 1985. On the other side of

Mid-1980s Soviet-Heroic war memorial, Riga

the Daugava river but on an axis with the Freedom Monument erected in the 1930s, it does seem like a pointed gesture, an assertion of Soviet power when it was becoming shaky. It is more dominant and vast in scale than the projects in Bratislava or Tallinn, though the symmetry and great open spaces are familiar from Vienna or Treptower Park – a great square, with two striving heroic figural groups (one of Red Army soldiers, one of Mother Motherland), another central obelisk (or rather a cluster of them) and a pool, unusually, with benches around it. The obelisks are very elegant in their way, formed out of steel, each of a different height, and each part culminating in a star (from the air, uselessly, you would be able to see that the whole complex is in the shape of a star). The obelisks, the best part of the design, are visible from afar. The statues are less inspired, examples of a very common genre – yet while it's hard to imagine anyone finding this helpful as a way of making them think to any degree about their wartime experiences other than that they were glorious (or, in case you were on the other side, not), there are a lot of fresh flowers left here, for reasons which may become clear when we look at Latvia's more recent memorial spaces. Seen on its own, it is an image of domination; in its historical context, it's more an image of *insecurity*, of a regime that no longer believed in itself.

Memorials in Russia itself, where there isn't a colonial aspect as such,

Integration of architecture and sculpture: Victory Monument, Leningrad

are often architectural–sculptural amalgams, reflecting the fact that land nationalization meant the possibility of creating integrated spaces of memory that were at the same time mundane pieces of city infrastructure. The main war memorial in St Petersburg, in the mostly Stalinist-Baroque Moscow District, is framed by two identical skyscrapers, on the model of Kalinin Prospekt, albeit a little more stiff, with a carefully modelled surface. They are supported, Le Corbusier-style, on thin pilotis, as are a series of shops arcing around them. This is the Soviet Union's take on the International Style, Modernism finally reclaimed as something positive rather than what happens when you strip the ornament off – but it retains monumentality, with the two blocks strictly symmetrical. From here, you must take an underpass to the war memorial which you can see directly in front of you, visible here as a red-granite obelisk framed by a red-marble crescent. Come out of the underpass, and you can see the uncanny symmetricality of the street, each side seemingly identical but for the shop signs and the movements of the people below.

The monument is appropriately subterranean: you are in the open air, but you must step down from the underpass to find it, flanked by concrete walls moulded to look as if they have been smashed into pieces. In the middle are some restrained Socialist Realist figures, as strong and muscular as always but hunched, huddled, starved; the red crescent around them features the gold letters '900 DAYS', referring to the length of time Leningrad was besieged by the Nazis; over a million people died, as they starved the 'excess mouths' of the city. Eternal flames flicker from boughs, and behind the figures are three tiny pine trees, placed in alignment with the obelisk. The red-stone crescent is broken in the middle and, behind, you see it is made of the same 'smashed' concrete as the steps, here broken in an obvious gesture of *architecture parlante*; it 'says' that the blockade was broken. Of course, it says little about the fact that the leaders of the city during the blockade were purged by Stalin within a couple of years of its ending, but this Victory Monument is nonetheless strangely un-triumphant, mournful. War is not glorious here. When you walk back up the steps onto the surface, two long, low Brutalist buildings are on either side, identical – and all this careful monumentalism suddenly evaporates, as a series of shabby prefabricated towers march their way out towards the forest. Turn around, and there is a sight to take the breath away in awe and in terror. The towers, the obelisk and two groups of figures, alternately downcast or celebratory, are placed on an absolutely precise, straight and symmetrical axis; two figures stand at the base of the obelisk, with '1941–1945' in gold letters at the top. We watched the sun go down here. It wasn't quite a 'white night', a mere 11 p.m. in late May. On this spot, the Soviets attempted to transmute the aesthetic preferences of Peter the Great into something symbolizing the suffering of ordinary people when faced with terror, starvation and atrocity – something which these monumental aesthetics obviously can't support, geared as they are towards domination and intimidation. The work strains to convey what happened, but it can only create a cartoon. Or can it?

ATROCITY EXHIBITIONS

In these giant, half-architectural sculptural groups, there are sometimes hints, or more than hints, of something other than glory and heroism – the horror from which it was inextricable. The hanged soldiers on the doors of the temple at the heart of the Slavin complex, the mute sense of loss in the Maarjamäe monument, are gestures at this; other monuments and memorials from the time make more of a conscious attempt to confront it. One memorial space which moves constantly between triumphalism and horror is the Museum of the Great Patriotic War, in the centre of Kiev. This is perhaps a random example, as there are museums of this kind in practically every city in Ukraine, Belarus and western Russia (though they have been unsurprisingly discontinued in the Baltic states); this happens to be the one that we saw and explored, in spring 2011. It is hard to see anything about it as typical, however, so ludicrously powerful and overscaled is it. You can see the central part of the complex almost anywhere within a three- or four-mile radius – one of the symbolic Mother Motherland figures that were erected on hills from Volgograd to Yerevan, a hard-eyed steel colossus holding aloft a sword and hammer-and-sickle-emblazoned sword. Although its scale and complexity suggest it must have been planned for some years, the Kiev Museum of the Great Patriotic War was completed as late as 1981.

It stands next to an enduring symbolic space of Ukrainian statehood, one of the few surviving structures that was established by Kievan Rus, the literate, advanced, Byzantine-influenced state that was the first 'Russian'

Mother Motherland casts her eye over Kiev

state of any kind, long before the rise of what nationalists regard as the petty tax collectors for the Golden Horde in Muscovy. This is the Kievo-Pecherska Lavra, a monastery on an escarpment overlooking the Dnieper, made up of a dazzling collection of golden domes, some spreading and Orthodox, some in tight collections in the much later Tsarist Baroque, and some of them reconstructed after 1989. There is another hill just next to the monastery, and on that the city's planners put the symbolic Soviet space. The contrast between the irregular concatenation of golden domes and the singular steel warrior queen probably did not please traditionalists. However, out of the two it's the Lavra where I was told to put my camera away, so certain rituals are more enforced than others.

On the ground, there is more happening than the sword-wielding figure apparently nicknamed 'Tin Tits'. Coming to it from the Lavra, the first part of the complex is an immersive sculptural group, hewn out of grey shutter-marked concrete, which has been shaped into a series of fragmented, clashing and crashing volumes. Here, there's an unexpected commonality with the ideas being thrown around at the time by 'Deconstructivists' in British, American and French architecture schools. For Daniel Libeskind, Peter Eisenman and others, modernity could be properly represented only by a disorienting, smashed-up space, one which Eisenman called, with typical portentousness, 'non-Euclidian', where walls, floors, roofs were no longer certain and clear volumes but deliberately unstable, or as unstable as you can make a fixed piece of architecture without it actually falling over. The horrors of the twentieth century were explicitly pointed to as 'inspiration', if we can call it that, and it is telling that each of them designed symbolic spaces in post-1989 Berlin, with Libeskind designing the Jewish Museum, which shuns and contorts against a sober neoclassical building, filling itself with rooms whose austerity or angularity are intended to at least slightly evoke the experiences of German Jews, a brave but surely foolhardy move; Eisenman's Memorial to the Murdered Jews of Europe is less didactic, but its succession of hundreds of stelae, placed on a slope, presents a maze which doubles as a place to contemplate the greatest crime against humanity in history and as children's playground.

There's no evidence that the designers of the Kiev memorial complex – F. M. Sogoyan, V. P. Vinaikin, V. Borodai and V. V. Schvesov – were remotely aware of this work, but they were clearly trying something similar – to disorient, to shock, to try and make the museum visitor aware that they are entering something which commemorates a period when normality and security no longer applied. You enter into it through an opening in the concrete sculpture, to find walls made up of huge, chopped-off slabs of concrete, whose shuttering marks imply trenches

Taking snapshots at the Great Patriotic War complex, Kiev

thrown together out of wood; the walls jut out, fall away, and form alcoves and cave-like hideaways. An unconcealed speaker, in a cantilevered concrete box that suggests they were at least aware of the South Bank in London, plays, on loop, 'The Sacred War', a terrifying deep-voiced bellow in march tempo that was one of the 'hits' of the war, and is a very long way away from 'We'll Meet Again'. It sounds like it was sung by the race of giants that populate the Socialist Realist universe, rather than by mere mortals. In those alcoves, triumphalism and horror coexist in the form of bronze groups, emaciated victims and musclebound saviours, mourning women and fist-waving heroes; when we visit, we find a few people are getting their photos taken with these. At the end of the concrete cave, an opening, and another bronze group of soldiers, rifles aloft, about to run towards the shaft of light.

When you emerge, you can see how this extraordinary sculpture is laid into a created landscape, which includes an artificial hill and a circular metal brazier for the eternal flame. A large granite-paved square leads to the museum itself, past some much more conventionally heroic bronze

Red Army men suspended on a long concrete float. You don't notice them first, however; you notice only that you're now at the foot of Mother Motherland, and that below her, built into the same composition, is the building – again, in an integration of architecture and landscape, with a rectangular building protruding onto the square, and the rest of it covered by grass, but for a circular, buttressed shaft for the statue, which has large windows implying there are exhibits inside. There are only two indications that the Soviet Union no longer exists: the eternal flame doesn't appear to be burning, and two crossed tanks outside the entrance have been painted in psychedelic colours. The easy, informal way people are using the spaces also feels quite un-Soviet, with children clambering over the bronze giants. There is another hint inside, when the Ukrainian flag flies in the place where a bust of Lenin once stood. Of the rest, I have a 1987 guide to the complex, and on its evidence every one of the exhibits and rooms is exactly the same as it was then.[27]

When we first came here in 2010, we didn't go in, too scared by the sculptural groups surrounding it, not in the mood to be subjected to a monumental programme of Soviet patriotic bombast; we circled round instead, following the stairs that run round it back to the city, and argued with each other about it. Back in Kiev six months later, we swallowed our reservations, bought tickets and entered the first room. The ironwork door to it has a hammer-and-sickle shield on it shaped exactly like the *Superman* logo. Inside these early rooms, dedicated to the first year or so of 'their' war (i.e. 1941, not the to-be-forgotten-about Nazi-sanctioned annexations and battles with Finland, Poland, Romania and the Baltic states in 1939–40), everything is murky, sombre-toned, to evoke the disaster and darkness of this period. As architectural design, it is ambitious, far more so than something like the Moscow Central Museum of the Revolution. There are glass cases containing artefacts, of course – newspapers, pamphlets, possessions – but everything is linked together as a sculptural diorama, suspended in a red-painted steel frame, on an abstract parquet floor; giant photographs of the taking of prisoners-of-war make up two of the walls. Maps, made as colourful sculptural reliefs, show how quickly the Nazis overran Ukraine, and their encirclement of Kiev. One diorama-sculpture shows photographs of murdered Soviet citizens on a stretched piece of greenish-brown canvas fabric and a wooden frame, evoking the camps of the defeated soldiers.[28] Another frame, shaped like something between a printing press and a miniature gallows, has hung from it two concentration camp uniforms; another is in a vitrine, with barbed wire run through it. These, it transpires, are authentic.

The next room, on 1943, shows a return of hurrah-patriotism, as Stalingrad turns the tide; over the door is a continuous bronze relief, with the busts of Red Army soldiers and straggle-haired Partisans waving their guns in the air; the flags of Partisans hang from the ceiling. The format is the same, though, with vitrines and more of these dramatic sculptural dioramas (by now often made up of guns or motorbikes) telling the story. It is some measure, perhaps, of the museum's success in achieving its aims that despite not being able to read Ukrainian (and with only Agata's primary-school Russian), the narrative was abundantly clear. That may also point to its problems – unlike in the 1930s, the Soviet authorities were no longer broadcasting their propaganda to the illiterate. You know without reading that, here, you are being physically informed of the Soviet war machine and its power, and the maps show the Red Army overrunning occupied Europe. What upends this, and makes it kitsch, is not necessarily the production of a narrative – this is indeed what happened, so why not – but the way that more obvious, 'realistic' representations of glory keep having to be thrown in. There are atrocious giant paintings of pitched battles and of the taking of Berlin, with a quality you usually expect from paintings sold on street corners to tourists – overwhelmingly literal panoramic depictions with a God's eye view. It is at this point, when you feel they are truly ramming their point down your throat, that it's hard not to think about the thousands of German women that were raped in the aftermath. If someone is screaming at you that they were heroic, it is natural to react with some suspicion. It is striking that when they are throwing together 'real' artefacts and these montaged artworks, the museum is moving – you cannot but be aware of the terrifying scale of the sacrifice that these people made, and, given that scale, it's not surprising that the architecture and design are not in 'good taste', but are angry, demonstrative. The inclusion of 'art', in the form of the paintings and some more bronze reliefs, cheapens it.

There are two endings to the museum, two Valhallas of the Red Army. The first is laid out in a long, curved room; as everywhere else here, the lighting is exceptionally important, going from the glaring yellow of the rooms on the Battle of Berlin to a dark, funereal tone, with tiny concealed lights. There is a wall covered with photographs of victims – some individual snapshots or passport photos, some entire assembled groups, often of women and children, as in the many Ukrainian villages whose populations were killed in their entirety. A long table stretches in between, without chairs, but with samovars and empty glasses. Trumpets hung from the walls suggest a celebration. There is a record player at the end. Sentimental, perhaps – a room for the commemoration of the dead as a victory party they all couldn't come to. But the scale, rather than making it risibly authoritarian, makes it moving – the reason why the table is so long is because so many were killed, so it has to stretch all the way around to accommodate them. And for somewhere so didactic, this space does not yell at you. What *does* yell at you is the last of the rooms, which is above this, in the buttressed rotunda that forms Mother Motherland's base. This is the Victory Hall, and its marble-and-glass rotunda features a mosaic frieze running round the top, so that you have to crane your neck to see it. Like the Zoloti Vorota Metro station being built at the same time, it shows a renewed interest in the Byzantine aesthetics of Kievan

A Soviet Valhalla, Kiev

Rus – with mosaics so dripping with gold that an oligarch might find them a bit excessive, every bit as opulent as any in the Lavra, in Hagia Sophia or Ravenna. As in Byzantine art, the figures are stretched and slightly abstracted, though here the inspiration seems to be comic books as much as Andrei Rublev. The Red Army does its heroic deeds and those in mourning are comforted, against a backdrop including the Kremlin and the Dnieper Dam. From one side of the wide glazed windows you can see the Lavra's domes, and on the other side an unseemly cluster of oligarchical high-rises. Ecclesiastical power, political power, financial power.

For Agata this was the limit, the point where she couldn't bear the Soviet Valhalla any longer, where its opulence and jingoism became suffocating. We both stared for ages at the mosaics, and she reminded me that I didn't want to go to the Lavra itself because I thought I'd feel uncomfortable with all the incense, genuflection and serious ritual of an Orthodox service (she did go, and found it wholly unscary). Being in this Soviet Valhalla is probably not unlike the experience of being in an Orthodox cathedral during the Soviet era, when they had been de-sacralized and were essentially used as nothing more or less than art galleries. In those, it was expected that you would enjoy and contemplate the beauty of religious art for its artistic qualities, and for what it said about society, rather than as part of a ritual. Here, too, the ritual has been discontinued, giving a false sense of distance. There were a few visitors wandering in and out of the hall in the time we spent there, and nobody was genuflecting or saluting, but wandering around wide-eyed and a little (but not too) shaken, as they would in a Libeskind museum. This is a 'doing' architecture; like the Soviet magic described by Marcuse, it is a 'performing' architecture, designed to accompany some sort of act. What it does, and what all the various rooms here do, is evidence of how, even this late, architecture in the USSR was an extreme, Pavlovian form of *architecture parlante*. Everything is symbolic, everything has a meaning, everything wants you to feel something, a relentless *Gesamtkunstwerk* of propaganda. The result is that it has become a museum of itself. But here it is, still surviving; apart from in the ex-Hapsburg lands of the West, which had a very different war, most Ukrainians would not dissent from this view of the Great Patriotic War, as something horrifying but necessary and ultimately heroic.

If that combination has a considerable degree of truth, however much the Molotov–Ribbentrop pact or the mass rape of German civilians might complicate the picture, it was applied elsewhere, in places where an ultimate glorious victory was much less obviously apparent. The famous Holocaust memorial spaces, Jerusalem's Yad Vashem aside, were erected in the aftermath of 1989, when Western Europe got to newly 'discover' its Eastern neighbours, and when travel to the camps and mass graves became much simpler. The Holocaust, however much it may have had considerable assistance from the governments of Europe (and hardly solely its east, see e.g. Vichy France's total collaboration with it), took place entirely on the territory of what was at that point Poland and the USSR, something which leads to the oft-used phrase, and offensive canard, that talks of 'Polish concentration camps'. The mass shootings by the *Einsatzgruppen* took place mostly on Soviet territory; the death camps were in occupied Poland. Large cities in both countries had ghettoes into which Jews were herded before being exterminated – Białystok, Łódź, Warsaw, Vilnius, Kaunas, Riga, Minsk. Anti-Semitism would recur, appallingly, in the post-war period – the Slánský trial in Czechoslovakia in 1951, Stalin's purge against the Jewish Anti-Fascist Committee in 1952, and Mieczysław Moczar's threats to Polish Jews in 1968 were breathtakingly cynical, depressing proof that anti-Semitism didn't need many actual Jews to continue; and hence there was mass emigration of Jews from both countries in the late 1960s and 1970s, and again after 1991. At the same time, reactionary popular memory – sometimes, as in the Baltic states, reactionary official memory – indelibly associates Jews with communism. However, this shouldn't suggest that the areas where Jews were massacred were not memorialized in the USSR or the People's Republic of Poland – they were, especially as even in the pogrom atmosphere of Stalin's last years anti-Semitism was always officially condemned. However, they had to be fitted into a narrative of 'glory' and, in Poland, 'martyrdom'.

In some places this move was easier than others – most clearly, in the memorial to the Warsaw Ghetto Uprising of 1943. This was erected early, in 1947, to the designs of the sculptor Nathan Rapoport, and it does refer to an indisputably heroic event. The Ghetto's inhabitants had mostly been deported to the death camp at Treblinka by the time it occurred, and the less than a thousand remaining took up arms, in a hopeless act that it nonetheless took the Nazis a month to suppress.[29] Notoriously, they fought alone, with only the most perfunctory co-operation from the Poland-wide Home Army. The memorial is unambiguous, and is remarkable among Soviet-era monuments for featuring explicitly religious symbolism, in the form of the menorahs that are placed at either side of its thick granite frame. Inset on each side of this large grey block are two bronze high-relief sculptures. The side facing the large square behind is completely Socialist Realist, pulled into a Mannerist composition of emaciated bodies, one carrying a child, others carrying grenades and knives; one is lying, crushed. On the other side, facing the street, is a classical mourning procession. It was here that Willy Brandt fell to his knees in supplication, on a state visit to Poland in 1970.[30] Elsewhere in the Ghetto are many other monuments, mostly created after 1989, but this is 'the' monument. It sits strangely here because it is not part of the Polish war narrative, but of an Israeli post-war one – there are always large Israeli tour groups in buses visiting. The Łódź Ghetto, too, has its monuments and memorials, though they are less a part of the itinerary. Both ghettoes were razed to the ground, and both are now poor, inner-city

Children's Camp Memorial, Łódź

districts made up of an uneasy mix of unfinished Socialist Realist *grands projets* and Modernist estates. In both cities, the outlines of the Ghetto are shown on the pavement, so that they are in a sense wrapped by a continuous memorial. But, within that, there are completely normal, working-class Polish districts – the one in Łódź, unsurprisingly, noticeably a lot poorer. Among the memorials there is one sculptural group on the site of a concentration camp solely for the incarceration of children; at any one point there were 1,500 children here, whose ages ranged between two and seventeen. Like the Warsaw Ghetto memorial, it is in some way integrated into the area around, a quite pleasant, almost Scandinavian district of Modernist blocks in green space, albeit one neighboured by derelict pre-war tenements and seedy Socialist Realist half-boulevards. In this 1971 design by Jadwiga Janus and Ludwik Mackiewicz, an elevated plaza features a curved, heartshaped structure made up of two metal wings, broken by the imprint of a starved child. Small, spiky stelae, running alongside the garages of the flats, carry the names of the death camps to which many of the children were taken. It is an eerie, original piece of abstract sculpture, but it's completely unable to give even slightly a sense of the horror of what happened here, and how could it?[31]

This is unsurprisingly even more the case with the death camps themselves. When we went to Lublin in January 2013 neither of us had ever visited any of their remains – we hadn't taken up the offer so frequently advertised in Kraków for package tours of 'Ghetto, Auschwitz, Salt Mine'. The death camp of Majdanek, however, is in the suburbs of Lublin, a ten-minute tram ride, and for some reason – not for the sake of this book – we decided to go there. It is most definitely not a place which it is advisable to visit, as we did, in temperatures of −10°C, but it is an open question as to whether it should be visited at all. Unlike all the other death camps, it is surrounded by the suburbs of a medium-sized city, on all sides. What announces the death camp to the suburban street is the Monument to Struggle and Martyrdom, designed by Wiktor Tołkin in 1969. It consists of a Monument-Gate, a Mausoleum, and a Road of Homage and Remembrance, which connects them, spanning the length of the camp, whose primitive wooden buildings are mostly preserved, unusually, since the camp was liberated by the Red Army before the Germans had the chance to clear away evidence, as they had to some extent in Treblinka, Sobibor and other extermination camps. It was funded by a

The Monument-Gate at Majdanek, Lublin

Polish institution called the Council for the Protection of the Remembrance of Combat and Martyrdom,[32] but, mercifully, none of the monuments pretend that there was anything heroic happening here.

The Monument-Gate is huge, and hideous, as it should be. It is entirely abstract, a scream of concrete and rubble suspended over a slope lined with rubble (which now has a sign in front of it to stop visitors from falling in), contorted forms which look like giant three-dimensional letters, intended to read as the Hebrew letters for 'Lublin', but cracked and smashed into illegibility – in its refusal of any consolation, any reference or any representation, it is less sentimental, less obvious, than the 1990s architecture of American academicians, although even then there's a question about whether or not tortured sculpture is of any use for the representation of actual torture, as if an unpleasantly dissonant experience is in any way comparable to those actual experiences; but this attempt at the impossible has more conviction than most. You can, if you want, walk straight from it to the Tołkin-designed mausoleum, but another pathway leads into the remains of the camp itself. Majdanek was, like the much larger Auschwitz, both a death camp where Jews were gassed, and a 'regular' concentration camp where political prisoners and deportees were kept. There are exhibits in the surviving huts, so cold that it must have been difficult enough not to simply freeze to death. They are sparse, laconic; and the doors are open, so that you can walk quite without thinking about it into a tiled room without realizing that you've walked into a former gas chamber. The signs, in German, have been kept, as have the watchtowers, like all of the buildings in a quickly hurried-together wooden non-architecture, with some brick in the crematoria. From here, we got to the mausoleum. I later found that the design was based on an ancient Slavic burial urn, which is perhaps inappropriate given that 60,000 of the camp's 80,000 victims were not 'Slavic', but the form is not didactic enough for this to be obvious. An inscription across its circular limestone cap reads 'Our Fate is a Warning to You'. Underneath that, unexpectedly and horrifyingly, is a mound of human ashes.

Although it's debatable whether any aesthetic, any kind of architecture, has a chance at what is, even at best, making art out of atrocity, it's arguable Soviet aesthetics couldn't cope with the Final Solution for similar reasons that Marxists of the time – with certain exceptions, such as Trotsky or Adorno – could not understand the reality of Nazi anti-Semitism. It was the norm to see it as a mere scapegoating that cloaked a new form of monopoly capitalism, rather than as a distinct phenomenon with its own, psychotically irrational, momentum. In much the same way, it resists being slotted into the Soviet narrative. The Holocaust did not involve 'heroism', and the victims and their families would be hard pressed to call any of it an act of 'martyrdom' – too senseless, too incomprehensible. To this there is one exception, perhaps. The story of the Minsk Ghetto is one of the least remembered of the era, and according to its main English-language historian that's because of its atypicality.[33] For diverse reasons – a less horrific experience of Stalinism than had neighbouring Ukraine, meaning Belarusians had internalized official Soviet values of 'internationalism', plus, perhaps crucially, an absence of any large-scale nationalism in Belarus itself – there was huge co-operation between the Ghetto, the rest of the city's underground and the Partisan movement in the forests. The Nazis' attempt to set up a reliable collaborative *Judenrat* to enforce their rule in the Ghetto failed, with its leaders consistently working with the resistance. Tens of thousands were smuggled out of the Ghetto to the forests. In the politics of history, they weren't useful to any side: too communist for the Americans, they were not left to fight alone so weren't much use to Israel; and in the USSR they were not officially acknowledged until the 1960s, because the resistance movement had not been officially sanctioned, unsurprisingly given that the local Party leadership had fled the Nazis with great speed. The many memorials in Belarus's capital include sculptural groups, Metro stations and, fittingly, an underground eternal flame. These memorials to internationalism survive partly because of Belarus's faintly neo-Soviet regime, yet its absolute leader, Aleksandr Lukashenko, publicly condemned Jewish tourists in 2007 for making a Belarusian town a 'pigsty', and asked 'rich Jews' to visit instead. Memorials evidently can't enforce politics.

Maybe, as the American architects who became the memorialists of the 1990s and 2000s made clear, it really is pointless to figuratively represent the unrepresentable. In that case, following Adolf Loos, who once claimed that 'architecture' in mausolea was one of the few occasions where it was justified, you can sometimes find more successful examples in the cemetery. At the main cemetery in Kiev, there is a 'Park of Memory', whose design is so abstracted and haunting that it was picked as a (back) cover image for one of the recent *Totally Awesome Ruined Soviet Architecture* books. We went looking for it in March 2011. The first thing we noticed in this big municipal cemetery was the complete and total lack of even the slightest maintenance. It is interesting to see what a cemetery looks like when it really isn't maintained. The Victorian cemeteries of the UK are full of picturesque delights such as ivy-covered headstones and trees growing out of the heads of angels, but the pathways are impeccable and the rubbish left by courting Goths is always thoroughly cleared up.

Here, however, in a cemetery where there are clearly some very recent graves, with fresh new headstones, all the pathways between are the setting for mud and trash, fighting for control of these routes. Rubbish of all sorts – the usual bottles, packets and plastic products, but with a large amount of toilet paper also scattered around, perhaps as an abortive means of clearing up the mess. The mud itself, congealing with the remains of the thawing snow, is of fairly apocalyptic proportions, necessitating wellingtons at the very least for all but the insensible or those promised fine avant-garde architecture and the warm glow instilled by a sense of achievement at the end of it. As if in response to this, several of the graves are marked off by low walls, which unfortunately makes negotiation of the place even more impossible. But after a few minutes, and having decided not to try and escape in the other direction, we got used to it, and admired the gravestones. Many of them are mini versions of the Soviet memorial genre, partly no doubt due to the need for secularized forms of remembrance. There are a lot of black and red marble or granite wedges, some of them carrying heroic images of those underneath; in some cases there are small statues of the dead, one in Komsomol dress. The 1970s grave of the Didichenko family is a small piece of concrete abstraction, two volumes held in tension. Later graves are more obvious, for obvious reasons – that is, they're crosses – and in some cases, wooden crosses appear to have been added later to 1970s and 1980s memorials. Earlier, pre-Soviet monuments of lesser rectitude can be found here too; a classical sarcophagus looking disapproving among these atheists.

Then we came to a clear main road, and in the distance what looked like what we'd seen in the glossy book. Our optimism was justified when we reached the entrance pavilion, a very sober structure compared with what comes next, but nonetheless recognizable as consciously thought-out architecture in a way that little else here is. Its forms initially seem very abstract – subtle curves and small windows, white render on concrete – but there is also an attempt here at a non-referential ornament. Over one doorway, the concrete suddenly bulges, curves and billows into some peculiar fleshly opening. This is the first indication that the Park of Memory's designers, the architect Abraham Miletsky and artists Ada Rybachuk and Volodymyr Melnychenko (who drew on their earlier, unbuilt competition project for a memorial at the ravine of Babi Yar), were concerned to evoke the sacred without using any obvious religious symbolism. Recent additions have no such compunction – the adjacent door to this is decorated with tacked-on, bright Orthodox icons.

Yet the original designers' more subtle symbolism is not removed, not yet – a bundle of concrete forms sits next to the sign towards the crematoria, and you notice something else. A rippling, flowing wall of concrete, enclosing a clearly very recent toy Orthodox church, its onion dome the pinnacle of a small, modest building that thankfully doesn't proclaim the Restoration as loudly as it might. It's that concrete wall that dominates, though, curving all the way round a small moat, accidentally forming a micro-acropolis for that church to sit on. Concrete it may be, but the wall looks completely organic, its curves so irregular that they can't possibly be the result of deliberate architectural intent. Although it's represented as wholly abstract in the coffee-table book we were using as a guide, it transpires that the concrete wall is an accident.[34] The bulging, curving wall was originally a huge relief sculpture, depicting the horrors of the twentieth century: of which there were many here, with the extermination of its large Jewish population at Babi Yar in 1941, or the famine of 1933, or the mass murders of the 1937 Great Purge. In the surviving photographs of the wall under construction, you can see all of this featured and evoked on the relief, a vast tapestry of pain that was here only for a couple of years before being replaced by the concrete abstraction we see here today. Somewhere, underneath it, the sculptures are still there and still recoverable. Even when at their most abstract, then, Soviet architects could not resist *architecture parlante*; and, sometimes, what they had to 'say' was not welcome.

The crematoria have a ceremonial approach, one which bypasses Christian iconography altogether and reaches back to the pagan. A hill fort, more or less – a great circus, a mound of earth, or rather of overgrown grass and the usual windswept rubbish, which you approach up a flight of steps; the tops of the cupolas are visible from here, a set of domes and flames. From the top of these steps, you see the crematorium buildings' tight circle surrounded by an earthwork fortification, stepped upwards for ease of access, planted with fresh flowers, hundreds of stones and little memorials. Or, rather, we noticed this somewhat later, as the crematoria are so compelling. There are three actual 'buildings' here, shallow structures which one could imprecisely call domes, were they not so organically cast. They face each other with perfect symmetry, sentries in worn, white-rendered concrete, their shells rising from doorways of roughly person height, swooping upwards and then down in a biomorphic, maternal curve. Guarding them in turn are purely sculptural, sometimes uninhabited concrete forms which flicker, twist and taper upwards and outwards, marking out the space of a memorial stone. The entrances to the three buildings take the organic metaphors and make it clear that the inspiration is human, not animal; if these double-curves resemble female body parts, the doorways appear as faces, with mouths, eyes, noses and even fancifully a glazed hairline. Sexual metaphors might seem bizarre and inappropriate in a space devoted to death, but they're

Two views of the Park of Memory, Kiev

abundant in the crematorium's inexplicable ancillary rooms and spaces, which feature vulval openings towards their pinnacles. Look at them from another angle, however, and they resemble a wailing wall of anthropomorphic forms, twisting and turning in agony, their mouths open in pain. The main moulded metal doorways, through which the mourners pass, are imposingly deathly.

Even without the sculptures, this is still a speaking architecture, as much as any other more conventional, more conformist Soviet public building. The atheistic sacred that these concrete forms aim to evoke is captured on one level by a frank paganism – metaphors of weeping and contemplation for death, evocations of sex and pregnancy for rebirth; and it is surely this conception of cyclical, carnal life that necessitates the newly built Orthodox church to stand guard, as much as the now freely expressed faith of the mourners. The designers evidently took extremely seriously the requirement to create a non-confessional, non-sectarian, even non-mystical form of sacred architecture without the recourse to the conventional forms of Soviet ritual, and the concreting over of the relief forces it to do so without recourse to any conception of the political or historical. That doesn't mean the latter are wholly absent. In a sense, what the designers were trying to do here is what Eisenman, Libeskind and those other 'architects of mourning' attempted with their volumes evoking war or the Holocaust; but there are no obvious triggers, no big dark room to be locked into in which to contemplate the cattle trains (or rather, here, no deep ravines in which to contemplate the *Einsatzgruppen*). At the same time, even with the relief sculpture which was intended to animate it left blanked out, this is impossible to conceive as a normal, straightforward space of mourning and commemoration. In all its abstraction, it could only exist in a city which has faced extraordinary suffering. It is abstract, but it is not mute.

ANTI-COMMUNIST MONUMENTS

There are many Museums of Communism in Europe, and they are at their most wilfully frivolous in cities that are regularly visited by Western tourists – in Berlin, where the GDR is two things, the Stasi and cutely clunky consumer goods; in Tallinn, where the Soviet Union is the KGB and cool pop-art adverts for products you couldn't buy in shops; and in Prague, where the museum takes the form of an attic full of tat pointedly advertised as being 'next to McDonald's'. Others have more serious ambitions – to provide spaces of public memory, or to set up new national narratives. Some of these anti-communist spaces are much more ambitious as architecture, and paramount among these is the Statue Park in Budapest, set up in the outer, outer suburbs of Buda in 1993, the greatest of what Agata Pyzik describes as the 'zoos' and 'monument graveyards' that can be found also in the Grūtas Park in Lithuania (better known as 'Stalin World'), or in the Park of Fallen Monuments in Moscow.[35] The last, looked over by a ludicrous Postmodern monument to Peter the Great and in front of the New Tretiakov Gallery, one of the most impressive high-Modernist buildings in the city, is particularly weird, given that – the decisively demounted Brezhnev and Stalin aside – most of its subjects can be found in abundance left around in the city. A few hammer-and-sickles, Lenins, Dzerzhinskys and such are 'fallen' here, but many more are still in their original place in the Russian capital – a ten-minute walk from the park and you'll spot in situ a Lenin as well as a Georgi Dimitrov, and can descend into a Metro station watched over by a heroic space-age worker couple. This schizophrenia is not atypical.

In Budapest, however, there really are no, or nearly no, communist

Anti-Stalinist satirical classicism at Budapest's Statue Park

monuments on show in the city centre, apart from the small obelisk near the parliament or the de-Sovietized liberation monument on Gellert Hill. The Red Army soldier that originally appeared below the goddess of peace in the latter can be found in the Statue Park. It is so far from the centre of the city, quarantined away in a green belt past even the *Plattenbau* blocks, that its original ambitions to be a memorial space for both former Eastern Bloc citizens and tourists seem unlikely to be fulfilled. There are adverts for it on the Metro, in English, and the bus stop for the only bus that goes there is also given a specially illustrated English signpost. The park was designed in 1993 by the architect Ákos Eleőd. The architecture is Postmodern classicism, not in the popular, kitsch, classicism-in-fibreglass sense so present in Moscow – though there's a fabulously horrible example of that in the new National Theatre in Pest – but in a more serious vein, with its porticos and pediments constructed out of industrial red brick as a literal stage set, demonstratively without actual buildings behind their façades, with the columns holding up nothing. Into these spaces are placed the removed statues, in a particular order, in a taxonomy much as we've tried to follow in this book – monuments to the Fathers of the Workers' Movement here, to the Workers' Heroes there, to the Red Army and Lenin elsewhere, and with a special place for the commemoration of the Hungarian Soviet Republic of 1919 and the 'counter-revolution' of 1956.

According to Eleőd, 'in order to build a counter-propaganda park out of these propaganda statues, and in order to faithfully follow the Dictatorship-like way of thinking and its inherited recipe, I had to create this park with more direct, more drastic, more up-to-date devices' – i.e. the emptinesses, the lacunae, the holes in the classical buildings have the role of encouraging criticality and thought, rather than just presenting a Stalinist horrorshow. It is placed on an axis, where flanking 'buildings' reveal, through the bare portico, the severed legs of Stalin; the only 'fake' monument here, made in reference to the destruction of the Stalin statue during the 1956 revolution. The only text, other than the plaques, is a poem, 'A Word on Tyranny', by the communist turned dissident Gyula Illyés. 'This park is about democracy,' Eleőd continues, because 'only democracy can give us the chance to think freely about dictatorships.' Does it elicit thought, or does it just elicit 'Wow' or 'What were they thinking?' 'Inevitably, in a tourist from another country, to whom dictatorship means nothing more than at most a reading experience [and here we are!], very different thoughts arise than in a person with a tragic past, who lived here, lived through hard times, carrying the drama of his own broken life under these statues into the park. But silence is common.'[36] Silence is indeed common, and so is taking lots of pics of yourself gesticulating next to these giant gesticulators. We did.

As the removal in Budapest has been so complete, or so indiscriminate – even Warsaw has more Soviet statues left in place – it can be a little unnerving seeing how every part of the twentieth-century socialist experience has been thrown in here. Marx and Engels of course, and it's a waste of breath maybe to argue how little they have to do with what happened in Hungary more than a half-century after their deaths; there's a lot of the Soviet Republic of 1919, which was hardly a Russian imperial project, as the Red Army couldn't then have got to Hungary even if it had wanted to, but was an indigenous Hungarian revolution, and one which had mass support in Budapest itself, and which was overthrown by the Romanian army, not by any Hungarian movement against it – and which was replaced by a violently anti-Semitic right-wing dictatorship. That doesn't make the monuments to it any less absurd, and its largest fallen monument, a 1986 sculpture of Béla Kun and the Magyar Red Army by Imre Varga, is indeed completely preposterous, a cluster of little leaping tin soldiers, deliberately thin and left un-fleshed out, which suggests that late 'real socialist' sculptors could do Postmodernism as well as any post-communist space of sober memory. But also in here is a monument to the 1,200 Hungarian volunteers who fought in the International Brigades during the Spanish Civil War, in a decent, abstracted bronze of three soldiers next to plinths with the battles they took part in, to the designs of Agamemnon Makrisz, in 1968. It forms part of the park dedicated to the 'unending promenade of workers' movement concepts'. There are monuments to the surely wholly admirable, selfless gesture of the International Brigades in most other countries that had a workers' movement – there is an equally large one on London's South Bank, and a smaller one in my hometown, Southampton, among numerous others. But, here, the International Brigades are just another part of a spurious promenade of fake heroism.

Perhaps unsurprisingly, then, alongside the transformation of communism into a horror-reservation, there's a conspicuous failure in the

Hungarian capital to commemorate Hungary's experience of fascism, which culminated in the extermination of 70 per cent of Hungarian Jews. In a country where the hard-right interwar dictator Admiral Horthy is immortalized and the third-largest party is openly neo-fascist and anti-Semitic, this matters. As an extant movement, Soviet-style communism is stone dead in contemporary Eastern Europe, bar maybe its undeath in the Czech Republic, Ukraine and Russia; but fascism most certainly isn't. And the sculptors who once designed glowering Lenins and muscle-bound workers now devote their talents to edifices representing the likes of Admiral Horthy, Marshal Józef Piłsudski, the Latvian dictator Kārlis Ulmanis and the Ukrainian fascist leader Stepan Bandera, none of them 'democrats' in any sane sense of the word. The statues are often in the same style, in the same red granite, on the same angular abstract plinths with realist busts and statues built in. Often, looking at one of the many looming bronze Piłsudskis in Poland, it's only the peaked cap and the more luxurious facial hair that make it clear you're not looking at a Lenin. Though the official ideology is to reject both 'totalitarianisms', in practice their conflation is very frequently packaged with the rehabilitation of right-wing authoritarianism.

If fascism's victims are ever commemorated in post-communist Europe, it's usually in the form of museums that put together the 'two totalitarianisms'. In Budapest, the central House of Terror (actually called this), is in the building on Andrássy út where the Gestapo and then the Hungarian secret police, the AVO, had their offices. In the Baltic states, there are museums to the 'Double Genocide', and the Lithuanian one is also in an office block that was used as a torture chamber by both the Gestapo and the KGB. On that level, the desire to place the two regimes in alignment is understandable, but what is the word 'genocide' doing here? Both Latvian and Lithuanian official histories use this term to refer not merely to the actual genocide of Baltic Jews – for which reason there are now nearly no Jews at all in such former 'Jerusalems of the North' as Vilnius, Kaunas, Daugavpils and Riga – but also to the genocide of Lithuanians and Latvians, which seems contradicted by the continued existence here of Lithuanians and Latvians. The term hasn't been wholly pulled out of nowhere, but refers to the mass deportations of potential 'counter-revolutionaries' in the Baltic states under Stalin's rule. These were appalling crimes under any possible interpretation of international

The Museum of the Red Riflemen/The Museum of Occupations, Riga

law, and many died in the transport to Siberia, but these people were not all shot in pits or gassed in vans and chambers. In fact, most survived. It is not the same thing. Nonetheless, denying 'both' genocides is illegal under Lithuanian law, so we'd best be careful.

A typical space for remembering the 'Double Genocide' is the Occupation Museum in the centre of Riga. We have come across this already, as the central building in the reconstructed Riflemen's Square, surrounded by contemporary and Stalinist interpretations of historical architecture. The building, originally the Museum of the Red Riflemen, was designed in 1969, by the architects Dzintars Driba and Gunārs Lūsis-Grīnbergs. As an exterior structure, it is harsh, with an almost windowless copper-panelled façade; in front of it is a statue of the 'Riflemen', appearing as superhuman sentries standing at the gates to the city, at the point where the main road bridge over the Daugava connects it to the centre. Because of that the museum is 'the' entry to Riga's Old Town, and accordingly its façade is often covered with giant adverts to the road. Before we can think about the building's current purpose, we need to know who these statues are, and what the museum was devoted to previously.

It was not devoted to the Great Patriotic War, during which Soviet-occupied Latvia was then occupied by the Nazis, but to the tens of thousands of Latvians who fought on the side of the Bolsheviks in the 'Russian' Civil War, between 1917 and 1921. They gained a reputation for ferociousness; after he survived an assassination attempt, Lenin's personal guard was a detachment of Latvians. Many later took high positions in the Party and state (including, notably, the 'organs') before being decimated by Stalin, who specifically targeted Latvians, as he did Poles and Germans or any other foreign-born communists during the purges of 1936–8. The Riflemen, made up of divisions which had gone over to the Bolsheviks during the collapse of the Eastern Front in the First World War, were not alone in Latvia in their enthusiasm for communism. In the Constituent Assembly elections of late 1917, the Bolsheviks took 72 per cent of the vote. Latvia, as one of the most industrially developed areas of the Russian Empire, had been one of their strongholds since 1905. A brief Soviet Republic was set up here in 1919, and defeated only by foreign intervention. So this is not a monument to an 'occupation', but to Latvians' widespread participation in the October Revolution, something which even nationalist historians do not dispute. Like all Soviet jingoist monuments, it is hard to connect the deeds – not always heroic, and civil wars tend not to be – and the unambiguous representation of these red-granite cybermen.[37] As a composition, it is very powerful. It is placed on one side of the low, intersecting volumes of the museum, and Riga Cathedral's spire emerges on the other side. The imposing asymmetrical alignment would be even more clear, but for the reconstructed Blackhead's House emerging just behind. It is, in the original, one of the Soviet structures that sets up a dialogue between 'heritage' as in great monuments, and 'heritage' as in the workers' movement, the state's official legitimation.

There are proposals to reclad half of the museum in mirrorglass and white tiles, so that its new purpose is more signposted, but at the moment the exterior of the Museum of Occupations is untouched, in contrast to the interior, where the occupations of Latvia by the Nazis and by the Soviets are treated oddly asymmetrically. In the fifty pages of the English-language catalogue, which gives a sense of the balance of the contents, there are just five pages on the Nazi occupation, in which there are three short paragraphs on the Holocaust, one of which is devoted to denying the existence of Latvian anti-Semitism.[38] Regardless, nearly all of Latvia's 70,000 Jews were killed, most of them before the Nazis even officially instituted the Final Solution at the Wannsee conference. There may perhaps not have been a 'history' of pogroms in Riga before the 1940s, but this didn't stop the Arajs Kommando, one of the most notorious collaborationist forces in occupied Europe, from doing much of the killing, here and elsewhere. The commando would later form the backbone of a Latvian SS legion, which the museum is at pains to point out was not involved in any atrocities, and was partly conscripted; glossy books in the shop show photographs of this rebranded 'Latvian Legion', their Swastika armbands proudly on display on the cover, along with apologetic commentary. Nearly everything is translated into English, as if they're very keen to make clear to visitors what happened here. If the Nazi occupation is skirted over, there is much, much more on how the Soviet occupation turned Latvia into an economic basket case and a colony, one where the Russian population – making up around half of the city's residents – still resist learning Latvian, and want Russian as an official second language. The museum is not about the past but about this present, and it is quite categorical about that. This is easily as gross as any Soviet instrumentalization of history, and it should be possible to say so.

There's little doubt that Latvia was treated in a colonial fashion under the USSR,[39] and the emigration of Russian workers was one facet of this, though it's doubtful they benefited from it much. There's also no doubt that under Stalinism Baltic peoples were subject to harsh repression, as were others, Russians included. But as the writer Otto Latsis, whose family had been communists since the 1910s, pointed out, even under Khrushchev Latvia's Communist Party was purged after it attempted a 'national communist' orientation, trying to limit Russian migration. Gratuitously, even harmless festivals such as the Feast of St Ivan were banned. So the use of the word 'occupation' is fair. But it is not fair to argue that both occupations were equal and equivalent. In the context of the Latvian independence movement in 1990, Latsis asserted that 'it is a ludicrous idea' to argue, as the official histories then did, that the occupation of Latvia was voluntary or caused by revolution in Latvia itself. 'Serious analysis shows there was no revolutionary situation at all, though there was a high level of discontent with the reactionary Baltic regimes . . . such arguments only make people realize that they are being treated as idiots.' He had equally harsh words for the notion that Latvia was still 'occupied' fifty years later. 'Am I not also being treated as an idiot by those whose talk of "occupation" stubbornly equates the events of half a century ago with those of the present? If there were an occupation regime in place today, even the mildest criticism would be forbidden.'[40]

So why the harshness, why the insistence that the Soviet occupation needs much more space and attention than the German? There is a slip of paper, in English, available at the entrance to the museum, which explains this. 'One of Latvia's greatest strengths, its welcoming attitude and openness to others, is becoming its greatest weakness, as others exploit that openness to change what it means to be Latvian in ways that subvert the nation and allow others to dominate it . . . now it is so obvious that no one concerned about Latvia and Latvians can afford to ignore it.'[41] What might this sudden change be? Conceivably, the election of a Russian-speaking mayor the same year, when the largest party in the parliament was a pro-Russian coalition that included post-communist parties such as the Social Democrats and the Latvian Socialist Party, the batter led by Riga's 1980s mayor, Alfreds Rubiks. This in itself was remarkable given that a large proportion of the Russian-speaking population are denied citizenship, having to pass a complex naturalization test if they want to vote in general elections. 'Changing what it means to be Latvian' is code for accepting that Latvian Russians are also Latvian.

So we have a museum that is extremely interventionist, as determined to make a polemical point as any under the USSR. History remains a tool, to be used according to whoever the enemy is at any given time. Estonia, too, has a similar citizenship regime to Latvia and an Occupation Museum, and typically for contemporary Estonia it's a much more interesting piece of architecture than you would find in Riga, a subtle, secluded neo-Brutalist building, a glass pavilion framed by steel diagonals, rising from a raw concrete base. Nearby is the empty space where the Red Army's less tasteful memorial, the 'bronze soldier', stood until its removal in 2007. The Estonian artist Kristina Norman notes that 'back then the education system was supposed to make "Soviet people" out of youngsters, today the aim instead is to produce an "Estonian-mindedness"';[42] in this context, 'the current political power constructs and redefines their historical, foreign and internal enemies for populist reasons. At the same time, they are carrying out a policy of the intensification of national identity, and in this process monuments have become visual instruments.' She recalls that her – Russian-speaking – parents voted for Estonian independence, as did 150,000 other 'Russians'. However, they did not get citizenship in the new state, unlike the descendants of anyone who lived there before 1939. In that context, the old Soviet monuments 'filled a gap that was left after the positive identity for the Russian-speaking population had disappeared'. When the Red Army memorial was removed in 2007, the rioting Russian youth targeted for particular violence a boutique/luxury office complex. The rioters were known to have come from microrayons on the outskirts of Tallinn. But these acts of 'class' were immediately subsumed into 'nation', with support from the Kremlin's youth movement, the 'Nashi', and chants of 'Russia! Russia!' The invasion of the microrayons into the tourist centre became the invasion of the Russians.

The maintenance of nationalism as the only acceptable frame is enforced on both sides; during the riots, President Toomas Hendrik Ilves was quoted as saying that, for Estonians, 'our people were not murdered by communists or Nazis, but by Germans and Russians'.[43] This discourse is ubiquitous in the Baltics. How to explain all the seeming evidence that in 1917 a lot of Latvians supported the Bolsheviks, and in 1941 many appeared to support the Nazis? The answer could not possibly be that factory workers in Riga were convinced socialists, like workers in St Petersburg, Berlin or Paris around the same time; it cannot possibly be that many young people in Riga, as in Vichy, Rome or Berlin, were adherents of fascist ideology. One recent Latvian book – translated, like so many in the Occupation Museum, into English – on wartime propaganda argues that 'the ideas of the Bolsheviks gained resonance' because 'they promised Latvian autonomy', and that while the Latvian SS 'technically fought against the allies, the majority of legionnaires did not wish to fight for Hitler and the Nazis, but rather against the USSR and Stalin'. Somehow it all seems to become acceptable if it's in the service of the nation. The result is not merely the existence of new spaces of memory – as politically pointed adaptive reuse in Vilnius or Riga, as bunker-chic in Tallinn, but also a spatial segregation, which even the casual observer can notice. Seldom did we hear Russian in the Old Towns of Tallinn and Riga, seldom did we hear Estonian in Pirita or Latvian in the Maskavas District; sometimes both cities can feel like a prettier Belfast. The memorial politics of these cities are, in this context, extremely undemocratic.

What makes the new memorial spaces in the Baltic countries so uneasy is that sense of special pleading, the attempt to at once conflate the two 'totalitarianisms' while exonerating their local auxiliaries. The rhetoric is always in terms of 'Well, you may have heard that we all collaborated with the Nazis' – (while, of course, most foreign visitors have no idea) – 'but in fact, we only did so because of the Soviets.' Obviously there's less of this touchiness in Warsaw, capital of the country that proudly didn't collaborate with either of the two totalitarianisms.[44] There are abundant memorial spaces to the Home Army, by far the largest of the three clandestine armies that resisted the Nazis (the other two forces, made up respectively of Polish communists and fascists, are unsurprisingly less remembered – though there are surviving plaques for the former, and graffiti stencils left by the young far right for the latter). Many were persecuted after 1945, and a small group of the Home Army formed Independence and Freedom, a partisan organization which fought on in the forests for some years. The Home Army's most famous action, the Warsaw Rising of August 1944, is central to post-1989 Poland's story of itself. Though it was of course directed against the Nazis, most sources agree it was also designed to secure the city so that the Red Army would be met by 'facts on the ground'. Perhaps unsurprisingly, then, the Red Army, bar its Polish units under General Berling, was ordered not to assist, and they watched the city burn from the other side of the Vistula.

Guidebooks like to mention how 'ugly' Warsaw's many war memorials are, as if the correct response to the suffering in this city would have been to erect something *pretty*. What is maybe more interesting is the way they try to create entire cityscapes of memorialization, in the Soviet manner – memorials as three-dimensional pieces of city, rather than as pieces of art you can casually walk past. And like Soviet monuments, this can make them rather silly – the first official memorial to the Warsaw Rising, built in 1988 mere months before the end of the system, has a combination of abstraction close to that cave-underpass that connects the Lavra to the war museum in Kiev – hulking concrete splinters through which bronze soldiers storm out. In a striking act of blasphemy against the national myth, the sculpture is known locally as 'Running for a bus'.

A gathering at the Sappers' Monument, Warsaw, on a 1985 postcard

All are huge, but some are less ideological than others – the Sappers' Monument, built in the 1970s, doesn't state whether the Sappers were in the Home Army or the communist People's Army, but it forms an ensemble with a riverside embankment. The combination of abstract plinth and hulking figures returns, as do some densely packed, tortured friezes, bulging out with angst and horror. The jagged plinths (representing in stone the risk of exploded mines) and the statue of a singular Sapper are one side of a complex which pulls an underpass leading to the river into itself – when you get to the other end, the memorial continues, more of the low-relief figures of resistance fighters, providing a dead end in front of the Vistula.

In the Warsaw Rising's dedicated museum, you get little sense that the Nazis might have been motivated by ideology in their extreme suppression of the Poles – specifically, racial ideology, with Poles regarded as 'subhuman'. It just 'happened' because they were bad people who wanted to suppress Polish independence. The museum spreads across an old factory that was badly damaged during the rising. A steel-framed watchtower has been erected, emblazoned with the ubiquitous symbol for 'Poland Fights', which you still find graffitied on every street corner, as if the war were still going on. And indeed, according to the museum guides, it is – Agata overhears one telling a group of schoolchildren: 'You think the war finished in 1945? No!'

The walls around the museum are decorated by Polish street artists, with murals on Solidarity, on the women of the Home Army, and some horror-cartoon images of fighting Poles. Nazis and Nazism are not depicted much here, either. When you go inside, though, the architecture of the museum is immediately redolent of the Museum of the Great Patriotic War, with dim, mood-setting lighting, dramatic montaged dioramas rather than mere objects under glass, and lots of machinery on display, with an aeroplane suspended across the old machine hall. All exhibits, as in Riga but unlike in Kiev, are captioned in English. There is a lot about the Molotov–Ribbentrop pact, and one tiny panel on the Ghetto rising of 1943. But it also has much more of the immersive museum spaces that a visitor to London's Imperial War Museum might recognize – a walk-in office of the underground, a bunker you can hide in. Its day-by-day charting of the rising and its accounts from participants is undeniably moving, and their courage and heroism are, again, indisputable, especially against such overwhelming odds. The photographs of these ordinary Poles taking over their city are emblazoned on the walls, and their joy, their obvious sense of liberation, is clear. But if the museum tells you how, it never asks why. Why did the Nazis treat Poles like subhumans? Who were they?

What did they want? It's almost as if to think about fascism would be to think critically about nationalism . . . And at the end, of course, we have Ronald Reagan commemorating the insurgents, John Paul II quoted reminding us that 'there is no way to understand this Nation without Christ', and rooms on the subsequent Soviet liberation/occupation. And here, in this room lit by a giant neon hammer-and-sickle, are panel profiles of Soviet collaborators. The implication is that the horrors did not really end until 1989.[45] But we hear once again that song which was blasted out on the way into the Museum of the Great Patriotic War, the enormous roar of 'The Sacred War', now repositioned to sing of occupation, not liberation. It may be a 'subverting' of the original use, but the results here are every bit as black and white and didactic as the spaces of Soviet memory.

So is there a way of remembering that is not somehow against a continuation of or a reaction to the jingoistic architecture of Stalinism? We came across two in particular which tried to do something different. One of them departs from the national, state-subsidized politics of memory for a remarkable transformation of a memorial space into property development – the 'Corvin Quarter', in Budapest. A large Baroque circus just behind Budapest's radial Haussmannian boulevard is, at first, a continuous monument to 1956. The big tenement blocks curve around a small cinema, which is covered with plaques for the revolution that had one of its main centres exactly here. Insurgents are commemorated with dozens of plaques, with biographies which aren't afraid to make clear how many of them and their leaders were communists; in fact, the only communists who have monuments to them surviving in the city are of course Imre Nagy, Pál Maléter, Sándor Kopácsi, and others who saw no contradiction between socialism and an insurrection against Stalinism. The dozens of memorials are in a wholly different aesthetic from Stalinist edifices, too, with cursive typography, the inclusion of photos and little portraits, and lots of crosses. A map shows you the Quarter and the battles fought there. Walk around it and you'll find that these are the only historical buildings left, as you suddenly find yourself in a new, shiny, Modernist shopping arcade, and then on a promenade lined by pristine luxury apartment blocks, exactly the same in style as any in Western Europe, with Trespa and brick cladding, little balconies and the like. The way it is all planned, from the memorial circus leading to the new development, appears to suggest that the culmination of the Hungarian revolution against Stalinism and Russian colonialism was luxury living solutions for the new European bourgeoisie. There are few places where the spatial link between nationalism and capitalism is quite so obvious, but here the Stalinist legacy has been truly left behind.

The other is unusual for its degree of contestation, its incompleteness, its inability and unwillingness to speak with one voice about the past – the series of memorial spaces dedicated to the Solidarity movement, in its birthplace, the Gdańsk shipyards. The first monument here was designed in 1980, and erected soon after – a triple cross dedicated to the shipyard workers who fell here in the wildcat strikes of 1970, when the army were sent in to suppress them with force. The crosses, designed by Bogdan Pietruszka, are of twisted and tapered steel, as raw and metallic as the ships; they are obviously religious in their symbolism, but on the lower parts of each cross, at eye level, are relief sculptures, depicting the workers and their struggle. Even after Solidarity, too, was violently suppressed at the end of 1981, the monument was retained, and after 1989 it was accompanied by various other memorial spaces, which seem only to have expanded as the shipyards have closed. An auto-rusting International Solidarity Centre, devoted to the histories of the trade union movement and anti-communism (not always the same thing, alas) was nearly under construction, described by Pyzik in *Poor but Sexy* as a place where you can 'see in a nutshell the results of the capitalist transition', a queasy historical joke, whose rusting and weathering do not only symbolize 'memory' but also inadvertently the disappearance of the shipyards themselves and the jobs that came with them. When we went there, a small fragment of the yard still existed, devoted now only to breaking rather than building ships; their red-brick sheds and immense pipelines and rotting infrastructure, constructed mostly when this was still Danzig, are abutted by wasteland. It's a goldmine for lovers of industrial design, all hard Hansa brick, twisted steel, skyscraping cranes and spindly gantries, blown by dust and crisscrossed by mud. The old entrance is still the way in, and you can just pass there from the street, past a kiosk selling Solidarity souvenirs.

The Gdańsk strikes in both 1970 and 1980 were initially caused by price rises for food, intended to make the system 'rational', like capitalism is, with prices decided by the market, not by what a worker can or can't

A 1981 postcard of the Shipyard Memorial, Gdańsk

afford. The Gdańsk workers' demands are emblazoned on the entrance to the shipyard, in full – in fact, what you see is the original text, scrawled in red and black onto a board. Aside from demanding amnesties for political prisoners and a free press, they include demands for fixed prices, for equal access to health care, and for the abolition of the special shops where those with access to foreign currency could buy things unavailable elsewhere. Demands for the restoration of the free market, let alone for 'shock therapy', are conspicuous by their absence. In fact, apart from the clause demanding freedom of worship, their programme would have been described anywhere in the world but Poland in 1980 as 'socialist'. Peter Gowan wrote of this apparent paradox at the time, 'Nationalised industry has entailed a number of social and economic corollaries: full employment and economic security; very low and largely stable prices for essential items such as food, housing, transport, etc.; rising living standards; a large and generally growing degree of social egalitarianism (in comparison with capitalist states); a lower level of work intensity; and, for a minority of the manual working class, prospects of social privileges and upward mobility considerably greater than under capitalism. Almost all of these phenomena are indeed registered in western bourgeois literature on the states of Eastern Europe, but they are mentioned overwhelmingly in the context of the supposed economic evils of these systems. Thus we hear an unending stream of scorn for the arbitrary prices, the slack work rhythm, the supposed absurdities of full employment in terms of rational use of labour resources, and so on . . . What is less often registered is that these supposedly irrational social features of the East European states are perceived by their own working populations as important social gains and rights . . . all the historical evidence of these states demonstrates that any attempt to tamper with these rights is liable to produce a political crisis.' Seen in this way, it almost seems as if the strikes were not designed to bring down communism, but to enforce communism on some very reluctant communists. The reaction to this in December 1981 stopped this as a possibility for good.[46]

Solidarity never spoke with one voice, including within it Catholics, Party members, dissidents, political prisoners, nationalists and even a few Marxists; its programme, by late 1981, was essentially syndicalist, calling for a 'self-managing republic'. Although nothing here suggests that syndicalism is remembered, there is a clash of memorials: the demands over the entrance, where in plain sight you can see exactly what it was they wanted, and how they didn't get it, either in 1981 or in 1989; the crosses, which make clear their devout Catholicism and their adherence to a Soviet iconography of labour; a concrete wall, decorated with memorial plaques

Tatlin's tower, Gdańsk shipyards

from all over Poland, a collection of messages of thanks to the Gdańsk workers for their role in liberating the country – one, depressingly, features a bust of Marshal Piłsudski, and one wonders how exactly they think this military dictator would have reacted to a mass strike on the Baltic coast. And, inside, there are remnants of more recent art projects, courtesy of the small Wyspa ('Island') gallery in one of the nineteenth-century warehouses. These include a miniature version, created by the artist Grzegorz Klaman, of Tatlin's Monument to the Third International, that Futurist dream devoted to international workers' solidarity, which has built inside it, instead of the hub of the world workers' revolution, a Corten steel bunker, a suggestive image of what that dream of international revolution eventually became, here in this international seaport. It all amounts to a confused, emotional but powerful statement of just how little of this struggle is clear and obvious, a contradictory rejoinder to all those univocal statements of national heroism, whether Soviet or post-Soviet. Still, if developers have their way, it'll one day be an unusually artistic entrance to a giant hypermarket.

IGNORANCE OF HIS MEMORY IS A CRIME

I will finish this chapter with two 'house museums', both dedicated to Georgian-born members of the Russian Social Democratic Labour Party, both of whom wrote some poetry. The first of these stands in between Dzhugashvili Street and Stalin Prospekt, at the centre of the small but historic Georgian town of Gori. Even a visitor unfamiliar with the most basic rules of town planning will have worked out that the entire town has been planned around this house museum. Stalin Avenue is a magistrale, its wide expanse lined with Tverskaya-style monumental apartment buildings (dressed with balconies and pinnacles in line with the Ottoman–Persian 'national form' in this part of the Union) on a scale which might seem excessive for a town of around 50,000 inhabitants, with a glass-domed neoclassical city hall larger than those of many cities ten times its size. At the end of the magistrale is Stalin Park, a pretty, symmetrical green space with a channelled stream in the middle, and at the end of that is the J. V. Stalin Memorial Museum.

Before we proceed to this place, some explaining needs to be done so you know why it manages to exist at all. A month after Khrushchev's (soon not-so-)secret speech of February 1956, rumours that Stalin had been publicly denounced reached Tbilisi. A mass wreath-laying at the city's Stalin statue escalated into what were by Soviet standards huge street protests of tens of thousands, carrying pictures of Stalin, demanding Khrushchev and his allies Mikoyan and Bulganin resign and that the Stalin loyalist Vyacheslav Molotov take over. The demonstrations spread to all Georgian cities and were, eventually, violently suppressed, with at least a hundred people killed when the Red Army shot at demonstrators in Tbilisi. Stalin, mocked by Khrushchev as the self-proclaimed 'father of the Georgians', was roundly defended by his co-nationals as a great national hero; but however much Georgian nationalists (such as the curators of Tbilisi's historically nonsensical Museum of the Soviet Occupation) might claim that this was an incipient movement for Georgian independence, its symbol and figurehead was the late Josef Stalin. This is paradoxical, to say the least, given that the main reason why Lenin requested in his 'testament' the removal of Stalin from his post was his brutal treatment of the Georgian Bolshevik leadership. Georgia was independent under Menshevik rule (with more than a little British assistance) from 1918 to 1921, and only Sovietized at gunpoint by the Red Army, at the insistence of Georgian Bolsheviks in Russia like Stalin and Ordzhonikidze. The newly installed local Georgian Bolshevik leadership, however, tolerated the Mensheviks and demanded federal rather than union affiliation to the USSR, as it was created in 1922. Stalin's crushing of the local communists helped define the Soviet Union as a (much more equal-opportunties) rebranding of the Russian Empire rather than the equal federation it could have been. Even this was a compromise with Lenin – Stalin had preferred to annex Georgia straight to Russia.[47]

For all his obvious contempt for local sensitivities, Stalin was still a Georgian, who spoke Russian with an accent, and allowed Georgia much the same freedom in matters of 'national form' as any other republic of the Union, and it suffered no more and no less from the Great Purge. For all that, the effects of Stalin's rule on his home town were more dramatic than most. The first part of the J. V. Stalin Memorial Museum accessible from Stalin Prospekt is a marble cube, in the cold, honey-coloured local stone, with white marble columns, top-lit with a square of yellowing

Encased in marble, the family home of J. V. Stalin, Gori

stained glass. This encloses a tiny little house, formed out of the same poor-quality bricks and cement as the flat expansions of contemporary Tbilisi, with a flimsy wooden balustrade to the street. This, preserved since 1936, is the house where Josef Vissarionovich Dzhugashvili, later Koba, later still Stalin, was born, to a cobbler and former serf in 1878, and where he spent his childhood. It is this tiny house (one of what would have been several like it nearby) which the entire town, having been demolished, has been rebuilt around – the living proof of how far Joe Stalin, working-class hero, had come from this shabby little house shared with his parents' landlord. There are few better indictments of Stalin's notion of what 'socialism' entailed than that. But if the house's preservation dates from his lifetime, the building behind it is posthumous – a massive museum to his memory, finished in 1957 just at the time when monuments to Stalin elsewhere started to be dismantled, as were the worst aspects of his system: the Gulag, the deportations, the purges, the quasi-medieval inquisitions, the absurd strictures on architecture, art and literature, albeit while leaving the political-economic system he created substantially intact. The museum building is a completion of the magistrale, a neo-Venetian palace with an airy colonnade, an ornamental attic and a heraldic tower at its corner. There is a certain sick irony in the fact that the world's two surviving museums to Stalin (there is another, smaller, in Batumi, also in Georgia) were built and preserved as a concession to a popular protest movement in a republic that has had and still has an often hostile relationship to Russia, and not as the legitimation of a Brezhnev or a Putin.

It is still a popular concession. Gori's oversized city hall boasted an oversized Stalin statue until 2010, removed by central government and apparently soon to be rebuilt at the instigation of the city council; attempts to close the museum are regularly blocked by the plucky locals. A gruff statue of the man stands in a niche in the railway station, another lurks in Stalin Park, another still is in the local war museum, and then there's the one at the top of the stairs in the anteroom of the main Memorial Museum – more Stalins, in fact, than you'll find at any of the post-Soviet statue graveyards, here in unironic situ. In them you can see that Stalin statues gestured less than Lenins: they present a relatively humble-looking chap with moustache, usually standing stiffly rather than pointing forwards. Aside from its impressive medieval castle, since Gori's industry collapsed along with the rest of the Georgian economy in the 1990s, the Stalin Museum is the only thing that would make anyone other than (in 2008, during the South Ossetia war) the Russian army come here. Inside the museum, we are encouraged to pay extra for an English-language guide – a well-made-up woman of around fifty who takes us up through the thicket of slender marble columns in the anteroom, up the red-carpeted stairs, to the museum itself. Gesturing with a thin metal pointer, her assessment of Stalin's life is full of numbers, facts and statistics – the year he was born, the amount of time he spent in Siberian exile, the amount of times he escaped, the awards he received, the amount of texts he wrote, the divisions he commanded, humanized only when she gets to a panel on Stalin's unfortunate family (some of whom, it transpires, were and are visitors to and supporters of the museum). These are not the numbers, facts and statistics you usually hear in conjunction with Stalin's life and work. The space itself is perhaps not quite as terrifying as it might have

Gifts for Comrade Stalin, Gori

been a few years before its 1957 opening, when Stalin was celebrated as a demi-god, but it is still, as you would expect, a shock. The first room, lit from above by gold-framed top-lighting, from the side by decorated stained-glass windows, and lined below with a patterned parquet floor, depicts his early life, revealing along with his rugged good looks and his youthful radical poetry (on sale in English translation downstairs) a remarkable collection of paintings of Stalin the boy. In one he is reading, idea-struck, from a book of poetry to his young friends, with Gori Castle in the background. After that, a room on his career as General Secretary, another on his time as Generalissimo, all full of artworks and curios (lacquerwork portraits, Stalin's fur coat, his chairs, his paperweights, etc., etc.), and then a circular, darkened room containing at its centre his death mask. 'There are many casts of this death mask,' our guide tells us. 'Each one is ten per cent smaller than the previous one.' This narrative of Stalin's life is, as you would expect in 1957 if you were an aggrieved young Georgian Stalinist, devoid of any mention of the mass incarceration, deportation and terrifyingly random, aimless murder of, among others, millions of entirely innocent Poles, Latvians, Chechens, Crimean Tatars, Ukranian peasants, Koreans, Volga Germans, Kazakhs, Russians, Georgians and, most of all, communists, who were jailed and killed at a rate surpassed perhaps only by Hitler. The narrative instead gives way to a series of wood-panelled, barrel-vaulted rooms, lit by Rococo chandeliers, a space shaped like a mini-Moscow Metro station, lined with glass cases containing gifts for Stalin, from Polish metalworkers, Chinese, Italian and Finnish communists, and a grain of rice upon which an Indian communist has written a poem of praise to Stalin, helpfully magnified.

From here, the guide can take you inside Stalin's extremely cramped childhood home, or through his personal bulletproof railway carriage. However, there is one recently opened room at the end of the main museum where you can see a mock-up of an NKVD interrogation room, with, we're told, authentic trenchcoats, a panel on murdered Soviet leaders (Zinoviev, victim of Stalin, on the same panel as Beria, victim of Khrushchev) and, meaninglessly, a panel on Russia's shelling and brief occupation of Gori in 2008, for which, for once, Stalin can't be wholly

Flying out of history at the State Mayakovsky Museum, Moscow

blamed. The museum of the 'great leader of the world's proletariat' stays resolutely local. Round the back of the station are streets of small houses that, aside from some Georgian-style balcony surgery, satellite dishes, cars and Orthodox memorial plaques to sons killed in South Ossetia, could be fundamentally unchanged from when young Dzhugashvili's house was round here. Seventy or so years of 'socialism' followed by twenty of capitalism haven't changed things here much, out of sight of that magistrale on the other side of the museum, where, as Engels wrote, 'the most scandalous alleys and lanes disappear to the great accompaniment of lavish self-glorification . . . but – they re-appear once again somewhere else, and often in the immediate neighbourhood.'[48] If this is what all that suffering was for, then why not reject it all?

The other house museum is the last of the memorial spaces to be built in the Soviet Union while it still existed. This is something called the State Mayakovsky Museum, dedicated to the 'Com-Futurist' poet, playwright, actor and draughtsman, born near Kutaisi in 1893, who would become the hero both of communist youth in the 1920s and of the young of the 'Thaw' in the 1950s and 1960s. It was built largely in 1990 and opened to the public then, although the last exhibit dates from 1993. It is built into the house where Vladimir Mayakovsky lived from the early 1920s until his 1930 suicide. House museums are an omnipresent genre in Russia and Ukraine, where a collection of someone's knick-knacks – always a desk, with their books on it – is either preserved or, more often, reconstructed. They're often a bit dull. You can tell the Mayakovsky house museum is going to be different when you see a red-painted steel polygon rammed into the side of the neoclassical tenement where he lived, avant-garde architecture of a far more pulp, pop, cheap sort than the Le Corbusian Modernism that actually got built in Mayakovsky's day. Enter, and you find what must be expensive artefacts – dozens of gorgeous books designed by Rodchenko and El Lissitzky, photographs of the man and fragments from his poems, architectural drawings from the Vesnin brothers, tens of posters, paintings, sketches, police mugshots, architectural fragments, smashed-up temples. They are placed in a vague, fragmented chronology, but as in the Museum of the Great Patriotic War, the priceless artefacts are not kept under glass but pulled into room-size dioramas connected by steel and wood frames and, here, wire mesh, making every exhibit an entirely original sculpture, a ludic pile-up, everything full of joy, imagination and experiment – far less a museumification of the old leftist avant-garde than any of the scrupulously curated exhibitions on them in the West.

As you go through these rooms, the exhibits seem not so much to have been constructed but to have been swept up by the wind and thrown together, clinging on to each other in a maelstrom which has been abruptly paused, as in a cartoon, so you can walk through it. It's amazing it all manages to stand up. At one point, little portraits of Mayakovsky and his colleagues on the magazine *LEF* are suspended in a wooden frame in the shape of a biplane, suspended from the ceiling. Look closely and there is actually a narrative here about Mayakovsky himself – childhood in Georgia, early membership of the Bolshevik Party as a teenager, imprisonment, dandyism, Futurism, Constructivism, his loves, his commemorations of Lenin, his travels through America and Europe, and his inspiration of left-wing artists and writers abroad. But the specifics feel less important than this explosion of creativity, this incredible release, with which the architects of perestroika have reconstructed the aesthetic experience of the revolution and its immediate aftermath. It's doubtful whether it's an even remotely accurate depiction of the actual experience, the grain of everyday life, in the 1920s; the grey room upstairs that served as Mayakovsky's study certainly suggests not. But what it does is convey an idea. It is the only revolutionary memorial of all of these we came across which argues that revolution might be a rather exciting thing, one that would transform the world, and transform space, for the better. Worth doing. Why not try it. But in the last room one of the broken images is a photograph taken in 1993, of the Russian parliament on fire.

Conclusion: Socialism Is

– The future is outside politics, the future soars above the chaos of political and social aspirations and picks out from them threads to weave into a new cloth which will provide the winding-sheet for the past and the swaddling clothes for the new born. Socialism corresponds to the Nazarene teaching in the Roman Empire.

– If one extends the parallel, the future of socialism is not an enviable one. It will remain an eternal hope.

– And in the process will develop a brilliant era of history under its blessing. The Gospels were not fulfilled and there was no need for that – but what were fulfilled were the Middle Ages, and the ages of reconstruction and the ages of revolution, and Christianity penetrated all these manifestations, participated in everything, acted as the guide and pilot. The fulfilment of socialism involves the same unexpected combination of abstract doctrine and existing fact. Life realises only that aspect of an idea that falls on favourable soil, and the soil in this case doesn't remain a mere passive medium, but gives its sap, contributes its own elements. The new element born of the conflict between Utopias and conservatism enters life, not as one or as the other side expected it – it enters transformed, different, composed of memories and hopes, of existing things and things to be, of traditions and pledges, of belief and science . . . Ideals, theoretical constructions, never materialise in the shape in which they float in our minds.

Alexander Herzen, From the Other Shore *(1851)*[1]

THE CATHEDRALS OF 'COMMUNISM'

It's customary for critiques from the left to reproach 'real socialism' for its regimentation, its statism, its bureaucracy, its subordination of everything to ideology. It is assumed in this that a 'real' socialism would be able to dispense with these things, and dispense, moreover, with the inheritances from the past that so obviously weighed upon the Soviet project – the legacies of combined and uneven development, of Tsarist authoritarianism, of Hapsburg bureaucracy, as you will – unlikely to have any purchase on a socialist experiment attempted under the ideal, Platonic conditions of a Western, industrialized country. Unfortunately, this has never actually occurred, and one of the most striking things about the history of socialism is that a fully developed capitalist class has never once been overthrown anywhere – with, at best, its destruction at the point of Eastern bayonets in East Germany or Czechoslovakia as close as it has ever come. The bourgeoisie's longevity, their staying power, their ability to transform their system into newer, leaner, if not necessarily fairer shapes, is way beyond what any twentieth-century socialist could possibly have expected. But in the ironic dialogues that make up his *From the Other Shore*, written in the aftermath of the failed French revolution of 1848, the Russian revolutionary Alexander Herzen suggested that any socialism which would finally emerge would come into being shaped by the inheritances of the past, by all the 'petrified crap', as Marx called it, that it should have shaken off. It would not follow any possible blueprint, but be coloured and shaped by unexpected and – if the example of the Middle Ages is to be taken seriously – exceptionally ugly forces. This could be a profoundly depressing conclusion, summed up by the Russian revolution's transformation into a ruthless personal despotism and eventually an inept gerontocracy; or it could be otherwise. Never mind the blueprints, what could be built with what we've got, with the materials that come to hand?

Looking at what they did build, with the materials they had to hand, it's hard to say that the problems with – or the virtues of – the built environment under 'real socialism' were the consequence of it being too 'capitalist', or not being socialist enough. Of course, the extreme spatial hierarchies of the jingoistic memorials, boulevards, palaces and secret policemen's castles of high Stalinism or of Ceauşescu were grotesque, for all their occasionally compelling architectural qualities, and their claim to being in the lineage of any idea of 'socialism' is astonishingly tenuous. Yet the immense housing estates, however much they were a negation of the Marxist idea of the 'self-activity of the working class', were nothing if not egalitarian, if not a total attack on the notion of urban hierarchy, with all the architectural compositions based on the refusal to let any one object take primacy at any given time, and surrounded with a sea of completely public, free space. Meanwhile, the most 'unique' buildings of the era were for the most part the most public buildings: the theatres, squares, 'wedding palaces'. The reconstruction of historic cities can be seen not so much as a wilfully reactionary project based upon a need to appeal to national nostalgia as a palliative for Russian colonialism, but a reaction to the realization that cities no longer had to undergo the process of continual rebuilding that came with rent-seeking and property speculation. And, most impressive of all, the Metro systems of the USSR or of Prague were a spectacular vindication of public space, of the transformation of the everyday, that went further than any avant-garde ever dared.

The claim that the problem was lack of 'socialism' in the sense of 'self-activity', of workers' control,[2] is also based on completely ignoring the experience of Yugoslavia, which had the most developed system of workplace democracy yet seen anywhere, and one which had a major role in the economy itself. The results, spatially, were a little more strung out, a fair bit more lively, but not fundamentally, intrinsically different from the more imaginative examples in the Soviet-dominated countries. What killed it, as with the states of the Soviet Bloc itself, was not so much bureaucracy as the International Monetary Fund, which picked off the 'socialist countries' as punishment for their running up of enormous debts, much as it punished non-socialist developmental regimes in Latin America and Africa for doing exactly the same thing, at exactly the same time, for exactly the same reasons. Yet while externally, for sure, 'real socialism' paid dearly for being integrated into the world market, whether that can always be the culprit for the successes or failures of what happened at home is less clear.

What seems to have been decisive – or what felt decisive to us, walking in and working in these spaces – was a strange ability to create impressive, socialistic public spaces with two provisos: one, a problem with mass production; and two, a problem with 'desire'. In trying to explain the Soviet libidinal economy, the Georgian-born philosopher Keti Chukhrov claims that its problem wasn't 'things' as such, but the creation of commodity fetishism.[3] Food, as any visit to a Polish milk bar can still make clear, was supposed to be filling and healthy, but no more than that – cheeses would not be based on the various exciting things you could do with cheese but on the essential 'cheesiness' of cheese, on what makes it cheese rather than what makes it something else. Cheese ought not to have 'attracted' you; you ate cheese because cheese was nutritious. Similarly, housing had to cater for a situation of shortage, so what was needed was housing constructed at speed, unromantically, as a necessity. These things were catered for by a strikingly undeveloped form of mass production, which created famously shoddy goods, at least in part because of lower worker productivity and the absence of any economies of scale; it is plausible that automation and computerization could have eventually solved this, but it is an unknowable possibility. The fact remains that the very mass production which the 'socialist countries' should in theory have been best at was the very thing they most conspicuously failed in. But only *individual* commodities were mass-produced, things you could consume – food, records, clothes, cars and the industrialized housing. Conversely, the most impressive permanent spaces – the Metros, the public buildings – relied on qualities of craft and an enjoyment of surfaces that was acceptable because not commodified or commodifiable. A Metro station, theatre, bathhouse, cinema or club could not be 'yours', in the way that even housing could. Some might argue that this is a parody of socialism, and they're welcome to. Economically, I can't agree; but politically they're emphatically correct that a democratically controlled socialism must surely have had different spatial results, with buildings and ensembles that don't feel quite so flung in people's faces, that are not quite so monolithic and dominating.

Today, socialism even as an idea, let alone as an allegedly developed fact, largely exists only retrospectively. Some in the early 1990s welcomed the demise of the 'socialist camp' (and the apparent defection of China) as a boon for the left, as now it would no longer be associated with a crumbling, dictatorial empire. It didn't pan out like that. The current world capitalist system – particularly its 'Atlantic' part – is sometimes compared to the USSR in the age of stagnation, where the system is obviously bankrupt, no longer able to fulfil its promises, but carries on in a form of economic sleepwalking: 2009 as a 1989 without a rival system to fall into the arms of. Ideologically this has some truth, but economically less so – the Soviet system fell because it no longer satisfied manager or worker, and capitalism can go on for some time making a tiny minority rich and a large minority comfortable. Yet places where its virtues and stability are less clear have seen capitalism threatened for the first time in a long while. There are today countries which are officially 'socialist'. Not only Cuba, every Western leftist's favourite, or North Korea as a persisting nightmare, but also the Latin American 'twenty-first-century socialism' of Venezuela, Bolivia and Ecuador; at the time of writing, a similar movement of 'twenty-first-century socialists' has just been elected in Greece, and may have been in Spain as well by the time of publication. China, too, has seen controversial attempts to bring back the slogans and practices of Maoism, ending in the deposition and imprisonment on corruption charges of its most prominent neo-communist leader, Bo Xilai.[4] Communism today may be merely the 'relentless criticism of everything that exists' on the part of academics, the 'real movement that abolishes the existing state of affairs' on the part of elective sects, or whichever other aggrandizing quote from Marx that a powerless left wants to cite to reassure itself over its own powerlessness – or it may still be something that existing social movements in power are consciously driving towards. What if the traces of socialism and of the socialist city can be found there, just as much as in protest camps, NGOs or squats?

THE THIRTY-YEAR NEP

Chinese cities actually have many of the components of the 'real socialist' city outlined in this book, only in a different order, with a very different history. There was Stalinist architecture, in the form of 'gifts from the Soviet people' like the Beijing and Shanghai exhibition centres – both once 'Palaces of Sino-Soviet Friendship' – and in indigenous efforts, such as the 'Ten Great Buildings' of post-revolutionary Beijing. These were strictly 'national in form, socialist in content', i.e. adaptations of Moscow models with Chinese traditional details, and can be seen in Beijing's main railway station, the Historical Museum, the Great Hall of the People, and so forth. This Sino-Soviet style was, before the Sino-Soviet split in the early 1960s, exported back to Europe, as in the Chinese pavilion at the Zagreb Expo site, or the Chinese Embassy in Warsaw, designed by Polish architects in a style combining Frank Lloyd Wright and Old Beijing. But, here, the immediate urban past that was being rejected by Socialist Realist architects was not 'Modernism' as a social democratic or even communist project to technologically improve the built environment, but the combination of slum squalor and luxurious Americanized architecture in Shanghai, or the fascistic stripped classical structures favoured by the American-backed regime of Chiang Kai-shek in Nanjing. Housing under Mao was functional, undemonstrative and unspectacular, but lacked the deliberate futurity of modern architecture. When 'Modernism' arrived in the 1980s it was already 'Postmodern', and capitalist from the start. But most of the things in this book – the neo-Baroque boulevards, the micro-districts, the grand public buildings, the impressive public infrastructure, the memorials to revolution – are present and correct, only first they are assembled in a different order, and second they *could* be seen as part of an ongoing project.

When I spent a couple of weeks in Shanghai and Nanjing in 2010, in the year of the Shanghai Expo, I couldn't get out of my head a theory about the People's Republic of China, voiced most recently in Boris Groys's intriguing, if historically nonsensical, *The Communist Postscript*,[5] that what seems like merely the administration of capitalism by an oligarchy which is a Communist Party in nothing but name, is actually a gigantic, prolonged version of the New Economic Policy embarked upon by the Bolsheviks throughout the 1920s – the use of a dirigiste, state-planned capitalism to build up productive forces to a level where the population has gone from being poor to being reasonably comfortable, after which the Communist Party could take command of this wealth and use it for the building of full communism, something which can, after all, in 'stage' theory only be achieved after the development of a mature industrial capitalism.[6] This is at least what Deng Xiaoping always claimed was going on, and maybe this was what Bo Xilai thought he was doing, albeit while putting his fingers in the till. And if this stage of 'building up the productive forces' has lasted thirty years – why not? Lenin, for instance, envisaged that the NEP would last a lot longer than the eight years it got before it was replaced by Stalin's forced collectivization, chaotic industrialization and total suppression of private commerce. In the NEP – as in contemporary China – land remained nationalized, industry essentially state-directed, banks publicly owned, and power held firmly by the Party. Both had a high level of strikes, public discontent and debate, which coexisted with heavy censorship and bureaucracy, and the absence of organizations – like free trade unions – that are completely independent of the state. If the USSR in the 1920s was 'socialist' or at least moving towards socialism, then why not China? After all, in Shanghai, 80 per cent of the economy consists of state-owned enterprises.[7] If we make what seems with good reason to be a rather extravagant theoretical leap, given the immense scale of worker exploitation, and see twenty-first-century China as a super-NEP, what could the future Full Communist China do with the hypercapitalist infrastructure, the gated communities, the skyscraping office blocks of Shanghai, the largest Chinese (and, in terms of 'city proper', largest world) city? If, as is often claimed, China is making the world's biggest investment in green technology, then what is it going to do with all those flyovers and coal-fired power stations, or those seemingly so capitalist skyscraper skylines? Except, look at one of those skylines from on high, and sometimes you will see something strange – in between and in front of the speculative glass towers, serried ranks of mid-rise blocks of flats, a set of Khrushchevian panel blocks built at the same time as the corporate headquarters.

Shanghai is a city usually associated with Chinese neoliberalism, with its 'opening to the West' and the creation of a new 'socialist' bourgeoisie, but it has a firm revolutionary pedigree, as historically China's foremost industrial city, as founding home of the communist movement, as centre of the abortive Chinese revolution of 1926–7, and as home of a Maoist attempt to revive the Paris Commune in 1967.[8] Yet Maoism's base was always rural, and this metropolis, built largely in the first half of the twentieth century as a colonial capital to the designs of French, British and American architects, was deliberately underdeveloped until Deng's Bukharin-like call to 'Get Rich!' It is laced with elevated roads, all built over the last ten years or so, at roughly the same time, but to rather more impressive effect, as the more obviously 'public' Metro system – which, on the Western European model, is pleasant, functional, aesthetically forgettable. By contrast, this system of flyovers, for the purposes of private vehicles, is monstrous, dominant. The friend who is showing me round tells me of a conversation he had with a Party member, part of the CCP's 'New Left', critical of the prospect of full capitalist restoration (which they see as a prospect, not a fact[9]). When global warming really hits, when

Khrushchevki and skyscrapers, Nanjing

the oil runs out, and the use of the car has to be curbed, what will the Party do with all this? Can it just ban people from driving? Will people accept it? Yes, was the reply, the Party merely lacks the will. So before I had even seen these constructions, I had in mind the idea of them cleared of the traffic which is too thick and dense even for their astonishing capaciousness, with bicycles and walkers making their way along these lofty elevated roads. They're one of the most impressive works of engineering I've ever seen, for the less than impressive function of moving the private car with its internal-combustion engine from A to B – though, at least for the moment, taxis are so abundant and so cheap, sometimes equalling the levels of private cars, that to call it wholly 'private' feels a minor misnomer.

After I had travelled along and under a few of them in a dazed, numb state once off the plane, the first of these flyovers that I really saw was in a working-class district in the north of the city, near Caoyang New Village, a 1950s housing development which my friend was showing to his students. The area around it was so impossibly dense, the width of its expressways so yawning, the clusters of towers so high, the Metro station toilets so abject (the PRC's inegalitarian public convenience policy is notable here – in an area where there are likely to be Westerners present the loos are impeccable, elsewhere they're infernal) and the crowds so massive that I simply gave up and went back to bed.

The flyovers too are hierarchical. While the flyovers in the centre have the smoothest-finished cream concrete you're ever likely to see, in the suburbs it's a much more standard material. They still tend to be rather dominant, but they're not meant to be looked at, and they travel through what is still a heavily industrial landscape, with huge factories on either side of the motorway. While some flyovers are meant for spectacle, these don't feel like they're meant for people at all, instead inducing the feeling of being a vulnerable fleshy part of a metallic network of freight, lessened only by the all-too-human aggressive driving that is ubiquitous here. There was one horrible moment on one of these expressways where various container lorries constantly overtook each other, manoeuvring into position to the point where it seemed as if they were actually intent on crushing the pathetic little car we were in. But many of the flyovers really are meant to be *seen*. Near People's Square, the former racetrack for the Europeans ('No Dogs or Chinese', as the sign ran), transformed after the revolution into a large public plaza, there's some sort of flyover convention, an intersection which is less spaghetti junction and more the intestines of a terrifying mythological beast. These sorts of organic metaphors tend to come to mind here, because there's little rationalistic or machinic about this place. The concrete itself is of the very highest grade, and there is planting running half way up the concrete pillars, an effort at civic beautification which is visible to the pedestrian more than to the driver. Presumably it is there as a gesture to 'The Harmonious Society', the official line of the CCP, replacing the Maoist fixation with identifying

Flyovers at the Huaihai intersection, Shanghai

and intensifying 'contradictions'.[10] So nature intersects with technology in a non-antagonistic manner, but it's far more like the engineers kept in mind the possibility that sooner rather than later these monuments will be obsolete, so made them pre-ruined, with picturesque vegetation creeping up them to simulate what they might look like when they've fallen into desuetude.

They also serve to frame the skyscrapers around, to delineate them, present them in their best light, to let them be seen from a contemplative distance, which gives a Futurist flash to what can often seem crushingly dense and badly made on closer inspection. Except that's the sort of thing only noticed later on – you don't notice the details initially. When I first saw the Huaihai intersection, I was absolutely frozen in awe, and then impressed by the fact that everyone else seemed entirely used to it, that it had become normal, just something you'd cross under on the way to work. There's a general ability to seem completely unbothered by what feels like a bloody steamroller of gigantism and force here which is admirable, although slightly worrying. The flyovers are the main event, works of public infrastructure more impressive than the baubles on top of the towers of capital. Their forcing through areas of already huge density necessitates an extra pedestrian layer being inserted into them – there are plenty of these intersections that have pedestrian walkways running across, blue steel and glass pedways sandwiched between the roads.

You eventually reach ground level among walkways cutting across neon-lit geodesic domes, skyscrapers with searchlights cutting through the ubiquitous fog, and some rather familiar corporate logos. This massive project of state-built infrastructure is the least trumpeted of the major public works in the city. There's the Metro, of course, with nine lines built in the time it takes to string a line from one side of Warsaw to the other, but there's also the Magnetic Levitation train. The Maglev might be the one area where the prolonged NEP of the People's Republic entailed doing something differently, where it put a genuinely advanced technology at the service of a public rather than private means of transport, but compared with these monuments to the hope, as right-wing hack P. J. O'Rourke puts it, that '1.8 billion people want a Buick', it seems paltry indeed.

In 1989, People's Square, before those intersections were built, was a place of assembly and protest; but it didn't see any massacres, apparently because of the constant presence of armed forces looming over the plaza.

The Shanghai authorities' handling of the situation earned them a prominent place in government – Shanghai's secretary, Jiang Zemin, became Party leader, and his 'Three Represents' became Chinese neoliberalism's numerical successor to Mao's 'Four Olds' and Deng's 'Four Modernizations'. The square is of course loomed over by dozens of corporate skyscrapers, but also by the far less interesting City Government building. Evidently the Party has little interest in emulating the capitalist delirium all around, instead providing something sober and bland, with perhaps a little hint of the Stalinist skyscraper style, denuded of ornament – a little like a cheaper version of the Hotel Ukraina in Kiev. Reach the Bund, the famous boulevard where the city meets the Huangpu river, and you find many non-socialist skyscrapers, usually designed by English architects in the 1920s and 1930s. Many of the Bund's buildings have the Red Flag flying from them, something which forces you into a minor double-take, realizing that it signifies something quite different here, or rather it does now. The Custom House's chimes play 'The East is Red' on the hour. The smaller, earlier public space here is where the notorious 'No Dogs or Chinese Allowed' sign once stood, but it did say something very similar in more polite language, and it now has two monuments to the revolution that ended that.

One of them is typical figurative hurrah-jingoistic Socialist Realism, with a bronze flag-waver on a red-granite plinth, and aside from a couple of curious snappers, lots of whom must be provincials up for the Expo, the large crowds entirely ignore it. The adjacent Monument to the People's Heroes, meanwhile, is completely abstract: it could be a monument to practically anything, and it could be admired by a Speer as much as a Shchusev – which doesn't stop it being a rather powerful sculptural object, its rectitude a contrast with everything around as much as its high-rise form is a complement to it. Whether it still conveys, as intended, the Chinese people's struggle against imperialism and capitalism is less certain.

Yet the architectural money shot, if you please, the thing that everyone in front of the Bund was taking photographs of rather than of the Bund itself (developmentalism winning an aesthetic victory over imperialism, there), was the skyline view. A clear vista like this is rare in Shanghai, because of the height of everything else and the ubiquitous smog, so when you get it it's all the more breathtaking. This is the skyline not of Puxi, the only built-up side of the Huangpu river until the early 1990s, but of Pudong, the area that is really an entire new town which sprang up from marshland after Shanghai was designated a Special Economic Zone – something the Chinese government originally refrained from, in order not to encourage the massively uneven development that made parts of Shanghai into one of the most modern cities in the world in the 1930s while horrifying poverty stalked much of the rest of the city, and of China. That the return to fully uneven development should coincide with the notion of the Harmonious Society is one of those ironies of history.

The skyline itself as the lights come on, like the expressways at night, is a joy that only a churl couldn't be in any way moved by, as if the Empire State Building couldn't be enjoyed because of the Dust Bowl (some *did* argue that, of course). To pick out details – the giant illuminated globes, Adrian Smith's smooth, tapering, gorgeously elegant World Financial Centre, the improbable declaration 'I Heart Expo' on the part of the Taiwanese Aurora company's offices, the pulsating lights extending even to the Expo-sponsored sightseeing boats (replacing much unsightly freight) . . . and, in the form of the Oriental Pearl TV tower, the curious feeling, once again, that you've seen the future somewhere before . . . that the future resembles very closely the past's idea of the future. It's Ostankino or the Berlin Fernsehturm with an extra spiked bollock. There's no time, evidently, to imagine a new idea of the future. The lights all come on between six and seven, but the concomitant of that is that they all go off at around midnight. The apparent reasoning behind this is derived from environmental imperatives – all that wasted electricity – but the effect is 'OK, you've had your fun, now go to bed.' The intended effect of the lights might be to present a vibrant and delirious techno city that never sleeps, but it's hard to be the city that never sleeps when you have to get up first thing in the morning for a day of hard, hard work.

SOCIALIST REALISM WITH CHINESE CHARACTERISTICS

Architectural periodization is completely meaningless here. In Shanghai there wasn't really a socially engaged Modernism along the lines of Berlin or Moscow in the interwar years, there was 'Moderne', i.e. Art Deco; and after the war Stalinist Gothick and unpretentious (but hardly Modernist) utilitarianism prevailed. Now, in the skyline, you can pick out everything from historicism to Pomo to Constructivism to Expressionism to serene Miesian Modernism, with the only logic seeming to be that rather chaotic notion of Harmony and Pluralism. There is one unacknowledged influence on the contemporary skyline, and that's Socialist Realist, or more precisely Stalinist architecture. The one fully fledged example in central Shanghai of the full-blown Stalin style still exists and is very much in use: the former Palace of Sino-Soviet Friendship, a 'gift from the Soviet people' just as much as the Warsaw Palace of Culture and Science – which of course bears the Polish acronym 'PKiN', or 'Peking'. China was never a satellite, though – like Yugoslavia it made its own revolution, and hence was reluctant to accept Soviet tutelage. After the Sino-Soviet split – caused, depending on what side you take, by Mao's crazy refusal to accept what a disaster nuclear war would be ('China will still survive!') or by Khrushchev's refusal to join it in anti-imperialist struggle, preferring a phone line to Kennedy when the Chinese government wasn't even allowed a seat at the UN. Either way, the Soviet response, removing all its advisers, engineers and materiel, was quick and vindictive. The building became the Shanghai Exhibition Centre, which still holds trade fairs and the like. It displays a typically Stalinist interest in symmetry, aligned around a great central tower 'supported' by columns, with a tall skyscraping spire surmounting the design, as ever of such a scale as to break any previously known rules of classical proportion. Isolate the tower and it could easily be the pinnacle on the Palace of Culture and Science, with the obvious difference that there is still a communist star in place at the top.

The unexpected fact is that the style lives on, now in a peculiar alignment with Modernist-oriented planning laws. Everywhere in Shanghai's southern suburbs are serried, identical towers, with south-facing aspects, generously proportioned windows and breathing space in between, and dressed with clearly machined ornamentation, whether the pitched roofs at the top or in the 'brick' coursing at the corners. It's not the crass, appallingly planned, architecturally illiterate, Zhdanov-goes-to-Vegas Yuri Luzhkov style, but something with rather more conviction and thought behind it; it comes out of a combination of 'market preferences' which elsewhere would be regulated (the ubiquitous south-facing orientation), and state edicts – the pinnacles that you find on every block, and which have such an effect on the Shanghai skyline, are the result of state policy, to stop extra floors being built on top, as they were in boomtime

'Top marques' at the former Palace of Sino-Soviet Friendship, Shanghai

Hong Kong. The result is a pictorial skyline, a 'city-picture', but it's the result of dirigisme leading to delirium, rather than a capitalist potlatch. What it really is, is Modernist spatial planning going classicist in detail. It's the wholly inadvertent successor to the likes of Andrei Burov's block on the Leningradsky Prospekt, which pioneered the use of prefabricated ornament in monumental construction. Much of contemporary Shanghai is the fusion of Burov's two preoccupations into a new architecture.

The block in the photograph below does this with more demented panache than any other I saw there – the sheer length and height of it, slathered

Prefab neo-Stalinist high-rises, Shanghai

in all kinds of prefabricated 'stone', with the particular approach coming very, very close indeed to the style of 1950s Moscow; except rather than the boulevard-and-courtyard approach, these are towers geometrically organized in parkland. It's one of eight identical towers stretching all the way past a main road in the southern suburbs. The lower, retail block in front is part of the same tabula rasa. Not far from here, you can find red-star-topped grand archways straight out of VDNKh, or department stores decorated in high reliefs based on Klimt – the 'Soviet' look is one of the many put into the mincer. The approach is redolent of that notorious photograph of a statue factory in the 1970s USSR churning out identical Lenins, the product of an ornamental production line – and mass production in 'socialism with Chinese characteristics' was mastered to the point where it is now the main supplier of commodities to the capitalist world system. Contemporary Shanghai is in many ways the fusion of the two architectures that contemporary urbanists find most uncomfortable – the repetition and lack of any 'street' in high Modernism, and the imposingly monumental, obsessively ornamental approach of high Stalinism. It is Le Corbusier meets Lev Rudnev meets neoliberal bling, the Stalinist city gone high tech, its pinnacles and swags slathered in neon. It's hard to think of it as even remotely 'socialist', it just throws communist aesthetics into its Postmodernist whirlpool like everything else.

'BETTER CITY, BETTER LIFE'

At the start of this book, we found at VDNKh, Moscow's Exhibition of Economic Achievements, a blueprint for the Stalinist city, which would be organized as if it were one continuous Expo. The Shanghai Expo of 2010 had similar ambitions,[11] and consciously presented itself as a compendium of potential future cities, advertised by a little blue creature called 'Haibo', grinning out from nouveau Socialist Realist ads all over the city, often accompanied by wholesome families. Its site extended across an area on the scale of a decent-sized industrial town, on both sides of the Huangpu, hence necessitating a Metro line to get from the Pudong side (the international pavilions, the bit in the magazines) to the Puxi side (the national and corporate pavilions); this trip comes free with your ticket. My friend suggested we meet outside Venezuela; the route there took me through Eastern Europe. I walked first past Bosnia, one of many retoolings of a basic shed design provided by the Expo authorities for free for those who can't pay for their own architects. These decorated sheds were more fun the less seriously they took themselves. In the context of demonstrative, good-taste high architecture, there was a certain relief offered by the kitsch painted box housing the pavilion of 'Europe's Last Dictatorship', Chinese ally and CIS state highest on the UN's Human Development Index, Belarus. It looked inspired in some way by the Belarusian Jew Marc Chagall, with a childlike, warped-perspective cartoon of an old East European city, with its spires and palazzos. It seemed the most popular of the East European sheds for the Chinese tourists photographing it. Nearby were the generically arty pavilion of Poland – popular, because offering free bigos – the cheap-looking green glass dome of Romania, and the Lego squares of the Serbian pavilion, which apparently 'derives specific code out of multitude'.

Venezuela, our meeting point, had far greater ambitions. Housed in a pavilion by Facundo Baudoin Teran, a dramatic but non-ingratiating

The Pavilion of the Bolivarian Republic of Venezuela, Shanghai Expo

sculptural creation, its clashing volumes centred on a steep staircase, in a manner which distantly recalls Melnikov's similarly politically charged Soviet pavilion at the Paris Expo of 1925. The Bolivarian Republic's pavilion is next to its comrade in Latin American Socialism, Cuba, but puts it completely in the shade – even within the limits of the free-shed genre, a hell of a lot more could have been done than their sad little red and blue box, which clearly showed the austere grip of the Raúl Castro regime. However, those of us who held out hope for twenty-first-century Socialism found a great deal to admire about the Venezuelan pavilion – in fact, its similarity to Melnikov and Rodchenko's presence in Paris in 1925 or El Lissitzky's in Cologne in 1928 is much more than an aesthetic matter. This was the only pavilion that seemed to have *political* ideas, ideas about the country it represented other than 'Here we are, we have a dynamic economy and really nice food, please like us'.

The pavilion made very clear that it took the official Expo slogan, 'Better City, Better Life', more seriously than do perhaps its originators, only expanding it out rather further, across 'Mejor Mundo'. The theme of the pavilion is, quite simply, 'Revolution' – and bear in mind here that the last 'revolution' in China, in the late 1960s, is now held in official governmental opprobrium. Here, as so often with the Bolivarian Republic, they *talk* such a fantastic fight that if I judged the place purely on this pavilion, I'd probably emigrate there at once. It all sounded more than just a little pointed. 'Everybody may get involved and take decisions in politics, economy and culture'; 'a country where all are included'; and, great to hear during the apparent End of History, 'a revolution makes everything move again'. Cut-out figures give testimonials on all the things the Bolivarian Revolution has done for them – stories of collective ownership, co-operatives, workers' councils, of expropriation, of non-alienated labour, told by construction workers, teachers, slum youth. My friend points out that 'nobody reads the signs on anything in the Expo', so it is perhaps a little misjudged in its heavily textual approach. He does find one gentleman reading them with great intensity, and asks him in Mandarin: 'So what do you think of all this talk of revolution?' 'It's great – but it'd be a long story to tell you why' was the response. 60,000 people were displaced from their homes to make way for the Expo.

Architecturally, too, it's more rigorous than most, its pleasures and surprises discovered through exploration and circulation rather than in an instant hit. The pavilion is a series of rooms with canted stairs going off at angles from them, and on the ground floor, open to the air, there are several definitions of what *Revolution* might be, printed on cotton blinds. It is, respectively, Individual Revolution, Collective Revolution, World Revolution. The central part of the Venezuela pavilion is where the freebies are given out – here, it's chocolate and coffee, and on the coffee tables are, in classic national-pavilion style, descriptions of the country's cash crops; and, in far from classic national-pavilion style, descriptions of its class and historical relations, like the role of the sugar industry in the slave trade. The aspect of the Venezuelan pavilion where all of this suddenly seems to be too good to be true is at the back end, where you get a lovely view of a steelworks, one of the few non-adapted parts of what was once the industrial centre of China's greatest industrial city. At the back of the pavilion are thousands of red, plastic flowers, with the following message: 'If the climate were a bank, it would have been bailed out by now.' True enough, but the Bolivarian Revolution's reforms and massive poverty reduction programmes have been paid for by oil revenues.

It was extraordinary, though, to find a place, a building, which argues that better cities and better lives aren't caused by throwing tens of thousands of people out of their homes, or by massive industrial exploitation. Finally, somebody seemed interested in a space that defined what socialism is, what it might mean and why you might want it, rather than one which interpreted it in terms of state power or historic heroism. That list of 'revolutions' is an inverse of Kołakowski's negations, his list of what socialism 'is not' – here are a whole series of suggestions of what it might actually *be*. Whether it accurately describes conditions in Venezuela I could not possibly say, and I doubt it – but how rare, how exciting, to see the city described like this, so far from either 'real socialism' or 'real capitalism', or China's current amalgam of both.

But for anyone expecting contemporary China to offer a viable vision of the future city, there was a pavilion dedicated to exactly that. The Urban Future Pavilion, heralded by a giant illuminated chimney-cum-thermometer, was housed in a converted power station. At its heart was a pile of giant books. In that stack you could find (though not read about) a litany of urban Utopias, many of those that Lenin had printed up and distributed in the first months of the Bolshevik government. Campanella, Plato, Francis Bacon, Charles Fourier, Thomas More – but also Lewis Mumford, Frank

What Socialism Is

Lloyd Wright and, remarkably, the Marxist geographer David Harvey's *Spaces of Hope*, sandwiched in just underneath *The New Atlantis*.

The explanation for this collection is found on the opposite wall: 'In yesterday's Utopia we find today's reality.' That is, they really were implying that contemporary Shanghai is the fulfilment of the hopes of generations, that they come to fruition here, in some manner; but this is

The Library of Utopia, Shanghai Expo

not meant as a statement of complacency, far from it. In the room with the stack of books are huge images of various urban Utopias, from Archigram's Walking City to the Ville Radieuse. There's a wonderful moment in the exhibit on Le Corbusier when, taking the place in an exhibition in Berlin or Warsaw where you'd find the usual hand-wringing denunciation of all the evils he wreaked on the innocent slums, there's the line: 'Sadly, Le Corbusier's ideas were never fully appreciated in his lifetime.'

Proposals are sometimes set against each other, but arbitrarily. On a screen, a 'Space City' is proposed by the Lifeboat Foundation, a Libertarian eschatological think tank. The organization was started after 9/11, and its aim is to preserve the human race, and the entirely unashamed telos of their plan for our survival is to colonize outer space. These really are people who think it's easier – and more desirable – to imagine the end of the world than the end of capitalism. Next to it is Eco City, which essentially appears to propose a 'sustainable' industrial revolution. 'We need to reinvent everything' is a criterion of Eco City. Near to that is Water City, which proposes that we grow artificial gills. And 'the views would be great'. The future cities in the Future pavilion rest on certain major assumptions, some more debatable than others. The first is that cities cannot remain as they are; the second is that they will face enormous challenges due to drastic global warming; and the third is that all ideas are of equal value, and that there is no need to set up an opposition between Space City and Eco City. Everything is equally valid – the barest hint of a contradiction and you suspect they'd start worrying they'd end up with a *revolution* on their hands.

So in the corner, not far away from the underwater aquatic city, was a model that summed up the sheer idleness of this, the idiocy of pretending that all contradictions can be resolved, that technical fixes rather than the conscious seizure of space can solve the mess we're creating for ourselves. It's a maquette of a gigantic energy-generating complex, and oil refineries go next to wind turbines go next to oil tankers go next to a cubic power station which goes next to pylons which goes next to serried cooling towers, just like those lining the charred landscape of the Yangtze river delta. There isn't the slightest hint that this energy-generating complex in its lurid, apocalyptic, radioactive green might lead to the situation described so cheerfully in Water City. Evolution, presumably, will decide for itself. The socialist city, communally owned, democratically run, consciously created, made by its inhabitants, dedicated to their own enjoyment and development, is the missing option, the void around which all these idly apocalyptic speculations revolve. We found all sorts of clues to it, fragments of it, abortive or not-so-abortive attempts at it, but we never found this city in the 'past', looking around Eastern Europe. We don't find it in the present, either, in the blare of China. It remains for the future to build it.

Acknowledgements

Thanks first of all to anybody who invited me to, walked me round or explained any of the places in this book: Liza Babenko, Edwin Bendyk, Konstantin Budarin, Sasha Burlaka, Christopher Connery, Matevž Čelik, Ivana Ivković, Gal Kirn, Kirill Kobrin, Marko Kostanić, Primož Krašovec, Sasha Kuridzen, Tor Lindstrand, Tomislav Medak, Douglas Murphy, Grzegorz Piątek, Goran Sergej Pristas, Hannah Proctor, Natalia Romik and all at The Knot, Kuba Szreder, Matthew Tempest, Twitter Maoists and to anyone I've forgotten, which I almost certainly have. Parts of the book appeared in a different form in *The Avery Review*, the *Calvert Journal*, *Culture Unbound*, *Dezeen*, the *Guardian*, and the *International Journal for Urban and Regional Research*: thank you to Jamie Rann, Justin O'Connor, Anna Winston, Mike Herd, Daryl Martin, Jacob Moore, James D. Graham and Caitlin Blanchfield for commissioning them. Thanks especially to those who helped me with this book at various points through conversations, arguments and suggestions (though the book's defects are not their responsibility): Michał Murawski, Oleksiy Radynski, Dubravka Sekulić and Jonathan Charley, who made some good, informed and unimpressed suggestions at an early stage, as did the attendees at a talk on the Moscow Metro at CRASSH, Cambridge, and another at Leeds Metropilitan University. The postcards, bar the one of Kalinin Prospekt, found in Oxford Oxfam by Pyzik, are mostly collected from the *Antykwariaty* of Pan Krzys in Zoliborz and Pan Marek in Grochów, to whom my thanks. Photographs are by the author, and most things described herein but not illustrated can be found at http://www.flickr.com/photos/8971770@N06/collections/; also, the collection of the Flickr user 'Socialism Expo' and the website ostarchitektur.com both proved very useful for research, so gratitude is due. The trip to Belgrade was funded by a visiting fellowship in the School of Architecture, Design and Environment at the University of Plymouth, to whom great thanks. Thanks particularly to my editor, Tom Penn, for his encouragement and work on the book, and for thinking anyone would be interested in such a book in the first place . . .

All my love and gratitude, most of all, for Agata Pyzik, without whom, nothing.

A Note on Names

Aside from pidgin Polish, I do not speak any of the languages of the countries visited in this book. Partly because of this, and partly for reasons of familiarity to the reader, I have not used a consistent transliteration system for Cyrillic, so well-known Russian, Serbian, Bulgarian and Ukrainian names are given in the form in which they are most likely to be known to an English eye – so Trotsky, not the more accurate Trotskii. In other cases, I've tried to be as accurate as possible.

Whenever possible I have tried to find the full names of architects, sculptors and others, in order to make them sound a little less like bureaucratic cogs. One thing that may escape the English reader is the number of female architects. Their proliferation in that place and time, on a far larger scale than in the West and often helming the most prestigious projects, is worth drawing attention to. They include Eleonora Sekrecka, designer of one third of MDM in Warsaw, Halina Skibniewska, architect of the Sady Żoliborskie estate, Helena Syrkus, pioneer Polish Modernist, Elena Nijolė Bučiūtė, architect of the Vilnius Opera and Ballet Theatre, Marta Stana, lead designer of the Riga Arts Theatre, Nadezhda Bykova, architect of the Brezhnev-era Moscow Metro, Tamara Chelikovska, who had the same role in the building of the Kiev Metro, Jasna Strzałkowska-Ryszka, who headed the team at the Warsaw Metro, Marie Davidová and Eva Břuschová at the Metro in Prague, and Anca Petrescu, the architect of Bucharest's Palace of the Parliament, to name just the most prominent.

City names and street names cause a problem given their many renamings. Again, I've opted for familiarity or, when appropriate, contemporaneity. So, for instance, when I'm writing of something built between 1924 and 1990 I refer to Leningrad, from 1914 to 1924 Petrograd, and at any other time St Petersburg. Names are often politicized in national as well as political fashion. Although there have been attempts for understandable political reasons – i.e. as a reminder that 'Ukraine is not Russia' – to make it the PC usage, I haven't referred to 'Kyiv' but to 'Kiev', not because of a preference for Russian over Ukrainian, but because it has been the accepted English usage for centuries; with less well-known

Ukrainian cities such as Kharkov/Kharkiv, I have used the Ukrainian names, but given that English-speakers don't refer to 'Warszawa', 'Moskva' or 'Beograd', it is odd to make an exception for Ukraine. Pre- and post-war usage is also problematic – very few before 1939, inside the Polish- and Yiddish-speaking cities of Lwów or Wilno and fewer outside them, would have referred to them as 'Lviv' or 'Vilnius'. Since these cities became the capitals of western Ukraine (de facto) and Lithuania these names have genuinely become the dominant international usage, and I've followed that. Street names are also used according to when we're talking about them – Grada Vukovara was built as Proletarian Brigades Avenue and so when writing about its moment of conception, that's what I've called it; similarly with Kalinin Prospekt/Novy Arbat or Tverskaya/Gorky Street, and their ilk. None of these usages are intended to imply adherence to any particular national cause. In the notes, all books with foreign titles are citations from parallel English translations in the books themselves, except those with Polish titles.

Notes and References

EPIGRAPH

1. Quoted in Anders Åman, *Architecture and Ideology in Eastern Europe during the Stalin Era* (MIT Press, 1992), p. 204.

INTRODUCTION: SOCIALISM ISN'T

1. Leszek Kołakowski, 'What is Socialism?', in *Is God Happy?* (Penguin Books, 2012), pp. 20–25.
2. And one didn't even need to visit to come to this knowledge – see his staggeringly ingenuous 1950 letter to *The Times*, on the propaganda magazine *USSR in Construction* – 'crowds of brightly dressed, well fed, happy looking workers . . . nobody who sees these publications will ever believe our tales of a half-starved population dwelling in Belsen camps under the lash of a ruthless tyranny'. Reproduced in R. Palme Dutt, *George Bernard Shaw: A Memoir* (Labour Monthly pamphlets, 1951).
3. On this generation – exemplified in the figure of Timothy Garton Ash – one witty account is J. Hoberman's 'Life in Czechoslovakia', on Philip Roth and others getting their love-amidst-the-secret-police kicks in Prague. J. Hoberman, *The Red Atlantis* (Temple University Press, 1998), pp. 121–39.
4. Agata Pyzik, 'Toxic Ruins: The Political and Economic Cost of Ruin Porn', in *Architectural Review Asia Pacific*, no. 128 (2012).
5. In *The Gulag Archipelago*, Solzhenitsyn recalls that after a wave of arrests of intellectuals at the end of the 1940s, a newly arrested inmate of the camps gave lectures on Le Corbusier to fellow prisoners. That's *in* the camps. See Alexander Solzhenitsyn, *The Gulag Archipelago*, vol. 1 (Collins, 1974), p. 603.
6. Hugh D. Hudson, *Blueprints and Blood: The Stalinization of Soviet Architecture* (Princeton, 1994), extensively documents the persecution of unrepentant Modernist architects under Stalin.

7. For instance, Jonathan Meades's insightful accounts of Nazi and Soviet architecture are notably devoid of the slightest sympathy with the politics of either. Both are in the anthology *Museum Without Walls* (Unbound, 2012).
8. For an example of this, see the monograph *Albert Speer: Architecture 1932–1942* (Monacelli, 2012), by the adviser to Prince Charles and planner of Poundbury, Léon Krier; here, despite the attempt to present the book as a neutral and brave study of the architecture of a supposedly great architect who was also a war criminal, the author's politics frequently leap out, Dr Strangelove style. Krier entirely fails to disguise that his enthusiasm for Speer coincides with a decided sympathy for an environmentalist variant of fascism.
9. Marx's long letter to the Russian revolutionary Vera Zasulich suggested that he envisaged that a transition to socialism could happen in some countries bypassing capitalism altogether, via pre-existing peasant communes; though he certainly didn't imagine that this would happen *first*, let alone *only* here. The 'Letter to Vera Zasulich' and its various drafts are available at http://www.marxists.org/archive/marx/works/1881/zasulich/index.htm. For an argument – soon to be heretical – that Marx knew very little about Russia and understood less, see the unorthodox Bolshevik and historian David Riazanov's 1918 *Marx and Anglo-Russian Relations and Other Writings* (Francis Boutle, 2003).
10. The classic text here is Trotsky's still highly pertinent 'Results and Prospects' of 1906, available along with a later, much more cantankerous and dated defence of the same theories in Leon Trotsky, *The Permanent Revolution* (New Park, 1982), though an excellent summation of it is given in the introduction to his *History of the Russian Revolution*: 'the privilege of historic backwardness – and such a privilege exists – permits, or rather compels, the adoption of whatever is ready in advance of any specified date, skipping a whole series of intermediate stages.' Leon Trotsky, *The History of the Russian Revolution* (Pathfinder, 1987), p. 5. Moreover, the massiveness of what Russian industry there was by 1917 – huge concentrations of high-tech factories with a huge labour force which remained islands in a mostly agricultural country – 'does not disprove this backwardness, but dialectically completes it' (p. 10), as 'in Russia the proletariat did not arise gradually through the ages, carrying with itself the burden of the past as in England, but in leaps involving sharp changes of environment, ties, relations, and a sharp break with the past. It is just this fact – combined with the concentrated oppressions of Tsarism – that made the Russian workers hospitable to the boldest conclusions of revolutionary thought – just as the backward industries were hospitable to the last word in capitalist organisation' (p. 11). The implication – not followed

through by the author – is that more 'even' capitalist economies were much less prone to socialist revolution. So it has proved. And ironically, this extreme unevenness pervaded the 'communist' landscape, and even more so its aftermath.

11. The best book on the revolt – perhaps the only historically reliable one in English – is Paul Avrich, *Kronstadt 1921* (Princeton, 1991).
12. The key text here is Engels' 1873 essay on housing, where he defines the term 'Haussmann' as 'breaking long, straight and broad streets right through the closely built workers' quarters and lining them with big luxurious buildings', a 'luxury city pure and simple', an attempt to design out barricade fighting, and an effort to 'create a Bonapartist building trades proletariat' dependent on the government. Friedrich Engels, *The Housing Question* (Progress, 1979), p. 71.
13. Profiled in Anatole Kopp, *Town and Revolution* (Braziller, 1970), and critically analysed in Ross Wolfe, *The Graveyard of Utopia* (available at http://rosswolfe.files.wordpress.com/2011/09/ross-wolfe-the-graveyard-of-utopia-soviet-urbanism-and-the-fate-of-the-international-avant-garde.pdf).
14. J. Hoberman notes in passing that 'in considering the region, one has to wonder whether Communism constructed the other European reality or whether this reality – as Lenin himself feared – had, in fact, made Communism what it became'. *The Red Atlantis*, p. 290. Rudolf Bahro makes a similar point in more typically dialectical fashion: 'The Hungarians have a long experience with what [their former Prime Minister] András Hegedüs described as "a system of organised irresponsibility". In the days of Maria Theresa, the Hapsburg army had a saying, "better do nothing, than do something wrong". This mentality prevails in any bureaucracy where the members are responsible to and dependent on only those above, and have absolutely no powers of horizontal cooperation'. Rudolf Bahro, *The Alternative in Eastern Europe* (New Left Books, 1978), p. 114.
15. This analysis owes much to Perry Anderson, *Lineages of the Absolutist State* (Verso, 2012). Anderson notes that there were two other empires which were influential across this territory – the Ottoman Empire, which dominated the Balkans and had a much more unplanned form of urbanism, informal and with less public or ceremonial space, and until the late eighteenth century the Polish–Lithuanian Commonwealth, which, while Baroque in its architectural tastes, was a realm dominated by vast serf-tended rural holdings that seldom embarked on large-scale town planning, with exceptions such as the Renaissance town of Zamość in eastern Poland.
16. On this continuing legacy, see Wolfgang Förster, '80 Years of Social Housing in Vienna', at www.wien.gv.at/english/housing/promotion/pdf/socialhous.pdf.

17. A comprehensive study in English is Eve Blau, *The Architecture of Red Vienna* (MIT Press, 1999).
18. Kaganovich quoted by Karel Teige, *The Minimum Dwelling*, trans. Eric Dluhosch (MIT, 2002), p. 94. On Magnitogorsk and its holes in the ground, see Stephen Kotkin, *Magnetic Mountain* (University of California Press, 1997).
19. For some remarkable analyses of the Soviet building industry and the exploitation of workers in even the most idealistic architectural schemes, see the chapters on Moscow in Jonathan Charley's essay collection *Memories of Cities* (Routledge, 2013).
20. 'The social strata [of Soviet managers] had some analogies to that of a nineteenth-century ruling class . . . somewhat fanciful analogies have even been detected in their aesthetic attitudes: a moralising literature, a strictly representational art, and an ostentatious architecture', E. H. Carr, *Foundations of a Planned Economy 1926–1929*, vol. 2 (Pelican Books, 1976), p. 470.
21. An excellent account of this abrupt attack on working class organisation can be found in Kevin Murphy, *Revolution and Counterrevolution: Class Struggle in a Moscow Metal Factory* (Haymarket, 2005).
22. Leon Trotsky, *The Revolution Betrayed: What is the Soviet Union and Where is it Going?* (Pathfinder, 1972), p. 286.
23. Bruno Rizzi, *The Bureaucratization of the World* (Free Press, 1985), p. 69.
24. Ibid., p. 97.
25. Maxim Gorky, 'Extracts from a paper read to the first all-Union congress of Soviet writers' (1934), in *Literature and Life* (Hutchinson, 1946), p. 140.
26. Gorky, 'A Talk with Young People' (1934), in *Literature and Life*, p. 145.
27. This had been underway since at least the mid-1920s. If the USSR began as a country so radically anti-nationalist that it didn't even include a territory in its name, through the course of the 1920s 'Soviet Russia' came to fill the void created by the absence of a Western European revolution – it 'became more and more openly the heir of Russian state power and attracted to itself traditional feelings of Russian patriotism, it claimed its mission in terms which conveyed to sensitive ears unmistakable echoes of the Russian past . . . The fulfilment of the eschatological promises of Marxism was delayed, like the Second Advent, far beyond the original expectations of the faithful; and, when this delay bred the inevitable current compromises with power and expediency, the process of degeneration from the pure ideal took on specifically Russian forms within a Russian context. Primitive Christianity decked itself in the trappings of imperial Rome, communism in those of the Russian national state'. E. H. Carr, *Socialism in One Country* (Pelican Books, 1970), pp. 31–2.

28. The best way of understanding this key concept is via Terry Martin's study of the USSR as an 'affirmative action empire'. In short, the 'form' of nationalism – costume, national literature, language, cultural signifiers – was vigorously encouraged and its exponents promoted to leadership positions, while the 'content' that usually comes with these – claims of national superiority, demands for separatism or independent states, even demands for federalism within the Union – were ruthlessly suppressed. As a result, the USSR had a rather essentialist liking for nationalist cultural expression, and a tendency to treat nations en bloc – which descended into collective punishment and ethnic cleansing in the case of border nations within the USSR like Poles, Volga Germans, Greeks, Crimean Tatars and Koreans, and then outside it, in the mass expulsions of Germans from Poland, Lithuania, Kaliningrad and Czechoslovakia, and of Poles out of Lithuania, Belarus and Ukraine, after 1945. That is, it was both unusually anti-racist and prone to shocking acts of systematic racialized violence. Terry Martin, *The Affirmative Action Empire: Nations and Nationalism in the Soviet Union, 1923–1939* (Cornell University Press, 2001).
29. Sergei Frolkin, *VDNKh: Exhibition of Economic Achievements of the USSR* (Planeta, 1969), unpaginated.
30. See Moshe Lewin, *The Soviet Century* (Verso, 2005), or Isaac Deutscher, *The Unfinished Revolution* (Oxford, 1967).
31. Rudolf Meidner, 'Why Did the Swedish Model Fail?', *Socialist Register*, vol. 29 (1993). His claim is corroborated by the comparative statistics on income differentials in Bahro, *Alternative in Eastern Europe*.
32. On the non-existence (until recently) of 'social housing' in Sweden, see Eric Clark and Karin Johnson, 'Circumscribed Neoliberalism', in Sarah Glynn (ed.), *Where the Other Half Lives* (Pluto Press, 2009).
33. It's worth noting here that the Eastern Bloc bordered countries which had major elements of 'socialism' in their economies and in public life – the extensive welfare states and hegemonic Social Democratic parties of Austria and Finland, or to a lesser degree West Germany, with its own Marxist tradition and 'co-determination' of trade unions and employers. The seductive mixed economy of capitalism tempered by socialism, beamed into the television screens of Eastern Europe, and directly experienced by Polish and Yugoslav gastarbeiter, was not the capitalism of Reagan or Thatcher. This was, however, the capitalism they would get after 1989.
34. Bahro, *Alternative in Eastern Europe*, p. 45.
35. That is, roughly until the 1980s. Paradoxically, the period between 1968 and 1986 saw more unorthodox East European socialists lose their faith in the possibility of a desirable non-capitalist society than any other era – even the

Stalinist one. Former enthusiastic Stalinists turned reform communists – including many names much fêted in the West, from Kapuściński to Konrad to Kundera, from Kołakowski to Kuroń – were largely by 1989 liberals or conservatives. The reasons are varied, although the cause can hardly have been greater repression, given the extremely mild nature of persecution compared with Stalinism – in the 1970s, dissidence meant an inability to publish, or at worst consignment to a mental hospital, as opposed to torture and certain death in the 1930s and 1940s. Perhaps more lax censorship made lip service less necessary, the suppression of even the mild reforms of the Prague Spring induced general despair – and horror at the antics of the American New Left helped push Kołakowski rightwards, for instance (as seen in the sad, mutually uncomprehending contretemps between Kołakowski and E. P. Thompson in the pages of *Socialist Register*). But, curiously, the Eastern Europeans chose exactly this point – with mass workers' protests shaking the system to its core in Poland – to decide the working class was no longer relevant; they chose the moment when the post-war boom collapsed under the weight of the oil crisis, when unemployment and homelessness returned, to decide that capitalism had proved its superiority. An alternative view is that some intellectuals disliked no longer being quite so important to power as they were under Stalinism – for a pugnacious assertion of this view, see the unrepentant Polish Trotskyist Ludwik Hass's 'An Open Letter to Ojasz Schechter', *Revolutionary History*, vol. 6, no. 1. Regardless, the upshot was that by the time Gorbachev came to power, there were few 'Party democrats' left to back him.

36. Václav Havel, 'Dear Dr Husák' (1975), in *Open Letters* (Vintage, 1992), pp. 58–9.
37. Havel, 'Stories and Totalitarianism', in *Open Letters*, p. 343.
38. Roy Medvedev, *On Socialist Democracy* (Norton, 1977), p. 399.
39. For an exceptionally intelligent, non-triumphalist analysis of the collapse, see Stephen Kotkin and Jan Tomasz Gross, *Uncivil Society* (Modern Library, 2010).
40. Hillel Ticktin, *Origins of the Crisis in the USSR* (M. E. Sharpe, 1992), p. 11.
41. Slavoj Žižek, *Did Someone Say Totalitarianism?* (Verso, 2001), p. 130. Similarly, in his recent account of Marx's *Capital*, Fredric Jameson makes an analogy between the forces behind the re-emergence of capitalism in 1989 and the emergence of capitalism itself in the eighteenth century: 'the properly capitalist farmer emerges in the person of a hitherto minor character, the bailiff of the estate. Like our modern post-socialist managers, he it is who *turns the activity of oversight into the status of ownership*, and exploits the land henceforth in accordance with the new "law of value"' (my italics). Fredric Jameson, *Representing Capital* (Verso, 2011), pp. 78–9.

42. This being an early-1990s slogan of the nomenklatura, cited in Boris Kagarlitsky, *Back in the USSR* (Seagull Books, 2009), p. 34. On the curious popularity of neoliberalism on the part of 'communist' academia and the elite in the 1980s, see Patrick Flaherty, 'Perestroika and the Neoliberal Project', *Socialist Register*, vol. 27 (1991).
43. Statistics here can be found variously in Kagarlitsky, *Back in the USSR*, Rumy Hasan and Mike Haynes, *A Century of State Murder? Death and Policy in Twentieth Century Russia* (Pluto, 2003), and Laszlo Andor and Martin Summers, *Market Failure: Eastern Europe's 'Economic Miracle'* (Pluto Press, 1998).
44. The ephemeral 'Soviet' republics of 1919 in Hungary and Bavaria, themselves built on workers' councils, called themselves the 'Räterepubliken' and, in Hungarian, 'Tanácsköztársaság'. The use of the Russianized 'Sowjet' for their system came later.
45. Vladimir Paperny, *Architecture in the Age of Stalin: Culture Two* (Cambridge University Press, 2002). A less poetic, empirical account of Soviet-influenced architecture during this period comes to strikingly similar conclusions: Anders Åman, *Architecture and Ideology in Eastern Europe during the Stalin Era* (MIT Press, 1992). In terms of 'urbanism', there is only one synoptic book, R. A. French and F. E. Ian Hamilton (eds.), *The Socialist City: Spatial Structure and Urban Policy* (John Wiley and Sons, 1979), which has a useful definition of what made Soviet-style cities 'an entirely separate category of urban settlement, (with)

    a generally much higher population density;
    a lack of a density gradient;
    a lack of any surface of land values assessable in financial terms;
    a lack of a determinable spatial differentiation of social groups;
    a far less marked spatial differentiation of function between one part of the town and another;
    a relatively low order of service provision;
    a distinctive employment structure, with a higher proportion of workers engaged in industry;
    a high degree of reliance on public transport; and
    as a framework to all the rest, the total concentration of decision-making in the context of development and urban change into the hands of the planners, and the elimination of individual decision or competition' (pp. 101–2).

    We will find evidence of much of this, though a lot is now irrecoverable.
46. The basis of a synoptic study of this territory is provided by Timothy Snyder, *Bloodlands: Europe between Hitler and Stalin* (Bodley Head, 2010). This

book is very useful reading for anyone casually interested in the period, for its mastery of sources, historical sweep, linguistic promiscuity and harshly readable style – but should often be taken with a pinch of salt, not least for its tendency to downplay or even ignore the less palatable aspects of the countries and regimes between the two big bad hegemons – as usefully pointed out in Dovid Katz's review in *East European Jewish Affairs*, vol. 41, no. 3 (December 2011). At worst, its lack of analysis and numbing accumulation of atrocity becomes, as one wag put it, a form of 'totalitarian wrestlemania'. Worth reading alongside Snyder is Arno J. Mayer's work on the Holocaust, *Why Did the Heavens Not Darken?* (Verso, 2010), which gives due attention to the influence of the area's pre-1930s history, and especially the bloody, frequently anti-Semitic counter-revolutionary wars of 1917–21.

47. Paul Fussell, *Abroad* (Oxford, 1980), p. 41.
48. Agata Pyzik, *Poor but Sexy: Culture Clashes in Europe East and West* (Zero Books, 2014).

1. MAGISTRALE

1. Bertolt Brecht, *Poems* (Methuen, 1976), p. 440.
2. Adam Jonca, *Idzie Wojsko* (Nasza Ksiegarnia Warszawa, 1976), p. 12.
3. A. Litwak, *Moscow* (Foreign Languages Press, 1960), p. 47.
4. Statistics on Tverskaya from Vladimir Chernov (ed.), *Moscow: A Short Guide* (Progress, 1979).
5. Walter Benjamin, 'Moscow' (1927), in *Selected Writings*, vol. 2, part 1 (Harvard, 2005), p. 41.
6. The Mayakovsky statue was the focal point of meetings of Moscow youth in the Thaw era, a sort of 'Speakers' Corner' eliminated in the course of the 1960s – see the many references to it in the accounts of 1950s/1960s hipsters in S. Frederick Starr, *Red and Hot: The Fate of Soviet Jazz* (Limelight Editions, 2004).
7. There are monuments elsewhere, however, most notably that by the great sculptor Ernst Neizvestny above the former camp at Magadan.
8. Demolished in 2012.
9. Aldo Rossi, quoted in the excellent account of the boulevard in Brian Ladd, *The Ghosts of Berlin: Confronting German History in the Urban Landscape* (University of Chicago Press, 1998), p. 187. For a dissenting view, see Stefan Heym's 1963 novel *The Architects* (Daunt Books, 2012), which uses the development of the Stalinallee (here as 'World Peace Road') as a way to satirize the Stalinist experience and the Thaw. Challenged by his Modernist-inclined wife, the cynical, Bauhaus-trained lead designer exclaims: 'You want

turrets, Comrade? I'll put up turrets for you. The authorities want World Peace Road to look like a cross between the Kremlin Wall and the Parthenon, with some Baroque thrown in? I'll build it to specifications . . . Why don't you investigate, as a Marxist should, the origins of our clients' bad taste? Look at the life these men led, the limitations of their minds, the power suddenly thrown into their hands; enquire into what shaped their sense of beauty, if any, and their dreams of the monument they wish to erect for themselves, and then you'll see, I hope, that World Peace Road could have been a lot worse than it is!' (p. 125). The plot hinges on the return of a Gulag inmate and Bauhaus colleague of the protagonist, who proposes to complete the road as a Ville Radieuse, which he imagines will be a modern, confident, agora-like democratic space . . .

10. Markus Sebastian Braun (ed.), *Berlin: The Architecture Guide* (Braun, 2011), p. 168.
11. 'Socialist Realist Palaces for the Common Man', in Cor Wagenaar (ed.), *Happy: Cities and Happiness in Post-War Europe* (NAi, 2004), p. 31.
12. On Alexanderplatz, see my *Across the Plaza* (Strelka, 2012).
13. See Bogdan Tscherkes, 'The Kreschatik', in Wagenaar (ed.), *Happy*.
14. The popular principle that 'if the Soviets said it, it must have been untrue' has often led to some doubt on this, but just to be clear – there is no serious dispute among historians that, as well as fighting the Soviets, the UPA also tried their best to create a Ukraine for Ukrainians through cleansing it of Jews (co-operating in the Nazi pogroms in Lviv, in 1941) and of Poles (massacring on their own around 100,000 Polish civilians in a campaign of 1943). On the Lviv pogrom, see Grzegorz Rossolinski-Liebe, 'The "Ukrainian National Revolution" of 1941', available online at http://defendinghistory.com/wp-content/uploads/2013/08/Grzegorz-Rossolinski-Liebe-on-The-Ukrainian-National-Revolution-of-1941.pdf
15. In this, they disprove one of Brecht's reassurances against Stalinism's 'excesses': 'at a time when petit-bourgeois conceptions of art prevailed in the government, Mr Keuner was asked by an architect whether he should take on a big construction contract. "The errors and compromises in our art will remain standing for hundreds of years!" exclaimed the desperate man. Mr Keuner replied: "Not anymore. Since the tremendous development in means of destruction, your buildings are no more than experiments, not binding recommendations. Visual aids for popular debates. And as for the ugly little embellishments, the little pillars, etc, put them up in such a superfluous way that a pickaxe can swiftly allow the big pure lines to come into their own. Put your trust in our people, in rapid development!"' Alas, the big pure lines turned out to be rather drab, and the ugly little embellishments

spoke much more of Soviet originality and otherness. See Bertolt Brecht, *Stories of Herr Keuner* (City Lights, 2001), p. 93.

16. A fascinating publication by this 'Maidan left' is Anastasiya Osipova (ed.), *Circling the Square: Maidan and Cultural Insurgency* (Cicada Press, 2014), which includes a useful map of the insurgency by Burlaka.
17. A good English-language essay on these lovely urban artworks is Ella Chmielewska, 'Material Errata: Warsaw Neons and Socialist Modernity', *RIBA Journal of Architecture*, vol. 15, no. 1. A good coffee table book, also with English translation, is Ilona Karwinska, *Polish Cold War Neon* (Mark Batty, 2011). The best place to see them, however, is probably the Silesian city of Wrocław, where a dozen or so of the prettiest and silliest signs are well-restored.
18. Jonathan Raban, *Soft City* (Harvill Press, 1974), p. 20.
19. Irrespective of its crass anti-communism and extensive 'but it's not real capitalism!' apologetics for its disastrous aftermath, Lucian Boia, *Romania: Borderland of Europe* (Reaktion, 2001), contains a balanced and informative account of the achievements and hypocrisies of 'Little Paris'.
20. Ana Maria Zahariade, *Architecture in the Communist Project: Romania 1944–89* (Simetria, 2011), p. 24.
21. Anders Åman, *Architecture and Ideology in Eastern Europe during the Stalin Era* (MIT Press, 1992), p. 137.
22. Stephen Kotkin and Jan Tomasz Gross, *Uncivil Society: 1989 and the Implosion of the Communist Establishment* (Modern Library, 2009), p. 78.
23. Quoted in Zahariade, *Architecture in the Communist Project*, p. 60.
24. For a comparative account, see Albert Fishlow, 'The East European Debt Crisis in the Latin American Mirror', *International Organization*, vol. 40, no. 2. Thanks to Charles Turner for the reference.
25. The details here, and elsewhere in this section, are taken from Mariana Celac, Octavian Carabela and Marius Marcu-Lapadat, *Bucharest: Architecture and Modernity* (Simetria, 2009), pp. 76–82.
26. I owe this point to Lucian Boia, *Romania: Borderland of Europe* (Reaktion, 2001), p. 291 – he suggests Bofill's Antigone housing project in Montpellier was the specific inspiration.

2. MICRORAYON

1. Miroslav Holub, *Selected Poems* (Penguin, 1967), p. 25.
2. This fact can be found both in positive accounts of the time, like the propaganda brochure *USSR: Welfare* (Novosti, 1973), and in negative accounts such as that of Florian Urban, where it is seen as proof of the lunacy of the socialist economy.

3. Most of the specifics in this chapter derive from Elke Beyer's fascinating, comprehensive essay on prefabrication and mass housing, 'The Soviet Union is an Enormous Construction Site', in Dietmar Steiner et al. (eds.), *Soviet Modernism 1955–1991* (AzW, 2011).
4. For the magical process of unslumming, see Jane Jacobs, *The Death and Life of Great American Cities* (Pelican Books, 1974), pp. 284–304.
5. Berthold Lubetkin, 'The Russian Scene: The Development of Town Planning', *Architectural Review*, May 1932.
6. Václav Havel, 'Stories and Totalitarianism', in *Open Letters* (Vintage, 1992), p. 343.
7. Roy Medvedev, *On Socialist Democracy* (Norton, 1977), p. 85.
8. Antanas Papšys, *Vilnius: A Guide* (Progress, 1981), p. 142.
9. Ibid., p. 145.
10. Ibid., p. 146.
11. Jerzy S. Majewski, *Landmarks of People's Poland in Warsaw: A Book of Walks* (Gazeta, 2011), p. 102.
12. 'Meduna borrowed not only the shape of the building but also the scale and placement of the reliefs over the central opening and the coffer detail within the archway'. Kimberly Elman Zarecor, *Manufacturing a Socialist Modernity: Housing in Czechoslovakia, 1945–1960* (University of Pittsburgh Press, 2011) p. 162.
13. For an interesting series of student projects on possible uses and transformations of these, focusing on the Tallinn microrayon of Lasnamäe, see Reedik Poopuu (ed.), *Lasn* (Eesti Architektide Liit, 2012).
14. Richard Cartwright Austin, *Building Utopia: Erecting Russia's First Modern City, 1930* (Kent State University Press, 2004), p. 54.
15. Ibid., p. 56.
16. Kirill Kobrin, *The Last European* (3am Press, 2013), unpaginated.
17. Peter Carlson, *K Blows Top* (Public Affairs, 2009), p. 147.

3. SOCIAL CONDENSER

1. In Joseph Sherman (ed.), *From Revolution to Repression: Soviet Yiddish Writing, 1917–1952* (Five Leaves, 2012), p. 144.
2. Wilhelm Reich, *The Mass Psychology of Fascism* (Pelican Books, 1978), p. 247.
3. Specifically, the 'Familistère' in Guise, which is profiled in Gillian Darley, *Factory* (Reaktion Books, 2003), pp. 67–9.
4. Anatole Kopp, *Town and Revolution* (Braziller, 1970), p. 141; the description is of the Narkomfin flats in Moscow, built in 1930.
5. On this see Rem Koolhaas, *Delirious New York* (Monacelli Press, 1997).

6. El Lissitzky, *Russia: An Architecture for World Revolution* (MIT Press, 1970), p. 43.
7. It should be noted that this didn't make it completely typical – Vilnius's status as the capital of a Union Republic meant that it could obtain resources for these projects better than the average provincial town. Even so, a city with similar status, like Riga in Latvia, did not create spaces this impressive; the talents, and luck, of Lithuanian architects are as much part of this as the policies they carried out.
8. All descriptions in this paragraph are based on information from Rūta Leitanaitė and Julija Reklaitė (eds.), *Vilnius 1900–2013: A Guide to the City's Architecture* (Architekturos Fondas, 2013), a particularly informed and prejudice-free work.
9. An account of the ceremony in a contemporary guidebook: 'The young couples and their accompanying family and friends are escorted by the master of ceremonies into the wide vestibule of ceremonial processions leading through the open suites to the entrance hall. The wedding procession goes through these ceremonial halls – this is the stately spectacle that has determined the designs and entire composition of the palace.' Antanas Papšys, *Vilnius: A Guide* (Progress, 1981), p. 137.
10. Let the record show that it was not appreciated by Nikita Khrushchev, who attacked the 35-year-old building for being 'as ugly as sin' in a 1962 speech on the awfulness of 'formalism'. Unlike his precedecessor, his opinions on architecture were not regarded as gospel, and modern architecture was immediately defended in the press. S. Frederick Starr, *Melnikov: Solo Architect in a Mass Society* (Princeton University Press, 1978), p. 236.
11. As with the Kennedy assassination, the jury is eternally out – for two contrasting accounts, see the confident assertion of guilt in Robert Conquest, *Stalin and the Kirov Murder* (Oxford University Press, 1989), or conversely Oleg Khlevniuk, *Master of the House: Stalin and His Inner Circle* (Yale University Press, 2008), whose trawl through the archives at least makes clear that however likely it was he dunnit, Stalin's culpability is not supported by any documentary evidence whatsoever.
12. They are a little more rare, though we found a few. Prominent in the centre of Moscow and St Petersburg is the retro-*stolovaya* chain 'Stolovaya 57', an oligarch-owned enterprise which has a combination of relatively very cheap food and ominipresent Soviet nostalgia, with the same old posters to be found in every branch.
13. Francis Spufford, *Red Plenty* (Faber and Faber, 2011), p. 146.
14. I owe this information to Elke Beyer, Anke Hagemann and Michael Zinganel, *Holidays after the Fall: Seaside Architecture and Urbanism in Bulgaria and Croatia* (Jovis, 2013), pp. 92–3.

15. Catherine Cooke, *Architectural Drawings of the Russian Avant-Garde* (MOMA, 1990), p. 45. Cooke was constrasting this with what she regarded as the far worse proposals in the mid-1930s to demolish GUM, the famous and still extant turn-of-the-century shopping arcade.
16. Leszek Kołakowski, 'In Praise of Inconsistency', in *Marxism and Beyond* (Paladin, 1971), p. 234.
17. See Gowan's pseudonymous 'The Polish Vortex', quite the best English-language analysis of Solidarity during its glory days, published under the name Oliver Macdonald, in *New Left Review*, no. 139, May–June 1983. Gowan argues that the church, 'far from being a militant centre of "anti-socialist counter-revolutionary mobilisation", was a settled, conservative and prosperous establishment without any active project for upsetting the status quo. In Poland's successive political crises, the episcopate had always proved its loyalty by appealing for calm and order in the cities, its message on social questions a mixture of calls for sober hard work and respect for the family combined with denunciations of worldly, secular (and pro-Western) lifestyles, as well as a strong appeal for Poles to love their country and build up its resources. There was no trace of radical democratic ideology within the episcopate.' However, he argues that the pope was more strongly inclined towards Solidarity, and 'encouraged a more dynamic and combative thrust within the working class' than the Polish church itself.
18. This information is from Ludwik Hass, 'The Tragedy of Solidarity is Its Advisers', *Revolutionary History*, vol. 6, no. 1.
19. This anecdote is courtesy of Gavin Rae's blog Beyond the Transition, at http://beyondthetransition.blogspot.co.uk/2010/09/thirty-years-of-solidarity.html.
20. *Architektura*, no. 5, 1980, p. 12.
21. Le Corbusier quoted in Hugh Pearman, 'Design for Living', *New Humanist*, March/April 2006.
22. Fr Tomasz Bojasiński, *Architektura*, no. 5, 1980, p. 17.

4 HIGH BUILDINGS

1. Leon Trotsky, *Literature and Revolution* (Red Words, 1994), p. 282.
2. The glassware designer Karel Wünsch claimed to have designed 'on the basis of Jung's theory of the collective unconscious'. As well he might. See the celebratory *Ještěd Phenomenon* (City of Liberec, 2008).
3. For a more in-depth analysis of this building and its histories, see my 'One Better Than Stonehenge: The Gosprom Building and Dzerhzhinsky Square in Kharkiv', *AA Files*, 62 (2011).
4. In Joanna Warsza (ed.), *Ministry of Highways: A Guide to the Performative Architecture of Tbilisi* (Sternberg Press, 2014), pp. 27–8.
5. Ibid., p. 42.

6. Andrew E. Kramer, 'Moscow Tries to Reinvent Itself as Financial Hub', *The New York Times*, 3 April 2013. Choice extract: '"Moscow was never going to be an international financial center," a Western banker working here, who was not authorized to speak for his employer on the matter, said of the effort. "That was a joke." So Moscow is setting its sights a little lower. Its biggest problem is to be taken seriously even as a regional center. The midsize companies in neighboring Ukraine or other former Soviet republics are choosing to go public in Warsaw. They are hardly bothering to look at the carefully laid out welcome mat in Russia. Kernel, a Ukrainian corporate farming enterprise, and Coal Energy, a Ukrainian producer of steam coal, listed in Poland, where a policy of investing pensions in the stock market helps the local exchange. The Warsaw stock exchange, in fact, has so many Ukrainian company listings it has a Ukraine index. Micex, the Russian stock exchange, has no such index because it has so few listings.'
7. Walter Benjamin, 'Moscow' (1927), in *Selected Writings*, vol. 2, part 1 (Harvard University Press, 2005), p. 43.
8. On Lissitzky, Stalin and the Garden Ring, see Karl Schlögel, *Moscow* (Reaktion, 2005), p. 23.
9. Bukharin, who had led a behind-closed-doors pro-peasant opposition to what he called Stalin's 'Asiatic' policies, described Stalin as the new Genghis Khan in a private communication (read nonetheless by the security services) with Lev Kamenev: Stephen F. Cohen, *Bukharin and the Bolshevik Revolution* (Vintage, 1975), p. 291. Valentinov is quoted in Alec Nove, *An Economic History of the USSR* (Pelican Books, 1978), p. 159.
10. Vladimir Paperny, *Architecture in the Age of Stalin: Culture Two* (Cambridge University Press, 2002), p. 248.
11. For a fascinating and incisive political-aesthetic analysis of the Palace (and its complex current status) by an anthropologist and architecture historian, read Michał Murawski's essay 'Inappropriate Object', *Anthropology Today*, vol. 27, no. 4, August 2011.
12. Agata Pyzik, 'In Latvia, Riga has become a ghost town', *New Statesman*, 22 August 2012.
13. On this battle of the TV towers, see David Crowley and Jane Pavitt, 'The High-Tech Cold War', in their edited catalogue, *Cold War Modern: Design 1945–1970* (V&A, 2008), pp. 174–8.
14. For an account of these events, see Stephen F. Cohen, *Failed Crusade: America and the Tragedy of Post-Communist Russia* (W. W. Norton and Company, 2001), pp. 124–35.
15. On the exhibition and its aftermath, see Sophie Pinkham, 'The Museum of the Revolution', *The Nation*, November 2013.

16. At the twilight of Stalin's rule, in 1953, Czesław Miłosz wrote: 'since everything is planned in a socialist economy, why not proceed to a planned satisfaction of the aesthetic needs of human beings? . . . even now one can see some progress. They are already erecting skyscrapers patterned after the buildings erected in Chicago about the year 1900 – it is possible that in the year 2000 they will officially introduce art forms that are today considered modern in the West.' In the event, that would take about two years rather than fifty. *The Captive Mind* (Vintage, 1990), pp. 68–9.
17. Lithuania, like Estonia and Slovenia, has managed to retain a more vivid and imaginative contemporary architecture than larger EU neighbours like Poland or the Czech and Slovak republics, let alone Russia, Belarus or Ukraine; projects from these three small countries appear in Euro-architecture magazines like *A10* much more than those from larger ones. It's a puzzle, but then all three were both unusually well-off and unusually educated in the 'socialist' period, as they are now.
18. Joel S. Torstensen, Michael F. Metcalf and Tor Fr. Rasmussen, *Urbanization and Community Building in Modern Norway* (Urbana Press, 1985), pp. 68–9.
19. Boris Kagarlitsky, *Back in the USSR* (Seagull Books, 2009), p. 6.
20. I owe this information to Bart Goldhoorn and Philipp Meuser, *Capitalist Realism: New Architecture in Russia* (Dom, 2006), p. 190.

5. METRO

1. V. I. Lenin, *Selected Works*, vol. 3 (Progress, 1977), pp. 590–91.
2. That's not to say they completely neglected the main late-twentieth-century form of international transport. One surreal aspect of Stalinist planning is Baroque airports, such as Pulkovo in St Petersburg; and much later, at Boryspil in Kiev or at Belgrade's Nikola Tesla airport, you can still find multicoloured realist-Futurist reliefs of heroic workers flying through the air.
3. Nikita Khrushchev, *Memoirs*, vol. 3, ed. Sergei Khrushchev (Penn State Press, 2007), pp. 178–9. I owe this reference to the Institute for Conjunctural Research. Also note Khrushchev's noting of Stalin's concern for this matter: ' "Comrade Khrushchev," he said, 'rumours have reached me that you've let a very uncomfortable situation develop in Moscow as regards public toilets. Apparently people hunt around desperately and can't find anywhere to relieve themselves. This won't do. It puts the citizens in an awkward position." This episode, trivial as it may seem, shows how Stalin, the leader of the world's working class, wasn't too busy to bother himself over as important a detail of city life as public toilets.' Nikita Khrushchev, *Khrushchev Remembers*, vol. 1 (Penguin Books, 1977), pp. 54–5.

4. Benson Bobrick, *Labyrinths of Iron: The Story of the Underground Railway* (Newsweek Books, 1982), p. 281.
5. Ibid., p. 275.
6. Ibid., p. 276.
7. On the 'organs', see *The Gulag Archipelago*, vol. 1 (Collins, 1974), particularly the accounts of interrogation and torture on pp. 93–144.
8. E. Abakumov, *The Moscow Subway* (Foreign Languages Publishing House, 1939), pp. 10–11
9. Egor Larichev and Anastasia Uglik, *Moscow Metro Travel Guide* (WAM, 2008), p. 5.
10. Khrushchev, *Khrushchev Remembers*, vol. 1, p. 87. He continues: 'I think it's probably easier to contemplate space flights today than it was for us to contemplate the construction of the Moscow Metro in the early 1930s.'
11. Larichev and Uglik, *Moscow Metro Travel Guide*, p. 20.
12. Valentin Berezin, *Moscow Metro Photoguide* (Planeta, 1989), p. 38.
13. Larichev and Uglik, *Moscow Metro Travel Guide*, pp. 66–7.
14. Abakumov, *Moscow Subway*, p. 20.
15. According to Andreas Trier Mørch and Juri Nikitin, *The Unknown St Petersburg: Architecture from 1917 to 1956* (Royal Danish Academy of Architecture, 2003), p. 98.
16. In fact, it was dictated by military spending. In his memoirs, Khrushchev notes with some regret: 'When I was the leader of the Party and the government, I decided that we had to economise drastically in the building of houses, the construction of communal services, and even in the development of agriculture in order to build up our defences. I even suspended the construction of subways in Kiev, Baku and Tbilisi so that we could redirect these funds into strengthening our defences and attack forces.' Khrushchev, *Khrushchev Remembers*, vol. 1, p. 545.
17. Tamara Deutscher, 'Introduction' to Isaac Deutscher, *Lenin's Childhood* (Oxford University Press, 1970).
18. Kost' Kozlov, *Kievskii Metropoliten* (Varto, 2011), p. 232.
19. One of many similarly exotic mosaics in the Georgian capital – for an English-language guide (with attached postcards!), see Nini Palavandishvili, *Lost Heroes of Tbilisi: Soviet Period Mosaics* (GeoAIR, 2014).
20. Thanks to Otto Saumarez Smith for this description.
21. G. M. Voskresenskii, *Kharkivskii Metropoliten* (Prapor, 1980), p. 59.
22. A. Merkulov, *Automation Serves Man* (Foreign Languages Publishing House, 1958), p. 74.
23. *Ibid.*, p. 149.
24. Ernest Mandel, *Beyond Perestroika: The Future of Gorbachev's USSR* (Verso, 1989), p. 53.

25. However, Warsaw does have several overground stations built between 1958 and 1974 in a highly stylish concrete-Expressionist style. In his edited collection on their designers, *AR/PS: The Architecture of Arseniusz Romanowicz and Piotr Szymaniak* (Centrum Architektury, 2013), Grzegorz Piątek points out that their avoidance of any hint of *architecture parlante* makes them very unlike both the Moscow Metro or the currently popular symbolic train stations of Santiago Calatrava. There is also, full disclosure, an essay by the author on the stations in the book.
26. Edwin Heathcote, *Budapest: A Guide to Twentieth-Century Architecture* (Ellipsis, 1997), p. 228.
27. Ctibor Rybár, *Prague* (Olympia, 1979), p. 51.
28. Radomira Sedláková, *The Prague Metro* (Futurista Universum, 2010), p. 15.
29. Who is interviewed (in English) in Jerzy S. Majewski, *Landmarks of People's Poland in Warsaw: A Book of Walks* (Gazeta, 2011), pp. 246–9. The (identical) 1983 drawings of the 1995 stations can be found in T. Przemysław Szafer, *Contemporary Architecture in Poland* (Arkady, 1983), p. 32.
30. On Bojović and Energoprojekt, see Dubravka Sekulić, *Three Points of Support* (Belgrade Museum of Contemporary Art, 2013).
31. That's at http://en.wikipedia.org/wiki/Riga_Metro.
32. Alec Nove, *An Economic History of the USSR* (Pelican Books, 1978), pp. 250–51. The statistics are from 1935 – the very year the Metro's first line opened to its appallingly housed public.
33. Khrushchev, *Khrushchev Remembers*, vol. 1, p. 90.
34. Larichev and Uglik, *Moscow Metro Travel Guide*, p. 24.

6. RECONSTRUCTION

1. Andrzej Bursa, *Killing Auntie and Other Work* (CB Editions, 2009), p. 28.
2. Simon Jenkins, 'The architect's ego is reconstructed as Moscow's Mayor asserts the lay view', *Guardian*, 27 April 2007. 'A stylistic self-confidence not seen in European cities since Victorian Britain . . . it is London, not Moscow, that has sold out architecturally to money and vulgarity.'
3. Quoted in Walter Benjamin, *Understanding Brecht* (Verso, 2003), p. 33.
4. The fact that a few houses in the old town were being rebuilt already before the full Stalinist takeover is both true and fundamentally irrelevant – the decision to reconstruct the entire historic city was a governmental one, and heavily contested by Modernists, some of whom emigrated as a result.
5. Marta Leśniakowska, *Architecture of Warsaw* (Arkada, 2006), pp. 73–4.
6. This is, it should be noted, not necessarily a consequence of post-1989 neglect – there is a late-1950s film from the Polish 'black wave' of critical documentaries which depicts the Old Town of Lublin in exactly this light.

7. Zygmunt M. Stępiński, 'In the Light of Our Experience', *Architektura*, July–August 1978, p. 36.
8. Pierluigi Cervellati, 'Innovation or Conservation?', *Architektura*, July–August 1978, p. 80.
9. Ibid., p. 80.
10. Ibid., p. 74.
11. *Architektura*, January 1980, p. 77.
12. Ibid., p. 53.
13. 'The rise in productivity due to the industrialisation of building techniques, which at first sight looks so significant, on closer inspection proves to be largely self-deception. Even today, in Thuringia, for example, traditional stone building can still be cheaper, even for a fairly large construction, than the same building in the hallowed style of prefabrication, and this is instructive, as the tricks of financial cost accounting are far more disturbing on the macro scale than on the micro.' Rudolf Bahro, *The Alternative in Eastern Europe* (New Left Books, 1978), p. 433. A similar point on the dominance of concrete in Soviet-era Estonia, a country abundant in high-quality wood, can be found in Adrian Forty, *Concrete and Culture* (Reaktion, 2012).
14. Florian Urban, 'The Invention of the Historic City: Building the Past in East Berlin 1970–1990', Ph.D. thesis, Massachusetts Institute of Technology, 2007, p. 204. The thesis can be accessed at http://opus.kobv.de/tuberlin/volltexte/2006/1204/.
15. Ibid., pp. 322–3. Urban notes that 'since [the Nikolaiviertel] does not claim authenticity, it leaves space for the imagination', p. 324.
16. Janis Krastins and Ivars Strantmanis, *Riga: The Complete Guide to Architecture* (ADD, 2004), p. 212.
17. Ibid., p. 219.
18. For a bestiary of sham replicas, see Clementine Cecil and Edward Harris (eds.), *Moscow Heritage at Crisis Point* (MAPS, 2007), pp. 78–81.
19. These, the first 'social housing' projects here since the 1920s, given that the housing projects of the USSR were (mostly) not aimed at a particular social class, are profiled in English in Karin Hallas-Murula, *Tallinn Architecture 1900–2010* (Museum of Estonian Architecture, 2010), p. 122. Typically for Estonia the architecture is quite pleasant, in its good-taste way.
20. Brzeska, the 64-year-old founder of the Warsaw Tenants' Association, was found dead in 2011 in the forests outside Warsaw, her body burnt. There is an account in English at http://libcom.org/news/housing-activist-found-dead-warsaw-08032011. Pensioners are often the victims of the privatization of communist-era housing, which they are usually informed of after the fact.

21. '. . . and just when they seem engaged in revolutionising themselves and things, in creating something that has never yet existed, precisely in such periods of revolutionary crisis they anxiously conjure up the spirits of the past to their service and borrow from them names, battle-cries and costumes in order to present the new scenes of world history in this time-honoured disguise and this borrowed language'. Karl Marx, *The Eighteenth Brumaire of Louis Bonaparte* (Lawrence and Wishart, 1984), p. 10.

7. IMPROVISATION

1. György Konrád, *The City Builder* (Dalkey Archive, 2007), p. 123.
2. This is A. J. P. Taylor, a sceptical aside on Isaac Deutscher's Marxist 'hocus pocus', see 'Trotsky' in *Europe: Grandeur and Decline* (Penguin Books, 1991), p. 175.
3. These figures are somewhat outside the purview of a book about things that still exist, but for 'Movement' and similar Soviet kinetic artist-architects, see Jane A. Sharp, 'The Personal Visions and Public Spaces of the Movement Group (Dvizhenie)', in David Crowley and Jane Pavitt (eds.), *Cold War Modern: Design 1945–1970* (V&A, 2008), pp. 234–41; and on Hansen and other more experimental architects of the post-war era in Poland, Yugoslavia and Czechoslovakia, see Łukasz Stanek, *Team 10 East* (Muzeum Sztuki Nowoczesni, 2014).
4. Miklós Haraszti, *A Worker in a Worker's State* (Pelican Books, 1977), pp. 141–2.
5. See Rem Koolhaas's 2006 film *Lagos – Wide and Close*. For a critique of this irksome ideology see Matthew Gandy, 'Learning From Lagos', *New Left Review*, vol. 33, May–June 2005, or by implication Mike Davis's *Planet of Slums* (Verso, 2006).
6. There is a website with an informative essay on the kiosks and photographs of them in various permutations – including being used as bus stops in Belarus – available at http://www.publicplan-architects.com/k67/k67_kiosk_project_information.html.
7. Rusudan Mirzikashvili, 'Everybody's Favourite', in Dietmar Steiner et al. (eds.), *Soviet Modernism* (AzW, 2011), p. 156. Conversely, for an optimistic take on these self-built extensions as 'the architecture of the future', see Joanna Warsza, Bouillon Group et al, *Kamikaze Loggia* (Georgian Ministry of Culture, 2013); and also Levan Asabashvili's essays on housing networks and the collapse of Georgia's infrastructure in Joanna Warsza (ed.), *Ministry of Highways: A Guide to the Performative Architecture of Tbilisi* (Sternberg Press, 2014).

8. For a sympathetic critique of the *Baugruppen*, see Adrian Jones and Chris Matthews's post at their blog *Jones the Planner*: http://www.jonestheplanner.co.uk/2014/05/berlin-baugruppen-mental-walls.html.
9. See Agata Pyzik, *Poor but Sexy: Culture Clashes in Europe East and West* (Zero Books, 2014), p. 75.
10. For an English-language history of FV, the umbrella group behind this scene, and their role in Metelkova, see Nikolai Jeffs, 'FV and the "Third Scene"', in Lilijana Stepančič (ed.), *FV: Alternative Scene of the Eighties* (Mednarodni grafični likovni center, 2008). He concludes that for these groups 'the issue was not socialism or capitalism, but rather the possibility of developing a cultural production – and above all a society – that would transcend both forms.'
11. Markus Bader, Oliver Baurhenn, Kuba Szreder, Raluca Voinea and Katharina Koch (eds.), *The Knot: An Experiment on Collaborative Art in Public Urban Space* (Jovis, 2011).
12. Tristan Sechrest interviewing Sierakowski for Open Democracy, at http://www.opendemocracy.net/can-europe-make-it/sławomir-sierakowski-tristan-sechrest/put-Václav-Havel-in-any-election-today-and-he-would-lose.
13. Dennison Rusinow, *The Yugoslav Experiment 1948–1974* (University of California Press, 1978), pp. 68–71.
14. Roy Moore, *Self Management in Yugoslavia* (Fabian Society, 1970), p. 11.
15. Ibid., p. 8.
16. Milojko Drulović, *Self-Management on Trial* (Spokesman Books, 1978).
17. Branka Magaš, *The Destruction of Yugoslavia: Tracing the Break-up 1980–92* (Verso, 1993), p. 97.
18. Ibid., p. 133.
19. Vladimir Kulić, Maroje Mrduljaš and Wolfgang Thaler, *Modernism In-Between: The Mediatory Architectures of Socialist Yugoslavia* (Jovis, 2012), pp. 124–5.
20. Dubravka Sekulić, *Glozt nicht so Romantisch! On Extralegal Space in Belgrade* (Jan van Eyck Academie, 2013), p. 20.
21. There were many forms of self-management. 'The entire collective', i.e. all the employees in a given BOAL, were 'obliged to meet five or six times a year' by law, but this often degenerated into a mere rubber stamp. More ambitious workplaces were more devolved at plant level, with for instance work groups of thirty people meeting and then voting. Either way, the system was open to, in the parlance, 'distortions'. Drulović, *Self-Management on Trial*, p. 63.
22. There was actually a programme of 'council housing' in Belgrade by the 1970s, largely to fill this gap: 'Acting on the solidarity principle,' writes Drulović, 'Belgrade undertook a drive to build flats for persons employed in enterprises which cannot set aside any resources for that purpose. Financed by city funds, with the help of credits from banks and the contributions of work organisations of up to one third of the cost, 2,000 such flats have been

constructed so far, and a further 10,000 should be completed over the next five years.' This could perhaps have alleviated the problem at least to a degree, had the IMF not stepped in. Ibid., p. 116.

23. Sekulić, *Glozt nicht so Romantisch!*, p. 50. The architects STEALTH. unlimited, in their work on Kaluderica, ask whether it's 'the top or the bottom of the philosophy and practice of self-management', in Simona Vidmar (ed.), *Unfinished Modernisations: Between Utopia and Pragmatism* (Umetnostna Galerija Maribor, 2012), p. 39.
24. Vidmar (ed.), *Unfinished Modernisations*, p. 39.

8. MEMORIAL

1. Octavio Paz, 'The Other Mexico', in *The Labyrinth of Solitude* (Penguin, 2005), p. 229
2. Quoted in Norbert Lynton, *Tatlin's Tower* (Thames and Hudson, 2009), p. 90.
3. There are penetrating studies of all of these and others in Gwendolyn Leick's *Tombs of the Great Leaders* (Reaktion, 2014).
4. Quoted in Patrick Hyder Patterson, *Bought and Sold: Living and Losing the Good Life in Socialist Yugoslavia* (Cornell University Press, 2011), p. 299.
5. A probably more symptomatic museum in this respect is the Belgrade War Museum, built into the Kalmegadan fortress. Its exhibits and dioramas about the wars on this territory from ancient times to the 1990s feature everything from abstract sculptures to heroic bronzes of Tito and an executed Partisan, with nearly all of it ending in 1945. The only post-Yugoslav exhibit is a small series of maps of the 'NATO aggression' of 1999, showing whence and how Belgrade was attacked. There is nothing, however, on the wars that preceded it throughout the 1990s, following the fictional official line that the Serbian government had nothing to do with the war in Bosnia, or the wave of atrocities perpetuated by Bosnian Serb paramilitaries.
6. Walter Benjamin, 'Moscow' (1927), in *Selected Writings* , vol. 2, part 1 (Harvard University Press, 2005), p. 36.
7. Dubravka Ugrešić, *Nobody's Home* (Telegram, 2007), p. 54: 'Why, they are the bulwark and the crossroads! Croatia has always envisoned itself as a bulwark. For a while, Croatia was the bulwark against the Turks (who would have taken Vienna were it not for the Croats), and then against communism (those Serbs, as everyone knows, were all communists). For Croats the word "Balkan" means "Serbian", "Orthodox", "the barbarian hordes". Croatia is renowned as a crossroads as well: not only as a maritime one but also a web of railway junctions and airline routes. The bulwark and the crossroads are fantasies of the state and the nation which have been disseminated with the

same melodrama of patchy argumentation everywhere, particularly when one heads in an easterly direction from Croatia. Bosnia, too, is a bulwark and a crossroads, and Serbia is too, of course. And don't forget Macedonia. A friend of mine who often travels to the southern states of the former Soviet Union has come across notions of the bulwark and the crossroads identical in every detail, cultivated by Georgians, Azerbaijanis, Armenians, Uzbeks, the Turkmens, the Kyrgyz, Tajiks and Buryats.'

8. See Domenico Losurdo, *War and Revolution: Rethinking the Twentieth Century* (Verso, 2015).
9. On this, see the introduction to Terry Martin, *The Affirmative Action Empire: Nations and Nationalism in the Soviet Union, 1923–1939* (Cornell University Press, 2001), or E. H. Carr, *The Bolshevik Revolution*, vol. 1 (Pelican Books, 1971), pp. 295–312.
10. See Agata Pyzik, *Poor but Sexy: Culture Clashes in Europe East and West* (Zero Books, 2014), p. 75.
11. This forms the subject of a short, apparently neutral, politically pointed film by the Ukrainian artist Mykola Ridnyi, which shows construction workers at work dismantling the representation of 'the workers', available online at http://www.mykolaridnyi.com/works/monument-platforms.
12. Slavoj Žižek, 'Barbarism with a Human Face: Lenin v Stalin in Ukraine', *London Review of Books*, 8 May 2014, essentially argues that it should have been eastern/southern Ukraine's 'anti-Maidan' tearing down Lenin's statues, given his role in ensuring 'Novorossiya' was part of a sovereign Ukraine.
13. For an account of this, see Agata Pyzik, 'Why Soviet Monuments Should be Protected', *Guardian*, 29 September 2014. I can attest her inbox at the time included outraged claims that Lenin 'killed millions' and that the Soviets killed '140%' of Ukrainians, among other highlights. Probably the most sensible and historically astute response to the Leninoclasm was in Zaporozhia, where the giant Lenin was simply dressed in Ukrainian national costume.
14. Reproduced in Alexei Tarkhanov and Sergei Kavtaradze, *Stalinist Architecture* (Lawrence King, 1992), p. 11.
15. The actor who plays Lenin in Eisenstein's film was denounced in the avant-garde magazine *New LEF* as resembling 'a statue of Lenin'. See Viktor Shklovsky and Osip Brik, 'The 'Lef' Arena', in *Screen*, Winter 1971/2.
16. For the interested, these two survivors are in Gorki Leninskiye just outside Moscow, and in Lenin's hometown, Simbirsk, still known by its Soviet name, Ulyanovsk. The English-language guide to the Central Lenin Museum (Raduga Publishers, 1986) lists a ridiculous number of Lenin museums in the Soviet Union and its satellites, dozens and dozens of them from Ulan Bator to Bucharest to Zakopane. It also lists several in the West, of which the one in Tampere, Finland, survives at the time of writing.

17. Herbert Marcuse, *Soviet Marxism* (Pelican Books, 1971), pp. 75–6.
18. The useful comparison here is to the Racławice Panorama in Wrocław. This intriguing folk-Brutalist rotunda in the city centre was designed in 1967 to rehouse a late-nineteenth-century panoramic painting originally on display in Lviv, depicting the great Polish radical general Tadeusz Kościuszko's (sadly pyrrhic) victory over Tsarist forces at the battle of Racławice in 1794. Though clearly for any Marxist the Englightenment-inspired democrat Kościuszko had 'progress' on his side in the war with Russian absolutism, any depiction of a victory over Russia was considered too politically risky; the panorama was only opened to the public in 1985, nearly twenty years after the building was designed. Still, in its Pavlovian lighting effects, pomp and solemnity combined with a localized Modernism, the building is very Soviet.
19. Cf. Jerzy Wilmanski, *Łódź: Miasto i Ludzie* (Wydawnictwo Łódźie, 1977), p. 71.
20. Usefully, Wikipedia has a chart of the various estimates from Western historians of the Soviet dead. The very lowest estimate is John Keegan's 14 million, of whom half were civilians; while historians who can hardly be accused of Soviet sympathies, such as Norman Davies and Tony Judt, give far higher calculations, of 28 million and 24 million, respectively, with civilians a majority in both. See http://en.wikipedia.org/wiki/World_War_II_casualties_of_the_Soviet_Union#Estimates_of_Soviet_war_dead_by_Western_scholars.
21. Richard J. Evans, review of Roger Moorhouse's *The Devil's Alliance*, *Guardian*, 6 August 2014.
22. This claim, regurgitated from Stéphane Courtois's *The Black Book of Communism*, is a historical nonsense. What it does is take all deaths that happened under 'communist' rule from 1917 to 1991 – from murder, famine, war – and ascribe them to 'communism'. Most of Stalin's victims were killed by the famine of 1932–3, for which Stalin and his regime are undoubtedly culpable, but in much the same way that any government in an industrialized country is culpable for famine – which they have been, often, as extensively demonstrated in Mike Davis, *Late Victorian Holocausts* (Verso, 2000). Following Courtois's logic and adding the deaths in Europe during the Second World War, for the outbreak of which Nazism was solely responsible, the deaths from Stalinism are vastly outnumbered. This is in no way to excuse Stalin, who would otherwise have been by far the most murderous European leader of the twentieth century, but there *is* a reason why the Soviets were chosen as the 'lesser evil' to the Nazis – because they were. In Poland, for instance, victim of both the two 'totalitarianisms', the experience is not comparable. Even given crimes such as mass deportations and the Katyn massacre, or the forcible imposition of a Soviet-dominated government, the Nazis' systematic destruction of hundreds of Polish villages, several cities and their inhabitants sits strangely with the Soviets' bankrolling and aiding of their subsequent reconstruction. In fact,

more Poles were killed in the war by Ukrainian nationalists than by the Soviets, which would perhaps be better remembered if it had been Ukraine that imposed an unpopular government on Poland for forty-five years.

23. The differences between the two events are blindingly obvious – in 1921, the Bolsheviks called upon countries which only months before had been at war with them to send aid; in 1933, Stalinists refused even to publicly acknowledge that the famine was happening, let alone ask for relief. Both famines, incidentally, occurred in southern Russia as well as in Ukraine. For a good, and conspiracy-theory-free, account of exactly how the mass murder of the famine of 1933 came to happen, see R. W. Davies, M. B. Tauger and S. G. Wheatcroft, 'Stalin, Grain Stocks and the Famine of 1932–33', in Christopher Read (ed.), *The Stalin Years: A Reader* (Palgrave, 2003).
24. On which, see Neal Ascherson's wonderful portrait of the various cultures to occupy the *Black Sea* (Vintage, 2007).
25. For a fascinating account of this removal and the events around it, see the Estonian artist Kristina Norman's book project *After-War* (Estonian Museum of Contemporary Art, 2009), which charts how the bronze soldier became an informal gathering point for the city's alienated, working-class Russian-speaking youth, and argues that there were good reasons why they took its removal as a direct attack on them. She claims that the monument was actually in the process of being domesticated and made informal by the Russian teenagers who congregated there to drink and lay flowers, and that its removal was determined by intra-Estonian political power plays.
26. The original design can be found (with English translation) in Alexandra Kusá, *Prerušená pieseň: Umenie Socialistického Realizmu 1948–1956* (SNG, 2012), p. 94.
27. Gavin Stamp, *The Memorial for the Missing of the Somme* (Profile, 2006), p. 84.
28. Vladimir Olshansky and Alla Filatova, *Memorial Nad Dneprom* (Kiev Misteshtvo, 1987); thanks to Oleksiy for the gift. The reader should bear in mind, however, that given the pace of change in Kiev at the time of writing, the museum may not remain in this form by the time of this book's publication. Who controls the present controls the past . . .
29. The mass starvation of Soviet prisoners of war is extensively discussed in Timothy Snyder, *Bloodlands: Europe between Hitler and Stalin* (Bodley Head, 2010), pp. 175–82.
30. In English, one powerful account is that of the Bundist and later Solidarity supporter Marek Edelman, *The Ghetto Fights* (Bookmarks, 1943).
31. This gesture is remembered by another plinth elsewhere on the square, but it's not quite what it seems. Brandt, as a member of the anti-Nazi underground and a socialist activist, had nothing to apologize for, unlike most of West Germany's industrial magnates. He was atoning where they wouldn't or couldn't.

32. To give some sense of the narrative this is placed uneasily into, the book from which I obtained the name of the artists is Tadeusz Czapliński and Jerzy Launer, *Places of National Memory in Łódź: Martyrdom and Fight, 1939–1945* (Łódźie Zakl, 1974). In what sense were these innocent, helpless victims 'martyrs' or 'fighters'?
33. This information is courtesy of an English-language guide for sale at the visitor centre: Maria Wisnioch, *Majdanek: Guide to the Historical Buildings* (Państwowe Muzeum na Majdanku, 2012).
34. See Barbara Epstein, *The Minsk Ghetto: Jewish Resistance and Soviet Internationalism* (University of California Press, 2008), among other things a useful corrective to Timothy Snyder's disgraceful treatment of the Partisans as mere provocateurs of the Germans in *Bloodlands*.
35. I owe this information to Oleksiy Radynski – see his essay on the subject, 'Scientifically Justified Artistic Consciousness: Artists and Architects in Late Soviet Ukraine', in Steiner et al. (eds.), *Soviet Modernism* (AzW, 2011).
36. See Pyzik, *Poor but Sexy*, p. 68.
37. Quotes from Ákos Eleőd are in the brochure *Statue Park: Gigantic Monuments from the Age of Communist Dictatorship* (Akos Rethly, 1995), unpaginated.
38. For a work that does, you need to turn to the greater possible complexity of film, not the univocality of monumental sculpture – see Juris Podnieks's elegiac, haunting 1980 documentary *Constellation of Riflemen*, which interviewed many of the survivors of both the war and the purge.
39. Valters Nollendorfs, Dzintra Bungs, Gundega Michele and Uldis Neibergs, *The Three Occupations of Latvia: Soviet and Nazi Takeovers and Their Consequences* (OMB, 2012), p. 28.
40. Attempting to explain this in the dying days of the USSR to the readers of *Izvestia*, then full of complaints about 'out-of-towners' moving to Moscow, Otto Latsis said: 'I invite Muscovites to imagine for a moment that "out of towners" [become] the majority population, and that Russian is heard less and less; that spokesmen have appeared amongst them who lay claim to these areas and even claim them as their own national property. This is how it is in Riga now.' Translated into English as 'Farewell to the Communist Party in Latvia', *New Left Review*, no. 182, July–August 1990, p. 157. An informed, unsentimental account of Baltic history can be found in Anatol Lieven, *The Baltic Revolutions* (Yale, 1994).
41. Latsis, 'Farewell to the Communist Party in Latvia', p. 158.
42. Paul Goble, 'The Growing Importance of Latvia's Occupation Museum' (Museum of Occupations, 2013), unpaginated leaflet.
43. Norman, *After-War*, p. 18.

44. Quoted in *After-War*, p. 70. This is not an exclusively non-Russian phenomenon – far from it. Boris Groys writes that 'Since class interests, along with Marxism, have vanished from the sights of current historiography, there are no "real" protagonists of history left beside the nations. Accordingly, it has now become characteristic for recent historical commentary on formerly communist-dominated East European countries to view communism as simply an ideological façade for Russian imperialism. Even if such an interpretation might seem corroborated by numerous facts, it should not be forgotten that in Russia itself the suppression of the Russian national identity was prosecuted not less but more forcefully by the apparatus of communist ideology. Besides the Russian Orthodox Church, the Russian philosophical tradition, and its historiography and literature from pre-Revolutionary eras were also largely banned or rigorously censored. So it is hardly surprising that the dismantling of the communist regime in the early 1990s was accompanied and spurred on by cries on the streets for "Russia! Russia!" In that period the anti-communist revolution in Russia was waged as a fight for national liberation – as a campaign to emancipate Russia from the grip of the Soviet Union and liberate it from the dictatorship of Soviet authorities. The civil war between the Reds and the Whites that first spawned the creation of the Soviet Union had been a war between the communist "International" and the nationalist "Russia": back then, the "International" won. But in the 1980s and 1990s, "Russia" got its revenge. For Russian nationalists today, anything connected with communism is automatically the work of others: Jews, Latvians, Georgians and so on. That, of course, does not mean that Russian nationalists take no pride in the achievements of the Soviet state during the communist era – except that these achievements are ascribed solely to the capacity of the Russian people to remain creative, resilient and victorious in the face of the ruinous communist dictatorship. Anything "good" that arose in the Soviet era is thus ascribed to the Russian nation's cultural identity; anything "bad" is seen as resulting from the anti-national project of communism.' Boris Groys, 'The Postcommunist Situation', in Ljubomir Micic, Frank Castorf and Haralampi G. Oroschakov (eds.), *Nach Moskau! Nach Moskau!* (Volksbühne, 2010), pp. 171–2.
45. This is broadly true, but not exclusively – see Jan Tomasz Gross's *Neighbours*, on the Polish-assisted pogrom in Jedwabne, 1941. In this book Gross has many interesting things to say on the persistent *Żydokomuna* myth, arguing that those who perpetrated the pogroms were equally likely to co-operate with *any* occupation, and did so with the new one in 1945.
46. However grim Poland in the 1960s, 1970s and 1980s was, to compare it either with the Nazi occupation or even the Stalinist years of 1948–53 is not

serious. But this comparison did have a political use – Kotkin and Gross note that Poland's unusually extensive opposition 'was possible only because the opposition had come to reject the idea of reform ("socialism with a human face") and instead to see the system as "totalitarian". At the same time, the Communist system they were challenging was the least totalitarian country in the bloc, with non-Communist values, public spaces, and even institutions.' Stephen Kotkin and Jan Tomasz Gross, *Uncivil Society* (Modern Library, 2010), p. 102. Yet official memory has enshrined the total equivalence of all these 'crimes against the Polish nation', with regular searches for reds under the bed. For a prescient account of the 'paranoid style' in Polish politics, see Andrzej Walicki, 'From Stalinism to Post-Communist Pluralism', *New Left Review*, no. 185, January–February 1991. As if unable to cope with the fact that the Party had begun the process of its own dissolution – surely impossible for a 'totalitarian' force – conspiratorial explanations had to be sought.

47. For an account of the results, see David Ost, *The Defeat of Solidarity* (Cornell University Press, 2005), quite the best book published on the post-Soviet working class in English, one which for once gives due attention to ideological factors in the apparent paradoxes of Eastern Europe's rightward shift.
48. The major text on this is Moshe Lewin's *Lenin's Last Struggle* (Pluto Press, 1975), pp. 43–64. This is vindicated and expanded upon in his later trawl through the newly opened archives, *The Soviet Century* (Verso, 2005).
49. Friedrich Engels, *The Housing Question* (Progress, 1979), p. 71.

CONCLUSION: SOCIALISM IS

1. Alexander Herzen, *From the Other Shore* (Oxford University Press, 1979), pp. 89–90.
2. Ticktin, for instance, appears to argue that workers' self-management could have solved the Soviet economic crisis, as if an equally intense crisis had not already destroyed workers' self-management in Yugoslavia at exactly the same time.
3. Keti Chukhrov, 'Sexuality in a Non-Libidinal Economy', *E-Flux Journal*, no. 54, April 2014.
4. For a justification of this view, see Yuezhi Zhao, 'The Struggle for Socialism in China', *Monthly Review*, vol. 64, no. 5, October 2012.
5. In fairness, Groys's suggestiveness and originality is sometimes more interesting than mere 'facts', and seldom more so than in this bizarre, ultra-abstract neo-Stalinist tract. He writes of China that 'Marxists have always believed that capitalism represents the best mechanism for economic acceleration. Marx frequently emphasised this, and employed it as an argument against

"utopian communism". The proposal to tame capitalism, to instrumentalise it, to set it to work under the control of the Communist Party for communist victory – this had been on the agenda from the October revolution on . . . However, the idea had never been finally translated into action because the communist leadership had never felt secure enough, and feared losing power through this experiment. In the 1980s and 90s, it felt strong enough, and risked the experiment. It is still too soon to judge whether this experiment has failed. In China, the Communist Party is still firmly in control . . . the model will be tested further – and may yet prove entirely successful.' Boris Groys, *The Communist Postscript* (Verso, 2009), p. 118.

6. Meanwhile, for an intriguing if outrageously historically lofty argument that China is not now and has never been capitalist, see Giovanni Arrighi, *Adam Smith in Beijing* (Verso, 2006).
7. That's more than double the rate for the country as a whole – see Richard McGregor, *The Party: The Secret World of China's Communist Rulers* (Penguin Books, 2012), p. 155, which quotes the local Party secretary: 'if you want to discuss who adheres most to socialism, wouldn't it be Shanghai?' This is of course 'socialism' in the Kaganovich definition. For an analysis of what this total state ownership of land and widespread state ownership of business means for the proletariat, see Julia Lovell's book on urban development and Western architects, where she notes that 'according to China's land management law, the state can requisition any land when it is in the "public interest"; the vagueness of this concept has led to widespread land-grabs that turn social housing and farmland into profitable commercial housing complexes, golf courses and amusement parks.' She notes with some bafflement that campaigners against this tend to invoke Chairman Mao in their defence. Julia Lovell, *Splendidly Fantastic: Architecture and Power Games in China* (Strelka, 2011), p. 48.
8. On this last, a typically Maoist combination of self-activity, mass participation and rampant, dogmatic authoritarianism, see Elizabeth Perry and Xun Li, *Proletarian Power: Shanghai in the Cultural Revolution* (Westview Press, 1997).
9. An English-language account of the Chinese New Left can be found in Wang Hui, *The End of the Revolution* (Verso, 2009).
10. See Mao Zedong, *On Practice and Contradiction*, introduced by Slavoj Žižek (Verso, 2007).
11. The best English-language account and description is the former cyber-theory guru and 'neo-reactionary' Nick Land's dizzy combination of advertorial and historical melodrama, in his *Shanghai Expo Guide 2010* (Urbanatomy, 2010).

Index of Places

General Index

About the Author

Owen Hatherley is the author of the acclaimed *Militant Modernism*, a defense of the modernist movement, and *A Guide to the New Ruins of Great Britain*. He writes regularly on the political aesthetics of architecture, urbanism, and popular culture for a variety of publications, including *Building Design*, *Frieze*, *The Guardian*, and the *New Statesman*. He lives in London.